SILENCE IS NO REACTION FORTY YEARS OF

IAN GLASPER

PM PRESS   Ei EARTH ISLAND BOOKS

ISBN: 978-1-62963-550-7 (paperback)
ISBN: 979-8-88744-000-2 (hardcover)
ISBN: 978-1-62963-695-5 (ebook)
Library of Congress Control Number: 2023930802

Cover and interior design by Welly Artcore
artcorefanzine@gmail.com

10 9 8 7 6 5 4 3 2 1

PM Press
PO Box 23912
Oakland, CA 94623
www.pmpress.org

Published in the UK by Earth Island Books
Pickforde Lodge
Pickforde Lane
Ticehurst
TN5 7BN
www.earthislandbooks.com

Printed in the U.S.A.

INTRODUCTION

I would have been fourteen or fifteen years old when I first heard Subhumans, and it was just what I needed at the time, because they grabbed me in a way that only a few bands have (Crass, Discharge, Rudimentary Peni, Voivod, D.I., Adam and the Ants, all take a bow too), ensuring that I'd be listening to them for the rest of my life.

It helped that I was a budding bassist as well, and Grant's bass runs on those early releases drew me in like a moth to a flame, challenging me to try to learn them. Indeed, I would even go so far as to admit I learnt to play bass by ripping off Subhumans' songs (not to mention the UK Subs and Flux of Pink Indians), plonking painfully along (well, two beats behind, most of the time) to their debut album, 'The Day the Country Died' (and as a sidenote, I later stole the title of that first album wholesale for my 2006 book on early Eighties anarcho punk, just because it was so evocative of that era).

They came along at a time when I was devouring Sounds, hanging on all the reviews in that venerable music paper, spending all of my meagre wages from three paper rounds on records each week. And they were one of the first bands (alongside Crass, Conflict, Icons of Filth and Instigators) that I hitched off to see, having adventures that would again stay with me all my life. One memorable weekend was spent down in London, jumping the tube, sleeping in a friend's squat and being chased by angry residents with baseball bats, whilst going to see three gigs across three nights – Subhumans, Sears, Icons of Filth, Mau Maus, Anti-System, Devoid, amongst others – which basically blew my tiny rural mind and helped pave the path I personally wanted to walk.

So, it was a very important time for me, and incredibly influential, my attitudes towards society and authority being forged at the same time as my musical tastes, and right at the centre of it all was the Subhumans. Musically and lyrically, they bridged the gap between serious anarcho punk, sneering fury and drunken fun, and I started going to see them live whenever I could.

When my cousin Mobs and I started our own first proper band, Decadence Within, it was very apparent Subhumans provided a major steer on what we were trying to do (we even called our first single 'Speed Hippy'), and of course we wanted to play with them. But as a new, unknown band, it was unlikely we were going to be invited to support them, so we just followed the DIY punk route of booking them ourselves (don't wait for it to happen – make it happen!). We got Dick's phone number off a Bluurg cassette cover or something (people didn't shy away from publicising their home address and phone number back then) and rang him up, literally 'out of the blue', to see if they could be tempted to come and play The Horse & Jockey pub in the sleepy village of nearby Colwall, which of course they did (it would seem they turned down very few gigs in the early to mid-Eighties). We sold about 150 hand-numbered paper tickets at £1.50 each, paid the band the moment they arrived (I was desperate to off-load the money before I got pissed and lost it!), and a great night was had by all. We also had Discarded Remnants of an Age No More opening up, who were a two-piece from Malvern named after a lyric by The Mob, another seminal band from that period.

Unfortunately, we lost that venue – as we did most venues we booked at in the Eighties – because of trouble (the next gig we did there with Lunatic Fringe and Foreign Legion was spectacularly violent) – so we then talked our good friends The Dismembered from Upton-upon-Severn in Worcestershire into booking Subhumans at the Upton Memorial Hall and having Decadence Within as one of the supports (main support came courtesy of the brilliant Depraved).

Little did we know at the time that the band were nearing the end of their first incarnation, and we would soon be attending their 'final' gig. When news broke that the Subhumans were splitting, we were obviously gutted, and determined to make the pilgrimage to their (approximate) hometown of Warminster for their last show. It was in the Athenaeum, a pivotal place for the band, as you will read shortly, which was a seated venue so there was only room for a hundred or so to jump about in front of the stage and everyone else would be twitching in their seat, or straining to see past the dancing throng. I was of an age and inclination then (eighteen) to squeeze down the front and be in the thick of it, and it was a bittersweet moment, hearing them play 'No More Gigs' as their last song (before the inevitable flurry of encores, of course) – 'sweet' because they were at their brilliant best, and 'bitter' because we would never see them play live again. Or would we…? If only we knew then what we know now! The world was a much smaller place in the Eighties, and no one could have foreseen them becoming the enduring global phenomenon they are today.

Dick went on to do Culture Shock, which was good, but for me not a patch on the Subhumans – my teenage brain couldn't cope with so much reggae, and deep down I just wanted them to churn out endless variations of 'Worlds Apart' (the album, not the song) ad infinitum, not really grasping the concept of artistic license and evolution (I mean, bands *were* allowed to evolve, of course… but only if their evolution remained aligned with *my* musical tastes!). Our good friend Decadent Dave booked them to play our then-regular local venue (also soon to have its doors closed to us, thanks to yet more mindless violence…), the Herefordshire House, up in the Wyche Cutting, on top of the Malvern Hills. A beautiful spot that we relished inundating with crusty punks by booking bands like Culture Shock, Antisect and Amebix there. What was *really* beautiful though was that Decadence Within always got to support!

Talking of which, Decadence Within often played a cover of 'Religious Wars' live (us and about a thousand other bands, to be fair), and we once played it in Bath when Dick was in the crowd (we nearly bottled it when we realised a *real life* Subhuman was in the building). He was very gracious when we spoke to him afterwards, but said we'd maybe played it too well, i.e. slavishly reproducing the original instead of putting our own stamp on it.

That was something we were also guilty of when we recorded a version of 'Joe Public' for Bus Station Loonies vocalist Chris Willsher's proposed Subhumans tribute album in 1995. The project ran aground somewhere though, and the song didn't come out until I revived it when my own label, Blackfish, did a Subhumans tribute compilation in 1999, the 'Still Can't Hear the Words' CD – by which time, Decadence Within had split but, joy of joys, the Subhumans were back together. Chris gave me all the covers that bands had sent in for the project, and I collected a load more, and it turned into one of my favourite releases I put out on Blackfish. I even put together an anonymous ('til now!) band called Human Error, with various old mates, to cover 'It's Gonna Get Worse' and 'Not Me' because I couldn't stand the thought of a) only being on it once, and b) those songs not being covered. Ever humble and self-deprecating, Dick insisted we subtitle it 'The Subhumans Covers Album' rather than 'The Subhumans Tribute Album', as he wasn't really comfortable with bands 'paying tribute' to them. It reeked a bit too much like pedestals and stuff.

Their reformation wasn't something that filled me with dread, as many a punk reunion was wont to do, because this was a band I still genuinely loved. I just hoped there would be new material! And there was… although we had to wait eight years for the 'Internal Riot' album to appear, and then a further twelve years for 'Crisis Point'. Yes, after being incredibly prolific in the Eighties, these guys now make Metallica look like they're in a hurry (although it doesn't help when your drummer lives in Germany…), but they like to take their time and allow songs to ferment, and test them out on the road a bit, so when they do drop, they're always worth the wait.

And, pound for pound, they remain probably the best punk band the UK has ever produced. I've never seen them do a bad gig, and there's hardly a song of theirs that I'm not thrilled to hear over and over again. In the wonderfully intimate scene of underground punk, their canon of material is rightly regarded as a cornerstone of invention, integrity and inspiration, yet they remain some of the most level-headed and approachable people you could ever meet. And when they agreed to let me write this book with them/for them/about them, I was overjoyed – it genuinely feels like the book I've been building up to writing ever since I put pen to paper and ordered my first cassette from Bluurg Tapes back in 1981. Over forty years ago now, but forty years made a little easier in the company of these timeless tunes.

IAN GLASPER, JANUARY 2023

1982, PHOTO COPYRIGHT © PAUL SLATTERY

ACKNOWLEDGEMENTS

Front cover art – Nick Lant
Front cover live pic – Christine Boarts Larson
Back cover live pic – Havie Martinez
Back cover line-up pic – Tony Mottram
Cover and book design – Welly Artcore

My sincerest thanks to these wonderful people for allowing this book to happen, and making it such a pleasure to work on:

The Subhumans – Dick, Bruce, Phil, Trotsky, Grant, Andy – for their time, patience and cooperation, and for granting me permission to do this in the first place. Hope you like how it turned out! Michelle for putting up with me ruining her and Dick's weekends, Kev Tydeman for invaluable assistance with pictures and scanning, not to mention his enthusiasm for the project, Steve Hyland, Rachel/Baz for the proofreading, Jock McCurdy, Mel Bell, Pete & Paula Roadie, Colin 'Colsk' Latter, Hammy, Semi, Mooney, Tab, Tez, Erika Ransom, Bill Markley, Julian Newby, Chris Knowles, Ruth Elias, Nut, Andy Owen & Gary Scarth, Chris Boarts Larson, Andy Nazer & Gavin Bagshaw, Graham Burnett, Chris 'Wheelie' Willsher, Jay Whyte, Chris Hill (TCB Photography), Sarah, Lee, Shannon Saint Ryan, Gizz Butt, Jaz Wiseman & Marc Freeman, Rob & Karoline Collins, Sean Forbes, Min Stokes, Nick Lant, Richard Newson, Rob Berends, Patrick O'Neil, Nick Toczek, Rob Challice, Paul 'Mo' Mahoney, Stu Pid, Paul & Stew Summers, Peter Jones, Steve Cotton, Pete Stennett, Steve Bemand, Neil Duncan, Dai Joseph & Anthony Tooze, Sned, Paul Slattery, Will Binks, Rich Pickett, Tony Mottram, Havie Martinez, Pete & Julie, Sean Harrison, Scotty, Decadent Dave, Claire Callaghan, Sickboy Photography, Albert Licano, Andrew Le Poidevin, Welshy & The Human Error, Greg Daly, Daren Locke, Welly Artcore, Konstantin Sergeyev, Damon & Vique at Pirates Press, Greet Druyts, Tony & Gaz Suspect, David & Lou & the Earth Island family, Ramsey Kanaan & PM Press, Tim Cundle & Mass Movement, Alexandros Anesiadis, Joel McIver & Bass Guitar Magazine, James Sharples & Fistful of Metal, Miles Hackett & Down for Life, Neil Cox, Chris Burton, Mobs, my bandmates in Zero Again.

Respectfully dedicated to the memory of the following lovely people:

Steve Lucas
Nigel Johnston
John Loder
Calvin Sewell
Dean Uzzell

Gone but never forgotten.

1982 LINE-UP, PICTURE BY TONY MOTTRAM

1998 BY CLAIRE CALLAGHAN

CAST OF CHARACTERS

SUBHUMANS

Andy Gale – first drummer, 1980 – 1981

Bruce Treasure – guitarist, 1980 – now

Dick Lucas – vocalist, 1980 – now

Grant Jackson – first bassist, 1980 – 1983

Phil Bryant – second bassist, 1983 – now

Trotsky (AKA 'Trotsky'!) – second drummer, 1981 – now

ASSOCIATES

Andy Nazer – vocalist/bassist, Self Abuse

Andy Owen – Chippenham punk promoter

Andy 'Tez' Turner – vocalist, Xpozez & Instigators

Bill Markley – drummer, Organized Chaos

Chris Knowles – drummer, Hagar the Womb

Chris Larson Boarts – Slug & Lettuce fanzine

Chris 'Wheelie' Willsher – vocalist, The Bus Station Loonies

Colin 'Colsk' Latter – Flux of Pink Indians vocalist and co-founder of Spiderleg Records

Damon Bebe – Pirates Press Records

Erika Ransom – Maximum Rocknroll contributor, merch seller on 2007 US tour, wife of Phil

Graham Burnett – New Crimes fanzine

Hammy / Semi / Mooney / Tab – the Instigators

Gary Scarth – vocalist, The Lumps of Merde

Gizz Butt – guitarist, Destructors, English Dogs, Janus Stark, Prodigy etc.

Jay Whyte – stand-in bassist for Subhumans, 2013 – 2016

Jaz Wiseman – bassist/vocalist, Virus

Jock McCurdy – guitarist, A-Heads

Julian Newby – vocalist, Stupid Humans; guitarist, Organized Chaos

Kevin Tydeman – friend and photographer

Lee – vocalist, The Lumps of Merde

Mel Bell – vocalist, A-Heads

Michelle Diwell – artist, writer, co-founder of Bluurg TV

Min Stokes – friend, flying instructor and Australian tour booker

Nick Lant – cover artist

Nick Toczek – punk poet

Nut – (first) drummer, Lost Cherrees

Patrick O'Neil – tour manager on the Subhumans' 1984 US tour

Paul 'Mo' Mahoney – vocalist (then bassist), Onslaught

Paul & Stew Summers – guitarist & vocalist, Shrapnel

Peter Jones – guitarist, Paranoid Visions

Pete Stennett – owner of Small Wonder Records

Pete The Roadie – er, roadie (and vocalist, Kicker)

Rachel 'Baz' Ridley – proofreader and Guernsey correspondent!

Richard Newson – AKA Winston Smith, Sounds journalist

Rob Berends – Paperclip booking agency, Holland

Rob Challice – bassist, Faction

Rob & Karoline Collins – tour management, driver & merch team, USA

Ruth Elias – vocalist, Hagar the Womb

Sean Forbes – Wat Tyler, Hard Skin, Rugger Bugger Records, Demo Tape Records etc.

Shannon Saint Ryan – friend of the band and occasional live keyboardist on 'Susan'

Steve Bemand – guitarist, Smart Pils

Steve Cotton – editor, Crisis Point fanzine & Art of the State photo blog

Stu Pid – vocalist, Contempt, Police Bastard and Sensa Yuma

Vique Martin – label manager at Pirates Press Records

LIVE IN L.A. BY ALBERT LICANO

MAY 1982, PHOTO COPYRIGHT © PAUL SLATTERY

CONTENTS

9/9/98, WASHINGTON DC - BY CHRIS BOARTS LARSON

Every story has to start somewhere, and I suppose Warminster Community Centre on March 16th, 1979 (which was Mother's Day, if you're really interested), is as good a place as any. Warminster is a small army garrison town of about 18,000 people, in western Wiltshire, a landlocked county in southwest England steeped in pagan history, and home to the ancient stone circles of Stonehenge and Avebury, not to mention eight white horses carved into its rolling chalk hills.

And that seemingly random date was when young guitarist Bruce Treasure made his live debut with his first band, Vermin. If you're wondering why that is of such significance to this particular tale, it's because Vermin only played two gigs before they became Stupid Humans, who themselves only played three gigs before they became Sub Human, and then the Subhumans. But let's not get ahead of ourselves, because to understand the Subhumans, we need to look at the environment these musicians grew up in, and the many weird and wonderful influences that fed their musical approach.

"My first punk gig was The Stranglers at Bath Pavilion, September 1978," begins **Bruce**. "I would have been about fourteen or something. But my first ever, ever gig was 10cc a few years before that, which was very inspiring too. Before punk I was more into prog. When punk first came along, I didn't really like it... I didn't really understand it – the Sex Pistols were very yobbish, and I didn't really like that. But my sister Lou, who's four years older than me, went out with a biker in Bristol... well, he was a Hell's Angel, really – and the Angels were really into The Stranglers. A lot of the bikers were, so I got into The Stranglers because my sister went out with a biker, and from there I got into punk – it was like my musical route into it.

"Getting there [to The Stranglers gig] was fun. Mike Bradbury, who was in some of the bands around here, including Organized Chaos, was an older boy who got me into pretty bad things like smoking – I had my first cigarette with him. He was a bit of a punk mentor, who got me into lots of punk bands, and I went with him to The Stranglers. We got to Bath on the train, and then we watched the gig, but didn't have anywhere to stay afterwards, so we pretty much stayed in a telephone box for most of the night. Until I phoned someone who knew someone else with a friend in Bath. But we were just so amazed by the gig, it didn't really matter where we stayed.

"I was a big fan of Penetration as well. I went to see them in Bristol, in April 1979. I even wrote about them for one of my English projects at school. We were just inspired by Sounds and the NME, and copying what they did. I went to see a lot of bands – The Skids, The Clash, Elvis Costello, Richard Hell... and The Damned, who were with The Ruts, which was one of my favourite ever gigs – I got *really* into The Ruts after seeing them with The Damned in Bristol. They pretty much became my favourite band, for sound, and guitar tones, and musicianship, and all that – probably still are really. I was big time into them.

"It's funny how people get inspired by music and they want to get their own band together, whether they can play anything or not. And I got together with Mike and a few other people. I wanted to play Stranglers' songs but, of course, I couldn't manage to play them. We might have struggled through the blues riff in 'Queen of the Streets' or something, off their first album, because everyone sort of learnt that one. Apart from that, I couldn't really play.

"I think I pretty much always *wanted* to play though, even when I was really young. My first guitar was a classical guitar, which my brother got me, because he played classical, and I had a few lessons, which I didn't really enjoy. And my grandmother was a teacher, so she taught me some of the reading music stuff – which I didn't like at all, because I was interested in rock, and prog rock, and all that. I had nothing in common with what I was being taught. The music I was listening to was stuff my elder sisters were listening to – one's ten years older, and the other's four years older than me. So, there was lots of The Who, Pink Floyd, King Crimson… as a consequence, I had quite a prog understanding at an early age, I think? But what really decided it was an Elvis Presley film, where Elvis hit someone over the head with his guitar, and for some reason, that really did it for me. I was like, 'Wow, that's really cool…'

"That would have all been going on in Mangotsfield, near Bristol, where I lived until the last year of junior school, when my parents split up, and then we moved with my mum to Bath, where we lived with my grandmother for a year. I remember that last year of primary school was when I was bought a Black Sabbath album and a Yes album for my birthday… I don't know if that's unusual for a ten-year-old? [laughs]

"After that year in Bath, we moved to Warminster, and I was very keen on trying to customise my acoustic guitar. But it being a classical, it didn't really customise that well, so I ended up destroying it, like you do. I hassled an older boy who lived up the road here until he taught me how to play guitar. I learnt a few chords, and when I learnt barre chords, that's when I got into the idea of being in a band. I felt like I could play enough by then. Some friends of my mum, who we lived with, helped me make a guitar, but that didn't work very well because it was just made out of chipboard. Eventually I got my first Woolworths guitar for Christmas, when I was thirteen or something, and that was lovely to have. But it was a standard sunburst, with horrible pick-ups, so I customised it [see the cover of The Mental/Stupid Humans CDEP] with some help from a guy in Warminster, Jim, who's been helping me out forever – he helped me put a better pick-up in it. I put the pointy headstock on it, and someone else helped me take the finish off and make it natural. I still go and see Jim a lot today, but he's disgusted with the state of my guitars now, because they're covered in crap…

"Amps were a problem too, of course – because they're so expensive when you're young. I had this valve amp, which was a converted radio, and I just used to get shocks off it the whole time. So that was a very nice present from somebody, haha! I ended up getting rid of that, and got this plastic five-watt thing – but then when you start doing gigs – like the first Vermin gig – you realise that no one can hear you…"

Eventually joining Bruce in Vermin were vocalist Julian Newby, bassist Nigel Johnston and drummer Andy Gale, everyone knowing everyone else through school and their love of punk and skateboarding.

"Andy was the only one who'd had any real lessons in the band," recalls **Bruce**. "He bought his drum kit in bits, which was quite amazing – every week there'd be a few more drums! I think he bought a floor tom last, and it was a slightly different colour because he couldn't get one that matched. But we didn't have any gear… I always joked that we only had Julian in the band because he had an amplifier. We were just so full of ourselves though… it was all that young adrenalin, I suppose.

"Vermin was my first band. Julian and Andy were in a band before that called The Castrators. I can't remember how I met them, but we all went to Kingdown [a comprehensive, secondary modern school], out by the army camp here in Warminster. I remember Julian used to work in a building yard opposite Kingdown, called John Wallis Titt's… yeah, I know, what a great name for a company! He used to dress all punky, and he was into skateboarding – he had a skateboard that he put metal mudguards on. It was a bit ridiculous; it was really heavy. A few of us were into skateboarding though… I certainly was. Ju used to skateboard to work every day, and I might have just met him when he was skating up the road. He used to write lyrics on his coffee break at work.

"We used to use the skateboards to transport our gear, because it was a long way to the community centre, so we'd put our amps on skateboards and push them along. Warminster never had a skate park or anything. When Subhumans did our first Bowes Lyon House gig a few years later [17/5/81], I remember being so impressed because they had a skateboard park right behind the venue. And that was the first time I'd ever seen one. I was really into it; I used to spend a lot of time looking at all the pictures in the skateboard books I had.

"I might have met Julian through Mike Bradbury. Mike was a bit older, and was in his year at school, so I think that was probably the connection. So much music came from Julian – he was into the Banshees, The Dickies, Punishment of Luxury, Eater… wow, I just loved Eater, and I heard them through Julian. Interestingly, [Subhumans vocalist] Dick was really into Eater as well… certainly their music anyway, not sure about the lyrics. Mind you, a lot of bands had bad lyrics back then, didn't they? Andy was really into Tubeway Army… so was Ju, so we all got into their first few singles, and the first album."

"I first met Bruce in 1979," recalls **Julian**. "I was above him at school. There was a little note on the board outside the headmaster's office that said, 'I'm looking for a singer!' And I thought, 'Oh, I could do that!' I had no idea who he was, but I looked him up, and he was from 'the Warminster hippy family', and I contacted him, to see

3

BRUCE, JULIAN, NIGE AND ANDY, VERMIN

JULIAN, NIGE AND ANDY

BRUCE AND NIGE, VERMIN

BRUCE

what he was doing. And he said to me, 'Have you got an amp?' 'Nope!' 'Have you got a microphone?' 'Nope!' 'What do you do then?' 'I don't know, but I want to be part of something…'

"I was already in a very loose band by then called The Castrators, but we were just hanging around really, it was more of an idea for a band… we didn't even know what alcohol was at that point, haha!

"I was really into Eater and Slaughter and the Dogs. I wasn't so much into the Pistols like everyone else seemed to be, although they were *there*, you know what I mean? I was more into Eater. And they were disgustingly terrible, haha! We used to go and see them up in London, and they couldn't play a gig without something going terribly wrong. I'd hang around up in Bristol with Beki Bondage, and her boyfriend at the time, Igor, and we'd go up to London, go to Carnaby Street and the Kings Road, get into nonsense with the mods… with our raggedy clothes and food colouring in our hair.

"But I was born and bred in Warminster, and went to Kingdown School. That was where I met Bruce. And we used to skateboard together… there was a natural progression with us. My skateboard had these big mudguards on it, haha! We became mates, and I'd go round his house, where we'd sit around listening to Cheech and Chong records.

"The one thing – the main thing! – we always said was, the best rule was no rules… so there *were* no rules. Everything was wide open; we didn't have to worry about any conformity. We could play whatever we liked; we had no idea what we were playing anyway, we just played it. We had no idea what we were doing at all really. Bruce had his stupid little guitar, and I had my stupid voice. He bought this guitar from Woolworths, and it came as a sunburst finish, and we just put a sander on it and shaved it all off… it was some sort of rebellious statement. But then things got a bit deeper as well."

"It was the last year of school, when I suddenly heard this band, the Sex Pistols," remembers **Andy** fondly, picking up the story, "And The Jam were about then as well, who I really liked, who were a slightly different thing, but it was the Sex Pistols who kicked it off for me really. And before long, a few of us got together at school and thought, 'Perhaps we could have a go at this?' That was with different people to start with… I can't actually remember how I first met Bruce. I think I met him after I left school, through a friend of a friend. But I didn't have any equipment. I was going round to Julian's house, and I was hitting this plastic chair, and they had makeshift guitars, and we started making things up.

"It was probably through my dad," he continues, when asked as to how he ended up drumming. "He played drums, so I was probably influenced by him. He didn't play a full drum kit; he used to play a side drum and things like that, in a skiffle band. And basically, that's how we got started, and once we started working to earn a bit of money, we gradually got some gear. I went as an apprentice painter and decorator, and started buying bits of a drum kit. Being an apprentice, I was on stupid money, a fraction of what a tradesman would earn, and couldn't afford a whole kit, so I bought it one piece at a time. I saved every spare penny I had.

"But I loved the drums, and just had a good sense of rhythm. People used to take the mickey out of me, saying I played like Animal from The Muppets, haha! I taught myself to play, just sat in my bedroom with headphones on, in front of my partially built drum kit, playing along to my records. I just tried to soak up how other people played.

"My father was in the army, which was how we ended up in Warminster [Warminster has been home to the British Army installation, Battlesbury Barracks, since 1965]. And the punk scene was quite big here. Although personally I never looked like a typical punk rocker at all, I was drawn to the excitement of it all, of being able to express yourself. I didn't feel the need to look like one, but I loved to get behind that kit and go for it.

"It was difficult for me, actually, being in a punk band, because my dad didn't like it at all. One of my singles was 'God Save the Queen' by the Sex Pistols, and I was blasting it out in my bedroom… of course, dad was in the army, a royalist, and came marching up the stairs, and smashed my record to pieces! He was not keen at all. He helped me move my drum kit around a few times, but he definitely wasn't keen…"

"I found my old school project where I wrote about the bands back then," **Bruce** admits ruefully. "We gave ourselves all these silly names – that I'm not sure I want in print, haha! We were so full of it. I was 'Willy Wombat', which was just ridiculous. And slightly embarrassing looking back… why did we do that? I suppose it was fun at the time, and it wasn't just *me* doing it."

With Nigel adopting the stage moniker of 'Yo Yo', Ju known as 'Plug' and Andy as 'Worm', Vermin saw the creation of at least one song that has stood the test of time…

"We had songs like 'Clinic of Doom', 'Get Off of My Back' and 'The Fuzz'… I still think about some of those songs today. We had eight in all, I think, and then Stupid Humans did some of those, and so did Sub Human, which Dick refers to as 'Subhumans # 1' in the family trees he does. Subhumans took on a lot of songs that we were doing in the Stupid Humans, but the only Vermin song that has carried on through all the bands is 'New Age'. That was originally a Vermin song.

"We were being inspired by everything," he adds, of the family trees that were produced of the interconnected Wiltshire bands at the time. "I found a really good cutting that I'm going to frame in the attic the other day; it's the original Sex Pistols family tree, and how they connect to The Clash and The Slits… there was about fifteen people in just one of those bands, and there's all this wonderful writing all over the family tree, about all the bands… and it came out in NME or Sounds. And I think everyone was inspired by it, to try and do the same. But they were proper bands, of course, and some of ours were just planned.

"I was always interested in arrangements. Even when I wrote 'New Age' – when I first started playing barre chords, and realised that the chords could go down, then it's nice

POGO PROMOTION

PRESENT

STALAG 44

PLUS

VERMIN + DISCO

AT

chapmanslade village hall

SATURDAY 21ST. APRIL

DOORS OPEN 7·30. BAR. £1·00

JULIAN, VERMIN

JULIAN AND BRUCE, STUPID HUMANS

ANDY GALE

KINGDOWN SCHOOL

if the bass goes *up*. Again, it seemed to make sense to me, and it's a good way to write music if things are going in different directions.

"When the Subhumans formed, we just needed some songs – so why not use the songs from the last band, at least until we had written some new ones… and that's what we did. Although Dick obviously improved them all; he came along and made much more sense of everything.

"But Vermin only did two gigs. Our first one – and my very first gig – was at the Sunday night disco at the community centre, down at the army camp in Warminster [the aforementioned Mother's Day bash]; they used to have a disco down there every Sunday. And we *had* to go to them, like you did, even though you hated discos. Andy's dad worked there, I think, so he got us that first Vermin gig. But we'd go there on Sunday nights and get them to play the odd punk record."

The second Vermin gig was at the Village Hall in Chapmanslade, three miles northwest of Warminster, on April 21st, 1979, with Stalag 44. A month or two later, Nige left, going on to join Stalag 44, making way for Herb to join on bass, and the band became the Stupid Humans.

Meanwhile, in nearby Melksham, Dick Lucas joined his brother Steve in their formative band The Mental during March 1979, and they played *their* first gig, in Winchester's Milner Hall, a few months later, on June 23rd.

"My earliest musical influences probably came from Ed ['Stewpot'] Stewart of Radio One on a Saturday morning," reckons **Dick**, "And my dad's record collection, which involved a lot of organ music, classical music, and a bit of The New Seekers, which he liked for some reason. So, I wasn't really exposed to pop culture until going to school, when I noticed people were singing Beatles songs – all these kids aged seven going around singing, 'She loves me, yeah, yeah yeah!' and I'm thinking, 'What's all that about? What does it mean? Where's it come from? What's going on?' I didn't have much clue about popular music as I grew up, and there wasn't loads of music in our house when I was a kid. Although our dad was in a choir, and our mum was the organist in the same church, so there was a *bit* of musical background.

"Then me and my brother Steve were packed off to boarding school, which was where we later formed The Mental. At boarding school, I got subjected to alternatives to pop culture, which were still mainstream, but included things like Black Sabbath and David Bowie's weirder stuff… that was the good bits. But in the meantime, you just got bombarded with all this pop stuff coming off the charts every Sunday, and stuff like that. It was a release, to check out the charts every Sunday, and some of it was quite good. Before punk rock, I guess my favourite bands were probably ELP, Yes and Black Sabbath – things that were either heavy, or complex enough to be interesting. I didn't realise then – until punk rock came about – that nothing they sang about had any element of surprise or challenge to the status quo… nothing made you angry or prompted you to question anything whatsoever. And that's probably the largely overlooked element of punk rock, that really made punk rock so important to people – it was saying something about things you could relate to.

"From the age of sixteen, I was listening to Alan ['Fluff'] Freeman on his Saturday afternoon Rock Show, and he played 'Bored Teenagers' by The Adverts, and I was like, 'Wow!' Not only were they putting all the heavy bits from a Black Sabbath album into a two-minute song – and sped up! – but they were singing about bored teenagers, and I was like, 'Yeah, I can relate to that!' And it was the same with The Clash and the Sex Pistols… a song like 'No Fun' was so good, because until then all the pop songs were about people *having* fun! Just the title 'Pretty Vacant'… what does it mean? It didn't matter; it sounded fantastic.

"So, I got well into the nihilistic side of punk rock – the joys of negativity, perhaps you wanna call it? Just irking people, winding them up, going against the grain… it just felt really good to be into that sort of thing. And you felt connected to the people saying these things, because like most teenagers – with the benefit of hindsight – you were feeling pretty alienated by the way your life was going. Especially in boarding school. And I say 'especially' because I went to one – I didn't go to grammar school, or whatever you call it – but have no doubt – well, *some* doubt – that my mental state would have been roughly the same, wherever I'd gone. I was just trying to find some sense of self-control: I was confused and annoyed at all sorts of things going on all over the planet, and didn't have much real clue as to the nature of how things work.

"Now, that clue came along a couple of years later, when I was leaving school, around about 1979, when I heard Crass, and Crass were singing about 'the system'… I didn't even know there was such a thing as 'the system' – was it some sort of collective noun? And the system was [quotes 'Banned from the Roxy' by Crass], 'School, army, church, the corporation deal, a fucked-up reality based on fear, a fucking conspiracy to stop you feeling real…' I wasn't instantly transformed into an anarcho punk there and then, but those four lines, beginning with 'Their systems? Christ, they're everywhere…' summed up for me – and still sum up – the essence of anarcho punk. And opened a door to a world where bands could say, 'We're punk rock, we take things seriously, and this is what is going on!'

"Until then, I'd never thought of the church as part of a system; I'd never thought of the church as anything apart from somewhere you got dragged along to when you were a kid. It was all God and Jesus, and I didn't believe it, wasn't interested in it, so whatever. But then you start to realise there are patterns in society, that are all about controlling the masses, to make the minority all the money, all the profit, all the luxuries of life that everyone else is supposed to be aiming for – which is why we're all set into the pattern of school, possibly university, get a job, succeed, get property, get married, have kids, retire

DICK, THE MENTAL

DICK AND STEVE, THE MENTAL

JUST ANOTHER MUZIK-BIZ SHATTERIN' FREE TOUR
WiTH HERE 3c NOW

AUGUST DATES

* 19 · COLCHESTER · ESSEX UNI ·
* 20 · MANCHESTER · SALFORD UNI ·
21 · OLDHAM · TOWER CLUB · with the FALL
22 · LIVERPOOL · PICKWICK CLUB with the FALL
* 23 · STOKE · KEELE UNI ·
24 · STROUD · MARSHALL ROOMS
* 25 · DEVIZES · CORN EXCHANGE
26 · BIRMINGHAM · SMALL HEATH PARK
* 27 · NORWICH · UNI · (THE BARN)   (PHONE FOR DETAILS)
* 28 · HIGH WYCOMBE · NAGS HEAD
* 29 · LONDON · COLL · PRINTING · ELEPHANT + CASTLE
* 30 · BRIGHTON · UNI · SUSSEX
31 · WATFORD · CAREY CLUB

AND ALTERNATIVE T.V. at all gigs with *

LIVE ALBUM "WHAT YOU SEE IS WHAT YOU ARE" BY A.T.V. / HERE · NOW ON SALE AT GIGS PRICE £1 OR MAIL ORDER £1·50 · GRANT SHOWBIZ · 67 · STONELEIGH ST · LONDON W.11 ·

1978 - HERE AND NOW AND ATV UK TOUR - THE DEVIZES
GIG WITH THE MOB WAS DICK'S FIRST GIG

THE MENTAL, BASINGTOKE, 1979 BY NEIL DUNCAN

and die. And if you can die as soon after you stop working as possible, they get the most out of you and pay you less pension… full stop, haha!"

Although Dick says he would have almost certainly 'turned out' the same way regardless of whether he went to a boarding school or an open state school, there is little doubt that his upbringing did shape his personality to an extent. How could it not?

"Yeah, there wasn't an end to the day… well, there was an end to the *school* day, when you stopped learning stuff, when the classes stopped. And then you'd go to the dining hall to have your tea, where you sat down with your tray, and then there was prep time, as they called it, which was an hour or an hour and a half to do whatever homework had been set that day. And then there was a bit of free time before you went to bed, which varied, depending upon how old you were.

"You slept in a dormitory with about twenty other kids, and when you got into the sixth form you got your own little cubicle, your own personal space, so you could get away from everyone else. And that's where I was trading punk rock bootleg tapes from, live tapes of the Pistols and The Clash, that sorta thing, making copies and swapping them for records and stuff. Bootleg records were a big thing – all still advertised in the back of Sounds and NME at that point, before they started clamping down on that sort of stuff. I'd get the homework out the way as fast as possible, and then settle down copying tapes, and covering my walls with graffiti and little notes, silly drawings of eggs, whatever.

"The thing that eventually became Bluurg Tapes, I originally called The Electric List, and came from that tape trading. There was lots of trading going on back then… each generation copy sounded worse than the one before it! I've still got all those in the garage, never got rid of any of them, although they've probably leaked oxide all over the place. But this was when I was still at boarding school; instead of doing homework or whatever, I gradually built up this list – The Electric List. Until I left school and called it Bluurg… probably after the sound you make when you throw up? And I went from bootleg stuff to local stuff – I just thought I'd make my own bootlegs of any bands I got to see. And no one cared about you taking tape recorders into gigs in those days… they didn't mind what you did really.

"There was not a lot of outlets for your own creativity at boarding school… although there *were* a lot of rules, and a lot of timetables. But there was rebellion of sorts. The masters had their own bit of the dining hall where they ate their food; they ate way better food than what we did, and whatever they left behind was still sat there on plates, for some reason not cleared up yet… until now, I've not really thought about that – but at 2 am, we'd be in there, getting all this spare food that was still sitting on their plates, not thinking that they must have been eating this hours ago and no one had cleared it up. What's that all about? Never mind!

"So, we'd nick whatever food was left, and take it back to the dorms and eat it. Just do naughty stuff… like smoking was really naughty, 'cos if you got caught, you got suspended – and if you got caught twice, you got expelled. They were pretty heavy on that sort of thing. Now and again someone would bring some booze in – that would be fun. But these were small rebellions.

"We were in a mini-society, 'cos we didn't go home from everybody at the end of the day. It wasn't like you might see some of your mates from school later on, down the disco, or anything. You're with your mates, and your enemies, basically the people you live with, all the time…"

And no girls?

"No, no girls! Although ironically there are girls there now, they've opened it out. But that was the main difference of not going to a normal school – we missed out on all that social and sexual knowledge until we were out of school. When I completely didn't know what I was doing – in that area, so to speak. Still, that sorted itself out.

"But it was all based on male hierarchy, and a male values system – there were several fights that were almost advertised… 'There's a fight going on!' Such and such against somebody else. And they were just fighting for more credit for themselves – if they could win a fight, they would have more sway over other people. There were a lot of fights going on. And if you were good at certain things, you had higher status… and by certain things, I mean contact sport – rugby, football… if you were good at those things, you were tough, you had credit. And if you were anywhere near intellectual, you were just a wimp, or whatever. Those that were actually *very* intellectual, rose above all that, ignored it, carried on and got, like, A+ in their exams, and probably went on to work for the Bank of England – who knows?"

You said in your interview for my 'The Day the Country Died' book that you *were* a 'wimp' at school – which I could certainly relate to. It was one of the things that attracted me to punk actually. Being a bit odd and downtrodden was almost a pre-requisite!

"Yeah, absolutely – I was persecuted… bullied… whatever the word is. I was in that weird place where you try to get on with the people that are pissing you off, just to make them stop doing it. I was in this small social circle with six or eight people, in the same dormitory anyway – and you can't really avoid people when you're sleeping in the same space – and you could say I was too sensitive. But that's a really shit excuse, because basically the sensitive people should be ruling the world, and not all these insensitive fucks. And people who bully people are just the worst scum in the world, so it didn't really help my view of everything – they don't get anything out of it other than seeing people upset or freaked out, and then they do it again, to make it worse. But I couldn't get myself into the head space that said you should fight back, to give as good as you get – some people just can't do it… I couldn't do it.

"And then punk rock came along, and provided me with something that connected me to all these other people that were into punk rock. Most of them were my brother's age – two years younger than me… people of my age were just sort of set in their rock ways, and they stuck with it, Neil Young and all that shit. But punk rock opened this door, instantly, to new friends, because we just liked the same music – it was brilliant. You could just jump about to it. And you could cut your own hair. This was in the Seventies, and everybody at boarding school wanted to grow their hair as long as possible, before they were stuck on the list of people that had to go and see the barber when he came round. I hated it – but when punk rock came along, I thought, 'Fuck it, I'll cut my own hair!' And then I spiked it up – and they couldn't do anything about it. The only haircut rule was to keep it short; they hadn't imagined people would go DIY and cut their own! There's a Johnny Moped song that starts off, 'One, two, cut yer hair!' It was an act of subversion!

"My first actual punk gig was during one of my school holidays in 1978; I went to Devizes to see Here and Now on their free tour of the UK. They played with Alternative TV and The Mob, and a couple of other bands I can't remember. Me and my mate got a lift with my dad, bless him, to Devizes, seven miles away, and got dropped off. My mate took one look through the door, shit himself, and walked seven miles back home again! Which I think was a turning point in our lives really – he never went to another punk rock gig again in his life, and I went to loads of them after that. It was free, which was nice – someone was passing a hat round – and loads of flashing lights… it was Here and Now, after all, so lots of people with long hair and Afghan coats, and not many punk rockers. I briefly saw Mark Perry stood outside the venue, this small hall, afterwards. I was just kinda blitzed by the whole thing.

"And then my dad came and picked me up. My dad was great. He took me, and several other people, to lots of places that we could only get to by hitching or buses, so often over the years, and he didn't like the music… 'Too many drums!', he said. He doesn't like drums in his music, which pretty much cuts out everything, haha! I offered to make him a boxset once, of everything I'd ever done, and he said, 'Oh, I wouldn't like it… too many drums!' He asked me if I'd been drinking once, when he picked me up from Trowbridge, and I said, 'Oh, a couple of pints…' And he said, 'A couple of pints? That's a *quart!*' But he didn't drink or smoke – which is why he's still alive at ninety-four…

"Ironically enough, although I was at the same school as my brother Steve, we didn't see each other much, which was annoying 'cos we kinda drifted apart, because we were in different 'houses'. We'd just see each other now and again. But we were both into punk rock, as were a lot of people his age, and – with the general message of punk rock being, 'Anyone can do this!' – we thought, 'Yeah, let's do this!' So Steve bought himself a guitar from Woolworths for £26 – bargain! Back when Woolworths had guitars hanging up on their walls for £26. He borrowed it off our dad, I think. Actually, Steve bought himself a bass, and was a bassist to start with, because his mate, Si – or 'Si Kick', as he called himself – was a guitarist [Steve and Si Kick had formerly messed about musically as first The Clones, and then Ed Ibble and the Plastic Sandwiches] and a chap called Tony

16

[Delvalle] was a drummer. He was a rarity because he actually had a drum kit. And there we all were: a punk band in this boarding school. So, we went to practise at Si Kick's parents' place, somewhere in the Basingstoke area, where the school was. We'd go over there every other Saturday or so, clear a space in the garage and make a right racket. And we invented all these pretty-okay songs… they were great to us anyway, just because they existed, and they had a start and an end, and I managed to write some lyrics to them. None of them were very good, and a lot of them were complete rubbish, but the ones that weren't complete rubbish ended up being The Mental songs.

"Before The Mental there were a few other things going on, but they were more ideas than bands that did anything, and only lasted a month or two. There were then seven line-ups of The Mental!

"And that all chugged along nicely, until we got to '79. I left school at eighteen; the rest of them left at sixteen… actually Steve got expelled. And we finally did our first gig in Winchester; Si Kick organised it… he organised most of our gigs actually. We had about eight songs, there were about twenty-five people watching, and it was in Milner Hall, which was run by nuns or something? No stage, just like a youth centre type place. God knows how Si Kick found this place for a gig, but he did.

"At that point, we had Toby on guitar as well; we had two guitars going on, and we were just awful… lots of feedback, the songs would stop and start again. And we played one song three times just because we knew how to play that one the best. There might have been one other band playing – Si had connections with local bands in his area. He lived in a town called Tadley, and there was The Urge, Kinetic Energy and another band called Level 5… I think? There's a band called The Irritations somewhere in my memory too. We did ten gigs anyway, and the first was just as we were leaving school.

"I didn't fit the 'front man' thing at all. I got embarrassed, because it was all collapsing around me. And I could only just remember the words – which wasn't too hard… you're only talking three or four verses max. It was pretty chaotic. Some gigs were better than others; some gigs were more like gigs should be – you know, you start and stop together, get through to the end of the set having played most of the songs right, and people like it. We played in Chippenham once, with Vice Squad… we got through one song and the guy turned the PA off! He just said, 'Sorry, you're crap, get off!' And that was it. We were like, 'What? We sounded really good!' I'm not sure PA guys should have that kind of power, haha!

"I couldn't play anything, which is why I ended up singing, I suppose. I was writing lyrics before I was singing – they were poems, but I thought, 'I could sing these, and call 'em songs, and get in a band!' There was a lot of drinking going on, and a fair bit of glue going on with some of the people… well, all of us, at some point, tried sniffing glue. It didn't catch on with me though – I even wrote down in my diary exactly what I was thinking whilst I was on the glue, so at least something came out of it. Even if it was

17

how to stare at the fireplace for twenty minutes and feel completely interested in it. But generally, you just got a massive headache and felt stupid. And I saw other people that were doing it, and thought, 'I don't wanna be like that…'

"I left school in June '79, and carried on living in Melksham. As soon as I knew Bruce, and got in the Subhumans, every weekend was spent in Warminster, but before that, two or three nights every week were in Trowbridge, for weekend drinking or the Wednesday disco and gathering of the masses! It would be Tuesday at the Conservative Club, across the car park from where I lived, who had an alternative disco every Tuesday night, where the mods and punks of Melksham would gather in their very small numbers, and stare at each other across the floor and dance about to their own music… that sort of thing. Very small town stuff, but that's how you learn about things, especially after being in boarding school for the previous seven years or whatever. I'd discovered there was a small punk scene in Melksham at these Tuesday night discos, and found out there was a disco going on every Wednesday in Trowbridge, which they all went to as well, so I went along with them, and made a load of new punk friends over there. That was a regular weekly hangout for the next year and a half."

It was at an Angelic Upstarts gig, at the Civic Hall in Trowbridge, on September 14th, 1979, that Dick and Bruce first met in person, sowing the seeds for their lasting musical collaboration.

"It was so rare for a national band that everyone had heard of to be playing Trowbridge, everyone was freaking out about it," **Dick** remembers, "So, I was very excited, and went to that, which is where I met Bruce for the first time, who I knew to be in the Stupid Humans. And it was like, 'Are you in a band?' 'Yeah! Why? Are you in a band too?' 'Yeah!' It seemed like *everyone* was in a band. And we got on really well. Bruce was calling himself 'Willy Wombat', for some reason.

"Steve had asked the Civic Hall if The Mental could support the Upstarts, but they said no. Oh well, we tried. It was Vice Squad, The Wall, and I think No Gods supporting… can't remember who *they* were though?"

"I remember Dick had his tapes for sale," says **Bruce**. "He was interesting, because he was selling, or swapping, tapes. And probably recording the gig too. As well as being in The Mental, of course."

"I had an old tape deck that I carried about with a microphone, trying to record the gigs I went to," explains **Dick**, "But the recording was usually just distortion. And that was where the idea of Bluurg Tapes later came from, these bootleg live recordings I used to swap. But Bruce and I just clicked because we were both in bands. And I think I'd heard of Stupid Humans from someone at the weekly Trowbridge disco, who'd told me that they were one of the best bands in the area, so then I went to check out one of their practices. I was well impressed and hung out and had a few drinks."

"There was a lot of violence and fighting at that Trowbridge gig," adds **Bruce**. "Mensi [from the Upstarts – RIP] got into an argument with somebody in the audience, and this person got up onstage and started walking towards him – and then Mensi headbutted him. And there was blood everywhere, and then the police came, which they always seemed to do back then… and then there was a riot!"

On September 23rd, 1979, The Mental recorded their first EP, the cheekily entitled 'Extended Play E.P.', onto eight-track tape somewhere in Reading, with Martin Maynard engineering. A self-released effort, each one in a hand-numbered photocopied cover (with Steve Lucas billed as 'Steve Collapsible'), it's an obscure but fun 7", featuring four tracks of simplistic fuzzed-out punk rock, reminiscent of Bristol's Court Martial (although *they* didn't form until a year later, so I should really say Court Martial sounded like The Mental?), but Dick's sneering voice was unmistakable even then. And the sing-song intro to 'Kill the Bill' (set to the tune of 'London Bridge Is Falling Down') – 'Harry Roberts is our friend, is our friend, is our friend, Harry Roberts is our friend, he kills coppers… let him out to kill some more, kill some more, kill some more, let him out to kill some more, Harry Roberts!' – was a regular anti-police chant of the time, Harry Roberts having shot dead two plainclothes policemen in Shepherd's Bush in 1966.

"The recording of the first EP had been farcical," admits **Dick**. "We went over to Reading, with Martin, and we just went in, ran through each song two or three times until we got to the end without fucking up, and he'd press record. Then he said, 'Right, we're going to have a break now…' and we went to the pub, because he wanted a drink, so we got half-cut before going back in to play them all again. Then we got a load of our friends in to do that 'Harry Roberts is our friend' bit for 'Kill the Bill'. And then we sorta mixed it, and it sounded okay, but it was straight in and make a noise – there was no thought about quality, not even from the bloke doing it, who didn't care.

"We invented a name for our own record label, Kamikaze Pig. We just doodled on a bit of paper and made that the cover, and slapped The Mental on the top of it. Si Kick had them made up somewhere; I think 700 copies survived the process… we asked for 1000, and got 700 back, and I don't know what happened to the others. Si Kick sorted it all out though; I never did ask him how he managed it… just through making phone calls, I guess. I know he scrounged the money off me to finance it! Rough Trade took it on, and sold the lot. John Peel played 'God for a Day' twice on his show. And I was like, 'John Peel! Yes!' Because I was a total John Peel addict."

Was he important in informing your musical taste?

"Very! At boarding school, in the late Seventies, I was listening to Radio Caroline, the pirate ship station [it was literally broadcast from various ships, to avoid the constraints of British broadcasting laws], where Emperor Rosko would play some punk rock, like the first Blondie single… even Blondie was punk rock back then. He was playing it at

COUNCIL START INVESTIGATION

By Stephen Hughes

LANDLORD Mr Gordon Ormston-Heron, organiser of a punk rock dance in Trowbridge which ended in a brawl, said last night: " Never again."

The dance in the town's civic hall, attended by 200 punks, erupted in violence 20 minutes from the end.

Fighting broke out, glasses and chairs were smashed, clothes pegs ripped down in the cloakrooms and obscene slogans daubed on the walls.

Two teenage girls have been bailed to appear before Trowbridge magistrates on October 11, charged with causing criminal damage.

Top of the bill at the dance on Friday night were the Angelic Upstarts, who have attracted a violent following in the past.

RUINED

Their manager Mr Tony Gordon admitted before the dance: "They do have a working class following which sometimes erupts in anger."

Mr Ormston-Heron, who runs the White Swan, said he was angry and disappointed that a handful of people had ruined a good night.

"It is the first time I have organised a dance and I will not have anything to do with punk in the future.

"I was let down by some bands at the last minute and the Angelic Upstarts were a last minute stand in. I knew nothing of their reputation. I am very disappointed and sorry it happened. Once again it was the minority spoiling things for the majority."

Mr Gerald Garland, chief executive of West Wiltshire

Hadrian Strutt, aged ten, Ivor Summers, 11, Darren Pendleton, six, and Richard Harding, ten, as British soldiers in the Zulu war on the Bishops Lydeard Primary School float.

Tips for success pay

Story: John Thorne   Picture: Francis Strothard

THE organisers of Bishops Lydeard village carnival had to say a big thank you to neighbouring Taunton carnival committee for the success of Saturday's event.

The Taunton committee secretary Mr Colin Critchard gave advice to the village secretary Mrs Thomasine Dart on how to improve the procession.

And the judges of the 19 entries were also provided by Taunton organisers.

The local Gulliford family swept the board in the walking entries which were up on last year.

Mr Nick Gulliford and his wife Bunty took first and second in the adult's fancy dress class as French Revolutionaries.

And their children William, aged ten, and Hermione, eight, won first prize in the group entries as French Aristocrats.

The procession was led by carnival queen Abigail Baels and her attendants Jane Waites and Janet Bellringer.

Fancy dress, under eight: 1, Somerset Cricketer (Ben Jowett), 2, Mare, Mary (Kate Jowett); Over eight: 1, Clown (David Clark) 2, Drunken Sailor (Les...

INVESTIGATION

By Stephen Hughes

LANDLORD Mr Gordon Ormston-Heron, organiser of a punk rock dance in Trowbridge which ended in a brawl, said last night: " Never again."

The dance in the town's civic hall, attended by 200 punks, erupted in violence 20 minutes from the end.

Fighting broke out, glasses and chairs were smashed, clothes pegs ripped down in the cloakrooms and obscene slogans daubed on the walls.

Two teenage girls have been bailed to appear before Trowbridge magistrates on October 11, charged with causing crimi-

YOUR MONEY AT WORK

Lager lure for the

THE MENTAL, TADLEY BY NEIL DUNCAN

the same time John Peel was, although I hadn't discovered John Peel quite yet, but then I did. And our dad had this reel-to-reel recorder, so I'd be phoning up from school, asking him to record John Peel, and then when I came home for half-term or holidays, I'd take all the good stuff from his show off the reel-to-reel onto cassette. I compiled about twenty cassettes of what I considered the best stuff John Peel played, including some of the sessions he did with bands. I wish I'd recorded his voice between the songs, because he did say some cracking stuff before playing something, but I cut all that out. Never mind.

"John Peel was a *major* factor in knowing which records to buy. At first, you'd just buy anything that looked punk rock, but then you bumped into a couple of singles that looked it but were shite. And you didn't have enough money to waste on shite records.

"Years later, just before Subhumans released 'From the Cradle to the Grave' [1983], I sent a copy to John Peel and asked if we could get a session, and he sent a postcard back saying that he was up for it, but John Waters, his producer, was not. So we were *that* close to doing a session. Even Crass had a session, so it wasn't the politics… maybe his producer was on an off-day?"

December 1979 also saw Andy taking part in a thirty-six-hour drum marathon at Warminster Youth Club, to raise money for the International Year of the Child. Three other local teenage drummers took part, Derrick Murray, David Stephens from Moskow and Bill Markley from Audio Torture and Organized Chaos.

"I remember it well," says **Bill**. "It was a straight thirty-six hours, but I only did thirty-three; I didn't quite get to the end. And my old man wouldn't come and pick me up, I had to stagger home, haha! Andy did the whole thirty-six! But we just kept drumming – the band even came in and had a practice with me, then went home to bed, and came back for another practice, and I was still going! The hard part was staying awake, but having two or three other drummers in there, we all kept each other going, helped each other out if we saw someone flagging. And we were allowed a ten-minute break every hour and a half, or something like that…. a quick comfort break. But we were only seventeen, and full of energy."

Friday 14th December was another especially pivotal date, as that was not only the first Stupid Humans gig – having renamed themselves after Nigel was replaced by Herb – but they were on the same bill as The Mental.

"Yes, that was at the Athenaeum [in the Warminster High Street], supporting Vice Squad, The Mental and Stalag 44," clarifies **Bruce**, "Which my diary assures me was excellent on our part, as I have given us '10/10', haha! It was an interesting gig though. The Vice Squad drummer [Shane Baldwin] nailed his drum kit to the floor, to stop it sliding around, but it made it really awkward for all the other bands, who couldn't move any of the stands. They did their sound-check, and then nailed everything down, and all the other bands had to use it as it was. And I'm sure [Vice Squad vocalist] Beki Bondage talks about that as being one of their worst gigs ever? There was a lot of problems with squaddies in those days, and it was a bit of a nightmare.

"Stalag 44 had some pretty neat songs. These were older people who knew what they were doing… who had proper amplifiers and stuff. Tim Waterman had a nice little valve amp, and actually knew about tone. We had a little dig at them in private, because we were very jealous and envious, so we'd slag them off, and try and get the dirt on them as much as possible, but they were really good, with catchy songs. I can still remember one of their songs, 'City Life', to this day. They were a great band."

"That one was quite eventful, a packed-out gig," elaborates **Dick**. "We played pretty well, if I recall – we at least managed to go through the whole set without stopping too long. There might have been some trouble there… it seemed a bit like there was some kind of trouble at every punk show. And Vice Squad had a bunch of skinheads following them around, which didn't help. Vice Squad were very big; they were in Sounds and Garry Bushell loved them."

"Vice Squad made the mistake of going out to the local pub over the road before the gig started," laughs **Andy**, "Which was where all the soldiers went, and all the bikers, so it kicked off. It spilled out into the street, and then into the Athenaeum when the concert started. It was all very tribal back then, it really was…"

"Well, you always felt like there could be trouble if you went into town, or if you went to the Chinese in East Street to get some food," concedes **Bruce**. "Punks were picked on… actually, everyone was picked on. It was just the climate of the time, I think. My step-father was having a go at us too – I mean, he thought it was fun, but everyone who came in the house had to have either a dead arm or a dead leg on the way to my bedroom. It was just a thing that had to happen, like a rite of passage! Which wasn't very nice, but it was what was going on."

That Vice Squad gig was also the first punk concert attended by fifteen-year-old Grant Jackson, who lived in Dilton Marsh, five miles outside Warminster, and would himself soon be playing alongside Andy, Bruce and Dick…

Not So Stupid

A sponsored 36-hour drum-in at Warminster Youth Centre during the week end is expected to have raised about £135 for the International Year of the Child.

Four teenagers took part and the two eldest, 17-year-old Andrew Gale who plays with a Warminster group, the Stupid Humans, and 19-year-old David Stephens, who plays with the Trowbridge group Moscow, lasted the full 36 hours.

Derrick Murray, 15, played for 18 hours, and William Markley, 14, for 33 hours.

The drummers, all members of Warminster Youth Club, kept going on hot dogs, sandwiches, beef goulash, tea, coffee and pop. They had a 10-minute break every hour.

The event was organised by the youth centre's youth and community worker Mr. Alan Chesters.

During the daytime, there was a steady stream of friends and parents, and helpers were present for the whole 36 hours.

Drum-in profits will be added to £180 raised by a 24-hour sponsored disco at the youth centre a month ago, and youth club members will be asked how they want the money spent in keeping with the International Year of the Child.

CHARITY DRUM MARATHON, DECEMBER 1979 (L-R): ANDY GALE, DERRICK MURRAY, DAVID STEPHENS (SEATED), BILL MARKLEY

WARMINSTER YOUTH and COMMUNITY CENTRE

Present a Punk Spectacular

In Concert

VICE SQUAD

plus

STALAG 44, STUPID HUMANS, MENTAL

at the ATHENAEUM ARTS CENTRE,
HIGH STREET, WARMINSTER

FRIDAY 14th DECEMBER 1979   7.30 p.m.

ADMISSION £1.

WARMINSTER YOUTH AND COMMUNITY CENTRE

PRESENT A

PUNK SPECTACULAR

In Concert

VICE SQUAD

WITH

STALAG 44,   STUPID HUMANS,   MENTAL

Friday 14th December 1979 – 730pm

AT THE:

ATHENAEUM ARTS CENTRE, HIGH STREET, WARMINSTER

ADMISSION (By Ticket or at the Door) £1

TICKETS AVAILABLE from: THE YOUTH & COMMUNITY CENTRE,
THE CLOSE, WARMINSTER, WILTS   (MORNINGS)

and   WILLIAM POWER LTD.,
THREE HORSE SHOES MALL, WARMINSTER, WILTS.

A new decade dawned, and it ushered in a grittier take on UK punk rock. The so-called second wave – or third wave, depending upon how you calibrate your punk history – was harder, faster and more political than what had come before in the Seventies. But there was no sense of hope, that such a calendar change might sometimes bring, especially as it had been preceded by the so-called winter of discontent, and the Eighties looked set to be even bleaker. With inflation at a whopping 14% and unemployment at 6% – both of them on the rise too, as the country headed for a crippling recession – and an Iron Lady drawing up battlelines from Westminster, there was plenty for punk bands to sing about, and plenty of kids taking up instruments to vent their frustration at their complete lack of any real prospects. There was a perfect musical storm brewing to match the political one sat atop the UK, and the Subhumans would find themselves sat squarely in its eye… once they coalesced that is.

"Stupid Humans did our second gig at Bath Trinity Church [Saturday 16/2/80], with Vice Squad and The Mental," recalls **Bruce**, "And it seems that Audio Torture did a short set as well, which was Grant's band, of course, who eventually joined me in the Subhumans. It was a terrible gig for us – everything went wrong – but we had our first payment, of £13! Although I've got a letter somewhere from the caretaker charging us for the things that had been damaged and stolen at the gig… almost in shillings and pence, haha!

"Then we played with Audio Torture at the Warminster Community Centre the very next day as well. According to my diary, I had to borrow Grant's guitar – he played guitar in Audio Torture, and then swapped to bass for Subhumans – because I had smashed mine up the night before in Bath… oh dear. We didn't get paid that night, but were apparently given free crisps…

"We thought we were so big though. We'd even sign our own cassette covers – why would anyone do that? [laughs] I even put 'Willy Wombat' when I signed! I have no idea why I would do *that*! It was a reflection of the times, and the music we were playing."

"My family had moved to Dilton Marsh, just outside Warminster on the way to Bath, when I was about four, and we lived there until I was seventeen," explains **Grant**, of his childhood. "I used to cycle into Warminster for school. We all went to Kingdown School, and you know, terrible teenagers and all that, punk rock was something we all got into. There wasn't much of a choice – it was either punk rock or disco, whatever… but it was that whole teenage thing of getting into everything, and it seemed like the whole world opened up for you. So, I'd cycle home after school, then cycle back into town to hang out with my friends in the evening.

"The Warminster punk scene was quite small, quite random, but thriving. It all seemed like good fun, and we thought, 'Could do with a bit of this!' I can't remember exactly where it *first* stemmed from for me, but it might even have been seeing the Stupid Humans about somewhere. Actually no, it was probably a year before that, hearing punk on the radio?

"But yeah, I played guitar in Audio Torture. I started playing when I was in the fourth year at school – whatever you call that these days? Punk was really exciting because you could play and be a part of it, if you wanted to. Audio Torture was my first band, with Billy Markley on drums, although I got even more into punk when I started hanging around with Bruce. He'd help you out, and I started buying second-hand amps and all the rest of it. Some kids were into football – much more so then – but we were into bands, for something to do. You'd meet other kids who could play something, and you'd form a band; it was that straightforward back then. But first and foremost, we were kids that hung out together, sneaking into pubs when we were fifteen and trying to buy pints of beer, and bands were secondary to that.

"I'm pretty sure Audio Torture practised up at Billy's house. We weren't very good, just basic punk, and we only played a few gigs, but it didn't matter – it was all about being in a band and playing and being a part of what was going on at the time. We recorded the gigs, but never went in a proper studio, so there might be a few dodgy tapes around, but luckily there's very little surviving music from Audio Torture. There was me, Billy, Mike Bradbury [vocals] and a chap called Piggy [bass].

"My first guitar was a black Les Paul copy made by Shaftesbury, so it was half-decent really, just bought from a second-hand shop, for £40 or something like that – several months' pocket money, haha! I think I wanted to play guitar because guitar seemed more glamorous than bass… it didn't matter that I wasn't any good at it. But when I joined Subhumans, Bruce was clearly a million times better than me, so I took up bass. Less strings… and I've always really enjoyed bass-led music, whatever it is."

"I grew up in Warminster, and was fortunate enough to go to school with Grant, at Kingdown," elaborates **Bill**, who after Audio Torture went on to Organized Chaos (and then Culture Shock… not to mention Eastfield, Citizen Fish and A-Heads!). "He was the year above me, as was Phil [the eventual Subhumans bassist], and Bruce was a couple of years above me. So, I met them all at school. We knew each other from both being at school together, and getting into punk at the same time as each other.

"I had a very liberated, open-minded mother, who was a great pianist, and who didn't mind me liking punk, because it was so different. It was angry but fun. The first record I really liked was 'Gotta Get Away' by Stiff Little Fingers – the structure made total sense to me. And it was the same with The Ruts, a great band making proper music. And it was the drumming I was really into. I started drumming when I came out the womb, haha! I was playing on the back of the sofa, on saucepans… I think I was nine years old when I told my mum I wanted to play drums, and she encouraged me. I did a paper round for like two years, saving up £3 a week, and my mum saved some money up as well, and we bought my first drum kit when I was fourteen. It had to be yellow… and yellow is still

27

STUPID HUMANS - AUDIO TORTURE - SIGNED CASSETTE COVER

MENTAL PRACTICE, FEBRUARY 1980

THE MENTAL, ALTON FOURMARKS, 23/2/80 BY NEIL DUNCAN

BILL MARKLEY, ORGANIZED CHAOS

my favourite colour. It was a little Premier Olympic three-piece; I had it at the end of my bed, and I literally couldn't wait to get up in the morning to play it again… forty-five years later, and I still have the same feeling, it's fantastic.

"I was just drumming along to punk records really, and then I met Mike Bradbury, who was just this nice guy in the Warminster scene. We were watching The Mental – Dick was a massive influence, who made me realise the power of lyrics – and we thought, 'Well, if they can do it, so can we!' He introduced me to Bruce, who was a big inspiration back then too; he was very clever and very musical. He came from a nice arty family. He was like, 'Oh, you've got a drum kit, let's have a go!' and he jumped behind it and started playing it perfectly straight away; he's such an amazing musician.

"And we were so young at the time – I was still at school when I was in Audio Torture. I was possibly the only kid at Kingdown with peroxide spikey hair. I got suspended for it, but they had to let me back in, which set a precedent, you know what I mean?

"Julian was a few years older than me, but very influential, with his two green Mohicans, leopard print trousers, leather jacket, piercings everywhere, skateboard… we were all big skaters – me, Nige, Julian, Bruce… and all those things drew people in, and then they got into the music off the back of that.

"Audio Torture was my first band, and we would practise in my front room. We did that Vice Squad gig in Trinity Church completely spontaneously! Stupid Humans were supporting them, so we all went along to watch the Stupid Humans – when we looked around, we realised the whole band was there. Mike went off somewhere and then came back and said, 'We've got fifteen minutes!' I was like, 'Really?' I was only a kid, but thought, 'I can do this…!'

"We got up on the stage, and I looked at the drum kit just before we went on. I'm left-handed, and it was a right-handed set-up; not only that though, the kit had been nailed down, to stop anyone moving it around. I was stuffed! So I ended up doing my first ever gig right-handed… the same beat for fifteen minutes, haha! But it went alright, with people dancing and having a good time, and that gave us the buzz to want to keep doing it."

"I always remember I had a big argument with Herb at that Community Centre gig [17/2/80]," continues **Bruce**, on the demise of the short-lived Stupid Humans, "And Mel [A-Heads vocalist], who was going out with him at the time, always says that's when I chucked him out of the band. I can't remember what happened, but *something* did…"

"I don't remember exactly when I got into punk," says **Mel**, "But I do remember the black-outs, when the telly channels went off, and they'd put videos of The Damned and The Stranglers on, and I can just remember thinking that was my kind of my music. I worked at Gateways [a supermarket chain] and there were a couple of other people there getting into it.

"That would have been '78 or '79, when I was a teenager. There was a local band, Moskow, and I quite liked them, and a few of the people who liked them liked the punkier stuff as well. And when I was at school, I used to hang around with this kid called Andy Smith, who turned up on my door step one day with Herb, who went on to be in Wild Youth, and he lent me a few records. That was an interesting time – I was listening to Pink Floyd, The Animals and 'Feeding of the 5000' all at the same time. Herb lent me Ian Dury's 'New Boots and Panties!!', which I'd never heard, and I remember putting it on when I was sat at the dinner table one night, and the plethora of swear words didn't go down well with my foster parents. Then a few years later, I started to go out with Herb and I came home in a pair of tartan trousers, and they said, 'It's time for you to go now!'

"I went to live with my mate Sue, and through Herb we met Dick, and his brother Steve. We all used to hang around Trowbridge Park. Me and Dick became good friends – I always felt like I had to look after him, because he was a bit fragile at the time. We used to go to the practices, and when me and Herb split up, I rang up Bruce and asked him for a practice tape, because I'd mislaid the first one I had. And I was coming over to Warminster to hang out. I started seeing Bruce and moved over here.

"I did join a band in Trowbridge, but there was only the three of us – me, Steve Hamilton [who will crop up again later in our story] and this guy Mike Coward, who's died now which is a shame. We didn't even have a name, but we had a few practices, and we ended up coming over to Warminster for a practice at The Globe, because Organized Chaos were practising down there. And that's when Jock and Nigel asked me to join the A-Heads…"

"Anyway, we started recording at Eclipse Studios," continues **Bruce**, "A four-track studio in Warminster, on the 21st of February, 1980, then we did a bit more on the 24th, and we mixed down on the 27th – the three songs, 'Drugs of Youth', 'All Gone Dead' and 'Try' [a great little punk demo, with 'Drugs of Youth' and 'All Gone Dead' slower than they were later recorded by Subhumans, with Ju's brilliantly snotty vocal delivery keeping the all-important energy levels in the red]. And we never played live as Stupid Humans again after that…

"The glue thing was quite bad, especially in Trowbridge. Herb had a bit of a glue addiction. And at the start of 'Drugs of Youth', we've actually got a 'sample' of him sniffing in and out of a glue bag. You'd see all the discarded crisp bags they'd been using around Trowbridge. Everyone was doing that sort of thing – if it wasn't glue, it was dry cleaning fluid or Zoff [adhesive removal liquid, immortalised in the UK Subs song, 'Lady Esquire', which itself was about sniffing shoe dye]. And of course, we had the old 'dingbat'… which was basically a bit of hash. And at the start of 'Drugs of Youth', the Subhumans version, Dick shouts, 'Dingbat – argh!' Somebody once wrote to us asking if he'd said 'Dick Barton!'"

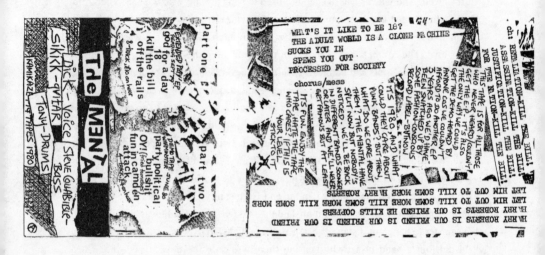

THE SECOND ISSUE OF
DICK'S 'SO WHAT?' FANZINE   BLUURG 1 TAPE

STEVE HAMILTON, 1980

STEVE, BRUCE, DICK — THE MENTAL RECORDING

"There *was* a lot of glue-sniffing in Trowbridge," confirms **Mel**. "I was anti-glue, of course; that's why I wrote 'Dying Man' [the first A-Heads single, released in 1982] – I thought they were all going to die… and of course, most of them are still in fine health, haha! A friend of ours, Dave from Trowbridge, sniffed glue for the longest time – but not now – and he's absolutely fine, nothing wrong with him at all. In fact, he's got a wicked sense of humour, none of his brain cells have disintegrated or anything, so I needn't have worried. It's like acid, where the odd person jumps off a building or something – it doesn't mean it happens to everyone.

"One of them once said to me, 'How can you be so against it if you haven't tried it?' And I thought, 'You know what? He's right,' so I tried it, and yeah, I could see why they wanted to do it, but I just thought it was so bad for you…"

"It was about then that Alan, my sister's boyfriend, became our 'manager'," **Bruce** continues. "He basically took on the job of sending all the demo tapes off. Stardust Records phoned us up… whoever they were? And we had a letter off EBG Records, who were considering the tape. We sent one off to GEM Records as well, who were the UK Subs' label.

"On April 12th, 1980, Julian informed me he was leaving the band. We had our last practice, and then went down The Fox & Hounds in the evening. He really wanted to play guitar, I think – he got the guitar bug from me, and I remember he went to see The Exploited, and was really inspired by Big John, so he went and bought himself a second-hand Flying V. He wanted to be a guitar hero rather than a singer to start with.

"According to my diary, we then asked this girl called Polly to come for an audition on the 17th – but she didn't turn up for that. She came round on the 18th, and Sub Human was born. Because we were minus Julian, who was a Stupid Human!

"I was coming up with a Sub Human logo in my school maths book. That's what I was planning after the Stupid Humans finished. To be honest, maths was the only thing I was any good at when I was at school. Although my maths teacher actually went mad and ended up in Broadmoor for murdering someone. She was a good teacher, but very strict."

"I'm sure Polly lived in Trowbridge," adds **Mel**, trying to shed some light on the mysterious vocalist, who lasted just one practice, "At the home just around the corner from me. She was pretty cool… bright red hair and stuff."

"If she did one rehearsal, that was it really," reckons **Bruce**. "We really liked the idea of her being in the band, but nothing really happened. She was a friend of Herb's, I think? I never saw her again after that one practice anyway…

"I saw the UK Subs at the Bath Pavilion, on May 3rd, who were great," he continues. "Nicky Garratt was absolutely an inspiration for me – I really liked his palm muting and his downstrokes. This was also when I was having my exams at school… I left school at the end of May. Dick was coming around a bit then, and I was going to watch Audio Torture practise quite often. Herb was fizzling out, for whatever reason, and Grant joined."

"The Mental went into Eclipse Studio [AKA 'Adrian's Place'], where we had recorded, to do their 'Shoot the Hostages' demo, on June 15th, and I was really involved in that. I sang on two of the tracks – 'Party Political Bullshit' and 'Oy (Fried Tomatoes)' – and I was getting involved in some of the music, giving them ideas how to do things perhaps. I liked to think I was a bit of a producer even back then. I was fascinated by recording. I got hold of two tape recorders and a reel-to-reel, and I was fascinated by overdubbing – I used to mess around with that all the time.

"On August 19th, Dick came over and recorded me, Grant and Andy doing all the Sub Human songs we had at that point. I was singing and playing guitar on that. We'd just written 'Parasites' and 'Minority', and we were doing Stupid Humans songs like 'All Gone Dead' and 'Ashtray Dirt', that Julian had written. We were also doing 'So Paranoid'… which was sort of about the police, but didn't go anywhere. Horrible lyrics, very cringey… and I'm not particularly proud of them. We'd lined up a gig on August 22nd with The Mental, but when we turned up at the gig, there were no amps left onstage, so we couldn't play. I can't remember where that was exactly, but it was a hall above a pub, and that *would* have been the only Sub Human gig, if it had happened…"

"In March 1980, I went along to another Stupid Humans practice," **Dick** recounts the story from his own perspective. "I'd heard that they'd almost got a contract with Stardust Records in London. After the practice I went to Bruce's house, and did an interview for this So What? fanzine I was planning at the time. I did at least six issues of So What?, but I can't recall the interview with Bruce ever appearing in it, so who knows what that interview was actually for – unless we were just being silly? There was a lot of being silly going on…

"The sixth issue was actually on a C60 [cassette tape], where I'd play a few songs and then talk about them. Terveet Kadet were on it, who were great – like Discharge, but better… tighter. They did some brilliant records – like one line per song… and then we played with them years later, when they were all grown up and hairy."

"I'm sure there *was* a Vermin or Stupid Humans interview in *one* of them," interjects **Bruce**, "And you interviewed Ju as well, because he was joking about the replies from the record companies, saying that one of them was written on a piece of bog roll. The So What? issues changed shape, didn't they?"

Dick: "Oh yeah. The first one was A4 size, the second one was A5… all printed on a photocopier at work. I'd sneak all these photocopies through – photocopiers weren't what they are these days, and the paper was all horrible and shiny. Number five was the smallest fanzine in the world, like A7. One of them had an interview with God in it, and an unfortunate interview with Adam and the Ants as well…"

When you say 'God', are we talking about the Dutch band, or the celestial being?

"The actual celestial being, of course," laughs **Dick**. "He asked me where I got his phone number from. It was all made-up rubbish really, but there was a review of the

WHY DO YOU WANNA FIGHT ⟨MVSIC⟩ BASS LIVE

SOCIETY DRUMS CHANGED, GUITAR ON CHORUS

ASH TRAY DIRT **.

KILLED ** ⟨ON CHORUS *⟩

DRUGS OF YOUTH. MIDDLE BIT. SORTED OUT

TRY DIFFERENT BASS LINE POSSIBLY. *

ALL GONE DEAD ** ⟨* ON CHORUS⟩.

FUZZ SCRAPED COMPLETELY.

FIRST AID WORDS TOTALY CHANGED, BASS LIN

NEW AGE TOTALY SCRAPED).

SID WORDS CHANGED *

GET OUT OF MY WAY * or **

VOCALS * POLY   GUITAR BRUCE
        ** BRUCE   DRUMS ANDY

STUPID HUMANS
MENTAL DEMOS CD

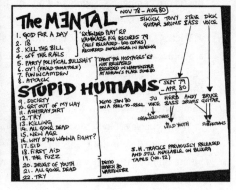

THE MENTAL, CHIPPENHAM BY NEIL DUNCAN

Stonehenge fest, complete with badly printed photographs. I'd give away ten copies and sell two, and that would be it. No one really knew about it. The art of publicity has never really been in my make-up – I just had fun doing it.

"So anyway, they were called Subhumans before I joined," he continues, "Although there was a short debate one afternoon at Bruce's, about whether to keep the name Subhumans – Bruce's mum suggested it could be 'Super Humans', but we thought 'Super Humans' sounded too much like showing off. She thought Subhumans was just too negative, but there were a lot of negative names for punk bands – and there was a lot of positive negativity, where negating things was part of a positive statement. It was where you started from, in a sense. 'I don't want to be part of this, therefore I'm anti-this…' There were loads of 'anti' bands – Anti-System, Anti-Pasti, anti this, that and the other. And there was The Exploited… The Damned… talking of which, Sex Pistols is a daft name for a band, don't you think? But you get used to it, don't you? [laughs]

"As for the second Mental EP – well, *demo* that was going to be the EP, but we split up so it didn't happen – it was recorded around July 1980, in Warminster, with some chap called Adrian, who'd set up this little studio there. And that was cracking, because by that time, we could actually play better."

The second demo was indeed a marked improvement on the first Mental recording; it was still endearingly (very) rough around the edges, but boasted a more powerful sound and focused approach, and it was a shame the band didn't get to release it at the time, although it eventually got released in 2007, along with the band's 'Extended Play' EP, as the 'Extended Play L.P.' by Demo Tapes Records, the label ran by Sean Forbes, of Rugger Bugger Records and Wat Tyler/Hard Skin fame.

"The Mental is so basic and raw you can't help but love it," reasons **Sean**. "The original 7" is impossibly hard to find and the demos were just as great, so it seemed like the honourable thing to do. Demo Tapes also released Culture Shock [Dick's next band after Subhumans]'s 'Reality Stop No. 44' demo on vinyl… the best thing they ever recorded and the soundtrack to the Brixton squatting scene of the '80s, along with Blyth Power's 'A Little Touch of Harry in the Night' and 'The Seaside' tape by the Cardiacs…"

"Steve called time on The Mental after this one practice," **Dick** gets our tale back on track, "And Si Kick just hit him in the face a few times… 'That's from me, and that's from Toby, and that's from Dick!' Then he shut him outside in the yard for several hours, before letting him back in and hitting him again. But he apologised for it, and they got on fine again. We did do another gig after that, but the seeds were sown. By August, Si wanted to go off and do something 'more mysterious', which was a bit weird – too many drugs! – and Toby pulled out of a few gigs we had booked… probably because he couldn't be bothered as no one turned up, no one liked us, and there was no money in it.

"Our last gig was at Crondall [a village in northeast Hampshire]… I thought it went okay," says **Dick**, before touching on a topic that scourged the punk scene in the early

Eighties: "I can't remember a lot of violence or anything, but generally, in west Wiltshire at least, and possibly a lot of other places, there were the punks, the mods and the bikers, these three subcultural tribes… and it was punks versus mods, until the bikers got involved, and the mods and punks would be more united, and the bikers didn't want to unite with anybody. They didn't make friends too easily… well, they did if there was only two or three of them – you could have a good conversation with them then – but if there was a lot of them, the tribal mentality was very solid.

"And the Eighties was everybody split into these different subcultures, and there was a lot of violence in the Eighties… a lot of broken phone box windows, and people throwing bikes off multi-storey car parks… supermarket trolleys in rivers, people running around smashing windows, and people being scared of the bikers. At Stonehenge festival, for instance – that really kicked off badly. In '79 or '80, when Crass were going to play, but didn't, and Colin out of Flux got hit in the head with a bottle whilst onstage. And there were rumours of all the Winchester punks ending up in hospital and stuff. There was a lot more of that then than there is now, and thank fuck for that."

Bruce: "It was terrifying really. I certainly found it terrifying, and I wouldn't have had the courage to go to London at that point, the stories you used to hear about the violence at the gigs there, from skinheads and everything…"

Dick: "There was a violent edge everywhere, which you sort of got into for the thrill, but you were also very aware that it was a fine line between the thrill of excitement – people breaking the law, and all the cops turning up – and ending up arrested, or beaten up, or in hospital… all that nasty stuff. Some people did get beat up pretty severely, and it was horrible.

"That eventually played out, because the culture changed and… well, we all got older and grew up a bit. But punk rock really did offend quite a lot of the public. It was still offensive to people back then… it's not offensive now, of course – you can do almost anything nowadays without offending anyone. Almost."

It's odd that punk offended bikers though, seeing as the two subcultures had more in common than not?

Dick: "It wound them up. We saw the bikers, and they were doing what we wanted to do – they were in this big united club, all doing the same thing, with this 'out of society' air to them. We were outsiders like they were, but we might have wanted a bit of the respect they got. They just didn't like us going into their pubs – like The Bear in Melksham, literally thirty yards away from where I was living. I'd go in there for a pint late of an evening, and they thought I was weird. They didn't beat me up or anything – but one of them slapped me really hard on the back once, because he saw I had sunburn. He was like, 'Alright, mate… bang!' And I thought, 'Ow… you bastard!'

"Me, Bruce and Mel were walking back from the chip shop to our house in Melksham one time – they were staying over – and these mods came over; they'd seen we had bottles

SUB HUMAN LOGO - DOODLED ON BRUCE'S MATHS BOOK

SUMA 3 17/8/80

C

B

1 PARASITES.
2 ALL GONE DEAD
3 ASHTRAY DIRT
4 MINORITY
5 DRUM SOLO
6 PARANOIO <SO>

7 MINORITY
8 PARASITES.
9 ASHTRAY DIRT
10 ALL GONE DEAD.
11 DROSS OF YOUTH
12 REGGAE JAM.

SUB HUMAN REHEARSAL TAPE - BRUCE SINGING, DICK RECORDED IT

THE STUPID HUMANZ

ANDY GALE BY KEVIN TYDEMAN

in our hands, and came over asking if we were out to cause trouble. I said, 'Right, you're the chief mod around here… and I'm the chief punk' – I had to make shit up, haha! You had to find common ground with your enemy, or potential enemy, before it got silly, or worse – 'We're both outside society, we do what we do, you dress like that, I dress like this, it doesn't matter what we look like, we both live on the same level…' I talked him into some sort of mutual respect; I had to think fast to get all that out – talking saves lives, haha!

"And then there were skinheads… and there were skinheads! There were the two-tone skinheads, and then there were the other ones, and the other ones were a nasty bunch. Certain venues like Skunx in London, where you'd never go again, because the skinheads turned up just to pick fights and hassle people. That too has thankfully vanished."

Apparently you took half of the Wiltshire punk scene with you to the last Mental gig?

"We did!" laughs **Dick**. "We hired a van, but our driver didn't have his driving license to show to the van hire guy, so our dad – much against his usual way of behaving… he was usually straight as a die, you know – went and hired the van for us, whilst we hid in the background, and then our driver took over from there, which was handy. This was from Petty's Van Hire, who were famous for how awful their vans were – he was cheap, but if you made it where you were going, you were lucky! Anyway, we drove back to Trowbridge from Melksham, picked up a load of punks, then a few more from Warminster… it was something stupid though, like twenty-one people in the back, and we drove to Hampshire. So, we took our own little crowd with us, which was nice – *and* Organized Chaos were playing with us, so it was a fun night.

"Anyway, Steve then declared it would be 'okay' if I wanted to have a go singing for Wild Youth [his new band, with Herb]. I'd just assumed that we'd carry on, me and Steve, but he wasn't sure that he wanted me to be the singer, for some reason. But I tried it, just not for long, before I decided to go off with Bruce, because me and Bruce had struck up a really good friendship… we just had excellent laughs, and this connectivity about punk rock. I had a choice really, Wild Youth or Subhumans, so I chose Subhumans…"

And did that cause any animosity with your brother, choosing the Subhumans over his band?

Dick: "Er, I don't remember any. It made sense really; he wanted to be the singer, he was writing loads of songs, both lyrics and music... we were both in bands still, and it didn't matter that we weren't together in the *same* band anymore."

"For me personally, I wanted to be the guitarist, not the singer," confirms **Julian**, of his defection from Stupid Humans to Organized Chaos, adding with a chuckle, "And Bruce taught me everything I don't know! No, he was my teacher, for everything, and I'll never ever forget that. He was a great guitarist – but don't tell him that, haha! He bought the first Marshall head we ever saw, and we all thought he was really clever. But yeah, I decided

I wanted to be a guitarist, and I was leaving the Stupid Humans, leaving Bruce to it, so we needed a new singer for the Stupid Humans. And that was where Dick came in, this scrawny little geezer [laughs] – but he was instantly the right person! He was perfect! It was obvious that things were falling into place... and Bruce went the Dick Lucas way, and I went the Organized Chaos way. He had the intelligent mates, who knew what they were on about, and I had all the mental ones, haha!

"We lost a lot of people to glue-sniffing, especially in Trowbridge, where it was very prolific; a few people dived off multi-storey car parks and died and all that. Organized Chaos wrote a song about it all, 'The Centre of Nowhere'. It was quite sad really. But it was a good punk scene in Warminster... it was definitely an 'us against them' situation. I wouldn't have had it any other way, even being chased by the bikers. But you had to take your chances. We had a police officer called '109', who took it upon himself to come and get us, but in the end, we trashed his car, and he got transferred somewhere else. So we won that day! We used to go around spraying on walls, 'Would the last person to leave Warminster please feed the pigs?' We broke into the police car park and sprayed that on the wall. But we weren't after any trouble really, we just wanted to be left alone. The CID didn't used to bother knocking on our front door – they would just go round the back and let 'emselves in. I remember we had a harpoon gun, but the police soon took that off us..."

"And then Dick got arrested, for stealing a policeman's helmet [on 30/8/80]," laughs **Bruce**, "And he joined the band around then, sometime in September."

"In August – well, the summer in general – Trowbridge Park was the place all the punks went, including myself and my brother," continues **Dick**. "The Melksham bunch used to go to Trowbridge a lot, and quite a few of the Warminster punks used to come over as well. It was a good 'punk rock central' place to be. And not that this was the most important thing about it all at all, but there was so much glue-sniffing going on in Trowbridge that there was an article in the Daily Mirror about it, and then Channel 4, or the BBC or someone, came down and made a programme about the problem of glue-sniffing, and Trowbridge became the glue-sniffing capital of the UK for a couple of weeks. It was weird. And they had a clip of Pagans doing a few songs in their film, because it was the punks who were doing the glue-sniffing, and the punks were going to see these bands... so Steve was up there on the telly, playing a couple of bars, and we were sat there with our dad watching it... wondering what our dad made of it all, haha!

"So, there was a lot of that going on, and a lot of drinking going on – a helluva lot. I'd leave work on a Saturday afternoon; I used to work most Saturdays, nine until twelve, and then I'd cycle back to Melksham, get the bus to Trowbridge, start the weekend in Trowbridge Park, and then go down to Warminster and see Bruce, or go straight to Warminster for practice... there was a Warminster-Melksham-Trowbridge punk rock

NOTE FROM DICK

GRANT, DICK, ANDY AND MEL 1980

BRADFORD-ON-AVON, ST MARGARET'S HALL

triangle going on, all this social interaction, drunkenness, parties, gigs, or just hanging out. Which all involved a lot of drinking. I won't say that everyone in the UK under the age of twenty at that point was drinking every weekend, but that's what it felt like.

"And there was one particular weekend, towards the end of August, and we were walking from one pub to another as it was getting towards closing time, and a fight had broken out outside The Elephant & Castle, and the cops were there. During the confusion, one of the cops lost their helmet – well, their flat hat – and I picked it up, because it was just lying there, right? And I put it under my jacket, then hid it in the nearby multi-storey car park. The next day, after work, I came to Trowbridge and then had to get from there, drunk as I was, to Warminster, to hang out with Bruce. So I went back to the multi-storey, picked up the hat, thinking, 'This will be a laugh... he'll like to see this!' I stuck it under my jacket and hurried to the train station, on the other side of town, to catch the six o'clock train... I realised I was going to be late and started running – and pulled the hat out from under my jacket and started running with it in my hand. Unbeknownst to me, these cops were running behind me, and this arm goes round my neck, and they hauled me over. They were like, 'Right, what's that? Are you going to hand that in?' And at this point, folks, always say, 'Yes, I'm going to hand it in at the local police station, because it's obviously not mine...!' But I said, 'No, I'm running for the train...' and the police station was in the other direction...

"So, that didn't do me much good, and I got arrested. And the [early Subhumans] song 'Trowbridge Park' came out of that sort of thing; it was about all the punks in the Trowbridge Park, and all the skins, and the mods – and the pigs! 'Kill the pigs, we'll all get along, drinking Kestrel lager...' It was a song for the times... which we later dropped, because it was a bit *too* local and a bit *too* of its time. Bloody good tune though!"

"The Stupid Humans fell apart, for whatever reason," adds **Grant**, "At the same time as Audio Torture fell apart, again for whatever reason. I was mates with Bruce, and we used to hang out, and jam – it was school days' stuff, so we were just bedroom jamming, whatever – and the next step was to form a band. We started off as a three-piece, but thought we needed a singer, and Dick was pretty cool, so we nabbed him. We lured him over to Warminster, and maybe The Mental was falling apart as well, so it all came together. Me, Bruce and Andy were just looking for what came next musically, but it was all driven very strongly by Bruce. He's always known that was his path, and always been into it.

"I bought a cheap Rickenbacker copy first, but then the next [bass] guitar I picked up was the one I've still got today – a Squire Fender Precision copy, which I tried out in London when we were up there for a gig. I tried out a Fender Precision, and then the Squire, which was a copy, and the Squire was far superior, it really was. It had a fantastic action on it, a better sound, and was a hell of a lot cheaper."

September 1980 was a key month for Subhumans. Not only did Dick join, cementing their first line-up, but they played their first gig a few days later.

Thankfully **Dick** has kept comprehensive journals all his life, and can recollect the exact details: "September, 1980, and I was maybe going to sing with Wild Youth, Steve's new band, with Herb from Stupid Humans on bass, Steve on guitar, and a guy called Ron from Melksham on the drums. But we had a really bad practice at the start of September – Ron was useless… Herb was useless – and I decided not to sing, and chose to go with Bruce instead.

"So I was 'verbally' in the Subhumans on September 11th, according to my diary – yes, 9/11! – and we had a practice the week after that, on the 18th… and did the first gig on the 19th! In between the 11th and the 18th, I'd been learning all the words to Julian's songs – 'Drugs of Youth', 'Killing', 'Ashtray Dirt', 'All Gone Dead' and 'Society' – and chucked in 'Mickey Mouse' and 'Minority' with those. It was at the St Margaret's Hall in Bradford-on-Avon… about 200 people turned up."

Also in the set that night was a little-played song called 'High Class Pits'?

"That was a song we soon dropped," admits **Dick**. "I don't even remember what it sounded like, or what the words were, but it probably wasn't very good, and that might have been the only time we ever played it?"

"Rob Challice [who went on to be in Faction, when he moved to London] wrote the words to 'High Class Pits', and Grant wrote the music," clarifies **Bruce**, "But we did play it for a while. That was one of the songs we were doing as a three-piece, before Dick joined."

Another song from those early live sets that was soon dropped was the amusingly titled 'Big Bastard'…

"That was an Audio Torture song," says **Dick**, before quoting, "'Big bastard in a flash limousine – drinks gin and tonic and worships the queen!' [laughs] It was about someone local who had a big car… probably a landlord.

"Anyway, Wild Youth started off the night," he continues, of the band's live debut, "With Steve singing and playing guitar, and then the Subhumans went on. We had to scrounge an amp off The Waiters, who were going on last, because ours blew up. Bruce's lead fell out of his guitar as he ran onto the stage all showman-like for the first song, strumming all these chords at the beginning of 'Drugs of Youth', and it all went quiet whilst he tried to get that back in. It was chaos, but we got to the end of the set.

"Herb from Wild Youth got into a fight with someone who was yelling at him from the crowd, and that didn't help. By the time we came off, the police were outside, and the gig was being closed down, so The Waiters couldn't play, or didn't want to play, or weren't allowed to play. The cops came along in bulk, and there were about ten people arrested, which got us in the Wiltshire Times. For a first gig it was quite eventful, and very memorable."

"I thought it might have been a good idea to run onstage playing the 'Drugs of Youth' guitar bit," smiles **Bruce** ruefully, "But the cable came out my guitar – that old chestnut… you soon learn to coil it through your strap. This was the sort of thing you do before you know what you're doing, haha! And we really didn't know what we were doing much. We were all wearing trench coats, or leather jackets… we must have been boiling hot."

"That first gig, in Bradford-on-Avon, went down really well," adds **Andy**. "It was pretty frightening though; some of the audience weren't the prettiest, haha! And if they didn't like you, they let you know about it.

"Stupid Humans was my first band, but we were always really busy; we soon had plenty of songs and offers of gigs. And that continued with Subhumans; Dick was a very clever chap, and he was good with the lyrics. And Bruce was brilliant at coming up with ideas. I could be tapping away at something, and he'd look round, 'Hang on a minute, play that again…' And Grant was a great bassist – as a drummer, you're always looking to the bassist, of course. I think we had a pretty good chemistry from day one.

"We were recording our practices on a Saturday afternoon on our little Philips cassette recorder, and trying to get our name out there. You could hear us practising all around town – it was open door, and you can imagine how loud we were in there. People would wander in to have a listen – you'd see these strange people come in and sit down at the end of the hall. And the word started to spread."

Ah yes, we really should talk about those Saturday afternoon rehearsals behind the Athenaeum, which were so key to not only the development of the Subhumans, but of the Warminster punk scene as a whole.

"What a great place, when you think about it [the Athenaeum building]," enthuses **Grant**, "This youth club in the middle of town that would open up its big old rooms for any kids to come and practise on a Saturday. As a kid you take everything for granted, of course, but that was a brilliant thing."

"Organized Chaos, A-Heads and Subhumans would be practising up there most Saturdays," continues **Dick**, "Sometimes in the week, sometimes on Sunday, but usually Saturday afternoons. When I was working, I had to get myself to Warminster, so I had to cycle home, then get the bus to Trowbridge and the bus to Warminster. So I wouldn't have got there until 2 pm if it was a Saturday. And they'd be broken up by visits to the offy [i.e. off license], to get some beer, or a pasty or whatever. Then it would depend if anyone had anything to do in the evening – but normally we didn't, except if we had to get back to where we lived. But generally, we usually packed up about half-five, went to the chip shop for food, and then went to the pub…

"The bands shared the space, and there grew to be a tiny crowd of local punks turning up to have a look at one band or the other. Which was sometimes annoying, because you wanted to concentrate on getting the songs right, but you were aware that you were also sort of performing at the same time. A bit of a weird feeling. Half the time, I didn't

WEST WILTS C N D
PRESENTS

LAST GIG BEFORE
THE HOLOCAUST

ANTI-
NUCLEAR
EVENTS
IN
FORE STREET

LIVE MUSIC
10 A.M — 6 P.M
(APPROX)
TROWBRIDGE
BANDSTAND

WITH

SUBHUMANS
E ORGANIZED CHAOS
WILD YOUTH

+ OTHERS

PROTEST + SURVIVE
TROWBRIDGE
SATURDAY
22ND NOVEMBER

NEEDLES
Winter Collection
FASHION SHOW
+
Pedro's Disco
at
The Old Bell
TUES. DEC. 9ᵗʰ 8-12 PM

£1

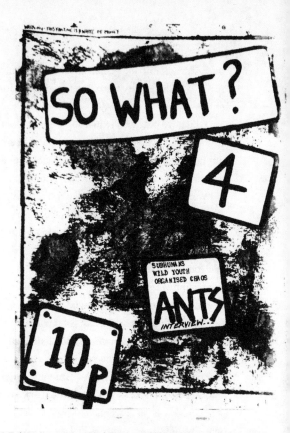

SO WHAT?

4

SUBHUMANS
WILD YOUTH
ORGANISED CHAOS
ANTS
INTERVIEW...

10P

THE FOURTH ISSUE OF DICK'S 'SO WHAT?' FANZINE

SCHOOL DAYS PICTURE OF STEVE AND DICK
FROM BLUURG 11 TAPE COVER

A WILD YOUTH   A SUBHUMAN

particularly know the people who were there – they sat there and watched, but I didn't really know who they were. Everybody was drinking anyway, and they didn't really say much…"

"I think we practised in just about every room in the Atheneum," reckons **Bruce**. "One of the rooms was orange, one was pale green… complete with curtains. There was a hut out the back where they had discos too, and sometimes we'd practise in there… sometimes we'd go downstairs, sometimes upstairs – all sorts really."

"We used to practise with them in the youth centre, in the middle of Warminster, on a Saturday afternoon," confirms **Bill**, "In these big rooms – you could fit two or three bands in one room, and we'd have Subhumans and A-Heads and us, all in there. And it was just a magical feeling of inspiration, because we all used to listen to each other and encourage each other and feed off each other. It was just a case of being in the right place at the right time, but it was still pretty incredible. And infectious – people would come across from nearby towns to sit in and watch.

"The youth centre was a real focal point, very important – and the guy who ran it, Alan Chester, was key. My mum had a lot to do with that actually – she worked down the youth centre sometimes, and she introduced us to Alan and told him we needed somewhere to practise. He was a lovely guy, a Brummie, a gentle giant; he said he would try to help us out, and he did. But we never gave him any grief down there – we treated it with respect. All we did was play; we never trashed it, or left beer cans everywhere… we cleaned up when we left, every time. Which was why it went on for as long as it did, because we really appreciated the place. I remember it closed for a bit to get some work done, and we had to practise in a church hall down the road, and that was when we realised how lucky we were."

"We'd be practising at the youth centre on a Saturday," recalls **Jock McCurdy**, the A-Heads guitarist, "And there was one guy who would cycle in every week from Shrewton, which is about fifteen miles away, just to sit in and meet everybody. And when the bands had a bit of downtime, we'd go shopping, or end up in The Ship & Punchbowl [a pub in Silver Street, which closed in 1984, and is now residential properties] – and that was a day out… which went on into the night. Like a free gig…"

"You could just wander in and take a seat against the wall and watch," recalls **Kev Tydeman**, an old friend of the band, and a keen photographer, many of whose pictures appear in this book. "You know, I was at school at the time, but could sit and watch Organized Chaos rehearse, and no one had a problem with it. It was great, and I'm sure being able to do that inspired and shaped some of the people present at that time. No one worried about you wandering through a door and sitting down to listen.

"And I was an outsider really, but they grew to be my mates. I knew Phil from school, and that's how I got to know Bruce, and I was in a class with Grant. But the one thing I always saw was that there were never any rivalries, never any animosity. Now we look back at it all and say there was a scene forming, but back then, everyone was just really pleased for everyone else to get on. Even with the [Warminster new wave band] Silent Guests – and who knows how you describe Silent Guests really? It was more like new romantic music; they were writing pop songs – but everyone was sharing gear and happy for everyone else."

"Yes, there was the Silent Guests too, who used to use the other room," adds **Mel**, "But they always seemed to be looking down on us lot. The drummer had been in a band called Animals and Men, from Frome, who were about at the same time as Moskow [a late Seventies post-punk band from Trowbridge]. They thought they were better than us anyway. We played with them at one of our first gigs, at the Regal Cinema, which was all very odd. I remember being backstage, and looking at their bass guitar when I walked past, and their bassist Wally – who later became our drummer – was like, 'Don't touch my bass!'"

"You did get times when the Humans would shut the door because they needed to work on stuff," concedes **Jock**. "Back then you couldn't send ideas digitally to each other, you just had to blow it out on a Saturday morning. Which was great for the kids turning up to watch, and then all of a sudden, a couple of months later it was like, 'Jesus, they're playing some big gigs now…' But we didn't really think about it too much at the time; it was just something that happened, something that naturally progressed, and kept progressing."

Kev is also keen to stress, "Alan Chester was the youth club leader, and he played an important part really. If he hadn't been so switched on, and hadn't cleared it with the Athenaeum to use the rooms above it, and hadn't turned up on a Saturday to open the doors – often on his own time – and hadn't had all these other ideas, like printing flyers and T-shirts, it would probably have played out quite differently.

"It was a pivotal building. It was a nice venue, and at the back of it, we'd have the Friday night disco, where all the punks would be standing around in the corners, in the dark, speeding like jets – as the saying goes [referring to 'Staring at the Rude Boys' by The Ruts], waiting for them to put on 'New York State Police' by the UK Subs, which would be your one track of the night, haha! And the rest of it would be 'D.I.S.C.O.', haha! But it was like any other town across the country – where else was there to go? Half the blokes dressed like Dexy's Midnight Runners, half the girls dressed like Bow Wow Wow. The pubs would shut at a certain time, or you weren't old enough to get in the pubs, and you'd be down the park after dark, listening to John Peel."

The band had a distinctive sound from the very start, even some of the earliest songs of a high enough quality to still be in the set forty years later, and immediately recognisable as Subhumans due to the unique style and sound of the delivery.

"Yeah, I guess so," agrees **Dick**. "Bruce had played with Andy on the drums in Stupid Humans, so they were in synch anyway, especially playing the old songs. Grant fitted in really quickly after Audio Torture, but it wasn't like it was his first band or anything, and he was very competent on the bass. And I'd been singing, and writing, for a while, so although it was possibly a bit hit and miss in places, we all gelled together quite quickly. Me and Bruce got on especially well together, and he had quite complicated ideas – it wasn't just like, 'verse, chorus, verse, chorus, end'; well, quite a lot of it was, but occasionally Bruce would suggest we try something unusual, and there was no debate about it. We'd just try what Bruce said, and it usually turned out really good. He would even write a few of the bass lines, or suggest what the bass could do in a part with his guitar. Bruce was a bit of a genius really; he had loads of ideas."

"A lot of the bass lines – or at least, the skeleton of the bass lines – came from Bruce," confirms **Grant**. "He was a massive musical driver; he had all these ideas and how they should fit together with the bass. We jammed together, and bounced ideas off each other, and all worked it out together, but ultimately Bruce was the main musical force. And he was the one who brought the reggae influence, although we were all into The Ruts, and they'd crossed over with a bit of reggae.

"Dick had a big book of words, and Bruce had a big head full of music, and we'd work through it when we came together. Before multi-tracks, Bruce had a reel-to-reel and would bounce tracks down."

"It was musical," states **Bruce**. "I was never into noise. I always agreed, and still do, with the punk idea that if you can play three chords, you should form a band – there's nothing to stop anyone making music. But when everyone started copying the same three chords in a certain way, it stopped evolving and became a thing. And when things become a thing, they become boring. And it lost the *initial* thing as well, which was to be yourself. But then again, everyone is influenced by someone, and when you hear a band that sounds just like another band, I hope it's because they really like them, and not just copying the blueprint because it's easier than doing something of their own."

There were a few months then before the band's next gig… which was November 22nd, 1980, and – surprisingly for the time of year – was open air!

"Yeah, it wasn't hot," laughs **Dick**. "It was on the Trowbridge bandstand, in Trowbridge Park; they had one of those things that looked as if you'd cut an orange in half, and then into quarters, and took a segment out of it and put a stage in there… like a half dome, that directed the sound out to the whole park. It was a CND [i.e. Campaign for Nuclear Disarmament] benefit gig, but only about seventy people turned up. Someone from the CND, whose name I forget, and his wife, got together with all the local punk bands to do this gig… it sounded pretty good, so we did it. It was a bit scary because it was open air, but it was a good crack."

"The main problem with that Trowbridge Park gig," adds **Bruce**, "Is that the punks were treading all over the flower bed in front of the bandstand, so we got into trouble for that… for standing on the flowers – sorry!"

The third and final Subhumans gig of 1980 was a fashion show, of all things, at The Old Bell in Warminster, on December 9th.

"Oh god, yeah, that was weird, very bizarre," remembers **Andy**. "How do you tone what you do down for all these people sat in nice neat rows watching you? The language and everything like that? You can imagine! Because most of them weren't punk fans. But we wanted to get the name out there, and it got people talking. We played a few of the more reggae-ish numbers, like 'Human Error' and 'Germ', thinking they might go over best."

"That was the first gig I ever went to," says **Kev**, "At the back of the Old Bell hotel, just this function room above a 'bistro' – although I'm not sure anyone, including the hotel itself, knew what one was at the time – called The Chimes Bar. Vanessa Treasure had a shop in the town, which stood out for its bright dayglo designs, and was throwing this fashion show to promote it. Subhumans played at the halfway mark. I remember listening to 'Germ' and possibly 'First Aid' properly for the first time. It wasn't a punk rock sweaty pit kinda vibe *at all*, but I guess that's pretty much how all bands start out?"

"Yes, that was a very unusual gig," **Dick** smiles. "Bruce's sister, Vanessa, made clothes, and she had hired out the hall above The Old Bell pub in Warminster, to put on a fashion show, to show off her latest creations… all these colourful clothes, a bit hippy-ish, I suppose. So, she and two or three of her best mates were wearing these dresses, walking around to a bit of David Bowie, and then they had her brother's band playing as entertainment – which was a bit odd, to say the least, haha! We only did five songs, and we chose the slower ones, like 'Germ' and 'Human Error', and we had a few claps…"

Looking at your gig diary, that was the first time 'Human Error' appeared in the set, and that was quite a departure from the traditional punk sound.

"Oh, totally," agrees **Dick**. "Bruce had made a little dub of the lead guitar line set to a beat, and we were all like, 'Wow, that's great!' It was so catchy, so I wrote some lyrics to it, then rang him up and read the lyrics down the phone, and he liked them. So yeah, songs were formed really quickly; we were writing a few a week."

Their youthful prolificity was still in its infancy, but it would stand them in good stead over the following year, when they would break out of Warminster and make an indelible mark on the national punk scene.

DICK BY MEL BELL

Not only did 1981 see the Subhumans start to broaden their horizons beyond Wiltshire on the live front, hooking up with many of the then-leading lights of the punk scene, it saw them recruit Trotsky on drums after Andy left, and release their first EP, 'Demolition War', that crashed into the top twenty of the Indie Charts at the end of the year.

Besides playing a few local gigs, at Trowbridge Court Mills and Kingdown School in Warminster that most of the band attended, the first few months of 1981 saw Subhumans releasing their 'Demolition War Parts I – III' demo on Dick's own Bluurg Tapes label. An hour-long collection of their best songs to that point, and one of the few places to check out long-since-dropped songs such as 'Trowbridge Park', 'Sid' and 'Pisshead', it was surprisingly decent in sound quality (Part I being a live recording of their fashion show set from a few months earlier, and Parts II & III recorded at youth centre rehearsals during February and March '81).

"The Trowbridge gig [21/2/81, with Organized Chaos and Wild Youth] was my twentieth birthday gig," reveals **Dick**. "There's been a few birthday gigs over the years, because there's nothing better to do on your birthday than play a gig. It was only our fourth gig, and we already had twenty-six songs to play…"

"And that gig at Kingdown was possibly a sixth form disco or fifth year leaving party," recalls **Kev Tydeman.** "There was a small room in a corridor, where the kids normally had their BCG jabs or 'nit' treatment – how very '80s! – that was where the band were before the gig, which was weird 'cos it was Grant and Andy etc. I think a teacher announced them playing and someone dipped the lights, and then put them straight back on full again? Which wasn't very rock 'n' roll…

"There was a mixed response from the vastly differing cross section of pupils, soon to be former pupils, and a gaggle of punks in the corner, but I like to think, like myself, it changed a few people's perceptions – possibly at the very cusp of their child to adulthood lives – and steered them in a different direction in some way?"

"We played 'Pisshead' a few times – that was just about being drunk," says **Dick**, of that first demo, looking through his old song book. "The lyrics went: 'My brain is all fucked up, and I don't really care; I can't take no more drink, I'm going to pour it on my hair; fill my lungs with smoke, fill my head with dreams; violent paranoia, nothing's what it seems! Leave me alone, I'm going to get stoned; don't know what I'm thinking, I'm gonna die drinking! Cut myself about, and no one understands; they think I'm going crazy, it's getting out of hand; getting so fucked up, getting so pissed; 'cos I know that when I'm dead, I won't be missed… I threw the bottles about, now look what I've done; I smashed up a police car, oh, the joys of having fun; the bastards know whodunnit, I'm the only one who's drunk; running down the street to the cries of 'get that punk!' So… not my most eloquent effort, haha!"

'Demolition War Parts I – III' was shopped around various record labels in the time-honoured tradition of trying to land yourself that elusive record deal, but they eventually hooked up with Spiderleg Records, the label ran by members of Flux of Pink Indians, through a more circuitous, fortuitous route. As with many things in life, how Subhumans made their all-important first step towards popularity was a mixture of desire, hard work and good fortune.

"I've got an interesting shoebox somewhere, full of the rejection letters," laughs **Bruce**. "We definitely had a reply from Clay Records… saying they weren't interested! Shock Treatment were one of the labels that *were* semi-interested before Colin and Derek from Flux said they wanted to release us on Spiderleg."

"I think Flux got hooked up when Graham Burnett from New Crimes put out a compilation tape," offers **Dick**. "He was very organised and it seemed like his New Crimes fanzine and tape got around to a lot of places. He used one of the songs from the 'Demolition War' tape on it, and Flux were on it as well, and that's how Flux heard us and got in touch."

"New Crimes fanzine ran from 1980 to 1984, and was started by myself, Chris Kemp (AKA 'Voss Trent') and Stephen Dobson (AKA 'Dr Pretorious') in Southend-on-Sea, Essex," explains **Graham**, "Although after the second issue it was basically just me. It was printed at home using a Gestetner duplicator, a process that involved typing or directly drawing onto special wax 'stencil' sheets that were then attached to an ink-filled drum. You would then load paper into the machine, turn a handle and print the pages one at a time in batches. This was a very messy business with very high paper wastage rates. The ink application on the first pages coming through the machine would be too thick and would smear or seep right through the paper, there would be a batch of fifty or so 'good' copies, then after that the ink would start to run low and be too light and uneven on the page so you'd have to refill the drum. The machine would also often jam and need to be unblocked, inevitably wasting even more paper, so unusable pages could often be as high as 40% in any print run. I also used to get ink all over my mum's dining room carpet so that didn't make me very popular...

"Then there was the tedium of collating all the pages and stapling them together which would involve organising a load of piles of paper on the dining room table and putting each copy together by hand, which was very labour intensive. I love that nowadays I can just email a PDF file off to a printer and they come back all nicely bound and collated in nice cardboard boxes just a few days later.

"New Crimes sold for 25p a copy which just about recuperated costs I think, although lots of copies would also be traded with other zine makers around the country and internationally. They were really proliferating around that time. Just about everybody and their dog seemed to be putting together their own zine around 1980 – 82; that felt like the real golden era for me, especially for 'anarcho punk'.

"Before that, I used to love being involved with the school magazine; I would write science fiction and horror stories, then after I left school, I became involved on the periphery of Bang, a local arts, poetry and music magazine. I would go to some of the editorial meetings so got some insight into that process, and also used to submit gig reviews to another local punk-orientated fanzine called Strange Stories that was produced up the road in Basildon. That would've been about 1978 – 79.

"There were also lots of independent record shops in Southend selling punk and post-punk records at this time, and some would have little sections stocking mags like *Zig Zag* and a few zines, so I'd pick up copies of *Jamming* and *Sniffin' Glue*, which were probably the first two true 'punk' fanzines I bought, and a little later on, go up to London on the train, to Rough Trade and Compendium Bookshop in Camden Town and come home with bundles of zines which I would fervently devour... things like *Toxic Grafity* [sic], *Rapid Eye Movement*, *Cobalt Hate*, *In the City*, *Vague*, *Ripped and Torn* etc., where I would learn more about bands like Crass, The Pop Group, Slits, The Raincoats, Joy Division etc. from a different 'on the ground' perspective than what was written by professional journalists in the *NME*, *Sounds* etc., and at some point I just thought, 'Hey, why don't we just do our own zine then we can put exactly what we want in it?'

"After the first couple of issues of *New Crimes*, I began to move away from covering local bands after interviewing Crass up at Dial House, and moving more towards focusing on anarcho punk bands and ideas, so quite a lot of those bands would send me demo tapes to review. At the time, the Subhumans were completely unknown outside of their own area, and Dick just sent me a copy of the 'Demolition War' demo to review. As I remember, it had a hand-drawn cover and a list of tracks written in biro... I may still have it in a box somewhere? Anyway, I was really impressed with their amazing energy, so gave the band a full-page feature in the zine.

"This was also the time of the 'cassette culture' revolution; people started having access to cheap tape copying facilities (in my case two cassette recorders in my bedroom linked together by a cable), so would make demos (or 'cassette albums' as we would rather grandly call them) which folks would trade with each other or sell really cheaply, often in exchange for 'a blank tape plus SAE' [i.e. a stamped, addressed envelope], a very democratic way of distributing your music, even if you couldn't afford the costs of making a vinyl record. So I decided it would be a good idea to put out a compilation tape of bands that had appeared in *New Crimes*, called 'New Criminals Volume 1'. It featured three tracks each by The Sinyx, Flux of Pink Indians, The APF Brigade and various other bands, one of which was the Subhumans. I sent a copy to all of the bands that had appeared, and a few weeks later got a letter from Dick thanking me for sending the tape to Flux of Pink Indians, as they'd heard it and were so impressed that they decided to offer the Subhumans a chance to make a single on the Spiderleg record label they had just set up. And the rest, as they say, is history! I still see Dick from time to time every few years and he still mentions it every time we meet up."

By that time, the Subhumans had played their first 'away' gig, in Worcester at the youth centre there, with Wild Youth, on April 11th, 1981, a less than auspicious occasion that only drew in thirty punters (**Dick:** "It was a typical youth centre gig – no stage, small PA... someone up there must have written to us off the back of the 'Demolition War' tape?"), but after a few more local gigs with the likes of Organized Chaos, they then found themselves opening for Discharge at the Bowes Lyon House in Stevenage, on May 17th.

"That was our first big gig really – 400 people... we were shitting ourselves," admits

SUBHUMANS

& WILD YOUTH

WORCESTER
YOUTH CENTRE
SATURDAY 11th APRIL
8→10·30 APPROX.
COST

SUBHUMANS
WILD YOUTH
ORGANIZED CHAOS

BRADFORD-on-AVON YOUTH CENTRE
THURSDAY ONLY
30TH APRIL 30P 7·45-10·00

ALTERNATIVE MUZIK PRESENTS

DISCHARGE
THE MOB
SUBHUMANS

SUNDAY 17TH MAY 1981
BOWES LYON HOUSE ST·GEORGES WAY,
MEMBERS £1·50 STEVENAGE
NON-MEMBERS £1·75 7·30-11·00PM

BLUURG

MAY 81 TAPE LIST NO 1

BLUURG 1 – STUPID HUMANS LIVE WARMINSTER
COMMUNITY CENTRE 17-2-80 (AVG QTY) +
3-TRACK DEMO FEB 80 (EXC QTY) – C60

BLUURG 2 – AUDIO TORTURE LIVE BATH TRINITY
HALL 16-2-80 + WARMINSTER C/CENTRE 17-2-80
(G/AVG QTY) – C60

BLUURG 3 – MENTAL 'EXTENDED PLAY' EP + JAN 80
DEMO + JUNE 80 DEMO (EXC QTY) – C60

BLUURG 4 – ORGANIZED CHAOS LIVE TROWBRIDGE
COURT MILLS Y/CENTRE 21-2-81 (G QTY) +
LIVE WARMINSTER CMTY CENTRE 9-5-81 (VG QTY)
+ PRACTICE JAN 80 VG C60

BLUURG 5 – WILD YOUTH LIVE TROWBRIDGE COURT
MILLS Y/CENTRE 21-2-81 (G QTY) +
WORCESTER Y/CENTRE 11-4-81 (VG QTY) – C60

BLUURG 6 – WILD YOUTH LIVE CHIPPENHAM TECH
8-5-81 (VG/EXC QTY) – C60

BLUURG 7 – SUBHUMANS 'DEMOLITION WAR'
PTS 1-3 (LIVE + PRACTICE) 24 TRACKS
(VG/EXC QTY) – C90

BLUURG 8 – SUBHUMANS LIVE WORCESTER
Y/CENTRE (VG QTY) 11-4-81 – C60

BLUURG 9 – SUBHUMANS LIVE WARMINSTER
CMTY CENTRE 9-5-81 (VG QTY) – C60

BLUURG 10 SUBHUMANS LIVE BATH WALCOT V. HALL 20-5-81
VG C60

STILL LIVING IN THE PAST Ⓐ /PUNK /SPECIAL BREW

SEND BLANK TAPE + 50P
OR C60 = 80P
C90 = £1.00   OTHER BANDS
                     WANTED   BLUURG

2 VICTORIA TERRACE MELKSHAM WILTS
                                  SN12 6NA

SUB HUM ANS

PETE THE ROADIE BY MEL BELL

Dick, "But we'd organised a coachload of people to go up there, so we brought our own crowd, who were all down the front cheering us on, which really helped. Organising the coach was a bit crazy – you'd make up little photocopied tickets, and probably charge about £3 for the whole experience… possibly not including getting into the gig, which you had to pay for when you got there. We'd pick up in Warminster, Melksham and Trowbridge."

Like almost every other punk rocker in the UK in the very early Eighties, the Subhumans were fans of Discharge.

"Oh yeah," agrees **Dick**. "The first time we heard Discharge, we were like, 'What? This is amazing!' Dead short, dead fast…"

"The first time I heard them was on John Peel, and I'd never heard anything like it," says **Bruce**, "But I was a bit disappointed at Stevenage… I think they had the Flux drummer playing for them – Bambi [i.e. Dave Ellesmere, also of The Insane] – and they were okay. I remember being very pleased with our gig though; we went down very well indeed."

"That was a cracking concert, the place was packed," says **Andy**, before adding proudly, "I actually lent the Discharge drummer my cymbals because his were broken. That's my claim to fame… then when I saw him playing my cymbals, I realised *why* his were all knackered, haha! We were on first, and we had quite a long set – it felt like thirty songs! – and it was scary, the biggest gig I'd done. But it went really well, we did alright. I was always a panicker; I needed a couple of pints, a bit of Dutch courage just to calm me down. I felt a bit sorry for Dick really, with the gobbing and bottles being thrown around – being a drummer, at the back, at least you had a little bit of cover. I don't miss having to clean my kit off the day after every gig. But that meant they liked you… I think."

"I just remember big hair," laughs **Grant**. "All of Discharge had big hair really, but Cal had especially massive hair. They had a great sound. That was a top day out, and it felt great to be supporting them."

The Discharge gig was also notable as the first Subhumans gig attended by Pete 'The Roadie' – *before* he became their roadie.

"I was born in 1963, in Bradford-on-Avon hospital, right next to Mike Bradbury, the future singer of Organized Chaos," begins **Pete**. "I grew up in the village of Heytesbury, four miles from Warminster. It was a typical rural upbringing – a hard-working family, who were pretty much self-sufficient. I was a shy kid, not really into music until 1976, listening to John Peel, Radio Luxembourg, and reading Sounds and NME. Punk rock just seemed right for me, an identity, and when I started going to my first gigs in '77 and '78, I was hooked. Live music was fantastic, and a punk crowd of hundreds of other kids just like me was amazing. I started going to gigs nearly every weekend, seeing the likes of The Damned, Ruts, Stranglers, Banshees and Wire. I started hanging out with the punks from Warminster, usually at The Ship & Punchbowl pub [closed in 1984 and now converted to flats, but then in Silver Street, and one of the oldest inns in the area, dating back to 1710] – they had punk rock on the jukebox in the lounge bar, and that's where I met the Subhumans.

"I actually went to the same comprehensive school as Bruce, Phil and Trotsky. Trotsky was in the same class as my younger brother. I didn't really hang out with them at school, but knew they were into punk. I got to know them more in Warminster pubs, and every Saturday afternoon they rehearsed in the local youth centre along with the A-Heads and Organized Chaos, which was absolutely brilliant. Punks from surrounding towns would attend; for the size of the town, the punk scene was fantastic.

"The first time I saw them live was at the Bowes Lyons House in Stevenage, with Discharge and The Mob – there was a bus full of local punks to go to the gig with Subhumans, and then I saw them again and again at local shows in Trowbridge, Bradford-on-Avon and Bath. And then they asked me to roadie for them – what a day! I didn't know anything about being a roadie; I couldn't change a string or a drum head, but I could carry stuff, and that's how it started. I think the first thing I learnt to do was putting the tape back on Bruce's Copycat [delay unit] after it had been kicked or pogoed on!

"The local Wessex scene was full-on. Warminster had Subhumans, Organized Chaos and A-Heads; Trowbridge had the Pagans; Bath was Smart Pils and Amebix, and the gigs were packed, all usually in the back rooms of local pubs. Thinking about it now, it wasn't just punks that came to the shows; it was a real local event, with different people from many walks of life turning out.

"There weren't so many fanzines at that time, and as far as places to hang out went, it was the local mall on a Saturday morning, and the park in the afternoon. Warminster was a military town, with soldiers everywhere, which I think made the civilian population stick together more. But everyone was proud of the Subhumans – they were playing all over the UK and were an integral part of the UK punk scene."

"It's my fault that Pete became a roadie," laughs **Mel**. "[Eventual bassist] Phil was originally their roadie. But Pete was such an ardent fan, like myself… we always said we were their No. 1 fans, and we went to every gig, at least until they went to America [in 1984] – Pete went over there with them, but I didn't. Anyway, Phil was always getting drunk, and I just said to Bruce, 'Why don't you make Pete the roadie?'"

"I did break a string at the Stevenage gig, and Phil did change it for me," recalls **Bruce**, "But the one I had just happened to be the wrong one, so I did end up with the wrong string on my guitar, but it wasn't really Phil's fault, haha!"

"Going out wasn't that great, because the squaddies liked to pick on the punks," **Mel** continues, on the subject of Warminster being a military town. "[My friend] Sharon got curry sauce tipped over her head once by a load of squaddies, and Tracy got her teeth punched out – but that was a few years later [during the late Eighties]. It was a different regiment back then – the Black Watch, or something like that – and there was some friction. But they were different times. We only used to go down The Ship & Punch Bowl and The Weymouth Arms in those days, although sometimes we'd come up The King Arthur; there were a few gigs in there."

"You did get a lot of grief in the early days," **Jock** continues. "I remember leaving the pub with Nigel one night, and we got as far as the Speedy Chef, by the town park, and turned around to see Nigel getting punched by a squaddie who didn't like the look of him.

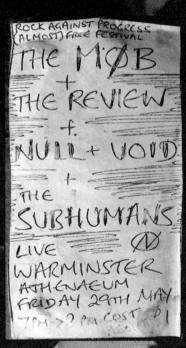

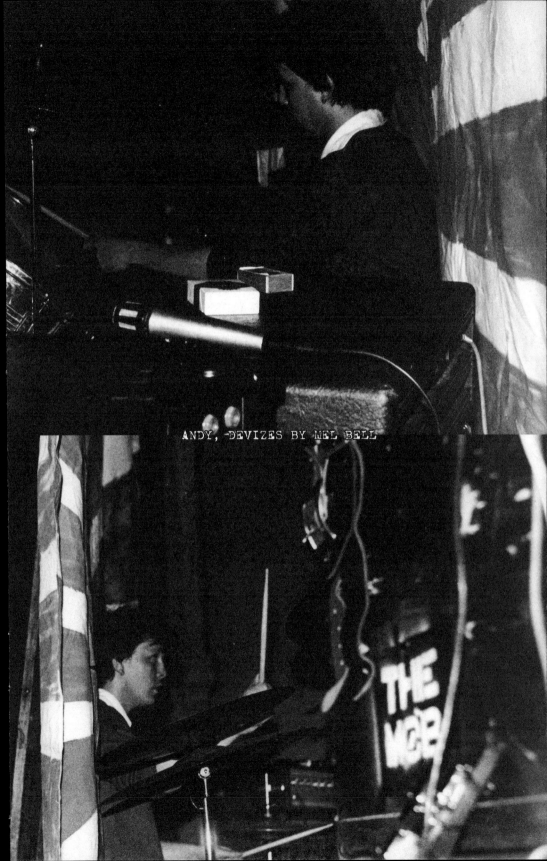

ANDY, DEVIZES BY MEL BELL

He was offended that Nigel was walking around town looking the way he did. This was at a time when all my old school friends were either fighting on Mount Longdon in the Falklands or were punk rockers in Warminster…"

"Again, it was a bit later on, and I'm sure he'll tell you about it," **Kev** recollects, "But a few of them cornered Phil in the park and broke his fucking leg – jumped up and down on it! And Phil didn't even look like a punk. So yeah, there were a few times when there were flashpoints, but we had a few pubs, and they had their own pubs; we kept to our own. And that was the easiest thing. The army was always ever-present, but if you stuck together, you could avoid trouble by and large. There was mainly argy bargy when there were girls involved, y'know?"

Jock: "Back in the Eighties as well, they were all full of bravado 'cos of the Falklands. And every couple of years, you had a new regiment here, and you had different regiments coming here all the time for training and stuff. We kept out of the centre of town, and went to places like The Ship & Punchbowl and The Weymouth Arms, where all the bikers were. But that was okay, because the bikers were friends of some of the guys that ended up driving us all around to gigs. They'd put their arms around us a bit and sorta said, 'If you need us for a gig, we'll drive the Bedford for ya!' Which they promptly rolled over on the road to Trotsky's house, haha!" [More on that later…]

Just prior to the Discharge gig, where The Mob also played, Subhumans had supported The Mob in Devizes, at the Corn Exchange, which led to a spate of gigs with The Mob during late May/early June 1981, in Bath, Warminster and Bradford-on-Avon – the latter also notable as being Andy's last gig with the band… and the one in Devizes as a near death experience!

"Bruce was taking his photography exam, and for some reason, he wanted me to take the photos, of them on the stage," explains **Mel**. "Anyway, The Mob had their backdrop on this really big, tall piece of wood – it was massive, and really heavy duty. And that is where I nearly killed the Subhumans…! They were playing, and I was onstage, taking photos, by Andy's drum kit, and I touched this piece of wood, and it was about to fall down. They couldn't see what was going on, but it was about to fall directly onto the band. Luckily, Josef Porter [from The Mob] saw me and came to my rescue just in time, but that was really scary, because it could've killed one of them…"

Bruce: "The Mob were a bit of an influence. I used to really like 'Shuffling Souls' [B-side of 'Witch Hunt'], that was one of my favourite Mob songs… and 'Youth' was pretty cool, 'cos of the reggae dub stuff. And they were really nice people, of course."

As for Andy leaving, and being replaced by Trotsky, **Bruce** recalls, "Andy left to join the A-Heads really, because they were going into the studio. He didn't like all the punky gobbing over his drum kit either…"

"And he didn't get on with all the members of the band apparently – at least according to my diary!" interjects **Dick**. "He said he got on with me, because I at least told him what was happening, otherwise there seemed to be a lack of communication going on.

Although I rarely saw him outside of the practice room; he didn't really hang out that much."

"He had better equipment than us, and he lent us his stuff for some of our recordings," continues **Bruce**, "Because Trotsky didn't have a very good drum kit. To lend someone your cymbals was a bit of a strange thing to do even then, but that's what he did... Andy's cymbals are on [debut album] 'The Day the Country Died' – apparently! Because geeky drummers have talked to me about this, haha!"

"We had this gig in Bath," recalls **Andy**. "There were loads of punks there, but then in came the skinheads, and it was horrendous. The police turned up. We went out to our van, which we'd hired for the night, and it had been kicked in. That wasn't much fun, but the majority of gigs I played with them were really good.

"Sadly, at the time when punk kicked off, we had a real problem around here, especially in Trowbridge, with glue-sniffing. Our [Stupid Humans] bassist Herb even got interviewed for a programme on TV about it. It was terrible really; there'd be people in the back of the van puffing away on it... but it never interested me. And it didn't worry me really – I liked to drink, they liked to puff on something...

"It didn't bother me until that last [Subhumans] gig I did, and it was the end of the night; all the lights were up and everyone was clearing up, and there were all these bodies passed out at the back of the hall, and a syringe on the floor. I was just miffed, because I thought those people had come to see the bands, but they were all as high as kites, and it could have been anyone playing. It got to me a little bit.

"And that did it for me really. It was exciting music, and exciting times, but me, as a person, I didn't want to see that. It frustrated me, all the glue-sniffing... I lost a few friends to all that, it just turned them – and what could those kids remember of the songs we'd played that night? I know they weren't all like it, but I'd made my mind up; I needed a change.

"That was one of the reasons anyway. The other was that I was doing an apprenticeship at the time, and weighing the band up against my future and what I needed to do... although in hindsight I wish I'd stayed with the band a bit longer, and seen what happened.

"It might have been a bit of a knee-jerk reaction, but I joined the A-Heads. It was a different style of music, a female vocalist for a change; they weren't as busy as the Subhumans with gigs, but we did an EP. Sadly I wasn't with them for too long either, before I moved on again; embarrassingly, I joined a disco band, called Rare Breed. The disco scene was starting to come in, and you had Oscar's nightclub [in nearby Longleat], and people wanted to dance. It was quite a successful band, but pretty boring drumming for me. It wasn't the same. We were starting to make good money off that band, but the singer got cold feet when things started moving apace, and just left.

"And then I joined a rock band, Salient Point, which was more exciting as regards drumming. We wrote all our own stuff, as did the disco band, but that was the last band I was in. I stopped playing drums sometime in the mid-Nineties. I started working shifts, which really messed me up; I couldn't go to rehearsals, I couldn't get to the gigs... and what can you do? You need to earn a living. And then you add girlfriends into the equation

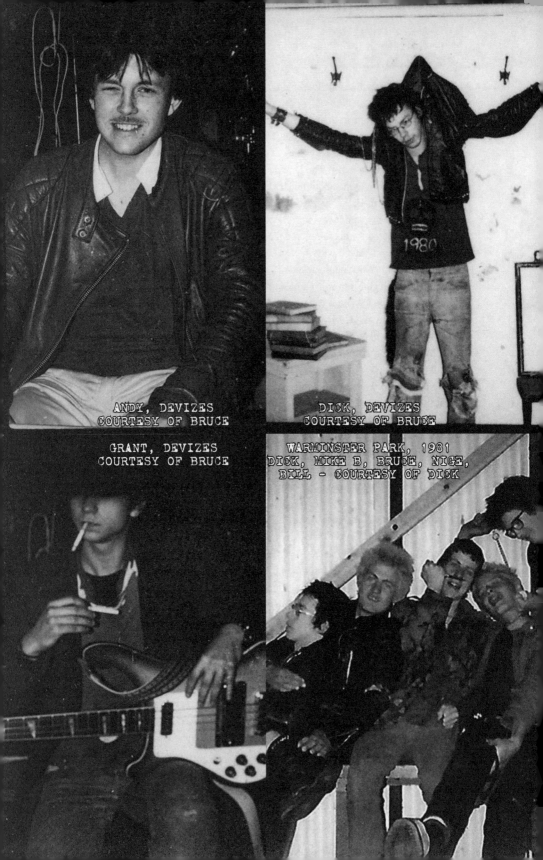

ANDY, DEVIZES
COURTESY OF BRUCE

DICK, DEVIZES
COURTESY OF BRUCE

GRANT, DEVIZES
COURTESY OF BRUCE

WARMINSTER PARK, 1981
DICK, MIKE B, BRUCE, NIGE,
BILL - COURTESY OF DICK

BRUCE, DICK, GRANT,
1981 - COURTESY OF DICK

ANDY, WARMINSTER YC,
1981 - COURTESY OF DICK

GRANT, BRUCE, ANDY, DICK, 1981 - COURTESY OF DICK

subhumans dick voice grant bass bruce drums
steve gtr...andy (drums) had left 2 weeks
earlier so this was the improvised lineup...
also a chance to do some mental songs.......

wild youth steve gtr/voice herb bass ron drums
possibly their best gig to date, and yet
again in front of a totally apathetic crowd

A WILD YOUTH   A SUBHUMAN

"When there's no more room in Hell, the dead shall stalk

MELKSHAM
YOUTH CENTRE
LIVE 15/7/81

① DRUGS OF YOUTH
ALL GONE DEAD
ASH TRAY DIRT
SOCIETY
NOTHING I CAN DO
MICKEY MOUSE IS DEAD
SID
PEROXIDE
KILLING
NEW AGE
ANIMAL
PARTY POLITICAL BULLSHIT
FUN IN CAMDEN
ATTACK

② LAST PUNK IN TOWN
SKINT
RUN FOR YOR LIFE
NATIONAL REACTION
NO CHOICE
CROWDS
PROBLEM PAGE
77 IS GONE
PLASTIC AGE
GLUE
SICK BOY

BLUURG 11

SUB HUM ANS   WILD YOUTH

BLUURG tapes Dick 2 Victoria Terrace Melksham Wilts

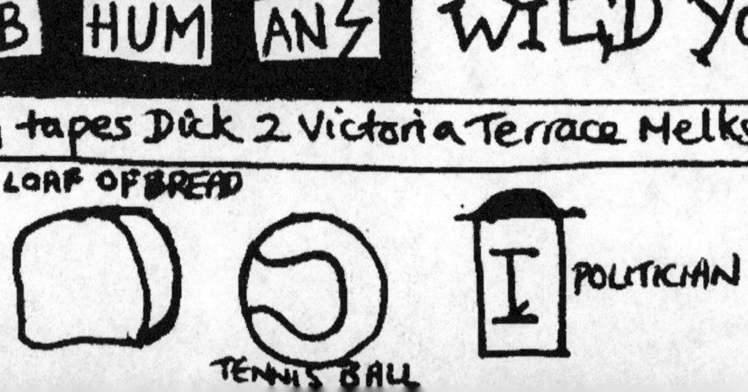

LOAF OF BREAD

TENNIS BALL

POLITICIAN

BORING
OBJECTS
OF OUR
TIME

TROTSKY, WARMINSTER YOUTH CLUB BY PHIL
GRANT - COURTESY OF JOCK MCCURDY

as well… my girlfriend at the time became my first wife – she came to one gig, I think, and didn't like it at all."

Andy was replaced by Trotsky, who the band members inevitably knew through their time at Kingdown School, although not before the band played one gig at the Canberra Youth Centre in Melksham [15/7/81] with Bruce moving to drums and Dick's brother Steve on the guitar.

"Yes, Steve played guitar, so Bruce could go on drums, because Andy had just left," confirms **Dick**. "Wild Youth were headlining, Subhumans were supporting, and we did three Mental songs at the end of the set – extraordinary gig really!"

"When Andy got his drum kit, piece by piece, I'd always have a little go on it, and I didn't find it difficult to do a basic pattern, you know?" explains **Bruce**, of his intuition for drums as well as guitar, "And I found I could do the coordination thing between the right foot and the right hand. I think that would have helped when I was writing songs, for sure. I later played drums in The Flying Fish Band with Steve as well.

"But where did we find Trotsky?" he laughs. "That's easy – next to the shed on the school playing fields, having a fag. In my school, there were only two drummers, in a school of about a thousand kids, because drummers were so rare in those days. So, when Andy left, it was like, 'Who else can play drums…?' And Trotsky was in the year below us. He always had his fag behind the shed at the top of the school field, because you weren't allowed to smoke at school… obviously. But we all tried it, and all got punished for it. He managed to find somewhere to go and do it.

"He looked like he wasn't into punk, because he had long hair, and wore a cut-off and everything, but there was just no choice – who else was going to play drums? So we invited him, and he came along and auditioned. I'm not really sure why he joined us in a way, because he was more into Ian Gillan and Black Sabbath… I don't think he was much into punk at all, but he needed a band like we needed a drummer. We did have some common ground with Black Sabbath though – we probably all owned Black Sabbath albums… although we all had different albums in our collection."

"I've still got 'Volume IV' and 'Paranoid'," confirms **Dick**.

Bruce: "I had the original one with the witch on the front, and Trotsky had 'Heaven and Hell' and 'Sabotage' – which is a great album… I got into that through Trotsky. 'Symptom of the Universe' and all that, very heavy stuff."

Dick: "There was a Hawkwind connection too. Trotsky and Bruce were both into Hawkwind, and [later on] Phil was into Hawkwind bigtime as well."

"I think we were going in a heavier direction a bit by then… certainly I was already getting away from punk a bit, in my head," ponders **Bruce**, before continuing, as regards what Trotsky joining changed in the band, "Definitely the personal chemistry, because he was a lot of fun. He had the same sense of humour as us really, lots of Monty Python jokes… I just remember him laughing most of the time. I'm not sure musically whether anything was better or worse than with Andy, to be honest. I think Trotsky would agree with me when I say, he was still learning, it was his first band. But he learnt very quickly."

"Subhumans *was* my first band," confirms **Trotsky**. "It was the summer of '81, and I was fifteen years old, still at school. I'd been playing drums for about a year and a half, just jamming a bit with my brother who played guitar – but I had no band experience at all.

"Bruce and Grant were the year above me at school. And Billy, the Organized Chaos drummer, was in my year. I knew of all those guys, and word got to me that Subhumans were looking for a drummer – a guy I knew from school told me this, and organised a practice in his mum's front room. So me, Bruce and Grant had a jam… I don't think Dick was there. And I got the job.

"I hadn't actually seen Subhumans live, but one of the first gigs I ever went to was The Mental with Vice Squad and Stupid Humans in Warminster. There were loads of fights afterwards with the squaddies. So, I'd seen Bruce play live with Ju in the Stupid Humans, and I'd seen Dick in The Mental with his brother Steve. I didn't really know them at that point, although I knew of Bruce vaguely, through school… Dick was from Melksham, of course, which was virtually foreign parts, haha! I was from the villages just outside Warminster, so I wasn't that involved in the scene.

"I was a metal-head really, I had very little punk knowledge. The first band that made me want to play drums was AC/DC. There was a [late Seventies, BBC] series called 'Rock Goes to College', and AC/DC were on there, playing some little college gig in front of about 500 people, and that absolutely blew me away – I was like, 'That's it! I want to play drums!' But yeah, I was into Black Sabbath and AC/DC… although I remember hearing 'Holiday in Cambodia' by the Dead Kennedys on John Peel, and thinking, 'What the hell is that? It's fucking incredible!' I remember it as clear as day, and that was, what? 1980? Hearing punk, and then playing punk, was a new experience, and it was great – something totally new. I listened to John Peel a lot… and the Friday Rock Show, of course, with Thomas the Vance!

"I don't like the 'hippy' word," he frowns, when asked about his distinctive look, that was certainly left field for the early Eighties UK punk scene, "Not only because of the punk attitude towards hippies, but most hippies were wankers anyway. I was more of a metal-head than a hippy. And I wore cowboy boots – which were impossible to play drums in, haha! So I'd end up drumming barefoot. We did look completely different… I obviously wasn't very punky, but neither were the rest of them really. And I never got any hassle for the way I looked either. In some scenes, if you didn't look right, they'd have you out back and do you over, but I got no hassle off anyone at all, I was just accepted as I was. The punk scene was such a welcoming place.

"At the time, there were so many bands in Warminster; that town produced so many musicians.

"Wally who was in the A-Heads was in Silent Guests. And before that he was in Moskow, around '78. He used to jam with my brother at The Shed [which was, quite literally, a shed on Trotsky's dad's farm, where Subhumans would later end up rehearsing too]. The first time I ever played on a drum kit was on Wally's kit… he had this massive twelve-piece drum kit, with double bass drums and eight rack toms – this huge thing. That was the first drum kit I ever touched. And when he sold it, I bought the main hub of it – and that was the kit I used for all the Subhumans gigs. I've still got a few bits of it left too; I never throw any gear away.

"I was self-taught, but after about four years or so, I had about ten lessons from this local guy – mainly because I wanted to learn how to read drum music. So I had to get lessons, because I didn't know anyone else who could teach me – none of the punk drummers knew how to read music. That was good, and I'm glad I did it, although I'm glad I didn't have the lessons when I started, because it's important to find your own style.

"Obviously my influences were very different to Andy's," he continues, when pushed as regards his style. "My top drummers of all time back then were Phil Rudd from AC/DC, Neil Peart from Rush… Phil Collins on the early Genesis stuff was technically fantastic… John Bonham… there are too many to list. I suppose my influences crossed over with Bruce's in many ways, because he was into the prog rock stuff like Yes, rather than stuff like the Dead Kennedys, for example. But having said that, when we played with the Dead Kennedys at the Central London Polytechnic in '82, we were first on the bill, and I watched the Kennedys from the side of stage, and watching [their drummer] Peligro was awesome, he was something else. Maybe I was just in awe at that first gig, because I saw them again a few years later, and he just didn't have it; he didn't have quite the same speed and precision."

"Trotsky was a very good drummer, despite being only fifteen when he joined," says **Dick**. "He does make it look effortless. He looks too relaxed. He does all this amazing stuff, but he's just looking around whilst he's doing it – not really breaking into much of a sweat but really pounding on the drums."

"Even though Trotsky listened to heavy drumming, he wasn't as loud as Andy," reckons **Bruce**, "It took a while – many years – for him to become 'the John Bonham of punk'! I remember Trotsky's drum audition with us. He'd bought some drums off Dave Stephens [the aforementioned 'Wally' from Moskow], who was one of those guys who once had a huge twelve-piece drum kit, and then decided to sell it off in bits. So when Trotsky came for his audition, he had a tiny little tom and a massive tom, with nothing in between – he'd ended up buying each end of this massive kit or something, so it looked funny. And when he played, he was very in control, but very fast… he was just different from Andy, but it worked.

"Again, he didn't have much time to learn our set. Just like Dick had to learn all those songs before our first gig, Trotsky had to learn all our songs before going in the studio, because we only had one gig lined up before we were in recording."

Grant: "Well, I knew Trotsky from school too – I probably bumped into him when going for a fag up the playing fields… as you do! Bruce was a year older than me, and Trotsky was a year younger. We got chatting, so we knew he played drums, and when Andy left, we immediately thought of him. There weren't a lot of drummers around back then, and we really liked the fact that he had a massive kit, haha! It was very impressive.

"Andy was a real sharp, hard, tight kind of drummer, and Trotsky was much looser… but not in a bad way – he was more expansive, I should say? A lot of punk bands channelled themselves into one specific style, but we left ourselves wide open, so we could mix and match whatever… we'd just jam, and pick stuff up, and turn it into something else… we used to really enjoy jamming together, as long as it broadly fitted with what all of us wanted to hear, and I'm sure that's what the band still do now."

"I was busy with Organized Chaos at the time, so I wasn't paying that much attention," **Bill** adds, contemplating the different dynamic the change of drummers may have heralded, "But they're very different people, Trotsky and Andy, and personalities have a big influence on a band. They've totally different styles in their playing as well – Trotsky was totally John Bonham, very powerful, very flowing, whereas Andy was very tight, very precise, really snappy and sharp, and reminded me of the first Tubeway Army drummer, who was brilliant – I still watch him to this day on YouTube. They both suited the band in different ways, but the dynamic of Trotsky's personality was probably the biggest difference."

Trotsky made his live debut at Kenny Fox's party on July 25th, 1981, an impromptu appearance and relatively low-key affair to break him in before they went into the studio to record their first EP for Spiderleg: "It was in a tent in his garden, with a band called Wasted Space, a bunch of real hippies from Trowbridge, and it was amazing. I had my first weed that night as well, so it was great...!"

"Kenny was one of our drivers from Trowbridge, a bit hippy, a bit mad, but very friendly," explains **Dick**. "He was good friends with Tony Carter, who was another one of our drivers, who was also a good laugh. They were older than us, very hippy-ish, with flares, purple trousers... but they had vehicles and free time. They weren't properly working – a lot of people weren't in the Eighties – and they could drive us, quite often at just a few hours' notice. For a lot of our gigs we only had a day, or a week, or a fortnight's notice... which is probably why so few people would sometimes turn up. It was all quite chaotic. The ability to make phone calls was quite limited – you had to have the right amount of coinage to use a pay phone, and you had to find a pay phone that actually worked, and the other person had to be in when you rang, because not many people had answering machines. I used to live with my dad, and I used to use the phone so much, he put a *pay*phone into the house, to make me pay for the calls there and then, because the bills were enormous."

Bruce: "That gig was in the back garden of Kenny's house, on the edge of Trowbridge, this terrace block. We've got it on tape somewhere, and I remember that gig very well as I was trying out a new effect pedal I had. I think we wanted to warm Trotsky up a bit, and it was an opportunity..."

Dick: "I think Kenny probably said, 'Can you play my party?' and we said, 'Yes!' Words like 'opportunity' didn't exist... we didn't take *opportunities* – all that 'new speak' came in during the Nineties, but this was before new speak!

"There was *a lot* of spontaneity going on at the time, without even knowing that's what it was – a lot of pre-planning didn't exist. There was one gig we had to go to in the early days, where I'd woke up, the morning after a party at a friend's house in Trowbridge, and this chap came in that morning to give me back my leather jacket, that I didn't even know was missing, but he'd grabbed it the night before to give himself a disguise because he was on the run from the pigs. I was like, 'Eh?' Quite extraordinary, but you had to take it in your stride, haha! Then I had to go running around Trowbridge, to find

DICK AND GRANT - COURTESY OF JOCK MCCURDY

DICK, SPUD, MEL - COURTESY OF JOCK MCCURDY

any one of our several ex- or current possible drivers, to get us to this gig that night. I forget where the gig was, but the point is, once we'd found a driver, we then had to find a van from somewhere – not a week before the gig, but on the day of the gig. And then get transport to get to the van, then get the van, pick up all the other band members... I think the gig was in London somewhere, and we got there three hours late, but it didn't matter. These things just sort of fell together half the time. It's amazing the amount of gigs that *did* happen, that came together despite the insanely momentary way they were often organised.

"Other gigs would be offered you at two days' notice... 'This band's pulled out...' or 'Someone's ill...', and you'd fill in, often in a faraway place, and if you could all do it, and we all could, usually, because no one was really employed. Or at least weren't in a job that they cared about enough to miss a gig. I actually agreed to a lot of gigs before I told the rest of the band. But it didn't matter, because no one had anything massively important that they had to do instead, like regular jobs. In actual fact, for the most part, I was the one with the regular job, at least until 1983, so I was blagging all the spare time off work that I possibly could. Then I had to apply a bit of planning, because I'd have to make sure I could get the time off. But I always managed to, by making back the time, going in on Saturdays or whatever – I always pulled it off.

"My job? Well, after I left school, and after a few months doing nothing as much as possible, my dad got me a job at Avon Rubber in the tyre test department; that lasted a few months, then he found me another motor-related job at Devizes Motor Company, where I worked from '80 – '83. It was there, in downtime and lunch breaks, that I wrote a lot of the early Subs songs. I remember, when my co-workers, whose daily conversation revolved around drink, women and cars, read the lyrics on the 'Demolition War' sleeve, they had a laugh along the lines of, 'Oh, Dick's gonna change the world...' 'Haha, fuck you!' I thought, and got back to work. The place hadn't had an upgrade since like 1930 or something, and when an electric till was introduced, it was chaos; no one could work out which buttons to push. I cycled to and from work [fourteen miles a day] until I was run over [more on that later], and left in '83 as soon as the first royalties from [debut album] 'The Day the Country Died' arrived [more on that later as well!].

"Anyway, I think we played twice at Kenny's place? The second time a brick came flying over the wall from a neighbour and hit Pete The Roadie in the head... and then the police turned up, asking, 'Who's in charge?' And of course, no one was."

Less than two weeks after Kenny's party, Subhumans were in Pickwick Studios, in nearby Corsham, with the house engineer Steve Collinson, recording the aforementioned 'Demolition War' EP for Spiderleg (August 8th, 1981). Colin 'Colsk' Latter, who had previously fronted The Epileptics before becoming the singer for Flux of Pink Indians, started Spiderleg Records with Flux bassist Derek Birkett, and the Subhumans EP was the first non-Epileptics release on their label.

"It started at a time when we'd already recorded 'Neu Smell' [the first Flux EP, released on Crass Records in July 1981], and it was quite easy to go and get records pressed yourself," recounts **Colsk**. "Before 'Neu Smell', we'd had '1970s' [by The Epileptics] come out as a 7" on Stortbeat Records; that was in 1979, and Stortbeat dried up after about a year. They pressed 2000, I think, and there wasn't going to be any more, they just disappeared. But one of the guys involved with them came to us and said he had the masters and he was happy to hand them over to us. So, Derek and I went to Mayking – we had quite a long relationship with Mayking, and coincidentally that was where Southern [the studio that distributed Crass] stuff was being pressed as well – and we pressed up 1000 copies, with white labels and a photocopied cover of the body in the woods... not too punky at all; I think I was in a bit of a Joy Division phase by then!

"And I can't really remember selling them there, but I've been told by some people that they bought them off me at Cambridge Station, so I reckon that when the Corn Exchange had gigs on, Derek and I used to just go up there and hang around and sell records, like people have done ever since, if you think about it. That was 1981, so we were Flux of Pink Indians by then, but we were still trying to keep '1970s' in press.

"We knew that 'Neu Smell' was a one-off on Crass Records; they only ever did one record with any band, and I don't think they had Corpus Christi [their offshoot label, that released the likes of Conflict and Icons of Filth] going at the time, so we set up Spiderleg for ourselves – almost accidentally. Not really as a record label as such, but more someone giving us some masters and going to a pressing plant – 1000 records turned up in a big box, and we went and sold them. We never sat down and planned, or had an office, or accounts, or anything like that.

"The second release was 'Last Bus to Debden' [also by The Epileptics], and Sid [the Flux drummer who was also in Rubella Ballet] must have been around at the time, because that was a title that he came up with for Flux, but we never used it. We weren't thinking about putting out any Flux stuff at that time, which seems a bit strange – and [the Flux debut album] 'Strive...' didn't turn up until [catalogue number] SDL8. Which was a year later. But it was because people started leaving the band after 'Neu Smell' came out – Andy left first, and then we thought Sid should just do Rubella Ballet, it was silly him doing both. Neil left about the same time, and then Bambi and Simon from The Insane joined us for a bit; they did quite a few gigs, but no records, and then we started turning down all these gigs that they would have loved to have played as The Insane, so we kind of fell out over that really. And [Epileptics guitarist] Kevin re-joined us.

"I was still living at home in Bishops Stortford, and that's where the Subhumans demo would have been sent – my mum's old address on the back of all those early Spiderleg records. And apparently it was a fanzine that sent it to me [the aforementioned Graham Burnett of New Crimes fanzine], not the Subhumans themselves. Derek was also living in Bishops Stortford – we hadn't moved out from our mum and dads', y'know – and with the little bit of knowledge we had from doing the two Epileptics records, plus getting to know the set-up at Southern Studios, and getting to know John Loder there, after doing 'Neu Smell' for Crass, we must have slowly got the idea to start doing other people's records as well. And we didn't do a Flux one until SDL8 – before that we did three singles with Subhumans, Amebix and The System...

GRANT, 1981 - COURTESY OF MEL BELL

SUBHUMANS MAP OF WILTSHIRE

DEMOLITION WAR AD

"We got to know The System through Dave and Simon from The Insane. They lived up in Wigan, and Dave – or 'Bambi', as we knew him – was also drumming for Discharge. And as much as I was into Crass, there was half of me that was just as much into Discharge… just as political, but less intellectual, which was where I was at, but more noise… *that* sound they had. Anyway, Dave was still in Discharge, and I was speaking to Cal, and we were going to organise a tour together, which would have been quite a crossroads as it were, because gigging with Discharge wasn't really the world of Crass. And that could have quite easily happened, but when Bambi left Discharge and came to play for us, that wasn't to be.

"Subhumans were one of the first bands who contacted us who we didn't know through Poison Girls, Rubella Ballet, the Fatal Microbes, Crass… Subhumans were a band we got to know on our own, completely separately, and it would have been from hearing that tape. It was something quite different. I remember when we first met them, they had this 50% punk, 50% hippy thing going on, which – as far as I know, and certainly not in Bishops Stortford, or even London – didn't really exist in 1980, 1981…

"We had turned up at Stonehenge as The Epileptics in 1979. Some of Crass had been involved with the festival from the beginning, in the Seventies, and they must have still had a connection there – them, and Poison Girls, and Here and Now really fitted into that scene. Anyway, we never played – we couldn't get onstage early enough, and I'd only booked the van for one day, so we had to go back that night.

"We went back there again the following year, still The Epileptics but just about to change our name to Flux of Pink Indians, which Crass thought was the most ridiculous thing they'd ever heard – they didn't get the name at all. Crass had been given a stage for the night, and they had quite a few punk bands. We came on about 8 o'clock, and it wasn't getting dark, because it was the longest day of the year, but it was getting hard to see what exactly was going on, and that was when we had the trouble with the bikers. They weren't happy at all that there were all these punk bands playing.

"And then we played again in '81, but at 4 o'clock in the afternoon; Crass weren't there that year, and there wasn't that many punks really.

"But there was a proper crossover scene going on in that part of the world, and the Southwest, with The Mob and Smart Pils and everyone. There seemed to be a strong connection between Stonehenge and the summer solstice and the music scene there. And when we first met Subhumans, Trotsky had his long hair and a Led Zeppelin T-shirt, Dick had his – as we used to say – 'wet sock' fringe… there was no spikey hair as such. We all thought it was quite funny – no one was supposed to like bands like Led Zeppelin anymore, but here they were, wearing the T-shirts and not giving two hoots what anyone thought. It was almost like a breath of fresh air."

"Corsham is between Chippenham, Melksham and Box [just under twenty miles north of Warminster]," explains **Bruce**, of their first formal recording experience. "Pickwick Studios was a transformed house, behind a laundry. Upstairs was the mixing room, and the playing room downstairs was probably an extension. They had a proper glass drum booth though, which they don't seem to have so much these days, which you could do the vocals in later as well. It was an eight-track studio.

"Steve Collinson was the resident engineer. It was owned by someone who had something to do with the label that released that A-Heads EP, which was TW Records… which stood for Track West. TW also released Silent Guests and did an EP by Animals and Men, which we all seemed to have… which was a bit weird.

"For some reason, when you recorded in those days, you brought all your friends with you to the studio, haha! So Julian was there; we wanted him to do backing vocals, I think, but he was there anyway…"

"Kenny drove us there," adds **Dick**. "Steve was there too [he did backing vocals on 'Society' and 'Drugs of Youth' with Julian], and Jayne, Mel and Julie…"

"Yes, all the girlfriends had to be there, for some reason… moral support?" ponders **Bruce**. "I think Andy lent us his drum kit – but you'll have to ask Trotsky to be sure – and we played it all live. It was done ridiculously fast, like in six hours, to record and mix it. We definitely didn't take too much time over it though – and by the end of it, the guitar was quite out of tune, haha! We started off in tune, and gradually went out of tune – which is ridiculous when you think about it now, you can't imagine doing it. But we were on a tight budget.

"It felt to me like we had a new drummer, and we weren't quite as tight as we were with the old drummer who'd just left, y'know? I think we could have done with a bit more time, but Spiderleg wanted the songs."

"To start with, we were planning on just doing four songs," elaborates **Dick**. "'Drugs of Youth', 'Parasites', 'Big Brother' and 'Who's Gonna Fight in the Third World War?' We were going to record them at practice in July, to send down to Spiderleg to hear, but we got too drunk and didn't have a very good take. We discussed going to Crescent Studios at one point… that was in Bath. That was like the 'big' studio in the area at the time, but it was probably too expensive for us.

"Colin rang me up, and he wanted 'Animal' and 'Society' on the EP as well. And he said we could have up to eight minutes on either side of the EP, so we could maybe do some more. We had that many songs, so for the first EP, we had a lot to choose from; we just had to debate, argue and agree which six songs went together the best, and the rest just had to wait. Songs just carried over – if they weren't on this one, they'd be on the next one, or maybe the one after that.

"We did the music first, and everything was pretty much first take, apart from 'Parasites', that we did twice. And all the vocals were first take, apart from 'Parasites' again, which took three goes. I didn't have much fun doing the vocals, because there were no effects on the mic at all, and I thought I sounded fucking terrible, which knocked my confidence a bit. I thought my voice sounded weak, but Steve made it sound much better when he mixed, by slapping various things on it.

"I wanted to sound like Iggy Pop, but I didn't. There's a scream on the EP somewhere, and I was trying to replicate the scream from the song 'TV Eye', where Iggy Pop does this amazing scream, and I wanted to do something like that, but couldn't, because my voice was too high or something."

Ever since they put you away
things haven't been quite
    the same
They cut off all your hair
And gave you a brand new
    brain

Now you~~ ...~~
They sent you to University
That was the next step up
Studying sociology
They gave you a ...
    plastic cup

Your new brain was voting
    well
~~...~~ ... were satisfied
They thought they'd done a
    miracle
But you had something to
    hide
They'd left a bit of your old
    brain
Stuck inside your skull
~~That bit that~~ ...
    Screwed up your culture
You ~~became~~ became an animal

And one night you
    were drinking
In the students bar
It was ~~just one pint~~
    2 ...
~~And it~~ ...
Your ~~...~~ brain got control
2 pints blew your animal brain
And your mind just went too
    for
~~You ... up all the tables~~
~~And~~
You murdered all the
    students
And took all you could get
Now you sit alone in
    a disco
Smoking cigarettes

~~Well did k you do,~~ well
~~... You got a brain new brain~~
What happened to
you with your brand new brain
So ...
~~...~~ what will they
~~they~~ ... get you ...?
~~Animal~~ - they're going to get you
~~Animal~~ - ~~...~~ when cos you went
    insane

'ANIMAL' - DICK'S ORIGINAL LYRIC SHEET

The government are real great to us
crawl in their slippers and let us die.
The holocaust won't last that long,
While turns to black in our sky.

[You build your demolition wall,
[Who the hell are you fighting for.

~~The corporations have to be fed,~~
~~You love us too they buy tons of lead,~~

You keep your peace with starving countries,
The combodiens have to be fed,
But You can't you see We've got our problems
Your taxing us to buy tons of lead.

Cuba can ~~not the~~ take our business over,
Because they have got no workers rights,
We've got a choice of three for our democracy
When their all wrong whats left to bite.

'PARASITES' - ORIGINAL LYRICS BY BRUCE

HUMAN ERROR

'HUMAN ERROR'
DICK'S ORIGINAL
LYRIC SHEET

Theres a ~~bit~~ bomb going ~~on~~ in Belfast
~~And the~~ Theres a war in Vietnam
~~Theres~~ There's a TV documentary
To help you understand

But the other channel is better
Becos it don't tax yor mind
Relax in the ignorance of yor home
As ~~nuclear~~ ~~they~~ destroys mankind

And the rest of the world has gone to sleep
Becos they couldn't care less
The world is going
So am I
Its such a fucking mess

There's a arms race in America
~~The~~ The race that no one wins
~~And the~~ ~~Somebody~~ ~~the~~ ~~Somebody pushed a button~~   If someone pushed a button
~~And stuck the planet them with pins~~   An accidental sin

~~Meanwhile back in suburbia~~ Meanwhile baby wonders
~~People~~ ~~Mummy feeds the cat~~   whats a nuclear war?
~~And baby says whats nuclear war?~~ ' And mummy says
~~Shut up you little brat~~!'   to tell the truth
                          'I'm really not quite sure

And the rest of the world ~~has gone to sleep just stayed~~
Becos they ~~did~~ ~~couldn't care less~~   ~~just~~ ~~at home~~ was ignorant
~~The world is going~~ didn't know more
So am I   The pamphlet sed
~~Its such a fuck~~ never just stay ~~in bed~~ at home
                 Avoid the nuclear war'

~~An the computer pressed a button~~
~~Som~~ The computer pressed the button
And the rain was full of lead
And more bombs ~~went~~ dropped on Belfast
And Vietnam went dead
The TV documentary
Outlined the possible cause
It was ~~Author~~ Just a human error
Becos man invented wars

And the rest of the world
stayed in their homes
~~And~~ Cos thats what they were
And the children cried too
Before they died
As they knew they'd never get to

Who's gonna fight in the IIIrd W/War?
There ain't no patriots no more
They all died out in the ~~2nd W/War~~

Who's gonna fight in the 3rd w/war?

~~The government~~ ~~come~~ ~~Gov~~

The government talk about conscription
Another ~~restriction~~ restriction
self imposed
~~Cos ~~everyone~~ ~~knows~~ ~~it just ain't right~~

Their excuse is no conviction
Patriotism its all fiction

Everyone knows it just ain't right
~~The natural law is live not~~
Don't we get the choice to live or die?
~~Alone turns of~~
They give us hardship all our life
And then we refuse they wonder shy

I won't fight for any ~~countries~~ ~~cause~~
Cos the country wouldn't fight for me
~~Put the unemployed~~
They can't afford ~~to pay~~ ~~security~~ the dole money
So they'll put the unemployed in the army ~~wars~~

14·2·81

'WHO'S GONNA FIGHT IN THE THIRD WORLD WAR'
DICK'S ORIGINAL LYRIC SHEET

BRUCE, DICK, MEL - COURTESY OF JOCK MCCURDY

BRUCE AND GRANT ON BOOZE CRUISE TO DENMARK, 1981

SUB HUM ANS

HISTORY/THE SUBHUMANS FORMED IN APRIL 80 AFTER THE STUPID HUMANS SPLIT WHEN JU LEFT/
POLLY REPLACED JU ON VOCALS BUT SOON AFTERWARDS BOTH HER AND HERB (BASS) LEFT/BRUCE
(GTR) AND ANDY (DRUMS) REPLACED HERB WITH GRANT FROM AUDIO TOTURE ANOTHER LOCAL BAND
WHO'D RECENTLY SPLIT/AND BRUCE DID THE SINGING UNTIL SEPTEMBER WHEN DICK JOINED ON
VOICE AFTER THE MENTAL SPLIT UP/THIS LINE-UP LASTED UNTIL JUNE 81 DURING WHICH WE DID
13 GIGS THE BEST OF WHICH WAS SUPPORTING DISCHARGE AT STEVENAGE IN MAY/IN FEBRUARY AFTER
SENDING OFF DEMOTAPES TO VARIOUS RECORD COMPANIES A SINGLE DEAL WAS OFFERED BY SHOCK
TREATMENT RECORDS BUT THEY WENT BANKCRUPT IN APRIL/FED UP WITH DISORGANISED GIGS AND
THE LACK OF STUDIO WORK ANDY LEFT IN JUNE AND JOINED THE A HEADS WITH WHOM HE'D BEEN
'ON LOAN' FOR THE LAST FEW MONTHS/TROTSKY A FIFTEEN YEAR OLD HIPPY REPLACED HIM WITHIN
TWO WEEKS AND WAS SOON UP TO ANDY'S STANDARD/MEANWHILE FLUX OF PINK INDIANS HAVING HEARD
OUR THREE TRACKS ON THE 'NEW CRIMINALS' COMPILATION TAPE OFFERED TO FINANCE AN E.P. ON THEIR
OWN 'SPIDERLEG' LABEL/THIS 'DEMOLITION WAR E.P.' WAS RECORDED IN AUGUST AND RELEASED IN
NOVEMBER DURING WHICH A SERIES OF GIGS TOOK PLACE WITH FLUX/THE E.P. HAS NOW SOLD 5000//////
7000

VIEWS/ANTIWAR/ANTIGOVERNMENT/ANTIAPATHY/WE OFFER NO SOLUTIONS COS WE DON'T KNOW ANY/
PERMANENT MASS CHANGE HAS TO BE A RESULT OF MASS COMMUNICATION AND THE MASS DESTRUCTION
OF IGNORANCE/SOCIETY IS ONLY A MASS OF PEOPLE WHOSE INDIVIDUALITY AND IDENTITY IS
GOVERNED BY THEIR WILL TO BE GOVERNED BY THE LAWS MORALS AND RESTRICTIONS IMPOSED ON
US BY THE SYSTEM/PERSONAL ANARCHY THE REJECTION OF THESE RESTRICTIONS THROUGH THOUGHT
AND ACTION IS THE STEP TOWARDS MASS REALISATION THAT HAS TO BE TAKEN BEFORE ANY PERMANENT
CHANGE CAN COME ABOUT/ANARCHY IS THE PRODUCT OF NIHILISM/DISBELIEF IN ALL WE ARE
CONDITIONED TO BELIEVE IN/FROM SCHOOL TO WORK TO COFFIN OUR MORALS AND IDEALS ARE PRE-SET
THROUGH PREVIOUS GENERATIONS' STANDARDS/NOTHING EVER CHANGES COS WE RELY ON THE
GOVERNMENT TO CHANGE OUR LIVES AND GOVERNMENTS ARE RUN ON POWER AND MONEY NOT EMOTIONS/
FOR THEM THE SYSTEM WORKS COS THEY WORK THE SYSTEM AND WE WORK FOR THE SYSTEM EITHER
THROUGH CHOICE OR NECCESITY/THE ALTERNATIVES OF SELF-CONTROL AND SELF-SUFFICIENCY ARE
FOR THE MAJORITY EITHER TOO REMOTE TO REALISE OR TOO MUCH OF A THREAT TO 'NORMALITY'
TO CONTEMPLATE/OUR MEAGRE CONTRIBUTION TO THIS GRADUAL FIGHT FOR AWARENESS IS THROUGH
SOME OF OUR LYRICS/INSTRUCTION OR SUGGESTION RATHER THAN UNJUSTIFIABLE VIOLENCE AND
TRIBALISM/WE MAY NOT SOLVE THE PROBLEM BUT WE REFUSE TO IGNORE IT/WE TRY TO PRODUCE SONGS TO
THAT ARE ENJOYABLE AND MEANINGFUL TO GET OUR IDEAS ACROSS TO AS MANY PEOPLE AS POSSIBLE
WHILST RETAINING THE ENERGY IN THE MUSIC/////@

"We just banged the reverb unit to get the bomb noise on 'Human Error'," laughs **Bruce**, "Which is why it just sounds like a Great British spring being bonged…"

"We did six tracks in six hours, which wasn't hanging around," continues **Dick**. "We ran out of money before we'd finished mixing 'Human Error', and had to scrounge around for an extra fiver to get it finished. It cost £85 in the end… [consulting diary] £10 from Trotsky, £10 from Steve, and £65 from me. Which we probably got back later on. And we were pleased with it, although also a bit worried about what people would think of it…"

"It was just a local studio," says **Grant**, "But because it was our first time in a *proper* studio, it felt very glamorous, even though it was a sleazy little dump! [laughs] But it was a great little place, and I preferred the sound from there, even though it was more basic, than some later attempts at Southern – that was a better production, but a very hard sound, whereas Pickwick had a much softer, warmer sound.

"It was a great time for us; it felt very creative, very productive, just being there, producing our very own record. Steve 'Splice' Collinson had a few good tricks up his sleeve too – he once got us out of jail when he spliced out a part of 'Religious Wars' [but more on that later]…"

"It all happened very fast for me," adds **Trotsky**. "It was my first band, straight in the studio, record out, touring… just in the right place at the right time, I guess. I used Andy's kit in the studio – probably at Bruce's insistence, because my kit didn't sound very good – and his cymbals. And when we went into Pickwick Studios, there were egg boxes stuck on the walls and everything, proper old style. We didn't spend long doing it, so it is what it is. Recording equipment and technology back then was very basic, but all things considered, I think we did alright. There are a few fluffs on the drums, with hindsight, which is a shame I suppose, but they help make it what it is. It's a bit naïve in places, but all our recordings are a bit like that."

Grant: "We were very lucky that Spiderleg picked up on us and did the first EP. Although we had quite a good local fanbase as well before that, which really helped. But we were lucky so many people were able to hear us, and liked what we were doing, and it all happened quite fast. And it was a fun thing to do, playing all those gigs, meeting different people, seeing new places… and have people actually want to come and see you and hear your music."

After committing the EP to tape (quite literally back then), the band then had a nerve-racking wait of several months for it to be released, during which time they started gigging further afield, albeit still quite sporadically, their new-found connection with Spiderleg helping them secure bookings.

"Yes, we did a trio of gigs in October '81 with Flux," confirms **Dick**. "Wigan, Nottingham and London. The London gig was at the Red Lion, and it was our first anniversary gig – we did seventeen gigs in the first year – and Rudimentary Peni played as well. Their gigs were rarities really; they didn't like doing gigs. Wigan was September 5th, 1981, on Grant's birthday… and I've written in the diary, 'Went over the road to get Grant a cigar and two bubble gums for his birthday!'"

"It was at that gig where Mel and Jane, or one of the other girls, decided to backcomb our hair," scoffs **Bruce**. "They even backcombed Trotsky's hair, which was just ridiculous... backcombing was still a thing back then."

"That was my first *proper* gig, at Trucks in Wigan," remembers **Trotsky**. "We ran a coach up there, so all the local punks could come along, which was a quality thing to do, and I think that was the first time I met Pete The Roadie. I was walking through Warminster and bumped into him, and he was after tickets for the coach to the gig, so we went to Bruce's and I sorted him out. Although I knew his brother, because he was in my class at school.

"They tried to punk me up for the gig! They were all saying, 'You've got to look more punk,' so Mel back-combed my hair, and basically gave me a huge afro... Bruce gave me some tie-dyed jeans, and I had these steel-toe-capped boots. When I was playing, because I had this fucking huge hair, the drumsticks kept getting caught in it, haha! So we didn't do that again."

It was their association with Spiderleg/Flux that had Subhumans 'lumped in' (which makes it sound like a bad thing, but believe me, it really wasn't) with the anarcho sub-genre within punk.

"Yes, I think it totally came from that," agrees **Dick**. "Spiderleg had a strong Crass connection, but we never set out to be an anarcho punk band at all. The majority of songs I was writing then were not political... they were angry against politics in general, but not on any thought-out level. They were socially aware songs, but there were a lot of songs like, I don't know, 'I Don't Wanna Die' – which was anti-war... anti a lot of obvious things that you would be anti if you had any thought going through your head. That lumped us in as a band that thought about their lyrics to a certain extent, so that became part of the anarcho punk scene, but we never actually went out there and said we were an anarcho punk band. Unless people insisted on putting us in either the Oi! camp or the anarcho camp, because everything got split down the middle a bit."

"But we would have been influenced by The Mob a bit before we got involved with Flux, and they were quite anarcho in their own way, weren't they?" reasons **Bruce**. "They had a commune at Seend, near Devizes, which was close enough we could almost walk there."

Dick: "We went round there a couple of times. And one of their old drummers was possibly going to drum for us, but it didn't happen – he said on the phone that he didn't think he could keep up with the speed of our music, or be as tight as Andy had been. And then Trotsky came long, and that died a death anyway."

Colsk: "We [i.e. Flux and Subhumans] started to play some gigs together, and we got to know them as very calm, straightforward and nice people really. Not OTT political, they had a sense of fun, a sense of humour in all their lyrics, which was a bit different to Crass, and Flux – where, when you wrote a lyric, every word had to mean something."

Dick: "Flux really did get us out of our locality and into the wider world – as well as putting our records out. Without them, who knows what would have happened?"

DICK, GRANT, BRUCE - COURTESY OF JOCK MCCURDY

```
 1) ALL GONE DEAD.......................................  J/B/ST.H/OCT89
 2) ASHTRAY DIRT........................................  J/B/ST.H/MAGGOTZ/AUG79
 3) DRUGS OF YOUTH......................................  B/B/ST.H/FEB80
 4) PARANOID............................................  B/G/JULY80
 5) PARASITES...........................................  B/AUG80
% 6) HIGH CLASS PITS.....................................  ROBGG/AUG80/L.P.OCT80/LIVE-1
% 7) MINORITY...........................................  D/B/AUG 80/AUG80
% 8) KILL MYSELF........................................  B/B/AUG80/DR.AUG80/SAME MUSIC AS M-MOU
 9) MICKEY MOUSE IS DEAD...............................  D/B/SEPT80/SEPT80
10) NOTHING I CAN DO....................................  D/B/SEPT80/SEPT80
11) SOCIETY............................................  J@D/B/ST.H./OCT79/@SEPT80/OCT80
% 12) TROWBRIDGE PARK.....................................  D/B/SEPT80/OCT80/L.P.JUNE81/LIVE-4
% 13) WHAT MUSIC?........................................  D/D-B/SEPT80/OCT80/DR.OCT80
14) SID................................................  J@D/B/ST.H./OCT79/@OCT80/OCT80
15) BIG BROTHER.........................................  D/B/OCT80/OCT80
16) ZYKLON B MOVIE......................................  D/B-A/OCT80/OCT80
17) ITS GONNA GET WORSE.................................  D/B/NOV80/NOV80
18) PISSHEAD...........................................  D/B-A/NOV80/NOV80
19) HUMAN ERROR.........................................  D/B/NOV80/DEC80
20) BIG BASTARD.........................................  MIKE/G/A.T./SEPT79/DEC80
21) SUBVERT CITY........................................  D/B/DEC80/JAN81
22) NO MORE GIGS........................................  D/B/JAN81/JAN81
% 23) TOTAL COLLAPSE OF SOCIETY...........................  D/B-A/DEC80/JAN81/DR.JAN81
24) SO MUCH MONEY.......................................  D/B/DEC80/JAN81
25) FIRST AID..Y.......................................  J/B/ST.H./JAN80/JAN81/
26) NEW AGE ...........................................  J@D/B/ST.H./MAGGOTZ/VERMIN/MCH79/@JA
27) KILLING............................................  J@D/B/ST.H./AUG79/@DEC80/JAN81
% 28) PEROXIDE...........................................  D/B/DEC80/JAN81
% 29) WELCOME BACK JACK...................................  D/B/DEC80/JAN81/DR.JAN81
% 30) GIRL ON THE ROXY L.P. .............................  D/B/OCT80/JAN81/DR.FEB81
% 31) T.V.D.............................................  D/B/DEC80/JAN81/DR.FEB81
32) ANIMAL.............................................  D/B/JAN81/JAN81
33) FALL APART.........................................  D/B/JAN81/FEB81
34) SONG NO. 35 .......................................  D/D-E-G/FEB81/MCH81
35) WHO'S GONNA FIGHT IN THE THIRD WORLD WAR?.........  D/B/FEB81/MCH81
36) GROW YOUR HAIR......................................  D/B/FEB81/MCH81
37) NO THANKS..........................................  D/B/FEB81/MCH81
38) TILL THE PIGS COME ROUND...........................  D/B/FEB81/APR81
39) DON'T DO THAT AT THE BREAKFAST TABLE...............  D/B/APR81/APR81
40) FORGET ............................................  D/B/MCH81/APR81
41) PROGRAM PARTNERS....................................  J@D/B/MAY80/@APR80/MAY81/DR.MAY81
42) GET OUT OF MY WAY...................................  J@D/B/ST.H./DEC79/@MAY81/MAY81
43) BIG CITY...........................................  D/D-P/JUNE81/AUG81
44) WORD FACTORY........................................  D/B/AUG81/SEPT81
45) WHAT'S YOUR NUMBER? ...............................  D/B/MCH81/SEPT81
46) EVERYDAY LIFF......................................  D/B/JULY81/SEPT81
47) I DON'T WANT TO DIE................................  D/B/AUG81/SEPT81
48) REASON FOR EXISTENCE ..............................  D/B/JUNE81/SEPT81
49) CANCER ............................................  D/B/MAY81/SEPT81
50) NOT ME ............................................  D/B/OCT81/OCT81
```

THE FIRST FIFTY SUBHUMANS SONGS - COURTESY OF DICK

Colsk: "We didn't really do a lot of touring as such with the Subhumans; I think The System did quite a bit of touring with us though. Subhumans felt like their own band really; they certainly didn't feel like they were just coming off of us, or needed anything from us. We just gigged with them when we were down their way – or vice versa.

"If you look at the early Epileptics stuff we did, you'll see there was still a sense of punk humour in the lyrics, which Subhumans still had, and always kept, didn't they? They were their own people, they 100% weren't copying anyone else. Whereas I know that we were copying Crass – we were quite young really, and we were heavily influenced by them, and then you had [Crass drummer] Penny [Rimbaud] producing us, who was twenty years older than us, someone with lots of great ideas, someone we looked up to. What went down on [first Flux EP] 'Neu Smell' was heavily influenced by them, but with Subhumans, that first EP, they weren't influenced by anyone; it was their own sound, their own vision."

"No, not really, I didn't like the way they sounded at all," offers **Bruce**, when pondering whether there was a Crass influence on the Subhumans' music. "Looking back on our first EP now, I don't think it was a very powerful sounding EP, and musically I really wanted us to get more powerful, which didn't happen until [third EP] 'Religious Wars' really. Because we were all still learning about how to get better sounds in the studio. But that first EP has a lightness and naïvety to the sound."

"It's very trebly," agrees **Dick**, "But part of that is because there's so many songs on a 7". We actually tried re-recording 'Parasites' up at the TW studio in Melksham in about 1983; we thought we'd have a crack at re-doing one of the songs, but we sent it to John Loder and he said, 'Nah, this is useless!' It wasn't that bad… but it wasn't the original, and once you've done the original, that's it, you're stuck with it."

Jock: "Yeah, when we were on TW Records, the label decided to create a new studio up at their place, and they got hold of this huge desk that Tears for Fears had done their first album on or something, and we thought, 'Great, let's give it a go!' Except the people operating the desk didn't know what the fuck to do with it! The Humans spent about a week in there, and I don't know what they did with the recording, but from what I heard, the mixing desk was the dog's bollocks, but the engineers there didn't have a clue."

Regardless of underlying influences, with Bruce's idiosyncratic style, Grant's tantalising bass runs, and Dick's delightfully scathing delivery (one of the best punk voices ever), all locked into Trotsky's rock solid rhythms, the 'Demolition War E.P.' was one of the most assured debuts of the period, entering the Indie Charts on December 12th, 1981, where it stayed for ten weeks, peaking at No. 13.

After the EP opens with the irresistible energy of 'Parasites' (that contains one of your author's favourite lyrical couplets of all time: 'A choice of three for democracy, and they're all parasites'), the high-speed numbers 'Drugs of Youth', 'Society' and 'Who's Gonna Fight in the Third World War?' tick all the boxes for thrashers without descending into genericity thanks to some frantic stop/starts and memorable choruses, whilst the most catchy track on offer, 'Animal', is basically deranged, driving rock 'n' roll, subverted by

Grant's almost percussive, clanky bass, and 'Human Error' brings everything to a most satisfying close with its poignant anti-war lyrics and chilled punky reggae vibe. As well as an endearingly quirky, crumbly guitar tone, Bruce also provided some great backing vocals, the perfect foil for Dick's frustrated exhortations, setting up a taut dynamic that would be explored further on future releases. It was an intense EP that could be – and still is – played to death without losing one iota of its breathless power. It also introduced the world to the now-iconic Subhumans skull and 'three box' logo, that have adorned tens of thousands of shirts around the world ever since.

"I had that idea of a skull singing down a microphone," reveals **Dick**. "Grant drew the original, and then I re-did it, and added some more cracks and detail around the teeth and that. And it might have been me that split the band name up into three boxes too. No real reason for it; it just divided into three groups nicely, with the hardcore 'S's either end. There might have been a bit of consternation about the Germanic 'S's, but Kiss did it… loads of bands did it. I tried it with normal 'S's, but that didn't have the same impact. And I wasn't going to let the fucking Nazis take over the shape of a fucking letter! And it's like the fish and Jesus… why should the fucking Christians have the monopoly on fish? Bollocks to credibility – I like fish, I want fish for my logo. People go, 'Does that mean you're Christian?' 'No, it means I like fish!' 'Do these 'S's mean you're a Nazi?' 'No, I like 'S's drawn with straight lines!' Honestly, the way people think…"

Jock: "I've watched Dick patiently explaining to someone who has cornered him about the two Germanic 'S's in the logo that they don't mean anything. That's annoying, I'm sure, especially if you have to do it every gig. And he does get this little crowd around him after every gig, especially in the States, having to explain and justify everything… but he never loses it; he's got so much respect for everybody, he'll give them his time to explain everything, often over and over again."

But let's not get ahead of ourselves just yet – the first (of many) US tours was still a few years away at that point. They finished off 1981 with a gig in Swindon at the Devizes Road Church Hall (the underground punk scene in rural areas utilised church and village halls a lot back then), with The Snipers in support (an Oxfordshire punk band whose 'Three Peace Suite' EP on Crass Records coincidentally entered the Indie Charts on the exact same date as 'Demolition War'), but their sights were already set on their next release.

SUBHUMANS

The year 1982 was an important one for the Subhumans. Not only did they release two more EPs, including a much-loved anthem that has endured for four decades since, but they recorded their debut album, the timeless 'The Day the Country Died', and did their first interview with the then-essential music paper Sounds. But it all started rather incongruously with another fashion show! It was in Codford, of all places, a small village seven miles southeast of Warminster, but pulled in 150 punters. The Subhumans only played four songs, one of which was 'Cancer', an unusual choice for such an event, given that it's an absolute mood-killer...

"Er, yeah, the opposite of a singalong chorus really," laughs **Dick**. "That song was just an observation that if you had cancer, then the normal societal thing to do, of offering someone who is upset a cigarette, would completely backfire. Which was entirely what that song was about... it wasn't because I had cancer or anything, or because anyone I knew had cancer. If you were looking upset, and someone offered you a cigarette... but then what if the problem was that you had cancer? The song's based on that thought, and nothing much deeper. But when you listen to it... 'No! I've got cancer!'... you think, nice one – put that one on at Christmas, haha! Singalong happy choruses were never my forte..."

Two days after the fashion show, they were off to London for the last weekend of January, to record their 'Reason for Existence' EP at Southern Studios. It was produced by Pete Stennett, who ran Small Wonder Records.

"If 'produced' is the right word for it?" questions **Dick**. "Basically him and [Flux bassist] Derek [Birkett] were in the studio, repeatedly telling us to go back and play it again, because it could be better. Whereas previously an engineer would ask us, 'Are you happy with that?', we were asking the producers, 'Are *you* happy with that?' Which felt completely the wrong way round... the band should be the ones saying, 'This is as good as it gets!' rather than someone suggesting we might be able to do better over and over again.

[Reading from his diary] "In between playing them over and over again, we'd go back to the mixing room, and Derek would keep making irritating generalisations like, 'There wasn't enough feel...' So there wasn't a very good vibe, not with Derek about – he was being too forceful, and it showed... we weren't relaxed enough. 'Go and loosen up a bit,' said Pete, and we thought, 'Get stoned!' So we did, and played disco versions of 'No' and 'Word Factory', and a slow version of 'Reason for Existence', before we crashed through them again... and it did us a lot of good, because they did eventually turn out better, but it was a long process. We didn't feel completely in control of our own music, which was kind of a weird thing, being *produced* by somebody else."

"It was also a very clinical sound, because it was a much better quality studio," adds **Bruce**. "Southern was twenty-four track, with much better gear, better microphones, and because John [Loder] had had all this experience doing Crass and other stuff, his engineering was very exact. I found it too clinical actually… I think we all did. Which is why we went back to Pickwick for the 'Religious Wars' EP."

Trotsky: "That was definitely a step up, a different world really. Especially with John there as well, who was very focused on what he wanted it to be like. He knew what he was doing, and he had all this fantastic equipment. It was definitely a different situation to working with Steve at Pickwick – we had to do what we were told! We just hired Pickwick by the hour, and Steve was just there to engineer it, so the band pretty much did what we wanted, and he helped us do it. With John, the studio was very much his baby, and he didn't want anything bad coming out of it…"

"It was heavy… a lot heavier than 'Demolition War'," continues **Dick**. "They captured the sound a lot better. It was going to be six tracks again, but Derek and Pete insisted that four would sell better than six, which seemed totally illogical. So we dropped 'New Age' and 'It's Gonna Get Worse' from the original list of songs."

"Thinking about Southern Studios now, it was such a good studio, it may have sounded too brutally honest for a second EP," offers **Bruce**. "It wasn't that it was a bad studio in any shape or form, but more that we weren't good enough for it yet.

"Pete Stennett even wanted to release it on Small Wonder, and we thought, 'Why not?' It was a bigger label, and I don't think we were unhappy with Spiderleg, or Southern, or anything, but just wanted something different…"

"We were just taking offers, and not knowing what to do about it," reckons **Dick**. "Derek wanted us to stay on Spiderleg, Pete wanted us on Small Wonder, and there was another label, who rang up Bruce's mum's house, and we went round to see them… I think they were called Skunk Records? Anyway, we went to this guy's house, and we were all sat in the front room, all the chairs facing the same way, with his mate stood by the fireplace, talking for quarter of an hour about music… Bob Dylan, Acid Heads, blahblahblah… he was talking and talking, and we couldn't figure out why we were being delivered this lecture – if we *were* being chatted up to join the label, it wasn't fucking working! It was a new label, and he really liked the 'Live at Bath Walcot Village Hall' tape I'd done on Bluurg – which was Bluurg 10, a cracking live tape – and he wanted to do a record with us. So there was that on the so-called table as well.

"In the end, we went round to see Pete Stennett, with our girlfriends, who insisted on coming with us, to talk about contracts, and he showed us this multiple page deal – we'd never seen one before, so we were like, 'What's all this?' But we supposed that was what was done, and he was still an independent label, y'know? We liked The Carpettes and Patrick Fitzgerald…"

"*And* he'd put out 'The Feeding of the 5000' by Crass," points out **Bruce**.

Dick: "Yes, he put out the original before it got banned, because of the first song, and John stepped in to help Crass set up their own label. So anyway, we looked over the contract, but it all ended badly a month later with a series of phone calls. I was insisting on the 'pay no more than' thing – about 90p by that point – but he was insisting it would have to be £1.50, the regular retail price, because he had his overheads… which to be honest, went over *my* head, because it was business talk, not hardcore, DIY, 'cheap for the punks' talk! So that fell through on that basis really, and we stuck with Spiderleg.

"The first EP had had 'Pay no more than 85p' on it… which is ironic seeing as copies of the first pressing of 'Demolition War' go for like £50 now. It's ridiculous… 'pay no less than'!"

"I can't remember much of it at all, to be honest," sighs **Pete Stennett**. "I *can* remember the band sending me their tape, and I arranged to go to Southern Studios to record them… most of the stuff I released I would co-produce with the bands, but I just didn't always mention it. The only other thing I can definitely remember is getting Dick to cough at the end of 'Cancer'."

Dick: "The 'Hello' at the start of 'Reason for Existence' was a suggestion from Pete as well. I can't recall his rationale for it… maybe he thought it would start the EP off well? But we B-sided it anyway."

"I'm not actually sure why it ended up on Spiderleg and not Small Wonder," says a bemused **Pete**. "It's a bit frustrating really, because I remember so much about other stuff I did, but my memory lets me down for that one. I was obviously impressed by the band else I wouldn't have recorded them otherwise. I knew they were something special… and that EP says it all really. But most of the time I was so busy running the record label and mail order; being in the shop all day and then going down the studio all night, it was a bit frantic, and all a bit of a blur – I didn't know what the fuck was going on really.

"I thought they handled it beautifully; they looked like they'd been in the studio all their lives. I can remember thinking they were such a good, 'together' band; they took it all in their stride really. I wouldn't have known they were newcomers, but then again, *most* of the bands I worked with had never been in the studio before.

"That was quite common in those days," he adds, when asked if he could remember sending them off to 'loosen up'. "I did a band called The Molesters, and the guitarist just couldn't do the rhythm, so we sent the band down the pub so he could do it on his own – and he still couldn't handle it. Nerves definitely got the better of some bands. We took Patrick Fitzgerald into a proper studio to do his 'Safety Pin' EP – first we went into a sixteen-track, and then we went to an eight-track place, but eventually we ended up in someone's back room on a little four-track studio, because he felt more relaxed then.

"I honestly don't remember that either," he continues, of getting at loggerheads with the band over the 'pay no more than' price-tag. "I obviously paid for the recording, so I don't know why I didn't release it… maybe it was just me being kind? It was obviously their decision, but it's a complete mystery to me, and always will be, and the only time it ever happened – everything else I recorded got released by my own label. But I'm just pleased to fuck it came out and people bought it, y'know?"

"Derek and [his girlfriend] Sue moved up to London, near Bounds Green, and Sue started working in the office at Southern," adds **Colsk**. "From '81, we were [Bishops] Stortford-based, but in '82 we started moving closer and closer to Southern. My girlfriend

ANARCHIST CENTRE LONDON
Sunday 10th — January 1982
SUB HUMANS
+ ORGANIZED CHAOS
+ VERTICAL HOLD
+ Lack of Knowledge

A COACH WILL BE GOING STOPPING AT MELKSHAM TROWBRIDGE AND WARMINSTER TICKETS £3.50 £1.50 ON THE DOOR

FOR MORE DETAILS PHONE DICK: 0225 702853
(MELKSHAM)

ALTERNATIVE MUSIC presents
SUB HUMANS
+ CONFLICT
PART 1
BOWES LYON HOUSE
ST. GEORGES WAY STEVENAGE
53175
SUNDAY 21st FEB.
730 to 10·45 PM
£1·50

THE CROWN
TIMBREL ST. FRIDAY 5TH MARCH
£1 ADM. 8-12PM
SUBHUMANS
WASTED SPACE...
THE PAGANS
BRITISH A HEADS
PROCEEDS TO NOAH'S ARK
PLAYGROUP

LACK OF INTEREST PRESENTS
THE MOB
SUB HUM ANS
THE A-HEADS
+ ORGANIZED CHAOS
REBEL DANCE
SATURDAY APRIL 10
7·30 PM
THOSE WHO CHOOSE TO IGNORE THE PAST ARE CONDEMENED TO REPEAT IT
TICKETS £1·25 adv 175 on the door FINISHES 10-30
RING O BELLS PUB
WIDCOMBE PARADE
WIDCOMBE BATH
the mob NEW SINGLE
NO DOVES FLY HERE OUT APRIL 7th

PHIL AND JULIA, TROWBRIDGE COLLEGE, 1982

DICK BY KEV TYDEMAN

Jude was a cleaner there too, when we moved up; then when Tim and Lou joined [Flux] after Kevin left, Tim worked there as well. So we became very tight with Southern Studios, and when Subhumans recorded there in '82, that was really the beginning of the relationship between Southern Studios and Spiderleg; before that we were just releasing older [Epileptics] recordings.

"Derek hadn't done any production up until that point, but from then on, he began to get involved in the releases, with Amebix, Kronstadt Uprising and The System, to have that kind of 'Penny role', where he's the producer for the band. But the Subhumans got on and did it all by themselves really."

February '82 saw the band return to the Bowes Lyon House in Stevenage, with Part 1 and The Disrupters in support, before they played The Crown in Trowbridge on March 5th, supporting Wasted Space alongside the A-Heads, Organized Chaos and the Pagans.

The short-lived Pagans are key to our story because they featured Phil Bryant on guitar, who would become the Subhumans bassist the following year. Bruce also joined the Pagans on drums, when their original drummer, Ronnie, left.

"I actually grew up in the Lake District," reveals **Phil**, of his childhood. "My dad was in the army up there, and we moved to Warminster in 1975, when I was eleven. I started at Kingdown School, and that's where my Subhumans story starts, because I was in the same class as Bruce, which is when we first met. I was one term late for the new school, because we arrived after Christmas. Even though we were only eleven, we had an instant connection through music; we both had older siblings who were really into The Who and Led Zeppelin, and all that kind of stuff. So we were both really into our music even though we were only little nippers. I was especially into The Who… the power of their music really hit me. The 'Live at Leeds' album was really heavy… it's not mod stuff, it's their heavy rock stuff, and it's got an almost punk power to it. So, that was a favourite album of mine, through my brother, and Bruce's older sisters knew all that too. Both of us knew all the words to 'Tommy', the rock opera, through our siblings as well. We had this instant connection because of music.

"So I already knew stuff like 'Space Ritual' by Hawkwind, and I really liked the power – it was crazy stuff to hear if you'd only been listening to chart music, this weird, heavy, drug-induced music. But I can remember, on the Queen's Jubilee, my family jumped in the car and went up to light the beacon on the Westbury white horse, and the Sex Pistols were on the car radio. And, as it did for so many other people, it just grabbed me straight away; it sounded so dangerous, and I got off on the energy and the whole vibe.

"All the local bands were at Kingdown. Me and Bruce were there, Grant turned up there, Trotsky, Jock from A-Heads, Bill from Organized Chaos… everyone except for Dick really. Bruce was playing guitar, but he was from a musical family – hippy mum, grandmother into piano and opera and all that stuff, so he was surrounded by creativity and music and was playing guitar from an early age. But I was from a pretty straightlaced family; my dad was in the army, which was much more conservative – I was really into music, but wasn't playing myself. Although I'd had a few piano lessons when I was, like, nine, but I was really disinterested at that point, as it obviously didn't relate to anything I liked musically. I regretted giving up later, once I did start playing, as I could see the value of piano and keyboards. But at the time, I was sat playing 'Three Blind Mice' in a creepy room with a picture on the wall where the eyes followed you around... it was *that* kind of piano lesson, haha! I didn't show much interest and my dad cancelled it.

"But I did really love music; it was all The Who and Hawkwind and stuff like that, and I was slightly in awe of Bruce, who was the musical one in my class. Bruce was really getting going during the last years of school, but I didn't actually start playing until after I left. He was doing his first band, Vermin, with Ju, and I was hanging around that whole crew. Sat around at Bruce's all the time, and there were all these guitars there, and I'd tinker about on them. I just thought I'd give it a go, and got myself a guitar, an acoustic, as I left school. Then I picked up a cheap Strat from somewhere, and got the Bert Weedon songbook, learnt a couple of chords and off I went...

"Punk had already come along by then, so it was probably '79 or '80 when I started playing. I went through a really big Jimi Hendrix phase from fourteen onwards, so I was listening to Hendrix at the same time as I was listening to the Sex Pistols. I was really into the power of punk, but I was into all sorts of music really, even some proggy stuff... some wide influences. Pink Floyd, a bit of Genesis... I never liked Yes or Rush really, although I know Bruce and Trotsky were into them.

"Anyway, after being in the Lake District, in this sleepy village by the sea [Bootle], coming to Warminster, where they had a transport café in the central car park, and shops and gigs and things, I liked growing up here. I made loads of great mates at school – people I still hang out with now, people I go way back with. There was a disco out at Longbridge Deverill on the weekends, the little village where Trotsky was from, and where the Subhumans used to practise later on, in The Shed, which was slightly too far to walk, so you'd get your parents to give you a lift out there. And then there'd be the usual underage drinking, and that weird mix of music... I did have some punky clothes then – an old school blazer with some paper clips on it, and 'Sid Vicious' written on the back, or whatever. Everyone would be sitting around through Rose Royce, waiting for 'My Way' by Sid Vicious to come on, or The Members, and the punky kids would get up. All the young punks would go to all the discos and sit there waiting for the four or five punk songs they'd play.

"So there was quite a little scene here. Everyone was playing in various bands, messing around with each other. I went to some of Bruce's bands' early gigs. They used to have a disco up the army camp, and Vermin were playing up there. And that was just amazing really – it was my first exposure to a live band, but seeing your mates play live as well... Andy was drumming, and he was a great player, really fast – I was pretty transfixed watching him. I was kinda hooked and thought, 'I wouldn't mind a bit of that action!'

"I'd got my first guitar, just as I was leaving school – I might have got an old acoustic off Bruce? – and hot on the heels of that, I got myself a CSL Strat copy and started noodling about on that. Within a few months, I felt confident enough to join in with other people, messing about with Bruce and jamming with Bill at the youth centre.

"When we finished at Kingdown, I went to Trowbridge College – with Bruce as well – and started hanging around the Trowbridge scene a bit more. Bruce had met Dick by then as well, and Dick's brother Steve, who I got on really well with, was doing Wild Youth. And I tagged along for the latter part of Wild Youth. They used to practise at Court Mills Youth Centre in Trowbridge. This was when they had Ronnie drumming, so before Bruce started playing with us. Herb was on bass, and me and Steve were both on guitar, and that morphed into the Pagans in early '82. Can't remember exactly why, but Ron probably wasn't available to drum for some reason, and Bruce was always up for drumming, so he gave it a go and the Pagans got started. At the time, it felt like a really big thing in my life – my first real band and everything – but looking back, it only lasted a few months really. But it was kind of life-changing for me, because that was when I first started playing gigs.

"I don't remember too much about that first Pagans gig at The Crown, it's all a bit of a blur, and I probably drank too much. I was just very happy to be in a band, doing gigs."

"The thing with The Crown in Trowbridge, there's a Nirvana connection," adds **Bruce**, tangentially, "It's one I always tell my students, haha! Scream [who Subhumans would go on to tour the US with, in 1985] had Dave Grohl drumming for them – although not originally, not when we toured with them. Anyway, Subhumans broke up, and Scream came over to do a tour in the UK, with Dave Grohl on the drums. They came here to borrow some equipment from us, or Culture Shock, and did a gig at The Crown. So, Dave Grohl played at The Crown in Trowbridge. After the tour, they went back to the States, and eventually split up whilst touring the West Coast, and Dave Grohl got stranded in Seattle – and that's where he met Kurt Cobain [and joined Nirvana]… that's how the story goes anyway."

Subhumans played the Wellington Gemini Club at the end of March with the preposterously named Orinj 'n' Yella Kurtain Rayles, before making the first of two appearances at the Centro Iberico Anarchist Centre in London on April 4th, supported by the A-Heads, Organized Chaos and Hagar the Womb.

"We played with them at a couple of gigs, and they were extremely wonderful and silly," recalls **Dick** fondly, of the Orinj 'n' Yella Kurtain Rayles. "One of them was called Jay, and he had a really thin Mohican, and did this great comic strip storybook called 'Ickabod Poo'. He did a whole series of them, properly printed, and they did quite well. The Orinj 'n' Yella Kurtain Rayles were based up in Telford, and their bass was one string on a broomstick, their drum kit was all these cardboard boxes… the guitar might have been plugged into something? Not sure! They had songs like, 'Wish I Had as Much Dole Money as the Queen', and it was all spectacularly silly. And colourful – lots of orange and yellow, and neon!"

"I'm a Londoner born and bred," explains **Ruth Elias**, vocalist with Hagar the Womb, setting the scene before sharing her Subhumans memories. "I got into punk at school, drawn in initially by the music and attitude when I was too young to go to gigs, and then got well and truly hooked when I could. The legendary Wapping Autonomy Centre was my weekly gigging universe, every Sunday night. It was a time when new venues sprung up in squatted empty buildings seemingly every week, and you could go out every night, dole cheque permitting. The Hags formed in Wapping, and I remember those years as part of the London anarcho punk scene with a warm fuzzy feeling of being alive and in the thick of it.

"I can't remember if I read about the Subhumans, in one of the myriad fanzines I devoured every week, before I saw them, or the other way round. But I saw the Subhumans so many times it's hard to recall exactly when was first – but they always stood out on a line-up, like all the worst crims, ha! They weren't just fast and furious like most of the bands we saw at the time; their performances were mesmerising, and their lyrics were on another level, poetic and poignant and beautifully written.

"When the Autonomy Centre shut, we all migrated to the Centro Iberico and became part of the 'regulars' there. We played there quite a few times – in the same way as gigs appeared almost by osmosis at Wapping… i.e. just through being there to ask. We had all seen the Subhumans by then, so were proper happy to get to play with them. We felt an affinity with them, as – like us, but in a different way – they also stood out from many of the bands we played alongside. It was refreshing to see their friendly, down-to-earth attitudes and lack of ego, impressions that anyone chatting with them will come away with. Maybe mixing with London bands so much made us aware of the jostling that goes on in trying to get higher up bills, more attention etc. – small fish in a big pool syndrome – and the Subhumans were separate from all that guff. I can remember dancing, and ending up with more bruises than usual, but courtesy of cider 'n' black, my memory doesn't alas extend to the finer points of their performance that evening. It's all a bit of a blur of non-stop gigging, partying and fucking the system from back then."

"I first became aware of Subhumans after getting a cassette release of theirs from Graham Burnett – or Jah Ov Jam as he was affectionately known back then! – of New Crimes fanzine," adds **Chris Knowles**, the Hagar the Womb drummer who also played bass in Cold War. "The Subhumans blew me away as soon as I heard them; I nearly wore out the cassette as 'Parasites' and the other songs featured were just so powerful, fusing anarcho punk lyrics with an energy and fizz – and dare I say it… tunefulness – of more traditional punk. They were not afraid to be rock 'n' roll and unserious, a characteristic that marked them out from some of the more serious po-faced anarcho bands. I don't remember when I first saw them live; we played with them a fair few times, and I've seen them countless other times as well… my memory from those days is a bit vague.

"I can't remember how we got the gig, but I do remember it was slightly less shambolic than the other gigs we played there [at the Centro Iberico], including one with only half a drum kit if I remember correctly. I also remember the massive kit Trotsky had – loads of drums, and set up really high as befits a great drummer… I found it difficult to traverse his kit. The Subhumans were great, they never failed to be good; they had quite a professional approach to gigging – unlike us, haha!

ITS GONNA GET WORSE

EP COVER IDEA

CHRIS KNOWLES, ORIGINAL Hagar the Womb DRUMMER

BiG CiTY

Well here we are in the big big city
Plenty of ways to spend your money
Getting ripped off its a way of life
~~You don't know watch that its help a knife~~ They'll grab you money on a skin flick etc
Tourist attractions ~~look at flick~~ ~~those points~~ look at that
Buy me a plastic policeman's hat
~~But there's a riot going on~~
~~P violence + hatred racist attack~~ But there's a riot uptown
And the boys in blue are wearing black   they're
                                                  fighting b
~~Go to a gig~~ The flying squad what a farce ~~fence on others~~
If pigs could fly they wouldn't need cars
~~what a big city there's so much~~ to do
~~Why don't you tell me something~~ new?
~~Pick on the~~ ~~pick on the push~~
Got control over us all
Scotland Yard + Berlin Wall

So give me a break - don't tell me
that life is great in the big city

Its all built on money + greed
They've got everything you'll never need

No No No No its ~~too~~ shitty
~~Lets get rid of the~~
Don't wanna live in the big big city

"Dick was always really nice to us, but I sometimes got the impression that the others didn't take us too seriously, though that may not have been true as I didn't really know the others, only Dick, to be fair. Dick has always been brilliant, and he fostered a great relationship with us. Considering how well-known Subhumans were, even back then, he has always been very down to earth, and playing with Subhumans always felt like a family affair.

"Me, Dick and Dan, the original Apostles drummer [and later in Look Mummy Clowns] once talked about a side project band, but it never actually came to fruition sadly, despite us making a few plans."

The 'Reason for Existence' EP was released on May 1st, and went to No. 11 in the Indie Charts, the four songs it contained sounding somewhat more simplistic than those on 'Demolition War' the previous year, but all the more catchy for it. As well as the dark, brooding and rather morbid 'Cancer' discussed earlier, the EP was uplifted by the bouncy 'Peroxide', a cautionary tale about using bleach on your hair, and the equally upbeat 'Big City', another cautionary tale, this time highlighting the perils of urban living, whilst the existential title track remains the ultimate 'four chord' punk song, raging against the apathy and mediocrity of modern life. The band's frustration with the police was evident through the cover montage and lyrics like, 'Flying squad? What a farce! If pigs could fly, they wouldn't need cars… got control over us all, New Scotland Yard, the new Berlin Wall…'

"We were as anti-police as anyone else of that age who had been arrested," reasons **Dick**, "Or who had seen their mates arrested, or were just wary of the cops, because of the threat of potentially being arrested, sometimes for something as innocent as having a drink in a public place, or gathering in numbers too great for someone else's perceived safety. It was a punk rock thing to be anti-police, in the same way as it was to be anti-war, anti-government, that sort of thing. There wasn't much detailed thought about it – it was just resentment at being told what to do, in this case by cops… but more or less anyone in uniform really – unless they worked in a supermarket!

"The police in an idealistic sense are there to keep people safe, to protect the public, rather than provoke the public into breaking the law. The cops have to go along with whatever laws the politicians make up, and that subdues any conscience they've got about what they're doing. And I don't think it should be like that. And then there's the violent side of the police, that doesn't often get reported in the news…

"Everyone says, 'It's the good old "British bobby" – they don't carry guns…' but they do actually; they're allowed to carry guns, in whatever circumstances they feel are justified. It's not as gun-happy as, say, America – yet – where more or less everyone can have guns, and an awful lot of people do have them, which is just insane, but that's going off topic a bit. Generally, the law is not there to be enjoyed, and the police are there to enforce the law. And the law can be very petty and particular about behaviour at certain times of night, and at certain volumes… stuff that isn't really doing any real harm. Just simple stuff like that can get you in more trouble – and the more trouble you get in with the police, the more likely your criminal record will affect your job prospects, your chances of getting a mortgage, owning stuff, renting things… businesses and people in charge will penalise you for something you've already been penalised by the law for doing. You get penalised twice – firstly you do your time, or pay your fine, but then you've got a criminal record that carries on penalising you down the line.

"So being arrested was something you seriously wanted to avoid. But you could find yourself in situations where you could easily be arrested for doing something you couldn't easily imagine would be an arrestable offence. Like when I found that copper's helmet that got knocked off his head – 'theft by finding'! You what? What happened to the old law of 'finders, keepers'? Apparently that's not a law, haha! But the 'Reason for Existence' cover is just a depiction of a lone person, bent over, head in hands, feeling generally threatened by society and authority – as represented by a bunch of cops.

"Anyway, Garry Bushell reviewed it in Sounds and compared it favourably to the latest Infa-Riot single," **Dick** continues, with some incredulity, given Bushell's preoccupation with Oi! "In fact, he said we knocked Infa-Riot into a 'cocked titfer'… as in 'tit fer tat', which was a hat – he was being all Cockney about it. So he liked it, which was nice, I suppose. And Derek even said he thought we could 'be the next Damned', during one phone call, haha! I didn't know whether he wanted to keep us, or get rid of us; it was getting a bit complicated, and we couldn't decide whether we should do an LP next, or another EP…

"I've got this royalty statement from the time, which came with a cheque for £106.36… we got paid 5.5p per copy of 'Demolition War' that got sold. We had to sell 1947 to break even. Then, for 'Reason for Existence', the studio time cost £500, so we had to sell 3000 of that to break even, but after that we got 9p per copy. There you go – that's how rich we were getting off those EPs, haha!"

"I wouldn't have been surprised if Subhumans didn't get any money from Spiderleg," admits **Colsk**, "But there wasn't any money made really – the records were being sold at the base minimum, and it was more about just getting the records out than recouping costs. Spiderleg and Southern was a bit of a strange set-up… there were no accounts, no money – although maybe accounts existed, via Southern Studios, and were offset against the production costs. We certainly never paid Southern a penny, and they never paid us a penny for any record that ever came out on Spiderleg.

"I seem to recall Amebix saying that they never got any money, and that we were living in a nice three-bedroom house in Bounds Green… which is the most ridiculous thing, because we were renting that house between six of us for £50 a week! I know what people were thinking, but there you go, it's strange where people get their ideas from."

"Listening back to the old stuff now has made me realise how Grant's bass playing was quite jolly," smiles **Bruce**, bringing talk back to music, "What I mean by 'jolly' is that he

bollocks 82 3/2

My mind was on overdrive
~~Heroin~~ Adrenalin overdose
Sleepless ~~insomnia~~
I could have sworn
All these words were

CRAP ALOT
TEABAGS

~~[crossed out line]~~

PEROXIDE

~~[Also]~~ She's out of trouble
~~She never got touched~~ cos
her hair was white
And the punx they all think she's alright

Peroxide girl with a false ID
lost and lonely she can't see
~~burnt out eyes~~
~~burnt out~~ + burnt out eyes
Peroxide head + blinded by so many lies

But ~~she~~ she's dyed her face
The Peroxide's soaked into her red

+ caught stealing in a shop
~~she told but she killed a cop~~ Stuck a knife in a passing cop
had to get a new disguise Becos nobody cares
~~Dyped~~ ~~bathed in~~ Peroxide?
What about — just a boring mess? P.P.! ~~Do they anything~~
Well what would do?
Dye yor hair!

her hair was ~~brown and boring~~
~~she~~ had never known success
~~At the~~ Saw the punx they didn't care.
~~walked around with peroxide hair~~
Now she's blind her face is red
Her

SUBHUMANS REHEARSAL, MAY 1982, PHOTO
COPYRIGHT © PAUL SLATTERY

SUBHUMANS WITH RICHARD 'WINSTON SMITH' NEWSON
(BOTTOM RIGHT) PHOTO COPYRIGHT © PAUL SLATTERY

was quite a happy, optimistic guy, so musically, even if I was doing something minor, he would do a little happy major thing. Like on the song 'Cancer', which is about as dark as you can get really, but he keeps doing these little happy bits, haha! It's so dark, in fact, that we don't play it anymore… well, we haven't played it in ages. I'd like to do it, because lots of people like it, but Dick has a reason for not doing it. You'd have to ask him… but it might be because he smokes, and he feels it's hypocritical?"

"It's mostly just 'cos of numbers – we've got so many better songs than certain songs," reckons **Dick**. "I don't remember ever vetoing playing 'Cancer' any more, but it might have happened. Possibly because it's a slow song, and live is much more suited to faster, more energetic songs."

You wouldn't have dropped it because you felt it was insensitive or anything?

Dick: "No. That song is not really about cancer anyway; it's more about the glamour given to cigarettes, when they're just not a glamourous thing. But I don't think we've ever dropped a song because it might offend people, or upset people… and hopefully I haven't written any songs that would upset people. I might have written a few that offend a few people, but that's part of the whole thing really…"

Certainly some punk bands back then wrote a few lyrics that they regret now… is there anything you're not particularly proud of now?

"Well, the word 'slag' turns up in 'Killing', and I don't particularly like singing that," **Dick** says candidly, "But I do like the song – it's got a nice atmosphere to it musically. I didn't write the lyrics though – that's my main excuse for it. Julian wrote it [it was originally called 'Killed'], and I was probably being a bit lazy when we first did it – I could have changed the words to something else, but now they're there on a record. A product of the Eighties. It's hard to tell exactly what it's about, but there's a practice tape of Stupid Humans from years ago, with Stupid Humans practising in Bruce's mum's kitchen, and Julian introduces it as, 'This one's called "Killing"'… it's about a prostitute…' I think it's about someone who gets so out of it they kill a prostitute?"

May 1st was a doubly significant date in the 1982 calendar for Subhumans as it was also the day they did their first interview for Sounds. Writer Richard Newson, who wrote under the pseudonym of Winston Smith (after the character in George Orwell's '1984', of course), travelled up to Warminster with photographer Paul Slattery to interview the band before sitting in on a rehearsal. That interview holds a special place in Richard's heart as well, because it was his first commission for the paper.

"A few of my music mates in the same year as me at school started buying punk records in late '76, but we were only fourteen," **Richard** begins the story of how he ended up there that fateful day. "Although we were unusual in that we already went to lots of rock concerts at the Hammersmith Odeon, seeing bands like Aerosmith and Thin Lizzy, most of us were a bit wary of actual punks. We didn't feel brave enough to start going to punk gigs until '78, by which time the Sex Pistols had split up and punk was very much old hat…

"Despite that though, we dived in and saw as many punk bands in '78 as we could, making up for lost time, belatedly switching to punky short hair and narrow trousers – which even then was still a big deal, risking trouble with the local teds and skins in the process.

"I stayed on for the sixth year, but by early '79 I'd had enough of school. The only subject I was interested in, or any good at, was English Language. I decided to leave and work at a music paper instead, doing whatever jobs turned out to be available. I thought this would be a good way in. So, in the February half-term, I made a list of all the music weeklies and their addresses, and got the tube up to London.

"At that time, I was buying Sounds, NME and Melody Maker every week, but Sounds was my favourite. As it happened, the first place to visit on my list was Sounds HQ at 40 Long Acre in Covent Garden, directly above the tube station. I walked in and asked the office manager if he had any work going. He said, 'Actually, yes, someone's about to leave a job in the post-room…' I couldn't believe my luck! After a quick interview, he offered me the role of postal clerk/messenger. I started working there in March '79.

"I loved the job; I filled the coffee machines first thing in the mornings, and the rest of the time I delivered post to and for the staff of Sounds. This meant I made friends with the writers, including Garry Bushell, who encouraged me to start writing and see if I could get something published. So, for the next couple of years, I followed Garry's advice. Amazingly, by May '82 I was writing for Sounds, using the pen name Winston Smith – because I'd just read '1984' – ironically setting myself up as the paper's 'anarcho alternative' to Bushell, who was closely linked with all the Oi! bands.

"And my debut trip as a Sounds writer was by train from Paddington to Wiltshire, to meet a new band I was excited about called Subhumans. I'd heard their 'Demolition War' EP, which I'd possibly bought purely because it was on Spiderleg, the label ran by Flux of Pink Indians, who I liked… but to be honest, I can't remember now.

"I'd raved about 'Demolition War' in the office, and at my first ever editorial meeting, I asked if I could interview the band. The editor Geoff Barton was impressed by my enthusiasm, and he gave me the nod to write an article on the band, which was my debut feature, and I think it was their first too. As it was going to be my first interview for Sounds, I kept the A4 sheet of typed meeting notes as a souvenir, and I still have this now. On the train to Wiltshire I was buzzing, and for some reason I knew instinctively that I'd get on well with the band; I've no idea why.

"I travelled down with Paul Slattery, who was a few years older than me. He was already a legend, as by then he'd been taking photos for Sounds for years, making his name during the original punk days when he'd taken pictures of the Sex Pistols and other bands, often down the front and in the thick of it at key punk gigs.

"Paul was as keen on Subhumans as I was, especially when we sat in on their Saturday afternoon rehearsal in Warminster, with a small group of their friends watching too. Paul and I were impressed by singer Dick's scruffy charisma and how tight and unusually *musical* the band's thrilling run-through was.

"And that was what set Subhumans apart for me when I first heard 'Demolition War' – they shared the anger and energy of the other early '80s punk bands, but what made them different was their trick of mixing this with brilliant melodies and intelligent lyrics, sometimes delivered in a rapid-fire style that left you stunned. The political side of their songs was sharp and focused, but equally they didn't mind sending themselves up or having a laugh. They were serious, but with a smile. Everything they did, they did properly, as well as they possibly could.

"The opening track of 'Demolition War', 'Parasites', was an instant classic, jumping out of the speakers, loud, furious, but catchy too. From the start, the band took the basic punk framework and built perfect, hook-packed mini anthems, weaving inventively around a thrashy core to make perfect blasts of rage that made you smile even as the songs snarled.

"I've never been able to work out why 'Parasites' and other such tunes aren't given the same respect as Buzzcocks' catchy punk gems, or the songs of other punk bands who are now celebrated in music history docs and played on 6 Music and other radio stations. Meanwhile, all those Subhumans classics remain loved only by the hardcore punk crowd... it's baffling!

"'Demolition War' was amazing in so many ways, breaking all kinds of punk rules, from Bruce's soaring, rock guitar solos, to Grant's propulsive, Lemmy-ish bass, often pushed up high in the mix; the spacey, phased guitar on 'Animal', the way the tracks were thoughtfully sequenced and faded into each other, and the record's thrilling mix of musical styles.

"Add in the fact that the band didn't *look* like punks, especially the fact that drummer Trotsky wore flares and happily displayed a Led Zeppelin patch on his denim jacket, and it becomes even more impressive, thinking back, that the hardcore crowd, with their strict ideals of punk purity, embraced them so wholeheartedly. I reckon the sheer exuberance and honesty of Subhumans won over any doubters; the band's blend of full-on energy and cracking tunes overriding any concerns about their deviation from the 'studs and leather' punk norm.

"As for the interview itself, what I remember clearly is that we did it at Bruce's parents' house, before the rehearsal, and I was struck by how 'hippy-ish' it was, with political posters on the walls, socialist books around the place and so on. I recall thinking how this must have played a part in shaping him as he grew up; it was all very different to my own conventional upbringing. Bruce's parents and mine couldn't have been more different, despite he and I being very close in age. I remember feeling quite impressed by this side of him.

"The interview went well, although I felt the band were a bit wary of me. As a mainstream music press reporter, I was meant to be 'the enemy', at least from a punk perspective at the time. Only writers from anarcho fanzines were to be trusted. The band wanted the photos to be taken at the rehearsal, because this would present them in a 'real' way. But despite this, they were also happy to pose for Paul Slattery when he asked them to do a 'normal' photo session..."

"There were definitely photos of us standing next to trees or something," laughs **Bruce**, "And there were some hats going on… and a scarf… which was pretty bad actually."

Just over a week after 'Reason for Existence' entered the Indie Chart, the Subhumans were back in Pickwick with Steve Collinson on May 9th, recording what many consider to be their finest moment, the 'Religious Wars' EP.

"It was a relief to get back to Pickwick, sound-wise at least," admits **Bruce**. "We got a much better bass tone as well. I think that was when Grant borrowed the engineer's Jazz bass, which sounded so much better than his P-bass [i.e. Fender Precision]. He used it on 'The Day the Country Died' too, with a bit of distortion on, which sounded really nice. Grant's P-bass was like a Squire or something, which was okay, but a bit dull.

"I was a bit of a Siouxsie fan at the time, and I was really into the effects – the flangers and the chorus – and there's a couple of creepy songs where she has this reverb and backward echo on her voice. And back then you had to turn the reel over so it was playing backwards and put the effect you want on, and then you record the effect onto another track and play it back. But I was really interested in all that stuff."

"But we weren't entirely happy with it at the time," says **Dick**, of 'Religious Wars'. "We went back and re-mixed it a couple of times. And there's that bit towards the end of 'Religious Wars' itself, where it stops dead and echoes off – and that was because Steve accidentally wiped out a few seconds of music. All of it. Because before that, it just went straight into the chorus, so we had to get inventive, and Steve said, 'Let's put an echo on the last note, and then quickly fade up what's left…' And that's why that track sounds the way it does – because of a cock-up. It took us three hours to fix it in the mix and get 'Love Is' to fade in…

"Like most teenagers, I guess, I had discovered 'love' was a byword for inconsistency and pretence via a string of failed relationships," he adds of the lyrical inspiration for 'Love Is', "Including the one I was in at the time! But other people's behaviour has always been an influence on me: the dehumanisation of school, the physical boundaries of male hierarchies and the ways up the illusionary ladders, the hidden misery, the timetabled existence... life and work post-school was just an extended version of it.

"As for other influences outside of punk's emergence? Certainly not literature – I read detective novels mostly... and I can't think of any role models or musical 'heroes' as such; musicians were so remote from real life."

"At one or two practises back then, we were inventing three or four songs," recalls **Bruce**, of their prolific song-writing in the early days, "But at least one new song would come out of most practises. I'm generalising a bit though – some practises we would spend going over old stuff. Then other practises, Grant would turn up so late, and Trotsky would have to finish early, so we'd go through 'Rain' ten times, and that was it!

"There was a place in Dilton Marsh, where Grant lived, in the village hall or wherever we went, and at one practice we got together 'Cancer', 'Reason for Existence' and

'Word Factory', all on the same day. When Grant was in the band, there's a good chance we were getting together elsewhere as well, trying out some ideas and doing some planning musically. I remember before we did the first album, we sat down and worked out how all the songs were going to go together. But a lot of rehearsals started with us jamming and messing around; there was quite a lot of natural feeling about it."

Dick: "And I'd be sat at the side, flicking through my lyrics, thinking, 'That bit goes over that…' And between us, we'd manipulate what was going where, we'd just try ideas out and cooperate until the songs came together.

"I don't really think about it much now though. Doing this book is the first time – possibly ever! – that we've really looked back on this stuff with any thought behind looking back at it, because we've got memories, in case people ask, but even those memories get smoothed over – they're basically just summaries that you keep saying to people in interviews. When people ask you the same things over and over, you soon get a nice couple of sentences up for certain aspects of what we did in the past, but then you go back through the diaries and talk about this stuff, and you realise how much detail you've been missing out over the years. But this is certainly the first time I've looked back in any depth at what we were doing in the Eighties… and a lot was going on!"

Winton Smith's first Sounds interview with the Subhumans appeared in the paper on May 22nd, with a strapline, 'Reason for Persistence', and helped boost the band's popularity overnight, such was the high regard people held for that publication. Here's a transcription of the text:

"We played in Bristol, right, and there were all these so-called hardcore punks roaming around, bloody ten-foot Mohicans and more studs than a bloody horse farm, and they're all going, 'Are you the Subhumans? Are you the Subhumans?' Yes, we are. 'You CAN'T be!'"

Dick is the Subhumans' singer, and like the rest of the band he isn't quite your average Sun reader's idea of a punk rocker …

Guitarist Bruce and bassist Grant have only about five studs between them, while Trotsky the drummer has long hair, a denim jacket with a Led Zeppelin patch sewn on the back, and… flares. The singer's gear is pretty punk rock in itself, but the hair, it kind of droops, and there's this strange long bit that hangs over his face like a wet sock, and well…

Do you think the punks express such disbelief because you wear glasses, Dick?

"It's because I wear glasses, because Trotsky's got long hair, because Bruce has curly hair, because Grant's got that hair… they think if you don't look like a hardcore punk, you can't be a hardcore punk band."

Rising triumphantly out of the ashes of the Stupid Humans, Audio Torture and The Mental came the Subhumans. The current line-up has been together since June 1981.

The Subhumans are becoming very popular. They've released two EPs on Flux of Pink Indians' Spider Leg label – 'Demolition War' and, more recently, 'Reason for Existence', which at this very moment is steadily climbing the indie pop charts.

They are not an ordinary punk rock group. The music available here is special. Deadly, shimmering, growling guitar, teasing, stunning musical dodges and chases, their name is deceptive. Sometimes the Subhumans stray into the more familiar territories of punk, pushing the four chord bashes too far, for too long, but this is unusual. On most occasions when they opt for thrash, they'll weave and twist around that basic framework, add ever so subtle, mesmerising little sounds, decorate and build upon their song, and come up with something new, something fresh, and something exciting.
Yet it's still punk – Subhumans punk . . .

Are you aware of your growing reputation and street credibility...? "No, tell us about it!"

Dick: "Well, I'm getting a lot of letters, because I put my address on the back of the first EP thinking, oh great, I'll get some letters for once! Now I can't stop them, and I'm months behind in answering them. A lot of people must think we're a bunch of cunts, but I do eventually get round to answering them, I mean I must have had 300 this year."

What sort of letters do you get?

"Most of them are just three lines saying, please send me some info, thought the EP was great. You get the occasional people who write long letters, and out of those there's the ones who tell you they're doing fanzines, and those that make it worth it really, the ones who offer constructive criticism."

What's the reaction been to 'Human Error', the fiery reggae-based number on 'Demolition War'?

Bruce: "We've only had one person who said they didn't like it. We were a bit dubious to put that on the first EP, or to put it anywhere, because it's slower. We thought it would be best to put it on the first EP because if we put it on the second it'd look as though we were copping out."

Reggae was very cool with punks at one time.

DICK AT BRUCE'S, 1982 BY KEV TYDEMAN

GRANT AND PETE BY KEV TYDEMAN

DICK AND GRANT, WARMINSTER YOUTH CENTRE
PHOTO COPYRIGHT © PAUL SLATTERY

Dick: "Yeah. I don't like it myself, this so-called 'real' reggae bores me to tears, the stuff John Peel plays all the time."

Bruce: "I like reggae a lot."

How did the connection with Flux come about?

Dick: "Well, when they were starting up Spiderleg, they heard our three tracks on the 'New Criminals' compilation tape, and they thought we were good enough to be put on a record.

"First of all, we intended to record 'Demolition War' on a cassette recorder and make it into an EP, but they said they'd pay the money back if we went into a studio, so we did that instead."

You've got strong views about keeping prices low, haven't you?

Dick: "Yeah, we intended to do an EP with Small Wonder, but just at the last moment I said can you put it out for 85p? They said no way, it has to be £1.05, which isn't so much their fault, because they've got a lot more overheads to see to than a small, totally independent company like Spiderleg."

The Subhumans are different. They sing of things most punk bands wouldn't even consider singing about, like ... 'Peroxide girl with a false ID/Lost and lonely she can't see/Peroxide hair and burnt-out eyes/Blinded by so many lies ...' ('Peroxide').

Are you slagging off peroxide?

Dick: "Not at all. No, it's just a made-up fantasy type story about this girl who dyes her hair and it goes wrong. Instead of going on her hair it goes on her face and she fucks herself up."

But the majority of punk bands wouldn't dream of writing something like that...

"Not nowadays, no. Because it's not considered hip at all. It's just a fun number, we've got to have some fun numbers."

Bruce: "I worked it out the other day. We've got 27 serious numbers and 20 fantasy numbers."

Is 'Cancer' a fantasy number?

'Smile – it's impossible / I – I feel disposable / You laugh and it fucks me up/ Fag? Has he woken up?' – ('Cancer').

I thought it was an anti-smoking song, but as you all smoke it obviously isn't.

Dick: "No, it's... imagine the situation where this bloke who's got cancer is sitting down at work on his lunch break with his mates, and he's feeling depressed because he knows he's got cancer, and there's these blokes trying to cheer him up by giving him fags. People think that fags actually cheer you up and, er, more so than... er ..."

Bruce: "Sweets."

Dick: "It's like 'Drugs of Youth', it's just a statement. It's not pro-drugs or anti-drugs..."

But how do you feel when you see punks sniffing glue?

Dick: "I don't like glue."

Bruce: "We don't agree with glue."

Do you deliberately try to bring something fresh to the confines of punk?

Dick: "No, you can't do it deliberately. You just come up with what you do, and it either works or it doesn't work..."

Bruce: "We try to keep the music tight, and interesting.... we've got a lot of bash-bash stuff, but we also put lots of little interesting bits in it."

Grant: "Bash-bash with a difference...."

In a musical area that grows simultaneously larger and more unexciting all the time, the individuality, sparkle and strength of the Subhumans is a rarely experienced treat. Does the sheer predictability of most of today's punk groups depress them?

Bruce: "Oh, the whole scene depresses me actually, musically it depresses me. Because they all say they don't want anything to do with politics..."

Dick: "Yeah, that is copping out if you ask me."
Grant: "What's wrong with it?"

119

Stratton Youth Club
Hyde Rd. Kingsdown

SUBHUMANS

+ Support

Friday 14th May

The Pagans +

Tickets £1-00

Sound

Admittance on Door

Depression

130 Tickets Only

Doors Open 7-30p.m.

WESTWOOD 82

STALLS FOOD

BAR

LIVE BANDS

SIGNPOSTED FROM BRADFORD-ON-AVON

AUG 14

FROM 3 TILL LATE

PONY RIDES

£2 IN ADVANCE

£2.50 ON GATE

KIDS'

PLAYGROUND

ALL PROCEEDS TO THE KIDS OF HINSLEY CENTRE

TICKETS AVAILABLE FROM: PEEWEES BAR T.BOWBRIDGE WON GO LUCK NOW CANAL TAVERN B-O-A

ADMISSION

ST.JOHNS AMBULANCE IN ATTENDANCE

UNDER 13 YEARS

KIDS FREE

Divers
Rhythm Section
The Sabhumans
The Bohana Mouse Band
The Marshall Howe Band
Max Headroom and the Car Parks
30,000 Frenchmen
(reforming for a one off gig)
White Spirit Blues Band

R.O.A.F

LACK OF INTEREST PRES.NTS

FLUX OF PINK INDIANS

SUBHUMANS

DEAD POPSTARS

FROM WEYMOUTH

SMART PILS

SUNDAY 18th JULY
CENTRE 69

Accept Nothing
Question Everything
Destroy Conformity

BE BIZARRE
REBEL NOW

PENN HILL ROAD,
WESTON VILLAGE,

To Live Outside
The Law
You Must Be Honest

DON'T JUST SPECTATE
PARTICIPATE

BATH.
7:00–10:30 £1·50

Not So Sub-Human

The rise of the Warminster-based and, Subhumans, has been given boost by a full-page profile in the pop music newspaper *Sounds* during the past few days.

Together since this time last year, Subhumans are one of several groups who have been able to find their feet and develop their style under the roof of the Warminster Youth Centre in The Close.

At the moment three rehearse here, the others being A-Heads and Organised Chaos, and a fourth "Silent Guests" have only recently moved on to more sophisticated facilities in Melksham.

Subhumans are Bruce (Treasure) whose home is in Vicarage Street, Dick from Melksham, "Trotsky" from Longbridge Deverill, and Grant who lives at Dilton Marsh.

Sounds describes their latest E.P. (Bruce says the spread could help to sell anything up to 10,000 copies) this way:—

"The music available here is special, Deadly, shimmering, growling guitar; teasing, stunning musical dodges and chases.....On most occasions when they opt for thrash, they'll weave and twist around that basic framework, add ever so subtle, mesmerising little sounds, decorate and build upon their song, and come up with something new, something fresh, and something exciting."

The youth centre's achievement as an inspiration to pop musicians, is partly a reflection of the demand for local practice facilities.

It is not particularly well-equipped and youth leader Alan Chesters has had to use his best diplomatic skills in the past to keep the peace with neighbours.

For some time now he has been searching for an annexe, preferably some way away from human habitation, so that he can give more young musicians a chance to follow in the footsteps of Subhumans and Silent Guests.

As things stand, he is having to turn budding talent away, and he says it is a fair measure of Bruce, Dick, Trotsky and Grant's determination that they made so much headway in such a desperately competitive business.

The centre, meanwhile, is running two highly-popular courses for its membership. A self-defence scheme for teenage girls, expected to attract about a dozen recruits, is currently catering for 40, and another 20 or so youngsters are meeting at Kingdown School each week for beginners' tennis tuition.

Dick: "Well… it's just the way they stress it. I mean certain bands, I've read in fanzines how they say all these bands who write about politics are idiots, that sort of crap."

Somebody once described you affectionately as 'hippy punks'.

Grant: "I can't see anything wrong in that."

Bruce: "Hippies are passive people, aren't they? Nice people hippies, always got on with them."

Along with the refreshingly sensible anti-war/bomb lyrics printed on the sleeve of 'Demolition War', there is a long complicated and utterly incomprehensible mini-essay. What are they getting at? Dick explains it to me …

"Ah yes, I remember writing this."

Surely it could have been made a lot clearer.

"Well of course it could have been made clearer, it's just that I love writing long complicated sentences like that!" (uproar)

But seriously, do you think any of your fans understand it? I didn't.

Bruce: "I didn't either. He's got an 'A' level in English, the bastard. He knows all these long words we don't understand."

Dick, do you ever worry that like some bands get labelled a 'Crass-band' you'll find yourselves labelled a 'Flux-band'? "Well yeah, quite a few people have lumped us in with Flux and Crass. I'm not particularly worried about that, because both bands are good. I mean it's better than being called an Oi band or something like that, which obviously we ain't… I think we're a 'Subhumans-band'."

Unpredictable, unpretentious, thrilling and new. The singer is perfectly correct.

Barriers will be broken.

"That first Sounds interview talked a lot about our appearance, how we looked really weird," says **Dick**, "And I was quoting people from when we turned up at our first Bristol gig, who were saying, 'Where are the Subhumans? You can't be them!' because we all had long hair or whatever. And that was referenced in the interview. The fixation point was that we were different from other punk bands. That was when my hair got called a 'wet sock'… that stuck!

"We didn't exactly get flak for looking different, but people were curious. A lot of people referred to us as 'hippies', mainly 'cos of Trotsky's appearance – long hair, Afghan coat, Led Zep patches... we weren't what people expected really. And it turned out that a lot of our basic outlooks on life, and war and peace and stuff, were of the same style as the hippies of twenty years earlier, but at the time, being called a 'hippy' was an insult, because hippies were derogated for being, uh, too 'out of it', lazy, enjoying themselves too much... everyone was jealous of them basically! And a lot of people's parents would have been of the hippy generation... in fact, you could have called Bruce's mum a 'hippy', and she was one of the smartest parents going!"

"Crass influenced us more with their political views and their 'pay no more than' stance than with their music, I think?" **Bruce** picks up on another thread in the Sounds interview.

"And they generated quite a lot of shallow following mentality in the local punk scene as well," ponders **Dick**, "Who all started wearing black and spraying the Crass symbol everywhere, but that came and went, and left behind a hardcore of people who'd got right into them and what they were saying. What they were saying was very new to the punk scene, because they were taking everything very seriously indeed. Up until then, the only anarcho reference kids had ever had was 'Anarchy in the UK', so they brought a new perspective. They made people think a bit more about how they were actually living, and what was going on around them, the structures of society... when you're young, things like 'hierarchies' were words for philosophers or professors – you just wanted to have a good time, and get out of your head, and if you wanted to play music, you just got your instrument or your pen and created something on the back of not much. But when you get a band like Crass come along, as a lyricist, it really fired me up, to see what would come out... not copying it word for word or anything, but they definitely had an influence on outlook.

"We had a foot on both sides of the divide, without really trying. We couldn't be as serious as Crass... they were *so* serious. Interestingly, if Crass had played bouncier music, I wonder how that would have turned out? Because their music put a lot of people off. It was very basic, and if you didn't like it, you weren't going to stick around long to listen to the lyrics. That's how music works – the tune is what pulls you in and gets you into the lyrics. It's rare that you get lyrics so good it doesn't matter what tune they're sang to."

"I think Dick understood the anarchy thing a bit more than me," laughs **Bruce**, "I had no idea what it was about! You'd sometimes give me letters to answer for the band, and they'd be like, 'Do you believe in anarchy?' or 'How long have you been an anarchist?', and I didn't have a clue."

"Oh yes, all those fanzine questions, like 'Are you anti-war?'" continues **Dick**. "Mmm, let's think about this one...! But we used to get a lot of letters... I think the most in one day was thirty-two, and it wasn't like emails popping up; these were proper letters by real people with all sorts of weird handwriting and doodles, and all these questions for fanzines. And I felt overloaded, so I thought, 'Why can't the rest of the band help out?' So, I started

DICK AND GRANT

DICK IN PICKWICK, RECORDING 'The Day the Country Died'
BY MEL BELL

DICK, NIGE, JOCK, BRUCE, WARMINSTER YOUTH CLUB BY PHIL

handing out a few letters, and Trotsky and Pete got hold of one, and the first question was something like, 'Are you anti-war?' And they put something like, 'No, but I've got an auntie in Cirencester...' They were just giving silly answers, so that didn't work!

"I used to add them up, and I'd get over hundred letters a week, and this was before I left work. The peak of letter arrivals was after [first album] 'The Day the Country Died' came out, which was – relatively speaking, for us – a massive success at the time. Record sales these days are pretty pathetic really. 'Demolition War' was only going to be a 1000 pressing, but then Derek rang up and said they were doing 2000, because they'd had pre-orders for 1000, and then it was 5000... first pressing.

"So, in the space of a year and a bit, we'd only done twenty gigs, but generated enough interest to sell 5000 records. What? That's how big the punk scene was, even on a smaller level – it wasn't on the radio, but it was all over the world.

"My opinion of reggae has developed a bit since that Sounds interview too," admits **Dick**. "That comment I made was prompted by not having heard more than Bob Marley and the hits, whatever. John Peel played quite a bit of reggae, and I just couldn't get into it. I just found it too slow, and I just couldn't engage with the whole religious aspect of a lot of it, all the Jah stuff... I still can't engage with that, to be fair, but each to his own and all that. I find it all far too... religious really! But mostly, that part of the brain that got woken up later was not engaging with the beat. At all. It was slow, it was very repetitive, it goes on... that's how I was thinking at the age of eighteen or whatever.

"When it came to Culture Shock [his band after Subhumans], and the reggae bass lines that Paul brought along, I soon discovered that you could skank it up a little bit, insert some punk rock now and again, mix it with a bit of punk and ska music, and as a singer, I suddenly had all this space to sing in. I started actually singing, as opposed to 'sort of singing but more or less shouting' all the way through Subhumans. With Culture Shock I could actually start finding and singing and holding notes, which was a great step forward for me, singing-wise. I realised it had the same amount of room for energy and passion as singing much faster, except this time you could hear what the singer was singing more.

"So my dislike of it was just where I was at that point. When The Clash did 'Police & Thieves', I thought, 'Hang on, what's this? It's a bit slow...' For me, it didn't have an edge, and most of the stuff I like has got some sort of edge to it. 'Bankrobber' was the same – a bit boring really.

"I should say right here though that a lot of dub reggae is in my top albums. A lot of the stuff Dub Syndicate did was amazing, and their 'North of the River Thames' album is my favourite album of all time. So it was just about mental musical evolution really."

The next few months waiting for the 'Religious Wars' EP to be released were notable as they played several gigs with the now-legendary Rudimentary Peni, not to mention further dates with Flux, and most importantly they recorded the aforementioned debut album, 'The Day the Country Died', in late June, although it wasn't released until early '83.

"Peni were still quite a small band, when we played with them in Welwyn Garden City [at the Ludwig Family Club, May 28th, 1982]," recalls **Bruce**. "They were on first, and they did the sound-check in their school uniform, because they'd come straight from school. I thought it was part of the act, playing in their school uniforms, but they'd literally come to the gig from school…"

"Then we played the London Musicians Collective [June 7th, 1982] with them," continues **Dick**. "That was the gig with the ultimate line-up: Flux of Pink Indians, Conflict, The Mob, Subhumans and Rudimentary Peni… that would get people excited these days! There was 500 people there, and it was £2 to get in, or something like that… maybe with a can of food as a donation, 'cos it was a benefit. So there were piles of baked beans and soup and all sorts just inside the front door.

"Their lyrics were really over the top," he continues, on the subject of Peni, "Really taking it to the extreme of cynicism – I loved it. I was like, 'Whoah!' I wouldn't write that myself, but I really like reading it. It was really warped, and introduced, or at least reinforced, the fallacy of male hierarchy… and all that stuff about the Pope and the Catholics…

"They had that line, 'Three-quarters of the world is starving…' so I was thinking, is that actually true? Given the population of the world, are three-quarters of them starving? I've never worked it out, so I don't know if it's accurate. But then they say, 'The rest are dead!' What? Oh my god! 'Overdosed on insensitivity…' What a line! 'Nail varnished to crosses!' It's fantastic, it's absolute poetry. Wonderful stuff, and it really got to the core of a lot of things, without being obvious. It was more like, 'Here's a statement – try and get your head around that…' Stuff like that was a major confirmation for my own head space… I wasn't the only one thinking warped-out thoughts. It was twisted and dark, and there was no let-up."

Although it didn't see the light of day until January 1983, 'The Day the Country Died' was recorded at Pickwick between June 22nd and June 26th, 1982.

"It was a frenetic time of year," smiles **Dick**. "It took four days – basically we recorded side one on day one, side two on day two, then mixed side one on day three, and side two on day four… more or less. We basically belted through the songs. As far as I remember, we had been at Stonehenge festival up until the day before we started recording, and we had to hitch to the studio, or get lifts off Trotsky's mum… my dad picked Andy's drum kit up from Warminster and dropped it off for Trotsky to use. Some of us stayed over there after day one, some of us came back to my place in Melksham. Corsham was about seven miles from Melksham, but we didn't have cars and still had to get there. Those that stayed over had the luxury of somewhere cosy to sleep and breakfast in the morning. Think me and Trotsky hitched back to Melksham?

"It was quite chaotic. Our girlfriends were all there, and they were fairly bored throughout the process, listening to the same songs over and over again, waiting for something else to happen, but they always liked to be where we were at – they even came

127

with us to see Pete Stennett to discuss the recording contract he wanted to give us. They insisted they came along, and it was a bit embarrassing really, because Pete wanted to talk to the band, not necessarily the band and their girlfriends. It was a strange time, haha!"

A strange time indeed, but one with some great gigs to be had. July saw Subhumans support Flux of Pink Indians three times, in Putney, Fareham and Bath, the latter gig at the Weston Centre 69 with local band Smart Pils opening up proceedings.

"I thought they were the best, tightest band I'd heard for years," says Smart Pils guitarist **Steve Bemand**, of the first time he saw Subhumans. "There was much mushrooms, and much cider, of course, but the band were sensational, and had the audience gripped. We were hanging round after the set chatting with the guys, and they seemed like kindred spirits. Dick was a total bright spark, enthusiastic and intelligent; Trotsky was a lovely guy, and an ace drummer; Bruce was a great guy, and a nimble guitarist, and Grant had this analogue, punky style of playing. We also grew very friendly with Pete The Roadie – he was a larger than life personality, and seemed like the non-playing member of Subhumans; he later roadied for Smart Pils on a UK tour [in 1987… your author's band Decadence Within went along as opening act], and a continental trip.

"Anyway, they were considered a proper together band as opposed to us lot, and many others locally, who were often a bit loose and untogether! But the punk scene was always a minority so they were, early on, slightly mythical, a cult band, and as far as I was concerned, setting a standard we could aspire to."

The 'Religious Wars' EP was released August 14th, 1982, and enjoyed a twelve-week stay in the Indie Charts, peaking at No. 7. The title track is an insistent earworm from the moment it bursts from the speakers, its chorus simplistic yet uplifting, buoyed by some energetic interplay between Bruce's driving guitar and Grant's roving bass runs. The desperately frantic 'Love Is' is elevated by subtly ambitious guitar runs, whilst 'It's Gonna Get Worse' remains one of the band's most convincing numbers, an explosive intro giving way to an intense high speed bass lick, with Dick spitting universal truths like, 'You can blame the fucking Tories, but every government's the same, they don't believe in the public good, just in their financial gain…' as if his life depends upon it. 'Work Experience' closes out the EP, and is propelled by thick syrupy bass runs with Trotsky's rock-solid rolls underpinning the jagged guitars.

"'Work Experience' may have been the first example of me singing harmony on a chorus," reveals **Bruce**. "Before that I was just doubling Dick's vocal live, where he would've doubled himself in the studio. I always liked singing in harmony – if possible, haha! I also always felt that the chorus would be 'brought out' more with a second or third vocal. It can be more powerful on the one hand, or more melodic on the other. In time, when Dick's voice got darker and lower, I used my voice to lighten the vibe a little too. Choruses are about singing along after all."

Dick: "'Work Experience' was just a good topical title; my job was a 'normal' one… but still fit my 'all jobs suck' mindset!"

"I borrowed a Jazz bass for some of the recordings," recalls **Grant**, "I think it was

128

[second bassist] Phil's actually – and sound-wise that was even better than my Squire, a bit growlier. It definitely had more depth to it. Although the thin bass sound on the first EP was more to do with the rudimentary recording set-up than the bass I played…

"I had a big 2 x 15 Peavey bass cab and a Marshall top all the way through my time in Subhumans. It was a transistor amp, not valve, so it didn't quite have the full Marshall sound, but it was fine for gigging, nice 'n' growly. I remember Pete was carrying my cab down the stairs at Warminster youth club once, and he slipped and fell – it bounced all the way down the stairs, and on him a few times! He's never been the same since… he was a little dazed, but he's full of life, that boy, haha!"

"I wrote that song with the generally fresh at the time information in my head that so many wars had been started throughout history because of religion," says **Dick**, of the lyrical inspiration behind the title track, "One religion fighting another one, all for the same apparent god. I was fairly anti-religion anyway, because of the structure of the church, and all the power the church has got – it's up there with government and business in terms of the power it's got, the land it owns, the money it's got… and the control it therefore has. But it's different from politics and business because it controls the mind. And it invests all its power into something that doesn't exist… all its power comes from people having faith and belief. The downside of not having that faith and belief, especially a few hundred years ago, was being persecuted, or tortured, or locked up, or set fire to. For being a disbeliever. Or a war would start because your whole country didn't believe in the same religion as the country next door. There's so much death and war that goes on because of religion, but it was generally not on people's list of the top enemies of freedom, and it should have been way further up.

"As regards the spiritual side of religion, I think everyone has got that anyway, but to put the source of spirituality up in the heavens, with one god or another, seems to be shirking your own realisation of your potential as a human being, and the power of the human brain, to be spiritual, i.e. kind, caring, and nice to things. And appreciative of nature. Nature is the closest thing to the concept of god that I can think of – that's where it all came from. But religious people will be like, 'Who invented nature though?' No, no, no, nature's just a word for everything we do – or don't – understand, and to put it down to one person is just more – overwhelmingly male – bullshit.

"There were probably lots of battles fought between pagan leaders over their religious beliefs as well, but generally paganism gives a lot of credit to nature, and a lot of reverence to the sun – and other stuff that does visibly, obviously, exist. It makes more sense to worship the sun than it does an invented character. But from a more twentieth century point of view, it makes no sense to worship the sun at all, because it's just going to be there whether you worship it or not. And you'll die whether you worship it or not… and the chance of an afterlife is just the same as believing in anything else."

The EP was also the first Subhumans release to feature artwork by Nick Lant, an artist that would become almost synonymous with the band, because he had such a distinctive style and didn't do art for any other band, so it was very much unique to Subhumans.

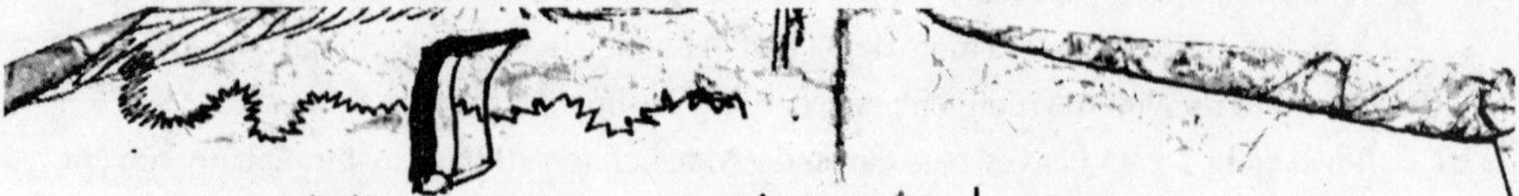

Working for money and the system to
You ~~believe~~ the dole queue made you worthless
taught
So now you're ~~enslaved~~ to a public machine
Getting somewhere is that what they mean?
Worthless – not enough money!

you wanted more & what did they say?
'you'll never sell yourself to anyone
Come back and try in 6 months time
Don't you know there's a social decline'?
Politics – dunnit make you mad?

you sed you'd look for another job
well try it sonny you won't get far
~~Do~~ as yor told ~~+~~ stop complaining
Being ~~to~~ conned is part of the training
~~Manage~~ Crash course – learning how to lose

I'd rather work for ~~no one~~ money
than just for something to do
But then why bother ~~why~~ working at all
Dyawanna stay totally normal
~~Normal~~

Ⓒ

WORK EXPERIENCE

Dick
21/1/82
Work

'WORK EXPERIENCE' - DICK'S ORIGINAL LYRIC SHEET

ove is a bastard / it ~~fuc~~ tears you
Just when you ~~thought~~ you didn't have apart
Couldn't give a ~~shit~~ fuck cos you g heart
And ~~it~~ suddenly everything brings you down
know how
Love is a bastard / it fucks you up
Makeup breakup totally messed you up
Lipstick stains and little ~~white~~ lies
Can you see the blood running ~~in you~~
outta my eyes?

Love is a bastard / It makes you cry
~~Get you~~ Do something wrong and you don't
Can't remember what you said   know why
~~Hang yorself from the end of yor bed~~
lie in the road and wish you were dead

And everything just gets you down

**'LOVE IS' AND 'IT'S GONNA GET WORSE'
DICK'S ORIGINAL LYRIC SHEETS**

ITS GONNA GET WORSE

1 I don't like the way I'm living
2 No-one gives me any choice
3 ~~They~~ They don't like the way I'm singing
4 ~~But all~~ I got is my fucking voice

5 I can't get a word in edgeways
6 ~~A~~ Surrounded by so many lies
7 ~~They~~ ~~Just treat us like the scum~~
8 We're th people they despise

10 Theres always g rising unemployment
~~Theres~~ always debates on nuclear war
Do you think that any government
Gives a shit what we stand for
Sometimes you wonder what to do
when you havent got no cash
~~Wel~~ Better start thinking what do
when your country turns to ~~gah~~

You can blame the fuckg Tories
~~Becos~~ ~~Rulernm~~
Bt every government the same
~~It could be a~~
They don't believe in the public goo
~~They~~ Just in their financial gain
~~And~~ then the bastards throw you out
And take yor furniture away
Becos you can't afford the rent
~~Becos~~
Becos unemployment dosn't pay

"He just wrote a letter, as people did in those days," explains **Dick**, "Asking for some more info on the band, and at the bottom of the letter was this little one-inch-square picture of a punk rocker's head with a Mohican, done in very fine pen.

"In theory, I should still have that letter somewhere. I kept all the letters I got sent; they're in bags in the garage – I don't know what to do with them. If I throw them away, I feel it's wrong, but if I keep them, I don't know what to do with them, so I just keep them, which *is* what I do with them! They're just there… for moments like this.

"Anyway, we were stuck for a sleeve, because quite often, doing the art for a record is a massive pain in the ass… you've got the record done, and it sounds fantastic… 'But what about the artwork?' 'Oh, fuck!' So, I wrote back to him, and sent him the lyrics to 'Religious Wars', and asked him if he could come up with some artwork for it… and then a few weeks later – it came through quite quickly – this drawing turned up in a 7" cardboard envelope, and it was like, 'Oh my god!' He just did it. Remarkable."

"I was born in Melton Mowbray, Leicestershire, on July 1st, 1965," **Nick Lant** goes back to his childhood, to set the scene. "I grew up in Hoby, a small rural village where the countryside was my playground (and is still where I'm happiest). My dad was a violent bully. The older and more independent I became, the worse he got.

"I'd loved music from an early age. My introduction to punk came via my best friend. He had a much older sister who periodically returned from London; I'd see her in the village and thought she looked magnificent, resplendent in bright orange spikes, shades, boiler suit and boots. I heard the villagers discuss her behind her back and inwardly rallied to her defence, my first heroine. She'd brought the music with her and left her brother with 7" singles that we played to death, and there began my musical education.

"But my access to music was difficult, as there was little money in my home. I got an old tape machine from somewhere and made do with snippets recorded from the radio. Upper school was the next step; it brought kids from a wider area together and so I met likeminded souls, just as post-punk and new-wave was being met by the second hit of bands like The Undertones and SLF, who were respectively the first live bands I saw.

"Mum shared a love of music and dared to bring a music centre into the home. I loved Ian Dury and somehow dad got to hear the intro to 'Plastic Patricia'… it didn't end well – I ended up with a final beating, fought back and was thrown out. Aged sixteen, I was living in a tent and working on a farm, but I was free.

"I created my own entertainment as a kid, I did a lot of sketching and doodling which taught me to draw. As my punk circle widened and my skills became known to my mates, I was asked to paint their biker jackets, becoming over-familiar with Airfix paints, band logos and sleeve covers. Often bored in school, I cartooned any material that accepted ink. At this point I didn't have any influences; I was either a copyist of punk band images or just knockin' out my own style of cartoon sketches. I never had any training and, given my childhood, I had little chance of university or art school.

"Being rural, I was initially isolated from any punk scene. The internet and mobiles didn't exist, so I occasionally wrote letters, fan mail I suppose. I loved the Subhumans;

they seemed approachable and had contact details on a cover. I was still in the family home when I wrote to Dick Lucas and typically my letter was illustrated with sketches. I was absolutely thrilled with his handwritten reply, complementing my work and unbelievably offering me the opportunity to draw their next cover, 'Religious Wars'. I was buzzing.

"I didn't get many opportunities to see them live. The first time was before I'd written to them, a gig at Retford Porterhouse. Early years and a great gig, but sadly memorable because a mob of mods on scooters attacked punks leaving the venue, and a running battle ensued through a multi-storey car park. The first time I *met* the band was a gig in Nottingham, I remember chatting to Dick pre-gig, over a tray of chips near the old Lace Market; I think that was the only time we met.

"Anyway, I remember knocking out 'Religious Wars' really quickly. If I look back at it, the work is naïve; I was young, but it perfectly sums up that early time in my life. I'd realised the nonsense of religion early on, rebelling against church, Sunday school and religious studies. It was only later that I learnt of all the harm perpetuated, and had no other course than anti-theism. I'm glad that was my first cover as my thoughts against all religions have only strengthened over the years.

"It's probably my least favourite piece that I did for them, even though it holds a special place as the first. Often a band's early work, or first album, is their best, but I don't think that's true for an artist. That cover reflects a teenager at work on a dining room table in an unhappy home in Leicestershire, but happy in his ability to comment against religion and in his remote connection to likeminded folk in Wiltshire. Its simplicity is its saving grace; it's just not an accomplished piece of work."

"Nick's art has been highly influential really," adds **Dick** appreciatively, "The amount of times it's been reproduced on jackets and T-shirts is insane. When I announced there was a 'The Day the Country Died' jigsaw coming out, it got over 800 likes on Instagram, which was 400 more than anything else, you know what I mean? So we took a hundred with us on tour in the States, in 2018 or whatever, and we sold like ten... you bastards! You all 'liked' it, but wouldn't fucking buy one, haha!"

August 14th saw the band headline the eclectic Westwood festival, which unfortunately wasn't as big a deal as planned, but they made the most of it, fuelled by alcohol and youthful exuberance.

"I went to a Wasted Space/Pagans garden party gig the night before, in Southwick [near Trowbridge]," recalls **Dick**, "And awoke with a pounding skull to get to Warminster YC for a practice. I got there on time, but Bruce was still asleep, so Grant wrote a set out; we only had time to practise one song in the end, 'Rain'... that and 'Adversity' were played for the first time at the festival.

"There were only 200 people there, not the 2000 that were rumoured. Peewee, the local pub owner, ran the beer tent, which was packed because it rained off and on most of the day. I hung out with the Trowbridge punks, and watched [local 'comedy band'] 30,000 Frenchmen, who were pretty hilarious – five or six straight-looking oldish blokes running

UNUSED NICK LANT ART

NICK LANT

WILTSHIRE TIMES, AUGUST 1982

LYNDA WHITE and Ginny Taylor take refreshment at the Westwood Festival on Saturday. More pictures inside.

40934A

Pop festival in the rain

CONSTANT drizzle failed to dampen the spirits of pop fans who attended the Westwood Festival on Saturday. And they were in good humour, according to organisers, despite the disappointly small number who turned up.

The musicians were praised for their high standards—and they all gave their services free in aid of the Winsley Centre.

A competition to see who came farthest to the festival revealed visitors from France, Germany, Holland and Finland. And one who travelled from Australia.

The organisers said Trowbridge's comedy band, 30,000 Frenchmen, performed an outstanding set; heavy metal fans were persuaded to leave the beer tent to listen to Marshall Howe,

the popular Rhythm Section were on top form and punk band the Sub Humans got critical acclaim from the audience ranging from "magnificent" to "diabolical".

Pee Wee's real ale tent was a popular attraction at the festival—providing shelter from the rain and refreshment.

'Child's

about in perfect silliness with perfect timing, doing songs like 'What's Gardening, Eh?' Grant crashed out very drunk, so Bruce and Trotsky had to drag him round the field to help sober him up before our set.

"We were on last at 11:15, and I remember feeling nervous in front of an unusual crowd and on a big stage. There was a great sound in the monitors and we played well. I couldn't see most of the crowd, but a few people leapt about at the front. 'Rain' was really powerful on its first playing – all the practising had paid off – and we ended with 'Human Error', just before midnight when we were going to get cut off. 'It's been the best Westwood festival this year!' I said, 'And it's all down to this man!' and pointed at Spike, the organiser, one of several very motivated Trowbridge area hippies/CND members a few years older than us, some of which were our occasional van drivers, or friends of Bruce's mum, or co-drinkers in Peewee's pub in Trowbridge."

Towards the end of August, the band did a long weekend around London, playing the notorious Skunx on the 21st, with the A-Heads and Organized Chaos ('notorious' for being frequented by violent boneheads), the Centro Iberico Anarchist Centre, with The Mob, A-Heads and Pagans, on the 22nd, then the Moonlight Club on the 23rd, with Faction supporting, who their old friend Rob Challice played bass for, and then the Red Lion in Gravesend on the 24th, with The Mob and Faction. Quite the weekend.

"We went up there [Skunx] with a chap called Tim, who had this bus, and he was pissed off, because his van got covered in swastikas and shit," sighs **Dick**, "And the tyres got punctured, and we had to pay him all the money we got, which was about £70, to cover the repairs to his van, or coach, or whatever it was, which got fucked up by the assholes at Skunx. That was a sad place."

"There was never a very nice feel to the gigs at Skunx," agrees **Mel**, "The toilets were flooded with piss, and there were skinheads everywhere. But other than that, I enjoyed the London gigs – I really liked the Centro Iberico... you used to meet all your mates up there. I don't actually recall there being too much trouble at gigs really, although there was a bad one at the Ring of Bells in Bath once, where there was a set-to with some rugby players...!"

"Rob Challice was a good connection," reckons **Bruce**. "He moved from Warminster to Kent, and then into London. I hadn't heard of Rudimentary Peni, Epileptics and Part 1 until Rob got into them and played them to me. I liked guitar flanger effects, from listening to the Banshees, and Part 1 seemed like an extreme version of that really. They were interesting. UK Decay were a bit like that as well... layers and layers of guitar effects."

"I must have met Bruce and Phil for the first time when we all started secondary school at Kingdown Comprehensive, Warminster, in 1975," explains **Rob**. "We were eleven, and thrown together in the same form group, 'Wylie 6'; Phil was always carrying a football, and Bruce had long hair.

"My family had just moved from Salisbury to Warminster; my dad was training for a career in the clergy. We lived over the road from Bruce, and one day I had to deliver some homework to him as he was off school. I knocked on his door for the first time and his mum, Jeanne, invited me in. It was like stepping into another world. I remember the house had an interesting smoky smell to it. Bruce had an attic bedroom with a train set and maybe a guitar in the corner. I was soon over there every day. Music was always being played in the house and it was full of interesting people. Bruce, myself and our mates were listening to the heavy stuff of the time: Hawkwind, Budgie, Black Sabbath, Led Zeppelin… but within no time we had discovered cider, pot and punk. We were probably more Stranglers than Sex Pistols, but we were listening to everything.

"In 1977, we had to move to Longfield, in north Kent, where my dad became a vicar. I wasted no time in finding the other school kids that were into punk. We started a fanzine, Enigma, and formed a band, Anthrax. At that time punk was morphing into various sub-sects: anarcho, Oi!, new wave etc. Through bands like Crass, Epileptics and Poison Girls we became politically aware and part of the 'anarcho' scene. We started travelling to Gravesend, Medway and London for shows, often to sell our fanzine and meet similar-minded folk and bands. Not all gigs were peaceful; there were often right-wing skinheads at the shows in southeast London and Kent, with them inevitably wanting to start a fight with us young punks.

"I kept in touch with Bruce and frequently visited Warminster. Bruce was into playing music and was starting to put together a band, Stupid Humans. When I was down there, we would often sit around in his room drinking and smoking. I remember coming up with joke band names and occasionally writing some lyrics. Around then I must have jotted down the lyrics, 'We're the minority and we're okay, we're the minority, got something to say…' [which later became the Subhumans song 'Minority', of course].

"On one of these visits Bruce introduced me to Dick and we hit it off. Dick was in the band The Mental at the time and wanted to know all about what was happening with the punk scene in and around London.

"1981 was a pivotal year for me. In May, Subhumans played one of their first shows outside the West Country at Stevenage Bowes Lyon House, supporting Discharge and with The Mob opening. A bunch of us travelled up from Kent to Stevenage on a Sunday evening to see this incredible bill. I was especially proud that my Kent mates were going to see my old West Country mates, Subhumans, for the first time. The venue was packed and Subhumans smashed it. I threw myself into the mosh pit. It felt life-affirming letting off steam, with the frustrations of a factory floor job and living in a rectory.

"A couple of months later, I was made redundant, and I decided to leave home. I moved into one of the squats in Brougham Road, Hackney. The Convoy [i.e. new age travellers] used the road and derelict bus garage as a 'safe' place to spend winter. Through that scene I got to know The Mob and various other bands."

"Trotsky and I would hitch up to London to see Motörhead or whatever, and we'd stay with Rob in Brougham Road," recalls **Kev Tydeman**, "And the convoy would be

DICK, WITH A-HEADS - JOCK, NIGE AND MEL, EBBW VALE
COURTESY OF MEL BELL.

PETE - COURTESY OF JOCK MCCURDY

TROTSKY, TREVOR'S TRANSPORT CAFE, WARMINSTER, 1982
BY PHIL

resting up their buses there, and Rubella Ballet would be there – I saw them playing in a bedroom in a house next door. It was a real hub of activity up there, and really broadened our horizons… the first time we came across a proper co-op. Those people were really active politically, and it was great to go from sleepy Warminster to that, to having a base you could stay in up in London."

"It was fucking dangerous there too," adds **Jock**. "They told me there was a rehearsal room down in the cellar… 'Oh, where is it?' 'Just follow the extension leads…!' And there'd be all these cables cobbled together, with no proper plug sockets or anything… but that's how it was, you just got on with it. And if you got an electric shock, you got an electric shock."

Kev: "That was the first time my eyes were opened to that real frontline of anarcho punk. Class War were operating out of that street, I think, although I didn't have much truck with that, but we [later – in 1984] went off to Stop the City from there. I became aware of punk as a movement, an ongoing thing with people trying to move things forward – being politically aware, and trying to do something radical about it."

"In May 1982, Subhumans played Welwyn Garden City with Rudimentary Peni," continues **Rob**. "I hopped on the train from Kings Cross. That night, the guys thought it would be a great idea to kidnap me and take me back to Wiltshire, and that's me in the van that night on the back of the 'The Day the Country Died' album cover. A couple of hours later, the van broke down in the middle of Salisbury Plain, and we were stuck there until daylight with a field of pigs for company.

"I was in a new band, Faction, still doing the fanzine and I started a cassette-only label, 96 Tapes. One of my housemates was the legendary JC, and together we bought a second-hand Ford Transit for £400 so we could get around to gigs and help move stuff from squat to squat. I started presenting shows at venues like the Centro Iberico.

"I booked Subhumans to play the Moonlight Club in West Hampstead that August in 1982, with Faction supporting, and it was one of my favourite Subhumans shows despite somebody stealing my leather jacket. It was a sold-out show and it really felt like things were starting to happen for the band."

"It was amazing how much we drank back then," laughs **Dick**. "At the Gravesend gig that weekend, which was the last of that series around London, I actually apologised for being so drunk at the end of the set. I tried to make it comical, by pointing at the barman and blaming him, but it didn't really work, although he did give us free drinks afterwards. We were getting sloshed before we played, which I don't remember doing – but because we all were, it probably didn't matter too much. It mattered more later on, when one or two of us did, and one or two of us didn't, because then the differences showed in competence. But in the early days, 'competence' wasn't really a word we concerned ourselves with too much…"

"My memories are all a bit hazy of most of the gigs," admits **Grant**. "I can just recall falling out of the back of the van in various car parks, and there being all these punks saying, 'Oh, here's the band…' Just the frantic excitement of being part of that scene as a teenager. What the gigs were like, I have no idea, haha!"

September 12th, 1982, saw the band back in Pickwick Studios, to record the track 'No Thanks' for the regional 'Wessex '82' compilation EP, that also featured the Pagans, A-Heads and Organized Chaos. In fact, all four bands recorded and mixed their contributions to the 7" on the same day, which would certainly have kept engineer Steve Collinson on his toes, and the EP was released a few months later, in December, the first *vinyl* release for Dick's Bluurg label.

'No Thanks' was an enjoyably upbeat – and cautionary – tale of a disillusioned punk rocker seeking fame and fortune in (and eventually being chewed up and spat out by) the music industry, its lilting bass intro and adventurous guitar flourishes typical of the Subhumans, but all the bands turned in great tracks, the pure aggro of 'Victim' by Organized Chaos perfectly counterbalanced by the melody-drenched 'No Rule' by the A-Heads and earthy pathos of 'Wave Goodbye to Your Dreams' by the Pagans, making for a very solid compilation that really helped put the area on the punk rock map.

"'Wessex '82' was all down to the Subhumans," says **Bill**, gratefully, "Well, Dick really – being so proactive, and thoughtful, and wanting to capture what was going on here. And rather than sell the band out, he started Bluurg, to do it himself. It was a magical scene back then, it really was. We were all doing our own thing at the same time, but all spreading the word. And that's what it's about at the end of the day: connecting with people."

"But the nice thing about having all your mates in these bands," reckons **Kev**, "Was you'd travel off with them, and you suddenly started feeling you were part of something bigger, and you'd get your mum or dad to drop you off at gigs in Bath, or Bristol, all these places you wouldn't normally go to at fifteen or sixteen."

"And it was great that, when A-Heads played a gig, Dick or Pete or whoever would turn up, to support," smiles **Jock**. "I remember going to Cumbria, and it was a proper day out, hire a van and drive all the way up there, and they were with us, in the background, just our mates – but when you got there, everybody was like, 'Ooh, it's Dick, or Pete…' We broke down on the way up, and it took us four hours to change a wheel, because I was turning the wheel nuts the wrong fucking way – and I worked in a garage! Somebody came over with a blowtorch and helped chisel the nuts off before pointing out, 'I think you turn the nuts the other way on this side of the vehicle…?'"

Kev: "But the thing is about Warminster, we're very aware we come from the forest, we live in rolling countryside, and that came across in that release. Phil was telling me that someone once asked him where all the studs and spikes were, and he said, 'But that's not where we come from…' Which is why when we did band photos, they would go and stand in a field – amongst the cows! And 'Wessex '82' with the Westbury white horse in the background… that was just part of the environment, and gave a feeling of where they were coming from. It was a nice juxtaposition, I think."

BRUCE AND MEL, BRUCE'S PLACE BY KEV TYDEMAN

STEVE L, WARMINSTER, 1982 BY PHIL

GRANT BY MEL BELL

Jock: "Most other bands would be up against a wall, with all the graffiti around them, which became quite predictable. Not one of them has got a tattoo either. And in some places, like America, where everyone's covered in tats, that surprises some people."

"That was just where we were," interjects **Grant**. "It might have been cooler to be leaning up against a graffitied wall, I suppose, but we didn't have any graffiti to lean on, I guess, so we just had to lean on cows…!"

Kev: "It was one of those things when we were in the van, coming back from gigs all over the place, and it might be 4 or 5 am, but once we hit the stones [i.e. Stonehenge], we knew we were home. And sometimes we'd just get out of the van on Salisbury Plain and enjoy the sunrise."

Jock: "The worst one for me was opening the side door of the van in Bratton – Dick was asleep and lay against the door. As soon as I opened the door, he fell out… five or six feet down onto the floor. I've never laughed so much in my life; it was comical, like something off 'Morecambe & Wise'.

"I remember they took us up to Ebbw Vale to play with them, and all of a sudden, you were meeting different kinds of people, who had a different way of doing things – like walking past you with penknives out and spitting at you during sound-check! I think we pissed the Humans off a bit that night, because we got these buckets of water and threw them over the guy who was spitting at us, and then they had to get up after us in all these floods of water… but it was nice to go from your safe environment to something completely different."

After a gig in Bath, and several in South Wales (including the Ebbw Vale gig just mentioned by Jock), with the likes of Amebix and Disorder, the band were briefly stopped in their tracks when Dick was involved in a rather serious accident on November 1st.

"I was working in Devizes, and I was cycling there and back, seven miles each way, every day," explains **Dick**, "So I was getting super fit, and had reached the point where I could go all the way up Caen Hill in Devizes, this big long hill, in third gear. But anyway, I got to the point in the journey where there was a brick wall, with no pavement, and traffic coming up, overtaking me. And a chap driving a van, who ran the scrap yard down the bottom of the hill, came past me, and for some reason couldn't avoid hitting the back of my head with his wing mirror. He reckoned I veered out into the middle of the road, but I reckon I would have been super careful *not* to veer into the road, because of the place I was at, with the wall… no one knows really. But I ended up in hospital for about three weeks, with a fractured skull, so the four or five gigs we had coming up over the next few weeks had to be cancelled. Although I was convinced, once I was actually conscious, which was about a week or ten days after the accident – up until then, I was pretty much delirious, and can't remember much about it – that I was able to do some of them. I even

144

convinced the nurses to get me a telephone, and I rang my dad up, who had been made redundant the same day I got knocked over... he was having a really bad November! 'Hello, Rich, are you alright?' 'Have you got Petty's Van Hire's phone number, dad?' 'Well, what do you want that for?' 'We've got some gigs coming up, and I need to hire a van...' 'Ooh, I don't think they'll allow you out to do that!' And he was right, of course, they wouldn't. But I was convinced that if I hired the van – because I was the person who always hired the vans – the driver would come along and I'd just jump in the van and off we'd go... but that wasn't going to happen.

"And the fuckers shaved me! I'd never shaved once in my life at that point, and the fuckers shaved me. I liked a bit of bum fluff on my face, and I'd cut it off now and again with a pair of scissors – totally normal behaviour for a fucking eighteen-year-old, haha! – and they shaved me without asking. I nearly screamed when I looked in the mirror!"

Mel: "It was quite bad really. I caught the train to Bath to go and visit him in hospital. I bumped into his auntie as I was going in, who had just been in to see him, and I said to Dick when I went in, 'Oh hello, I just saw your auntie...' And he was like, 'Why didn't she come to see me?' It was the knock on his head, or the morphine or something, but I thought, 'Shit, he's not all there anymore, this is really bad...!' He was ringing up and arranging gigs, and ringing Petty's Van Hire and everything..."

Dick: "One of the cancelled gigs was a local one, over in Lavington, which was going to be Subhumans, Organized Chaos and A-Heads, and because Subhumans couldn't play, a new band called The Flying Fish Band played – which was Bruce on drums, my brother Steve on bass and yet-to-be-Subhumans-bassist Phil on guitar... a band that had come out of the Pagans, who had come out of Wild Youth, and so on. That was their first ever gig, which I missed, so I was quite annoyed about that. And they raised some money and bought me a present... a 'Mickey Mouse' it says in my diary, but I can't remember what it was... obviously not a real mouse, nor a plastic version, 'cos I wouldn't have liked that, but it might have been an ashtray, because I *have* got a Mickey Mouse ashtray somewhere! *And* they bought me a Blitz LP, which I thought was really nice of them."

"I couldn't even say how many gigs the Pagans did, before it became The Flying Fish Band," elaborates **Phil**, "But it was probably only six or seven, although we did do a recording. We jumped in on a Subhumans session over at Pickwick – they'd booked a few days to record something for a compilation [the aforementioned 'Wessex '82'], and we managed to get in on the end of that. The Rolling Stones were playing in Bristol at the time – Ashton Gate – and Herb said, 'Sorry, guys, I can't make it to the session... I'm off to see the Stones in Bristol!' So Steve ended up playing bass on it.

"But Steve was an amazing, talented, very natural musician, and was always messing

SUBHUMANS

"REALITY IS WAITING FOR A BUS" [   ]

SATURDAY AUGUST 21st — Skunx, 415 CITY ROAD LONDON EC1 — + A-HEADS + ORGANIZED CHAOS + RESISTORS — £1·50

SUNDAY AUGUST 22nd — CENTRE, 421A HARROW ROAD Nr WESTBOURNE PARK LONDON W9 — + The Mob! + A-HEADS + PAGANS — £1·00

MONDAY AUGUST 23rd — MOONLIGHT CLUB 100 WEST END LANE LONDON — + flux of pink indians + FACTION — £1·50

TUESDAY AUGUST 24th — RED LION CRETE HALL ROAD GRAVESEND — + the MOB + FACTION — £1·00

WEDNESDAY 25th — FLIXTON ROOMS, FLIXLAND NORWICH — + ?? — £1·50

SUBHUMANS + CORRUPTION + POLITRIX AT THE CENTRAL HOTEL 27 SEPT

ADMISSION £1·00

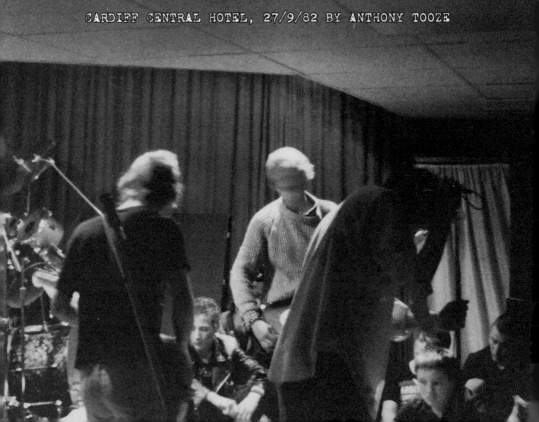

CARDIFF CENTRAL HOTEL, 27/9/82 BY ANTHONY TOOZE

CARDIFF CENTRAL HOTEL, 27/9/82 BY ANTHONY TOOZE

around on the bass anyway, so he did a great job on it. Steve was a multi-instrumentalist, and just had this insatiable desire to learn all things musical really. In fact, later on, towards the end of Subhumans, I ended up sharing a place with him in Holt, over near Trowbridge, and by that time he had a sitar as well! And he was learning to play trumpet and violin… he was just insatiable when it came to learning new stuff, creating new sounds.

"What pissed me off at the time was, we were just getting going with the Pagans, but he wanted to move forward and do different stuff all the time. We were doing alright, and people seemed to like it, but Steve was already on this quest to branch out musically – which is why Pagans morphed into The Flying Fish Band within a year. We were all still into punk, but also into old hippy music like Gong and Kevin Ayres and Here and Now… Steve had John Martyn records and stuff like that.

"I guess you could say we were a hippy punk band. And there was never any thought given to trying to do something to be popular, haha! We were hanging around at Peewee's in Trowbridge, which was where we used to drink at the time – half the people in there were punks, the other half were hippies, into Roy Harper and smoking dope and everything.

"Steve had spikey bleached hair early on, but by then, he had moved on. And that was what he kept doing for his whole life: moving on to the next thing… doing poetry, doing art… doing more and more new music. He was great at the acoustic stuff, and he did quite a few gigs as Steve L. later on.

"He was always getting into something else, and he eventually got into gardening, landscaping and organic farming.

"We just did a few gigs with The Flying Fish Band… maybe three or four. That was me, Bruce and Steve, just the three of us, although the Subhumans driver Tony Carter joined us for a while as well, but we never did any gigs with him. He was like a real Gong fan, so he would play what we called 'the old glissando bar'. We had a bunch of practices out at The Shed, and we would record all these jams. One of them was when the guy came to read the electric meter the same day, so that jam ended up being called 'The Day the Electric Man Came'! But we had great fun doing that band."

"I eventually came out, completely knackered," **Dick** says, of the slow recovery from his accident. "My muscles were aching from lying down for three weeks. They showed me the x-ray of my skull, with a big crack down the middle… a quarter of an inch either way, and I could've been dead. And then within five days, I got the phone call asking us to play with the Dead Kennedys, because apparently, of the list of bands they wanted to play with them in the UK, none of them could make the gig. We had a practice, where I didn't feel like singing much, and we did the gig, which went okay, although I was aching all over still.

"My girlfriend thought I'd changed, from having a cracked skull. And because I'd had an epileptic fit whilst in hospital, I wasn't allowed to drive any motorised vehicles for the next two years. Not that I had a car anyway. And I had to take these little white pills, which they'd started giving me in the hospital by telling me they were 'pep pills'… I was a bit annoyed that they hid the fact they were anti-epileptic-fit pills until just as I was about to leave the hospital. 'Oh, you need to take these pills for the next two years…!'

"After that, the only major effect was the adjustment of my smell – not the way I smelt, but the way I smelled with my nose… everything started to smell the same as everything else, and it was a really unpleasant smell. And that was a fucking nightmare – some nights I couldn't get to sleep, because every time I breathed in, this smell would just be there, and kept me awake. I went a bit mental with that. We were on tour, and I got a bit drunk – as you do – and I bit Trotsky through his leather jacket – as you do. Playfully, of course. Which is possibly not connected to the accident, but just something one does when out of one's head in Holland. It eventually sorted itself out, although I never got my sense of smell back completely.

"The other consequence of all this was I stopped riding my bike to work, and got the bus there. Until the bus times changed, and I started getting a lift with someone else who worked there. And then 'The Day the Country Died' came out, and we had a royalty cheque – and I quit work. We had like a thousand pounds each, because it had sold 10,000 copies in a month or whatever, which was an insane amount of money at the time… before that I'd never had more than a hundred quid, despite working."

"It did knock your spirits a bit though; you got a bit more serious after that," interjects **Bruce**. "For a while. Which you would do, wouldn't you? It might have been the end of the silly songs…"

"Oh no, no, no, not having that!" protests **Dick**. "You say things like, 'It makes you re-evaluate your life…' but it doesn't when you're twenty-one or whatever. I wasn't thinking in those terms at all. You think like that when you're fifty-something, because you have less life to live, and more people you know have started dying… but at that age, you just wonder what you missed while you were away. Not much apparently."

Bruce: "You said you were eighteen earlier, when you were talking about shaving…"

Dick: "I was twenty-one… but that's the effect of the accident, forty years on – I get my eighteens and twenty-ones mixed up! Anyway, as for songs written after the accident – 'Think for Yourself' was the first one… 'A combination of work and rest, keeps your head in a total mess…' then 'Joe Public' and 'The Price of Fame'… never sang that one. You know what? I *had* stopped writing silly songs at that point…"

Bruce: "Told you!" [laughs]

Dick: "But I might have stopped already by then anyway…?"

GRANT AND TROTSKY
BY KEV TYDEMAN

BISHOPS STORTFORD
TRIAD   DOWNSTAIRS

SUB
HUM A N S

A-HEADS

THE BURIAL

ANIMUS

EMERGENCY

THURSDAY 23rd DECEMBER 7·30
£1-50 ON THE DOOR
BE YOURSELF - COS THERES ALWAYS
SOMEONE WHO WANTS YOU TO BE
SOMEONE ELSE

RIDGEART '8

ZIEP'S PROMOTIONS UN-LTD. PRESENTS:

AT
STAC
DEANERY ANNEXE
BERNARD STREET
SOUTHAMPTON

OCT
12TH

SUB
HUM ANS

+ SUPPORT...

8.00
£1.25
£1.00 DOLE CARD
HOLDERS

The London gig with Dead Kennedys mentioned above was on November 26th and sparked a bit of controversy...

"Derek, who was the main man at Spiderleg, was fucking hardcore, and very set in his ways," reckons **Dick**. "We played that gig with the Dead Kennedys, at the Central Polytechnic in London – it was the Dead Kennedys, MDC, Serious Drinking and the Subhumans [on first, before Serious Drinking], and it was £3 to get in, which was double what we'd normally ask people to pay to get into a gig. Because we were associated with Spiderleg, people were hassling Derek, because we had done a gig that was £3 to get in – and he was thinking of dropping us off the label because of that! And he also called Dave out of MDC about it, who were doing all the dates with the Dead Kennedys, and they pulled off the rest of the tour because the prices were too high. Whoah!"

"I think that was the tour where they played the Bath Pavilion," says **Bruce**, "Where I went backstage and talked to Jello about getting us on. And then someone pulled out of the gig and that's how we got on. At very short notice."

The band's last gig of 1982 was two days before Christmas, in Bishops Stortford, but for some reason they only played six songs after going all that way, so not the most satisfying end to the year.

"Yeah, that was at the Triad in Bishops Stortford, which was Colin [from Flux]'s hometown," confirms **Dick**, "With Burial, A-Heads, Animus and Emergency. And we were headlining, so the gig must have over-ran for us to only do six songs? I hate it when that happens!"

Bruce: "Driving all the way to Bishops Stortford to play six songs... that's terrible, haha! But unfortunately it used to happen quite a lot."

What *was* significant about the gig at the Triad was that it was their fiftieth show. However, things were soon going to get much busier in 1983, as they spread their Wessex noise overseas.

SUBHUMANS LINE-UP PIC, MAY 1982
PHOTO COPYRIGHT © PAUL SLATTERY

The year 1983 was pivotal for the Subhumans, as it saw them not only release their debut album and undertake their first international touring, but also get themselves a new bassist, Phil, when Grant decided to leave, arriving at their definitive line-up – which has remained stable to this day.

They ushered in the New Year in style with a well-received headline set at the Stevenage Bowes Lyon House, with support coming courtesy of The Destructors and Virus, a gig that Graham 'Gizz' Butt, lead guitarist with The Destructors, remembers fondly.

"I remember when I *first* heard the Subhumans too," **Gizz** recalls. "The Destructors were playing a lot of seriously good shows all across Cambridgeshire and East Anglia, and had built up a pretty huge following, 'The Death Squad'. There was a character named Alley Rat who always stood out; facially he looked like Justin Sullivan of New Model Army, but his leopard spot hair and painted studded jacket made him a punk pin-up. And he was dating one of the Peterborough punk princesses, Sara Hudson. He invited me to his bedsit on Whitsed Street, a dank, dark, smoky pit, and over piping hot teas we rummaged through his record collection. There were some things I'd never seen before, all very curious, like The Epileptics, Rudimentary Peni… and the Subhumans. The 'Demolition War' EP was placed on the turntable, and what I heard was a fresh, raw sound that had a lot of personality. It was up-tempo, the sound was sharp and youthful, yet professional and tight. The guitars were tough and not over-fuzzy, and the high-pitched vocals had a twang. They immediately had *something*; you could hear Sex Pistols, Honey Bane, UK Subs, Stiff Little Fingers, The Ruts, and a touch of Crass. It was musically ahead of its time compared to some of the other punk bands that were fashionable in the early Eighties.

"And it was on January 2nd, 1983, that The Destructors played with the Subhumans at the Bowes Lyon House, Stevenage, a good vibe venue that attracted a loyal punk following. It was an exciting time as the Subhumans had shot to a high level of popularity, because they had a magic about them that had been sorely lacking from newer UK bands – which accounted for the growing interest in American bands at the time. The Destructors shared the dressing rooms with the Subhumans, and shortly after our set, Dick approached me with a black marker pen and asked me, 'Can you write "FISH" on the back of my white shirt?', to which I consented. I've seen pictures of him wearing that shirt since – that's my claim to fame right there! But yeah, the Subhumans always were, and still are, a vastly superior punk band. Good old boys!"

A week later, they were back in London, headlining at the Moonlight Club with Conflict and Naked in support. It was a huge night for them, as Richard Newson, still writing under the moniker of Winston Smith, was there to interview them for Sounds

Alternative Music Present A New Years Bash With

SUBHUMANS

+ DESTRUCTORS

+ BORN B.C. + VIRUS

SUNDAY 2 JANUARY '83
7 30 ~ 10.45

Admn: Members ~ £1.50
Seperate Beer Bar ~ Over 18's

Bowes Lyon House
St. Georges Way, Stevenage, Herts.
Telephone: Stevenage 53175

JANUARY 22, 1983 40p

PAT BENATAR in colour · JIM STEINMAN
HYPOTHETICAL PROPHETS · THE WAKE

sounds

ANIMAL KINGDOM
The Subhumans uncaged!

again – and this time they were going on the front cover (one of the first colour covers the popular music paper would run), to promote the release of their 'The Day the Country Died' album, that had been reviewed in the paper that very day.

"They'd only actually agreed to me writing a Sounds cover story if the front page had a live image taken at that gig at London's Moonlight Club, with the crowd visible in the pic," reveals **Richard**, "So they still had that 'no sell out' punk attitude going on. We did the interview in the Moonlight's dressing room, and despite their reservations, they were still the same friendly bunch I'd met the year before.

"It was unusual to have a live shot on the front page [taken by renowned rock photographer Tony Mottram], possibly even a first, and it was rare for the cover to be in full colour. I'm not sure if this had or hadn't happened before, but Sounds certainly stood out from the other music papers that week.

"Anyway, back in May '82, I'd been very happy with my first Subhumans interview, and thinking about it now, they must have liked it too, because they let me interview them again for that January '83 cover story, when 'The Day the Country Died' came out. The album was absolutely stunning, and I gave it a well-deserved rave review."

"We played with them less times than you might think," ponders **Dick**, on the subject of Conflict, the main support band that night. "And the amount of contact we had with some of those bands, like Conflict, Peni, Flux… well, not so much Flux, because they were involved with the record label and everything… but it might surprise some people. We'd be separated out by promoters to headline different gigs – 'This week we'll have Subhumans, next week The Exploited, the week after Conflict…' So you'd only bump into each other at larger multi-band gigs that only happened once or twice a year. And then of course it was always so busy at those gigs, with ten bands playing, and everyone running around trying to figure out what gear they were using, what to put in the set-list, meeting people, socialising, that it was rare you could sit down with, say, Colin Conflict and have a really good conversation. In fact, the first decent – longer than two minutes – conversation we had was in, like, 2011, way after we'd all been going in our youth, so to speak.

"And the first time I properly met Steve Ignorant was when we eventually played with Stratford Mercenaries in Bristol, and he said, 'About time really, ain't it?' But that's the way it falls. And then the other month, Michelle did an interview with both me and Steve down at Rockaway Park [a truly alternative new live music venue – and so much more – just south of Bristol, run by Mark from The Mob], just chatting away, not so much an interview as just a chance to sit down and talk about what we thought about hippies and punk rock in the Eighties and progress, or the lack of it. And that was us finally having a really good half-hour conversation about stuff… it's almost like you have to set these things up to make them happen.

"But I imagine the outside perception might have been that all those anarcho punk bands lived together, hung out together, drank together, shared their ideas… nah, it didn't happen like that. Although I know Crass and Conflict had quite a close relationship, but they were in the same area, I guess.

"I liked Naked," he continues, this time reflecting on the opening band that night at the Moonlight, who would play with the Subhumans ten times in total, and have Dick release their 'One Step Forward Towards Reality' EP on Bluurg (also in 1983). "They were a fantastic band, that I was more than happy to release on Bluurg. They had a nice way with music, and a strange singing style – Chris had a really original voice. That's my favourite speed of punk rock really – not too slow, not too thrashy…

"Them and The System were the two bands who just did the best demo tapes, better than anything they went on to record afterwards… everyone was talking about them when those demos were doing the rounds because they were the dog's bollocks. I remember when The System's actual album came out, it didn't sound as good as the demo versions, but that's the nature of music, isn't it? The first version you hear will rule over any other version you hear later on, even if it's a shit recording. I remember when we tried re-recording 'Parasites' in Lysander Studio in Melksham, where TW Records sent their bands, and it sounded professional and good and proper, but it didn't have the 'thing' that the first one had – because it wasn't the first one, and that's all there is to it."

Appearing on the front cover of Sounds, one of the most popular music papers of the time, was a big deal, and proof positive that the Subhumans were held in high regard as one of the UK's leading anarcho punk bands. Two weeks ahead of the interview running though, Winston Smith gave 'The Day the Country Died' a rave four-and-a-half star (out of a possible five) review, that ran in the January 8th issue and helped the album smash into the Indie Charts the following week, storming in at No. 3.

"We got that high in the Indie Charts with 'The Day the Country Died' because we sold the first 10,000 very quickly," reckons **Dick**. "It was about the speed they sold more than anything – if you sold 10,000 in a week, you might be in at No. 1, and then straight down to No. 50 in week two!

"Yes, it all happened quite quickly. It was a bit, 'Wow! What's going on?' It was constantly surprising that so many people had heard of us and turned up at gigs. Because, apart from Sounds, we weren't getting that many interviews – it was all word of mouth."

Ushered in by the disconcerting sound of static and what sounds like a bomb dropping on you, the album opens with the urgent 'All Gone Dead', a jaggedly menacing number built around an insistent descending bass line and an evocative post-apocalyptic lyric ('There are no banks left, they all went bust, and the Houses of Parliament are just a pile of dust…'). It careens into the irresistibly up-tempo 'Ashtray Dirt', an anti-smoking song penned by Julian for Stupid Humans that has since been dropped by Subhumans, seeing as two of them smoke. 'Killing' and 'Minority' keep the momentum rumbling along, with their jaunty memorable choruses, before 'Mickey Mouse Is Dead' kicks in with its unmistakable staccato intro that bursts into the album's first bona fide thrasher, and one of the band's most enduring tracks.

DICK BY TONY MOTTRAM

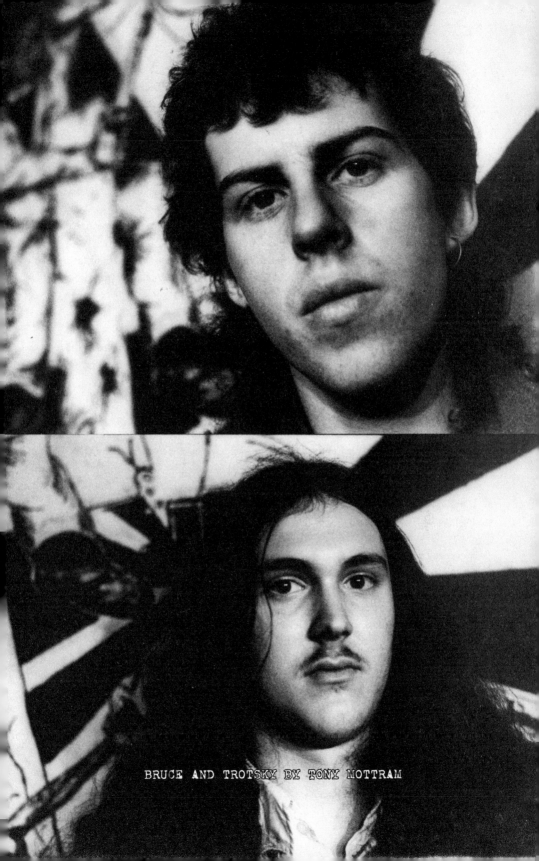

BRUCE AND TROTSKY BY TONY MOTTRAM

"Here's a missing verse from 'Mickey Mouse Is Dead'," reveals **Dick**. "'If you laugh too much, they think you're insane; you'll end up like Mickey Mouse, in a television grave; so after you have died, they'll find another one; the state control the TV, to make sure you're having fun; but the people have all died, along with Mickey Mouse; the humour isn't needed in the system's concrete house…' And it was probably the words 'system's concrete house', that don't flow at all, that made me think, 'Sod it!' Or we might have got to a point in the song where the others said, 'That's long enough, we don't need any more words…'"

'Nothing I Can Do' is another fast one, neatly counterpointed by Grant's hyperactive rambling bass runs, with Dick's lyrics examining nihilism and apathy from both a personal and political perspective ('There's a great big hole in my back door, and everyone expects a nuclear war…'). It's followed by arguably the album's two strongest tracks, that close out side one, 'Dying World' and 'Subvert City', both of them slower paced and atmospheric. 'Dying World' has an almost hypnotic cyclic riff, with Dick dropping a spectacularly powerful metaphor in the opening couplet ('There's a hole in the bottom of the earth, where the blood pours out at the end of the day') which sets the compellingly downbeat tone of the whole song. The poignant acoustic strains of the 'Subvert City' intro are then smashed to one side by the huge pugilistic verse riff, that bears more than a passing resemblance to 'Troops of Tomorrow' by The Vibrators.

"And here's a missing verse I never ended up singing for 'Subvert City': 'In a silent court room lined with rifles, female subverts screamed out loud; dying breath of the anarchist party, last defiance of the laughing crowd…' Who knew, eh?" laughs **Dick**, before adding:

"It doesn't seem to bother anyone that 'Subvert City' sounds a lot like 'Troops of Tomorrow' by The Vibrators. We were like, 'That sounds a bit like this… but it sounds great, so let's do it!' I think if you look hard enough, you'll eventually find something in any Subhumans song that sounds like something else from the history of music. Everything you listen to is an influence that will in some way or other seep through into what you do, and that's how it carries on. That's what ideas are for really."

"There's bits of everything that comes up in Subhumans stuff," admits **Bruce**. "Some music you hear, and you either include it in your stuff and don't realise you're doing it, or it's so good, you just have to steal it, you just have to! It's like, 'This is such a good riff, I just have to play it…' But then, when the band gets hold of it, it doesn't sound like it anymore.

"I worked out pretty early on that I like certain chord sequences… very simple ones, just going up and down a tone by a major chord… I never really analysed it, but I really liked doing it, and that's all over the Subhumans material. But also the minor stuff, like 'Subvert City', which is very obviously a minor scale and a minor interval. And yeah, I really liked the second Vibrators album, 'V2', and was influenced by it quite a bit… and probably stole a few riffs off it, haha! Dick was a bit older, and he liked the Vibrators' first album, 'Pure Mania', more."

Side two of 'The Day the Country Died' opens up with three of the band's punkiest songs, the furiously intense 'Big Brother', a reflection on the insidious nature of state oppression (that even references Dick's favourite drink of the time – lager and lime – in the cheeky backing vocals), the pleasantly melodic 'New Age', and the raging defiance of 'I Don't Wanna Die' ('The system kills – but it won't kill me!'). A tantalising excerpt from 'Song No. 35' then opens into the mesmerising bass line of 'No', one of the album's highlights, its undeniable power coming from Dick's passionate lyrical exhortation, that sees him laying himself bare for the listener: 'No, I don't believe in Jesus Christ, my mother died of cancer when I was five; no, I don't believe in religion, I was forced to go to church and wasn't told why…'

The mood isn't lightened much by the ensuing 'Zyklon B-Movie', which has some weighty subject matter at its heart, albeit given an imaginative sci-fi twist.

"It's one of those songs that I really don't want anyone to ask me what it's about, because I've never quite worked it out myself," laughs **Dick**. "I just remember being in a cinema, and imagining gas rising up from under the seats… and then you had this wordplay, between 'B-movie' and 'Zyklon-B', and where that took me, and Zyklon-B was obviously the gas used by the Nazis… 'If this is the first film, then what could come next?' It's like a warning against fascism, in a very obscure, lateral way, and it's also a bit of a horror movie in a song."

That unpredictable and irreverent approach to writing lyrics is one of the many things that differentiated the Subhumans from the other anarcho punk bands – after all, you wouldn't have Crass or Flux singing a song like 'Peroxide'…

"And you wouldn't have Toy Dolls singing 'Reason for Existence'," counters **Dick**. "We were somewhere in between, and had all these different angles. We did get labelled an 'anarcho' band, rather than labelling ourselves as one… but *we* just thought we were a *punk* band. It was partly due to us being on Spiderleg, which was Flux's label, because there was this family tree of Crass releasing Flux, and Flux starting Spiderleg and releasing Subhumans, Subhumans doing Bluurg and releasing Instigators, then Instigators doing Peaceville… there was a nice family tree going on there.

"I hate labels though, and we were just as much Toy Dolls as Crass, if people had to put a label on it. We were a bit of both, because there were some silly songs in there, and we're still playing them now. And people still love them. I wrote a lot of silly songs, but then I started writing more serious, more thought-out songs, and got a lot more pleasure singing those. It's just good fun to sing 'Peroxide' or 'Animal' or 'Germ' or 'Nothing I Can Do'… and there's a nice intensity about singing 'Reason for Existence' or 'Evolution' or 'Labels' or 'Apathy'… and so on and so on. If the music wasn't there, it would not be the same at all. Without the music, it would just be poetry, and wouldn't have anywhere near the same passion in it."

Thankfully a light-hearted song is up next in the album track-listing, the endearingly silly ode to intoxication, 'Til the Pigs Come Round', but the album closes out with two

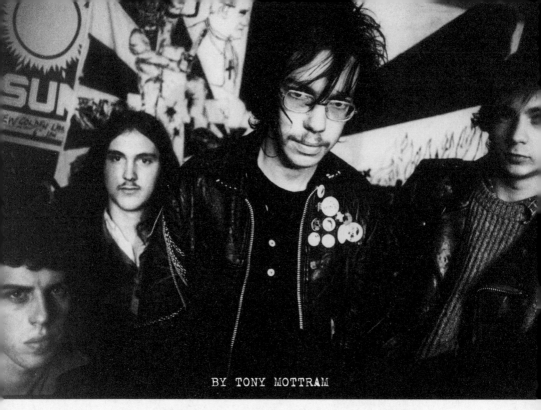

BY TONY MOTTRAM

'MICKEY MOUSE IS DEAD' - DICK'S ORIGINAL
LYRIC SHEET

Mickey Mouse is dead
Got kicked in the head
Cos people got too serious
They planned out what they said

They couldn't take the fantasy
They tried to accept reality
They analyzed the laughs
Cos pleasure comes in halves

The purity of comedy
They had to take it seriously
They changed the words around
Tried to make it look profound

And now the comic's in the pub
The comedian gets on the stage
Pisstaking people for a wage
People laugh then
The people think he's great on the TV
But the laughter turns to HATE!

Mickey Mouse is on TV
And the kids stare at the screen
But the pictures are all black n white
And the words don't mean a thing
Cos mummy's got no money
And daddy is in jail
He can't afford the license
And she can't afford the bail

But the people have all died
Along with Mickey Mouse
The humour isn't needed
In the systems concrete house

The fear of being sussed
for what they really are
the fear of being laughed at
When you go too far
They call it paranoia
You can't laugh it away
Until you come to realise
That everyone's the same

But people hide their problems
Under faces of contempt
They hide them til it kills them
And no one is exempt

If people laugh too much
They think your insane
You'll end up like Mickey Mouse
In a television grave

So after you have died
they'll find another one
critics the State control
the people think he's great, the TV
to make issue of having fun

So the kids out on the road
their minds have all gone cold
Cos Mickey Mouse is dead
They shot him thru the head
With ignorance + scorn
They believed in something new
They read the papers watched the films
And thought they knew the truth
But really deserves
No matter what you believe
there's always another idea
And it's based on fear

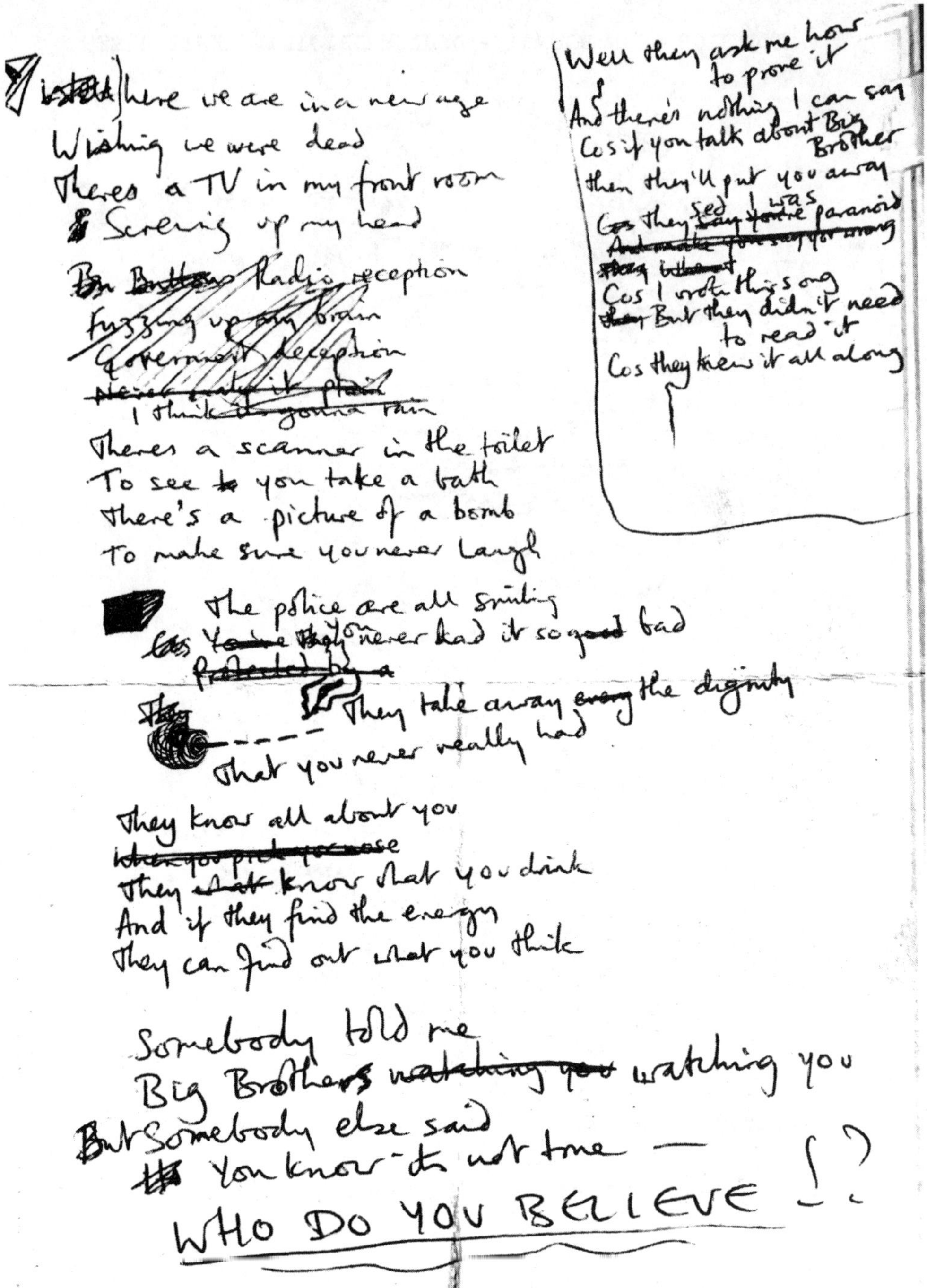

here we are in a new age
Wishing we were dead
Theres a TV in my front room
Screwing up my head

Radio reception
fuzzing up my brain
Government deception
I think its gonna rain

Theres a scanner in the toilet
To see you take a bath
There's a picture of a bomb
To make sure you never laugh

The police are all smiling
Cos you never had it so bad
They take away the dignity
That you never really had

They know all about you
They know that you drink
And if they find the energy
They can find out what you think

Well they ask me how
to prove it
And there's nothing I can say
Cos if you talk about Big
Brother
then they'll put you away
Cos they sed I was paranoid
Cos I wrote this song
But they didn't need
to read it
Cos they knew it all along

Somebody told me
Big Brothers watching you
But Somebody else said
You know its not true —
WHO DO YOU BELIEVE !?

'BIG BROTHER' - DICK'S ORIGINAL LYRIC SHEET

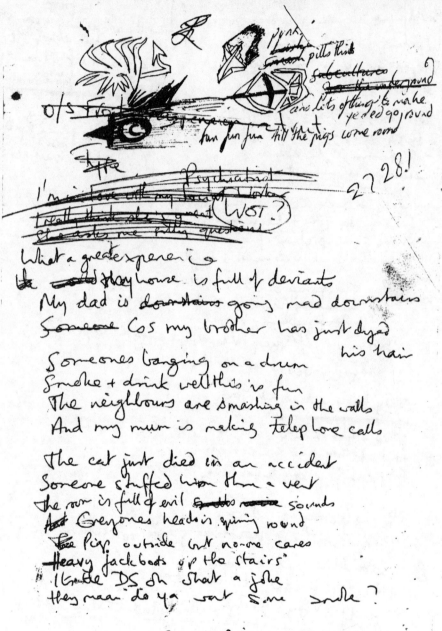

SUB-HUM-ANS
AHEADS
ORGANIZED CHAOS

BATH VIADUCT 14/1/83
8 til 12 — WITH BAR.
ONLY 50p on door.

GINA SHCK 83

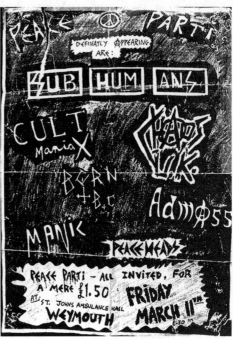

PEACE PARTI
DEFINATLY APPEARING ARE:

SUB HUM ANS

CULT ManiaX   CHAOS UK

BORN +B.c.

ADMASS

MANIC   PEACEHEADS

PEACE PARTI - ALL INVITED, FOR A MERE £1.50 AT: ST. JOHNS AMBULANCE HALL WEYMOUTH   FRIDAY MARCH 11th

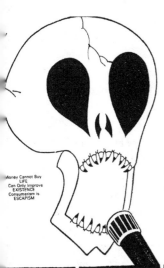

Money Cannot Buy
LIFE
Can Only improve
EXISTENCE
Consumerism is
ESCAPISM

External actions don't
betray internal thoughts
True feelings are
never shown
LIFE IS A SHAM!
Why can't we be honest?

AD-NAUSEUM
DISORDER
AMEBIX
ANTI-SECT

SUB HUM ANS

FRIDAY 4TH MARCH 7·00≫11·PM   £1·50

VIADUCT HOTEL MONKTON COMBE BATH

NEAR THE UNIVERSITY. TEL, LIMPLEY STOKE 3187

Ⓐ CHRIS 83 Ⓐ

powerful songs loaded with pathos, 'No More Gigs', a timeless rumination on the nature of loss, and the immensely powerful 'Black and White', that paints a bleak picture of a depressed UK in the early Eighties ('Broken through madness, hate and boredom; UK – a disunited kingdom!') that is sadly completely relevant to this day.

When asked about the picture of Trotsky with all the police behind him on the back of the album, **Dick** recalls: "That was a gig where the cops came along to break it up, but didn't. That was the gig with Flux, Conflict, The Mob and Rudimentary Peni [Camden, 7/6/82]. It was £2 to get in, or £1.50 if you donated a tin of food for the needy, and every band played for half an hour. Which was ace. The cops turned up, walked around and then left again. The picture was taken post-gig, judging by the look on Trotsky's face…

"And the picture in the middle that's sideways… that's Julie, Mel and Jane – that was Grant's girlfriend, Bruce's girlfriend and my girlfriend, who all came to the recording of the album."

On the album credits, it says 'original bass lines by Andy' for 'Zyklon B-Movie' and 'No More Gigs', which prompts **Dick** to comment: "I don't actually remember the process where Andy got hold of a bass and invented any tunes, but maybe he did that with Bruce?"

"Andy used to come and sit in my bedroom, I guess when he was catching up on band news," explains **Bruce**. "He often picked up a bass guitar, and just noodled. He thought of the 'Zyklon B-Movie' riff, which became the guitar introduction bit in the song. Somewhere there is a recording of Andy playing it, with me on guitar and Dick doing some poetry, sort of 'pre-Zyklon prose', about the subject. That would be gold dust – I've got to find it!

"I don't remember Andy writing 'No More Gigs' though… but he probably did. It's his noodling style. I do remember him writing the 'Pisshead' bass line as well – I've got a recording of both of us doing that too. Andy was also convinced that the middle bass bit to 'Sonic Reducer' by the Dead Boys was recorded while the drummer played on the bass with sticks – there's a musical urban myth for you!"

"They're all great in their own way," ponders **Grant**, when asked to name his favourite Subhumans release. "I really like 'The Day the Country Died' though, which is admittedly a bit patchy in places, but it was the first one we did, and on the whole that was a massive boost for us. I think the best songs are probably the less obviously punk songs, like 'Subvert City' and 'Black and White', which were a bit different to what everyone else was doing at that time. We weren't trying to jump on anyone else's bandwagon, we were just doing our own thing. We were lucky in that Dick had very clever, imaginative lyrics, and Bruce had tunes tumbling around in his head – and tumbling out through his fingers – all the time."

"Grant and I worked out how we wanted 'The Day the Country Died' to run before we even went in the studio," reveals **Bruce**. "We were quite organised, in a musical way; we were thinking how things would flow into each other."

166

Grant: "And how things flow together on an album is so important. Albums then – much more so than now – were something you'd sit down with… you'd take them out the cover, get all excited about them, and play them from start to finish… and there'd be a theme and a feel to them. Listening to music felt like it had more value back then than it does now, and at that age, music is such an important part of your life – it's the key to the little subculture you're discovering. You were discovering how to be a teenager, and music was a massive part of that. I don't know how it is for kids these days, because music isn't quite so big a part of it, and it's all so much more corporate… when was the last youth-led musical movement?"

"I suppose it was 'another Subhumans record', but it was also *the LP*," **Dick** explains how big a deal it felt for them at the time, "The LP that we had been dreaming about doing and everything. We'd been joking about it for years, how it would be a concept album, triple-gatefold sleeve and everything, haha! And we insisted on the gatefold cover with John Loder, because we wanted it to be this big *thing* that opened out in front of your face when you listened to the music."

"You can file 'The Day the Country Died' next to 'Feeding of the 5000' by Crass," **Pete The Roadie** exclaims, before adding with a laugh, "And Kicker [Pete's current band]'s 'Not You'! If you are in a shit mood, or for some unknown reason fed up with punk rock, just put 'The Day the Country Died' on, and I guarantee you'll be pogoing around and singing along by the end of it. And the lyrics are still just as relevant, especially after this virus and lockdown stuff."

And let's not forget the importance of the Nick Lant cover art, capturing the zeitgeist of the time with its lurid depiction of a protesting punk rocker shot through the head by a leering cop with a smoking rifle, against a backdrop of dubious priests, doomed soldiers, burning buildings and ballistic missiles. It was an evocative summary of many of the issues that were keeping punk lyricists awake at night during the Eighties (and sadly every decade since), and it's adorned countless thousands of T-shirts, jackets and patches since it appeared in all its monochrome glory in '83.

"The art for 'The Day the Country Died' didn't take that long either," recalls **Nick**. "It's so long ago now, I really can't recall how long it took me, but remember having no space and working covertly on the family dining table. I drew it to size, so once finished I put it in a vinyl sleeve and blue-tacked it to the dining room wall to self-critique, then forgetting, or perhaps leaving it purposely for my dad to see at mealtime. The cover was lucky to survive his reaction, but his inevitable criticism was enough to know I had things about right.

"And yes, it's an iconic one. It was a great feeling the first time I saw it reproduced, painted on the back of someone's leather jacket, as that was how I'd started, copying other people's art and now here was mine being copied. I never had any thought of the work being iconic though; it was more about the present and that was satisfying enough, both at the time and in reflection.

DICK AND BRUCE BY MEL BELL

"I remember someone at school, a punk and reggae DJ and John Peel devotee who we all looked up to, telling me that Peely had played a track the previous night and mentioned the cover. I learnt how it felt to be on cloud nine that day.

"I got free remit from the band. I felt thoroughly privileged to be sent the lyrics before any of my mates even knew a new release was imminent, and best of all, Dick sent me a tape of all the tracks, I think to assist me with the cover. I don't remember being told to keep it to myself, but I did, and that's a treasured memory."

Winston Smith's second interview with Subhumans ran in Sounds on January 22nd, 1983, two weeks after his album review, and one week after 'The Day the Country Died' entered the Indie Charts. It carried the headline 'Mickey Mouse Is Dead', and looked superb, thanks to Tony Mottram's brilliant photos of the band. Another Tony Mottram live shot of Dick and Bruce, looking suitably feral, graced the front cover of the same issue, with the strapline 'Animal Kingdom – The Subhumans Uncaged!' It was eye-catching stuff, and the interview saw the band wrestling with the dichotomy of punk rock and popular success, and even talking about the writing of their second album, 'From the Cradle to the Grave', almost a year before they recorded it. Here's a transcript of the interview:

In a smoke-filled room… sit the Subhumans – arguably one of the very best (punk?) rock groups in the country. Their new album, 'The Day the Country Died', stands pretty much alone in its field as a work of, if not brilliance, then a thrilling new musical outlook, and on occasions, a quite rarely found power.

The LP is the Subhumans' fourth record – including three EPs – and marks the end of a twelve-month period in which they've achieved more than most bands manage in an entire lifespan.

Most heartening is their apparent unawareness of their own potential. This could very well be for the better; or perhaps a lot of people are simply getting worked up about nothing…

Do you still get a thrill, do you still get a buzz, when you have a new record coming out?
Dick: "The thrill is still there, but it's not so much the thrill of having it come out anymore as it is the thrill of the reactions people give you from when they've bought it, that always stays there – the thrill of having people appreciating what you're doing; I don't think that will ever disappear, because that's really what you're doing it for, in one way."

Was there a conscious attempt to create a kind of Rock 'concept' feel to the album?
Dick: "No not at all, that is largely your imagination, which isn't an insult or anything, because you've made it into something it wasn't intended to be, but that doesn't mean to say it's not, perhaps it is, I dunno. I don't even know what a Rock fucking concept is!"

Aren't you glad to be alive
Got your brain taken out ~~then~~ you see s
Learned to respect your mum + dad
~~And~~ in itself it ain't so bad

~~Dick~~ Silence is no reaction ← ①
~~Silence~~ is just ~~matters~~ ~~reaction~~
~~Riot~~ ~~at least its~~ (at least it improves /your /mind)

Violence — that one word caption ← ②
~~Abolition~~ ~~the one~~
~~One word~~ say
Can you — ~~change~~ it ~~with~~ just /one /word ← ③
~~Attitudes~~ ~~From apathy~~
~~# * P~~ ~~Attitudes~~ ~~from~~
Unspoken — ~~statistics~~ that ~~go~~ /unheard ← ④
the sins

~~this system~~ black + white /   1 government
~~policeman~~   2 bullshit
system   3 black + white
                    4 fight

look thru — this broken window   ①
~~faces they act so~~   go
                                    one
From normality — into the   ghetto
Reasons — are always ~~shoved~~ / i /side
pushed
~~England~~ — the day the country died
died
lied

'BLACK AND WHITE' - DICK'S ORIGINAL LYRIC SHEET

Broken – thro hate + boredom
~~madness~~
UK – ~~a new dig this no disgust~~ } last 2
a disunited kingdom } 2nd verse

Enquiries – ~~if~~ ~~I~~ ~~edit~~ but no solutions
~~Pitbull~~ ~~propaganda~~ faceless – empty illusions ?
~~Flag~~

1 hour
45 fucking
minutes
2/1/81

Black
+
White

'BLACK AND WHITE' PART 2 – DICK'S ORIGINAL LYRIC SHEET

'DYING WORLD' – DICK'S ORIGINAL LYRIC SHEET

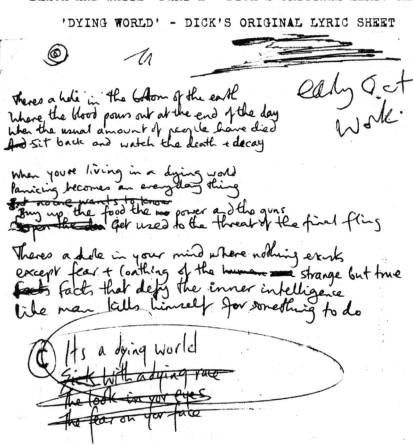

Eddy got
Work.

Theres a hole in the ~~bottom~~ of the earth
Where the blood pours out at the end of the day
When the usual amount of people have died
~~And~~ Sit back and watch the death + decay

When you're living in a dying world
Panicing becomes an everyday thing
~~But no one wants to know~~
Buy up the food the ~~no~~ power and the guns
~~open the do~~ Get used to the threat of the final fling

Theres a hole in your mind where nothing exists
except fear + loathing of the ~~human race~~ strange but true
~~facts~~ facts that defy the inner intelligence
like man kills himself for something to do

Ⓒ Its a dying world
~~Sick with a dying race~~
~~The look in your eyes~~
~~The fear on your face~~

How did you feel about the criticism in the album review?
Bruce: "I think there are too many 'fucks' on it."

I felt they could quite easily be replaced by words which would convey what you're saying with far more effectiveness. . .
Dick: "Yeah, possibly but I mean things like that reflect the temperament of your mind when you're actually writing the song, and not when you're performing it or doing it on an LP, by that time the lyrics may have lost their original anger."

And as for your dwelling repeatedly on 'The System'?
Dick: "Well. I see what you mean, but saying 'The System' is like, instead of listing a load of things which seem to be a part of the system, instead of saying 'Religion, school, work, parents,' it's quite easy to lump it under the name of 'the system', which may be wrong, but when you start taking that word apart you've got all the different aspects of it, and it usually ends up being a different song for each aspect. But yeah, if you keep going on and on about it, then again, it loses its meaning; it becomes something to shout against, but nobody really knows what it is."

And similarly on a post-holocaust society...?
Dick: "Well, that's important... I feel that's important. I mean something like war and... nuclear this that and the other, is a very probable threat to our existence in the next 25 years or whatever you want, you know?"

Can your singing about it stop it though?
Trotsky: "As for actually doing anything... as for actually avoiding it, I can't see that it's going to do any good at all, but the least you can do is make people realise the threat is there."
Dick: "Yeah, that's just it. The whole idea is to make people think, y'see? I mean four people can't change the whole bleedin' world, and that's bloody obvious. Some people think they can, and we know we can't, because it's so... it's logical, isn't it? But if you can get a crowd of 200 people and make just ten change their minds about something you're singing about, then I think you've done a good job, and that's what we're trying to do."

They're going to see bands singing about the same things as you every night.
Bruce: "It depends how the bands approach it, I mean if you go right over the top and every song's about it, then it can get boring, and you just forget what it's all about anyway."
Dick: "When I write a song about war, I don't think, 'Right, we'll put this on a single and it'll sell a lot because it's against war,' y'know? Because you're becoming more and more aware of the fact that there are a lot of bands singing about the same thing, therefore

you've got to be somehow better for them to buy your single instead of everybody else's, which is where the music comes in.

"From my point of view, being the singer, you want to sell records so you can get any messages in the songs across to other people. I mean apart from that there is the actual personal satisfaction that you're actually doing something, instead of just pissing around watching television, being on the dole and doing nothing all day. You're actually in a band, you're creating something, you're proving that you can do something, you know? People are so ready to put down everybody between the ages of 15 to 20-odd, because they reckon they're all violent juvenile delinquents, and we're not."

What exactly is the difference between you and 'juvenile delinquents'?
Dick: *"Intelligence. It's the intelligence to know that smashing a window isn't going to change anything, but trying to make people think might. I'm not saying it will, but then I'm not saying it won't.*

"It's better to be positive and useless than negative and useless. If we can make some people think and change their minds about something, no matter what it is, then we've done some good."

Was I right in assuming 'No More Gigs' is a love song?
Dick: *"'No More Gigs' is about being in a state... just about being in a state where you're not getting any gigs, and people trying to do something but not having the means to do it, very basically. It's a very depressive song actually, I probably wrote it when I was pissed off; I can't remember."*

Bruce: *"Yeah, but it's great because it's emotional; I think the only good band is a band that strikes an image, either a bad image or a good image; it's the in-between bands that aren't really worth listening to, lyrically or musically. If you listen to something that really hits the mind, either because the music's so tight that it amazes you, or..."*

Dick: *"You see, if you can write a song and have music with it that does get to people... it's like 'Religious Wars', I don't know anybody who doesn't like it. There's something about it, I don't know what it is. Half of it's just the notes you're singing..."*

'Mickey Mouse Is Dead' I think, is about comedy being taken too seriously...
Dick: *"Yeah, Mickey Mouse being representative of the simplest form of humour, i.e. someone does something and you laugh at it because it is a funny act, and now it's all sarcasm and criticism and inflection, all this sort of stuff; and people are totally paranoid about what they think, in case what they're thinking is the wrong thing to think. They don't laugh at things that aren't being laughed at by people who they think are superior to them. People just base their lives around paranoia and illusion these days."*

So it's not simply about comedy, but life in general?

DICK, 1983 BY PHIL

GRANT, PETE'S FLAT
WARMINSTER, 1983 BY PHIL

JOCK, PETE AND DICK, EN ROUTE TO AN A-HEADS
GIG IN CLEATOR MOOR BY PHIL

SUBHUMANS

AWOL
OUTRAGE
WALKING DEAD
BLACK EASTER

AT

AVALON HALL
ANDOVER

26TH MARCH (SAT.)

£1 ADMISSION

DOORS OPEN 7:30 P.M

"STARRING" Ha Ha Ha Ha EXISTED

SUBHUMANS
DISORDAAARGH
CHAOS U.K.
AMEBIX NAPALM DEATH
ANTISECT

ALL AGES ADMITTED £1.50 PAY ON DOOR
WHY PAY MORE?

SAT. 9 APRIL 1983

AT THE UNION CLUB
TRENT BRIDGE
NOTTINGHAM

NO BAR - BRING YER OWN

BRING OWN BOOZE! ALL AGES SOFT DRINK BAR ONLY £1.50

SUB HUM ANS

DISORDER

AMEBIX

ANTISECT

NAPALM DEATH

SUBHUMANS PROMOTIONS AT THE

UNION CLUB
TRENT BRIDGE
NOTTINGHAM

INFO (0602) 602.915 6.P.M TILL 10.15 PM

SAT. 9th APRIL 1983

SUB HUM ANS

XTRACT
TWO FINGERED APPROACH
CORPSE

at the FALLOUT SHELTER

MELTHAM · YOUTH · CLUB
meltham mills road, meltham,
Nr HUDDERSFIELD. (OPPOSITE DAVID BROWNS)

Saturday 14th MAY

- Buses -

320/321 From HUDDERSFIELD John William Street
(opposite St.Georges Sq.) or Chapel Hill
(Top or Bottom) to MELTHAM MILLS (opposite David Browns)
366/367 From HUDDERSFIELD High Street
(opposite, Bus Station) or Manchester Road
(opposite Acres) to MELTHAM
BUS STATION (Five minute walk)

ALL BUSES 30p AFTER 6.00p

NO AGE LIMIT

£1- on the door

7.30' Till 11PM

BANDS ON WELL BEFORE LAST BUSES SO DON'T WORRY ABOUT THE TIME.

Dick: "That's the meaning I've put on it since I wrote the song, which is quite often what I do. I often find that I've written a song and it's got a damn sight more meaning to it than I thought at first, which is strange, I suppose."

So do you see yourselves as breaking down barriers in any way?
Dick: "Well you obviously do, because you keep saying so..."
  Grant: "What's the barrier?"

The barrier that says a punk band mustn't write about comedy and love (for a start)...
Grant: "We sing about what we want, and if that's breaking down a barrier, then we're breaking down a barrier, but we didn't look at it like that."
  Dick: "I've always thought – until the beginning of that LP review, that said 'to label the Subhumans a 'punk' band would be a burden on them' and all that, it's like almost putting us out of the punk thing, and that is weird, because I've always thought of myself as being a punk and being in a punk band, and, er, I still think that. You see, it would be better in a way, if we sounded like all the other bands and still sounded like we do now. Do you know what I mean?"

You wouldn't like that, would you, if there was nothing original going for you?
Dick: "I can see what you mean, but when we started, we never thought, 'Wow, this sounds really different to everybody else!' It was only when we started getting letters through saying, 'You're fucking brilliant!' and this sort of thing, that we started thinking 'Fucking hell!' You know?"
  Bruce: "We're all getting better on our instruments, we're bound to, but the message is still there. We all still think the same, whether we get brilliant on our instruments and start producing... well, you know."
  Dick: "I don't know if you do think the same; you may think the same basically, but you just get more paranoid, this is what I do anyway. The more people that take an interest, and the more people that phone-up and write letters... and then you start getting criticisms and things coming out – 'Why did you do this? Why did you do that?' Questions that no-one would ask you, except for someone who doesn't know you; and then you start getting really paranoid, because there's so many elitist rules that you can't break, or else you're doomed, you know?"

But you have broken a lot of those rules, that's my point.
Bruce: "That might be the barrier."

Exactly.
Dick: "I suppose it is..."
For what reason was the one word 'THINK' written all over the inside of the album cover?
Dick: "Well, that's what most of the lyrics were intended to make people do – Think.

Think for themselves, think about what the songs are saying... I say some of the songs, I mean if you take something like 'Til the Pigs Come Round', you could think about that all night and you wouldn't get anything out of it." (laughs heartily...) "No, but if they could think about things like 'Black and White' or 'No'..."

Thing is, I've thought an awful lot about some of the songs and got completely the wrong idea, haven't I?
Bruce: "Well, it still makes people think, whatever it is they're thinking about..."
  Trotsky: "This is it, y'know? I mean everybody's hair is growing all the time..."
  (Bruce doubles up with laughter...)
  Dick: "I suppose quite a few lyrics are obscure, but they're just whatever comes into my head, y'know? I mean you haven't seen nothing yet; I've got some songs that are so obscure even I don't know what they're about."
  Bruce: "We've written this big long track, which is about twenty minutes long. It rounds everything up, 'From the Cradle to the Grave'; it's still nowhere near ready."
  Dick: "It's about 110 lines long, seven pages or something, and it just goes through everything, from A to B and back again..."

Very Rock Grandeur.
Dick: "Well yeah, if you want to put it like that, maybe it's another barrier being broken down, but we don't see it like that. We see it as a fucking challenge... I'd like Tommy Vance to play some of our stuff and see what the reaction would be like, because the state of people's minds concerning punk bands is..."

Which is why I said it's a burden nowadays – the tag.
Dick: "It is a tag, but it's wrong, or in our case it's wrong. It's like saying all mod, or all heavy metal, or all anything is crap. It's just bullshit, you can't say that... and that is created by the fucking music papers, and it works because people are so used to building barriers between themselves that they enjoy doing it. And that is where things start to fall apart, where people won't talk to each other because they look different."

Can you explain your concern about appearing on the front of Sounds?
Dick: "It's just what the front cover of... well, any music paper represents to the average person. Unfortunately, when they see someone on there they presume, wrongly, that they're all rock stars; that they've all got loads of money and so on. It's just the image it presents, which is generally only there because it's a front page. I don't think it's going to do us that much good; I mean it is the actual words we say in the interview that matter more, much more than a photo on the front cover. We don't want to be thought of as superior to anyone else, because we're not. We don't want to be put one step above the people we're trying to bloody talk to, because that defeats the object, doesn't it?"

177

"That *was* weird really, it seemed to happen within a couple of weeks," smiles **Jock**. "You had the Sounds interview and a couple of other bits 'n' pieces in a really short period of time… I can remember Mel saying to her mum, 'Oh, Bruce is on the front cover of the paper!' And she was like, 'Why? Has he killed somebody?' It was amazing actually, because we all bought Sounds, the NME and Melody Maker anyway, but all of a sudden, your mates were on the front of it!"

Bruce: "It was lovely to see us on the front cover. I was working when that came out, and someone I worked with came running in, 'Look, Bruce, look! You're on the front cover!' They were very excited by that."

"When 'The Day the Country Died' was released in early 1983, and the Subhumans were on the front cover of Sounds, it was no longer a word of mouth thing," offers **Rob**. "A number of things set them apart from the anarcho bands at the time and it probably explains their longevity. They wrote songs with hooks. They are great musicians, and Bruce is an excellent rock guitarist. There is humour in Dick's lyrics and you can find stuff to relate to. I was listening to 'No More Gigs' recently [during the 2020 coronavirus lockdown] and thinking, 'Shit, this is happening now, there are no more gigs!' 'Mickey Mouse' could have been written yesterday too. And I really want to go to that party in 'Til the Pigs Come Round'! They have always been a West Country band, and they have stayed true to what they are, just a great punk band."

"The first big gig of theirs I remember was the 100 Club," adds **Bill**. "I don't think we played, but I went up and watched, and can remember thinking, 'Wow, these guys are getting really big!' It was that village mentality, and all of a sudden, I realised that these guys, these mates who I'd grown up with, were a fucking big band. They were playing London, which was a big deal anyway, but they packed out the 100 Club, and it was a realisation, and an amazing night. Everyone went mad to 'Religious Wars'…

"One minute they were playing The Crown down the road from me, the next they were on the front cover of Sounds. It was brilliant – and inspirational… like, 'I was sat with 'em drinking last night – they're on the front of Sounds today! And they're no different to what I am?' And the beauty of it is, it never changed them. I've been playing in bands with Dick for nearly forty years, and he's just the same, never lost that attitude."

"I was still working at Devizes Motor Company," says **Dick**, explaining the seismic impact the LP release had on his life at the time, "And John Loder rang up there one day – the only time he ever rang up there – and said, 'Dick, you're a star! This is amazing! It all joins together fantastically!' He was well happy with it. It turned out really well. It came out in January '83, and by February '83, I'd left work, because John had sent us a royalty cheque for £1000 each. I'd rarely owned over £100 in total – when I started working, I was on £25 a week, which went up to £33 by the time I left… it was a pittance, and most of that was spent on Special Brew and bus tickets. So I told my dad I was leaving, and he said, 'I thought you might…!' And I told them in work I was leaving, and they said,

'Yeah, we thought you might… you haven't really been with us since the start!' Which was bollocks, because I'd done all the shit work, all the thinking, always covering for the boss's brother, covering his ass for all his mistakes, making endless phone calls rectifying wrong parts he'd ordered. The best of it was, I didn't even own a car myself; I couldn't drive, I'm not mechanical, so I was just relying on my wits, ordering spare car parts. I hated it. And I was cycling to work and back every day, until I got run off my bike – that was fourteen miles a day, five or six days a week, in all weather… I was keeping fit at least?"

The same weekend the album stormed the Indie Charts, Subhumans played the Manchester Gallery (on January 16th, 1983) with The System, and were paid a visit by a celebrity snooker player of the time – although not to partake of their music…

"There was a very famous Irish snooker player of the time roaming around one of the gigs in Manchester trying to find some drugs," laughs **Jock**. "He was convinced we'd have some because we were a punk rock band!"

"Yes, that's absolutely true," smiles **Dick**. "We were playing The Gallery in Manchester, and a few of us were sat upstairs in a darkened space, doing an interview with someone for a fanzine, and a chap comes in, and said, 'Anyone got any speed?' 'Er, no, sorry mate…' and off he went, and I looked at Bruce, and said, 'Doesn't he play snooker?' Then he came back through a few minutes later, and it *was* him… and I guess that's why he was called 'Hurricane', haha!"

"It wasn't serious all the time," continues **Bruce**, on the sly thread of humour that ran through the band and everything they did. "There *was* a lot of humour, even though we were usually bracketed in with the serious bands."

Dick: "We were always joking, there was a lot of wordplay… just silly things. There was a run of factory and company jokes – stuff like, I used to run a gate factory, but I'm thinking of opening up into another field… I used to run a phone company, but we had to bring in the receivers… there were loads of them."

Bruce: "I don't think it's unusual with people of our age. You put four or five people in a van and there's going to be humour. We had a lot of cushion fights in the back of the van as well. We had a lot of nervous energy."

Dick: "I remember Grant bought a tomato in a brown paper bag. He ate the tomato whole… and then he ate the bag, haha! It was just silly things to do… it wasn't like we were sat there reading newspapers! We'd sit and list band names – and foods – beginning with certain letters of the alphabet… turns out the easiest letter is C. There's hundreds of them. We can run through them now, for the next hour, if you like? Cauliflower…"

Bruce: "Whenever we went round a corner, we'd get ash and cigarette butts on our heads, because everyone used that top bit of the van – the guttering bit – to put their bloody fags out. We were all smoking, so the van was full of smoke."

Dick: "We'd make up sentences one word at a time, going round everyone."

Bruce: "It doesn't happen these days though. We still have a sense of humour, but we're more content to just be quiet. None of that messing around anymore!"

ORIGINAL INSTIGATORS LINE-UP, BEING
INTERVIEWED FOR THIS BOOK, APRIL 2021

TROTSKY, 1983, AT SOUTHERN

HERE WE ARE IN
A NEW AGE
WE WERE DE
MY FRONT RO
UP
RE IN THE TOP
TO TAKE A BATH
THE A OF HIROSHIMA
TO NEVER LAUGH
AN TOLD ME
E YELSE D
AND SO TCHING YOU
RIGH TS NOT TRUE
WHE YOU BELIEVE
WHEN ICE HAVE
IM GONE CRAZY
N YOU JOKER

SUB
HUM ANS

UNUSED BADGE DESIGN

GRANT, DUTCH TOUR - COURTESY OF JOCK McCURDY

DUTCH TOUR - COURTESY OF
BRUCE TREASURE

DOORNROOSJE
GROENEWOUDSEWEG 322
31 mei avonds!
èntree FL.7
PROGRAMMA ?
SUBHUMANS
AHEADS
HOLLANDS GLORIE
KROESE REBOP néé
DOORNROOSJE
DOORNROOSJE
BEKYK 'T MAAR

Jock: "One of those stupid things you'd do in the back of the van – like see how many times Grant would piss! – was see how many times Trotsky could wrap his own hair around his nose… and it was 36."

"They all got on really well," confirms **Pete**. "The humour in the van was non-stop, *lots* of Python, Young Ones, Mr Jolly and much tour madness. The Membury service station on the M3 became a place of homage, because it had The Pole of the Great Lord Snern (it was a radio mast!), and you won any game in the van if you saw a bishop driving an orange Beetle (you never did!). Everyone seemed to get on with it, and the gigs were fantastic, playing with such bands as the A-Heads, Organized Chaos, Pagans, The Mob, Conflict, Flux of Pink Indians, Faction, Amebix and Smart Pils.

"You know, I never really saw the band argue, not even on long journeys home along the M3 and M4 in cold, uncomfortable vans. If you did complain, you usually got a resounding chorus of, 'Do you need some sympathy? I wish I was you! Do you need a pillow and a blanket and a tour story?' You just got on with it."

Dick: "We were all big Monty Python fans, and could quote entire scenes, especially Trotsky… it fitted with our broad sense of humour – which was Pythonesque! Imagine that – having a sense of humour that was so original, you get your own adjective, 'Pythonesque'… fantastic!"

Bruce: "We had a running joke about having a beer garden on the roof of the van. We wanted that to happen so much, we were always imagining what it would be like, to just go up a ladder and have drinks on the top of the van! And we had a silly van that we bought… Eddie Van Human! It was a tall-top Transit, and *almost* looked like it had a beer garden in its roof – it had this see-through Perspex roof, so you had borrowed light in the back. But Grant bought our *first* van. It was orange… and didn't last very long."

Dick: "Is that the one that Tony tipped over? We'd played up north somewhere, and got home about 6 am, and he was driving back from Trotsky's place, having just dropped me and Trotsky off, along this dark country road. Tony was knackered, having been driving all night, and he went up the verge, and tipped the van over on its side. He rang us up having just left us and said he'd tipped the van over."

January 29th saw the band back in Southern Studios, recording four tracks for their 'Evolution' EP, which would be released later that year – on Bluurg, not Spiderleg, but more on that later.

"I personally think 'Evolution' was the best-sounding record we did," reckons **Dick**. "Hearing the songs blasting out of the enormous speakers at Southern at very high volume was just mind-blowing. That arrangement was not as original as you might think either, and one person writing for a French fanzine sussed it out almost immediately, haha! No one else has though, so I'll leave it at that… in case there are repercussions, and a particular band might want some sort of royalty payment! But you know what it's like when you hear something on a record and think, 'Oh my god, what if that was sped up?'

And Bruce being Bruce, as soon as he heard it, he figured out what the notes were and – boom! The thing is, there's only a certain amount of notes, and they're bound to start sounding like other bands' tunes after so many years of tunes being written.

"And when it comes to reggae, bass lines are shared amongst everybody. No one ever says they sound like anyone else's tune, even though they do, and some of those bass lines have been used countless times over the years – because they are good bass lines! They're not 'nicking' it, they're sharing it. I love that about reggae, how no one is all precious about the bass lines, even though they pop up all over the place. In all other cultures, you'd have to be so aware of 'ripping off' anyone else, otherwise they'd take you to court – what's all that about?"

"I went into Southern Studios with Subhumans when they did the 'Evolution' EP," adds **Pete The Roadie**, "And I did bad backing vocals on 'Not Me'. Some members of Crass were outside the studio working as well. The studio was great, but a bit boring after a while – as studios are! I think I did go back again for another one of their recordings… but didn't stay long."

In early February, they had a weekend in London, playing first at the George Robey with Organized Chaos and Lost Cherrees, and then the next night at the prestigious 100 Club in Oxford Street with the A-Heads and Organized Chaos in support. They would go on to play the 100 Club a further eight times over the next few years, always headlining.

"The George Robey gig was one set up by us," recollects **Nut**, the original drummer of Lost Cherrees, "And it would have come about from just a simple phone call: 'Can you play on this date?' 'Yes, we can…' All done and dusted! I had Dick's phone number from interviewing him previously for my fanzine, Hit Ranking. It may or may not have been that gig, though I know it happened most times we played with the Subhumans, but I think they turned up late as their van had broken down on the way to London. Despite that, they played a blinder. We'd played the Robey quite a few times and we'd had some varied turnouts, but it was packed on that night. Back then, some punk bands could sound great on record and a bit ropey live – and vice versa – but the Subhumans were a cut above in musicianship, and certainly proved it that night.

"Once we'd done some gigs with them, we got to know them, especially Dick, and he expressed his interest in releasing something from the Cherrees. I think at that point, we would have released our first EP, 'No Fighting No War No Trouble No More', on Riot/ Clone Records, and I don't think Bluurg had released anything on vinyl at that point, only cassette tape?

"If my memory serves me correctly, Hit Ranking put together a compilation tape called 'Pah!' and I followed it up with 'Hmmm', which had some live tracks from Subhumans on it. In those days I taped every gig I went to or played at; there was a tremendous amount of trust in the punk community then, and you could just leave a cassette recorder

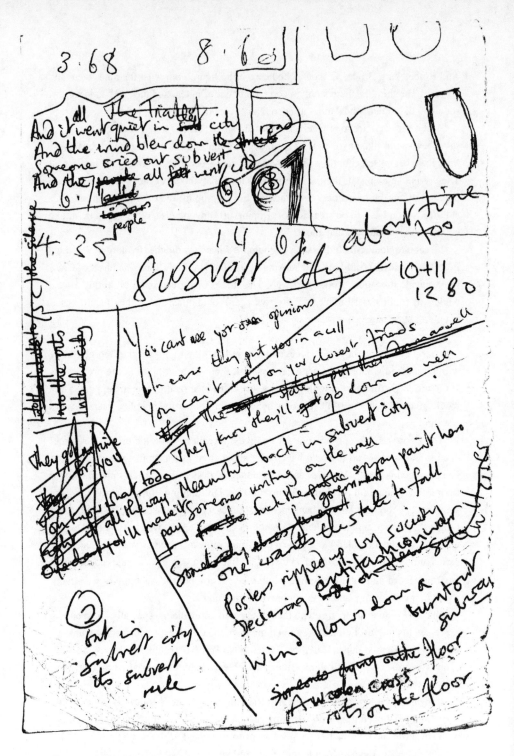

'SUBVERT CITY' - DICK'S ORIGINAL LYRIC SHEET

Inside a courtroom lined with rifles
~~Trial a party like jury instant~~
Female subverts ~~stand~~ screamed out loud
~~Defence~~ Dying breath of ~~the~~ anarchist party
~~one last~~ last defiance of the laughing crowd

~~At~~ originally
Ritual slaughter of ~~living standards~~
~~the~~ religious dogma enacted
~~Martyrs suicide~~ ~~to~~ living standards
were dying morals
a state ~~controlled~~ suicide
mass

The dying breed of ~~poor~~ subversity
Crept into the underground
The state police just left them there
Blockade holes and gassed them down

But 10 years later they emerged
~~As Mutated~~ As Mutated minds
so full of hate
Tried again to change the system
But ~~this time round~~
It ~~won't the same~~
It was too late
there was no system left to change
~~too~~ the people ran the entire land
The subverts became politicians
~~took had the u got~~ the upper hand

'SUBVERT CITY' PART 2 — DICK'S ORIGINAL LYRIC SHEET

at the back of the venue, press record and pick it up at the end of the night. Anyway, Dick then asked to put out a Lost Cherrees tape on Bluurg and we put together all the demos and live tracks that we had, and that ended up as the 'Nothing New' tape [BLUURG 25]."

"There was definitely a sense of things getting bigger," adds **Kev**, of the 100 Club gig, "Whether it was over a couple of weeks or a couple of months. But jumping out of the van in Oxford Street, to see a huge line of punk rockers outside the 100 Club, which you just didn't see at gigs very much, drove it home a bit. And they [i.e. the band] were all still young – eighteen or nineteen – and *adults* were coming to see them. There were queues of adults, in their late twenties and thirties, wanting to see them, which seemed incredible at the time."

A trip up to the Union Club in Nottingham on April 9th, 1983, was for one of those many 'line-up to die for' gigs the band played in the early Eighties. They were supported by – wait for it! – Chaos UK, Amebix, Disorder, Antisect and Napalm Death. It truly was a great era to be into punk in the UK, as these stacked – but affordable – bills came up with delightful regularity.

"Napalm Death were added at the last minute, as always," chuckles **Pete**. "It was only £1.50 to get in, and totally packed out, of course."

May '83 saw the band undertake a short tour of Yorkshire, taking in Brannigans in Leeds and the Palm Cove in Bradford, both with Anti-System and the Underdogs supporting. A gig at the Fallout Shelter in Meltham Mills had Xtract, Corpse and Two Fingered Approach on the bill, before they returned to Bradford for an eventful gig at The Vaults with Instigators and Convulsions opening for them (Instigators had also opened up the Palm Cove gig three days earlier).

"At that time, I was running regular punk nights at Brannigans in Leeds on a Wednesday and at the Palm Cove Club in Bradford on a Thursday," explains **Nick Toczek**, the promoter of that run of dates, and a renowned punk poet and writer, "Usually featuring the same bands on those consecutive nights in the two adjoining cities. That week, I'd headlined Wiltshire band the Subhumans, supported by three top West Yorkshire bands – the Instigators, the Underdogs and Anti-System. On tour at the time, the Subhumans had one gig in the northeast on the Friday night before heading back down south, passing through Yorkshire. Having no gig on the Saturday night, their singer and organizer, Dick Lucas, had asked me to find one for them in Bradford or Leeds. So I booked them into The Vaults Bar in what had been the cellar of the Alexandra Hotel on Great Horton Road [Bradford], although by then the hotel itself had been demolished, leaving only its historic and 'protected' façade. My proto-punk band Ulterior Motives had played several gigs there in the late Seventies and early Eighties.

"The place was run by John and June Farquhar, him a wily negotiator, her tough and business-wise, but both of them fair and kind with those they chose to work with on a regular basis. They were friends of mine then, and they remain friends to this day. I've

186

good reason to like them – The Vaults bar became not only one of the key sales outlets for my Wool City Rocker fanzine whenever bands were on there, but also my second office; it was where I met and interviewed many featured bands, reviewed their gigs, and relaxed after selling copies at gigs elsewhere around the city.

"The Vaults, a two roomer, with no windows and its walls painted black, was at that time a dingy dive popular with bikers, local bands and a bunch of older men who'd been regular drinkers there for years. The single entrance was at the downhill side of the hotel and led directly into the front bar, at one end of which was a narrow passage that led into a much larger back room. While some gigs were free, most had a door-charge of a couple of quid. This was taken at a desk set up at the back-room end of the passage. The old men and some of the bikers, if they were in the room before the gig started, could stay without paying. That was part of the deal.

"The Instigators were keen to gig with Subhumans, as were young local punks The Convulsions. Although it was short notice, I knew I could publicise this gig at the Brannigans and Palm Cove gigs and felt sure that The Convulsions would bring a local crowd, so it was viable and I booked it. What never occurred to me was that, after a couple of years with few bands down there, the bikers – most of whom styled themselves as Satan's Slaves – would see it as an intrusion on their territory.

"There was a good turnout for the gig and, although there was no real trouble, the ensuing intimidation terrified some of the younger punks. The bikers, most of whom were old enough to be the parents or even grandparents of the punks, did a bit of barging and shouting and threw a few glasses and bottles into the front-of-stage crowd, but luckily no one was injured. If they'd really wanted to make trouble, things would've been far worse. In the end, the gig went well, with the Instigators set recorded and subsequently released on Dick's Bluurg cassette label – which also released several of my own albums.

"Whilst all of this disruption was going on, I tried to calm things down. The main man behind the hostility seemed to be a stocky young Satan's Slave called Billy. Away from the music, beside the pool table, I tried hard to reason with him. His response was to pull out a knife and lunge at me with it. I stepped to one side, the blade missed me, and he stomped off. Later that evening, when things had quietened down, I spoke to him again, asking to see the knife. He showed me it. The thing was long enough, wide enough and certainly sharp enough to have done some harm if it had found its mark. He'd calmed down by then and we talked for a while. At the time I wrote a weekly column in the local free paper, The Bradford Star. He told me the name of his chapter of the Satan's Slaves and said that if I mentioned them in my column, we could call it quits.

"I did refer both to him and his chapter in my next column, relating the key details of our encounter and adding jokingly that I'd no idea what this group did, but guessed that they held Tupperware parties and did flower-arranging. I don't think Billy was amused. I was walking through the city centre the following week when a motorbike pulled up

JC, DICK AND TONY CARTER BY PHIL

STONEHENGE, NIGEL JOHNSON (NO SHIRT), THEN CLOCKWISE
- GRANT, PETE THE ROADIE, TROTSKY AND BRUCE

DICK AND BRUCE, 1983

'EVOLUTION' - DICK'S ORIGINAL LYRIC SHEET

Out in the garden
~~Out in your~~ room there's a little white rabbit
Like Revlon torture for your clean little habits
As you wash your hair ~~and~~ keep it clean
You get to wonder why Vaseline's green
And forget about the silent animal screams

Out in the ~~fields~~ garden there's a little white ~~bunny~~ dog
Shampoo in your eyes ~~is not so funny~~ like a burning fog
But it's tried and tested so you won't go blind
~~tested on animals~~ for the ~~blind~~ good of mankind
~~for that~~ your shining hair so many have died

~~And~~ Out in the garden there's a little white cat
And you're ~~catching~~ cancer as you smoke that fag
~~like cigarettes and the cure~~
When all they ~~find~~ the cure you ~~say~~ choke
When enough ~~animals~~ cats have died of smoke?
and ~~they say~~ that animals go for the throat

And the monkeys in the zoo they hide
Cos ~~they're~~ in the name of ~~science~~ so rare
they removed their brains
And to think that man evolved ~~for this~~
Civilised savages ~~down from the~~ from the ape
down from the trees beast
~~Cos~~ the animals who ~~animal rape~~
~~that~~ ~~are dying they~~ run these laboratories

EVOLUTION

23·4·82

Nork-Attik

beside me. 'You Nick Toczek?' asked the rider. When I confessed that I was, he added, 'Message from Billy: there's a contract out on you.' And he rode off.

"Several days later, I went into the city centre branch of NatWest Bank and joined the long queue. By an extraordinary coincidence, standing immediately in front of me, in all his leathered glory, helmet in hand, was Billy himself. Unable to resist the opportunity, I tapped him on the shoulder. When he glanced back at me, I said in a voice loud enough for everyone in the bank to hear, 'Hi, Billy, I'm told that, having not managed to stab me with that knife of yours, you've now put out a contract to have me killed?' Everyone was staring by now, and Billy actually blushed before whispering, 'Shut up… just shut up.' I did so, but that queue was moving very slowly indeed and, as the pair of us gradually shuffled forward over the next ten minutes, we shared a silence which I enjoyed immensely!"

As alluded to by Nick, the Instigators were a superb melodic punk band from Dewsbury, who so caught Dick's ear, he would release several tapes, an EP and two LPs by them through his Bluurg label, and they would support Subhumans no less than fifteen times during the early-to-mid Eighties.

"I think we first met them at the Vaults Bar gig, didn't we?" begins Instigators drummer **Paul 'Hammy' Halmshaw**, "Which Dick put out as the 'Instigators – Live at Bradford Vaults Bar' tape on Bluurg [BLUURG 27]. I'm sure that was the first time we ever played with 'em [it was actually the second]. Dick went up to [our vocalist] Semi that night, and said, 'I love your voice! There is no god! There is no god!' [quoting the Instigators' song, 'The Church Says']. And he ran up to me saying, 'There is no god!' as well, and I think it was that night he asked if we wanted to do a record. I think it was as quick as that. But first he said he wanted to do the live tape. You [guitarist, Simon Mooney] did the cover, didn't you? 'Cos there was loads of splatters on it, so it had to be you…"

Mooney: "That was the single cover with the splatters…"

Hammy: "No, you did the tape cover too, 'Live at Bradford Vaults Bar'. Anyway, I'd probably written to Dick beforehand, ordering their tapes off him or summat like that, because he did Bluurg Tapes, which was before I started to do Peaceville Tapes. We were 'in' with Flux of Pink Indians, if you remember; we supported them in Huddersfield, which was our first ever proper gig. For me, the plan was to try and get on Spiderleg, Flux's label, because that was nearer to Crass, and Subhumans had been on Spiderleg, before they went on to do Bluurg."

Semi: "'Demolition War' was on Spiderleg, wasn't it? That's my favourite ever record. I think I was about fifteen when I got it, and it was the best thing I had ever heard. 'Society' was a real fast punk track, but then you had 'Human Error' which had ska/reggae undertones. Everything about that EP is immense, and the lyrics made me think about quite a lot of things. I never saw them live until the first time we supported them, so I was quite proud to be on the same stage as the Subhumans."

Hammy: "Yeah, I wanted us to be on Spiderleg; I thought that was our way in, but it never happened. Then Dick asked us if we wanted to do a single after that first gig we played with them, I'm sure he did."

"They were all brilliant musicians," adds **Mooney**, before admitting, "I definitely ripped them off. When you're young, you take influences from everybody. They were one of those bands that I hated sound-checking after too, because they were so good."

"Can you imagine me going on after Trotsky, for fuck's sake?" laughs **Hammy**.

"So many bands back then just weren't very tight," chips in bassist **Tab**. "They were sloppy, and everything merged into one. But Subhumans were effortless. No matter how bad the sound system, it seemed like they could come in, not touch anything, not tune up, and go straight into something, and they instantly sounded immense. And they had the songs... stuff like [1985 EP] 'Rats' was just so powerful."

"The thing is with the Subhumans, they were proper musicians," reckons **Mooney**. "They probably grew up listening to Deep Purple and King Crimson. Well, I'm guessing that's what they grew up with..."

Hammy: "They were a lot older than us musically, although they might not have been in age."

Semi: "They would have been five or six years older than us? But a lot more mature in terms of influences..."

On May 27ᵗʰ, 1983, the Subhumans headed to Holland for six gigs, their first overseas touring experience, and one that would open their eyes as regards their international appeal.

"That was all put together by Rob [Berends] from Paperclip, and the A-Heads came with us," explains **Dick**. "Nick Toczek was with us too. We were blown away by the food and the accommodation – they fed you when you arrived at the venue, and put you up in the venue... this was unheard of, and nobody did anything like that in the UK. The rest of Europe did that too, and because bands were going over to Holland, Germany and France and seeing it, they started saying, 'This happens in Europe... do you think we should start asking for some food?' You felt a bit cheeky to start with, because venues just didn't do that, but there were more DIY organisations running the shows over there – they weren't run by people who were twice as old as us and only doing it for the money! It was great – you could get drunk as fuck in the bar until 2 am, crash out in a bunk bed upstairs, and wake up to breakfast before you left for the next gig... just amazing treatment."

"I started booking at the local Nijmegen youth centre/rock centre, Doornroosje [translates as 'Sleeping Beauty'], in '79, as a volunteer, two years after the punk rock explosion," begins **Rob Berends**, "And in this town, little had happened on that front, just a few shows here and there. But early in '79, I called the venue and said, 'Are you interested in a militant band from the UK, who have anarchistic, pacifistic, feministic lyrics and dress all in black, in Mao style?' I was talking about Crass, of course! And the owner of the venue asked what music they played – and when I said, 'Punk rock!', he was like, 'Oh no, we don't do punk rock here...' Click!

"Me and my friends – actually there were two separate groups of us – decided we were going to speak to this venue and tell them, 'Listen, we all love punk rock, and we have to go to Arnhem, or Amsterdam, or Eindhoven, to see these bands – and we want to see them in our own town...' And we bumped into the other group, and were like, 'Oh, you are here too', and we started working as a team, ten or fifteen of us. They called us the Punk Rock Committee, and we got given a Saturday night slot – whoah! And that's where it started.

"We started booking Dutch bands first, but we started doing foreign bands as well quite soon after – Joy Division in January 1980... The Ruts in early 1980... and we started cooperating then with likeminded venues elsewhere in the Netherlands. And we started bringing bands to the Netherlands on tour, working with booking agencies in London who were offering us new alternative bands – and that's when the Paperclip Agency started, in 1981.

"Subhumans were one of the first. And we were wondering how we were going to get in touch with them. We all had different jobs in the collective, and I was mostly the man on the phone. We tried to rotate jobs, but that was the best one for me. So, I contacted the wholesaler in Amsterdam, who worked at the local record shop and local pirate radio station, which was highly political... having a job was a bit weird in the '80s. Once a month you'd fill out a form and get your money, and then you'd do loads of other stuff, haha! Anyway, they told me they got the Subhumans records from Southern Distribution, so they gave me a number for them, and I spoke to John Loder, and he was like, 'Yes, Subhumans – they run their own label, Bluurg... here's Dick Lucas's phone number!'

"We always drew an audience, in Nijmegen for instance, of around 200, and it didn't really matter what bands we put on, because it was a scene. It was a big scene of musicians, all interested in new stuff, and all our friends, and there was a very cool atmosphere. It's hard these days to find anything similar, in bigger venues, in newer buildings. And Subhumans fitted the bill for us in terms of their music, their lyrics, what they stood for, and if they were bringing over A-Heads as well, they were going to get 150 or 200 people coming out. We didn't charge a high ticket price, but we always broke even – we were actually the best working group in the Sleeping Beauty as well, financially... which wasn't an aim, but the other groups booking there wasted money. And we didn't. So, it basically worked because they fitted the scene at the time.

"I loved what they did musically, and loads of us had their singles, because I made sure the record store had plenty of stock and they were played on the radio. They stood out, because they were really good, both in terms of music and lyrics, and everybody loved them as people as well. I remember they stayed at my place – if bands accepted it, we would offer them private accommodation, rather than a B&B or an economy hotel. I lived in a house with six bedrooms, with six people living there, with a shared kitchen and bathroom, and they stayed with me. And they were totally unhappy with the food we cooked for them – they wanted curry, haha! And they cooked us all a curry."

"I remember he put fish in a salad," says **Dick**, incredulously, "And I remember eating it, thinking, 'This tastes a bit weird?' And then he said, 'Ah, us fish must eat each other…!' He's a nice chap, but that was a bit of a bad moment, so we stopped eating it, because it was obviously fish and we were very obviously vegetarian – and had sent that info ahead of us. But some people thought vegetarians still ate fish… in fact, some 'vegetarians' still apparently ate chicken, and just didn't eat red meat!

"The Melkweg was a really big gig on that tour. Someone handed me this pipe before we played, and I messed up a couple of really obvious bits of lyrics in the set, so Bruce had a go at me afterwards. That was a life lesson – don't get stoned before you play…"

"The thing I was most scared about was booking them at the Melkweg [the Milky Way] in Amsterdam," continues **Rob**. "My brother had soon joined Paperclip Agency after I started it, mainly because my dad wanted us to work together, and this was the first time we had put a punk rock band into the Melkweg. The booker there was an old hippy, mainly into world music, but he got the vibe, and he liked the Berends brothers, so he booked Subhumans for us. And we were quite nervous about it, because it was in Amsterdam, it was at the Melkweg, and you never knew if there was going to be trouble. We had a good turnout – 500 people perhaps? – and there *was* some tension in the hall. But my brother and I were kneeling behind the two PA stacks onstage, looking at each other, watching the audience, keeping an eye on the front of the stage, and we'd decided we were going to act immediately if anything happened… the Berends brothers fighting the riot police or whatever, if needs be, haha! But there was no issue whatsoever.

"In Amsterdam, they also played squats on return visits – there was Van Hall, the Emma, the Wijers – but a lot of us were in squatter groups, so it all made sense. They were the first punk rock band we brought over, which paved the way for Instigators, Hagar the Womb, Blyth Power… even Major Accident! I think they did five or six shows on that first tour, something like that, and all of them were well attended. They did well. They got better, of course, as they got more well known. And they broke a few punk rock rules, like having songs that were almost twenty minutes long – I still think 'From the Cradle to the Grave' is one of the best lyrics I've ever heard…"

"I remember their funny little beers," laughs **Bruce**. "They gave you them in these little glasses, and used a spatula to take all the foam off. They weren't very big, so gone in a second and you wanted another one! But they do wacky things in Holland... like put a car in a bar, haha! It was just so amazing. They'd never do that in England, would they?

"And I remember hearing Thomas Dolby's 'Hyperactive' really loud in a bar in Holland, and thinking, 'What the hell's that? It's amazing!' Because for some reason I

ƵUB HUM ANƵ

FACTION

AFTER DARK

SUNDAY 21st AUGUST

Grange Youth Centre (Nixon Drive)   Admission £1.50

WINSFORD   7.30 p.m. — 11.00 p.m.

BRUCE DRUMMING FOR THE
A-HEADS, 1983 - COURTESY
OF JOCK MCCURDY

GRANT, DICK AND BRUCE
BY MEL BELL

SUBHUMANS WITH BLACKY
FROM SUBVERT SINGING,
COURTESY OF BLACKY AND SNED

TROTSKY

hadn't heard it yet in the UK. I was also surprised so many people came out to see us, because a lot of them wouldn't understand the lyrics, and a good 50% of it is about the lyrics, isn't it…?"

"I'd never left England before… I don't think any of us had?" adds **Trotsky**. "It was pretty awe-inspiring really, to be playing in Holland, especially as we were all so very young. We were shown phenomenal hospitality – all the beer and food you could want, and a place to sleep… and it's still like that. As opposed to England, which is still shit in that respect. It's one of the reasons I'm living over here in Europe now; I'm really glad I got out when I did with Brexit and everything. And it's only going to get worse, the more isolated it'll become, the longer it goes on.

"We toured with Holland's Glorie; they were really good, very polished… and had a very nice drum kit, haha! Rob Berends did the tour for us, with his brother Ruud, this huge, tall, gangly Dutch geezer. After one gig, Ruud and Rob were staying at the same hotel as us, and there was a convention in the hotel of the tallest people in Holland… it was full of all these giants, they were fucking huge. And Ruud got invited to attend because he was so fucking massive, haha! I remember this one guy turned up in a Mini, and he had a Perspex bubble on top to see out of when he was driving, like a small Popemobile! That was funny…"

"Going out of the country was definitely a new experience for me at that sort of age," agrees **Grant**. "I'd just bought an orange Bedford CF [van], so we took that over there, and the first time I ever drove it – because I didn't have a licence when I bought it – was in a field at the back of this youth centre in Holland. I was absolutely out of my head, and there were punks all over the roof of it.

"I seem to remember the gigs were pretty good, but my most enduring memory of that trip was of us just being kids going wild, being silly, and having a lot of fun. Not a lot of responsibility shown or taken… just young kids doing their thing.

"My van eventually ended up on its side at one point – coming back from a gig and dropping the gear off at The Shed. The driver fell asleep and ended up in a ditch. But the van survived – it sat at The Shed for a bit, until I eventually took it up to Yorkshire, and it rotted gently up there before I sold it on."

"They asked us to go to Holland with them, and we got as far as London before we ran out of petrol!" laughs **Jock**, of the A-Heads. "And Nigel had to thumb a lift on the side of the M4 to the nearest petrol station and walk back with a can – just enough to get us to the next garage. Dick was in a panic, and everyone else was cracking open another beer…

"When we finally got out there, about five in the morning, the tour manager dropped us off where we were staying, which had no roof on it. Subhumans were staying down the road – in a place with a roof, haha! But we all got up the next day, and were thinking, 'Where is everybody?' And the Subhumans were off rehearsing somewhere, whilst the rest of us found some pot. And that was the difference between them and us – the first day in Holland, they were rehearsing, and we were drinking and smoking somewhere. And it showed in some of the performances too…

"But it was great, all in the van together, having a laugh, turning up in all these different cities. The other band on that tour, Holland's Glorie, were amazing, really tight. Which in turn inspired the Subhumans to up their game, the same way they have to in America, because all the support bands are so tight, and there's nothing worse than being blown offstage by the support bands. So that motivated them into being as tight as possible."

"That first European tour was bloody brilliant," enthuses **Pete**. "We had to get passports, of course, we were going to Europe – every roadie needs one! I don't think any of us had been on the cross-channel ferry before, and I can't remember who drove, but the first stop in Holland was for chips and mayonnaise – bit weird, but never mind. Onto the first gig, which was a Sosjay protest in Hengelo, with Alerta and Zowiso, and we then went on to play Nijmegen, Zutphen, Amsterdam, Groningen and Hoorn. Apart from the first gig, the rest were with A-Heads and Holland's Glorie, fantastic times. We couldn't believe we were getting food and free beer at the gigs, although later, when we were putting on our own gigs in England, we realised that we could do this too. The squats were awesome, defended like fuck... I can remember asking if the punks in Nijmegen were bikers – they said no, and that the bike helmets were for when they were defending the squat against the riot police... and then they laughed at me! But we made good friends, and good contacts for future tours – I still know people from that tour to this day..."

"To us, it was the least we could do, to give some proper hospitality," says **Rob**, of the free food and drink the band enjoyed so much. "It was just natural for us, because we didn't know any other way. Belgium and Switzerland were the same... Germany was a little less good – it was better for the bigger bands, but not so good for the smaller bands. It was only when I started working for UK acts, and booking UK dates for touring bands through UK agencies, that I learnt how shite it was there in the Eighties, haha! Subhumans told me about this as well. I can't remember where they said it was, but they played somewhere for £300 and a couple of beers... maybe a sandwich, but probably not. The place was packed, and it was a good night, and they went to see the owner to collect their fee, and the owner said they had to go and see one of the bouncers for their money. And when they asked the bouncer for the money, he said he would throw them out of the venue – and they didn't get anything! But we did everything DIY... and, although we didn't recognise it at first, we also did DIT. Because these days, people say, 'DIY, DIT', but we *did* do DIT! Do it together."

Upon their return to the UK, Subhumans played gigs in Wells and Bournemouth, as well as their second gig at the 100 Club, this time with Naked, Lost Cherrees and Lack of Knowledge in support, before playing an impromptu set at the then-annual Stonehenge festival (the last instalment of the festival was the following year).

"Yes, we played Stonehenge, next to the van," confirms **Dick**. "Julian and someone else from Organized Chaos went back to Warminster in the van and got a generator, and we played twenty-seven songs... the longest set we've ever played. About fifty people watched us, and it was great fun. We played every song we had – including a song called 'No Two People', which we only ever played twice… and I can't even tell you what the words to that were? That's a rarity – I don't think there's *any* recordings of that song at all."

"I attended two of the festivals," remembers **Kev**. "The first time, when the Subhumans played, was low-key to say the least. We all arrived in the now-familiar blue parcel van, driving into an alternative universe of crusties, hippies, new age travellers, convoy, tricksters and dealers. A guy ran up to the back of our – moving! – van to offer us LSD and Leb [i.e. Lebanese cannabis] and to welcome us to Stonehenge!

"The festival was like none I'd ever been to. To be honest, I think the only festival any of us had been to prior was Reading, which was terribly well organised, with actual toilets and bars. There was, however, a good contingent of crusties and anarcho punks. The Subhumans played in a space near our tents between a few cars, their set publicised by word of mouth and a few hastily written flyers. I definitely seem to recall a flyer… Dick may have brought some with him?

"It was late afternoon, through the by-now-battered old WEM speaker stack Bruce owned. A small generator provided power. A decent crowd assembled, swelled by passers-by; we had mates who were bikers, so it was a real hotchpotch of people.

"We stayed there a few days, which was a great team spirit kind of thing. Pretty much everyone we knew from the Wiltshire punk scene was there: Organized Chaos, members of the A-Heads, and wider alternative types. Trotsky and I hitched home, others stayed longer. Warminster is only thirty minutes away, so someone was always coming or going, mostly to buy drugs, I recall!"

"I must have seen them there, but I can't remember!" admits **Mel**. "Tony, who used to drive the band, used to sell me and Dick these Lebanese hash cakes, haha! One day he didn't have any though, so Dick and I went to this Tibetan tent, and they sold us these cookies. Hawkwind were playing that night, and I really wanted to see them, but all I remember is falling over, and Dick and Bruce looking down at me, thinking I was dead or something! I wasn't very good with things like that, and I had to go to my tent to sleep it off… I'm more of a drinker."

"I first bumped into a couple of Amebix at Stonehenge," adds **Dick**, as an aside. "Prior to that I'd only heard of them, maybe heard half a song somewhere. They were very tall, with bones in their hair and everything – totally looked the part. Quite scary really, in a sense. Musically… I dunno! I'll start with Black Sabbath, because I always start with Black Sabbath when any sort of metal gets involved, but just a lot harder… less intricate. It was the sort of music I wasn't instantly into, because I preferred it sort of thrashy, but I did appreciate the fact that they were doing something not many other bands were doing. They were consistent, and powerful."

"That Bournemouth gig, at St Andrews Hall, Boscombe [June 11th, 1983], was the first time Self Abuse supported Subhumans, and only our third gig," recalls Self Abuse bassist/vocalist **Andy Nazer**. "We used to go there whilst still at school to the 'Supersonic' disco on a Saturday night. I'd first gotten into the Subhumans around 1982, off the back of my friend Rich Waterton, who had bought the early EPs on Spiderleg Records. I recall us getting stopped in the street by a passing plod [i.e. police] car in sleepy, leafy Christchurch, whilst we were wandering along playing them from a boombox. They pulled over and asked us what we were up to, where we were going and whatnot. Fun, fun, fun, fun, fun 'til the... well, you know!

"Anyway, the gig was organised by the opening band Parasites, and was originally going to be at a different church hall venue a few miles away, but that fell through for some reason, so Rich W. and myself went and booked it at St Andrews Hall instead. The Mad Are Sane were meant to be playing their debut gig that night as well; unfortunately, their guitarist Ash didn't show up, so they didn't play, which was a shame as we were all really looking forward to seeing them.

"Studio 95, where we recorded our 'State of Mind' demo, had just relocated from central Bournemouth to a new studio next to St Andrews Hall, and the owner was out with a decibel meter complaining about the loudness coming from the hall. And we were only using a vocal PA! Luckily the gig proceeded without any other bother and was very well attended; Subhumans played great, even though Dick had to battle somewhat with being able to hear himself through the PA. That turned out to be the final gig held at St Andrews Hall though..."

June 18th, 1983, was the date that the 'Evolution' EP entered the Indie Charts; it stayed in the charts for an impressive seventeen weeks, peaking at No. 4. It was the first Subhumans release not on Spiderleg, being the second vinyl release on Dick's Bluurg Records after the 'Wessex '82' compilation EP mentioned previously, a relatively simple transition though, seeing as both labels were bankrolled and distributed by Southern.

"I'm sure that Bluurg was through Southern as well, but you'd have to ask Dick," offers **Colsk**. "If you think about it, what Derek and I set up with Spiderleg, through Southern, was nothing that special that someone like Subhumans couldn't just do themselves. After the album, I remember Derek saying to them, 'You should just do your own label through Southern...' I remember Dick shaking his head, like, 'What the hell? Why?' sorta thing. He couldn't see the advantage of it really. But he would have known John Loder a bit, and Southern, and from then on, that was it. An accountant would have looked at that and said, 'You're bonkers – they're the best-selling band on your label!' But finances never came into it; me and Derek never once had a conversation like, 'They're an earner, we need to keep them on the label 'cos they're bringing in money...' We just didn't think about it – all we thought about was that people should do their own thing. And there was no reason why they should come to us to go to Southern, when they could go straight to Southern themselves. The same way that Crass did with us really, at least until they set up Corpus Christi, a label that would actually do second releases by bands."

The title track of the 'Evolution' EP is an intensely frenetic rant against the injustice

flying fish band

+ THE ERGOT BABIES

+ INFAMY

+ JUSTIN, DICK AND WALLY (?)

THE VIADUCT HOTEL
LIMPLEY STOKE
ON FRIDAY 20TH MAY 8·30pm
ADMISSION -80p.

PHIL AND BRUCE, FLYING FISH BAND ERA

STEVE, PHIL, LIMPLEY STOKE, 1983

of vivisection, built around a twelve-bar boogie ramped up to breakneck speed, whilst 'So Much Money' revolves around a rather sassy bass line. 'Germ' is also bass-driven, a bouncy cogitation on the nature of viral infections, more than apt in these COVID times, and the EP closer 'Not Me' is a ball of indignant punk rage, especially its fervent final couplet, 'Who's gonna fight the system? You? Me? Or fucking no-one?'

"The thing about non-digital communication in the early Eighties, you would get these paper leaflets in with your letters, and the BUAV [British Union for the Abolition of Vivisection] and Animal Aid were sending out a lot of leaflets," **Dick** explains the anti-vivisection sentiment of 'Evolution', "And a lot of them were coming through with letters from people wanting tapes, and a lot of this information was coming up on stalls at gigs. That really opened my eyes, and made me a confirmed vegetarian, where I'd previously been a sort of 'halfway house vegetarian', giving all this stuff up but still having a sneaky sausage roll – but that was it, I was like, 'Come on, you're either going to be vegetarian or you're not…'

"And then there was the horror stories of vivisection, and the uselessness of it all, the amount of animals being killed, the LD50 test and things like that… it was communication of that information more than witnessing it that got me – and the rest of the band, come to think of it – to be vegetarian. All around the same time, around mid '82 or something.

"So, communicating facts does have an effect. I was going to do a sheet on the inside of the EP that would list all the companies that tested on animals, so I wrote to the BUAV for such a list, and they came back to me saying that the list was too big, but they sent me a list of companies that definitely *didn't*, and I put a few of those in instead.

"I thought it was important to be very specific for a change. A lot of my songs are not specific; they're semi-fictional, semi-realistic slices of outlook, but that was one song that was specifically about vivisection. And only one – because I thought, 'I've said it now…'"

The EP boasted another superb Nick Lant illustration on its front cover, of a deranged vivisector, his pockets stuffed with syringes and scalpels, about to administer yet more misery to captive laboratory animals, whilst the background depicted the Animal Liberation Front, activists committed to ending such atrocities.

"As I matured, my work became more considered and detailed," says **Nick**, "Consequently it took longer to produce 'Evolution' and [fifth EP] 'Rats'. I'd become more interested in the anarcho punk scene and I'd got politicised."

At the end of June, a gig at The Roxborough in Harrow-on-the-Hill with The Disrupters, Faction and Lost Cherrees was opened by an obscure band, Four Minute Warning – the first band of Sean Forbes, who would go on to play in Wat Tyler and Hard Skin.

"I *absolutely* remember playing that gig at the Roxborough with the Subhumans," says **Sean**. "At that point, Four Minute Warning had befriended the Lost Cherrees and whenever they had a gig we asked to play as well, and we got ourselves some choice gigs, including this one. The gig was a massive deal for our band, but – like lots of gigs in the '80s – it was actually pretty average, and people were very indifferent to Four Minute Warning. Hindsight is a wonderful thing though, and now I totally understand why people were indifferent – Four Minute Warning were pompous anarcho punk and very, very poor at playing.

"We missed some of the Subhumans' set as we had to get the last train home with a full backline… and yes, that did include drums. Great days like that live long in the memory! The early releases by Subhumans remind me of a time and place, and that young naïvety that would change the world, and the only thing to be frightened of was nuclear war. Life was much simpler back then, and we didn't have a care in the world… apart from was Colin Conflict seen eating in KFC?

"I bought the first Subhumans 7" the week it came out. 'Pay no more than' hand-stamped on the sleeve, skulls and lots of anarchy signs… what's not to like? In the late '70s and early '80s, I was a Crasstafarian. So nearly every record I bought had a black and white sleeve with 'pay no more than 50p' on it, and a bit of bum fluff. I used to save my dinner money from school and go to Earth Records in Aylesbury and buy two or three 7"s every Friday. Most of the bands I'd never heard of, but because I had spent all my money on them, I played them until I fell in love with them. That happened for years, and I can still sing every track on the Public Disgrace 'Toxteth' EP, Death Sentence's EP on Beat The System Records, Annie Anxiety and others, to this day."

On July 27th, 1983, Subhumans recorded the live tracks 'People Are Scared', 'Everyday Life' and 'I Don't Wanna Die' at Feltham Football Club, for their next release, the 'Time Flies… But Aeroplanes Crash' 12" EP. A few weeks later, on August 5th and 10th, to be precise, they returned to Pickwick to record the studio tracks for that 12", which wouldn't be released until the end of the year.

"'Time Flies…' was originally going to be a live record," explains **Dick**, "So we recorded this gig at Feltham Football Club in July '83 [with Naked and Lost Cherrees supporting], but the recording was a bit naff, with most of the songs sounding weak compared to the previously recorded versions. So we only used 'People Are Scared', because we hadn't recorded it, and we didn't play it much – the jammy bit at the end was never the same twice, but it was a good version, so we kept that, but we never recorded it properly… although I quite like the fact that there's only a live version released. Similarly, we never did a recorded version of 'Everyday Life', which is kind of a pity, because that was a good, underrated track. And with 'I Don't Wanna Die', it's hard to make that song suffer from a bad recording, because it's so fast and basic and in your face."

"I think the Feltham Football Club gig was the best time we ever played with Subhumans," reckons **Nut**, of Lost Cherrees. "We played some great gigs there, and it was rammed again when we put Subhumans on, who had decided to bring down a

203

R ising Free avec:

V.I.S.A. présente :

Subhumans
Faction
Bérurier Noir
D & V

Samedi 8 Octobre
de 18 a 22 heures
22 RUE PALI KAO
métro: Couronnes

35f

VISA:concept

R ISING FREE

V.I.S.A. présente :

avec
subhumans, faction
berurier noir, d&v

VISA concept

35f

samedi 8 octobre
de 18 a 22 heures

✴22 RUE PALI KAO✴   Mét. Couronnes.

ROB CHALLICE WITH DICK, PARIS, 1983

BRUCE, IN THE VAN, ON THE WAY TO PARIS BY PHIL

DICK AND TONY CARTER - DRIVER & IMPRESSIONIST BY PHIL

mobile recording studio to record their gig. That was also the night that Dick stayed over at my house – or rather my mum and dad's – as the Cherrees were recording the next night, for our second single, 'A Man's Duty, a Woman's Place', and it wasn't yet decided who we were going to record it for. Dick wanted it for Bluurg and Colin [Jerwood, from Conflict] wanted it for Mortarhate… we were so in demand that record companies were fighting over us – yeah, right. Anyway, Dick kipped on my bedroom floor and awoke to find my mum had washed all his clothes and cooked him breakfast! She was worried about the state of his clothes, and I was mortally embarrassed as she'd probably just destroyed all my punk credentials. Punks washing their clothes? It's all over! He still remembered this when I spoke to him at the 100 Club years later."

"But it's a strange record," continues **Dick**, of 'Time Flies…' "We didn't know what it was going to be, so it came together in bits and bobs. It was originally going to be a live album, and then a live 7", but that didn't really sound good enough. Of the studio tracks, 'Get Out of My Way' and 'First Aid' were leftovers that could have made the first LP; they were old Stupid Humans songs, so we thought we'd record them."

Subhumans never seem to waste a good song – they might eventually crop up on a record years after they were initially written.

"That's part of the process of choosing which songs should go on which record," reckons **Dick**. "Any song that wasn't in your own top ten in your head might not get used. With 'First Aid', for example, Phil loves it… but I just think it's okay. I think it's a bit nonsensical, it hasn't got any massive meaning, so I can't really get passionate about it. So it was on the 'lower end' of my list of songs to do immediately, so to speak. Whereas a song like 'Reason for Existence' – or 'Evolution' – was instantly, 'Yes, that's on the next record!' They just had an immediacy, a newness, a uniqueness about them… or whatever it is about a song that makes it 'good'.

"'Work-Rest-Play-Die' was an interesting one, because it was written to that actual tune in my head when I was at work… that sort of sea shanty tune, and I said, 'Why don't we just do *that* tune?' And it is easier to write a song if you have a tune already in your head to write it to, so the scanning stays equal through the verses, that sort of thing. It doesn't happen very often – I usually write the words down without any tune or beat in my head whatsoever.

"'Somebody's Mother' [a song they wouldn't record until late '85] was written to a Rezillos song going around in my head called 'It Gets Me'. Listen to that song, and you'll hear the entire structure was totally ripped off from The Rezillos. That was handy! Then even later, 'Charity' by Citizen Fish was written to 'Penny Lane' by The Beatles in my head… sometimes having a tune in your head can help a song happen quicker.

"And, of course, there was 'Susan'," he continues, returning to the subject of 'Time Flies…', "Which was an experiment. I'd liked piano ever since I was a kid – in fact, it was about the only thing I could get a tune out of. And our friend Steve Hamilton had written a song, and he wasn't in a band, so he asked if we wanted to use it? And it was an odd song, because it was about one person… it was like a miniature one-person 'Cradle to the Grave' really… you know – this is shit, don't worry you'll get over it… and she kills herself. There was no happy ending to it, but it reflected a lot of the standard mundane shit that people, especially young women, were going through in their existence, taking pills because they were feeling depressed, trapped in a shitty job, and so on. So it was a fairly Subhumans-esque song in the first place, and I had this tune on the piano, so I put it to that to see if it would work, and it did."

Bruce: "Steve was a friend of Dick's – well, a friend of ours – from Bradford-on-Avon. He used to wear a raincoat… there was a point in history when people wore long raincoats, and got into goth music! And he was one of them. He was mad on The Fall. And he was obviously a lyricist, because he wrote 'Susan', which has grown to be one of our most popular songs."

Dick: "Curiously enough, and by complete coincidence, if you speed up the piano line to 'Susan', you get an approximate version of the bass line to 'Ashtray Dirt'."

The second half of August saw the band hitting the road for a dozen dates with Faction as main support; a tour primarily booked by Rob Challice, they started at the Queens Hotel in Wolverhampton on August 17th, with Submission opening, and ended up at a sold-out Fulham Greyhound in London on September 1st. Along the way, they played several hot spots for touring punk bands, like The Marples in Sheffield, Brannigans in Leeds and Jilly's in Manchester, but they also made time to play a cowshed in Upper Weeg!

"We played Newtown Church Centre after Wolverhampton, and then we had a day off. And someone asked us if we wanted to do a gig in this old lady's cowshed," laughs **Dick**. "She lived out in the countryside, lots of old stone buildings and trees… all very communal living, and just a bit weird. A few local punks, about a dozen people in all, turned up to have a look, haha! And we played [Flux of Pink Indians cover] 'Tube Disaster', which we didn't do very often… mainly 'cos I couldn't remember the words, or make out what the words actually were. Yeah, that was an odd one, in the middle of nowhere, all these big farm buildings, and one to do the gig in. Then this lady's son, or nephew, he was about twelve, nicked all the badges off my jacket. Little brat!"

It seems that at one point the band would play literally anywhere they were asked to?

"At that time, yeah," confirms **Bruce**. "It was only later on, when we got a bit more serious, that we got a bit more selective."

"We would basically play anywhere we could," agrees **Dick**, "And sometimes we'd just lose money… due to circumstance, depending upon how many people showed up. There were no guarantees back then, and we didn't feel known enough to demand a figure for playing a gig. Eventually we started saying, 'We'd *like* fifty quid', or a hundred quid, or whatever. But I think the most we ever got for a gig in the early days was £200 once at

207

the 100 Club. And that was rammed, and £2 to get in, so they made their £800, and we got £200, haha! But it didn't really matter that much at the time. I remember Charlie Harper was at the 100 Club, and he gave us some solid advice about doing gigs for more money."

Bruce: "There *was* sometimes an issue with being paid – at all! So Dick had to introduce his 'piece of paper' as he called it, which was basically a contract. We had to have a band talk and agree to do that, and it was just an agreement where someone would promise to pay us what we'd agreed…

"Our principles have always been a strong point though, and they've stopped us from seemingly selling out. Because we *haven't* sold out. Although at some point we did have to start thinking about income and all that. In fact, when 'The Day the Country Died' came out, we even had to go and see an accountant…"

"Well, we got this tax bill in the post," adds **Dick**, "That estimated we'd earned £6000 in a year; we were like 'Whaaat!?', and we had to get an accountant to prove we hadn't!"

Bruce: "We all found that rather funny. The first thing that happens when you go and see an accountant, the accountant says, 'What equipment have you got up to this point?' So we had to list all our equipment, so he could figure out how much we'd paid out before we started the band. I made Dick buy the echo unit, because he didn't have anything else to buy… bloody singers, haha!"

On August 27th, there was an unfortunate incident on the way to the Gateshead gig, which resulted in Dick going to hospital and the band playing the gig without him, and various guest vocalists from the other bands and the crowd getting up to have a go at Subhumans karaoke.

"We were on our way from Bradford to Gateshead, and we stopped to get some petrol," explains **Dick**. "There was the four of us, and a friend of ours called Fred, who was part of this trio – Fred, Cardigan Man and Tim – who were from Mansfield and Barnsley and used to hitch around the country to watch us… a funny little trio. Cardigan Man's real name was Brian, but he had this big long cardigan hanging off him. He got beaten up once by a gang of skinheads in Bedford, because he'd shaved his head, but he'd left two sideburns on, so they beat him up because he hadn't done it properly. But that was skinheads for you, in 1983 at least.

"So, Kenny was driving, and Fred was with us, and me and Fred were sat behind the driver's seat. It might have been a Volkswagen van, but it was one of those vans where the engine is on the inside, between the driver and the passenger, with a cover over it. It was steaming away, and Kenny was like, 'We've got to let the steam out of the radiator…' As he did that, he realised the cap was too hot and he couldn't control it, so he was shouting, 'Ah, everybody get out, I can't hold it!' But me and Fred got the full brunt of this boiling water that came spurting out all over the van. It went all over our legs, and it was really painful, so we were trying to find the nearest tap to spray cold water over them. But it was still hurting a lot, and getting worse, so someone called an ambulance, and me and

Fred had to go to hospital. And the rest of them carried on to Gateshead to do the gig at The Station…

"We were sat in this hospital, which was virtually empty – just me and Fred sat looking at each other. And my leg was starting to feel okay, until they came along and popped the massive blisters, that were six inches long and three inches wide, and peeled the burnt skin off, and *then* it really started hurting. But they covered it in cream and wrapped it up in bandages, and I got picked up the next day, to go to the next gig, in Sheffield.

"Fred didn't come with us, because his legs were worse than mine. Mine were bad enough, but his were burnt to fuck. We still had Sheffield, Nottingham, Leeds, and then finally the Fulham Greyhound, to do, so every day, wherever we were going, I had to go straight to a hospital, to have my dressings changed and my leg cleaned up. It wasn't like we were regular bathers on tour anyway, and with legs like that, covered in blisters, I was in a right state. I stank. And it was very painful.

"I thought I could maybe do a Val Doonican and sit on a bar stool to sing, but that lasted maybe half a song in sound-check; I felt a right twat and thought, 'I'm not doing this!' And actually, you just got into it and ignored the pain, it was alright; the worst thing was afterwards, and getting the bandages changed. 'Ow, my leg hurts,' became the standard van cliché for the rest of the tour.

"But it was never like we got ill much when on tour, despite all the drinking and stuff, but that's the advantage of youth. Or, if we were ill, it didn't matter – anything short of getting your legs severely burnt, you just carried on regardless. There's been plenty of gigs where I've had a bad cold before the gig, and more or less sweated the cold out during the gig. So I think gigs are actually good for your health… it's just the going to them and the partying afterwards where things go wrong."

As previously mentioned, and in the true spirit of 'the show must go on', Subhumans blundered through a set with guest vocalists, a set that saw Pete The Roadie, Blacky from Subvert, Scruff from Hellbastard and Semi from Instigators all jump up and sing a few songs each.

"I think we did our set and we were waiting for the Subhumans to turn up," recalls **Semi**, "And then they did – but without Dick! I think it may have been Bruce who asked me to sing a couple of songs with them, but not sure which tracks it was. I definitely sang 'Society', 'Parasites', and something else… a few other singers got up as well. The audience seemed to be dancing along to it all, so it can't have been that bad. I was too excited to really notice though. That was quite a big thing for me, because they were one of my favourite bands. In fact, I'd go so far as to say, that was definitely in my list of highlights from my short singing 'career'. And then they went on to do backing vocals on our album – happy days!"

"I'd be going off to Subhumans gigs even when the A-Heads weren't playing with them, and – probably because of my hippy childhood – I used to hitch everywhere,"

TROTSKY, PHIL AND DICK
COURTESY OF BRUCE

TROTSKY IN PARIS
BY ROB CHALLICE

TROTSKY, MEL, PETE, TONY
CARTER AND DICK BY PHIL

remembers **Mel**, who hitched all the way up to Gateshead for that gig. "I planned to leave at six o'clock in the morning, as there was bound to be some lorries going up there, but I didn't wake up until nine. But I'd planned to get there for six in the evening, and I remember getting into Gateshead just as it was chiming six! So I made it… but it wasn't so great, because they'd had van problems, and the radiator had overheated and Dick had been burnt and was in hospital. The gig still went ahead, but Dick wasn't singing, and it was a bit of a strange gig… a *very* strange gig. I think Faction played as well – who I joined later on, after A-Heads split.

"Gateshead was the furthest I ever hitched to see them, I think? And then I had to hitch back because we had a gig in Bournemouth. We stayed in Gateshead that night, and then went down to Sheffield – where we stayed with a girl called Becky, whose dad was a part-time magician, going by the name of Corky, and treated us to a magic show in their front room – he was making balloon animals for us and everything! Then they played Barnsley, or somewhere like that, and I hitched down to Bournemouth from there for the A-Heads to play Capones with Self Abuse.

"But hitching around was great back then – you'd see the same faces at gigs… like Fred, and Cardigan Man, and Chris from Bath, who all used to go everywhere to see them as well."

As if the tour hadn't been eventful enough already, the gig at the Fulham Greyhound was Grant's last gig as the Subhumans bassist, and his decision to leave the band hadn't really been openly communicated at that point.

"Well, at the end of the Fulham gig, which was a great gig, Grant put his bass down, walked up to me and shook my hand," frowns **Dick**. "I thought, 'Uh! What's that about?' I didn't get it at all. And then a week later Bruce was on the phone, telling me that Grant had left and Phil was going to be the new bassist. That was a bit weird, and I was a bit disappointed that Grant hadn't mentioned it. It was a decision he'd told Bruce about, and that was that; he went off into the night. And the handshake was a goodbye without me even knowing it. But never mind.

"I had no idea it was coming. Maybe he didn't want me to be even more freaked out than I already was with my leg thing going on. But that eventually healed up and scabbed over a few weeks later. It was a long process.

"So, Bruce sorted out Phil as the new bassist. They all knew each other way better than I knew any of them – Phil and Bruce were both in Warminster, and knew each other from before anyway, but Phil had been our roadie before he became our bassist. He was guitarist in the Pagans and The Flying Fish Band, both with Steve, my brother. I didn't know him very well, but in those days, you didn't know anyone that well really. They were either good people… or not, and most people were good people on the face of it. When you're nineteen, the unifying thing is having a laugh and music. Anything else – like emotional responses or subconscious archetypal memory transcendence – doesn't come into it until you're *way* older than that… well, until you're about sixty and making it up!"

"Phil and Bruce were always jamming a lot anyway," adds **Mel**. "Phil was a guitarist really, and was always playing his Frank Zappa-y stuff. The Pagans were great. Steve was brilliant, very talented; he wrote such good songs. I did have a chat with him before he died [Steve sadly passed away in 2011], and asked if we could cover one of his songs ['Wave Goodbye to Your Dreams']. He was very well liked. At his funeral, they planted a big circle of trees, with a big Saracen stone in the middle, which they'd dragged across the field and everything."

"My head was in a different space to where the band was, and it just felt the right time for me to do my thing," reckons **Grant**, of his departure from Subhumans. "I enjoyed being in the band, enjoyed doing all the gigs… I was just in a slightly different head space. And being so young, I didn't know how to bring things more around to my way of thinking, so leaving just made more sense to me.

"My last gig was at the Fulham Greyhound. I'd been ruminating and ruminating, and I think I'd said something to Bruce, but not to anyone else, and then I left. But not in a bad way; it was very amicable, because I loved every minute of being in the band. I must have spoken to Bruce and let him know what I was thinking, so he could line Phil up to replace me.

"To tour America is definitely something I would have liked to have done," he ponders, when asked if he picked the best time to bow out, "But I don't regret leaving when I did, because it was the right thing for me to do at that time. I got to crank the bass up until it was probably *too* loud on 'Time Flies' – there's a couple of songs on there where the bass is quite heavy, like 'Word Factory' – and I helped jam up some of the ideas for [second album] 'From the Cradle to the Grave', but left just before they recorded it.

"There's one recording I'd really like to have – we did an ace version of 'Adversity' and 'Rain' at a practice up the youth centre, these really killer, sharp, tight versions, and I'd love to get a copy of that tape. I like the atmosphere and dark edge of those songs, almost alternative rock rather than punk, if you know what I mean?

"After leaving, I went up north and went back to college, doing graphic design. I moved back in with my family, who had moved up there when I was sixteen or seventeen, but I'd stayed down here, dropped out of college and messed all that up, because I was too busy enjoying myself. I bought a little sports car up there, and stripped it down and sprayed it… then brought it back down here when I came back south a few years later. I'm an engineer now, working in construction."

"I'd been hanging out with them all at the youth centre long before I joined on bass," explains **Phil**. "I'd actually designated myself as their roadie, and it does say 'Thanks to

Phil The Roadie' on the back of one of the singles. So I was a self-appointed roadie… just a hanger-on really, getting into gigs free, haha! And then I was jamming around with Bruce all the time, doing the Pagans and stuff, so when Grant left, I'm not sure if I suggested myself or whether Bruce asked me, because we were hanging around a lot at the time doing music anyway.

"Although I wasn't playing bass in the Pagans; I was a guitarist, but thought, 'I'll give that a go!' Only recently did I find out that Bruce just said, 'Phil's going to be the new bassist…' He didn't ask Dick or anything. But thankfully nobody objected. Because I was a big fan – a really big fan. I can remember being sat in my bedroom at my mum's house, listening to the 'Demolition War' EP. I thought it was fantastic – I loved the energy of it – and I used to love watching them play.

"There were always basses hanging around in Bruce's bedroom, so I'd be messing around on them. He had an old Hondo, this Japanese Rickenbacker copy, which was a horrible thing to play. So, I didn't end up using that one, but Wally from A-Heads had a decent bass which he lent me for some practices. Then we heard from Steve Collinson at Pickwick Studios that his mate had a bass for sale over at Wilton, near Salisbury. I took the bus over with Bruce to this guy's little cottage on the A36, liked the bass and bought it.

"That was in 1983, and that's the same one I use now! It's a 1971 Fender Jazz bass, and I paid 175 quid for it. I haven't got very long fingers, and it had a really slim neck, which I found really comfortable to play. It had been mutilated slightly, and had the original bridge pick-up taken out and replaced by a bass Humbucker – possibly a DiMarzio – which looked a bit strange, but gave it quite a unique sound, really punchy. I don't look after it really, I don't polish it or anything like that; it's got years of grime on it. When I bought it, the original finish had been removed and it had been badly varnished, so back in the Eighties it had a natural-wood look which I never really liked. But a few years after we'd split up, I painted it black to punk it up a bit. I just used a can of Halford's car spray paint, haha! And that's how it still is. I had no real reverence for what a brilliant old instrument it is…

"I can't remember what amp I was playing back at the start; it could have been anything! I didn't have any real idea of tone, or how to get a nice sound, and I was probably turning up and using other people's stuff. But eventually I did buy a Marshall 100-watt Super Bass and a 4 x 15" cab, which was huge… has anyone even heard of a 4 x 15 since? It was loud, and really heavy, but didn't even sound that great. My ideal tone – which I always wanted, and still do – is that of Jean-Jacques Burnel from The Stranglers. I love that growly sort of tone, but back then, I didn't really know how to get it. It was a bass – I just used to plug it in! You can hear all the notes on the records though, so it worked alright, but I do go for more of that growly sound these days.

"I'd just finished college and was working at an agricultural engineering place, where Ju worked as well, in the stores – I was just doing odd jobs for them to start with, and they

SUB HUMANS
A HEADS
WAR TOYS

ADMISSION ONLY £1·20
DEAD ROSE
THE XROX

FRIDAY 25th NOVEMBER
COLLINGWOOD HOTEL
VAULTS BAR. ILFRACOMBE

COACH LEAVES TORRI Sq 6·30 BIDE,
TANTONS 6·45 BARN, Royal NORFOLK 7·00
COACH FARE FOR ALL STOPS IS £1·00

Bridgwater Animal Rights Society
PRESENTS!!
THE
SUBHUMANS
spying for britain
No OBLIGATION
AND EXIT 22
AT PURITON VILLAGE HALL
Tickets £1-50 (NR. BRIDGWATER)
AT DOOR
FRIDAY 9th December

LABORATORY ANIMALS
DESPERATELY
NEED YOUR HELP NOW.

ALTERNATIVE MUSIC PRESENTS A NIGHT OF FUN AND FROLICS WITH:

SUB HUMANS
THE A HEADS
ORGANIZED CHAOS

DYING MAN

"REALITY IS WAITING FOR A BUS"

SUNDAY, 11th DEC.

7.30pm
ADMN:
£1·50 members
£1·75 non-members.

Bowes Lyon House
St. Georges Way, Stevenage, Herts.

seperate beer bar - over 18's.

LONDON OXFORD ST. 100 CLUB
BLUURG RECORDS
PRE-XMAS BASH
SUB HUM ANS
A HEADS
Nick Toczek
+ Steve L
NAKED
instigators
[IN NO PARTICULAR ORDER]
THURSDAY 15th
DECEMBER 83 ENTRY £2 BRING AN OBSCURE RELATIVE!

BRIDGWATER, 1983, PHIL - WITH PETE ON SOUND DESK
ANDOVER, 1983 BY RICH PICKETT

TROTSKY, TONY C, JC AND FRED, PIC BY PHIL

offered me a proper job. I was far from any kind of success at Trowbridge college, being infinitely more interested in playing punk gigs and drinking at Peewee's than studying, so I'd half-flunked my exams and didn't know what I was going to do. Anyway, they offered me an apprenticeship as a draftsman, and then the band came up, and straight away they told me there was a gig in Paris and the possibility of an American tour. So I joined the band, knowing full well that touring was on the cards… I was only nineteen, we were all really young.

"When Grant headed up north to Yorkshire, I left home and moved into his old room, downstairs from Pete, in Silver Street, Warminster. I loved living there, playing my bass for hours on end, learning the songs – I knew I had to put in a lot of work to fill Grant's shoes. Being in the centre of town, mates were always popping in; there was lots of drinking and smoking and hanging out on the flat roof with the friendly bikers next door. Good times."

As mentioned in the intro, your author virtually learnt to play bass painstakingly – and painfully! – working out Grant's busy bass lines on the early Subhumans records, and those runs are hardwired into my style now.

"Exactly!" agrees **Phil**. "I did the same, because I ended up learning all those songs to play when I joined, and they really influenced my playing and got engrained in my style. So that influenced stuff I wrote later on. And we were trying to push boundaries with what we wrote, but as time's gone on, I'm equally happy going '1234, 1234…' You know, playing straight chugging stuff rather than being really complicated all the time. And that just reflects how my own personal tastes have gone – I get impatient listening to stuff that's complicated for the sake of being complicated. I'm more into the overall feel of stuff."

"I remember Phil learning really quickly," adds **Bruce**. "He learnt to play the guitar listening to Hendrix. We were at college together, very keen. Phil was very optimistic too… when I say 'optimistic', I mean he was another very jolly kind of guy, like Grant really. Maybe it's a bass player thing? I think I'm a pessimistic guitarist, haha, and Dick was definitely pessimistic at the time. So we needed some sort of balance. Trotsky was always very positive, always laughing, smiling – he's such a funny guy.

"In a way, it's a bit surprising that Phil – and Trotsky – wanted to get involved with a punk rock band really… although the band was going in a slightly non-punk rock direction, as I was getting more and more into prog rock stuff, and some of the stuff Trotsky was into, like Rush. I was really into Alex Lifeson's guitar sound; he does that thing with the chorus, and that's why I got into that chorus guitar sound… well, I use a flanger as a chorus basically. And I got into the echo unit, and things like that, as well. I was actually starting to move away from punk quite a lot; in fact, I'd pretty much stopped listening to punk around about that time."

Phil played his first gig on October 8th, 1983, an auspicious live debut as it was in Paris at the Usine Pali Kao, with Faction, Berurier Noir and D&V in support.

"I also booked that Paris show for Subhumans, and put Faction and D&V on with them," says **Rob**. "It was a memorable weekend; the gig was at the Pali Kao, a legendary squat venue. We had a sparc day hanging out at the promoter's house and drinking cheap French wine. Later on, a handful of us did an interview on air at Radio Libertaire, which was based up on Montmartre. I do not know if we made any sense to the French listeners though, as we were giggling too much…"

"I was used to travelling around with the band, having been in the van with them lots of times before, but it was the first time I'd been abroad with them," reveals **Phil**. "They'd been over to Europe once already, with Grant in the band, but it was all new to me. Faction came over as well, from London – Mel was singing for them at the time. We did what we used to do all the time back then: we arrived early in the afternoon, the day before the gig, I think, and went and bought loads of red wine. None of us could hold our drink anyway, and we got absolutely hammered. When I look back at anything I wrote about those times, the Eighties, it was all about drinking – and we'd do a gig as well! There wasn't any professionalism, or any focus on staying together enough to do the gig… although there must have been to some degree, because we would always play alright – but a lot of drinking went on.

"Anyway, on that first day, we all got really hammered, and quite sick as well, on all this red wine. And we stayed at this flat with these nice people, with steps going downstairs to the basement where we were sleeping. They had a big presentation case on the wall, divided up into hundreds of little compartments, full of all these tiny models and things. There was some chrome handle thing at the top of the stairs, that looked like it was fixed to the wall, after drinking so much anyway – but it wasn't. I put my hand on that, and it was free standing, and I fell down the stairs and knocked the whole lot over. I was in a pile at the bottom of the stairs, with hundreds of things all over the floor! Which was a good start to my time in the band…

"But to be honest, it was a continuity of my behaviour as their roadie as well. I was a pretty useless roadie, and by the end of the night, I was usually pretty drunk. Actually, at one of the earlier gigs – the Westwood festival – we were unloading the gear down the stairs at the youth centre, and I dropped Grant's bass cabinet, and it landed on Pete's head. It was a big 8 x 10 Black Widow bass cab, and it flattened Pete. Pete actually didn't come to the gig because he had such a sore head.

"So yeah, I was a shocking roadie. I was their only roadie in the really early days, and then Pete came on the scene pretty soon after, and I showed him how *not* to do it, haha! He was way more accomplished as a roadie than I ever was.

"Dick was just sober enough to go and do a radio interview that night, and the gig the next day went great, despite us all being hungover. I really enjoyed it, and felt pretty confident doing it. A stand-out moment though was our driver, Tony Carter, who was a real character and used to do impressions, getting up to do a few at the end of our set – of Liberace and Jimmy Hill! Which we all thought was hilarious, but no one in Paris knew or cared about who they were, haha!"

A few days later, between October 10th and 14th, Subhumans were back in Southern with John Loder, recording their second album, 'From the Cradle to the Grave', which was then mixed during December '83, but wouldn't be released until the following spring.

"On 'From the Cradle to the Grave', Bruce was playing bass, because Phil was that new, he hadn't practised it," explains **Dick**. "Grant ironically had been in the process of learning it when he left. Bruce had invented more or less all the music for it, and suggested to Trotsky what beats it should be, and suggested to me where the lyrics should come in… he more or less had the whole thing mapped out in his head."

"Yeah, I was jumping in right at the last minute," confirms **Phil**, "And to my regret – but it was just timing – I didn't have chance to really learn all those songs and get really competent at them. It was all written when I joined, I had nothing to do with any of it. And John Loder was a stickler for quality – he was definitely about getting the best sounding record rather than keeping me happy, that's for sure. Which is why Bruce played the bass on loads of it. It was too much of a rush for me to learn those songs, especially [the epic sixteen-minute title track] 'From the Cradle to the Grave', and *especially* having never played bass before I joined the band. I definitely played bass on 'Adversity' though, and some of the other shorter songs… 'Waste of Breath', perhaps?"

"I don't really know why we didn't just put the recording back a few months until Phil had had chance to learn the songs," admits **Bruce**, "But there you go… it turned out okay! That album was really interesting to record, because it was the first time I'd double-tracked guitars, the first time I used a raw Marshall… and I had a new guitar, so I was using a decent guitar with a Humbucker pick-up in it – but it was in the neck position, so completely wrong really, but I was still learning. If you listen to it, it's not very distorted, it's quite clean. But with the two tracks, it works."

"I can't remember any issues; it was quite a smooth transition," says **Trotsky**, of Phil taking over from Grant on bass. "Grant was a bit more of a simple, straightforward player than Phil, perhaps?

"That was Bruce's nod to prog rock," he then adds, with a chuckle, of the title track. "We recorded it in three parts, rather than one long song, and then joined it together, and in a way, that's how we play it live – by thinking of it as three, or more, shorter songs, just played without stopping. There's so many different bits in it, you kinda have to do it like that."

On November 5th, 1983, not only did Subhumans play their 100th gig, at the High Town Recreation Centre in Luton, with Karma Sutra and Nightmare in support, but their next release, the 'Time Flies… But Aeroplanes Crash' 12", entered the Indie Charts, reaching No. 8.

The opening salvo of two old Stupid Humans songs, 'Get Out of My Way' and 'First Aid', is a perfect way to kick the MLP off, punky to the max, everything sounding tight, powerful and intense. The more mellow 'Word Factory' trundles along on the back of a throbbing, and exceptionally catchy, bass line, before the first of three live tracks, the unnervingly prophetic 'People Are Scared' ('Nobody says anything on buses, and it's not the noise the engine makes – you can watch them all, staring nervous, sit at the back, it's the safest place…') even capturing some spontaneous jamming that perfectly illustrates the band's musicality.

"Well, no one's getting on buses these days [post-COVID] apart from the habitual, and the daring, and the very poor, and then you can't understand what they're saying anyway, as they're covered with face masks," reasons **Dick**. "But that's the way it is in this country, in general – speak when you're spoken to, be polite, and keep yourself to yourself if you don't want to get into trouble. Those are some of the mainstays of how people get brought up in this country. Politeness... and every person is an island... the great British reserve. I spent a lot of time travelling everywhere on buses; it was my means of transport."

Hence one of the tracks on 'From the Cradle to the Grave', 'Reality Is Waiting for a Bus'?

Dick: "Well, that came about following a phone call I had with Dan out of The Apostles, where I had mentioned something about reality, and he had scoffed and said, 'Reality is waiting for a bus!' And I thought that was a fantastic song title and went from there. Because the reality of the way people interact in this country, generally, in the terms of being polite and subservient to elders and all that sort of thing, as observed by the teenager I was, is totally summed up when you're waiting for a bus. You're surrounded by strangers, and nobody is making eye contact, and everyone was in their own world – and this was in the days before people had headphones on, as an excuse to keep themselves to themselves, and everybody was doing the same thing – waiting for this bus. And it occurred to me that the whole structure of society is based on this reliance on something, and the freedom to get really upset when the bus turns up late, or later and later, and you get more and more upset and you want a refund. It's kind of how the system works – it makes you hang there waiting for something you deserve, and makes you feel grateful when you actually do get it, just because it's turned up in the end. It keeps everybody in line.

"This analogy doesn't go too deep... if you analyse it, it falls apart eventually. But it just occurred to me that waiting for buses was a fairly good realistic example of how people get on, and how we are basically subservient to rules, regulations and timetables – the whole structure of compliance."

Then the listener is treated to the first big surprise of the 12", a haunting piano and vocals piece, punctuated by some dramatic guitar chords and telling the tragic tale of the fictitious Susan Strange, before two more raucous live cuts and the ridiculously bouncy – not to mention astute – aforementioned 'sea shanty' singalong, 'Work-Rest-Play-Die'.

"It was a total departure for any punk band, having a piano at the start of the song and then nothing much else, with the piano being the featured instrument," says **Dick**, of 'Susan'. "It was highly unusual, so no one knew what to make of it. I was just paranoid that people would think we were just scraping the barrel and fucking over our crowd because they wouldn't expect this sort of thing, but entirely the opposite happened and 'Work-Rest-Play-Die' and 'Susan' are some of our most requested songs now. Which is interesting. So people *have* got into them."

And the band have even managed to play 'Susan' live in more recent years, which is something they didn't do back in the Eighties.

Dick: "Well, when we can, which is very rarely. There's a chap called Shannon, who's from Preston but moved to LA years ago – *decades* ago, but has maintained his accent, which is nice – and he's very good on keyboards. He will sometimes bring his keyboard to a couple of gigs, and we'll do a quick sound-check to make sure the keys are all balanced in the monitors, and we'll play it. When he learnt it, he even learnt all the mistakes – there are tempo shifts that shouldn't really be there, but it was just played live on Bruce's grandmother's piano, and recorded on one of those old cassette players where you pressed 'play' and 'record' at the same time. It was all very basic. But it's quite extraordinary doing it live, especially in America – I looked down and there were a few punks doing a slow-motion mosh pit, going round in a very slow circle. Strange, innit?"

"I think we [A-Heads] were touring with them the first time they started doing it, which was about 2010," recalls **Jock**. "Shannon started setting up his keyboard, and I was like, 'What's going on here?' 'Oh, we're doing 'Susan'…!' And everyone was like, 'Wow!' The place literally exploded when they played it."

"That song always stood out for me, with Dick's piano work," admits **Kev**. "That was a really stripped-back track, and wasn't aimed at their punk fanbase… but I'm a faux-punk anyway, haha! There was nothing I particularly listened to – I got into the whole rave scene, and that wasn't because of the music; it was all about the people, and I enjoyed the party and the energy of being there. So I'm no expert on punk, but for me, the Subhumans – with their spikey hair punk rock following – playing a song like 'Susan', it was such a different thing to anything else coming from that scene at the time, which is what attracted a lot of people to it."

Indeed – even though it's far from being their most essential release, 'Time Flies… But Aeroplanes Crash' is as eclectic and intriguing as the band's collective musical influences, without ever losing sight of their punky grass roots.

"John [Loder] didn't like it much though," adds **Dick**. "He didn't think it was really our style, and we were a bit iffy about it too, to be honest; it wasn't the best thing we ever did, but certainly one of the most unusual. Not sure why we didn't ask Nick Lant for something for the cover, but we just found a picture of me with the word 'fish' sprayed on my back and thought, 'That'll do!' We were terrible at artwork until Nick came along…"

On December 12th, they played Puriton in Somerset with No Obligation, Spyin' for Brian, Organized Chaos and Exit 22. Shrapnel from Briton Ferry (near Neath, in South Wales) were the opening band that night, and it was the first of ten gigs Subhumans played with Shrapnel, whose second demo, 'Restricted Existence', would be produced by Bruce, and released by Dick through Bluurg.

"We got into punk around 1978 – when we were thirteen," begins Shrapnel guitarist **Paul Summers**, "Because of hearing and reading about bands like The Clash, The Damned, X-Ray Spex, The Fall and Sex Pistols. In early 1980, we saw The Clash on the 16 Tons Tour at Cardiff Sophia Gardens, and inspired by that, and the DIY ethic of bands like Crass and Discharge, we decided to put our own band together, which we did around

1981. After starting Shrapnel, we hooked up with several other local likeminded people – there was a very healthy punk community in South Wales at the time – and got involved in organising gigs locally with the likes of Armistice, Skull Attack, Nux Vomica and The Secluded. We were also involved with a fanzine called 'Smiling Faeces', which was the brainchild of Martin Hoare, a friend of ours whose nickname was 'Slag'."

[Author's sidenote – I corresponded with Slag for several years, and he was a very amusing, artistic character, decorating the envelopes of his frequent letters with daft doodlings. His nickname was 'Slag', and mine was 'Slug', which no doubt raised the eyebrows of the posties dropping off our little missives…]

"Another friend of ours, the legendary Neath punk, Simon Neads, told us about the Subhumans," continues vocalist **Stewart Summers** (Paul's twin brother), "After he'd seen them play a gig at The Camden Musicians Collective in London, with – amongst others – Flux of Pink Indians and Rudimentary Peni. He said we should really check them out because they were great.

"We then went to what I think was their first Welsh gig, at the Central Hotel in Cardiff on September 27th, 1982. The band were brilliant, a cut above a lot of other stuff that was around at the time, so it became a bit of a mission of ours to see them whenever possible, and we started hitching all over the country to go to their gigs."

"They played The Sandfields Youth Centre in Port Talbot a while after the Cardiff gig," recalls **Paul**. "That was organised by a collective of punks from Port Talbot, and was a great line-up with the likes of Disorder, Amebix and the A-Heads also on the bill. There's a picture of original bass player Grant on the back of the 'From the Cradle to the Grave' LP taken outside that gig, as you can see the old BP chemicals plant in the background."

Stew: "Anyway, the first time we actually played with them was at Puriton Village Hall, near Bridgwater, which was where we met Phil, who had recently replaced Grant on bass, for the first time. That was probably the worst gig we did with them too, as it was marred by some aggro. Some of the locals were obviously out looking for a fight; they certainly took a disliking to us Welsh punks, and I remember someone beating somebody up onstage as the Subhumans were playing. We got out of that place pretty sharpish…"

Subhumans rounded off 1983 with another gig in Stevenage, a more local gig in Swindon, with their old pals Smart Pils, and two further London gigs, including their fourth appearance at the 100 Club, with A-Heads, Naked, Instigators and Nick Toczek in support, the band as always supportive of their friends and wider punk rock family.

The ominous Orwellian milestone of 1984 was just weeks away, and it would see the Subhumans unveil their ground-breaking second album and tour America for the first time.

STEW AND PAUL, SHRAPNEL

George Orwell's Thought Police may well have been skulking at the threshold, but not even that could stop the Subhumans railing against Big Brother at the Ludgershall Memorial Hall on January 7th, 1984, their first gig of the year – and their 109th, if anyone's counting (and if you are counting, save yourself the bother and turn to our Gigography appendix…!). AWOL, Organized Chaos, A-Heads and Black Easter were in support, and 150 souls braved the Wiltshire winter to witness that raucous rural spectacle.

A week later, they were in Nottingham at the Colwick Vale Social Club with A-Heads, Naked, Instigators, Scumdribblers, Contempt and the notorious Seats of Piss.

"I think that was with Sic Boy Federation as well," says Instigators guitarist **Mooney**, "And [vocalist] Dead Boy Hendrix stuck the microphone up his ass!"

"You can't get much more punk than that," laughs **Hammy**. "He was a window cleaner – he used to clean the windows at Earache Records! It was the night their drummer threw up on himself, he were that drunk, and just carried on playing. Mind you, I was as drunk as he was, but I didn't throw up…"

Soon after the gig, Bruce was producing the Instigators' first 7" EP, 'The Blood Is on Your Hands', for Dick to release on Bluurg – it came out in May, and made it to No. 21 in the Indies. Despite it being a scintillating slice of tuneful punk, it didn't have the easiest route to your turntables.

"We had to record that first single twice," groans **Hammy**, "The first attempt was fucking shit."

"We drove down to Warminster in my old blue van," recalls (first) Instigators vocalist **Semi**, "One Friday night, and it was absolutely hammering it down. Two of the band were in the back, lying on top of the Marshalls, all the way down to Warminster."

Hammy: "We finished work at half-five, and it were a five-hour drive, and we stopped in Avebury for a pint, in that pub in the stone circle."

Semi: "And I wanted to be home Sunday night, so we needed to leave about one in the afternoon, but we ran over and didn't leave there until about ten – we got home about seven the next morning!"

Hammy: "It was absolutely fucking shite, that recording! We recorded it in Corsham, where the Subhumans recorded, and it was fucking shit."

Mooney: "I remember staying at Bruce's flat. Mel from the A-Heads was there, and Trotsky turned up. They were just getting back from the pub when we arrived. Trotsky got the blow-backs on, and we got fucked. We were getting pissed until well late, then slept on the floor in sleeping bags to get up at nine o'clock to go to the studio."

Semi: "I can remember feeling rough when I had to sing."

Hammy: "That was the worst studio we'd ever been in. I think Dick's still got the recording somewhere… hopefully he's buried it,"

Mooney: "Did they say it wasn't good enough then?"

Hammy: "Yeah, they just said it were shit, and we had to do it again. So we did it

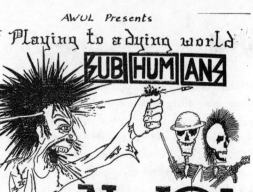

AWOL Presents

Playing to a dying world
SUB HUM ANS

AWOL

A-HEADS + ORGANIZED CHAOS

LUDGERSHALL
MEMORIAL HALL.

SATURDAY,
7th JANUARY. 1984

DOORS OPEN, 7.00 P.M.   COACH ENQUIRES:-
                         ALL
                         ANDOVER. 59093.   ADMISSION. £1.5

SUBHUMANS
ORGANISED CHAOS
SHRAPNEL
NUX VOMICA

AT RAIL AND TRANSPORT CLUB (STATION RD) PORT TALBOT
ON FRIDAY 20th JAN. DOORS OPEN 7PM Admission £1.50

"SQUAT THE LOT" PROMOTIONS PRESENTS:

CANADA'S FINEST PUNK BAND

D.O.A.

SUB HUM ANS
TOXIC SHOCK

SCREAMING
WILD SPREAD. SPANGLES

THURS.
23rd FEB

2 POUNDS
ON THE
DOOR.

ALL PROCEEDS TO GO TO THE VANCOUVER
FIVE DEFENCE FUND AND BRISTOL
PEACE CENTRE (1 PICTON ST. MONTPELIER)

TRINITY HALL OLD MARKET, BRISTOL.

SUB HUM ANS
EXIT-
STANCE
+
CRUX
+
THE RABID DOGS

£1.50

AT THE
RICHMOND
BRIGHTON

DOORS OPEN 8PM
STARTS 8·30 PROMPT

15th MARCH
A CELEBRATION IN HOPE OF PEACE + FREEDOM.

MAKE TEA NOT WAR
PRESENTS

in Woodlands [Wakefield], because we'd used it before, for [the track] 'Old Soldiers'. Marcus [Featherby, from Pax Records – RIP] took us there for [his compilation LP] 'Bollocks to the Gonads'… Mau Maus had been there before us, so we knew it was alright."

Tab: "The Subhumans liked Woodlands so much, they came back up to record something themselves the following year…"

Bruce: "I remember the Instigators all eating granola, and I was like, 'Bloody hell, what's that?' They were like proper vegetarians, and knew what to eat, haha!"

There was another notable gig at the 100 Club on February 21st, where Subhumans were supported by The Sears, Steve L., Smart Pils and Shrapnel. The more astute reader might be able to see the common theme running through the billing.

"Yes, that was a night billed as 'An evening of bands beginning with 'S'," confirms Shrapnel guitarist **Paul**. "That was a cracking gig all round, some great music, plus a member of the Smart Pils sorted out several of our entourage with some top-notch LSD. And in keeping with the 'S' theme of the night, someone shouted out 'Sheep shaggers!' at us before we'd even played a song – fun times indeed."

"I do believe our band *were* on LSD, so I sadly recall very little of the gig," admits **Steve Bemand**, of the Smart Pils. "We were all on a heady mix of drugs. I recall Richard's kick pedal broke away from the bass drum near the beginning, and Merlin – our friend and trusty roadie – sat in front of the full force of the kick drum, and held the ear-splitting unit in place for the bulk of the set! Such loyalty was great, but seemed well above the call of duty…"

"We travelled up in the old ex-delivery van and promptly went the wrong way up Oxford Street," recalls **Kev Tydeman**. "This meant we were treated to the sight of maybe sixty or so punks lined up outside, sitting on the pavement. I remember being quite impressed by this, because normally you got to a gig, it was empty for the first hour, and then gradually filled up. The 100 Club was rammed from the word go. Staff were saying they hadn't seen it that packed for a long time; rumour was going round that there were more in than for a recent 'secret' Rolling Stones gig, but I'm guessing that was just common gig-style bollocks that normally got whispered, as by the end of the night I was told it was since a recent Style Council gig, which was possibly more accurate. Either way, there was sweat running down the walls, a proper 'tropical heat' gig.

"Getting the Subhumans on, Trotsky and I stood on the lip of the stage watching a group of four lads, stripped to the waist, all spiked hair, pouring cooking oil over themselves. This, it turned out, was so they could slip around easier in the mosh pit. I believe people pay good money in certain clubs across the road in Soho to watch that sort of thing, haha! I remind you – we were all quiet kids from the country and not accustomed to such behaviour. However, it was a storming gig; Pete The Roadie and I spent the entire set pulling the monitors back out of the crowd and launching punks off the stage, all in good spirit."

"I always liked The Sears," reveals **Bruce**. "For me, it was more about the musicality of a band, and I liked The Sears because of Corny – she just had this amazing voice. I was a

BRISTOL TRINITY HALL, 23/2/84 BY PAUL 'MO' MAHONEY

SCAMMONDEN DAM, WEST YORKSHIRE, 1984 BY PHIL

HINTON ST. GEORGE - COURTESY OF ANDY NAZER

big fan of Pauline from Penetration, and I think Corny was as well, because she sounded like Pauline a lot of the time; she had a very pure voice. Their guitarist Dave [RIP] had a great sound too… and all the band members were really nice, which always helped.

"I always found Flux's sound a bit disturbing really, because it was so chaotic," he warms to discussing some of the other bands they played with regularly, "And not in a way I could listen to for very long. The Mob were a bit like that too, come to think of it. There were a lot of guitarists that, like me, were taking a long time to find their sound, and they were using all these pedals that were screeching and feeding back all the time. And between songs all you could hear would be this horrible feedback, and it was very chaotic. The Epileptics were the same when I saw them play at Stonehenge… the sound was terrible.

"I had a Copycat tape echo unit," he tries to explain his own guitar sound. "The echo side wasn't great, because it was always getting damaged, and when the top got a bit bent, the tape wouldn't go round properly and stuff like that, but it also boosted the guitar signal before it got to the amp, so it was working as a pre-amp. It was giving a lot of extra gain before the signal reached the amp, which is how I managed to overdrive a Marshall which didn't have a distortion channel – I did that using the output volume on the Copycat.

"I've since learnt that, with the Echoplex in America, which is their rough equivalent of a Copycat, but much more complicated, people liked the pre-amp stage so much that you can now buy a pedal that replicates it – you can buy a pedal with just one knob on it, and all it's got is the pre-amp from the Echoplex in it. And it sounds great!

"But I tried all sorts of distortion pedals and overdrives… I didn't get into the Marshall thing, where I ditched the distortion pedals and just went for overdriving the Marshall, until we did 'Religious Wars', and it sounded much better. The first amp I had – a Sound City amp – just wouldn't overdrive at all, even though it was a valve amp, it was so clean.

"My theory on it now, with guitar at least, is that you need to have an element of inefficiency in the chain. In other words, don't go for a hard plectrum, super quality pick-ups, a really high tech amp and high tech speakers, because it will sound really hard and horrible, as everything is going to be so efficient. So, my pick-ups are a bit saggy, and I've got a pre-amp that boosts it all, and my amp is pretty good, and I've got some speakers that I really like… and I go up and down through the chain, which makes it a bit warmer. Otherwise, it sounds too harsh, or too far the other way, and it sounds all sluggish. You know, Celestion speakers are not that good, but if you do something hot before it, they sound *really* good. That's my latest theory on it anyway, haha!"

March 29th, 1984, was an important date for not just the band but the political protest movement in the UK. It was the date of the second Stop the City demonstration in London (there had been a smaller 'warm-up' one the year before, on September 29th), which sought to draw attention to the ruthless manipulation of poorer countries by the conniving capitalist corporations of the western economies. Members of the Subhumans were in attendance, and their experience not only further politicised them, but directly influenced one of their best-loved and hardest-hitting songs, 'Rats'.

"'Rats' was one of the few songs I wrote about something specific, about an event,"

Dick elaborates. "I've so far managed to avoid naming names of politicians in songs, because they come and go quite quickly and they're all relatively the same. And by not naming them, you avoid dating the song instantly. But 'Rats' was written about the Stop the City marches that were held in the centre of London in 1983 and 1984. They were protests against the exploitation of so-called Third World countries in terms of money and profiteering by the Stock Exchange and the banks, so the protest was held right in the middle of what's called 'The City' of London, which is where all the banks and the stock market are.

"We're talking about thousands of people – a lot of them punk rockers, hippies, alternative types – all turning up, dressed up, making a lot of noise… bells, whistles and drums, that sort of thing. It was an angry party atmosphere, and it was just really refreshing. It was one of the first protests I'd been to that wasn't a CND march, and it felt slightly more relevant, more 'everyday' than a protest for nuclear disarmament. That was a one-subject protest, but this was against the exploitation of people across the world by the people who press all the buttons and control all the money – it was about the very hold that money and profit and greed have got on society in general. It felt more urgent to be there. I went up there on my own, and met up with lots of people. I remember the band Karma Sutra from Luton were there.

"At one point, people were being violently thrust around by the cops, and I overheard one of them say, 'If you act like rats, you'll get treated like this…', which became a line in the song and is the reason the song's called 'Rats', which may not be an obvious name for a song about protesting against capitalism."

When the song was recorded, the band used a sample at the beginning of the actual noise and chanting from the march, which Dick recorded himself.

Dick: "Yeah, I took a little tape recorder with me and just recorded the sounds for a couple of minutes – I like recording things, I've tried to record all sorts! But yeah, I thought that would be good for something, especially the old 'Fight war, not wars' chant. It was a good crack, it felt quite united… it wasn't so much a march as we all just gathered. All the workers were staring out of their office windows several floors above us, and there were just thousands of colourful people chanting against their existence. It felt good."

"The Stop the City marches are something I remember clearly, more for the sense of 'something' happening, the movement now going forward," adds **Kev**, who attended the September '84 Stop the City protests, which coincided with a gig for the Subhumans in London with likeminded anarcho punk bands the night before the demo. "Trotsky and I arrived with Dick and a few others from Brougham Road, but quickly got divided off around Threadneedle Street. I clearly remember thinking this was big, bigger than expected, and the moment everyone sat down in the road to literally stop the city, the ripple of applause and shouting rolling around the streets as a wave of sound was incredible.

"Trotsky and I found ourselves corralled into a small pedestrianised area, with lines of police horses either end, with their backs to us. The whole mood had changed, the horses were slowly walking backwards squeezing the protesters into a smaller 'kettled' area.

STOP THE CITY 1984 BY STEVE COTTON

STOP THE CITY 1984 BY STEVE COTTON

"I remember being quite concerned as horse arses pushed up against us, but there was a sudden scuffle, I saw a police helmet on the floor, and the police line broke; Trotsky and I went running through the gap. This all set the tone for the gig at Dickie Dirt's Warehouse in Coldharbour Lane, with Conflict and Toxic Waste. Against the backdrop of a city in tension, sirens and stragglers from Stop the City, Dickie Dirt's was a large abandoned clothing warehouse. Dark and damp, the mood was serious. It felt like proper protest; boots on the ground had taken place in the capital, and we'd taken part. The Subhumans were definitely more urgent and angry with the set, and the crowd likewise. It was a heavy mood; this was political, this was pushing back, and for someone from a small market town in the country, it seemed significant."

"I'd been to the fourth Stop the City the day before," recalls **Steve Cotton**, then editor of Crisis Point fanzine, and nowadays responsible for the Art of the State website/archive. "The cops were everywhere and I'd been stopped pretty much as soon as I exited the tube station near Bank. A WPC had rifled through my bag and found a fat-tipped marker pen, and said that if I went any further I'd be arrested. So I moved away but then caught up with a group of protesters and joined them – safety in numbers, or so I thought.

"The police were everywhere and driving vans at protestors, and I mean *directly* at protestors, with the intention of skittling a few. We walked around, grouped together and chanted for a while, but nothing like the previous protests was on the cards. I left for home in the end, but I'd been given a flyer for an amazing-looking gig the following night, a benefit for the bust fund for the protestors who had been caught. The gig was in Dickie Dirt's in Brixton – an ex-cinema that was used as a branch of a discount clothing store, before it had been taken over by squatters. Down on the flyer were Subhumans, Conflict, Toxic Waste and Stalag 17… I think it might have even mentioned Chumbawamba too, but I've long since lost it.

"I went to the gig on the back of my mate's new motorbike – he was worried about it being stolen, so ironically, we parked it outside Brixton police station! Inside the gig it was like another world; it felt like something was really happening. I remember during one of the bands, a guy on the left-hand side of the stage playing with a large knife like he was going to slash himself; I was so transfixed, it made it hard to watch the band.

"Like all of those squatted gigs, stage times were pretty fluid, so I went upstairs to have a look around. In amongst the usual stalls of BUAV leaflets, there was a whole raft of Animal Liberation Front material; there was the normal stuff like Supporters Group forms, but also manuals on how to do stuff like make non-electrical incendiary devices that could be used to set fire to fur departments in retailers. Nowadays, just possessing a manual like that could probably land you in jail, but I took one anyway.

"Of course, the Subhumans were amazing – they always are – but there was a different atmosphere. It felt like we were under pressure. For me, it felt like things were closing in and it was getting serious. There was a feeling that you had to be doing something, anything – or you were just getting in the way."

With their second album, 'From the Cradle to the Grave', due to come out whilst they were on tour in the USA, the Subhumans thought they should at least be able to play that epic title track live, so they blagged their way onto a Hagar the Womb gig at the Leeds Bierkeller on April 4th, 1984. A-Heads and Naked were the main supports, but punters who turned up early were treated to the first public airing of Subhumans' said proggy masterpiece.

"We scrounged our way onto it via Nick Toczek," reveals **Dick**. "We just said, 'Can we play *just one* song at the beginning of the gig...?' Ha! We went all the way up there to play the one song too – all because we needed to practise it live before we went to the States..."

"That was the first time I'd heard it, at the Hagar the Womb gig in Leeds," confirms A-Head guitarist **Jock**, "And Mel had to man the echo button for when Dick shouts 'Bastard!' in the middle. We all high-fived each other when she got it right, haha!"

Ruth Elias from Hagar the Womb picks up the story: "The Bierkeller gigs were put on by the 'Legendary' (yes, with a capital 'L') Nick Toczek and Ginger John. Those gigs were always memorable due to the wide variety of bands they attracted from all over the world – we played with Black Flag there the month after! – and for getting us out of the London soup. I can vaguely remember another blistering Subhumans performance, although my fondest memories of those Bierkeller gigs was staying at Nick or John's afterwards, where the party carried on. And when it came time to sleep... well, we have several photos of various Hags and Subhumans wedged into sleeping bags (not together!) on a piece of floor. There was silly behaviour in the morning like jumping on bags when their occupants were still sleeping, or shouting in sleeping ears and running away. I have to say the various Subhumans didn't hold it against us pesky Hags, and we loved them even more for it."

Pete The Roadie: "The first time Subhumans played 'From the Cradle to the Grave' live was in Leeds, and it was a great gig, to maybe 300 people. Then just nine days later we were at the Olympic Auditorium [in LA] with MDC, Red Scare, Tourists and New Regime – with 3000 people or more... it was mental."

However, just the day before the band were about to fly out to the States, the trip was almost jeopardised by an unfortunate brush with the law... over a box of McVitie's Jaffa Cakes.

"After an afternoon of boozing down the pub, me, Pete, Billy and Nigel called into the local Spar shop," explains **Trotsky**. "En route to our next destination, we were stopped by the cops and asked about the theft of a packet of Jaffa Cakes from the Spar. Of course, we denied all knowledge and then refused to give our names and addresses... so they nicked us all! We were hauled into the dungeons of Warminster police station for a couple of hours – with the sound of dripping water, scuttling rats and clinking chains, haha! I explained that they had to let me and Pete go, as we were going to the US the very next day. And they did release us... once we realised a US tour was more important than our ID info. It even made it into the local paper, the Warminster Journal; it was major news in a small town. As for who stole the Jaffas...? It wasn't me, honest guv."

BRUCE AND JELLO BIAFRA, SAN FRANCISCO, 1984 BY PHIL

BRUCE, PETE, DICK, TROTSKY, TROPICANA HOTEL, LOS
ANGELES, APRIL 1984 BY PHIL

"Oh yes, I remember it well," admits **Pete**. "It might have been Bill who nicked them, but I was there. I think it was the shop in Imber Road, which I ended up living above? Anyway, we spent a few hours in Warminster nick, which was a bit worrying – but it all turned out good in the end…. hmmm!"

That first US tour, which ran from April 13th until May 20th, was a very important moment in the band's career, as it ultimately helped set them up for the success they enjoy in the States to this day, but at the time it was just the next adventure for four young musicians having the time of their lives.

"We called it the USAT4 tour, with the 'Anarchy A' in the middle, which looked pretty neat," says **Dick**, of that ground-breaking trip, before explaining how the opportunity arose in the first place. "We were recording 'From the Cradle to the Grave' at Southern, and John got a phone call from Gary Tovar, who ran Goldenvoice, who put on punk shows in several large venues over there; it wasn't on our normal level, it was much bigger than we were used to. Anyway, he wanted to know if the Subhumans could go over there to play some shows for him, and on the back of that John said he'd ask us, and we said yes without thinking – as you would! We'd never flown anywhere… we'd hardly been out of the country. So John got to work on that, and organised the rest of it with different other promoters across the country. I'm not sure who he talked to, but he did all the work and made it happen, and I'm pretty sure the whole thing was financed by doing the West Coast shows for Goldenvoice, and we made our way across more or less the middle of the country to the East Coast, stopping off in strange places like Salt Lake City and Kansas.

"It was like, 'Oh my god!' We couldn't believe it was happening. I think Grant was a bit upset that he left about a month before we got offered it. John was brilliant and sorted out the work permits, such as they were in those days, and he booked the flights and came with us. Well, he didn't do the whole tour, he stayed on the West Coast and Patrick [O' Neil, who you'll meet shortly] drove us the rest of the way.

"We hired the usual cheap van from Petty's Van Hire in Melksham, which being cheap was also dilapidated, and broke down about ten miles out of Warminster, in the middle of nowhere. We were all slightly hung over from drinking the night before, and Pete got out the van and spewed up all this lager and black, so there was purple puke everywhere. I walked down to this solitary house, sheepishly knocked on the door and asked if I could borrow their phone – I rang John up, who was absolutely freaking out, saying 'You have *got* to get to the airport! If you can't get another van, get a *taxi*…'

"Of course, we were like, 'Get a taxi to London? It'll cost hundreds of pounds…!' But Petty came out with another van, and we got ourselves dropped off in London and made our plane. Where we were happy to find out we could smoke at the back, so we all lit up, and there were free drinks, so we all had them. And we were soon totally pissed up, but it was all new, and we'd never been on an aeroplane before.

"I lost my watch in the toilet. I think I took it off to wash my hands for some reason, and left it there, so I drew a picture of a watch on my wrist, and it said 'Time to say cheese'

GOLDENVOICE presents

SUB HUM ANS

FRIDAY the 13TH!

OLYMPIC AUDITORIUM

backstage pass

SUB HUM ANS

Live Export tour

USAT4

LOS ANGELES, 1984 BY HAVIE MARTINEZ

LOS ANGELES, 1984 BY HAVIE MARTINEZ

in the little circle. Every time someone asked me what time it was, I'd say, 'Cheese!'

"We got through customs when we arrived, and we were completely knackered and drunk, and then we got taken to this hotel – we had never stayed in a hotel before, and certainly never seen a hotel with a *swimming pool*. We had never seen palm trees before, had never eaten pizza before… nor chilli flakes – which was fantastic! Whoah, chilli flakes on a pizza seemed like total heaven, which may seem daft to people reading this now, but just imagine living a life where there was no pizza, to suddenly discover that there was such a thing… toasted bread, with all these tasty things on top, and hot melty cheese on top of that… and then add chillis on top, with all the fire and wakefulness they bring to the chemicals in your head – fantastic!

"Massive streets, massive cars, everything was huge, everything was lit up all the time, no one went to sleep, everything was noisy, people were shouting in the street at 2 am… so it was all brand new.

"We went for a meal with Tim Yohannon from Maximum Rocknroll, and [Dead Kennedys vocalist] Jello Biafra was there, and Ruth Schwartz [from Mordam Records] was there… maybe Martin Sprouse [also MRR] as well. We went to a Chinese restaurant, with the big round table that turned in the middle, and none of us had ever eaten like that before. We were a bit gobsmacked… culture shocked really."

"My first impression when we got to America was basically, 'Wow, it's just like it is in the films…!'" laughs **Trotsky** (Trotsky laughs *a lot*). "It was exactly like 'The Streets of San Francisco', which I suppose it would have been – because it *was* San Francisco! But it was surreal for us, like landing on a different planet. The whole vibe at gigs was so… intense, compared to doing gigs in England… people were so much more into the vibe of it all, rather than just going out to get pissed on scrumpy cider. The whole atmosphere was totally different, and quite intimidating, I suppose, for four boys from the West Country, haha!

"We were travelling in a car with Patrick O'Neil, who was a nice fellow… it was quite bizarre to later discover he was a bank robber! I remember we played with a band called Red Scare, and they wanted to charge us for using their drums… which we thought was a bit arsey. It didn't seem very punk to us – they looked very punk though. I think that gig got broken up by the cops anyway.

"I remember playing with Blast 'cos they had this huge chrome drum kit… I tend to remember drum kits more than anything else…"

"It was mind-blowing really," concedes **Phil**. "I'd never flown before, and I don't think I was the only one. But then I'd never been abroad or anything before I joined Subhumans. John Loder came with us as self-appointed manager, and we'd never had a manager before either, but he'd arranged it all through Goldenvoice over there. They were putting on a few big shows, which were financing the rest of the tour basically, and they were doing that for a few UK bands at the time, which was great. Without that support, those bands would never have made it over to the States. And that sowed the seeds for our later years, giving us this – speech marks! – 'legendary' status, which we are forever grateful for.

"We stayed at the Tropicana Motel when we arrived, and we didn't know it at the time, but that's like a legendary rock 'n' roll haunt, which all seemed very glamourous to us because it had a swimming pool and everything. It all seemed amazing at the time."

Pete: "It was hot, big and America – fuckin' fantastic."

"In my diary, I put stuff like, 'Wow, you can drink as much coffee as you want, and they keep refilling it!'" continues **Phil**. "We'd been watching 'Starsky & Hutch' and all this American TV in the UK, so were kinda familiar with the aesthetic of it, but going there and seeing it, especially back then, was pretty crazy. There were all these huge gas-guzzler cars everywhere, and it looked like something out of the movies or off TV. You go there now, and everyone is driving a Nissan or whatever, and it's lost a lot of its character. But staying at the Tropicana, it felt like we were on a movie set, which I think John might have done deliberately, just to give us a kick.

"The first gig was at the Olympic, and there was 3000 people there or something, and I was just standing at the back, thinking, 'Wow! I was working at John Wallis Titt in Warminster a few months ago, and we practise in a cow shed in Longbridge Deverill – and here we are in LA, headlining in front of 3000 people…!' It was completely mind-blowing. I actually really enjoyed it, although Bruce was a bit stressed out. Everyone was in a different head space when they arrived there, and everyone handled it in different ways, but personally I enjoyed the buzz of playing it myself. It was completely crazy – I'd never seen anyone stagedive before, I'd never seen a circle pit, or anything like that. And unlike our scrawny English punks back home, a lot of these were high school jocks who'd been working out and surfing and skateboarding in the Californian sun, smacking each other in the face… it was sensory overload.

"We didn't know a lot about the rules over there. We got given a couple of cases of Budweiser, which we thought was piss after English beer, and I went outside the venue, and opened my beer up and started drinking it, right in front of the police – not knowing it was illegal to drink on the street. And this huge cop came over, pulled the can out of my hand and says, 'You've sure got some balls, son!' I was like, 'What? I'm from England!' And he said something like, 'Well, you're in America now…' and poured the cans down the drain! The police there had a real reputation for violence, especially at that venue, so everyone was amazed I didn't get totally mashed by the cops. I was really lucky… it was probably my English charm. [laughs] Flipside fanzine were there, and they filmed the show, and did an interview backstage; it's all on YouTube, which is nice, as I've never been any good at keeping records, and it's great to see that."

"We flew out Thursday 12th, and the first gig was the 13th, the next day, at the Olympic Auditorium," explains **Dick**. "We drove the van *into* the venue, it was that big, and you parked in front of the stage. The venue was usually set up for wrestling matches, it was huge, the capacity was like 3000. It was so big, it blew our minds a bit – I mean, we managed, but I was hanging onto that mic stand like it was my root to reality. Everyone was going nuts… more nuts than we'd ever seen a crowd go before. There were also more bouncers than anywhere else, ever, both on and offstage.

"Although I don't remember any mass outbursts of violence during that first US tour,

LOS ANGELES, 1984 BY HAVIE MARTINEZ

TROTSKY - OLYMPIC AUDITORIUM, LOS ANGELES
AND SAN FRANCISCO, 1984 BY PHIL

MARTIN SPROUSE AND JOHN LODER, SAN FRANCISCO, APRIL 1984

there was lots of macho behaviour and posturing and whatnot, because there was just a lot of that everywhere in those days. But because we didn't sing about things from a 'street level', we maybe didn't attract people who thought having a fight was part of a good night out… and thank fuck for that.

"We stayed a lot of the time in the backstage room, having a drink and feeling fairly isolated from this huge event stuff that was going on, until it was time to play. I've seen clips of it, and it was pretty much an average Subhumans gig in terms of performance – we didn't play especially better because of the size of the crowd, and we didn't play especially worse because we were nervous or anything. It was a pretty big stage; we only took up about a third of it… we didn't want to be too spaced out from each other, so we stayed roughly in the middle. And there were rows and rows of seats, as well as this big floor space, so there were people going all the way to the back – it was pretty insane, so you didn't think about the insane bits and just concentrated on playing the songs. And trying to avoid the bodies that were constantly flying past you into the crowd.

"Then I had my jacket nicked, which I was really upset about. I'd taken it off and left it by the drums halfway through the set, and someone nicked it. But Maximum Rocknroll put out a message on the radio, saying the jacket had been nicked, and asked if whoever had it would return it to a gig a couple of days later, and a bunch of about ten skinheads came up to our van when we were parked outside this gig with the jacket, saying that they'd got it back, but I later found out it was probably one of those ten that had nicked it in the first place. They'd taken a couple of chains off it, but at least I got it back…

"Perkin's Palace was another one, in Pasadena, almost as big as the LA gig, which we later realised was used in the 'Spinal Tap' film. The routing was a bit crazy – we went all the way to Denver with Patrick, and then we came back to San Francisco for a gig three days later… then we had a day off and were hanging out with Jello, who took us to a beach and this very large, ornate cemetery – he drove us about, talking almost non-stop about local politics – he really impressed us with his knowledge and memory, he seemed to know everything about the local scene and US politics, and he talked *a lot* – we felt fairly inferior when it came to knowing stuff!

"America in general was more brightness, more volume, more size, more density, more intensity… everything was bigger. We just weren't used to it, and we stood out because of our accents, and, as we drove across the country and got out of the major cities, because of what we looked like, we had a lot of 'Where you guys from?' when we hit the rural areas. And Pete – with his foot-long Mohican – was getting photographed left, right and centre… a lot of people had just never seen anything like it.

"We played a fire station in Harrisburg with TSOL. There was no stage, and only twenty people turned up, but we were surrounded by fire engines… it was a totally memorable gig because it was so unusual; we were playing in a *fire station* – it wasn't a venue at all. We had a spate of gigs with TSOL… they had a lot of bandanas going on… in fact, Bruce had a bandana at that point – it was a bit of a bandana phase."

"We started with that huge gig, then we went up the coast to San Francisco with MDC, who were instantly a really friendly bunch," recalls **Phil**. "John knew Jello and the

Kennedys and stuff, so we met up with them. John hooked us up with Patrick O'Neil, who had been a road manager for the Kennedys, so he was going to tour-manage us... we didn't know at that point he was a heroin user. We were still young kids on that tour, none of us were even old enough to drink legally in the States. We didn't have a van; we had this thing called a Dodge Caravan, with a roof box on top, and we were borrowing a lot of the gear as we went. And we headed off cross-country, playing smaller club shows after the massive LA gig... but it was still a few hundred people every gig.

"And it's amazing how quickly the unknown becomes familiar. After about four days, we had the hang of it all. It's an amazing country to travel across. None of us had driving licences, but Patrick's legs got fucked up and he wasn't in a good way physically, so he was like, 'You guys have got to drive... have any of you driven before?' So I said I'd worked on a farm and could drive a tractor, and I'd driven the Dodgems at the fair, haha! And we all took a turn – we drove hundreds, maybe thousands of miles, between us – illegally! – because we had to get to these gigs. And luckily, we never got stopped... at least not while we were driving. I remember driving 100 mph through Utah, along a dead straight road that stretched as far as the eye could see. We did get stopped once with Patrick behind the wheel, and there were loads of drugs in the car, but the police didn't search it – which is just as well, because that would have definitely cut things short!

"And TSOL were a great bunch, fantastic musicians... we really enjoyed being around those guys. They were really professional, and we were picking up on a lot of that from playing with these serious bands, and it was probably about that time that *we* started to take it more seriously too. I'm sure it rubbed off on us, and we started to take a bit of pride in what we were doing... you don't want to look shit compared to another band, do you? Especially when you're the touring headliners! Personally, I was impressed by the professionalism and how tight those bands were."

"Yes, the standard of musicianship was fucking mind-blowing," agrees **Trotsky**. "Coming from England, where a lot of people couldn't play very well – and that's not a criticism, because at least they were getting out there and doing it – but going to America and playing with all these bands who were just on a different level, that taught us a lot. It certainly taught me a lot about playing, and not to be afraid about being technical. There was always a bit of pressure not to be too fucking clever because 'it wasn't punk', and that's just a dead end, y'know? Some of those American bands were much more adventurous... and they all had better gear as well, haha! Did they have more money than us, do you think?"

"I grew up in a dysfunctional and at times chaotic household," reveals **Patrick O'Neil**, as to how he ended up tour-managing Subhumans. "My parents were intellectuals and self-absorbed narcissists; my mother a liberal social worker, my father a Marxist professor of linguistics. There was always music playing in our house, but it was folk music Bob Dylan, Odetta, and Joan Baez. I was listening to The Rolling Stones, Humble Pie, Steppenwolf, and Ten Years After. Because of my father wanting to learn and study languages, we lived all over the place, moving every year: Iceland, Faroe

SUNDAY APRIL 15th

FROM THE U.K.

SUBHUMANS

MIA

SPECIAL GUESTS

ALL AGES

WITH "TRIAL" AND SATYAGRAHA

$4.50 ADVANCE $6 DOOR

TICKETS

3747 W. PACIFIC AVE.

TOWER (WATT AVE. and BROADWAY stores)
AFTERMATH RECORDS
THE BEAT RECORDS
ESOTERIC RECORDS
SPIRIT RECORDS
TICKETRON
FOR INFORMATION 453-8503

▼ CLUB MINIMAL

SUBHUMANS

angst • X-TAL

TREASON • MJB

Sleeping Dogs

Ap 24 at the On Broadway

435 Brdw

$3°° @ Door

8:00 PM sharp!!

For further info
398-0800
821-2648

the lake where it all begins

When 'sink or swim' is the choice you get
You cannot swim forever
You need support to keep you alive
US FISH MUST SWIM TOGETHER

FROM THE CRADLE TO THE GRAVE:

SubHumans
ANGST
SLEEPING DOGS
=X-TAL=
MJB
TREASON

APRIL 24
ON BROADWAY
435 BROADWAY
8:00 PM
TUES.
$3.00

FOR MORE INFO CALL 398-0800 OR 821-2648

littlest patients

...US FISH MUST SWIM TOGETHER.....

for Helmköf, who weighed 940 grams when he was born, is being treated at the Cleveland Hospital Intensive Care

LOUD Presents:

SUBHUMANS

LIVE- DIRECT FROM ENGLAND

with

album out soon!

7 SECONDS

starting their summer tour

and

Special Guests

Thurs., April 26
8:00 p.m.
Alumni Lounge-U.N.R.

ADMISSION: $5.00 / $4 w/ASUN id

ALL AGES WELCOME • NO ALCOHOL (sorry!)

may 14

&T.S.O.L from Calif.

+ SPECiAL GUEST

SUB HUMANS

produced by ZABO. INTERNATIONAL LTD.

4177 St. Dennis

CARGO

U.S. TOUR TICKET STUB

1984 U.S. TOUR SHIRT
COURTESY OF PETE THE ROADIE

SUB HUM ANS

MULTI-DEATH CORPORATIONS

Dicks

THE TOURISTS

NEW REGINE   RED SCARE

FRI 13 APRIL

OLYMPIC AUDITORIUM
1801 S. Grand L.A.

PATRICK O'NEIL
U.S. TOUR 1984

Islands, Germany, and in the States, Wisconsin, Oregon, North Carolina, and finally Boston, Massachusetts. I was always that new kid that looked and talked different. Some countries I didn't know the language, parts of America I had the wrong accent. It was the '60s, and I had long hair when the majority of Americans were still sporting crew-cuts and supporting the Vietnam War. Us kids were left to fend for ourselves—we were being raised by nomadic wolves. When I was thirteen, my parents split up… we were living in Boston, and my life got even more chaotic; I was running the streets, doing drugs, and creating mayhem.

"Not so surprisingly, from all that moving and having to fend for myself, I never felt like I belonged anywhere. From an early age, I was always the outcast and never fit in. As a reaction – or maybe survival – I turned to making art. I drew comics and illustrations, and at seventeen I got a scholarship to the San Francisco Art Institute. The year was 1976, and two things happened: punk and heroin. The SF Art Institute was a breeding ground for punk bands like The Avengers, The Mutants and The Readymades, and in the same North Beach neighbourhood were all the clubs, like The Mabuhay Gardens – or 'The Mab', Savoy Tivoli and The Stone. Every night a ton of bands like The Dils, Crime, The Nuns, Negative Trend, VKTMS and DOA – from Canada – were playing. But really it was a Ramones show, with local band Crime opening for them, that really fucking amazed me. The energy was raw and intense, and I knew I'd finally found my tribe and a place where I fit in. The next day, I cut off my long hair and started using more drugs.

"I had friends that were working at clubs. My best friend Chris Grayson was the soundman at The Mab; he later went on to work for Dead Kennedys, TSOL and Red Hot Chili Peppers. He'd put me on the list and I'd get in free every night, then Ike the bartender would slide me free drinks. One night, the promoter Dirk Dirksen was short-handed and needed an extra body working stage for a Flipper show. I got hired. It was anarchy, and I loved it. Not long after that, Microwave, the Dead Kennedy's road manager, hired me on as a roadie for local shows and tours. Then I started working for TSOL and did my first cross-country tour, of the USA and Canada. By the '80s, I'd quit my dismal day job, managing logistics and transportation for these massive conventions around America for some fucked-up pyramid scheme corporation, and started working full-time touring with bands.

"Mike Vraney was the manager for Dead Kennedys, TSOL and Tex and the Horseheads, and he booked tours. John Loder contacted Vraney to book a US tour for a new UK band, Subhumans, and to hire a road manager, someone that knew the United States and had toured. Vraney contacted me and I was hired. It was my first tour as a road manager.

"So, it's funny that you're asking me about being Subhumans' 'roadie/driver', which is what Subhumans always referred to me as – and apparently still do. I don't know if it was an anarcho punk issue, of not wanting to be associated with the business end of the corporate music industry, shit like hiring tour management, but I wasn't their 'roadie' – I was the road *manager* for Subhumans' first American tour. I just happened to be the driver because no one else had a driver's license, or knew how to navigate America, and I didn't carry or set up any gear – because they didn't have any.

"Back then, I'd introduce myself as their 'road manager', and Dick would cringe – he just couldn't deal with that title – and say, 'No, no, he's our driver...' But then drivers don't collect the money at the end of the night, deal with promoters, call ahead to secure the gear, pay all the expenses, keep books, navigate customs and get the band across borders, and rent hotels. It was a long tour though, almost two months, and I just gave up worrying about a job title and let Dick call me a driver, but it still annoyed the hell out of me. Maybe it was ego? But really it was my first tour as a road manager, and I was proud of rising up in the ranks from roadie to running a tour... plus the pay was better!

"They also brought Pete The Roadie along for the tour. Only Subhumans didn't have any gear, other than Phil's bass and Bruce's guitars. We borrowed amps and a drum kit from the other bands. Part of my job was calling ahead and making sure that was all worked out. It says a lot that American punks were not only willing to lend gear, but were stoked to let Subhumans use their gear. As we all know touring is hard on instruments. To have another touring band say, 'Sure, you can use our gear,' was an honour. Not once was this ever a problem.

"Subhumans were *tight*. I was ten years older than all of them, so I got called Uncle Pat. They were vegetarians. Back then I was a meat eater – oddly enough, these days I've been vegetarian for eighteen years, a vegan the last few years. We talked shit, and joked a lot. Fortunately, our political views were spot on... not that I professed to know shit-all about UK politics, other than Thatcher was the female version of America's poor excuse for a president, Ronald Reagan.

"And then there were drugs. I was strung-out on heroin for the majority of my time on the road. Usually, I'd kick my habit right before a tour and then stay somewhat clean off drugs. Yet as the only one that was driving, and gigs in America being so far apart, especially in the western states – averaging about 500 miles a night after playing a show – I'd fall back on doing speed for long drives, and then being a junkie I'd want to come down and score some heroin along the way. I think I kept my drug use secret for the most part – a lot of the bands I worked for didn't know – but I could be wrong. And except for the time we got pulled over in Utah, and I stashed a small zip-lock bag of drugs in the dashboard heater vent in front of Dick, I don't think the subject ever came up. And we never talked about it. There was a lot of drinking, mainly beer, but even then, none of them seemed to have a problem.

"Subhumans were touring for 'From the Cradle to the Grave', which had just been released in the States and was not that well known – yet. However, a good number of people had heard 'The Day the Country Died', and all the earlier EPs. But if you were to judge the audience from all the Subhumans T-shirts and logos on the back of cut-off black denim jackets, there was definitely a buzz. A good logo can get a band recognized – just look at the Misfits, Crass, Dead Kennedys and Black Flag. The word 'Subhumans' broken down into three black rectangles is classic. Add on the screaming skull and mic, and now every punk is a walking billboard supporting your band. I still see a lot of Subhumans gear on a lot of young punks here in LA today.

"Anyway, one of the first shows of the tour was a huge chaotic mess at Perkins Palace

247

DICK WITH TIM YOHANNAN, MRR, SAN FRANCISCO, 1984

PHIL, SAN FRANCISCO, 1984

PETE AND BRUCE, SAN FRANCISCO, 1984

TROTSKY, USA, 1984 BY PHIL

in Pasadena, Los Angeles, with Youth Brigade, MIA and Dr. Know. It was mayhem. LA shows are legendary for massive pits and violence. Dick was upset with the stage crew kicking the shit out of stage divers. It was a tough introduction to America.

"There was an amazing show in a loft in Baltimore. Subhumans were at their peak and it was a small show, all local kids. The opening band had these huge fog machines; the band was called Fear of God, hence the fog. There was endless free beer. I think it's a testament to a real band when they play a killer show in front of a small audience. We'd been on the road for over a month, and the band had played almost every night at bigger clubs with bigger audiences, and here we were in some DIY loft show in some shithole neighbourhood, and Subhumans killed it.

"At a show in Montreal, Subhumans played with TSOL and at the end of the night we all jammed together. I played bass for a ska/reggae song. We all just had fun, and I always wondered if it was an influence on Dick for Citizen Fish?

"There was a night in Salt Lake City where a pimp shot a hooker in the room two or three doors down from us in a scummy motel. I don't think the band even woke up because everyone was so tired. I went outside and saw the cops and ambulances. I went back inside and saw that a bullet had gone through the walls of the bathroom. I cleaned up the mess so the band wouldn't know. America can be violent. But I didn't want the band to stress about it. We were staying in some really bad parts of the cities we played, because we didn't have much money, and when we weren't staying at people's homes, we were in scummy hotels.

"The band got screwed out of playing NYC on their first tour. Vraney was trying to use them as leverage with Chris Williamson at Rock Hotel to get TSOL on the bill, but Williamson didn't want TSOL There was a big argument and instead of just letting Subhumans play their own show, Vraney refused. I didn't know this until later. I was really disappointed that we weren't playing a New York gig – I mean what US tour doesn't play NYC? But Williamson had a grip on hardcore punk shows in New York, and if you didn't work with him a lot of the other smaller promoters wouldn't touch you. I know the band was disappointed as well, but we ended up staying at a friend of mine's place in the Lower East Side, playing all night in his practice studio, drinking beer and eating pizza.

"It was bittersweet when I dropped them off at JFK airport and said goodbye. The tour was over."

The following accounts were written by Patrick for his book *Anarchy at the Circle K: On the Road with Dead Kennedys, TSOL, Flipper, Subhumans… and Heroin,* which was published by Punk Hostage Press in LA. These excerpts were cut from the end version of the book during the final edits, but Patrick has kindly given permission for them to be used here, as they capture some of the behind-the-scenes moments of that first Subhumans US tour, and it would be a shame for these memories to be consigned to the cutting room floor. They are also an insight into the tedium of touring – bands are only onstage for an hour a day, and the rest of the time is spent travelling, eating and sleeping (or if not actually doing the latter two, stressing about *where* and *how* to do them). The life expectancy of a band is often inextricably entwined with how well they manage this endless downtime, when they are forced to co-exist regardless of mood and circumstance.

It's late afternoon. We're in the low rolling hills of the Midwest with long stretches of grassy expanses bordering strips of forest and distant farms. Not quite the used East Coast look to which we're headed, and quite the opposite of the desolate untamed desert and Rocky Mountains we'd been through last week. At some point we have to stop for food and gas. But we're in no hurry. We've two days off, and plenty of time to get to the next show.

Everyone's awake. We're all sort of talking, or just staring out the window, shit you do on endless long drives. Of course, we've all got cigarettes going and the van is full of smoke. I've got the seat pushed all the way back, which is annoying to whoever is behind me. But this affords me to relax and put my right foot up on the dash. I'm sort of scrunched down, my head barely above the window like a lowrider. When I turn to glance at the passing vehicle on my right, I see a muscle car full of jocks. All three of them staring at us, one's even got his mouth wide open in surprise.

I'm always acutely conscious of what our appearance must be like to Americans out here in the middle of nowhere. The circles I live in, this is how we look. Cities like San Francisco, New York, Los Angeles, Chicago, it's no big thing. But then here we are, Bum-Fuck USA, and I'm staring at three all-American kids and they've got their windows down screaming at us. The one in the back seat is almost all the way out of the car, waving his arms and shouting.

"Hey, man!"

"Uncle Pat?" says Pete the Roadie, his two-foot tall Mohawk pressing against the van's ceiling. "Why they yellin' at us?"

I ignore them, and keep driving. Their Camaro swerving dangerously close.

"Pull over!" yells a big corn-fed blonde-haired dude, as he pounds the side of his door with his fist.

What I can see of him he looks huge, probably a football player, or worse a wrestler. These guys are somewhat aggressive, and I'm mentally calculating what my options are if this all goes sour. If we do get run off the road, can I get to the lug wrench under the back seat of the van? Or how I can possibly hurt one of these guys first, just to make a point. I'm thinking if we do get into an altercation, none of the Subhumans are going to do shit, other than getting pummelled to the ground and stomped on.

"Pull over!" screams the driver, and then he holds up two unopened bottles of beer. "Let's party!"

Now this is a different matter altogether. Never one to turn down a free beer, I'm considering it. But still, I don't trust these dudes.

"Go ahead," says Dick. "Stop, suss 'em out, see what they're on about."

"A lager be brilliant right now," says Bruce.

The politeness of English people always floors me. I'm kind of ashamed I'm so mistrustful. But I'm an American. These are my people and I know what they're capable

TIM MYZE PRESENTS

From ENGLAND

SUBHUMANS

RED SCARE

KILLROY

more core in '84

Fairmount Hall
3760 fairmount ave.

upcoming: 5/10 Twisted Roots, Kommolly TX · 5/15 The Cramps · 717 Black Flag · 5/18 Suicidal Tendencies

Friday April 27 8pm

GOLDENVOICE presents

SUB HUM ANS

YOUTH BRIGADE

M.I.A.

DR. KNOW

AND

iconoclast

SATURDAY APRIL 28th

AT PERKINS PALACE

ADV: $6.50 / DOOR: $8.

Dr. George W. Crile, famous vivisectional experimenter, tells in his book, Surgical Shock, of experiments on 148 dogs. "I turned some of them, and set fire to them. I cut others open and poured boiling water into the cavity, held their paws over Bunsen burners, crushed the most sensitive organs of the male dog, and broke every bone in his paw with a mallet, in others, I poked out their eyes with a tool and then scraped the empty socket."

SAT. APRIL 28th GOLDENVOICE PRESENTS AT PERKINS PALACE 129 N. RAYMOND PASADENA!

The ENGLISH

SUBHUMANS

AND

YOUTH BRIGADE

PLUS

M.I.A

AND OF COURSE

DocturKNOW

AND EXTRA BONUS

ICONOCLAST

YEE HAW

$6.50 ADVANCE
$8.00 AT DOOR

available at Ticketron, and these record stores

Zeds · Long Beach · Middle Earth · Downey · Toxic Shock · Pomona · Record Shed · Laguna · Vinyl Fetish · Hollywood · 2nd Time Around · Hollywood
Bionic · Licks West · Gavel · Huntington Beach · Flipr · Anaheim · Newport · Na Na's · Santa Monica · Spider · Gardena · White Sky · Seal Beach
London Exchange · Newport · Moby Disc · Sherman Oaks · Canoga Park · Pasadena · Rhino · Westwood · Claremont · Power Hollywood

THE SUBHUMANS U.K.

A CHURCH PICNIC

GROUND ZERO   LINDBURGH'S BABY

ST. STEVENS AUDITORIUM 2123 CLINTON
1 SHOW All AGES 7:00
MAY 3rd $5.00

CLARK

BRUCE AND DICK, U.S. TOUR 1984

of. Plus, I'm responsible for keeping everyone out of harm's way. I don't really like jocks. I fucking hated them in high school, hate them as much as skinheads, and these guys aren't coming off as much different. So yeah, I've a bit of my own shit to deal with here too.

We pass a highway sign indicating a rest stop. I give the jocks a thumbs up and then point at the oncoming exit. The kid driving guns it and swerves into our lane in front of us. We both take the off ramp and pull over by the restrooms.

"Dude! Where y'all from?" *screams the blonde hair wrestler, as he hands me a beer.*

The other two jocks are grabbing more beers from a cooler in their trunk and passing them around. Now I'm less worried about them, and a little more about the Highway Patrol catching us all drinking. I mention we should perhaps get out of sight of the Interstate, maybe over in the picnic area by the meadow. Pete the Roadie grabs a soccer ball some punks at a club in Denver gave us, and we all head that way.

"What're y'all doin' here?"

"On tour, mate."

"Tour?"

"Playin' shows."

"You guys in a fuckin' band!" *yells the one who was driving.*

The jocks are excited. They appear incapable of just talking calmly, and yell every word that comes out of their mouths. Maybe what I first took as aggression is just them being amped up and normal. It's just how they are.

"Dude, that's fuckin' rad!"

"Who're you, dude?"

"I'm their road…"

"He's our driver."

We start kicking the ball around, out in this lush grassy field. Everyone's running and laughing. One of the jocks tries to take the ball from Bruce, and he deftly sidesteps him and keeps going. There's an odd game of keep the ball away from the jocks, and it's funny to watch these skinny-assed punks rocking the soccer ball in between these huge guys.

I sit down on a picnic table and light another cigarette.

"Where you from, man?" *asks the kid who was driving, as he sits down and hands me another beer.*

"San Francisco? You?"

"Des Moines. That's in Iowa."

"Knew that," *I say.*

"San Francisco like they say it is?"

"Don't know what they say it is?"

"Music, clubs, parties, women, Golden Gate Bridge, cable cars…"

"Ah, yeah, sure."

"Wanna get out there some day."

"You should, man."

"Hey, gimme your number. I get out California way, I'll call ya. You can show me all that cool Frisco shit."

For a second, I'm thinking *fuck this guy, don't want him showing up in SF and calling me. Then I consider what the fuck it'd be like to be stuck in Des Moines. Probably all there was to do is be a jock, drink beer, and drive a Camaro.*

I write my number on a piece of paper and hand it to him. *This guy is never going to show up, so what harm can it do?*

"What's your name, dude?"

"Patrick."

He borrows the pen and writes my name next to the phone number.

"Got a last name?"

"O'Neil."

"You Irish?"

Tired of kicking the ball, everyone's sitting around the picnic table talking shit. The jocks are definitely in awe of these guys. Subhumans don't even notice; they're just smoking cigarettes, drinking beer, bullshitting, and having a good time. The jocks want to know what the band thinks of America and do they like it.

"Bloody huge, mate."

"Food sucks."

"Good looking girls."

I realize I'm witnessing a strange mishmash of conflicting cultures meeting head on. The age difference is only a few years between the two groups, but the knowledge and experience Dick and the rest of the band have is much more worldly than the three Iowans. Once again, I'm grateful for where I live and those around me.

The light changes as the sun heads down into the hills to the west. The beers are gone and we have to get back on the road. We say our goodbyes and pile into the van. The kid who's driving promises he'll call when he gets to California. The Camaro peels out leaving rubber.

"Good blokes."

"Can't play football worth fuck all."

"Beer was brilliant, though."

Here's a typical conversation from the road at a nameless coffee shop in Wyoming.

"Tired of eatin' eggs," says Phil.

Bruce points out the window. "Uncle Pat, couldn't we go over there, get a cheese roll?"

"Over where, McDonald's?"

"Right, instead of eatin' here."

"They've only got burgers, nothing vegetarian, 'cept fries."

"Think they'd make me a cheese roll, if I asked?"

"What the fuck's a cheese roll?"

"Roll, cheese, vegetable bits." Pete the Roadie puts his hands together as if holding a soft ball.

"A cheese sandwich?"

"Right. I guess?"

255

TUES. MAY 8

HBG, PA.

TRUE SOUNDS OF LIBERTY

FROM L.A.

AND FROM ENGLAND

SUBHUMANS

WITH HBG GUESTS TOM TERRIFIC

$6 SIX BUCKS

SHOW STARTS 8 PM

PAXTONIA FIRE HALL

RT 22 (JONESTOWN RD) TO RT 22 INN (TURN RIGHT AT JOHNSON ST.) 2 BLOCKS 125 S. JOHNSON ST.

COMING MAY 20 KRAUT

THE JOCKEY CLUB Presents

LEXINGTON'S $LUMLORDS w/ M.O.T.

MAY 4

MAY 5 OPEN/TBA

MAY 10 england's SUB HUMANS w/ T.S.O.L.

MAY 11 PLAN 9

bpd ose syl tci cpna

MAY 12 GetSmart w/ libertines

MAY 18 OPEN/TBA

MAY 16 VIOLENT FEMMES w/ BPA & libertines

MAY 19 die Kreuzen

MAY 25 from minneapolis P.J. & the TERRORISTS w/ G-SPOT from texas

MAY 26 OPEN/TBA

Look for: Dickies, Faction, Minutemen, Black Flag, Negative Approach, Addicts

633 YORK ST. ONLY 3 MIN. FROM DOWNTOWN VIA CENTRAL BRIDGE

Monday MAY 14 8 PM

ENGLANDS SUBHUMANS

BRING I.D.

TICKETS: $7.00 ADVANCE ONLY DUTCHYS · 1587 · ST. LAURENT UNDERGROUND · 372 · SHERBROOKE WEST

info-288-0578

CARGO 4177 ST. DENIS

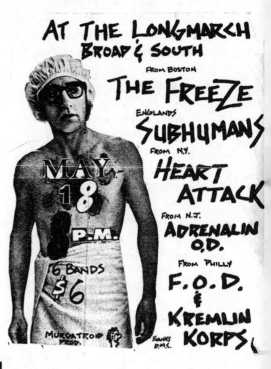

AT THE LONGMARCH BROAD & SOUTH

FROM BOSTON THE FREEZE

ENGLANDS SUBHUMANS

FROM N.Y. HEART ATTACK

FROM N.J. ADRENALIN O.D.

FROM PHILLY F.O.D. & KREMLIN KORPS

MAY 18 P.M.

6 BANDS $6

MUKOATROID PROD.

THANKS D.M.S.

PATRICK O'NEIL

DICK IN MONTREAL, 1984 BY PHIL

"A good veggie roll be brilliant," says Trotsky.

"What the fuck's a veggie roll?"

"Veggie fry up be even more brilliant," says Phil.

"Mushrooms 'n' beans," sighs Dick.

"McDonald's ain't gonna make no cheese roll."

"Think they'd suss it out, if I ask nice." Bruce looks sad. As if McDonald's not wanting to make him a cheese roll is the worst thing imaginable.

"You go over and ask. They gonna tell you to fuck off."

"They'd do it at home." Bruce is convinced I'm always lying or lazy, and is constantly challenging everything I say.

"Dude, we're in fuckin' Wyoming."

"Everywhere we go it's the same food," laments Phil.

"Welcome to middle America, pal."

"Pat, why you eat meat?" Subhumans are all vegetarians. One might even say militant vegetarians.

"Why you call me Pat?"

"What should I call ya?"

"Patrick. My name's fuckin' Patrick."

"Your name's fuckin' Patrick?"

"Pat, what's your surname?"

"What the fuck's a surname?"

"You know, I'm Dick Lucas. Lucas, surname."

"Oh, my last name? O'Neil."

"You Irish?"

"Uncle Pat's Irish." I can't tell if Trotsky likes that I'm Irish, or is just surprised.

"Pat, why you eat meat?"

"I like meat. Tasty shit."

"Not right."

"Not right?"

"Fuckin' starvin', where's our wait staff?" Pete the Roadie is always starving.

"Why you guys all vegetarians?"

"Bloody waste of resources," says Dick.

"What is?"

"Feedin' all that grain to cows."

"Could feed the entire planet instead, leave the poor cows alone," says Trotsky. He's the only one that doesn't berate me for eating meat, and I've occasionally caught him eyeing my cheeseburgers.

"Ain't gonna happen."

"Why not?"

"I'm fuckin' starvin'." After Pete the Roadie, Phil is the next most starving Subhuman.

"Cattlemen and butchers aren't gonna stop selling and killin' cows. Farmer's ain't giving away grain to feed the hungry."

"Want some toast 'n' jam," moans Pete the Roadie.

"Fuckin' hungry," Bruce tosses the menu aside.

"If everyone stopped eatin' meat, they would."

"Ain't gonna happen."

"You boys ready to order?" The waitress, her pen poised on a check pad, gives us a questioning look.

"That'd be brilliant, love."

"What can I getcha?"

"Cheese omelette."

"Yeah, make that two."

"You've a cheese roll?"

"A what, sweetheart?"

"They don't have cheese rolls," I tell Bruce. *"Get a grilled cheese."*

"Just make it an omelette. A cheese one."

"Any chance of fried mushrooms?" asks Dick.

"Y'all from England?"

"Yeah, they're from England," I say.

"Y'all musicians?"

"We're Subhumans."

"Y'all a band?"

"Yeah, they're English, they're a band."

"Martha, get over here." The waitress waves another waitress over to our table. *"I knew y'all was musicians."*

"I'm fuckin' starvin'," groans Phil.

"Where y'all from?"

"The UK."

"What's that?"

"They're from England."

"Who're you?"

"I'm their road man..."

"He's our driver!"

"Y'all the next Beatles?"

"Y'all look more like Rolling Stones."

"Be brilliant if we were Genesis," says Bruce.

"Phil Collins sucks," I say. It's an ongoing argument, especially when we're driving and Bruce wants to control the radio.

"He's fuckin' brilliant."

"So, five cheese omelettes?"

"I'll have the steak and eggs."

"Uncle Pat!"

"Bloody rare, eggs over easy."

"Anything to drink?"

KANSAS, 1984

You paint yor leather jacket
But it comes off in the rain
And the more you cut yor hair
The more it grows again
And the badges you pin on yerself
fall off or start to rust
And the more they take the piss
The less people you can trust

WASTE
OF
BREATH

Wrk
201081

You dont know who you might have been
Or what you now should be
Or what you ought to sloganize
Or why you wanna be free
And then you start to panic
Cos the inspirations there
But yor not sure how to use it
Anyway no-one seems to care

Yor the classic all round failure
Who never seems to win
~~No self respect and that~~ You'd like to write a book about you
But know how to begin
Its the story of yor life
And the end of its yor death
and every word thats inbetween
Is ~~andoo~~ just a waste of breath

'WASTE OF BREATH' - DICK'S ORIGINAL LYRIC SHEET

"Cokes."

"Can I get some coffee?"

"Sure thing, hon."

"How far we got to go, Uncle Pat?" asks Dick.

"It's 'bout hundred and fifty miles to Denver."

"So, what's that?"

"Two, three hours."

"Be hard pressed to drive three hours to a show back home," says Trotsky.

"Three hours? Run right into the bloody sea, mate." Phil laughs, reaching for his Coke.

"Dude, America's fuckin' huge. Takes three days to drive all the way across."

"Ya know Uncle Pat, sometimes I don't believe it. Figure you pull over at night while we sleep, then start driving again right before we wake. Can't be that bloody enormous."

"We've been driving for days," says Trotsky.

"I'm fuckin' starvin'."

"Still got thousands of miles to go."

"Still want a veggie roll."

"Enough with the fucking veggie rolls."

'From the Cradle to the Grave' came out whilst the Subhumans were touring the States, and rapidly climbed to No. 2 in the Indie Charts upon its release on May 12th.

"I think 'Cradle…' has got to be my favourite," reckons **Trotsky**. "I think that's the best one as regards content and general feel, and it was at a really good time, a really good point for the band. Everything was happening, and we were firing on all cylinders…"

They certainly were. It opens with one of the most exuberant instrumental intros you'll ever clap ears on, that instantly commands the listener's attention and segues into the insistent ebb and flow of the high-speed 'Forget' and the choppy laid-back vibe of 'Waste of Breath', which has an irresistibly catchy chorus.

"We call the opening instrumental from 'Cradle…' 'The Horsey Song', because it sounds like the Lone Ranger galloping off into the distance – or something like that," smiles **Dick**, "But we didn't want to actually call it 'The Horsey Song', so we just used the double quaver symbol, or crotchet, or whatever that note's called – well, those two notes joined together. Look it up, folks!

"'Forget' was just a screwed-up teenager's semi-love song… you know, confusion and teenage angst. And 'Waste of Breath' was one of the bounciest songs we ever wrote, but had *the* most nihilistic, pessimistic lyrics… 'your whole life is just a waste of breath!' Jeez! And people jump around and sing along to it. When I wrote it, I didn't think it was that good, because there was no uplift at the end. But then, I was very cynical about a lot of things. A mixture of paranoia and cynicism were my main two emotional states…"

'Where's the Freedom?' is the first hint of the sonic expansion the band was embracing, a lurching stop-starter posing profoundly pertinent questions about the truth of emancipation ('We're going nowhere, in vicious circles we gyrate… we reject the system, but put another in its place…'), although it's swept aside by the frantic attack of 'Reality

Is Waiting for a Bus', Dick's clipped, high-speed vocal delivery perfectly encapsulating the existential crisis at the heart of the lyric.

The band's zany sense of humour then comes to the fore on 'Us Fish Must Swim Together'; what at first appears a daft conceit is actually a heart-warming suggestion as to how modern existence *could* look, if we all might make do with just a little less. Coupled with Bruce's simple rhythmic strumming and a deliciously sing-song melody, its seemingly naïve utopianism is both infectious and genuinely uplifting.

Which is the polar opposite of 'Wake Up Screaming', a fictitious cautionary tale about the dangers of hard drugs built around a brooding Sabbath-like riff that coils ever tighter until it explodes into an eruption of punky unease ('I dream in slow motion, and I wake up screaming'), a sonic psychodrama that lives long in the memory.

"'Wake Up Screaming' is written in the first person, with the word 'I' going all the way through it," muses **Dick**. "There's a few songs like that. And again, that was entirely made up from an imagined point of view... about somebody whose friend died from overdosing on drugs. Imagining how that might feel. Because there was a lot of people trying a lot of different drugs... I hadn't tried many, but it was just like a horror film, an imaginary story, about how that would feel, and the nightmares that would ensue from it."

"We don't do that song very often now, do we?" interjects **Bruce**. "Because it's a slow song – and we don't do many slow songs... there isn't room to do too many slow songs, because it does have the set-dragging effect. But I like it; it's a great song, and it's always good when we *do* do it."

"I had a pet goldfish when I was a teenager," continues **Dick**, on 'Us Fish...', "But the rest was just based on loose theories that fish were colourful, independent, didn't drop nuclear bombs on each other, and were individual, and sort of represented the way we could live... so it was all comic idealism really. Nothing too serious. I didn't eat fish... and I wasn't religious. That's always annoyed me, that the fish symbol, which is basically a fish with a couple of lines through it to make an anarcho fish symbol; people think I nicked it off the Christians, or that I was a Christian. Er, no, read the lyrics... 'No, I don't believe in Jesus Christ...' Remember that bit?

"It winds me up that something representing fish is so attached to Christianity, they almost own it! But they *don't* own it, and I like fish, and that's a good fish symbol. I just generally like fish... it's an easy word, you can't misspell it, and the song 'Us Fish Must Swim Together' put it into words. The catalogue numbers for Bluurg Records went 'Fish 1', 'Fish 2' etc.

"We've got two fish in our pond. I find them fascinating and relaxing to watch, and I don't think it's particularly cruel to keep pet fish. Whether or not they have a memory of three seconds, who knows? Another theory says they have a memory of up to six weeks when it comes to recognising people's faces. But how the fuck does anyone know for sure?"

Bruce: "I started messing about with some classical guitar. On 'Us Fish Must Swim Together', there's a finger-style pattern on it. That's going back to my 'tune a day' classical days when I was nine or ten! Just doing a bit of finger picking really..."

263

OK lets start at the beginning
When fishes roamed the sea
they swam around before anything else
In 10 million years B.C.

Then one day they decided
To evolve into vertebrates
And a few came out of the water
And got drunk to celebrate

Soon, well when I say 'soon' I mean
A coupla million years
They evolved into various quadrupeds
With legs and things and ears

And about a trillion aeons ~~years~~ later
They went all civilised
And ~~built~~ lots of bombs and council flats
that reached into the skies

~~Meanwhile underwater~~
~~The fish didn't care~~
~~As their ancestors were laughed at~~

The moral of this tale ~~till is this~~ you see
~~is we are all~~ descended from the fish
And if we progress much further
We'll end up in the shit

We're starting to destroy ourselves
With pollution war + greed
When ~~all we need~~ food + sex + water
Is all we really need

When sink or swim is the choice you get
~~You cannot~~ swim forever
~~You need support~~ support to keep you alive
Us Fish Must Swim Together!

'US FISH MUST SWIM TOGETHER'
DICK'S ORIGINAL LYRIC SHEET

Hooray
etc
X !
11-8-82
Attik
+
camp
team
!

Diary 1984

databay

BIG JOHN IS WATCHING YOU

DICK'S SKETCH OF JOHN LODER

Side A of the album closes with two more rather downbeat tracks: 'Adversity', a scathing observation on the captivating power of advertising, driven by a powerfully minimalist bass line, and 'Rain', a violently pounding meditation (oxymoron alert!) on depression and obsession, synonymous with a band unafraid to take chances.

And talking of taking chances, whatever possessed them to do a sprawling, complicated sixteen-minute song for the B-side anyway? A true masterpiece, it has to be said, incorporating so many contrasting styles and moods and quirky twists into its ambitiously convoluted arrangement.

"Well, firstly, because I had written it!" laughs **Dick**. "It was written over three days at work in spare moments, from birth to school, I just carried it on through, until the day you die, and the message was – unless you wake yourself up, this is more or less how your life is going to be. You'll be exploited, and told what to do, and you'll obey all the rules… you might join the army, that was one job that was available for everyone, and Warminster was an army town, and there were a lot of squaddies out there who didn't like the punk rockers… it was just a cynical, fairly nihilistic outlook on a life that someone could easily go through, and a lot of people do go through. If not all of it, then bits of it. Especially the schooling bit – 'if you're too intelligent, they'll cut you down to size, they'll praise you 'til you're happy and fill you full of lies…' I think that is the way education works; it stops the brainiest people from excelling too much, and rejects the thickest people until it can't raise them any higher, so their lives are fucked up, because no one cares about those with less 'intelligence', and the ones that have got it are seen as a threat who might challenge the way things are. So everybody has to more or less fit into the middle bit of society, and follow the patterns, if they want to get on. School, university, job, retirement, plus marriage, kids, house ownership, pension… all these things are patterns that you're taught happens in our version of society. Not globally at all, but the western 'white world' version. Which has a major influence on the planet, unfortunately, more than, say, the Amazonian one.

"And it just went on and on, page after page, and I said, 'Look, I've written this song, but it's really, really long…' Bruce got into the idea then, because he had all these ideas that were hanging around that he hadn't used in songs yet, and they were a bit rocky, so they didn't fit in our normal two-and-a-half minute songs. And over a few weeks of practising, we nailed all the bits together and sorted out the structure – it was like doing a very large jigsaw, and it worked out well.

"It was quite an achievement in a way, because no one in the punk world seemed to have done it before, not to that extent anyway…"

"I was really into the 'Relayer' album by Yes," adds **Bruce**, "Which had a twenty-minute song, 'The Gates of Delirium', taking up one whole side of the album, and I wanted to do something like that because I thought it was such a cool thing to do. And Dick had this huge long set of lyrics, which were too good not to do something with – he had this massive song just waiting for music."

Your author remembers being inordinately excited when the band started playing the intro to 'From the Cradle to the Grave' at a gig. I thought, 'They wouldn't dare… would they?' But they did!

"It *is* a long song to put in the set," concedes **Dick**, "And that's usually the reason we don't do it. Well, either that, or we haven't played it for a year, and not everyone is confident they can get all the way to the end! There was one version we did in Salt Lake City that, due to a fairly excessive amount of gin that got drunk…"

Bruce: "By me!"

Dick: "… there were four or five bars that went missing. We got through to the end okay, but a chunk of it got lost somewhere!"

Bruce: "I like doing it. Phil's the sensible one, and he sometimes says, 'If we do it, that's three or four other songs that people won't hear…' And he likes to be kind to the audience…"

Dick: "But when we *do* do it, a lot of people go, 'Oh my god, I can't believe I just heard that! Thanks for playing that for us!' People really like hearing it."

Bruce: "I remember we played it at Rebellion a few years ago, and it was a highlight of the set."

"All their records stand up; it's difficult to find a favourite," reckons **Jock**. "You might skip the odd track here and there, but you'd always go back to them in the end. If pushed though, I think my favourite is 'From the Cradle to the Grave', because of what it is, how long it is… and because Bruce was influenced by The Pretenders halfway through it, haha! When he was drumming for us [i.e. the A-Heads], people would come up to us and say we were starting to sound like Rush, and Mel would say, 'Blame it on Bruce's record collection…'"

"I didn't hear 'From the Cradle to the Grave' when it came out for a few months, because we were so busy with Organized Chaos," says **Bill**. "I was kind of oblivious to the fact they'd released it, but when I heard it, I thought it was incredible. It was the production that blew me away. Our stuff was always rough as hell, some bootleg or something, done in someone's kitchen, and then you listened to that, and it was, 'Wow!'

"But they were always very serious about what they did. Bruce was always like that, even as a teenager. They set a standard, and were an inspiration – if you had a talent, and you could do something like music, you could take your thoughts and message and make everything bigger. Whereas we were more like, 'What will be will be…' And I'm still like that – I'll turn up at a gig with no drum kit, and have to use the house kit… 'Right, let's see what I can get out of that!'"

Unfortunately, what is a truly visionary album, exploding with unfettered creativity, is wrapped in a rather uninspired cover. The album's popularity is certainly based on its musical and lyrical content and not its aesthetic qualities (or lack thereof).

"The cover was described by Seething Wells [i.e. NME writer Steven Wells – RIP] as 'the most boring record cover in the history of record covers…' or something like that," frowns **Dick**, before admitting, "And I didn't like it either. I mean, I couldn't think of a cover for it, and for some reason we didn't ask Nick Lant. We were thinking that a collage would maybe do the trick… armies and death and bombs and nuclear explosions, and all the other stuff that life consisted of according to our rather nihilistic worldview, but

267

Well they take you from your mothers womb
And put you in a school
~~They~~ taught you how to run your life
By ~~using~~ following the rules
They told ~~not~~ you not to pick your nose
Or disrespect the queen
Scrub ~~clean~~ your teeth three times a day
Keep your mind + body clean
~~Empty your soul of all ideas~~
~~So they can~~

Save up all your pocket money
Cos nothing is for free
And you better trust your ~~mum and dad~~ parents
Cos there's no-one else you see
So when they send you off each day
Remember ~~that~~ ~~it's right~~ what you're told
You may think you don't need teaching
But you'll need it when you're old
And if you're too intelligent
They'll cut you down to size
They'll praise you til you're ~~really~~ happy
Then they'll fill you full of lies
Cos intelligence is threatening
And genius is sin
If you could ever see through them
They know they'd never win
So they channel your ability
Into the right direction
If you're ~~rich~~ good enough and ~~nice~~ good enough
You can be a politician
On the other hand if you're too thick
They'll tell you that you're lazy
They'll put you down and wind you up
Until it drives you crazy

Bigotry
radicalism
army
N-Ireland
unemployed
prison
police

jilted to Germany
or maybe N-Ireland

They'll say you ought to learn a trade
To help you ~~in~~ your life
Success is written in 3 parts
A job a house a wife
They'll say that school prepares you ~~on~~
for the ~~coming~~ world outside
Well it certainly gives you bigotry
and a patriotic pride
Racism and sexism
~~the foundation of~~ ~~from father~~ teacher
~~unto class~~
From school to work ~~to~~ remains
Are you white + middle class? the same
You'll learn that ~~bad men~~
~~And good young guys dress in white~~
And good men dress in black
And the patriotic pamphlets
In the playground says that's right

'From the Cradle to the Grave' PARTS 1, 2 & 3
DICK'S ORIGINAL LYRIC SHEET

②

And thats girls were made for ~~anything~~ house-work
And boys were made to fight
And the naughty pictures on page three
Makes everything alright

And so from school to the outside world
These morals you will take
And unless your can ~~refuse~~ reject them
You'll ~~only~~ have your mind at stake

~~They~~'ll give you a decision
When you get to ~~18~~ too
The right to ~~choose~~ vote for someone else
Who says he cares for you

$$\frac{\begin{array}{r}3\,1\\4\end{array}}{12\ 4}$$

10·5·82

who says he cares for you

But the ~~only~~ thing he cares about
Is getting to the top
By conning you with empty words
That promise you a lot

But the end result is slavery
To a false set of ideals
You'll be tempted to believe them
Cos they'll seem so very real

The slavery of attitudes
That make make you keep in line
Subconsciously devoted
To the morals of the time

And when you end up on the dole
Which you very likely will
They'll offer you a brand new trade
learning how to kill
~~They~~ Why don't you join the army?

Be a man + not a fool
There's ~~worth~~ someone else to think for you
He's just like there was at school

They'll promise you isolation
from the murders you'll commit
In the name of god + country
they can get away with it

They'll feed you full of orders
And promise you rewards
like busting up your family
By sending you abroad

A holiday in Germany
or Iceland or Hong Kong
Make money being useless
Well it seems it can't go wrong

← 11·3·82

But then its off to Northern Ireland
Where you'll practise what they preached
You'll shoot to keep yourself alive
And kill to keep the peace

And then it won't be so much fun
~~You shoot~~ As you hear the wounded crying
Cos foreigners can't speak English
So you don't know what they're saying

But when the children call you 'bastard'
~~then it'll be time to at think~~
~~But the~~ You'll
~~With you~~ it'll make you think again
~~That say~~ when you cannot tell the difference
between animals & men

~~Beca~~ animals don't wear uniforms
But they kill as you do you
But ~~it to~~ the army kills for money
And the animals kill for food

Its the basic degradation
In the name of ~~god + count~~ what is right
Become something you never were ~~and~~ different
~~And create the glory~~ ~~to~~ fighting
~~And feel guilty till you feel~~ ~~the~~ ~~not natural to fight~~
Cos your father ~~it~~ will tell your sonny
You must do what you are told
~~having done it~~
And you'll say the same thing to your kids
when you're 82 years old

And unless you can react against
the bullshit from the start
Your government will rule your mind
And your mind will rule your heart

You'll conform to every social law
~~and with~~ And be the systems slave
from birth to school to work to death
from the cradle to the grave

12·3·82

that didn't come to anything. And Bruce came up with the 'baby in the hand' picture, and thought it would be good if the baby was in the hand on the front, and then wasn't in the hand on the back, and then have this field with a few cows in it as the background... and because none of us had anything more concrete than that, we went, 'Okay!'"

Said 'baby photo' was borrowed from Arthur Wragg's 1946 illustrated version of 'The Lord's Prayer'.

"I'm sure we mentioned where it came from on the back of the record," ponders **Bruce**, "But we never asked permission to use it. I hope it's not still under copyright or anything, haha! We were bloody useless when it came to record covers – we were always scratching our heads. And when they said, 'What have you got?', I found this picture by Arthur Wragg in one of my mum's old books. But we're not religious in the slightest, so I'm not sure why we used something from a book called 'The Lord's Prayer'. My mum wasn't religious either, so it might have been my grandmother's, and got passed down to her – it was '2 and 6' [i.e. two shillings and sixpence, the UK currency in the Forties] when they bought it!

"Anyway, Sounds or someone thought it was the worst album cover ever – and it *is* pretty terrible [laughs]... it's got loads of cows on the front!"

"'Kev's pressed on with something', they said, and that 'pressing on' was my interpretation, and getting a photo of the Wessex landscape in," recalls **Kev**, who captured that atmospheric – not to mention, notorious – cow picture, before explaining how he came to be taking it in the first place:

"I got into photography through my father, who was a keen amateur photographer. He'd learned in the army, and he always said it was an easy option out of other tasks, but that kinda backfired when he found himself in Korea in '52, armed with just a small Rolleiflex camera...

"So I was always around cameras, 110 compacts then, at Trowbridge tech, following my father's mistaken footpath, taking photography as an easy option! However, in an era where everything seemed disposable and urgent, it was rare to see someone at gigs and parties with a camera other than a cheap compact. So, I started taking my camera everywhere. Film was cheap, and the alchemy of the darkroom was known to me. I shot constantly and consistently badly, with a few successes in between. And there was a joy in giving prints to everyone, and to documenting the bands coming out of Warminster.

"Anyway, I'd only heard the 'Cradle...' title track played at rehearsals, which by then were over at Trotsky's parents' house, quite literally with the gear set up in the corridor between the front room and kitchen. Was there a discussion about the sixteen-minute title track, and the departure or progression of the sound? I cannot remember. However, awareness of the physical geography of where this sound was coming from – Salisbury Plain and the ever-present army, Avebury, Stonehenge, and that history – all fed into the feeling that wide-open spaces and earthliness should figure. So, I was up at 4 am, tripod in hand, one summer morning; I walked out toward Longbridge Deverill/Five Ash Lane, found a field and waited. Up came the sun, and several badly exposed photos later, the main image was done.

"Pete Roadie and I had tried out a few ideas: a quite literal take on the cradle and the grave, taking some photos in a graveyard over Kingston Deverill, which didn't work, prior to a re-think. The cover ended up a bit of a sprawling mess though, to be honest. A lot of photos, like the walls of Dick's Bluurg office – an almost indecipherable collection of messages, postcards, memos and photos, reminiscent of a stereotypical detective's wall tracking a serial killer in the movies – is lost to lyrics.

"I particularly liked the photo of Pete with a box on his head, with the word 'Reality' written on it, standing at a bus stop – how more literal an interpretation could you have? – but that's now lost to blocked lyrics too.

"When it was released, we were staying with Nick Toczek in Leeds. Steven Wells was also living at Nick's, and told us the cover was the worst pile of shit he'd ever seen. Faint praise indeed, ha! That said, the cover does capture both where the band came from and, I believe, a shift in their musical landscape. As an aside, I've overheard the cover being discussed on more than one occasion, with people hypothesising that the front cover photo could possibly be a nuclear explosion, and the child in hand represents Mother Earth dying and being reborn? Whatever you want it to be, it can be, I guess…?"

Mid-June 1984 saw Subhumans back in Europe for ten days, playing two gigs in Germany and four in Holland.

"I woke up in a panic two days before the tour," recalls **Dick**, "As we'd just found out we had to have a green card for the van that proved it was insured to travel around Euroland, but then John [Loder] phoned up, and said he could include our van on his policy, that was already covering Crass and Conflict, and we could pick the documents up in London on the way to the Dover ferry. I said I'd send him a 'Mental' EP, which he'd been wanting for ages, as a thank you.

"Eddie Van Human overheated four times on the way to London, and we nearly missed the ferry. The thermostat was fucked or something, and it was really hot in the back of the van; sun and heat and drugs and vodka and orange turned from fun silliness to overheated heads and engines. Once we got off at Calais, Kenny was driving around roundabouts the wrong way, and he and Phil in the front were getting wound up because the only map we had was a simplified one from the Sealink [ferry] guide. We were driving around in circles until we ran out of fuel outside a petrol station in Antwerp; it was six in the morning, so we had to wait for them to open, but at least we managed to pick up a map…

"It was a *long* drive to the first gig in Hamburg, and then it took ages to find the youth centre we were playing once we got there. Me, Pete and Trots were outside in the rain, changing clothes and erecting Mohicans and talking to various people, when suddenly there was a massive bang on the side of the van. I thought someone had thrown a rock or a bottle, but there were no rocks or glass lying around, which was weird. Then someone told us it was just a pissed-up heavy metal freak banging his head on the van! The gig went alright, I suppose, despite someone actually throwing a bottle at the stage when we were on – though the guy who did it then gave me a drink a few minutes later.

"We did the Wutzrock Festival on that tour, which was a bit like Westwood really, lots

271

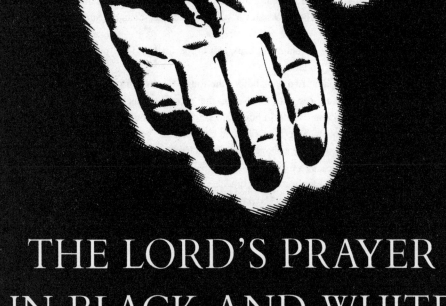

ARTHUR WRAGG'S 1946
ILLUSTRATED VERSION
OF THE LORD'S PRAYER

THE LORD'S PRAYER
IN BLACK AND WHITE

WITH DRAWINGS BY
ARTHUR WRAGG

donderdag 21 juni | donderdag 28 juni

SUB HUMANS (U.K. PUNK) + support

THE ALARM

THREE JOHNS

f 7,50 en lidmaatschap | *f* 10,00 en lidmaatschap

PARADISO

VOORVERKOOP AUB-TICKETSHOP / NWE MUZIEKHANDEL / RAF / BOUDISQUE

SUB HUM ANS

SOUND CITY (ROXY)

WAR TOYS

+ CONTORTED VENGEANCE

PLYmouth

are we nearing

ARMAGEDDON?

NO, But this is the next best thing...

THURSDAY 28th JUNE £1-50

DOORS OPEN 8-30

SUB HUM ANS

CVLT MANIAX

ORGANIZED CHAOS

SELF ABUSE

FRIDAY 13th JULY

£1-50p

WESTBURY YOUTH CLUB

He can't 'go for it'

MAINLINE MUSIC PRESENT

SUB HUM ANS

MASS OF BLACK

AND

SEARS

MONDAY 16TH JULY

£1.50

DUCK & FIRKIN, BOLTON

BRADSHAWGATE

of tents and stuff. There was free beer and food – well, lukewarm rice, but it was food nonetheless – and we had a Germany vs. England football match, which we lost 5–3. We ended up going on first, even though we had initially been told we would be headlining, but it didn't matter really, as it looked like it was going to rain later, and it was nice to get on before the neighbours called the cops about all the noise! Bruce nipped offstage mid-set to have a piss, haha, but the sound was excellent, and the crowd really got into it; it was a good gig in the end."

More UK gigs followed, including Oldham with Mass of Black (whose demos were both released by Bluurg) and The Sears, Bolton with Mass of Black again and Instigators, and the Winton Continental Cinema in Bournemouth with Self Abuse, Atrox and The Mad Are Sane.

"The Winton Continental was known as the local down-at-heel sex flick venue, although they did show other kinds of movies too," laughs **Andy Nazer**, from Self Abuse. "Greg Gwyther from the rock band Surge – later of local glam legends Poze – took it upon himself to book a string of mostly punk gigs there, the first being the previous June with the Cult Maniax, Admass from Weymouth and Self Abuse. Providing the PA system for the Subhumans gig was Andy Roger, who later played keyboards in Self Abuse for a couple of gigs and many years later would go on to join Here and Now. The turnout for the gig was really good, although Dick had to admonish the crowd along the lines of 'Don't wreck the venue or you'll have nowhere for us to play…' as some of them were trying to break seats up during their set, due to the nature of the venue. Luckily nothing too untoward happened, or got broken, as the venue was used again later that summer for a couple more gigs.

"As a band, the Subhumans were – and still are – really nice, friendly guys. Dick's lyrics were thought-provokingly great and the music was, well, off the chart. I always thought of them as kind of an 'anarcho Ruts', musically way ahead of the usual blocky, barre-chord merchants… not that there is owt wrong with that, of course! And it has to be said that the track 'From the Cradle to the Grave' certainly put them in a new light for me when it came out… who else could do a song as epic, rivalling even 'Curtain Call' by The Damned in running time?"

At the end of July, Subhumans returned to Southern Studios for three days to record their fifth EP, 'Rats', which would be released on Bluurg just before the end of the year. They tied in another 100 Club gig whilst they were down in London, with Naked, D & V, Steve L. and Blyth Power in support.

"Yeah, I loved that," says **Phil**, of the 'Rats' session. "I still find it mind-blowing how quickly everything happened, y'know? The Flying Fish Band were sort of noodling around, and suddenly I was in a gigging band, not having played bass before, off to the studio for 'Cradle…', then a gig in Paris, then touring America, and then we were recording the 'Rats' EP. It had only been a matter of months, but I listen back to my playing on that, and I was in the groove already. I felt like a real Subhumans bass player by then.

"[Lead-off track] 'Joe Public' was a song they'd been working on since before I joined, but I was at the youth club when they were practising it, and because I was a Hendrix fan, I remember Bruce asking me how to do the Jimi Hendrix 'Hey Joe' bit in the middle. So I was at their practice as they were writing that one.

"We were really into taping stuff, all the time; we taped everything on this old tape recorder. Bruce had that up in his room, and we'd get drunk and smoke, and then sit around jamming, having a laugh, doing really stupid stuff... but we'd record it as well. They were dubbed 'The Pisshead Tapes', and it was just unfiltered sixteen- and seventeen-year-olds being stupid really. And we carried that over to practises as well, and any ideas would be captured, and we'd listen back to those tapes later on, so stuff stuck around, and got used eventually.

"Then it was just a case of Dick being able to keep up and writing enough lyrics. Over the years, that's always been the thing really. We never had any shortage of tunes or anything, and Dick would get his song books out; the music was never written for a particular Dick song – we'd come up with some music, and he'd find something that fitted to it. As time went on, in the later years, when Dick was writing a lot less, we'd sometimes have the music, and he would write something to fit the song. Or he'd take some bare bones he had and modify them, or whatever. But back then, in the early days, when he was young and prolific – like everyone! – he'd flick through his song books and pick something."

"Phil had played on some of the A-side of 'Cradle...', but 'Rats' was the first record where Phil was really involved in making the songs up," confirms **Dick**. "Although 'Joe Public' and 'When the Bomb Drops' were written when Grant was in the band, so it was half and half. But Phil was well settled in – at the deep end! – by that point.

"We had a chap that John knew called Paul Ellis come in to do the keyboards at the end of the song 'Rats'. I thought the end section would sound really good with keyboards over it, because it sounded to me like Cleopatra entering Rome or something – really grandiose. It wasn't punk rock, but fuck it, it sounded really good. It got *too* grandiose at one point, I seem to remember, and we had to bring it down a bit, and Bruce added layers and layers of feedback and stuff. So, some parts of songs happened in the studio."

After the ambitious 'Cradle...' album, there were clearly no limits to the Subhumans' creativity, at a time when a lot of bands were seemingly scared to step too far outside their chosen/allocated box.

"I'm not sure if that is true or not," counters **Dick**. "I'm not sure they were so much scared to step outside the box as just comfortable inside the box? Or possibly, to be blunt, they just didn't have the ideas that would take them outside the box... all these influences of bands that weren't punk rock in their background like we had. It's a mixture really – plenty of other bands did take it outside the box that was standard punk rock, but others stuck to formulaic punk rock because they really liked it, or they were really good at it... the Ramones did pretty well, and they *really* stuck to their box!"

Trotsky: "When we were recording 'Rats', John Loder, who was engineering, suggested I might find a snare drum hit on a record that we could sample as he didn't like the sound

WESTBURY YOUTH CENTRE BY MARC FREEMAN

BOURNEMOUTH, WINTON CONTINENTAL BY GAVIN BAGSHAW

of mine – a Premier 2000 6½" steel shell. I dutifully trawled my record collection and found a perfect snare hit which could be lifted, from 'Bonzo's Montreux' on the Led Zeppelin album, 'Coda'. So, feeling very pleased, I took it down to Southern for the next session... and John hated it. 'It sounds exactly like yours', he said. Consequently he lifted the snare from 'Let's Dance' by David Bowie, haha!"

Between August 1st and 20th, the Subhumans embarked upon eleven dates around the UK that were rather bizarrely billed as The Exploding Egg Tour, and as usual, it was 'eventful' on more than one occasion.

"It was called 'The Exploding Egg' tour because I had drawn this picture of the Subhumans skull coming out of an egg," explains **Dick**, "Like the skull was being hatched. So I had this picture and thought we could call the tour that, just so we had a name for it really... although I think that was the last time we ever gave a tour a name, haha! 'I've got a name for a tour... we better do one!'"

"I remember some of those dates well, especially the overwhelming feeling of relief at just getting out of Warminster and the generosity of others," says **Kev**. "I watched the film 'Pride' a while back; there is a wonderful scene where the gang of protagonists travel to the small mining town they are supporting, and after a night out, you see them all divided up to stay at various people's houses in the street. That seemed to happen a lot to us. On another occasion, we found ourselves hunkered down in a garden shed... possibly the most uncomfortable night ever? Dick, Phil and I in sleeping bags at the end of the garden, Dick grinding his teeth and talking in his sleep! However, there was still a big old breakfast by 'mum' in the morning, and offers of washing to be done etc.

"That tour saw the Subhumans play Gateshead, a gig that came to be remembered more for the violence witnessed than the music played. How it began...? I'm not sure we were even there at that point; we'd been staying with friends and playing football in the tennis courts most of the day. The venue was in view of the Tyne Bridge, what was probably an old factory or mill at some point. The hall was quite big, up several floors, and accessed by the main stairs or a fire escape off the side of the stage. There was a lot of fighting and people got injured by being hit with metal-framed chairs scattered around the sides. There were bloody footprints across the floor, and a chap I came across in the bathroom was bleeding badly from his face being slashed.

"Fights happen at gigs, but not often at Subhumans ones that we had ever seen. This was something I hadn't really experienced before, and considering we came from a town where squaddies would regularly beat seven shades out of each other and any local stood nearby most Saturday nights, this was something completely different. There was an ambulance outside the building, but they refused to come in, so the injured had to be taken out to them. The atmosphere was pretty heated and confused. However, it was decided to get the band on quickly, to either disperse the crowd earlier or at least quieten them down.

"I remember being crouched at the front of the stage, doing what had now become a nightly ritual, of keeping the monitors on the stage and clearing the diving/dancing punks off the stage in the kindest way possible. This tactic worked and I could feel the tension drain; the crowd were up for it, and it turned into a really good gig in a way, albeit with a nasty undercurrent not welcomed or needed at a punk gig where everyone should be pulling together."

"I was heading to watch the Instigators… actually I did a bit, really good," says **Dick**, in the diary entry he donated to Sned's excellent book on the Gateshead Station, 'From the Garage to the Station and Beyond: Stories from the Gateshead Music Collective 1980 – 1988', which was published by Amorphous Press in 2021. "I went to the bog and a bloke was there, holding his head, dripping with blood. He said a skinhead had done it, and thought it was a knife. Oh fuck! Walking the five yards back to the hall, two others passed me, holding their heads or blood-stained T-shirts – what the fuck? Rumours flew and grew, and in the hall it was slowly nearing Armageddon. The Instigators stopped playing, and the lights came on, to reveal about five people causing 99% of the trouble. One anaemic crophead, two skins, one Mohican and a girl, with one arm in a sling – providing loads of useful excuses for the others to get on the defensive. It got frightening indeed, as the white-haired one started challenging *anyone*, 'one at a time' – don't stare at him! – and scraps were happening all over the place. The Instigators played another two or three more, and I went outside to relay the scene to the others.

"When the Instigators finished, the lights came back on. Meanwhile, I saw Toot [the promoter – RIP] on the stairs giving lectures about violence to some poor bloke who'd been beaten up. Toot was very angry; in the hall, he tried to get the bastards out, and ended up scrapping himself, with the Mohican bloke. Meanwhile *everyone* wanted stardom by yelling things down the mic: half inflammatory and detrimental, half sussed and positive. Now and then, one of the fuckheads got up, trying to justify themselves.

"We had to get the gear sussed out onstage, a long process, which took about fifteen minutes 'cos of everyone on the stage – had to use persuasion and force to get them off. One bloke got well narked 'cos the bloke I was trying to get offstage was his mate – and he was looking for trouble. Violence breeds violence. Being 'Dick of the Subhumans' comes in quite useful at times like this! It was like I was the only person left who could talk to them and keep them calm without getting hit [the ones onstage, that is]. And it seemed the only factor left to unite people was us, and the fact we hadn't yet played. One of the fuckheads actually started off that angle, with chants of 'Subhumans!' all over the place. Tune up and go... but it takes so *long* – Bruce even freaked out at one point down the mic; I rarely see him so wound up. The sound was brilliant and we played like fuck, a really good gig in fact, but for the violence. Rather than lecture, I let the words do the job… 'Can't Hear the Words' reached maximum relevance. The crowd flew about, and there were no other fights. The pigs came round at eleven, so we only played for twenty-five minutes or less. Soaked in sweat, half elated, half at a loss for words.

"Talking to Toot afterwards, we agreed the main problem was the lack of cohesion and unity against such fuckheads. Three hundred people, and less than ten can instigate the destruction of all the good vibes of a gig. It's a terrible state of the human mind, analogical to the arms race and the people who control it. Place cleared, one arrest, packed up. We went back to Newcastle and stayed at Paul's place, No. 41, up four flights of stairs

SUB.HUM.ANS

exploding egg tour

BRISTOL AUGUS-20TH

TRINITY HALL
+ VARUKERS
+ MAU MAUS
+ ORGANIZED CHAOS
+ ONSLAUGHT

AUGUST
1st WOLVERHAMPTON · QUEENS · + SEARS + CONTENT
2nd ROCHDALE · YOUTH CENTRE · + MASS OF BLACK + POTENTIAL VICTIMS
3rd HULL · TRADES + LABOUR CLUB · + CULT MANIAX
4TH GATESHEAD STATION · + INSTIGATORS + FREAK ELECTRIC + FACTION + PHANTOMS OF THE UNDERGROUND
5TH GLASGOW · KELVIN CENTRE · + TOXIC REASONS + LAST RITES
8TH } EITHER — EDINBURGH · STRADA'S · + TOXIC REASONS + LAST RITES
9TH } BOTH
12TH SCARBOROUGH · RUDIES · + SEARS + ?
14TH BRADFORD · PALM COVE · + ?
19TH GLOUCESTER · JAMAICA CLUB · + SEARS + SHRAPNEL
20TH BRISTOL · TRINITY HALL · + VARUKERS + MAUMAUS + ORGANIZED CHAOS + ONSLAUGHT
(MORA GIGS TO BE ADDED)

Scottish International Management Present

THE SUB HUMANS
PLUS
TOXIC REASONS
& LAST RITES

AT THE
KELVIN CENTRE
1073 ARGYLE STREET GLASGOW
Mon 6th Aug
at 7·30
TICKETS £2·00
FROM: VIRGIN RECORDS, GLASGOW
RIPPING RECORDS, EDINBURGH
Bus travel: Nr 169, 42, 44, 57, 64.

MEMBERS NOTICE

THE ATTIK

PRESENTS

SUB HUM ANS

WITH
MASS
OF
BLACK

exploding egg tour

BONSALL ST. HULME
15th WED 8·30 £2=
AUG.
MEMBERSHIP 10P

DAILY MILLION
FORWARD WITH BRITAIN ★

The Curse
of The Rat

SUB HUM ANS

SMART pils

THE
Aheads

STeve L

organised
chaos

£1·50

Trowbridge
court
mills

Sept 14
FRIDAY
7:30 pm

RATS £1
OUT
SEPTEMBER.

Steve Rapport

SUBHUMANS: a well-ordered occasion

'Humans' lib

SUBHUMANS/
D & V
100 Club

THE 100 club is *not* a wonderful place, I'm afraid. Tonight it seemed mainly full of the sort of punks who make you wish that punk *was* dead, all mock meanness and outrage. I mean, heavily studded jackets — really, really frightening, eh?

So it's a strong sign of the communicative powers of D & V that they actually get people to listen to their set, as it defies all the preconceptions punks usually have about support bands. With Andy on drums and Jeff on vocals, they build up a hypnotic and insistent atmosphere which — unbelievably — manages to increase in force through the set with no let-up.

The fact that they convey such a wide range of emotion and subtlety within what should be such a limited framework is a pointer to a real power that should soon blossom into luxuriant and warped flowers. Which is a roundabout way of saying: one of the best concerts of the year!

It seemed a bit strange for the Subhumans to be playing the 100 Club with tickets at £3, since they have shown themselves to be one of the more committed of the new punks. On the plus side, they did manage to slide in 40 punters free. Well done. This time around — tighter after their 300 date US tour? — they gave savage airing to their peculiar brand of Glastonbury punk — more Hawkwind than Sex Pistols — that has given them such a stable position in the damaged brains of thousands of glue sniffers everywhere. Time flies, aeroplanes crash, but the Subhumans keep on hovering. Excellent, in their mutant fashion.

TIBET

THE PRICE IS RIGHT

JUST TO put a few things in perspective about Tibet's review of our gig at the 100 Club a couple of weeks back, mainly the "£3" door price he quoted. Our gigs rarely go above £1.50 and the 100 Club at £2.15 (was) one of the few exceptions. On arriving at the gig we were shown a letter from the owners of the place saying a minimum entry fee of £2.50 had had to be imposed. At such short notice we had no choice but to carry on and make as many people as possible aware of the reasons for such a price (hence this letter). Prices at gigs mean as much to us as Tibet thought they did, and his mention of that one price will have no doubt led to several misconceptions about our attitudes. Prices like that one will never be repeated.

Apart from that, he could have mentioned the other three bands playing, used a photo that was a *bit* more relevant than the Leytonstone gig in '81 and to categorise all punks as 'glue sniffers' with 'damaged brains' is the lowest level of bigoted journalism possible.
— **Subhumans**

25-8-84

in an estate block of flats. Me and Pete stayed up watching 'Young Ones' videos. Tomato soup. Slept on the sofa."

"Another date on that same tour found us in Bathgate, just outside Glasgow," continues **Kev**. "For some reason there was a local beef that suddenly – possibly – involved some Exploited Barmy Army nutters spoiling for a fight with the Subhumans. The upshot of this was quite a tense gig in a small claustrophobic venue that we were all glad to get out of. I remember Bruce and I ducking behind his double guitar case – was that Bruce's Jimmy Page phase? Actually, I can't remember if Bruce ever had a double neck guitar, but the metal flight case one came in was very useful as a makeshift shield as we parted, as there was talk of a knife, and someone outside with a shotgun on their motorbike! Someone had smashed the windows of the van, and we left very quickly.

"Before playing in Glasgow itself, being bored, we all headed down the park and were being stupid, probably playing a game of 'Truce' – which was like 'Tag', only more painful. This is when we first came across the phenomenon of skinheads drinking Buckfast… how very sophisticated. Later that evening, after the set, surrounded by a group of menacing-looking skinheads, one pointed to us and said, 'We sees you all, in the park, playing around like a bunch of knackers, but you's is alright, great gig!' Phew!"

The final gig of The Exploding Egg Tour was at the Bristol Trinity Hall, with Mau Maus, Onslaught and Organized Chaos, and it was unfortunately marred by more trouble.

"Well, I saw the Subhumans quite a lot back in the day, especially at Bath Walcot Hall," recalls **Paul 'Mo' Mahoney**, who was then vocalist of Onslaught. "Sadly though, my memory merges it all into one, so I don't remember too many details, but that Trinity Hall gig was particularly violent, with one girl getting her face opened up by the usual thugs that frequented the gigs there. I think it was actually my first gig as Onslaught's shouter, and we had a knife chucked up onto the stage. I later found out that 'Danny the punk' grabbed it off someone, and was looking for somewhere safer to put it – shame that [Onslaught guitarist] Nige chucked it back! Subhumans were fantastic, of course, but they always were, and always are."

Six more gigs were undertaken in September, three of them in London – including the aforementioned Dickie Dirt's Warehouse gig with Conflict, and yet another date at the 100 Club (they virtually had a residency there in the early Eighties…), this time with The Sears, Legion of Parasites and Wartoys. The band then toured Ireland in early October, with Shrapnel in support (whose 'Restricted Existence' demo Bruce had produced only the month before), *four* of the seven gigs being at the Youth Expression Centre in Dublin.

"That all came about because, by that point, we'd become quite friendly with the band and their roadie Pete, as we'd seen them loads and played a few gigs with them," explains Shrapnel vocalist **Stew**. "We saw they were touring Ireland, and asked if we could also play out there with them. Dick said if we could get out there, we could do the gigs – though I think he was genuinely surprised when we actually turned up, ha! It was a brilliant experience for us; the Irish punks were super friendly and we went down really well in front of the Subhumans' crowd. Being in Belfast at the time was a real experience; the whole city centre was cordoned off at night and the only people around were the punks who were going to the gig. We got stopped and searched by the RUC on several occasions, which was a bit hair-raising for us, but the local punks just took it in their stride. The Subhumans were a pleasure to be on tour with, and we got to see them play a blinder every night; we all certainly knew how to enjoy ourselves and we still occasionally bump into some people on our travels who were at those Irish gigs and they are remembered very fondly."

"Dick was releasing stuff by other bands he knew and liked on Bluurg by that point, and again, as we'd become friendly with the band, he offered to release our demo," continues Shrapnel guitarist **Paul**. "Bruce offered to produce it too, and fair play to him, very kindly came to a studio in Tonypandy, South Wales, with us to do the recording. By 'producing', I mean Bruce made some great suggestions to us about the songs we were recording, which we of course, being stubborn young punk rockers, completely ignored. A fun time was had by all though, and we were completely blown away that he had made the effort to come down to help us out."

"I was born in Surrey, spent my very early childhood in Sunderland and moved to Ireland in 1973, just before my seventh birthday," begins **Peter Jones**, the Paranoid Visions guitarist who booked those Irish dates. "I got into punk pretty much as soon as it hit the Irish shores, although I would have been way too young to go to any gigs and, by the time it hit our mainstream, it was well into 1977 or 1978. By then, the punk bands that we got to hear were already signed to major labels and were on television and in magazines, so to me those bands were equally as unattainable as the likes of Yes were to the punk trailblazers. So, when Crass came along, a band who seemed to be the biggest cult band on the planet – genuinely underground, and offering a true spirit of DIY and alternative music and networking – it spoke to me in volumes. This felt like something I could identify with, and felt like it was *my* scene and *my* bands. I hoovered up the entire scene, buying up everything on Crass and Spiderleg and Corpus Christi – amongst many others – as they appeared, and buying fanzines I would read about in MRR or other fanzines. It was on the back of that that I started conversing with bands in the scene, writing and communicating and buying by mail order from the likes of Xntrix, All the Madmen and many other DIY cassette and vinyl releases. One day I received a letter from Poison Girls' Richard Famous telling me that they were playing in Dublin… I went on my own, aged about fourteen or fifteen at that stage – my first gig – and got to meet Richard before the show. The resultant discussion about how and why he played music was my spark to make a concerted effort to get a band together. A few weeks later, I met Deko, who had a band called Insane Youth, and he told me that they were splitting up and forming a new band, so I joined on guitar there and then… forty years later we are still stubbornly at it!

"As they were one of the Spiderleg bands, I had immediately bought the first few Subhumans singles as and when they came out. Then I saw a review in one of the fanzines I had of an early demo that Subhumans had done – probably 'Demolition War Parts I–III'

DICK BY PAUL MAHONEY

TROTSKY BY TWIG

GATESHEAD - FOOTBALL WITH FACTION AND LOCALS
1984 BY PHIL

WEDNESBURY, 1984, OUTSIDE ONE OF THE SEARS' HOUSES
SEARS BASSIST NICK JARDINE SAT ON THE PAVEMENT

– so I sent off for it, not realising I was buying it from Dick directly. After that we just stayed in touch, and have continued to do so ever since.

"Inspired by Bluurg, we had already done our first three cassettes on our own FOAD label. We were very keen to do a 7" single and thought it would be great to do it with Crass, Corpus Christi or Bluurg, so I asked Dick if we could put the tapes out through him and he agreed. Listening back to those tapes now, I hear the sound of a band with a lot of ambition musically, playing way above our abilities and trying to create a sound that contained elements of all the music we liked. The recording on the first tape was pretty poor, as we were way out of our comfort zone; the second one was inspired by 'Feeding of the 5000' and its 'live in the studio' approach, and sounds a lot more realistic albeit pretty poor audibly, and the third one is still the best. Musically it was quite advanced for a bunch of kids, and the recording quality wasn't bad at all.

"Anyone who has been to Dublin will be aware of the uber trendy Temple Bar area of the city. Back in the early '80s though, any stag parties that ended up there were clearly lost. It was a run-down part of the city, owned by Dublin Bus, who had some sort of long-term plan to turn it into a huge bus station, I think. That meant that the whole area was full of second-hand shops, rough-as-fuck pubs and anyone who wanted a cheap and nasty short-term month-on-month business organisation or art studio. For example, this was the location that the first, and at the time *only*, gay community space was opened, in 1979. A friend of ours, Brendan, was involved in a co-op venture to create the Youth Expression Centre, a space that included a café, rehearsal rooms, martial arts dojo, advice centre and venue. Greg, who was the keyboard player in Paranoid Visions, was asked if we fancied rehearsing there, and two of the other old school punks, Harry and Jody, who were mates of Deko, suggested that we could try to sort a gig there. So, from that seed, I contacted Dick and asked if they fancied playing over here on a Friday and Saturday. He said it sounded great, and contacted the people at Warzone in Belfast. The idea was for them to come over on the Friday, play two nights, head to Belfast and play another two nights, then go home via Dublin again. So, we suggested they played another two gigs on the way back as well. I remember Dick ringing me and saying – and I quote – 'One of the band has accidentally implied to a Welsh band called Shrapnel that they can come and play with us…' I didn't at the time, but I do now, suspect that *he* was the member of the band that promised this, haha! So, Shrapnel came along for the ride too.

"Over those four gigs, literally every punk band in Dublin that we were aware of played. Paranoid Visions – obviously, Vicarious Living – Niall McGuirk's band, who would go on to start the Hope Collective who put on tons of gigs in the '80s and '90s, Systems Agents, Mr Doom and Mrs Gloom, the Roisin Sheerin Dancing Lizardmen, The Golden Horde, and perhaps a couple of others. The latter band did a cover of 'Television Screen' by The Radiators [From Space], which nearly made Dick collapse, as it was one of his favourite punk songs. When it came to the following week, after the Belfast jaunt, it turned out that The Fall were playing the TV Club, a big venue, on the Friday, and we all wanted to go, so we switched the Friday show to Thursday.

"The significant thing about those gigs was that gigs in the UK always seemed to end up with a fight, as did gigs in Dublin for that matter, but here was four nights with an average attendance of about 300, with no security, no bouncers, no bar, no age restrictions, no limit to people bringing their own alcohol and yet… no violence whatsoever. On one of the nights, the police arrived to see what was going on. Brendan was, unlike the rest of the audience, a hippy type, and on this particular night he was mashed out of his mallet on mushrooms, and had put his long hair in a pony tail going down the front of his face and was sporting make-up… which must have looked great to him in the mirror at the time. Anyway, he elected to reason with the police. His argument was solid and it's quite impressive that they accepted it; it went something like this: 'We've got about 300 people in here, they are all absolutely shitfaced, many are underage and everyone is as mad as fuck, but they are having such a good time. Do you really want to ruin the buzz and send them all out into the streets in that state, in an area full of buildings with windows in them?' So, they left us alone, but put a parking ticket on Shrapnel's van as they went past!

"Another significant thing was that, since they were playing four gigs in the one town, they ended up playing literally every single song that the band had, including a few off the 'Worlds Apart' album that hadn't been recorded yet."

"It was a bit mad playing four gigs in the same venue," interjects **Dick**. "At one of them, there was something – we think it was piss – coming out of the toilet that was on the floor above, leaking onto the drum kit in drips… another one I can't remember too much about, because we were drinking the poitín [pronounced 'po-cheen', it's an Irish moonshine] that we had just discovered the existence of, and was very, very strong stuff."

As was often the way with the DIY punk scene back then, a relatively 'big' band coming through your town could often be the catalyst for a slew of bands to form in their wake, and this trip by the Subhumans was no less inspirational.

"It was enormously important for Irish punk," concedes **Peter**. "Effectively it kicked off the DIY scene here, and collated all of the underground bands, and lovers of the underground bands, together in a unity that lasted for decades."

Dick then produced a single for Paranoid Visions that was intended for release on Bluurg, but never happened.

"Yes, not long after all this was going on, we had also hooked up with Blyth Power and All the Madmen," explains **Peter**. "It's all a bit hazy, so forgive me if the timelines are a bit skewed, but from my memory we wanted to do a 7" single and we were hoping to do it on Bluurg. We had been offered the chance to do something on Corpus Christi, but that whole thing was falling apart at that point, I think, and the channels weren't properly followed through. So, we asked Dick if he would help produce the record for us. We organised a gig through Pete The Roadie in Warminster, with The Sears and Bannlyst [from Norway], and then headed to London the following day to record a single in Empire Studios. Dick produced the three tracks for us, and then headed back to Warminster, and a few days later we played with them and Blyth Power in the Fulham Greyhound, a gig promoted by Rob from All the Madmen. I was overawed by the size of the venue, and realised exactly how big Subhumans were by then. In the audience were our friends from Dublin, My Bloody Valentine, who even though they were well on their way to

SUBHUMANS

LIVE AMESBURY SPORTS CENTRE SATURDAY 15TH September

DO EASY + OPERA FOR INFANTRY £1·25

'RATS' EP OUT EARLY OCTOBER BLURG RECORDS FISH 10 // 'STOP THE CITY' LONDON 27TH September

IRENE'S 21ST BIRTHDAY PARTY.

THE **SUBHUMANS** FROM LONDON.

PLUS + TOXIC WASTE

TUES · OCT 9TH 7·30pm.

FERN LODGE DOAGH RD. N'ABBEY

ADM. £1

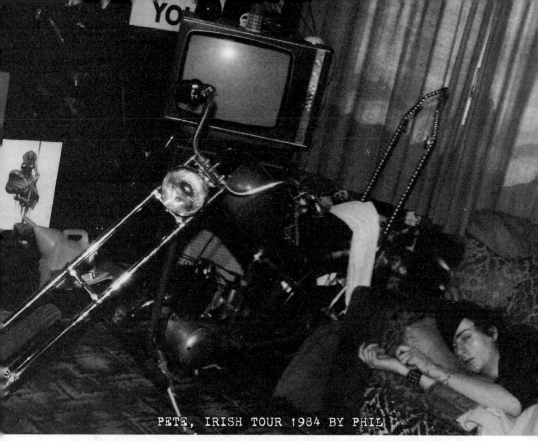

PETE, IRISH TOUR 1984 BY PHIL

**DIRECTIONS - PRE-INTERNET - SENT BY JACK, POTENTIAL
VICTIMS, ROCHDALE YOUTH CENTRE, AUGUST 1984**

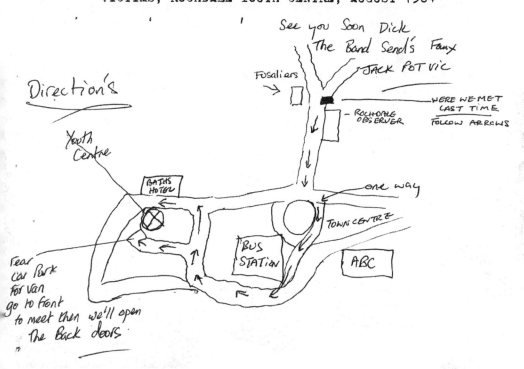

becoming famous, all paid to get in! Following on from the gig, we all agreed that the single needed a remix, but the studio had deleted the files so we couldn't, and Dick also said that he didn't want to release any more singles as they were always losing money. That's when All the Madmen stepped in and agreed to release a 7" if we recorded a new one, which we did."

The week after playing the opening night of Nick Toczek's new venue Adam & Eve's in Leeds on October 17th, with The Sears and Steve L. in support, a Swedish tour ensued, organised through the DIY punk network that was by then in full effect across Europe.

"That was eight gigs… and a bit chilly," deadpans **Dick**. "We took the ferry, which was an overnight trip, and there weren't many people onboard. Me, Pete and Trotsky got very drunk, and there was a Monopoly game onboard to keep people occupied, so we started playing that – and that lasted thirty seconds before it got all covered in beer and thrown around everywhere. I'm not proud of this, haha! I think I fell over into a pot plant?

"The gigs were good, but weren't overly attended. We had 120 in Malmo, 160 in Stockholm, 180 in Norberg… but they felt like sizeable crowds for that time, in that place. That was our usual crowd in 1984, about a hundred people in most places – then we might get 300 in London, or 200 in Bristol. I think it was set up by Per from Charta 77, but he might not have. He definitely did a Citizen Fish and Charta 77 tour a few years later, so maybe I'm basing the thought on that? Inevitably it would have been set up off the back of someone writing to us saying, 'We can set you a few gigs up in Sweden – do you want to come over?' There weren't many phone calls being made to Europe, because they just cost too much… you could barely afford to phone anyone at home, let alone someone over there. So, a lot of things were set up by the gradual exchange of letters. Which meant everything just happened at a slower pace, and it could take several months to set up a tour.

"Anyway, there was a lot of space over there, and a lot of trees and woods. This is going to sound daft now, but a lot of wooden venues… just lots of wood everywhere, haha! And strong drink – proper good beer, none of this rubbish we've got over here. And in Sweden, in the Eighties, if you wanted to buy some booze from the off-licence, it was only open one day a week, on a Friday evening. We went to one once, and there were six people behind the counter, and six queues going all the way to the door where you came in, with over twenty people in each queue. Because that was the one time a week you could buy booze. And it was very expensive… hence there was a whole subculture of brewing your own – a lot of people were drinking homebrew.

"Asta Kask and Charta 77 were very good bands. The crowds were fairly uncertain as to whether they liked us or not, and generally shuffled around, occasionally going a bit mad towards the end of the set. But that would happen almost anywhere really, unless you'd played there a few times before. It's not like now, where you can look people up on YouTube and get into them before you go to the gig and everything. You might have heard a band's records, and read about them in a magazine, but you wouldn't have been able to see them live until you were actually there yourself.

"It's easy to imagine that everyone went wild at all the gigs, but that was far from the case – just at some of them.

"I see we played a song called 'Out of Reach' on that tour, which we'd apparently played three times before, but I couldn't even begin to tell you what that sounded like. I don't even know if there's a recording of it anywhere. Maybe the tune was used for something else?"

After returning to Belfast for a one-off gig with Disorder at the Labour Club, and playing another 100 Club gig with Instigators supporting, Subhumans had their 'Rats' EP released in early December. Entering the Indie Charts on December 8th, 1984, and quickly climbing to No. 2 again (they unfortunately never quite made the coveted No. 1 spot, 'Rats' kept off the Nop of the pile by Depeche Mode's 'Somebody' single), it was arguably their strongest effort to date, powerfully produced and savagely tight. Opener 'Joe Public' was a well-aimed swipe at the only-semi-fictitious Mr Average, clinging to his outdated concepts of patriotism and class stereotypes, the band's furious execution of a rather complex arrangement pretty much flawless. 'Labels' remains one of the band's fastest, most intense tracks, raging at people's obsession with convenient pigeonholing, but they couldn't resist some lightening stop/starts punctuating some tasty bass runs and Bruce's demented soloing, not to mention a light-hearted bouncy breakdown in the middle to counterpoint the relentless speed.

"We never thought to deliberately set ourselves up as any sort of '-ist' or '-ism' band," reckons **Dick**, explaining the lyrical nuances of 'Labels'. "We weren't too keen on being called anarchists because we knew that certain parts of our behaviour made us completely *not* anarchists. Not that we were being complete arseholes or anything, but if Crass were anarchists, which apparently they were, we didn't feel that we were doing the same things they were. We didn't live together in a commune, we didn't all share exactly the same values...

"We didn't mind being bracketed in with Flux and Crass and that, because we were on the same label, and we definitely shared the same attitudes about obvious stuff like the nature of violence, war and animal rights – but we didn't feel we were completely in that bracket... because we also had songs like 'Til the Pigs Come Round', and 'Nothing I Can Do', and 'Peroxide'... there was a whole bunch of songs that were not obviously written by an anarchist band. They were written by a punk band, which is what we were.

"So being a 'punk band' was about the only label we liked having. Although we didn't like labels at all, because it did split people into groups. It gave bands perceptions that they didn't even know they had... people would follow one band because they said this, and they wouldn't follow another band because they didn't say that... and most of the time they were splitting hairs.

"At the time, I blamed Garry Bushell for a lot of that division of the whole scene after the initial wave of the Pistols and The Adverts and the Buzzcocks. Then Crass came along, and more or less at the same time, you had the Toy Dolls, Discharge, The Exploited, Cockney Rejects... who had a very original sound, so were influencing a

SUB HUM ANS FRÅN ENGLAND

EVOLUTION

+ CRUDE S.S.

FEAR OF WAR CHARTA 77

FOLKETS HUS NORBERG

27 OKTOBER KL. 21 30:-

OMEGA TRIBE

SUB HUM ANS

LiMBiC SySTEM

Plus
BEER
BAR
STALL
D.J.

BOWES LYON HOUSE
ST. GEORGES WAY. STEVENAGE. 353175
SUNDAY NOVEMBER 11th 1984

£1·75 members
£2 non members

7·00-
11·00-

discount vouchor!

SAT.
8th DEC.

SUB HUM ANS 40p off

look mummy clowns!

FLOWERS IN
THE DUSTBIN

INTERACTION
15 WILKIN ST., N.W.5
NEAR KENTISH TOWN TUBE OR CHALK FARM TUBE

ADMISSION
£1.30
WITH THIS
CARD.

whole bunch of other bands. And they were tied into the Oi! scene. But to me it was all punk rock. When punk rock started, Wire were a punk band, Eater were a punk band, and you would never see the two bands on the same gig, but they were both punk bands. It was just a general word. Punk rock just meant that it wasn't any of the other commercial stuff. And therefore, it didn't really matter what it sounded like. But then suddenly Garry Bushell in particular took bands' attitudes and confined them to one side of this coin or the other. And the Oi! bands didn't like the Crass bands, and the Crass bands didn't like the Oi! bands, because ironically both sides thought the other side were full of fascists. The Crass bands were 'fascist' because they all wore black and were really hardcore about what you could or couldn't say or do, and the Oi! bands were 'fascist' because they were racist and went around beating people up. Both of those descriptions were archetypal ones, and they fitted for journalistic reasons so they could stir things up. I didn't like that going on at all. They were both completely wrong… well, partially right, I suppose, because on the anarcho side of things, there was a certain self-assuredness that would take a lot of argument to get through, and they *weren't* right all of the time, and on the Oi! side there were a lot of racist skinheads and arseholes that fucked up gigs, and fucked up people's head spaces, just for the sense of camaraderie they claimed they got from it, or unity in the name of nationalism… there was a lot of borderline dodgy stuff going on.

"And that's part of the growing process. But you had bands like The Business, who were straddling both sides – their politics were all about unity, anti-racism, and the music was very street level, and there were plenty of bands like that, but it took a long while to filter through to the consciousness of both sides, for them to realise they were not on either side, if you know what I mean?

"So, there was a lot of labelling going on. And we were just as guilty of labelling bands one way or the other. It was an easy way to divide things up. Because one of life's lessons that you get drummed into you is that you've got to be part of something. And being part of something often included *not* being a part of its opposite thing. The fear of being different is something that is taught to us, and fed to us through the media a lot. And even the people who realise it are affected by it – no one is innocent, but at least realisation of the process going on helps you stop yourself short of becoming a part of it. Stops you making assumptions about people. It's a kind of idealistic way to go about living, but at least it's peaceful and non-violent – even if you're wrong about how nice you think someone might be,'cos some of them turn out to be complete twats anyway! But I'm more into giving people the benefit of the doubt than them being guilty until proven innocent…

"People used to call us 'hippies' – mainly because of Trotsky and his Afghan coat and long hair and Led Zep patch… which was fair enough really. A lot of people thought we were a 'peace punk' band. Some people thought we were crusties, before the term 'crusty' really existed, and other people thought we were in a different bracket altogether. Which was ace, because that's where we wanted to be really – not bracketed. And the diversity of tunes that Bruce has invented kept that 'non-bracketed' situation going, because he was coming up with all sorts of stuff, and he wouldn't often settle for a 4/4 beat throughout the whole song. Sometimes it would go into places where it was really hard to sing over… some bits in 'Cradle…' were really hard to get the words to fit neatly to bars, and the music would change two-thirds of the way through a lyrical line, but it all came together by the end so everyone stopped at the same time. Those things had to be really worked at.

"I went through the lyrics to 'Joe Public' in my head the other day," he continues, "And it's quite a confusing song as to who Joe Public actually is, haha! It's just about this notion that there's a Mr or Mrs Average out there, representing the thoughts of the entire country… it's just wishful thinking, because no such person actually exists. When the papers say, 'The public think this…' and 'The public think that…', they are way off the mark – they're actually saying they *want* the public to be thinking like this! And they can forge some sort of connection with their readers.

"It's the manipulation of the masses into a thought chain. They especially do it during elections. They don't want Labour to win any election, so they portrayed Jeremy Corbyn as an anti-Semite, which couldn't be further from the truth… they portrayed Michael Foot as a doddering old git… they portrayed Kinnock as a loudmouth idiot, y'know? And this mass mind control by the media actually works, which is why they do it. And Murdoch especially – he's up there with whoever is Prime Minister, he pays them an early visit or two, and he lays down the law… 'If you do this, if you do that, then I'll support you…' And consequently 'If you don't, I won't, and then the public won't either, because we're feeding out to them what Joe Public has to think…'

"I've always hated the whole flattening out of individuality into a mass emblem of what people are like, the streamlining of character and personality into this mass blob with apparently the same opinion – which is unfeasible and irrational and just doesn't exist."

And that unfortunately still goes on today, thirty-five years after you wrote the song…

Dick: "Well, this is it. Most things of this ilk that get sung about are sort of aspects of psychology, and national characteristics in this case, and they don't change overnight… they don't change over a few decades. They are just this sordid underbelly that persists, and the whole process of changing anything like that is to keep saying that it does exist, pointing out that it's actually there, because information – and communication of that information – is the only way to make people realise. And realisation is the only way to make any real change in people's attitudes – towards each other, but initially towards themselves, towards what they've been thinking, what they've been taught… what's right, what's wrong, what's outdated. From there to how they look at other people – are they really as bad as they seem, or are they just misinformed? It's labelled idealistic, but it's also pretty practical as well, because you can't just get up and say, 'Right, I'm taking over this newspaper!' Because that ain't gonna happen. You can't say, 'Right, I want the whole city, town, village, street, whatever, to vote this way…', but you can pop around and have a chat with your neighbour and see what they think. And if they think diametrically opposite to you, the least you can do is explain politely the way you think, and that might just change a few ideas they have in their own heads. It's a slow process, but if you multiply one person doing that by a hundred, or a thousand, or a million people – take your pick – it becomes a bit speedier. It's still a gradual process, but it has been

PHIL, FERRY TO SWEDEN, 1984

PHIL, BRUCE AND DICK BY KEV TYDEMAN

SUBHUMANS

BLUURG RECORDS

2 VICTORIA TERRACE
MELKSHAM WILTS

0225
702853

BAND: the SUBHUMANS
VINYL: "RATS"
A 4 TRACK E.P.
LABEL: BLUURG RECORDS
CAT. No: FISH 10
DISTRIBUTION: the CARTEL
RELEASE DATE: 28th September 84

tracks:
- JOE PUBLIC
- LABELS
- WHEN THE BOMB DROPS
- RATS

their peculiar brand of Glastonbury punk — more Hawkwind than Sex Pistols

The music hovers around the area of a mutated version of folk music.

qualities you expect from good punk: cutting guitars, energy, conviction.

who have taken a corpse and given it the breath of life. The time has come for the people who think that bands like the Subs et al have little to offer except token outrage to start to redefine their attitudes.

THIS IS THE 6TH E.P. BY THE WILTSHIRE-BASED SUBHUMANS, FOLLOWING CLOSELY ON THEIR INDIE-CHART-TOPPING 2ND LP 'FROM THE CRADLE TO THE GRAVE' AND CONTINUES TO UPHOLD THEIR REPUTATION FOR NOT BEING "JUST ANOTHER PUNK BAND" — WITH THE JUXTAPOSITION OF ECCENTRIC THRASH AND THEIR SELF-STYLED "OFF-WHITE REGGAE" THEY MAINTAIN A BROAD MUSICAL OUTLOOK WHICH RAISES THEM ONE STEP ABOVE THE RAPIDLY DETERIORATING 'PUNK SCENE' — AS EVER THE LYRICS ARE HARSH BUT CONSTRUCTIVE, CUTTING DEEP INTO THE REALITIES OF CONSUMERISM, TRIBALISM, WAR AND EXPLOITATION WITHOUT FALLING INTO THE TRAP OF MERE CLICHED REPETITION — THESE ISSUES ARE ONES THAT CONCERN US ALL, AND THE SUBHUMANS' DIVERSITY OF STYLE IS DESIGNED TO REACH MORE THAN A STABLE PUNK AUDIENCE IN ORDER TO MAKE THEIR IDEALS MORE WIDELY HEARD — TO MAKE MORE PEOPLE THINK RATHER THAN DISMISS SUCH IDEALS AS THE DERANGED RESULT OF THE CURRENT 'PUNK SCENE' AND ITS MANIFESTATIONS — WE HOPE YOU'LL LISTEN TO THIS RECORD WITHOUT THE PRECONCEPTIONS INHERENT IN THE MISLEADING LABEL OF 'PUNK' — NOT JUST ANOTHER PUNK BAND!

happening, and is happening right now. People get angrier and angrier, and one day they wake up and they complain, they protest. At best, they will do things positively that are against the status quo, as it is, and change it for the better.

"A fine example would be vegetarianism, and then veganism. There's now whole shelves in supermarkets dedicated to vegan products, which is incredible to see, especially for someone who has lived through decades of it being almost impossible to get anything that was even vegetarian. Now it's just all over the place, which is brilliant. People say, 'Oh, they've commercialised it!' Well of course they've commercialised it – that's how they sell things. But you can now buy it when you want it, instead of cutting off your own arm and leg to avoid starving between finding anything to eat. And that is literally the supermarkets following the will of people who want to give up meat. For once it's the right way round, where what the people want produces a corporate reaction to fit, rather than a corporate dictatorship telling you what you apparently want, which is the usual way things happen."

On the flip-side of the EP, as well as the incredibly powerful title track, inspired by the Stop the City demonstrations discussed earlier in this chapter, 'When the Bomb Drops' is a mellow reggae-ish number, which gradually builds into something more upbeat and driving before climaxing in the inevitable explosion sample that was something of a staple for the genre. There were a lot of bands writing a lot of songs about the threat of imminent nuclear devastation during the Eighties, all fired up by incredibly disturbing TV programmes like 'When the Wind Blows' and 'Threads', that had really contributed to an oppressive zeitgeist.

"A lot of bands were singing about nuclear war, and the threat of annihilation, and CND were high on people's conscience, with local CND groups organising benefits and such," agrees **Dick**. "It was very much a nightmare we hadn't known about beforehand. Well, we'd heard about Hiroshima and Nagasaki, but didn't really realise that the threat was continuing, or the sheer amount of warheads on the planet, and the fragility of the situation, where a leader could just give an order that could set off the end of the world.

"First of all though, the lyrics to 'When the Bomb Drops' don't even fucking rhyme, haha! I think it's the only song I've ever written that doesn't rhyme? But it was about the threat of nuclear war existing, and everyone being unaware of it, either wilfully or otherwise. And ironically everyone is really happy, it's a bank holiday or whatever, and suddenly – voomf! Gone! And that *could* happen. So, the underlying message was to wake up and realise there was still a threat.

"Bruce was developing all these progressive ideas and deliberately veering away from the usual 4/4 beat on which most punk rock – and most other music! – is based," continues Dick, commenting on the band's startlingly rapid musical evolution. "He was interested in testing the boundaries about what made a good song. That bit in 'Joe Public' towards the end was a deliberate copy of 'Hey Joe' by Jimi Hendrix – because the word 'Joe' was in the title, and we thought, 'Well, why not?' We'd put little things like that in now and again, that were knowing nods to other things. Bruce had lots of good ideas, like stopping unexpectedly, and then returning to that place after veering off into something unexpected. And that worked really well, especially when combined with the way the

298

words were being sung. Like in 'Reality Is Waiting for a Bus', each verse comes in on the third word, rather than the first word, which would have been much more obvious. Quirky little bits like that add to the songs and keep them vibrant."

The Subhumans were riding the crest of a wave, releasing brilliant records, playing exciting gigs and generally having the time of their young lives, seeing the world off the back of the music they were creating. As 1984 rolled into 1985, and with their third album and a second US tour in the offing, what could possibly go wrong?

RATS

Dirk Crack
from London 30/9/83

There is a sense of enterprise here   We fought the law
~~the~~ the attitudes that conquer fear   And no one won
Stability togetherness
~~Against a world in such a mess~~
~~If you get nicked give a false address~~
The feelings cannot be suppressed
United ~~we~~ stand but so do they
~~Hand in hand we'll have our say~~
~~Gun in hand they~~ the forces of the law
~~Against~~

Hand in hand we had our say → United we ~~stand~~ stood but so
Hands in handcuffs dragged away   do they
To cheers of hate and victory

Coordination was not so good
But everyone did just what they could
Unarmed Against ~~a with such~~ inexperience
We had to use our common sense

The papers played the whole thing down
~~And pushed the~~ Said there was nothing to worry about
~~We fought the law~~ but no one won
The rats were all gone underground
But we'll be back again next time round
If you act like rats you get treated like this
Said the policeman like we didn't exist
~~He'd lost his head of silence~~
When the force of law has lost its head
The law of force is what you get

'RATS' - DICK'S ORIGINAL LYRIC SHEET

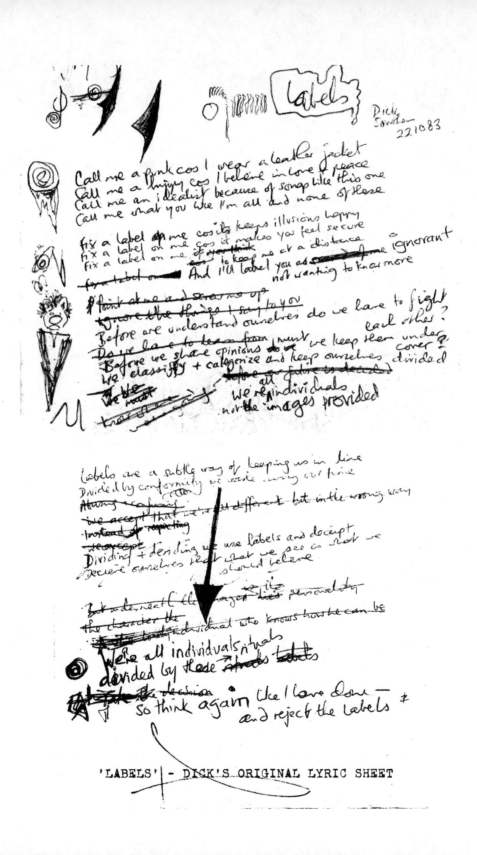

Labels

Dick Sawdon
22.10.83

Call me a punk cos I wear a leather jacket
Call me a hippy cos I believe in love & peace
Call me an idealist because of songs like this one
Call me what you like I'm all and none of these

Fix a label on me cos it keeps illusions happy
Fix a label on me cos it makes you feel secure
Fix a label on me to keep me at a distance me ignorant
And I'll label you as not wanting to know more

Before we understand ourselves do we dare to fight each other?
Do we have to learn must we keep them under cover?
Before we share opinions we classify + categorize and keep ourselves divided
We're individuals not the images provided

Labels are a subtle way of keeping us in line
Divided by conformity we waste away our time
we accept that different but in the wrong way
Dividing + deciding we use labels and deceipt
Deceive ourselves that what we see is not we should believe

We're all individuals divided by these labels
So think again like I have done —
and reject the labels

'LABELS' — DICK'S ORIGINAL LYRIC SHEET

The year 1985 started off quietly enough on the face of things, with Bruce and Dick travelling up to Castleford in West Yorkshire to produce the debut Instigators album, 'Nobody Listens Anymore', at Woodlands Studio, which would be released later that year, in August. The experience obviously impressed them, because they would return to Woodlands to record their next album a few months later.

The first Subhumans gig of 1985 was in Carlisle, at the Stars and Stripes, supported by Nightmare, on January 28th; it was the start of a short run of dates built around a gig they'd been offered on the Shetland Islands, 100 miles north of mainland Scotland – the most northerly part of the UK.

"We sailed from Aberdeen and it was an overnight boat, a long ferry trip to get there," recounts **Dick**. "A chap called Jeff convinced us it would be a good idea to do it, and we had 250 people turn out [at the Mossbank Hall, with John Bibby's Dog in support]. We had a druid chap called Tim, rest his soul, who came with us on that trip, because he was well into ancient monuments, stone circles and all that, and there was one up on the Shetlands that he wanted to go and see. So he came with us, and was filming, and for some reason he managed to convince us to run around this stone circle, in between the stones, for a few minutes whilst he filmed us. That film is luckily long gone, although I do have a photograph that I took… it all felt a bit ridiculous, but how many bands do you know who've ran around the stone circle on the Shetlands?

"It was great up there though. No one locked their doors, no one robbed anyone, because everyone knew everyone else, and it was really old style. The accent was like Scottish, only more Scottish than Scottish, very deep and broad, and we found it really hard to understand anyone, which was a bit tricky and very embarrassing. But lovely people.

"We played Carlisle on the way up to catch the ferry at Aberdeen, and after the Shetlands gig, we played Aberdeen, and then Leeds, Oldham, Warwick…"

"When we played with them at Oddy's in Oldham," says **Semi**, of the Instigators, "I can remember watching them do 'Cradle to the Grave' as a warm-up… that's still one of the best pieces of work – ever!"

A week later, they were heading up north again, for gigs in Sunderland with Toxic Waste, and Sheffield with Chumbawamba, before they played the 100 Club again on February 21st, with Blyth Power, Steve L. and Mass of Black in support. It was to be the last time they played the 100 Club during their original Eighties incarnation.

"That was a birthday gig!" reveals **Dick**. "I was in the habit of trying to arrange gigs for my birthday, especially if it fell on a weekend. But at the last few gigs we did at the 100 Club, Ron [Watts], who ran the place and did the door, put the price up without telling anyone. It would be £2.50 when we got there, and then people would be coming up to us and telling us they'd been charged £3. So, I'd find Ron and ask him why he was charging £3, and he'd say it had always been £3, and I'd be like, 'No, it's been £2.50 ever since you started talking about doing this gig…' Then I'd be pushing him on the guest list thing, because there'd be people outside who I knew really well who I didn't want to pay the inflated price…

"In the end, we got fed up of playing there because of all the price gouging. I mean, it was a good place to play, the crowds were fantastic, and it was a really good gig to do, but we were getting shafted money-wise. He rang up and asked to book us again, and I said, 'Actually Ron, we kinda decided we don't want to play there anymore…' And he was like, 'Fuck you then!' and put the phone down… so that was the end of that 'discussion', haha!"

The very next day, Subhumans played the Red Lion in Gillingham – a town in Dorset, fifteen miles south of Warminster as the crow flies – with Organized Chaos, Virus and General Belgrano. Virus put the gig on, and their bassist **Jaz Wiseman** recalls it fondly, primarily because of the positive inspiration Subhumans provided for his own musical endeavours:

"Living in a remote part of Wessex back in the early 1980s wasn't the easiest for teenage punk rockers; the point where Dorset, Somerset and Wiltshire meet is a backwater even today, a place where attitudes towards anyone who looks and thinks differently is usually met with violence and hostility. The established punk bands of yesteryear might venture to Bristol, Bournemouth, Exeter and occasionally Salisbury, but the landscape between these compass points was devoid of punk gigs unless you were prepared to put something on yourself, which in itself exposed me to the purest DIY punk ethic you could get. Punk gigs happened in pub backrooms, skittle alleys and village halls, with the bands standing in the audience and being approachable. There was no stardom or rock 'n' roll bullshit; we were all the same, which was invigorating.

"Virus were from north Dorset, and we were deeply unpopular in our immediate surroundings, where we were in danger of being suffocated by the army of mods, skinheads, scooter boys and bikers – many of whom had previously been 'punks' – but there were two beams of light that could lead us away to more sympathetic horizons. Across the border in Yeovil, Somerset, were The Mob; they had left for London, but had inspired many in their wake, although our relationship with the remaining Yeovil punks was tricky as they considered us, quite rightly, to be young upstarts. Over the hills of Mere Down and the Deverills and into Wiltshire was Warminster, a hive of DIY punk rock activity with the A-Heads, Organized Chaos and the Subhumans, and the locals there welcomed us with open arms.

"We were aware of things going on in Warminster as early as 1981, when a friend at school told me about a band that his mate was drumming for who were releasing a record soon. That band quickly became known to us as the Subhumans, and they were part of

SUB HUM ANS

+ SUPPORT
Tickets
£2·00

TUES 29ᵀᴴ
JANUARY
1985
at the
VENUE
GLASGOW

8-12 P.M.

TICKETS FROM A1 SOUNDS SAVOY CENTRE

SUB HUM ANS

DEPRAVED

FRIDAY
8ᵀᴴ
FEB.

8.00 pm
—
11.30 pm

THE SEARS.

SUB HUM ANS

EVOLUTION

from Ireland

and Also.......

+ TOXIC
WASTE

Phantoms
of the
Underground

16ᵗʰ feb 7:30

AT THE BUNKER
SUNDERLAND £1:50 on the Door

NO GLASS BOTTLES PLEASE

SUB HUM ANS

D & V
CHUMBAWAMBA
7-11
SUN 17ᵀᴴ FEB
The Leadmill Sheffield

£2   OR   £1·50

Live... SUB HUMANS

AT THE COLWALL "HORSE AND JOCKEY" INN

TICKETS FOR SALE RING IAN (LEDBURY ████) OR KEV (LEDBURY ████)

+ DECADENCE WITHIN
+ DISCARDED REMNANTS OF AN AGE NO MORE
+ THE CROWS

ON FRIDAY 1ST MARCH 1985

FROM 7·30 – LATE

£ 1·25   BEER NOT FEAR   BAR UNTIL 12·30

COLWALL FLYER AND PHOTOS BY IAN GLASPER

this explosion of hundreds of new young punk bands releasing records at that time. Their first two EPs were great, but the penny really dropped for me when I bought 'Religious Wars' on the day of release and played it constantly for days afterwards – it remains my favourite EP of theirs to this day. From that point on, there was an urgency to see them live, that happened not long after, and more importantly a drive to get our own band together and try to do a gig with them.

"In all honesty, we were shambolic and didn't get our act together until the end of 1984, and then we organised a gig with the Subhumans in our local pub in February 1985. The landlord was reluctant to let us do a gig, but gave in after my constant badgering... and in the end it was the busiest his pub had been in years, with punks from all the remotest parts of Dorset, Somerset and Wiltshire descending on Gillingham. The landlord made a lot of money that night, so much in fact that he wanted us to do it again, but for me the enduring thing was us becoming part of a wider scene and going elsewhere. The Subhumans returned the favour later that year, picking us up one day and taking us off on an adventure to a gig in Plymouth. I'll be forever grateful to them for letting us in, and being such down to earth, fun and friendly guys."

On March 1st, the Subhumans played a gig very close to your author's heart – at the Horse and Jockey in Colwall, as mentioned in the introduction to this book. My band at the time, Decadence Within, were instrumental in putting the gig on – it was only our fourth (and the Subhumans' 208th, if such stats float your boat), but quite a key moment in our local scene. The buzz leading up to the gig was palpable. Colwall is a large village (actually reputed to be the largest in the UK) nestled in the shadow of the Malvern Hills, and the thought that Subhumans would be playing there was blowing people's minds. I had put my phone number (well, my mum and dad's actually, as I was still living at home) on the poster as a contact for tickets, and punks from all the surrounding areas were ringing me up to buy a handful of tickets each so they could bring a carload of mates over, but there was a fair amount of scepticism that it was even happening. Decadence Within were a brand new band with no music out – how the hell had we persuaded Subhumans to come to our little corner of the Shire? Simple – we rang them up and asked them nicely, in the long-established tradition of entrepreneurial DIY punk! I had quite a few folk asking for reassurance that they'd get their £1.50 back if Subhumans didn't show – but of course they did.

Local bands were also queueing up to support, and people were even talking about *forming* bands so they could play. One local band, The Dismembered, definitely formed as a result of that gig (possibly *at* that gig), and they booked Subhumans to play Upton-upon-Severn, a sleepy riverside town in Worcestershire, six months later, with themselves opening the bill.

Everybody who was into punk for miles around – and a few that weren't, just out of curiosity – was there; in fact, we'd sold all our advance tickets, and were told we couldn't let any more in on the door, but things were a bit more relaxed in the Eighties, and the landlord (thinking of the bar takings) took us to one side and basically said to shoe-horn 'em in. The place was packed, and everybody was drunk – including/especially the bands – and everybody had a great time, singing along to some of our favourite songs. Yes, there were a few scuffles, with petty inter-town rivalry boiling over here and there ('My postcode is better than your postcode…!'), but it was essentially a unifying occasion. And a great reminder of what punk rock is all about – there are no 'stars' in the punk scene, we're all in it together, and a genuine punk band *will* come and play your town, and won't price themselves out of a few intimate gigs for the grassroots fans when they can.

After a small gig at the Oxford Co-Op Hall, and larger shows at the Salisbury Arts Centre and Fulham Greyhound, the Subhumans headed north to Castleford, where they recorded their third album, to be titled 'Worlds Apart', with Neil Ferguson at Woodlands Studio between April 10th and April 16th. Their hosts for the week were their good friends, the Instigators.

"They liked Woodlands so much when they came up to work on our album, they came back up to record something themselves," explains Instigators guitarist **Simon Mooney**. "They came up for a week, and needed putting up between us."

'Gators bassist **Tab**: "Dick stayed at my house when he was up to record at Woodlands. We would go out in Dewsbury, after they were done in the studio."

Drummer **Hammy**: "They also stayed with Simon Robinson, my friend from college – and they were always in The Poacher [a pub in Dewsbury]. We used to just go down the studio in Castleford and hang around with them. That was not long after we did 'Nobody Listens Anymore', and they liked how that turned out so much, they came up to do their album there. Then Neil [Ferguson] did the Chumbawamba album after them, and Chumbas asked him to join the band, and he became a megastar [he produced 'Agadoo' by Black Lace]!

"I remember Dick going in The Poacher, and there'd just been a blood bath in there. We'd talked to Dick about The Poacher loads, and we took him on a Friday night, just after they'd finished their recording session, and someone had just been glassed in there – and there was blood everywhere. I remember thinking, 'God, he's gonna get a right impression of this!' It was unheard of in The Poacher that there was even a fight, let alone someone getting glassed."

"We had our single on the jukebox in there, didn't we?" recalls **Mooney**, before adding, "I don't think they [i.e. Subhumans] had the same affection for the band after our line-up changed completely. It was that first line-up they liked, that caught their attention. I don't really know why they [Bluurg] did that second record [1986's 'Phoenix'], because it was a completely different thing."

Hammy: "But they were lovely people, all of them."

COLWALL, HORSE AND JOCKEY BY IAN GLASPER

DICK AT HIS BIRTHDAY PARTY, WARMINSTER, 1985 BY JAZ WISEMAN

RECORDING 'WORLDS APART' WITH DICK'S WOMBLE MASCOT BY PHIL

"'Worlds Apart' took absolutely ages to record," **Dick** picks up the story, "Because we recorded it between Woodlands in Castleford and Southern Studios again… because John wasn't entirely happy with the sound of some of it. So we remixed four or five songs at Southern, about three months after recording it in Leeds – 'Straight Line Thinking', 'Powergames', 'Carry on Laughing' and maybe 'Someone Is Lying'? I can't remember why John insisted it needed remixing, and to this day Bruce still thinks the guitar isn't loud enough on the whole album.

"It was quite a complicated album to record… lots of different styles, a bit of acoustic guitar, an anvil sound in 'Carry on Laughing' – well, not a real anvil, but some old piece of metal Bruce found. The intro isn't exactly '1, 2, 3, 4!' either; it's more like settling down to a book than… well, it's more of a 'listening' album than a 'dancing around' album, put it that way."

Indeed, the intro isn't '1, 2, 3, 4,' it's '33322', a bizarre title Phil inadvertently gave it when he was trying to get his head around the timing.

"That was my way of remembering it then, but I can't work it out now, when I listen to it," laughs **Phil**. "It's actually my least favourite thing on the whole record, because the start of it kinda feels a bit lumpy to me. Don't tell anyone [too late, Phil!], but I played that with my thumb at the start, to get a percussive feel to it.

"I love the whole record once it gets going, but I don't think we played the intro that well, looking back. It gets better once it gets going… and I do love the outro version of it at the end. That was the John Entwistle coming out in me, very inspired by The Who's 'Live at Leeds'.

"Musically I really enjoyed playing all that stuff like 'Get to Work on Time'… I was playing through that the other day, and it's crazy stuff, quite complicated and involved, but it still works as a song, without sounding too indulgent."

"We were practising at The Shed by then, this area in a large barn owned by Trotsky's parents," continues **Dick**. "Well, it was his dad that used it, working on old cars and things. We had quite a good space there – it had lots of junky stuff in it… I should probably say it had lots of stuff that was junk in it, rather than 'junkie stuff', haha! And an old piano, that I bought for about ten quid, and was pretty out of tune.

"We had a lot of fun practises at that place, and because it wasn't the youth centre, we didn't have to share it with any other bands, so there was no one stood there watching us practise, which for all its good intent was sometimes a bit off-putting.

"We had a lot of *silly* jams there too. There was even a non-band formed, which was named after an anagram of Subhumans… Shaun's Bum. I have a tape somewhere of Shaun's Bum's 'greatest hits', because I was still recording everything I possibly could. And there was some pretty good silly songs we did, which at best were like some Mothers of Invention style. All wacky stuff – we did a version of 'How Much Is That Doggy in the Window?' It was all made-up nonsense really… I'd basically make up lyrics, and Bruce would make up a tune… Phil and Trotsky would play along, and sometimes it was absolutely the most fun you could possibly have. All on various quantities of cider. It was very silly."

"I'm from a family of farmers, and my uncle had this big shed on his farm," explains **Trotsky**, "And we used to practise in one part of it. It was cold, dirty and horrible, haha! The downside of practising in the youth centre with all the kids in there was that you couldn't concentrate; it was difficult to focus on writing songs, because it felt a bit like you were doing a gig. Some bands might have found that pressure good for them creatively, but for me it was a bit stifling."

"Yeah, Woodlands had connections to that 'Agadoo' record," elaborates **Phil**. "The bass in the studio had been used on 'Agadoo'. I did have a mess around on it, but don't think I used it in the end... otherwise the 'Agadoo' bass would have helped create 'Worlds Apart'! [laughs]

"I had plenty of free rein to come up with stuff," he continues, of the writing process for the third album, "But Bruce definitely had bass ideas for some of it, especially the early songs we worked on. A lot of the early bass lines that are well known were from all over the place, as well as Grant. Bruce came up with some of those ideas... even Andy Gale came up with a few. Everyone was always chipping in. But when Bruce comes up with something, he has a pretty good idea of what he's after.

"And by the time we got to 'Worlds Apart', that was completely down to Bruce and I jamming ideas, and some of those ideas were bass line-driven to start with, y'know? It was a real mish-mash in that sometimes stuff would be completely spur of the moment; other times people came up with stuff on their own, and some of it was pre-formed ideas we'd worked up between us. We were practising on a real regular basis back then, at least once a week. None of us could drive though, so Dick would come over on the bus from Melksham, and we'd get a taxi over to The Shed with our guitars – we left the rest of our equipment out there."

"Yes, a lot of the time," confirms **Bruce**, when asked if he came up with most of the music, "And I'd have ideas for what the bass and drums could do as well, and it usually sounded okay when we tried it. It was the same with the arrangements – not all of the time, but I'd often come up with the ideas... and usually the rest of the band would go with it. I was lucky to have people in the band that appreciated what I was coming up with.

"I used to like practising, and then I'd go away and think about what we'd written all week, different ways of doing things, and then we'd try it out at the next practice. And I'd listen to them, because we used to record the practices, so the songs would be evolving. Well, they'd be evolving in my head, maybe not in everybody else's.

"We also had the luxury back then of doing a couple of tours playing the songs before we recorded them, which I think is always the best way to do it. Once you've got new songs – it's nice to have new songs in the set, and if they're not on a record yet, they're classed as a 'new' song – it's best to play them for a few years before you record them,

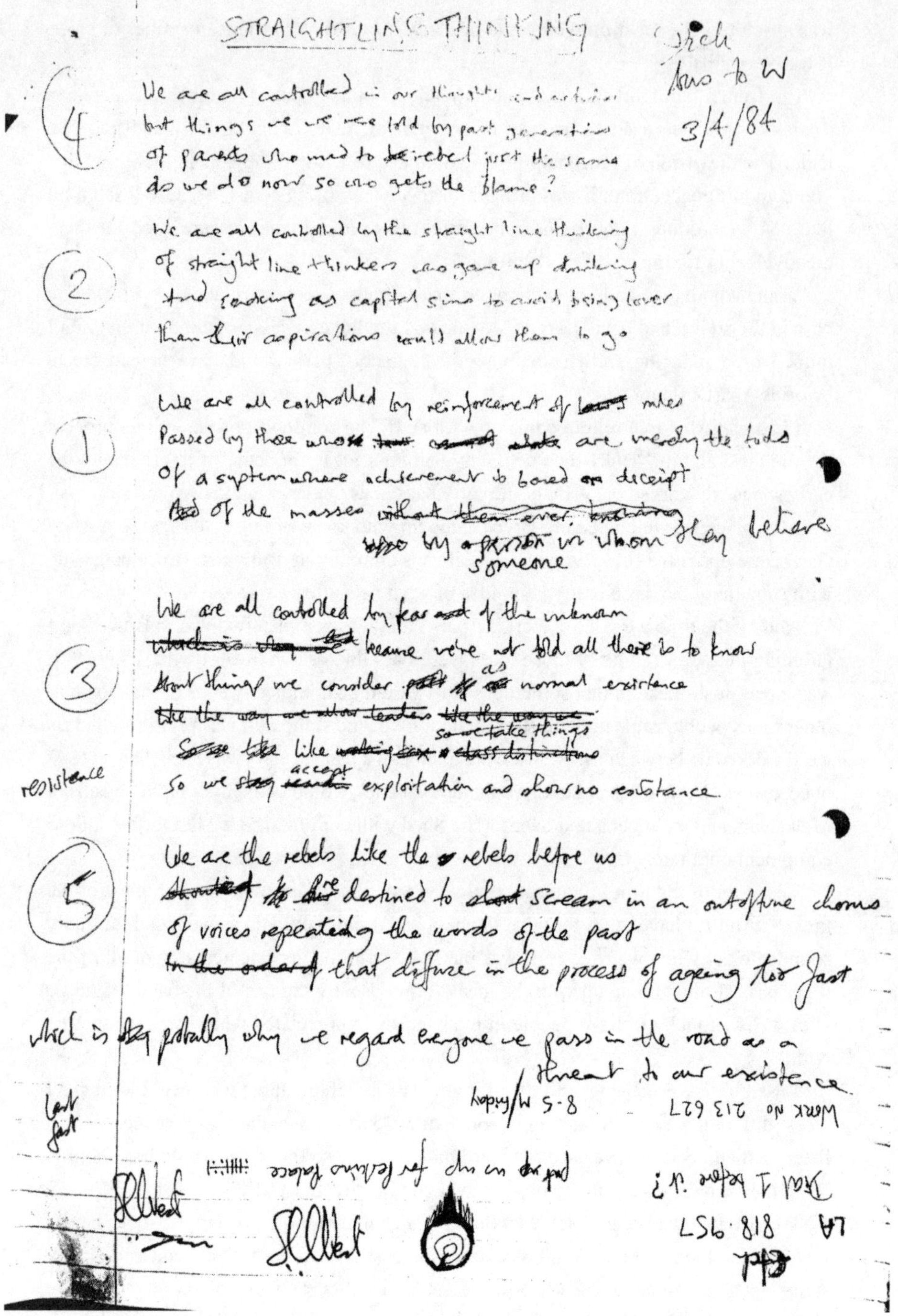

STRAIGHTLINE THINKING

Dick
bus to W
3/4/84

(4)
We are all controlled in our thoughts and actions
but things we were told by past generations
of parents who used to rebel just the same
as we do now so who gets the blame?

(2)
We are all controlled by the straight line thinking
of straight line thinkers who gave up drinking
and smoking as capital sins to avoid being lower
than their aspirations would allow them to go

(1)
We are all controlled by reinforcement of rules
Passed by those who are merely the tools
Of a system where achievement is based on deceit
Of the masses by someone in whom they believe

(3)
We are all controlled by fear of the unknown
because we're not told all there is to know
About things we consider as normal existence
some take things like class distinctions
resistance
So we accept exploitation and show no resistance

(5)
We are the rebels like the rebels before us
are destined to scream in an out of tune chorus
of voices repeating the words of the past
that diffuse in the process of ageing too fast
which is probably why we regard everyone we pass in the road as a threat to our existence

last
past

Work No 213 627
8-5 M/Friday
LA 818 957

'STRAIGHTLINE THINKING' - DICK'S ORIGINAL LYRIC SHEET

RECORDING 'WORLDS APART' BY PHIL

DICK BY KEV TYDEMAN

so you get them bedded in and you know what you really think of them… and what the audience think of them too. And you make sure you know them properly yourself. I hate the idea of writing songs in the studio… why would you do that?"

"We tend to record live initially, with a guide guitar, which sometimes gets kept if it's useable," reveals **Phil**, of the recording process, "But Bruce is really big on detail, and he knows exactly what he's after both sound-wise and playing-wise, so he takes some time with his overdubs and everything. He will generally go back and re-do his guitars, and have two guitar tracks going anyway. The main thing is to get a good drum take, and anything else, if you can keep it, is a bonus. For 'Worlds Apart', we were no doubt hoping to keep most of the bass takes, but I get pretty bad studio nerves, so I'm sure I would have ended up doing loads of drop-ins. I've got better over the years, but I do get that 'red light fear' when they start recording me. Although I'm a bit more chilled out these days, because we tend to work with friends, like Steve Evans who engineered the last couple of records, which is a lot less stressful than doing it with complete strangers and stuff."

Prior to leaving for another month-long US tour, Subhumans – and Steve L. – played Warminster's Christchurch Hall, a party for Sharon, their ex-drummer Andy's sister. Andy's disco band Rare Breed were also on the bill.

"Far from being just a practice gig pre-US-tour, that was a proper party gig," reckons **Dick**, "In as much as we messed up a load of songs, messed about with other ones – which is more or less the same thing, I guess – and had a lot of fun and silliness! I conducted a panel team to answer the question whether we were gonna play 'Human Error' or not? And we *did* play it. I was actually getting the words right… until 'Work-Rest-Play-Die', which was a real laugh – getting my voice in tune at the start, collapsing with laughter before I'd finished the first verse and starting again, forgetting the words and singing, 'There's a bucket at the bottom/of my garden I've forgotten/all the bloody words again/yeahyeahyaay!' It was a very 'out of it' evening!"

That second tour of the States started in New York on April 23rd, and took in twenty-four gigs in total, culminating in Sacramento on May 25th, a co-headline trip with Virginia hardcore band Scream (although Subhumans headlined the majority of the gigs).

"And what a lovely bunch they were," says Dick of **Scream**. "They had everything organised… although a couple of gigs got cancelled while we were there, and one got moved, but it was a very enjoyable tour. We started off in New York, then went south, down through Richmond to Florida, and then after playing in a place called Hollywood, which is actually near Miami, we set off on a fifteen-hour drive to Newport [Cincinnati] – to play in front of eighty people two days later. Then we played Cleveland, Pittsburgh, Detroit, Chicago and Madison, then headed off to Denver, which was a thousand-mile drive. If things had gone to plan, we would have got there at 10 pm, just in time to go onstage, but the rocker, or the cam shaft or something, went on the journey, and we spent two and a half hours at this garage in this very small town getting it fixed, which meant we missed the gig. So then we had a day off in Boulder, Colorado, and then we had to drive to LA, which again was a massive journey, that took two or three days.

"On the way, the van broke down again, so we had to hire a large U-Haul truck. Whoever was driving, and whoever was sat next to them, were fine, but the rest of us – and this was both bands – were sat in the back of this large truck, which had a roll-down door that we had to roll up to let the light in, but that also let the fumes in. So we were getting fumed out during these long journeys, and I got the flu, or some approximation of flu, for a couple of days. How we all basically survived, I don't know.

"At one point, we hired another van for a couple of days, and someone whose house we stayed at shut the side window of this van by hand, and did it a bit too hard, and as it closed it smashed inwards. So we had to pay for that, and get rid of that van. Most tour problems are caused by transport – if you're only going to do one thing right, make sure you get a good bloody van. Mind you, even a lot of good vans will start to suffer if you drive them flat out for a thousand miles every week, which never helps. On a different tour altogether, we put petrol in a diesel van once, and that didn't help either. But the tour with Scream was very good; they were very affable people, and we got on really well – they had the same sort of tastes in music, the same sort of attitudes towards things… and they were a very good band."

"They were a big influence on us as well… the Americans are such good musicians," concedes **Bruce**. "When you go there, you realise just how lazy we are over here… or how serious they are over there? Scream were really into The Damned… when we toured with them, they would sometimes do covers of songs from 'Machine Gun Etiquette'. And I was really into The Damned too; I think 'Strawberries' came out just before Phil joined the band, and we all got into that. But the one before it, 'Machine Gun Etiquette', was great as well."

"I can't say they organised every gig, but it seemed like it," continues **Dick**. "Joey P., their manager, sorted a lot of it. He was in this band called Pea Soup with Ian MacKaye and about four others, who we saw play in Washington, where they all lived. It was a mixture of jamming and funkiness and other strange stuff… costumes onstage, completely out there… it was quite bizarre."

"I thought Scream were fantastic," agrees **Phil**. "They were such an amazing band, and I loved watching them every night. That was a real treat for me, and they were all really great guys too – a bit older than us, and more experienced; we were still very young, although we probably felt older than we were by then. We travelled together, and they had a fantastic sound engineer with them, Joey P., who was a big part of the whole DC scene, Dischord and all that lot, and a great sound engineer. He was a *professional* engineer as well, even though he was doing the punk scene and working with those guys – partway through the tour, he took a couple of days off to go and engineer an Abba gig somewhere! Or someone like that anyway. But he was doing our sound every night, just because we were friends of Scream.

U.S. TOUR FLYERS, 1985

BRUCE SKATING, SAN FRANCISCO, 1985

"And Pea Soup was this James Brown tribute act, which they did just for a laugh – it was some of the guys from Scream, and Ian MacKaye [from Minor Threat and Fugazi] was in it… Joey P. was in it – he was the front man, so he was doing all the stuff with the mic stand, doing the splits and everything. So we saw them do that at the 9:30 Club in DC, which was a funny start to the tour.

"We felt like old hands by then. We'd just recorded 'Worlds Apart', and felt much more confident musically. We were excited to be playing new songs, and the gigs went great. We got to play with the Kennedys again as well, at this really great place called The Farm in San Francisco. It was only a year since we'd last been there, but things were moving so fast, and so many things had changed just in that short time… it takes us ten years to do an album now, haha!"

"I remember when we arrived in the US for that second tour, we got picked up by Scream in the tour van which both bands were to travel in," adds **Trotsky**. "I think it was an Econoline with a loft built in the back, so a bit different to the previous tour when it was just us and Patrick in a car. Plus this time we had a backline!

"Scream had a good open-minded attitude about music; when they picked us up, they were playing a tape – CDs were still in the future – of Vivaldi's 'The Four Seasons'! I think they were a bit surprised that we didn't look too punky when we got in the van, but they were a great bunch of blokes with a good sense of humour. Kent [Stax – drummer] was an awesome player, so relaxed when playing even the most technical patterns. He told me he'd been playing for twenty years or some such figure, and I was like, 'Wow, that's *ages*…' I'd been playing for about six. He'd recently become a dad, and every now and then he'd say, 'Wanna see my baby?' and pull out a photo of his kid – he was very proud. He also liked trains...

"Lee Davidson, or 'Harley', was a funny guy, and introduced us to the word 'gnarly' to describe, well, almost anything really! [Bassist] Skeeter was great, a really nice guy, as was Joey 'Pea', their sound engineer. [Vocalist] Pete and [guitarist] Franz were a bit more reserved, especially Franz, but they were friendly and put up with us. It felt like they were a bit apart from the rest of us… maybe because they were brothers?

"I don't remember too much of the tour, to be honest; I guess that, after the one the year before, this time was more like going over old ground and not so new and exciting, but I do remember the van breaking down in the middle of nowhere, and we were getting a little nervous of the locals as it neared sundown – think 'Deliverance', haha! We ended up hiring a U-Haul box truck, where two or three people could sit in the front, and the rest of us were in the back with no windows, in total darkness... for hours."

A few weeks after returning from this triumphant American jaunt, Subhumans were playing the Conservative Club in Chesterfield, with Chumbawamba supporting ("They were amazing," reckons **Dick,** adding, "We were pretty much blown offstage by them, I imagine? It would have felt like it, I'm sure…"), but it was their next gig, at the Chippenham Liberal Club, on July 6th with Organized Chaos, Smiles and Lumps of Merde, that was to have more significant repercussions for the band – and not in a positive way.

"I'd just turned sixteen, and our big local band the Subhumans were coming to our market town of Chippenham to play," remembers **Andy Owen**, now a Chippenham punk promoter himself, and vocalist for The Liabilities, who was in attendance that fateful night. "Conflict were meant to play but couldn't make it. The gig had been sorted by our mate Kev Woodward (RIP). It was at the Liberal Club on Station Hill, which was where we all went anyway because there was often an indie disco on there. So they were kinda used to us. But what they, or we, didn't know was how mental it was gonna be. So, gig day… the venue was ready, bands arriving, and lots of people. We went for pre-gig beers, and if I remember correctly, we were in The Black Horse drinking with the Subhumans. I remember someone writing across my jeans, 'Us Fish Must Swim Together'… I wonder who wrote that, eh?

"I also remember three punks from Sweden coming over. They were nice lads, and had never seen the Subhumans, so they were buzzing. Kev's band, The Lumps of Merde, started the show. My mate Steve had been taken to hospital in an ambulance pretty much before any bands had started; he put his hand through a window and cut his wrist. They had to strap him to a wheelchair as he was kicking off, not wanting to leave – and so it began!

"There were loads of punks, and loads of skinheads, which was where the problem was really, as the skins just wanted to kick off. Those Swedish punks got a kicking. The bands got threatened if they wouldn't play. At one point, we really thought the Subhumans wouldn't go on, but I don't think they had much choice in the end.

"I'll keep things kind of brief because loads went on. Kev got whacked, the bogs got smashed up, I had a scrap, my mate came back with his wrist bandaged up, the Swedish lads fucked off, and the pigs turned up. The skins barricaded the doors chanting, 'Kill the Bill', 'A.C.A.B.', and all that. Pete The Roadie got nicked for trying to charge the police the entry fee to come in! Fuck knows what happened to all the bands? We had riot police out and police dogs, the power got cut off. Arrests, fights, tears, laughter. Me and my mate Lecky tried to do a runner down the fire escape, only to be met by coppers with batons. We went back in, where the skins were still causing mayhem. The coppers tried to nick me, but a skin jumped in. He got nicked and I got off, haha! It was tense as fuck that night, a proper '80s showdown. The bands were good though. A few of us got onstage to sing along to 'Animal', but basically our night – and the bands' – was ruined.

"It took me over thirty years to get the Subhumans to come back to Chippenham. Thankfully they have played again here twice now – so ta, Trotsky, who agreed to play Chippenham again after all those years. I think that night in '85 really did his head in."

"We were well hyped up for the gig," adds **Gary Scarth**, vocalist for The Lumps of Merde. "It was my first ever gig, sixteen years old, and supporting Subhumans! Our

SUBHUMANS UK
SCREAM NY

worlds apart tour USA'75

WHERE → CLEVELAND UNDERGROUND

WHEN MAY 8
HOW MUCH $5

WITH: RAW POWER (ITALY)
& THE BREAKOUTS (SAN FRAN)

ALL AGES

GOLDENVOICE presents.... FROM ENGLAND...
THE SUBHUMANS
SCREAM
CAUSTIC CAUSE
JUSTICE LEAUGE
+ JOHNNY AND THE DINGBATS

SUN. MAY 19
SUN VALLEY
SPORTSMAN'S HALL
11050 LARNE
INFO: 818-767-9273

DOORS OPEN AT 7:00

NO BAD VIBES ALLOWED

TICKETS $7.00 AT DOOR...

ZERO O

— B. OTIS - 85

DEAD KENNEDYS
SUBHUMANS U.K.
FRIGHTWIG
SCREAM
THE BREEZE!
SEA HAGS

FRI. MAY 24 SAN FRANCISCO
THE FARM 1499 Potrero (415) 431-1524

FRI. JUNE 28th
SOCIAL DISTORTION

THE DEAD KENNEDYS
FRIDAY MAY 24 SAN FRANCISCO
THE FARM 1499 Potrero (415) 431-1524

TELETRON

GBH FRI. JUNE 14 8pm sharp!

415-431-1326

tickets are $6.50 adv. $8.00 at don
prices increase to help keep...

N RRZ GOLDENVOICE PRODUCTION

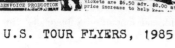

U.S. TOUR FLYERS, 1985

CLEAR & DISTINCT IDEAS PRESENTS
DEAD KENNEDYS
RETURN FROM ENGLAND
SUBHUMANS
w/guests
FrightWig
BLAST
AND JUNK WAFFLE

SATURDAY MAY 25TH

CREST THEATER
1013 K STREET, SACRAMENTO
INFORMATION: 444-3133

GOLDENVOICE PRESENTS:

SAT
MAY
18

FROM THE U.K.

SUB HUM ANS

WITH

FROM DC

SCREAM

AND

PLUS

FIRST STRIKE 8 PM

BAD RELIGION   ILL REPUTE   DETOX

OLYMPIC AUDITORIUM   1801 S GRAND   LOS ANGELES

INDULGEPRINTBWILL

U.S. TOUR SHIRT, 1985

GENVOICE PRESENTS

UB HUM ANS
Rats

TROTSKY, U.S. TOUR, 1985

DMR PROS PRESENT: WED 22nd MAY 6-10PM

SUB HUM ANS $4 DUDE
SCREAM BLAST
BONELESS ONES 956-
3315 MABUHAY 443 BROAD

SCREAM
BAD RELIGION
17th
RBRA

SCREAM
SUN MAY 19
SUN VALLEY

SAT MAY 18th
OLYMPIC AUD

bassist Kev organised it… he was a few years older than us. We all met up during the day to start the shenanigans, a few beers before load-in; we were caught up in the moment.

"The place was filling up. Pete The Roadie was on the door… £1.50 o.n.o., and a donation to the ALF. I think £75 was raised in the end? There were loads of punks and skins from all over the place, getting rowdy. We'd only had two practises, and we really were shit, but people joined in the fun. Jay Whyte jumped up onstage with us, and what a laugh we had… who would've thought that years later he would become the Subhumans' temporary bassist for a while? I remember coming offstage, relieved that we'd got away with it, and then it was party time, a few more beers.

"At some point, Dick from Subhumans found a piano out the back, and started playing 'Susan' on it. Anyway, the atmosphere was pretty charged. Barney [guitarist Mark Barnet] hit Kev. And Organized Chaos had to stop playing when Melksham punk Ecky got set on by the skins. All hell broke loose soon after."

"We pushed the tables up against the door to stop the police getting in," laughs **Lee**, the other singer in Lumps of Merde, "And Subhumans carried on playing. I remember Dick singing, 'It's 1985, and the pigs are outside', instead of 'It's 1984, and there's gonna be a war…'"

"There was a lot of warring factions back then," sighs **Bruce**, "And I didn't want us involved in any of it really. We weren't an Oi! band, and we weren't a football band, so I don't know why anyone would come out to see us just to cause trouble – we didn't really have a violent following. Crass would have people fighting the whole time they were playing, which always seemed weird, although I suppose Steve Ignorant came over as a bit Oi! in his delivery sometimes… I remember Silas saying that he went to see Crass in Bristol, and there was so much trouble, Steve said, 'If you don't stop fighting, we're going to do the whole set again!'" [laughs]

Thankfully July also saw some very successful and well-attended gigs, including the Fulham Greyhound gig with Blyth Power and Paranoid Visions, previously discussed by Pete Jones, as well as Leeds and Gateshead with Instigators, and Dudley with The Sears and Contempt.

"Two van loads of us went down from Stafford," recalls **Stu Pid**, who would himself later sing for Contempt, not to mention Police Bastard, English Dogs and Sensa Yuma. "We were all excited to see the Subhumans at last, and it meant a trip down the M6 to the famous Sugarhill Club in Dudley, which was where Daz Russell [who now books Rebellion] used to book before The Mermaid. None of us knew quite what to expect; we'd picked up 'The Day the Country Died' when it was released in '83, and everyone had all the words perfectly engraved in their head, but something changed in us all that night. What we witnessed was a togetherness as one: punks from every part of the Midlands had made their way there, and we were *all* singing those words that made us what we are today.

"Not long after that, it was a trip to the tattooist to get 'The Day the Country Died' done on the top of my arm, where it has proudly sat to this day. It was also the beginning of a great friendship; although we hadn't met personally, we soon would. 'From the Cradle to the Grave' became our bible; with all the songs sounding different, which made every track identifiable, we were asked to think, and question everything…"

The Subhumans then played at the Brambles Farm Peace Festival, on the outskirts of Waterlooville, on August 11th, which like so many well-intentioned events of its kind was more than a little shambolic.

"I went down two days earlier than both the rest of the band and Organized Chaos, who played before us on the 11th," says **Dick**, "Sleeping in a communal bender, on a diet of apples and cheese, and trying to avoid the torrential rain by smoking pipes and hanging out with the hilarious Shrapnel chaps. Poison Girls played a good set, although the site became a mud pool, and the best way to keep your feet dry was to wear dustbin bags over your socks. It was very cold and windy at night, and a lot of the 1000-strong crowd left on the Sunday, which was the day we played.

"DIRT came on, but the PA was shit," he recounts, referring to his diary entry for the weekend, "So the vocals were nowhere to be heard, and in the end they just fucked about. Antisect and Polemic did better, but the vocals were awful again. Bruce took over control of the PA and made some sense of it. Organized Chaos were good, with Spud re-joining them for the second half of the set. There were two cops on the entrance, who told us to turn it down when we were onstage, so we took the drums out of the PA. But a quarter of an hour later, an old bloke came over and said his grandmother across the road was ill and couldn't get any sleep; I told him we couldn't turn the drums down, and anyway it was only going to be a few more minutes… well, half an hour! Everyone seemed happy afterwards, and the crowd disappeared into the night, and each other's tents…"

John Loder did a partial remix of the 'Worlds Apart' album at Southern on August 19th and 20th, although – despite originally being scheduled for a December release – the album wasn't released until early '86, by which time the band had split up – *and* had already recorded the posthumous release, '29:29 Split Vision'. They were seemingly prolific even in death.

"I think John Loder only remixed one track, 'Straight Line Thinking'," hazards **Bruce**, "Pretty much on his own, and we let him get on with it, because it seemed to be going okay. But everything else was done up at Castleford. We were always having mixed feelings about Southern; we weren't completely convinced with what we recorded there… I dunno what it was really."

'Straight Line Thinking' is actually one of your author's very favourite Subhumans songs, propelled by some stirring vocal harmonies that perfectly capture the song's desperate sadness, of being trapped in a self-fulfilling prophecy.

"They were Bruce's idea," reveals **Dick**, "And every time we played that live, we had to be very careful to have that harmony ready to go from the first verse, because it starts off with singing and not much else going on. The writing of that particular song was

LIBERATE THE ANIMALS
presents
SUBHUMANS
UPROAR
ALL PROCEEDS to THE A.L.F ORGANISED CHAOS
SMILES + THE LUMPS OF MERDE
(LIBERATE + DISTORTED ABORTION)
AT THE LIBERAL HALL CHIPPENHAM JULY 6th 1985 7·30PM

UPTON MEMORIAL HALL, 1985 BY IAN GLASPER

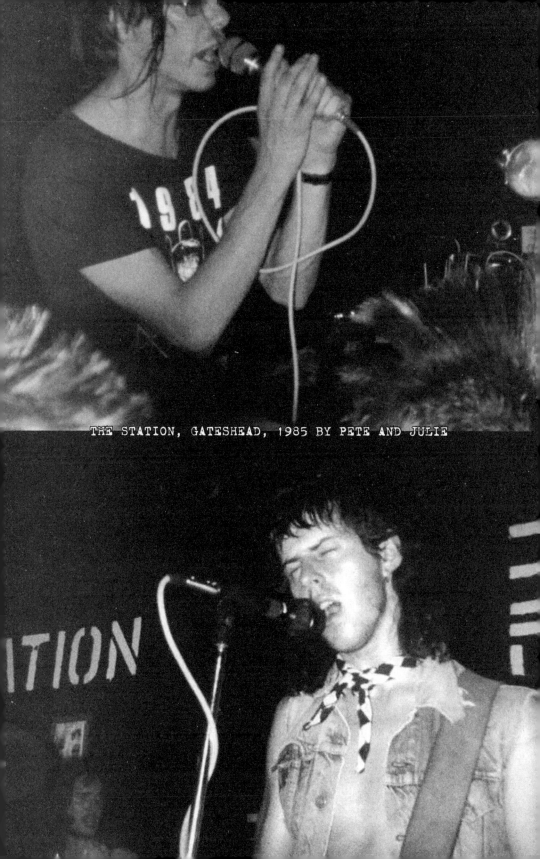

THE STATION, GATESHEAD, 1985 BY PETE AND JULIE

influenced by Rudimentary Peni, because I was amazed at how he could sing so many words without drawing breath. And I thought, 'Right, don't write four sentences for four lines, just write one sentence for four lines...' And it was the case that it was difficult to get through to the end of the verse without breathing, because each verse was one long sentence..."

"I like doing that song live," adds **Bruce**, "Although it's a lot of effort for me and Dick, doing those harmonies. And I think the guitars could have been louder on it. I was getting a bit obsessed with drums at the time, and getting a good drum sound was more important to me than getting a good guitar sound. I felt like I'd got my guitar sorted by then – it had taken ages to get there, but I was happy with that, I had the set-up I liked – and I was just very enthusiastically into the drums. So, I was concentrating on that, and I think the guitar was a little bit quiet – but it still seems to work okay.

"Once we'd worked out that it sounded so good, and that was what we were going to do forever more, we always did two guitar tracks," he continues. "Everybody does it now and doesn't even think about it, but at the time, you didn't always do it... you might only have an eight-track recorder or something, and you didn't have enough tracks to waste one on another guitar. And we were all influenced by the Discharge album, where he was clearly doing that – because when you stereo split guitars, it just sounds great... it sounds like a chorus effect. And you don't need to have the guitars very loud either – they just sort of fill in the gaps then. That's what we were doing from 'Cradle...' onwards."

"But yeah, we'd already split up by the time we recorded 'Split Vision'," continues **Dick**, of the aforementioned posthumous recording, "Although we hadn't *really* split up if we were still recording... but that's the loose nature of falling apart – which was apparently already in motion just after the US tour. Although I've searched through my diaries, and I can't find any specific point where we had definitely decided we were going to split up.

"I get the inference from a couple of comments that I was holding out, not believing that we would split up, whilst at least Bruce and Phil were thinking we probably should because we weren't really getting anywhere, we weren't making enough money and the whole punk scene seemed to be dying around us. And those feelings weren't helped by the fact that we came back from all those amazing gigs in America to play that Liberal Hall gig in Chippenham, where everything went wrong – the PA was crap, there were young kids drinking vodka and smashing windows and puking up everywhere, and then the cops turned up and stopped the whole thing happening. It was a chaotic mess, and I can remember Trotsky in particular saying, 'Fuck this, this is ridiculous...'

"I'd started booking a European tour though, so he said he would do that and then he would quit. So, we rolled on a bit further, and did these European dates in September..."

Said European trek ran from September 11th until September 29th and took in eight gigs in Holland and four in Germany (although eight were scheduled). Some of the Dutch gigs were booked by Rob from Paperclip again, and even he noticed the disillusionment bubbling to the surface in the band.

Rob: "Yes, during that last tour I booked for them, I remember we were having a good chat backstage, about society and politics, and Bruce started saying how he thought the band should become more accessible to reach a larger audience with their music… I can't remember what expression I would have had on my face, but it wouldn't have been one that said, 'Oh yeah, that's a really good idea!'"

"Well, I always wanted to do that," says **Bruce**, somewhat nonplussed, "And I still want to do that now! Doesn't every band want to reach a larger audience? We've always been a little held back by our principles, by not accepting every offer that's given to us – but that's also what's kept us going this long as well. When we do tour, we decide on the ticket price, as part of the deal, and try not to play things that are too expensive. But I've always been ambitious – musically. It's kind of a shame we never had anyone who got us more radio play, but we just haven't done it. We would have loved to have done a Peel session, that would have been really amazing. We just didn't get an offer."

"That tour featured yet again the total chaos of the van dying on us," **Dick** picks up the tour story again. "We had a big blue van called Eddie Van Human – as you would! – and we started off in Holland, where we did about six gigs. Then we left Venlo, in Holland, having looked up on a map where our next gig was, in Homburg – not Hamburg! – and it was only an hour and a half away, so we could relax a bit. We were sat around, eating food, drinking beer, and then set off at a leisurely pace for Homburg. Once we got there, we asked someone where the youth centre was that we were playing, and there wasn't one in Homburg. So we got the map out and had a look, and saw in the index at the back that there were about *five* Homburgs in Germany! There was no Google or anything back then, so I had to dig out the letter from the bloke who organised it, and we worked out from his address which Homburg it was… and it was over a hundred miles away. We jumped in the van and drove really, really quickly towards Homburg – so quickly in fact, that there was all this smoke pouring into the back of the van. There was a little crowd still outside when we got there at midnight, and lots of cheering, even though it was too late to play and everyone was leaving the gig, and it was quite embarrassing telling them what had happened. They even tried to pay us, but we refused to take anything more than the petrol money.

"The next gig was Freiberg [on September 24th]. The venue, Fabrik, was next door to this big disused building that they wanted to squat, and the gig was basically to throw the police off, a cover job that we didn't know about – the gig was held as an excuse to have a load of people gather in one place, this big squat venue, where a protest was planned. The squat was due to be closed, and they obviously wanted to keep it open. No one had told us this, but you'd be going up the stairs to the top of the building, and you'd notice, 'Oh look, there's a supermarket trolley full of bricks…how odd!' The idea was for the

BRUCE AND DICK BY KEV TYDEMAN

TROTSKY, DICK AND BRUCE BY KEV TYDEMAN

EXIT

COURTESY OF JOCK McCURDY

first band to play the Fabrik, and then everyone would go across to the squat and we'd play there, but none of us were into that idea, as it was highly likely we'd get arrested and put on file forever, so we decided to play first, before everyone went to the squat. After we finished, sat there very sweaty, some guy in a black balaclava announced the move to the squat next door, and I went outside to change my T-shirt, only to see everybody chanting at all these cops, who had come out of nowhere – probably tipped off. The police had surrounded the place and had riot shields and everything; it looked like a very inflammable situation. A big barricade was built at the entrance, and the police were firing gas into the building. When I went out to have another look, a petrol bomb was thrown, and a big cheer went up. The cops were using torches and cameras and getting as many photos of the front-liners as possible.

"We stashed the gear under the stage, and then the cops beat down the door and stormed the building using CS gas. Everyone ran to the gig room at the far end and opened the windows and breathed through handkerchiefs until most of it had dispersed. There were about seventy people stuck in the room, with about twenty riot cops guarding the exits, but in the end, they let everyone file out, past loads more cops. We told them we were English and needed to load our gear out, and one cop even helped, haha!

"On the way to Karlsruhe, loads of fumes started coming into the van, which needed a new engine, because we had driven it so hard trying to get to Homburg. A friend of ours, Jan, towed Eddie back to a garage in Freiburg where his mate worked – the plan was to fix it not dump it, because we liked the van – and we found out that we had cracked the head of the engine… it was, as the mechanic said, 'Kaput'! But Jan had a van we could borrow, bless him, so the plan was that we were going to do the rest of the tour in his van, and then swap them over once ours was repaired. It got us as far as a car park in Melksham, where I was living, and broke down, so then we had to pay for that to be fixed, and pay for Jan to come over in ours to collect it. But first they needed us to send a new engine out for our van, which was going to cost us £300 – which was a fucking fortune in 1985. Against our better judgement, we sent the engine out there and they repaired it, then Jan brought it back for us… and crashed into a taxi in Dover! Which didn't help… it was all very costly. It was a good van though, and we'd looked after it… although we should have put more oil into it and then the head might not have cracked! Tear gas and broken vans and everything – it was a final nail in the coffin really."

"The best tour vehicle we ever had was Eddie Van Human," **Pete The Roadie** recollects fondly. "It was a blue box Transit van, and we had a three-piece suite in the back, which would slide around with the equipment. We took that van to Europe a few times, it was mental. And then it became part of the barricade when that squatted gig went very wrong in Freiburg. I was trying to load the van after being tear-gassed by bloody big German riot cops, and poor old Eddie Van Human was part of the barricade… mmm, not good. And then they arrested our Dutch roadie!"

Dick: "We also decided not to do the final Hamburg gig, as it was too far from Duisburg and totally in the wrong direction. Holga, who had booked the tour, needed some convincing about this though, and kept saying it was too late to cancel it. We were all fed up and wanted to go home by that point, and then we couldn't do Osnabruck because Phil had gotten ill, and had been throwing up all night. We had to find a doctor for him in the end. It was all very chaotic, and there were lots of bad moods and arguments about what to do, but we decided to do Bielefeld and Duisburg because, apart from anything else, we needed the money. And then we had the Hamburg people on the phone, pleading with us to do the gig, because they had so much at stake on it, and I had to justify our decision to them, and explain the vibes in the band – which was hard."

Once they had limped back to the UK, the disheartened Subhumans played three more gigs before they split – Adam & Eve's in Leeds with Brigades, Organized Chaos and Shrapnel on October 23rd, and the Fulham Greyhound on October 31st, with Steve L. and Instigators, a gig that was billed as the 'Dead Fish Funeral', before bowing out with a hometown gig, in the Athenaeum Theatre on November 10th, with Steve L. and Organized Chaos in support.

"I can remember it being super packed, super hot and super sweaty," says **Andy 'Tez' Turner**, who was by then fronting the Instigators, of the Fulham Greyhound gig. "I even seem to remember some people passing out, and of course there were a lot of people upset that, 'This was it...' Little did they know [spoiler alert...]! But I don't think any of the band were particularly down about it; sometimes things just run their course, and they were a band that was always ploughing ahead, so they maybe felt trapped artistically by then?"

Essentially back where they started once they got to the final Athenaeum gig, they were also alongside the people they started out with, which was a nice way to sign off for a band that always cherished friends over popularity, despite the success they had enjoyed. Your author was proudly in attendance (after huddling outside in the cold for hours in a sleeping bag, to make sure I got in okay), and whilst the Subhumans were on brilliant form, and there was so much affection for them in the room, it was all ultimately overshadowed by the sad fact that one of our favourite bands was seemingly no more. There was a sense of inevitability they would have 'No More Gigs' as the last song in the set (although it *was* followed by a slew of encores), and Dick's introduction for it was suitably dry: "We thought it might seem pretentious to end our last gig with a song called 'No More Gigs', but then we realised it would be pretentious to even think it was pretentious...!"

"It was a seated theatre," says **Dick**, incredulously, "So you put 275 people in it, and it looked full up. There were two or three rows of people stood at the front, and everybody else had to sit down... bit of a daft place to have a gig really."

"I can't remember there being many gigs – mostly folk or classical – at the Athenaeum, let alone noisy, crash bang wallop punk music," confirms **Kev**, "So it was of great surprise

SUBHUMANS
EUR**open mouth surgery**

— HOLLAND —
SEPTEMBER 85
11th AMSTERDAM · EMMA ©
12th GRONINGEN · VERA
13th ALKMAR · PARKHOF
14th BELGIUM HEXSTRATEN · SAUUES DE BRUXBURY
17th NIJMEGEN · DORADUCA FABRIKKEN
19th ZUTPHEN · DEBARAK
20th STEENWIJK · DEBUZE
21st ROTHERDAM · ARENA
22nd VENLO · BAUPLATZ
— GERMANY —
23rd HOMBURG · JUGENDZENTRUM
24th FRIEBURG · AZ IM EXIL
25th DARMSTADT · CULTURHALLE
26th GOTTINGEN · AZ
27th OSNABRUCK · OSTBUNKER
28th BIELEFELD · A.J.Z.
29th DUISBURG · ESCHHAUS
30th HAMBURG · ??? ???

HOLLAND
ROB 080239322
GERMANY
HAUGR 076138194l

3RD LP
"WORLDS APART"
OUT IN
OCTOBER
(PROBABLY!)

(PLYMOUTH ZIGGY'S)

SUB HUM ANS

VIRUS

live onstage concert performance situation

FRIDAY AUGUST 16th   £2

PLYMOUTH ZIGGY'S

SUB HUM ANS

WO. 11
SEPT.

Disgust

ENTREE F.6,—
AANVANG 21.30

EMMA VAN DIEMENSTR.6 A'DAM

SUBHUMANS
(G.B.)

13 (vrijdag!)
september
PARKHOF toegang
f5,—

ZAAL OPEN 20.30 u

PETE, MIKE BRADBURY - ORGANIZED CHAOS, DICK, BRUCE,
AMSTERDAM, 1985 - MARTIN, THE DUTCH ROADIE FROM
ZUTPHEN WITH BLOND HAIR IN FOREGROUND, PIC BY PHIL

PHIL, HOLLAND, 1985

that the booking was allowed, although by then, there *were* a few radicals involved in supporting the centre. However, cometh the night, cometh the hour, with the foyer full of leather jackets and the street outside strewn with cans, there was a fair few ushers looking nervous. I'd been involved in a few volunteer things there previously, and had about then started to become interested in theatrical lighting, so I knew some faces, and spent a fair part of the gig telling the staff that everything would be alright… probably!

"Once the Subhumans were playing and everyone was going mad, I noticed a staff member trying hard to politely ask people to not jump about, and mind the seats, looking very concerned. I took them aside and said something like, 'Take your hands off the wheel and let it go, nothing bad will happen, I know this lot…' They did not seem that reassured, but retreated to the foyer; I followed, and found several staff huddled at the back, peering out with a mixture of horror and bemusement. To their credit though, in the foyer afterwards, the staff were in general agreement that everyone had been surprisingly polite, and that the toilets were clean – should that have been a concern? – but it was not really something they were keen to try again for a while."

"I was obviously disappointed when they split," reveals **Mel**, "But because they'd been to America, I wasn't as disappointed as I would have been if they hadn't gone to America… if that makes sense? Because I'd seen every single gig, and then they went to America, and I hadn't after that. But it was still disappointing.

"I can't remember whether I helped with the lights at that one. Because occasionally I would get behind the mixing desk and help out, not knowing what I was doing, but helping with the lights or putting a bit of echo or reverb on Dick's vocals here and there. I was back there at some point during that Athenaeum gig – but can't remember why!"

"It was fucking sad," remembers **Pete**. "'Sing, brother, sing, we've got no more gigs' felt so relevant – it was bollocks, I went home feeling shit."

Sean Forbes: "I saw them hundreds of times, but I guess the last gig – first time around, in Warminster – was a bit emotional. It felt like the end of an era. Little did we know [spoiler alert again!] that era would raise its ugly head many more times. Coincidentally I also helped put on the 'last' Culture Shock gig at the Fulham Greyhound, which never actually happened as there were too many people and a load of travellers stormed the doors. Oh, how we miss those glory days!"

Dick distributed a candid flyer through his Bluurg mail orders, explaining the reasons behind the band's break-up from his perspective, proffering musical differences and a growing divergence over approach, but everyone had a slightly different take on what precipitated it.

"I remember some definite things," begins **Bruce** carefully, "Like Trotsky saying that if things didn't improve, if we didn't start getting some better paying gigs, so we could do it properly, then he was going to leave the band. And I remember a meeting in Phil's parents' garden… in fact, that's what I always think about when I think about that decision.

"We probably wouldn't have done it if we knew then what we know now. But then again, the scene wasn't going very well in the UK and Europe… it was good in America though, and we could have probably carried on. But punk was not really there anymore. And I felt that us being labelled the way we were, we couldn't really go any further in that mould.

"We were trying to be a bit more professional, but I think we felt that if we were going to get anywhere further, it would have happened by then. Which was very naïve of us, because two US tours wasn't very many really. And we didn't realise until we got back together all those years later that we had created this sort of legendary status over there. And maybe it was because we *did* break up that we created that sort of status for ourselves? Maybe we had to break up to build up that excitement around the band?

"Crass had finished as well. It was just dying. And we needed to think how we could make a living. We were quite young, and trying to make a living off the band… we definitely weren't making enough money to live, that's for sure. But we were trying."

"We were flying high after the tour with Scream, and they were such a friendly bunch," reckons **Dick**. "And the third from last gig on that tour was the Olympic Auditorium, in front of 3000 people, and to come home from that to 80 people and the cops turning up… 'So this is where we're at!' I mean, I thought things were going along fine overall, and didn't really believe it could end. I also remember having a sort of band meeting in Phil's parents' garden, where we discussed it… I couldn't say when exactly, but it was after America and before we recorded 'Split Vision', and we just went around in circles. Bruce thought we should progress, and maybe our music should get heavier, or something like that. I was wary that other bands, like Discharge, had tried to progress in similar ways, and no one liked the results. We'd sort of reached a stalemate.

"So originally, after those last three gigs we did, it was more like, 'We are taking a break…'; at least that was the angle *I* was putting out to people in letters and that. You know, 'We're taking a break from gigs, let's see what happens…' Even then I couldn't really face up to the concept of splitting up. And we also had these songs left over, which became 'Split Vision'. There was never really a final cut-off point, because we were still mixing 'Split Vision' in July '86 – by which point, [Dick's next band] Culture Shock had been going five months. Everything overlapped; it was a very untidy end. But we stayed long enough to tidy it up, and we remained friends – there was no bitterness. So that was good."

"After some of the high points of the American tours, we hit a slump," agrees **Phil**. "Dick always totally believed in it, and wanted to keep going – he was like, 'Why stop?' – but for the rest of us, we'd just done quite a few gigs that were disillusioning. There'd been lots of trouble at various shitty little English gigs, people gobbing and fighting and the police turning up, and musically we couldn't see where it was going, with all these other bands edging towards crap metal. It felt like the roots of where punk had come from were fading away, and apart from Dick, the rest of us were questioning whether we

2 Victoria Terrace
melksham
Wiltshire
UK

Oct 85

SUBHUMANS

worlds apart

THIS IS NOT THE COVER, AS IT HAPPENS...

Subhumans answering machine...

① WORLDS APART

OUR NEW LP HAS BEEN DELAYED ALREADY A LOT
AND RELEASE DATE IS STILL UNCERTAIN....
SO HERE'S WHY!
ORIGINALLY PLANNED FOR SEPTEMBER RELEASE...
ARTWORK COMPLETED FINALLY IN LATE AUGUST...
3 TRACKS REMIXED IN AUGUST...
MASTER PRESSING BEING DONE EARLY OCTOBER...
ROUGH TRADE USA ARE LICENSING IT, THIS ENTAILS
A FURTHER DELAY AS THE UK RELEASE 'BY AT LEAST
4 WEEKS - OTHERWISE UK COPIES WILL BE SOLD AT
EXORBITANT PRICES IN THE USA - (AS IMPORT) -
THEREFORE EXPECT IT OUT IN DECEMBER -? - SORRY IT
TOOK SO LONG!
IT WILL HAVE 15 TRACKS AND WILL COST £4 - THE
PRICE RISE ACCOUNTS FOR OTHER RISING PRICES, FALL IN
RECORD SALES, COLOUR SLEEVE, ALTERATIONS IN OUR
DISTRIBUTION SETUP ETC. - IF YOU THINK ITS A RIPOFF
THEN THAT'S OK ?!!

② GIGS

WE'RE TAKING A LONG BREAK FROM GIGS FROM NOVEMBER
ONWARDS - AS SOON AS IT MAKES NO BOLLOCKS OUR
INDIVIDUAL IDEALS CONCERNING GIGS - MUSIC - PUNK-
ATTITUDE ETC. WHICH OF LATE HAVE SHOWN TO BE EQUALLY
DIFFERENT - SO THE FOLLOWING 3 GIGS WILL BE OUR
LAST ONES FOR SOME TIME...
Oct 23 - LEEDS ROOM 4 EVER. + INSTIGATORS GENT + CHUMBAS
(WHO WERE PAST DANCERS + MANAGEMENT - NO MORE SHIT
BY THE WAY.)
Oct 31 LONDON FULHAM GREYHOUND + INSTIGATORS + STEVE L.
Nov 10 WARMINSTER - ATHENAEUM ARTS CENTRE + ORGANISED
CHAOS + STEVE L.

MORE THINGS

AN 'EP/LP' WILL BE RELEASED AFTER 'WORLDS APART'... ITS LOT 4 EP'S ON ONE LP FOR £3 TO COUNTERACT THE EXTREME
PRICES + UNAVAILABILITY OF OUR EP'S IN EUROPE + BEYOND WHERE A 7 CAN COST UP TO £3 --- THIS IS NOT
CAPITALISING ON PAST SUCCESSES AS A RIPOFF - NO UNRELEASED TRACKS ETC AS SUCH YOU GET THE, YOU BUY IT! -
THE NOTSENSORS, 'BLOOD IS GONNA FLOW' EP WAS NOW BEEN RE-PRESSED (5-20 ONLY) --- THEY ARE THE LABELS
NATIONWIDE (EX FLATS, OBSCENE, INTERNAL FORCE, CIVILISED SOCIETY? SCREAM SCREEN FILE WILL BE ON
A BELGIUM COMPILATION LP. MEANWHILE WE GOT IT ALL TOGETHER... LITTLE SUGGESTIONS ARE WELCOME!

FRIDAY 1st NOV
with BLYTH POWER
3 JOHNS
MARK RILEY CREEPERS
UPSTAIRS AT THE CLARENDON

THURSDAY 31st OCT
the SUBHUMANS
& INSTIGATORS
STEVE L
£1.75
FULHAM GREYHOUND

SATURDAY 2nd NOV
THE ASTRONAUTS
KARMA SUTRA
Wat Tyler II
GOD WHITE HORSE - BRIXTON

hey ho let's go oo

POP STAR
BILLY
DOESN'T
LIKE THE
SYSTEM

FRIDAY NOVEMBER 15th
THE NEUROTICS
(BRIAN NEWTOWN)
and
THE EX PUSK
AT WOOD GREEN ARTS CENTRE
FEBRUARY RD - 20 THURS
£3.00 THE DOOR

WEDNESDAY 6th NOVEMBER
HAGAR
the
WOMB
& Wat Tyler II
CLARENDON BASEMENT

---

side itself life describes...

sing brother sing....

tempo changes than previously. At

SUBHUMANS

STEVE L.

ORGANISED CHAOS

SUNDAY 10TH NOVEMBER 1985

warminster
athenaeum arts centre

DOORS OPEN 7-30
EARS OPEN 8-00

£1-80 / £1-50 with dole card

WARMINSTER ARTS CENTRE

SUBHUMANS

Sun 10th Nov   7.30 pm
Tickets £1.75   £1.50 (Conc)

*Late-comers will not be admitted
until a suitable break in the programme.*

DEAD
FISH
FUNERAL

SUBHUMANS
INSTIGATORS
STEVE L.

thursday
31st oct

london
fulham greyhound   £1-75

DICK (TOP) AND PETE THE ROADIE (BOTTOM) AT
THE FULHAM GREYHOUND BY CHRIS KNOWLES

should even call ourselves a punk band. Were we still a punk band by the time we wrote some of that 'Split Vision' material…?

"There were also the practicalities involved, of trying to support ourselves doing it, as well – because we *had* been supporting ourselves… well, making just enough to keep going, but it was hard, and actually not possible to sustain. So, we were weighing up all these things – how could we be more successful as a band, and make more money, without being too commercial… it was all stuff that Dick wasn't very comfortable with, as he was happy with his punk roots, but the rest of us were thinking about that sort of stuff. We were definitely disillusioned, and things felt like they were winding down at the time… at least punk as we knew it. I think it might have been Trotsky that first said he actually wanted to call it a day.

"Not to be too corny, but it was like a star that shone really brightly and then burned out, because all that stuff happened so quickly and intensely during a few years, and then suddenly we weren't getting the same buzz off it. Except for Dick, who I think would have carried on, no matter how it was going, because he still loved it."

"Personally, myself, I wanted to do something else," concedes **Trotsky**, "Something a bit different musically, I mean. And at the time it did feel like the punk scene was dying off a bit. It all felt a bit… tired. Coming back from the US in '85, where we'd done a really good tour with Scream, all these amazing gigs, and then we played that gig in Chippenham, which was just fucking abysmal. And I was like, 'What the fuck are we doing? Why are we still playing gigs like this?' It was just sad really.

"So I said I was jacking it in, and the rest of them didn't seem to want to find a different drummer, or carry on if it wasn't that same line-up – and that was that! Once that spark has gone, and it's not as good as it was, it's best to leave it…"

The band's last act of defiance – or last gasp, if you prefer the fish analogy – was to record their final (new) release of the Eighties, '29:29 Split Vision', at Southern between December 14th and 17th, although it wasn't mixed until the following year.

"We split up before we did it… which does sound very odd, and I'm not sure I understand it myself," ponders **Bruce**. "We obviously liked making records! We wanted to get more musical really… not exactly mainstream, but we wanted to at least find a 'stream' where we could get a bit more popular perhaps? I don't think Dick disliked the new stuff we were writing, but maybe he didn't like it so much when it got too fancy either? We all really liked songs like 'Somebody's Mother'…

"We were still practising, because that was something we liked to do. We had split up though, and had agreed to carry on and record the new songs we had. It was a bit of a mish-mash of what we had left, I suppose."

"We had these songs left over, and thought we might as well record them," confirms **Dick**, "Which included stuff we'd been inventing and practising that ended up on side two of that record, stuff that to me seemed like an indication of what was setting into

338

the band in terms of musical differences, so to speak. Whilst I certainly liked what I liked, I didn't actually like much of side two of that record. The song 'Worlds Apart' was six minutes long, and Bruce was doing all these fiddly bits, and it was all getting a bit jazzy and odd for my tastes. And then there was the song 'New Boy', which was basically acoustic, with just me and Bruce and a few weird notes in it… and I felt quite embarrassed doing that song. But I told myself, 'Don't be embarrassed – it's an odd song, but they're good lyrics…' We never played either of those live.

"The songs on side one were as old as the hills; they'd been around for ages but just hadn't quite made it onto previous albums. You could assume from that fact alone that they were almost second division songs, which they kinda were – they weren't our best songs, else they would have been on previous records. Apart from 'Somebody's Mother', which was another new one, which we did play occasionally, and I think is really good.

"I think it was during the recording of 'Split Vision' that Trotsky cut his hair off, which was quite a shock – and a metaphor, of course, for the split."

"It was and it wasn't, y'know?" adds **Phil**, when asked whether it was weird recording 'Split Vision' posthumously. "We were all still really happy to meet up and everything… in fact, me, Trotsky and Bruce had carried on knocking around doing some music together. I think Grant even came along and had a few jams with us, but nothing really gelled at the time. We definitely had no firm idea about what we wanted to do, we just wanted to play some music, so we didn't gig or anything."

"And it was called '29:29 Split Vision' because twenty-nine minutes, twenty-nine seconds was originally the length of the album," explains **Dick**, "Although it turned out to be a bit longer than that, according to the CD player, but by the time we knew that, it was too late to change it – and it sounded good anyway…"

Bruce: "It was certainly better than the alternative names we'd thought of for it. I think Grant had the idea of 'X10' [it being their tenth 'official' release] as a title?"

The year 1985 had been tumultuous for the Subhumans, who were no longer together as a result, but they had two new releases scheduled for the following year – one of them being possibly the strongest record in their entire catalogue – and the band members were already looking to the future. So it wasn't the end, far from it, and as the old saying goes, what you lose in the fire, you may find amongst the ashes.

WARMINSTER ATHENÆUM, 2021

BRUCE, WARMINSTER ATHENÆUM, 1985 BY PHIL

WARMINSTER ATHENAEUM, NOVEMBER 1985

Subhumansions - 2 Victoria Terrace - Melksham - Wilts - England
Nov 85

No news is good news

(Subhumans fall apart shock horror probe)

We've now decided to disband for various reasons explained below and this handout has been done to save me writing it all out loads of times to all those who write to us and deserve to know why etc — sorry its rather impersonal but there's a lot to say so I'd rather write it once only instead of re-living it all every letter I write —

(WHY?!)

over the last year (and especially the last 6 months) we've grown apart in our attitudes concerning punk/protest/music/money — the majority opinion in the band was that we had reached our peak of "success" and also the maximum number of people possible within the punk scene, and with our past records and image could not reasonably hope to ever reach beyond the confines of the 'punk band' image in order to be accessible to a wider audience, no matter how varied our music became — much discord arose over suggested ideas of unrestricted prices for gigs and records, discarding our faster tracks in favour of slower more rock-orientated music, and other things that contradicted our present ideologies, all put forward as alternatives in order to reach more people, get off the bread-line etc — Several disorganised violent gigs reinforced these attitudes ('anarchists' smashing toilets etc) and in July Trotsky said he'd leave in October after a tour of Europe (that was already organised) — Rather than get a new drummer we have had to conclude that with so many contradictory ideas amongst us it would be impossible to reach a compromise, and therefore have called it a day — — After 5½ years of pushing the pen on behalf of the band in lyrics statements letters and interviews it has evolved into a situation where the Subhumans 'image' is more-or-less one persons line of thought (mine) rather than 4 persons — and so as I've grown with it, over the years others in the band have grown away from it, especially in political and punk-musical terms — so the split is partly the result of my obstinacy and refusal to compromise to the extents suggested, and partly the result of a desire for change after so many years of consistency — change in musical and social terms that, for most of the band, the Subhumans could not achieve — if we carried on through compromise it would only get worse and the same mental differences would create the same problems all over again —

We plan to record and release another EP in the future so as not to ✳ entirely waste our remaining unreleased tracks, and the 'Worlds Apart' LP will be out 2nd week of December — BLURG records and tapes will continue as long as people buy the records! Individual plans are uncertain but I at least intend to continue in one form or another (anyone need a singer?!) —

final predictable but necessary thanks list (of course!) — eternal thanks (pulls out peeled onion, violins etc) to John Loder, Derek + Colin, the Mob and the Trowbridge + Warminster punks who got us going in the first place; Grant, Andy, Pete the Roadie, all the drivers, Eddie the van and all the people who got us gigs, went to them, bought the records, read this piece of paper and generally supported us for so long —

Sorry + thanks

Dick
Subhumans

✳ 8TRACK
MINI LP
NO RELEASE DATE YET

DICK'S STATEMENT ON THE SPLIT, NOVEMBER 1985

On the face of it, it was a sorry time to be a Subhumans fan, with the band having just broken up, but there was much to celebrate as well, because their third album, 'Worlds Apart', was released in January, and sold enough copies to get to No. 2 in the Indies when it charted on February 1st, 1986. Its success was well deserved, because it is arguably the band's finest moment; it may lack some of the youthful energy of 'The Day the Country Died', and the focused attack of the A-side of 'From the Cradle to the Grave', but its maturity is undeniable. And 'maturity' doesn't have to mean slowed down and mellowed out (although there's an *element* of that too); here it means the band were competent and confident enough to take their musical quest to its logical conclusion, paying no heed to what was expected of them. Ironically, because it was released after they split (but let's not forget it was recorded nine months earlier), it sounds for all the world like a band completely comfortable in its own skin and at the peak of its not inconsiderable powers.

After the slightly underwhelming '33322' intro discussed in the previous chapter, 'British Disease' kicks in with Bruce's choppy, jagged guitars counterpointing Phil's clamorous bass runs, but the driving punk rhythms are offset by some dramatic doomy hanging notes, not to mention some snappy stop-starts and a disconcerting disregard for traditional timings. And over this fascinating musical backdrop, Dick contemplates everything that is amiss with our insular little island.

"'British Disease' was written shortly after the riots in 1981, in Brixton at first, but then they spread all over the country," explains **Dick**. "It was quite a new thing to us at the time, being young and that, and it was quite exciting – you thought something might change, that the basic gut reaction was finally coming through, albeit in violence rather than street protests. It was boiled-over anger that had escalated, anger about the way people were being treated... mostly at the way that non-white people were being treated. At the way the police treated minorities as some kind of second-class citizens. People were being murdered, and they got away with it – the victims would be blamed for their own murder... it was incredible. If a white person got murdered, there were investigations and trials and uproar, but if a black person got murdered, it was an accident, or self-inflicted, or self-defence [by the perpetrator]. This happened over and over again, and as a result, non-white people were seen as the problem – and it fed into the inherent racism that's been around in this country since the days of the empire and all that... when we went across the world enslaving everybody in the name of white superiority.

"And that hasn't gone away. In fact, it's fired up more now than ever before with Brexit. For a while, maybe sometime in the Nineties, it seemed like it was getting a bit better, that we'd all grown up a bit and became nicely multi-cultural, and there was an acceptance of being in Europe... I thought it was fucking brilliant being in Europe – it made total sense. And you realise these things because you are in a band and you go on tour around Europe, and you see what it's like over there – it's cleaner, it's nicer, it's

POSTCARD FROM INSTIGATORS ON TOUR OF SWEDEN, FEBRUARY 1986

the new album by
the SUB HUM ANS
is called

"WORLDS APART"
and the sleeve
looks like this :

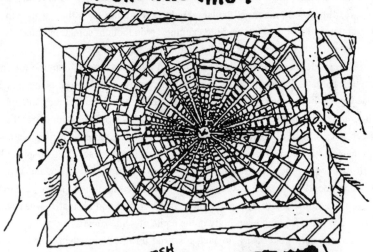

SEND $10 CASH (INCLUDES air mail
to. BLURG 2 VICTORIA TERRACE.
RECORDS MELKSHAM · WILTS · ENGLAND
YOUR LOCAL RECORD STORE IS PART OF THE SYSTEM · SUPPORT THE ALTERNATIVE

WORLDS APART AD

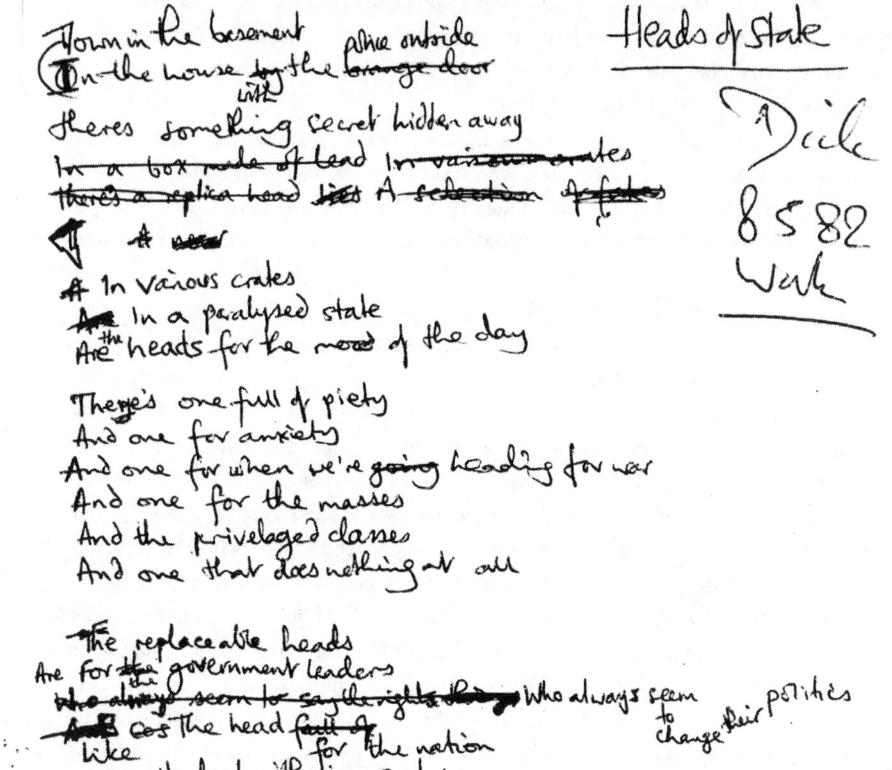

Down in the basement ~~the outside~~ she outside
On the house ~~by the orange~~ door
with
theres something secret hidden away
~~In a box made of lead In various crates~~
~~theres a replica head~~ ~~its~~ A ~~selection~~ ~~of false~~

A ~~new~~
~~A~~ In various crates
~~Are~~ In a paralysed state
Are the heads for the ~~most~~ of the day

There's one full of piety
And one for anxiety
And one for when we're ~~going~~ heading for war
And one for the masses
And the privileged classes
And one that does nothing at all

The replaceable heads
Are for ~~the~~ the government leaders
~~Who always seem to say the right thing~~ Who always seem
~~And~~ Cos the head ~~full of~~ to change their politics
like for the nation
Doesn't deal with immigration
Cos patriots + riots don't mix

And when the head for the day
Says I'll do it this way
Just remember also the replaceable head
Cos then they get elected
the decisions are rejected
~~And then forgetting~~ Contradicting what they sed
Completely
~~Cos~~ Don't trouble politicians / they don't make their own
~~they And~~ Cos they haven't even got their heads screwed on   decisions
~~And maybe one day~~ its all a load of bull / and the basements
~~And with~~ And state policy is what they base it on getting fun
For everything thats sed / its just another load
But then ~~maybe~~ And the politicians words can be replaced
But then maybe I am wrong / I mean this is just a song / MAYBE ITS JUST
~~OR~~ IS IT JUST that politicians are 2 faced?/THAT EVERYONE'S
TWO F

'HEADS OF STATE' – DICK'S ORIGINAL LYRIC SHEET

more colourful… the cops are sometimes more pragmatic. People generally haven't got this underlying tendency to want to control everything, and be in charge; they don't feel that sense of national superiority that the British have got, which has been assimilated culturally over the centuries since the empire.

"Of course, not everyone in Europe has the same positive outlook, and there are right-wingers and fascists in every country, who want to claim their own country back for themselves, and all that stupid shit. But they exist everywhere, and that's the mindset of the lonely and desperate, mostly male, people that just can't find satisfaction in any other way, except through fear and control of others. That's what nationalism is – it's drawing up the fences and being scared by the world, basically. For whatever reason.

"'Ignorance is the British disease…' It's like, just close the gates on thinking too hard about anything, outside the little square you live in – your job, your house, your partner, your retirement plan… that sort of thing. It's a reaction against how people follow the media for their information and don't think outside the little bubble that forms in their heads. Especially the tabloid newspapers, and most of what comes out of the TV as what they call 'news'. A lot of people take everything at face value, and believe exactly what they read – they let the media do their thinking for them. And a lot of people prefer it that way, because if they're not directly involved in being poor, or in a riot, or in situations that lead to riots, then they'll just accept it as fact. And it's going on somewhere else anyway, so it doesn't concern them. Generally, people don't like politics; they don't want to have to worry about things they can't change. And those that do worry about it undervalue their own potential to be part of the change that's needed, because it's all down to human behaviour and societal patterns. Most of us are kept in line – more or less – by rules and regulations and the archetypes upheld by the media and the way it gives us information about what's apparently going on…"

This is a powerful theme that Dick has explored in his lyrics many times over the years – how societal pressures connive with well-established authoritarian entities to keep us in our obedient little pigeonholes… and before you know it, you're gone, so what's the point? But that's what 'they' want us to think. Some of us are so entrenched in the fabric of this ubiquitous 'reality', it's just easier to embrace it.

Hence the spirited rant of 'Apathy', and its irresistible singalong chorus which is a firm live favourite; the song might have international readers scratching their heads at references to British institutions such as 'ITV' (a mainstream TV channel), 'The Sun' (a populist tabloid newspaper) and 'Ford Cortinas' (a popular British car in the Seventies and Eighties), but there's no mistaking the meaning of, 'Bombs? War? Famine? Death? An apathetic public couldn't care less!' The song skilfully explores a whole range of dynamics and ends with a deliciously cocky 'Huh!', which the band can be heard discussing in the studio after the final note has died away.

"We weren't sure whether we wanted to keep it or not," divulges **Dick**. "It was a bit too rock 'n' roll! And by leaving in me saying, 'I'm not too sure about that', that qualified it a bit, haha!"

346

'Fade Away' is the first truly mellow song on the album, its laid-back reggae verses built around a bouncy, descending bass line. "That was more of a Phil thing," reckons **Bruce**. "He wasn't afraid to bring his influences into the songs. Well, we were all bringing influences in around about the writing of 'Worlds Apart' – I was bringing in rock stuff, but Phil was even bringing in more funky stuff, because he was into that at the time."

"Yeah, I was listening to all sorts," agrees **Phil**, "And throughout our catalogue you can hear evidence of our diverse influences, from Stevie Wonder to the Rezillos and Hawkwind. I remember I was still quite into Hawkwind in the early Eighties; I'd been to see them with Vardis in Michael Eavis [who founded the Glastonbury Festival]'s barn in Pilton, Somerset. Then the next night was the same line-up, but at the Hammersmith Odeon. And I really liked the albums they were putting out at that time, 'Levitation' then 'Sonic Attack'."

And it's Phil's exquisite bass run in the middle of 'Fade Away' which segues the song from some nebulous soloing from Bruce into its rousing climax, which is one of the most stirring moments on the record, Dick imploring us all, 'So live your life, in fear of no one – we must have our say, before we fade away'. Bruce's perfectly pitched harmonious backing vocals help add great emotional depth to this section, as well as many others on the album.

'Businessmen' is a more straightforward punky number, similar in some of its jaunty feel to 'Apathy', but even here Subhumans mix it up, a rumbling chorus and some clever juxtaposition of vocals over instrumental 'stabs' ensuring nothing about any of this is even remotely generic. It's a nice little palate cleanser before the deceptively ambitious 'Someone Is Lying', which employs a suitably machine-like staccato riff to deliver its cautionary tale about industrial accidents, and the inevitable subsequent cover-ups, although cascading guitar scales and subtle crescendos sweep the story along to a truly progressive finale.

"Oddly enough, no," replies **Dick**, when asked if the song was written about a specific incident, like Chernobyl for example. "That song falls into the small category of personal lyrics written about something that didn't happen, but *could* happen to someone else. It's about people working – and dying – for the power industry, all the way from coal to nuclear, and it's about the by-products from the industry being buried underground and leaking into the mines. You can't just bury this problem forever; it will come out in the end. And I turned it into a personal thing, by writing, 'Someone is lying – and father is dead...' Which might have seemed like a strange line to write because my dad wasn't – and isn't – dead. So, it felt weird writing that, because it wasn't true, and when you write something like that, it really should be true, shouldn't it? Like in the song 'No', when I say, 'My mother died of cancer when I was five', that *is* true, and I wouldn't have written it if it wasn't. But here I am, years later, writing, 'Father is dead', but basically it was a personal story of a fictional father. And it wasn't about a specific incident, just the possibility of it happening.

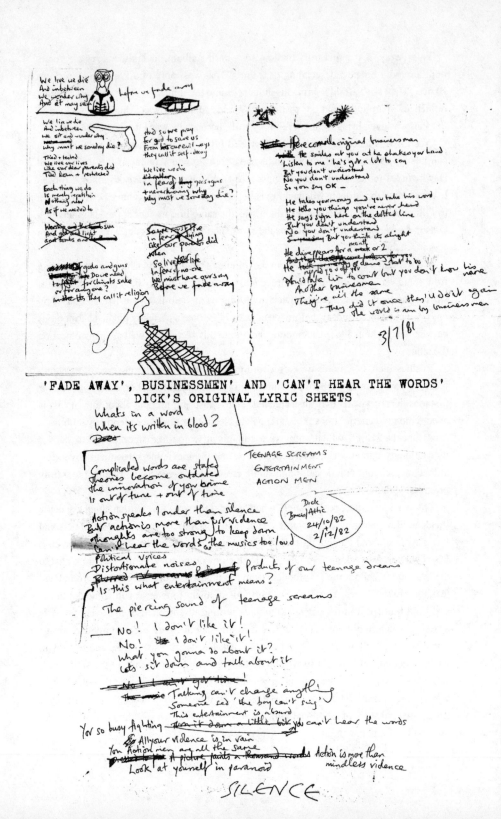

'FADE AWAY', BUSINESSMEN' AND 'CAN'T HEAR THE WORDS'
DICK'S ORIGINAL LYRIC SHEETS

GATEFOLD

166 FISH 12" BLACK
GATEFOLD SLV INNER

'WORLDS APART' GATEFOLD ARTWORK FOR PRINTING

CULTURE SHOCK, MALVERN, 1986 BY DAVE THOMAS

"The other song like that is 'Wake Up Screaming' [on 'From the Cradle to the Grave'], about a friend dying of an overdose, which again didn't happen, but could easily happen to anyone. It's a short leap from it not happening to imagining it happening."

Side A is brought to a brooding conclusion with 'Pigman', a pro-vegetarian song based on another of Dick's clever word plays – this time the disturbing concept of the 'family butcher'; the sickening tradition of consuming dead flesh is skilfully deconstructed with minimal precision ('Guilty conscience stews away in the kitchen…'), whilst Bruce's atonal guitar solo echoes the screams reverberating around the blood-soaked walls of the abattoirs so many of the public would prefer to forget existed, as they are a grim reminder of the brutal price paid for a fleeting burst of taste on the tongue.

Side B reveals some of the band's growing disenchantment with the punk scene's often small-minded prejudices and violent vagaries, and opens in high octane fashion with 'Can't Hear the Words', the pounding pummelling of the music (briefly brightened by a lightening freeform jam in the mid-section) seemingly intent on delivering a most pertinent message, 'Action speaks louder than silence, but action is more than just violence… all your violence is in vain, you action men are all the same…'

"It was just trying to reclaim some space for lyrics," offers **Dick**, "To gain back some importance for the words in punk songs, instead of it just being about the music. Which does make us go to gigs, and we all jump about, but there's all the excess energy and hormones and fights breaking out – and sometimes you feel like you're singing to a brick wall and nothing's getting through. And sure, if I wanted the words to mean more by themselves, I'd be a poet, or do lectures, but that ain't gonna happen because the music's great fun too. I just wanted to redress the balance a little bit, and say that words are a bit more vital; it's not just the music, and words should ideally make a difference. Or at least help towards something positive. That song was also – mostly, in fact – about fights breaking out at gigs where the bands playing were anti-violence, but when I say, 'Talking can't change anything,' that is very tongue-in-cheek. I can't actually remember where that song started… some songs just start with a title, and then I see what happens."

"Myself and Mel would look at each other and say, 'There's no point in trying to replicate that,'" adds **Jock**, on the eloquent power of Dick's lyrics, "So we [the A-Heads] sang songs that were social observation, with a bit of 'Hammer House of Horror' thrown in. I remember when we wrote 'Not Last Night but the Night Before', up at Bruce's flat in Vicarage Street after a night in the pub, we had a notepad that we passed around and everyone wrote a few lines of it – and you'll find that the most intelligent lyrics on that song probably came from Dick, haha! But they [Subhumans] never tried to ram their opinions down people's throats. And yeah, there was no way we were going to go anywhere near that, because you had the likes of Dick, and Colin from Conflict, doing that sort of thing so well, making people think…"

'Get to Work on Time' is more light-hearted and quirky in feel, with Bruce's wailing

350

guitar perhaps representing the dreaded alarm clock, or even the factory siren, that summons you to the workplace, where you're forced to shelve all the things you *want* to do and concentrate on things you *have* to do, for fear of ostracization. It's a scathing reflection on how modern society has painted us into cheerless corners, brilliantly observed albeit firmly anchored to the period it was written in by reference to 'the wages in the brown bag, underneath the name tag' (yes, we were still paid weekly in *cash* in the Eighties) – but this is no nostalgic time capsule, as the sentiment remains more valid than ever. Our work/life balance has never been more blurred and skewed.

"'Get to Work on Time' was written to the tune in my head of the Bob Dylan song, 'Subterranean Homesick Blues'," reveals **Dick**. "If you've got a tune in your head, there's your free structure to write lyrics to… it's quite handy. Years later, 'Charity' by Citizen Fish was written with 'Penny Lane' in mind – even though I don't own a copy of 'Penny Lane', it sort of sticks in your head."

The band's dogged determination to push the proverbial envelope is no better demonstrated than by the next two songs, 'Carry on Laughing' and 'Straight Line Thinking'; the latter was discussed in the previous chapter, but 'Carry on Laughing' equals it in the sheer delight it takes subverting genre expectations. There are very few punk bands – now, then or ever – who utilised acapella sections and such mind-boggling time changes (Nomeansno being a notable exception to the rule).

"That song was so complicated that we didn't actually play it live much after a while, and we more or less quietly dropped it," admits **Dick**. "People would be saying it was too tricky, or they weren't quite sure how it goes, and then it's 'We need to practise it first…!' And that can be the death of a song when it comes to playing it live – and that's what happened to 'Carry on Laughing'."

'Ex-Teenage Rebel' tells another oh-so-familiar story, of those vocal activists who set out to change the world, only to be beaten into submission by the fists of conformity ('The strength of us all could demolish the wall… but you chose to walk through the door…'). The song conjures a measured intensity, punctuated by moments of exquisite melody, before it hunkers down for an atmospheric dub/ska finale, much of its power coming from the delicate interplay between Dick and Bruce's vocals and Trotsky's powerhouse militaristic drumming.

"You would hear that so-and-so wasn't coming to the local disco anymore, because he had joined the army, or joined the police, and when you're eighteen, you're like, 'You what?'" elaborates **Dick**. "I have a specific person in mind still, this one person who joined the army, who had been a 'punk for life' type character. One week he was like, 'I'm punk rock 'til the day I die', and then the next… well, obviously he wasn't! I hated that false, macho strength thing, people showing off and then turning around and doing something completely diametrically opposite to it. That really used to piss me off, so I wrote a song about it, and extended it out to broader terms, talking about staying together in the beliefs that make people punk rockers in the first place."

CULTURE SHOCK ON TOUR WITH SCREAM

NEWPORT, WALES, 1986 BY WELLY ARTCORE

The closing track (if you discount the instrumental outro), 'Power Games', continues the band's critique of the so-often elitist punk scene, decrying mindless violence for superficial reasons such as fashion, some roving bass and a memorable guitar hook breaking down into some disconsolate – yet ludicrously catchy – reggae, loaded with pathos ('One man's hand is another man's fist, and so the power games still exist…').

"That was written about the pathetic macho nature of the scene," bemoans **Dick**. "It's about the punk scene because that was the scene we were in, but the same thing can be applied to any gathering of mostly male people in one spot, and the ensuing sight of some people being all macho and basing their existence on hierarchies of who looks more punk than somebody else who looks less punk than them, and the demarcation of other people, who are in the same scene, in the same club, watching the same band. They just need to feel superior, and they will take the piss and blank people out. And a lot of people got into punk rock in the first place because they felt alienated, so to feel alienated in the scene is just despicable and ridiculous. Being in a scene doesn't mean you have to support every aspect of it; there are unsavoury aspects to every scene, I imagine, and it's best to call them out. And punk rock, to its credit, is possibly the only scene to call out its own deficiencies. Because who else is gonna do it? Everyone else thinks it's *all* shit anyway. Punk rockers themselves don't think it's all shit, but they acknowledge there are shit elements, like standards of behaviour or whatever, that need calling out. That's the whole point of punk rock – for me, at least – it can do that. We don't want it to be self-*policing*, because that's a horrible phrase, but it needs to be self-regulating. There has to be way more give and take.

"I'm as guilty as any other teenage mind-set punk rocker of setting up barriers, including the Crass punk/Oi punk barrier. Although that was set up for me, by Garry Bushell and various other writers from the music papers who liked to create a scene within a scene – at the cost of disparaging other scenes within the scene… that also got invented by them! There was no such thing as 'Crass bands' – there were just bands that sorta sang about things along the same politically inspired road that Crass were on. And there were bands that didn't. There was just too much division. That's what the song 'Labels' was about too.

"A lot of the songs are written directed at the person writing them – directed at myself. In some of my songs, I'm telling myself off for being susceptible to doing the very things I'm writing about that shouldn't be done. Because it's part of the evolution of your character, to let these things out. If you feel like you're doing something wrong, the best way to express it is to suggest to other people that it's the wrong thing to do, because you know it is. I could write a song saying, 'I'm a shit bag, because I treated so-and-so really badly last week, and now I'm really depressed…' but that's for solo male artists of a certain age that go on to get platinum discs for doing so, but fuck that weak shit, haha!

"Part of your self-defence mechanism is not to go out there and say you're defective – a better way to channel that is to write about it in the third person, not the first person…

write about the problem, not the fact that you've got the problem. The fact is that some of those songs are reflections of my own insecurity at the way I've been led to think about certain things, and the way I've been led to think is wrong. And you get the realisation as you grow up that it's wrong, and you feel guilty because you've been thinking like that, but the guilt is coming from accepting responsibility for what other people are responsible for. You just have to cut the chain, and a) not send that shit thing you've been doing out any further into the world, and b) pull yourself up and tell the world that it's wrong. The process leading up to telling the world you think something is wrong – in your opinion – is full of self-recrimination, but to write songs saying you're full of self-recrimination is just a bit defeatist, and doesn't lead to any better feelings."

Overall then, 'Worlds Apart' is very slick, very eclectic, and very profound, both musically and lyrically – the album where the band got everything just right.

"I think we hit a sweet spot with 'Worlds Apart'," agrees **Phil**. "We had such diverse influences, in Bruce... Trotsky... all of us – it was quite a mixture between us, and we were really into trying to push boundaries, whilst still keeping the energy. And it sometimes got quite intricate, but it worked on that album. Whereas on 'Split Vision', even though it was recorded just after the band had split, it felt like we pushed it a bit too far with the prog stuff. It got a bit wanky, haha! Obviously some people love it, and I still enjoy listening to some of it, but I really love 'Worlds Apart'.

"Some of the songs are pretty hard to play, so – partly out of laziness – we don't play them, as it would be an effort to all get together and relearn the songs. I got my bass out at home and was playing along to a few of them, working them out again, and songs like 'Get to Work on Time' and 'British Disease' are a real bass workout, y'know? 'Fade Away' has got a little solo-y bit in the middle, although we still do that one live quite regularly. So there's a few of them we still do.

"Funnily enough, a lot of people in the States particularly like 'Worlds Apart', a bit more than over here perhaps. Sometimes, the people in the band get their own ideas about what people want to hear... but no one's gone and done a poll or anything, haha!

"It is my favourite Subhumans record, to be honest. A lot of how you feel about a release is down to where you were in your life at that time, and I had just started my journey with the band. I had got bedded in, and was able to influence the writing, and there's a lot of me – my character – in those songs, especially in how I was interacting with Bruce at that time. Me and him were very in tune with each other at that point."

"It was definitely more developed than the first one and a half albums," agrees **Dick**. "Side two of 'From the Cradle to the Grave' was fairly well above our capabilities, but we did it anyway, and it was quite unusual we did it. And a lot of the songs on 'Worlds Apart' are of the same complex type, where they're not 'bash, bash, singalong!' We don't actually have that many 'bash, bash, singalong' songs, although a couple of choruses caught on here and there, like 'Religious Wars' and 'I Don't Wanna Die', but I didn't

'SPLIT VISION' PHOTO SHOOT, LONGBRIDGE DEVERILL, 1986
BY KEV TYDEMAN

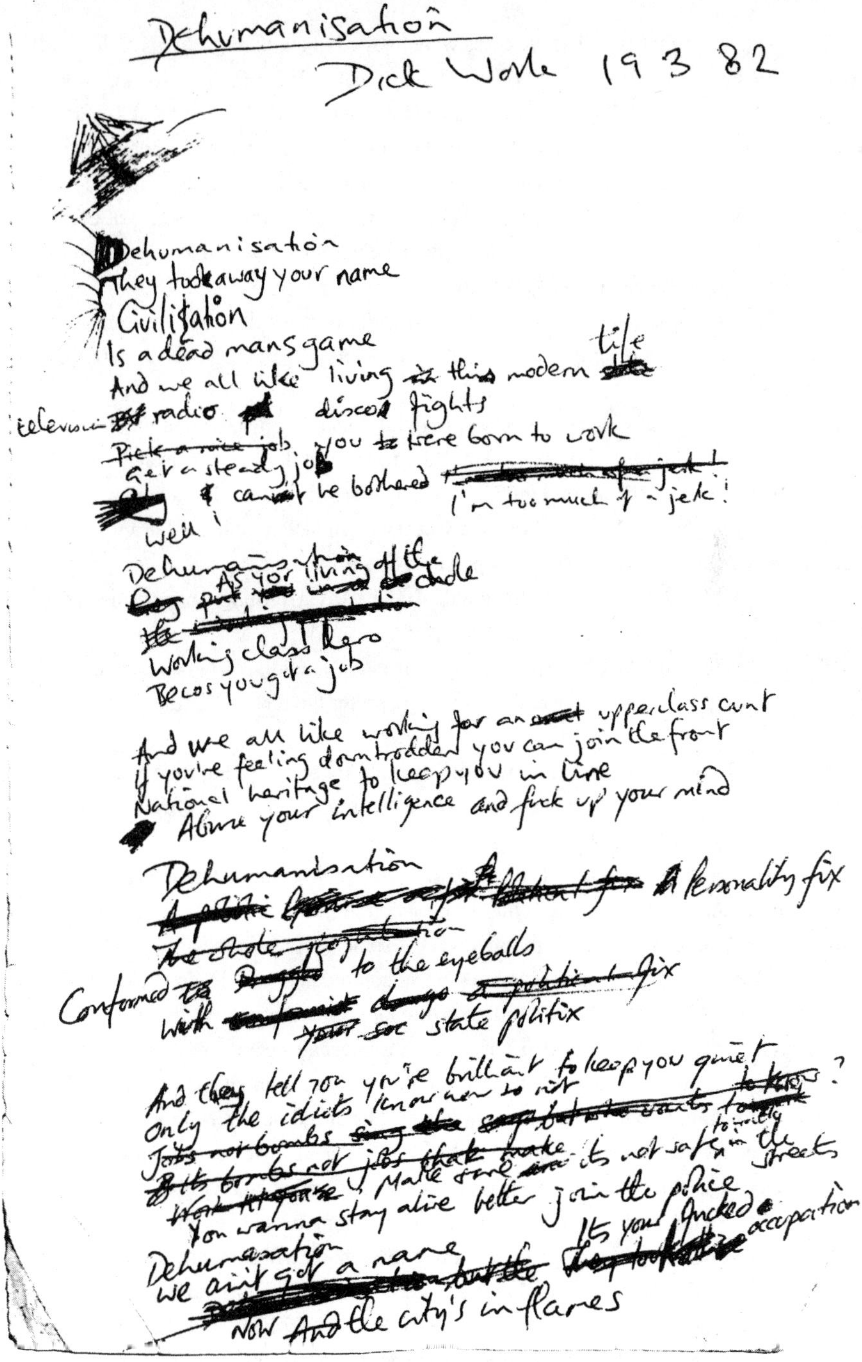

Dehumanisation
Dick Work 19 3 82

Dehumanisation
They took away your name
Civilisation
Is a dead mans game
And we all like living ~~in~~ this modern ~~life~~ life
television ~~&~~ radio ~~&~~ disco fights
~~Pick a nice job,~~ you ~~were~~ were born to work
Get a steady job
~~~~ & can't be bothered ~~~~
I'm too much of a jerk
well i

~~Dehuma~~ ~~As for living little~~ dude
~~the~~
Working class hero
Becos you got a job

And we all like working for an ~~~~ upperclass cunt
If you're feeling downtrodden you can join the front
National heritage to keep you in line
Abuse your intelligence and fuck up your mind

Dehumanisation
~~A politic~~ ~~~~ A Personality fix
~~The state~~ ~~~~
Conformed ~~~~ to the eyeballs
With ~~~~ state politix

And ~~they~~ tell you you're brilliant to keep you quiet ~~to riot~~ ?
Only the idiots know how to riot
~~Jobs not bombs~~ ~~~~
~~its bombs not jobs~~ ~~~~ its not safe in the streets
~~Work~~ ~~Make sure~~ ~~~~
You wanna stay alive better join the police
Dehumanisation
We ain't got a name ~~~~ Its your fucked occupation
~~Now~~ And the city's in flames

really write a lot of choruses. The choruses were insisted upon, that had to exist, that had to have lyrics written for them as add-ons to the original lyrics. Like the 'No, no, I don't like it' [in 'Can't Hear the Words'], which is a great chorus, but I didn't write it as part of the original song, until it was decided it would be a good idea to have a chorus in there. 'Just a couple more lines…!' But choruses can be quite hard to write, especially if you have a song that starts at the beginning and ends at the end, and there's a series of events over a passage of time linked to each other, you have to find a chorus that relates to each part of the song, which can be really difficult."

One of the beautiful things about 'Worlds Apart' is that, although the songs are complicated, they sound simple – they're so well played, the listener forgets how complicated they are.

Dick: "Yeah, musically there's all sorts going on, lots of stop-starts and weird beats, and it took some getting used to. Where it starts to flow, and you know exactly what's coming next. And with 'Carry on Laughing', we never really got used to it, and we were always having to think, 'Hang on, how many beats are in that complicated drum bit…?' And we didn't want to wing it, so we stopped playing it live."

Bruce: "'Worlds Apart' was really good. And it *was* a turning point really, very musical."

"I'm not so fond of 'Worlds Apart'," says **Trotsky**, candidly. "There's a couple of really good songs on there, but overall, I definitely prefer the feel of 'Cradle…'"

The album looked distinctive too, with its gatefold inner sleeve adorned by the best piece of art Nick Lant did for the band, and some old art of Dick's on the front and back covers.

"That was a picture I did when I was at school," says **Dick**. "In fact, that was the only good picture I did at school. I was in this art project thing, which wasn't a regular school class, but you had to do it one afternoon a week – some people did metal work or wood work, and I did art. The teacher did show me in some detail how to do broken glass, showing me how it would crack in different directions and that sort of thing. Anyway, there's broken glass in this frame that someone's holding, and a person has fallen through into the centre of all these tall buildings. At the time I didn't rationalise it out as regards the meaning behind it, but basically, it's how we're balanced on a very fragile place, in control of our own environment, and once that fragility breaks, we're doomed and we'll be surrounded by concrete and urbanisation – too much of that and we'll be swallowed up and we'll lose our basic human nature. Something along those lines anyway.

"That picture went up in a small exhibition at the school, and someone who was two years above me said, 'Ooh, that would make a good album cover…' And later on, it did! So, I was very happy with that. The inside artwork was a brilliant Nick Lant creation, definitely one of his best, depicting a rich businessman controlling and destroying the planet."

"How do I feel about that art now?" ponders **Nick**. "Forever grateful for the opportunity and very glad to have played a part in our subculture. And there wasn't any connection with any other band. If my style had appeared on other covers then I think it would have detracted from its connection to the Subhumans, and those covers would have suffered as a result. It was brief and very much of its time, a proper punk rock DIY ethos; it stopped where it did and retains whatever 'power' it had as a result. To have just one bit of my work referred to as 'iconic' is a very lovely thing, and to have got a message across back when there was no 'information highway' is a fine reward."

Bluurg also released the 'EP-LP' around the same time (Fish 14), which as the name suggests was the first four EPs compiled onto one album. Ever mindful of being accused of cashing in or selling out – or both, if indeed they are different things – the band were at pains to highlight in a statement on the (rather shoddy, thrown together) cover of the initial pressing – in nine different languages, no less – that there were no new songs on the album, that everything had been made available previously, and the primary reason behind the release was to offer a cheaper means of hearing the material than paying the extortionate import prices the individual EPs were attracting at the time.

The band's posthumous MLP, '29:29 Split Vision', was mixed by John Loder and Julie Anne Jonan between February 14th and 16th, and then finished off on July 5th and 6th, although it wasn't released until the end of the year, by which time all of the ex-Subhumans members were playing in new projects of differing kinds. In fact, Dick's next band, Culture Shock, had already recorded their first demo, 'Living History', before John Loder had finished mixing '29:29 Split Vision' – they recorded it in April '86, with Wally from the A-Heads, and Dick released it straight away through Bluurg Tapes (BLUURG 66). It was quite a departure from the Subhumans – and why not? – being heavily grounded in reggae, ska and dub, although there was plenty of punk energy and attitude there too, if you could get past the lack of power chords and fast songs. And the band were soon doing their first gig, at a local house party in Berkeley – a village just outside Warminster – on April 18th, 1986.

"We played in the kitchen," smiles **Dick**, before elaborating: "I wasn't exactly waiting about to see what happened next. I was still hanging around with the same people, except me and Bruce weren't hanging out as much as we had done previously. I don't remember socialising much with Bruce after the last gig… well, certainly not after the 'Split Vision' recording. He invented a band called The Switch. I was still going to Warminster though, and hanging around in the pubs, and that's when Nige came up with the idea of getting together with his mate Paul, who had just moved up from Cornwall and played bass, and was much inspired by reggae and dub tunes. Organized Chaos had just split, so Bill was a freed-up drummer. Nige also had time on his hands because the A-Heads had split up… there was a lot of splitting up going on! So, I just gave that a go really.

'SPLIT VISION' PHOTO SHOOT, 1986

TROTSKY, DICK, KEV TYDEMAN AND BRUCE, 1986 BY PHIL

PETE THE ROADIE, OUTSIDE HIS ANTIQUES STORE,
WARMINSTER, CIRCA 1990

EARLY CITIZEN FISH PHOTO, TAKEN AT 1A HIGH STREET,
WARMINSTER BY BARRY CALLAGHAN

"I did have a practice with a guy called Andy and his band, but I can't remember what they were called. That didn't go very well though, because the music was a bit new wave and poppy, and I didn't really feel inspired by it. And I didn't know them very well – if at all – whereas I knew Nige and Bill already, so I knew what they played like. Although, as it turned out, Bill's Organized Chaos–style drumming was not featured in Culture Shock hardly at all – it was a completely different kind of beat… for *all* of us. It was a massive departure.

"And if you'd asked me, 'Do you like reggae, yes or no?', I would have said, 'No, not really!' Because I didn't like much of it… but when you're singing to it, it's a whole different ball game. And we started off playing local pubs, once or twice a month, and it got up and running in much the same way that Subhumans did."

"Culture Shock was a massive change after Subhumans," agrees **Bill**, "And for me, after Organized Chaos, as well as for Dick. That was totally enlightening for me, and was down to Paul Taylor. Don't get me wrong, because we were listening to a lot of reggae, but he came up from Cornwall, and he was a lovely person, a very strong character, who knew what he wanted, and he got hold of Dick. He was a brilliant reggae bassist, and I was a punk, so I didn't think about it – I just played what came naturally, something off-beat, and it just worked. It was never a punk band trying to play reggae… it was just Culture Shock, and still is. And because we all lived at 44 [East Street, Warminster] – well, apart from Dick, but he was over all the time – we could just jam whenever we wanted, and that was all we did. We didn't work or anything, we just played, and all these other musicians would swing by and jam with us. And it's really important to have a scene or environment like that, where people can express themselves."

"I was just doing some stuff without Dick, but still with Trotsky and Phil," explains **Bruce**, of what the other ex–band members were doing. "And I was mixing the second Instigators LP ['Phoenix'], so I was helping Dick with that in April. I was also keen to get Grant back in a band with me, and that did happen with what became The Switch. That was very prog rock, but not a total departure from Subhumans… I think the rockier aspects would have fitted in? There was one riff that I was very excited about, and I was playing it in the studio when we recorded 'Split Vision', and it went on to be a Switch song. But we didn't gig and record until after I'd got a whole new line-up, although I kept some of the ideas Phil and I had come up with.

"But I was very naïve – I thought it would be so easy to just find some more musicians and carry on. I didn't recognise the value of Dick – I had no idea he was going to become a legend, not really. Obviously I valued him though, and what he did with Subhumans. Dick got into Culture Shock, and we kinda split apart, and didn't have much to do with each other. It's almost embarrassing how little we had to do with each other in fact…

"So, I began searching for other musicians, placing all sorts of ads around the place… I even put an ad in the job centre in Bath – which was where I found the members of The Switch. And the rocky stuff was good, I think, but it went off in all directions, a bit like the Subhumans' long songs do, but more prog rock. Grant came back from where he'd been living in Yorkshire and played keyboards. That went on for a year or two."

'29:29 Split Vision' was released in late 1986 and, as intimated by the labels on either side of the vinyl that proclaim 'Old Side' and 'New Side', is definitely a release of two halves. The 'Old Side' features five tracks (one of them actually relatively *new* when it was recorded, but let's not split hairs) that basically continue the trajectory Subhumans were on up until the end of side A of 'From the Cradle to the Grave'. 'Somebody's Mother' is immediate and infectious, albeit a bit of a traditional rocker, until it takes an off-kilter left turn at the mid-point, whilst the other four tracks are more simplistic and revel in their punky energy: 'Think for Yourself' is lifted by some exuberant bass runs, 'Walls of Silence' is a snappy number, railing against the insidious ways we are controlled by faceless systems, 'Heroes' seems to be a furious rant about well-intentioned musical activists selling out to the man (complete with sarcastic rock god guitar solo... if a guitar solo can even be 'sarcastic', that is), and 'Dehumanisation' incorporates exhilarating thrashy sections with rapid-fire tempo changes to denounce the mind games played on us all to keep us toeing governmental lines ('They'll tell you you're brilliant to keep you quiet, "Only idiots know how to riot..."').

On the other hand, the 'New Side' seems to pick up the wildly creative baton the band started whittling for themselves with the title track of 'Cradle...' and really started to carve into shape with 'Worlds Apart'. In fact, the first song on the 'New Side' is indeed entitled 'Worlds Apart', and is an eight-minute prog workout, all meandering bass and noodling guitars, veering dangerously near to rock opera territory in places; it's incredibly clever, and the lyrics are superb, but it's never likely to figure high in a Subhuman fan's poll of their favourite tracks by the band. Although it's likely to be higher in such a poll than the next track, 'New Boy'; a slow-burn mainly acoustic track that alternately explodes into jazzy noise, it's so far removed from the joyous punk of the band's earlier releases as to be barely recognisable. But at least it makes the closing track, 'Time Flies...', feel like light relief, although even that winds down for a claustrophobic third act, albeit with a chink of hope peering through the grim introspection ('Don't take everything for granted – exist as if each moment was your last!').

Whilst not a bad release by anyone's standards, and there's no faulting the playing or the production on it, '29:29 Split Vision' is stained in every pore by the jaded cynicism of a band who has just split up prematurely, fractured by external forces beyond their youthful ability to control.

"By the time we split up, which was when we were writing side two of 'Split Vision', some of the songs Bruce was inventing, like 'Worlds Apart', were well outside my comfort zone to sing to," admits **Dick**, "And 'New Boy', at the time, was the one Subhumans song I didn't like at all. I thought the words were good, but Bruce insisted it was a good idea to have almost no music in it, and it all comes across as a bit too... empty? The music on side two of that record is very much 'musician's music'; there's some really unusual stuff going on, but in terms of catchiness and bounciness and firing up a crowd, it's hard work."

PHIL, WITH RICHARD THE ROADIE, U.S. TOUR, EARLY NINETIES

PETE, TROTSKY, TIM CLAWS, CITIZEN FISH U.S. TOUR 1991

PIC: SUSAN MOORE

THE SUBHUMANS
THE VENUE, NEW CROSS

I'M a bit unsure about how to approach The Subhumans. Do I concentrate on how, if at all, Dick's lyrical style has changed over the years or alternatively scour the music for hints of the fine bands that were to come, namely Culture Shock and Citizen Fish. Or do I just dye my hair and drink 20 cans of Special Brew? Dilemmas, dilemmas...

The thing is with The Subhumans there's still a massive void between band and audience. Dick is not an anarchist, of this I'm sure, but the thugs, skins and tramps rally round his band's moniker as if it was meant literally, rather than ironically. And yet they still sing along with his every, well-formulated, positively intentioned word. Strange. So what's he saying? Initially each song sounds like a battle cry, a call to arms to the surplus people, a furious demand for immediate change, but it becomes clear that while anger is part of the reaction, well-reasoned argument, humour and forceful melodies are the driving elements. Songs such as "Pig Man" and "Adversity" succeed through argument rather than aggression, "Somebody's Mother" benefits from sounding like something from Rocky Horror, and "Flight For Freedom" and "Society" recall the searing energy of both Snuff and Dead Kennedys. These songs are literally anthems, the lyrics, words of wisdom to be written on squat walls.

It's not until the final part of the gig, however, that it becomes clear just how spot on The Subhumans were. "Who's Gonna Fight The Third World War", now horribly relevant, turns that battle cry into a fearful cry from the soul, while the epic "From The Cradle To The Grave" is one great plea for sanity. It's up to you whether you regard this one-off reformation as unfortunate timing or a bad omen. Either way, it's time something should be done.

IAN WATSON

MELODY MAKER, January 12 1991

1991 VENUE GIG REVIEW

"Well, I don't know whether we want to let all our secrets out really," laughs **Bruce**, of their far-reaching influences, "But we were all into a variety of bands, and even where we were all into one band, like Black Sabbath, we would be into different albums. And we were into prog... like ELP, although we were into different albums again. We might have all agreed on one Yes album though? But this was all before punk, of course, and when punk came crashing in, we had to hide all our prog records, haha! And pretend we weren't really into them... until later on, when we got them out again."

"Some of the stuff on 'Split Vision' is definitely self-indulgent," agrees **Phil**, "Which we all laugh about now. And that's one thing about the band – we don't take ourselves too seriously. We all really enjoy having a laugh, and have a great sense of humour... which also comes through in Dick's lyrics. Mind you, when you look back at 'Split Vision' in the context of the time, a lot of bands were going down a really wanky metal route as well, and there was this feeling that punk had kinda died in the UK by that time; it was all a bit depressing, and that played into the band splitting."

"I liked the 'Split Vision' album, because the sound was so good," counters **Bruce**, "And I really like the song 'Somebody's Mother'. It took us all that time to finally get a balanced sound... even the 'World's Apart' album is a bit weird actually. It depends how you listen to it, I suppose, but the guitars were quite quiet, and the drums were really loud. 'Split Vision' had a much better sound."

And if the music on side two wasn't confusing enough for you, the record was released in another 'love it or hate it' sleeve, that was arguably a tad too pretentious for the Subhumans.

"We were exploring the theme of the countryside again," reckons **Kev Tydeman**, who took all the band photos for the cover. "At that point there was a small cottage industry over at The Shed, which was the large barn – for want of a better word – over Longbridge Deverill, where Trotsky's parents had some land. Yes, we took over a large *barn* – how much more 'country' could you get? None of that deprived, inner city grime, twenty-four-hour off-licences and graffiti-strewn underpasses for us.

"Wally [A-Heads], myself, Trotsky and his brother Martin built the stud work, and partitioned off three spaces: one as a rehearsal room, one a dark room, and Martin set about building a recording studio and making/producing flight cases.

"The '29:29 Split Vision' cover was a similar 'no discussion' concept to 'Cradle...' really. We were way ahead of our time, proper Turner Prize anti-conceptualization there. The photos were taken outside The Shed, in the next field, incorporating a random metal frame found lying about. At that point, I don't think there was anything band-wise or message-wise left to portray.

"There was some awkward shuffling of positions and the usual laughs. I had been playing around with hand tinting and colouring photos, and had an idea to add some colour somewhere, possibly the background. Times had moved on tech-wise and colour printing on covers was now readily accessible and affordable.

"In the image, I like to think that the theme of the countryside, the land and wide-open spaces was once again subconsciously explored. None of the Warminster bands really left the area, no one upped sticks for the city etc. Indeed, even now, everyone is either living nearby or they return regularly. However, the fact Dick is effectively hidden or separated from the other members has probably caused some late-night bar-room discussion amongst the more cerebrally inclined, possibly with the aid of a bottle or two. But whether there was more to it – the recordings or title – regarding the Subhumans splitting up, or other empirical musing, you would need to ask them."

And the identity of the mystery cat that turns up in some of the photos of the band on that release? "Ah, that was Me Au," reveals **Trotsky**. "That was the farm cat, who would insist on slinking/cat-walking in front of us for every photo! Cats are sooo vain…"

Over the next three and a half years, Culture Shock would play just over 200 gigs, and release three albums – 1987's 'Go Wild', 1988's 'Onwards & Upwards' and 1989's 'All The Time' – with bassist Paul being replaced by Jasper from The Rhythmites in early '89, and the band playing their 'final' gig (they reformed in 2013) at the London Queen Mary College on January 19th, 1990, with The Rhythmites and RDF.

It was as the band were splitting, under the pressure brought to bear on various members by fatherhood and the associated pecuniary responsibilities, that Trotsky tried out on drums, which indirectly paved the way for Citizen Fish to emerge from the demise of Culture Shock (think 'more ska, less reggae').

"I did jam with Phil and Bruce straight after Subhumans," says **Trotsky**, "But it didn't come to anything really; it was a bit too proggy… it definitely wasn't a punk band, haha! But that wasn't a direction I wanted to go in either. I was in some howlingly horrendous bands after that – which I won't mention. I did a few gigs with those bands over the next four or five years before I joined Citizen Fish.

"I was briefly in a soul and blues covers band in Bristol, for a year and a half or something. We were called The Cartwrights, and it was good; I had a lot of fun. It was definitely something completely different to Subhumans though. We didn't do many gigs, but we got good money when we did play. Then Dick asked me along to a Culture Shock practice in Warminster, because Billy had left, and we had a jam in 44 East Street. Then we went back to Pete's flat and had a talk around it, and it went from there. I was a bit too rocky for them really. Then Nigel jacked it in [he sadly died a few years later, in 1993], and Citizen Fish grew from the remains – I was with them for fourteen years, I think? We went to the States a lot, and it was much more hardcore touring – smaller gigs, more intense… we did one tour that was six and a half weeks, and I vowed I'd never do that again, haha! That was too much."

Never ones to let the grass grow under them, Citizen Fish – the line-up rounded out by guitarist Larry – played their first gig just three weeks after Culture Shock's last, on February 10th, 1990, at The Weymouth Arms, Warminster, with Tiny Giants supporting and a crowd of fifty or so turning out to check them out.

367

BRUCE AT THE VENUE, LONDON, JANUARY 1991

JAY WHYTE AND DICK, 1996

PETE AND PAULA ROADIE, NYC, NOVEMBER 1996
BY CHRISTINE BOARTS LARSON

"It was a full-on 'local test'," admits **Dick**, "And basically we had to play up to Culture Shock standards... not quite, but it was a good start. We did another 92 gigs that year, and 420 in our first four years! It's easy to forget just how busy we were."

After their 'Free Souls in a Trapped Environment' debut LP was released later in 1990, Larry was replaced on guitar by ex-Subhumans bassist Phil, and between all those gigs, they somehow found time to release five more albums during the Nineties: 'Wider Than a Postcard' (1991), 'Flinch' (1993), 'Millenia Madness (Selected Notes from the Late 20th Century)' (1995), 'Thirst' (1996) and 'Active Ingredients' (1999).

Meanwhile, **Bruce** was taking a slightly quieter, but still fiercely musical path, for very personal reasons: "I was trying to get away from the cannabis scene completely. Partly because I was having a really bad experience because of cannabis. I was having heart problems... in fact, Dick commented about me acting weird in the studio once because I was having these problems. And I always thought it was a reaction to cannabis, because I'd been smoking for a few years, but I found out years later that it was a heart problem – and now I've got a pacemaker. I missed one of the BOB Fests actually because I was in hospital having my pacemaker fitted. But I had a very nice 'Get well' card signed by everyone at the festival.

"So, I was really prickly about that whole drug scene. I also didn't like the crusty scene... because that reminded me of hippies, which reminded me of drugs, which reminded me how I was feeling. And it took me a long time to get over that, y'know? When we started playing again, and we were playing squats, I was like, 'Oh no, here we go again...' But really that was more to do with me than anything else.

"Anyway, I thought I'd start anew, no more punk stuff, no more crusty stuff – just play the music I really like, do some local gigs – and get famous, of course! Because those local gigs would obviously be so brilliant, haha! So we [The Switch] did some local gigs, and we didn't get famous, and we fell apart. Our first gig was October 30th, 1987, at the Central Club in Bath. The bass player, Alan, is still in a band with me to this day though, and he's been a great friend and musician all the way through actually. And there was Dave, and Jeff on drums, and that line-up lasted two gigs.

"It was always difficult for me mentally to connect back to punk with both these projects. Although The Switch, with me singing, felt more like a connection – it was a bit like The Wipers. Also, I was quite into Pixies and Throwing Muses at the time too. We auditioned Beth Gibbons once before she joined Portishead! We even had some writing sessions with her; she has an amazing voice. I got some practice tapes somewhere. It was May 1988 when The Switch auditioned her; she sounded like Janis Joplin and blew all the other singers that we'd tried right out of the water! Something didn't click though. She was waiting for Portishead really.

"So I carried on, with me singing, and the bass player and the drummer, and it got a bit more punky, with shorter songs, with choruses and stuff. It was still called The Switch, but 'version two' really.

"We did our last gig on Boxing Day, 1989. We did actually play with Culture Shock at one gig, which was interesting… although I got the impression that Dick really didn't like us."

Then, out of the blue, the Subhumans reunited for two back-to-back gigs at The Venue, in London's New Cross. These shows took place on January 2nd and 3rd, 1991, with Zygote supporting on the first night, and Instigators on the second. What prompted this brief reunion is not entirely clear, but what *is* certain is that it was a massive treat for fans of the band, no doubt some of whom thought they'd missed their chance to ever see them live. And because the love for the band was so apparent in the room, it may even have paved the way, or at least planted an early seed, for their permanent reunion in 1998 – although the verdict remains out on that as well.

"It's very likely that John Loder had something to do with it, as we were still working with him and Southern in Culture Shock," suggests **Dick**. "I don't actually think anyone bar John could have persuaded us that it was a good idea! What justification he would have given to persuade us to do it I can't imagine? But those gigs were pretty good.

"The first night, for some reason, they put tables in front of the stage, to keep people from getting onto the stage – but it just meant that people ended up getting on the tables instead, which meant that everyone from the third row back couldn't see what we were doing…"

"That *was* definitely a one-off, but it was amazing!" enthuses **Trotsky**. "It was sold out both nights, absolutely fucking rammed; it was phenomenal to do two gigs like that, back to back. And it was very inspiring to see that people still wanted to hear us play."

"Those gigs were funny really," **Bruce** ponders. "I really wasn't into doing them, and can't honestly remember why we did. It didn't feel like the right time to me… although it didn't do any harm. And it felt so much better when we got back together properly when we did, and in a way, it feels like we eventually got what we deserved in the end… you know, a steady stream of gigs when we want them, and decent money – and Dick became legendary, haha!"

"They felt more like a footnote," concludes **Dick**, "Two gigs in the same venue, that were probably seven out of ten in terms of sound and performance. At the end of the second gig, someone was going around asking us all if we would ever reform again, and I think me and Bruce said, 'No', but Trotsky and Phil said, 'Maybe…'"

Having seemingly scratched their itch to dust off those songs again for a while, Subhumans went back into hibernation for seven years, and the band members continued on their alternate musical journeys. As if holding down the beat for the industrious Citizen Fish wasn't enough, Trotsky even managed to find time to dep for some other bands.

"In the '90s, I was on tour in the US with Citizen Fish and Cringer, from the Bay Area," says **Trotsky**, recounting some of his related musical endeavours after Subhumans returned to a back burner. "Cringer's drummer was Kamala, and she was at that time with

Dick, en route to a gig; they were messing around in the van when suddenly there was a loud crack, and Kamala was sat looking in shock at her hand… her finger was broken. So, I was asked to play for them for the rest of the tour, plus two or three gigs back in the UK, supporting Thatcher on Acid and Nausea [NYC]. It was an interesting time, and not only because for the first few gigs Kamala would sit by my hi-hat with 'idiot cards', with 'ride' or 'hi-hat' or 'toms' written on them, so I knew what to play. Although I must say, it did help… a bit. Sadly, Lance, their singer, has since passed away; such a lovely bloke.

"I guess it was early '90s when I was asked by Steve, of Freedom Fighter from Amesbury, if I wanted to play a gig with Freedom Fighter and this guy called Dan-I. Dan-I [real name: Selmore Ezekiel Linford Lewinson] was living in Salisbury and was a full-on Rasta, who had had a top-thirty hit in 1979 with a song called 'Monkey Chop' – just think 'Shaft'! He was an interesting character, and when we first met, he was very impressed with my lion head belt buckle, which was copper and had gone a little green… 'Ahhh,' he exclaimed, 'Green lion!' This I guess secured my position as drummer for one gig in High Wycombe. That was regular reggae, with a bit of convoy crust. I believe he has passed away now, too? [He sadly has, back in 2006.]

"I did a tour of Ireland with Decadent Few from London in the mid-'90s, doing the '3Ds'… drinking, drumming and driving – but not always in that order! They were a lovely bunch of people; I just found out that Womble the bass player died last year [2021], he was such a nice bloke.

"Also, in the mid-'90s, me, Phil and Jasper were asked to play a gig in London as backing band to Chris from RDF as his usual band were unavailable. This duly happened and was known as the Radical Dance Fish gig!"

Meanwhile, **Bruce** recounts what was happening back in Wessex: "Eventually I found a singer that I liked, with good political ideas, and we called ourselves Family Fruit Bowl. That started around February 1992, and we played our first gig in Monkton Combe School, just outside Bath, and lasted until August 1993. And we did another twenty gigs locally – pubs, schools, halls – but didn't get anywhere. That was when I started to realise it's not always easy putting together something that's good. I always knew Dick's lyrics were good, but I never knew how important they were until much later on.

"I also got into writing and reading music, because after Subhumans broke up, I decided to teach a bit more, and I *can* do it, but I find it a bit of a struggle. I struggle with it as a concept, because it seems to stop you being creative really. I do a bit of reading even now – in fact, I play in a little string trio as well these days, playing guitar with a violinist and a cello player. We do all these classical pieces and things… it's alright, it's something different."

The BOB Fest was something that lurched into life in the mid-'90s as well, and has endured ever since, and remains a festival very close to the hearts of the Subhumans and their associated bands.

"That stands for Bremen, Oakland and Bath," explains **Dick**, for the uninitiated. "It started off in Bath, mostly under the inspiration of Pete and Paula over here, and the

Oakland punks, who were obviously over in Oakland. It just developed around inter-band relationships, and bands touring, like us touring in the States, and European bands going over there, and US bands coming over here, who were all friends of friends. And there were a couple of marriages and relationships set up between countries, so to speak, and talk turned to organising a festival, and giving it up to a year to plan it out – 'Everyone come to Bath, and maybe next year, we can do Oakland or Bremen...'

"Oakland happened later on, because it was a lot further to go for the European bands, and a lot more expensive to get to, but it did happen in all three places, several times over. It started in the mid-'90s... in '93, or '94... or '95 – which is what mid-'90s means really, haha! And it took a lot of organisation. It was theoretically open to any band from those three places to play, but we extended the borders a little bit, and the Restarts got involved, and a couple of Bristol bands, just 'cos they were good mates basically. People put a lot of energy into keeping that going. You'd have between one and four different venues putting on gigs, and an art show where people could show off their paintings and all that, and a football game could happen... but mostly it was a string of gigs, over the course of a weekend, or a week. With the same people, with the understanding that more people would get involved as it went on... friends of friends, and people that moved into the area, and whatnot. Lately it's moved to every two years instead of every year – people just haven't got the availability or the funds to do it. Or they can't get away from work, or families, or whatever.

"The last one was in 2019, just before COVID came along, back in Bath, at the football club just over the road from me. That was very successful, the weather came out for us... the last time we did it in Bath, the temperatures were fucking sub-zero in April... and no one brought a coat!"

And it would be a chilly Bath that would host the long-overdue and hotly anticipated Third Coming (as opposed to the Second, because that had already happened in 1991) of the Subhumans, early in 1998...

The year 1998 was when Subhumans finally reformed, and despite originally being billed as another 'one-off', it thankfully turned into something permanent, and since then the band have been together far longer than their original incarnation, and have undertaken way more touring. They haven't been so prolific on the studio recordings front – quite the opposite, in fact – but we'll get to that in good time.

"You probably need to ask Dick, Phil and Trotsky about the reasons for the reformation, because they were together as Citizen Fish," reflects **Bruce**, "But I know they were getting asked a lot, 'When will Subhumans get back together?' And in the end, for whatever reason, they thought, 'Well, why don't we do it? So many people seem to want to hear us again…' So they approached me, and it was at a time when I wasn't in any bands. In fact, I was playing drums, and I'd got into jazz, so I was playing jazz drums – but I was very pleased to be asked to do it again. Because I was really missing it… I'd been missing it for a long time. In fact, I was probably a bit despondent about music. But I'd had kids and a family and was teaching guitar, then teaching drums as well, so had been very busy. I was definitely ready for it when they asked, and it was really nice to do. It was a big job for me to get back into playing again, and that first US comeback tour was a bit of a shock to the system, but we're very fortunate that we had another chance to do it.

"From a wider perspective, punk needed to get going again, didn't it? Which it did, I suppose – via grunge? We probably wouldn't have got back together again if there hadn't been enough interest; someone had to offer to do a tour for us, and think there was a market for it. And thankfully Americans like English bands. They don't like all English bands, of course, but if they do like you, if you manage to make your mark, you're always going to have an audience there. I wasn't so sure about it over here, because I didn't have such positive memories. Really, we could play London and get a good crowd, but towards the end of the Subhumans, we weren't really playing big places in the UK. We'd gone from playing to 3000 people in LA to 100 people in Chippenham. And there was a fight. *And* it was so foggy we got lost on our way out of Chippenham."

Chippenham seems to loom large in the collective subconscious of the band, as the proverbial straw that broke the back of the unfortunate camel, so maybe their getting lost on the way home from that sorry night wasn't just in the literal sense.

"I'm not sure who first had the idea to reform in 1998," says **Dick**, of a far happier moment in the band's timeline. "I think it was either Phil or Trotsky, and we were all playing together in Citizen Fish. And yes, people were always asking us if Subhumans would reform. When Citizen Fish first started, we put the logical statement 'ex-Subhumans' on posters… if we didn't put it on there, the promoters would put it on there anyway, to get more people in. And I think there was a fair amount of people who were disappointed when they came, because they didn't like the ska element – they didn't think it belonged in or near punk rock. Which is a shame, because I think it all works well together. But three people in the band were in both bands, which is why people made the comparison. 'Who do you prefer?' 'Subhumans – they've been going much longer and we know their albums backwards… Citizen Fish are new to us and they've got this weird ska stuff going on!'

"Other people – usually those who weren't so affiliated with Subhumans, or at least didn't know us that well – really liked the whole ska punk thing, and got well into it. Operation Ivy started in the late Eighties, I think, about the same time as Culture Shock, and their album was mind-blowingly good. Of course, Culture Shock didn't go to America the first time round, but Citizen Fish did – a lot.

"But Subhumans were all still active musicians. It wasn't as if anyone had died, or had an accident, or given up on music. It was all completely feasible, and of course, when we did have a practice, it was like, 'Oh my god!' It just all came back like that. And it felt that good to do it again after a break of seven years. So we pushed the rock off the top of the hill, and it's been rolling along ever since."

"It might have been either me or Trotsky," continues **Phil**, on who actually suggested the reformation. "After the first split, it was like this sacred thing that we should never touch again… you know, 'Don't even *mention* getting the band back together again!' But then we did the two gigs at The Venue, and I forget the reason we did those, which was a bit odd, just the two gigs back to back, but they went well.

"And then in 1998, for the reformation that's still going on now, I think me and Trotsky were mulling it over. We'd toured a lot with Citizen Fish and we'd had varying levels of satisfaction and success… Trotsky was particularly disillusioned with some aspects of touring with Citizen Fish. So we were just chatting about it, and we probably just decided it *wasn't* sacred, and maybe we could do it again, and maybe we could run the two bands alongside each other."

And the ongoing interest in Subhumans was apparent when touring with Citizen Fish.

"Oh god, yeah," agrees **Phil**. "People were always asking about it, so we knew the interest was there. Me and Trotsky were both doing shit, part-time agency work, driving around, delivering fridges and stuff, and trying to make ends meet in between Citizen Fish tours, because that wasn't enough to support us, so there were practicalities to consider. And we thought it would be great if we could live off doing music again… or at least do a bit better. But I don't want to make it sound like it was a decision just for that, because we definitely all missed playing together, and all missed doing Subhumans gigs, because it's definitely a real buzz playing those songs live.

"It's amazing really, and we feel very fortunate, compared to a lot of other bands, because it sometimes feels like every night is a good night for us, y'know? We don't have many bad ones, put it like that. We're very grateful for it, and it's such an amazing thing,

PHOTOS BY CLAIRE CALLAGHAN

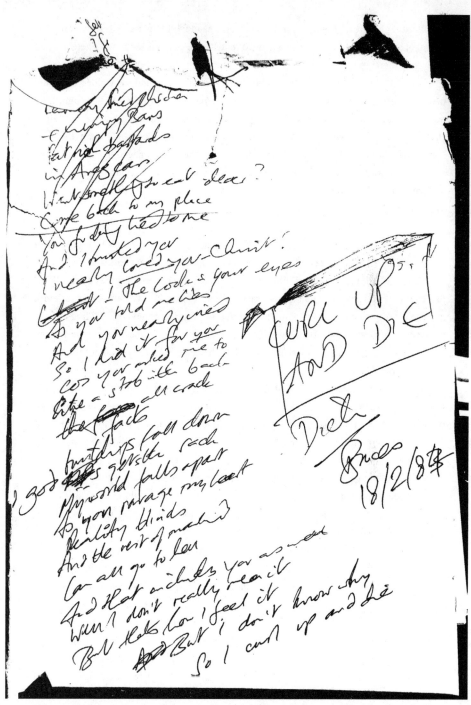

'CURL UP AND DIE' - DICK'S ORIGINAL LYRIC SHEET

that we still pull great crowds – although we have as much fun playing to sixty people, if that happens, as we do at the bigger ones. We just love playing, y'know? There's a real chemistry there."

"So I chatted to Phil about getting Subhumans back together, and we decided to try and persuade Bruce," continues **Trotsky**. "He was playing a gig with a jazz band in a little pub in Warminster, on a Sunday afternoon or something, and it was a bit like The Blues Brothers, because we were like, 'We're getting the band back together!' [laughs] We had a word with him after his set, and he was into it, and then we managed to persuade Dick as well… although he was like, 'It's just a one-off tour!' He was saying that all the way through the first US tour back… and over twenty years later, we're still on that 'one-off tour', haha!"

The band played their triumphant comeback gig at a packed-out Porter Butt in Bath on February 20th, 1998, with Zero Tolerance and Ex-Mass supporting them.

"We did a 'fish party' in the Porter Butt, and that was amazing," smiles **Dick**. "It all just came flying back – we had a few practises beforehand, but we hardly had to revise anything at all, which felt great. And then we set off properly around the UK five months later, because we thought, 'That was good!' We thought we'd do one more tour in Europe and one more in America, but we just carried on, because it was too good not to really.

"The Porter Butt gig was with Ex-Mass, which was George and Spider's band after Zygote, and Zero Tolerance. And it was just amazing. Right from the first song, 'It's Gonna Get Worse', we were just blown away really… it was something else, after all those years. I just remember that moment inside my head, thinking, 'Good grief, who would've thought this would be happening?' We went down a treat, and it felt so good to be doing it again. And when we were practising, we barely had to refer back to what we were playing… it gets imbued into the soul, it's there forever.

"The idea expanded from doing a few gigs in the UK to doing three tours, one of the UK, and one in Europe and America, which we did, and then to stop, which we didn't. Because why would you stop when it was all going so well?"

Before they headed out on tour though, the Subhumans re-recorded three old songs during June 1998 for the 'Unfinished Business' EP, bolstering the track-listing with a brand new instrumental and three early Eighties recordings that also featured Grant, and even Andy, so it was ironically a very retrospective release despite it ushering in a new era for the band. Whilst it's a fun listen, and I remember being very excited to pick it up after no 'new' Subhumans releases for a dozen years, it definitely feels insubstantial compared to the rest of their canon, and is widely regarded as a stop-gap curio.

"We'd just got back together," explains **Bruce**, "So we found a few old songs that we'd never recorded – 'Glad to Be Alive', 'Curl Up and Die' and 'What's Your Number?' – and then we just took some bits from old Southern Studios sessions, some funny stuff, and Dick wanted to have 'Song No. 35', the original version with Andy drumming on it, because he really liked Andy's drumming on that, I think. And we did the little instrumental, messing about with numbers... I like numbers in music, very much so.

"I'm not exactly sure why we did it really, but we clearly put it together so we had something to sell at the gigs – we'd just got back together again, and we didn't have anything new out. It was almost not worth doing really, but we needed something new. 'Glad to Be Alive' was a song we got together, but dropped, because it wasn't really good enough. But then we got it back together, because we were short of material for 'Unfinished Business'... we just didn't have anything really! So we went back through the old stuff, which is why 'Unfinished Business' is a bit of a mish-mash. The only new thing was the little musical piece ['864321'] we were messing around with. So called because it was going through eight bars, then six, then four... it was just a very sort of mathematical thing really. It seemed to make sense to me... and it *seemed* to make sense to everyone else!

"'Trowbridge Park' was a good tune, and Dick's singing was fabulous," he adds, when considering some of the old songs that could have made the cut, "But it would have needed reworking quite a bit – I don't think the chorus had enough of a musical difference to the verse? There was something that never really caught about it. Trowbridge was brilliant though, a great meeting place for us all.

"We recorded it in Phil's flat in Warminster, before he moved to Spain. He had a little recording studio – we used to practise up there – and he engineered it himself. And then we started to write again, but it was difficult to write because the other three had been used to writing together as the Fish, and I was coming in, as a bit of an outsider almost, but also wanting the quality to be the same as it was in the old Subhumans. And I felt it was becoming too much of a punk band, because that was what we were supposed to be doing, and it just needed a bit more creativity. So, it took a bit of working out how it was all going to happen."

"About the time that I joined Citizen Fish [1990], myself and my partner at that time [Claire Callaghan – contributor of a number of photos to this book] landed ourselves a huge flat above a 'gentlemen's outfitters' on Warminster High Street, that Jock from the A-Heads had previously lived in," elaborates **Phil**. "It was dirt cheap, had two whole floors – about thirteen rooms in total – but the place was unheated and freezing in winter, with just a few portable gas heaters dotted about. We'd end up living there until 2004 when we moved to Spain. Over the years, loads of friends lived there with us at various times – including Grant from Subhumans and Sid from Organized Chaos – and bands we were on tour with would stay there: Cringer, Spitboy, and Gr'ups... their exotic American aesthetic attracting quizzical, intrigued glances from the Warminster locals!

"On the top floor, I made one of the rooms into a practice room, then knocked a hole in the wall and installed a window looking through to a studio control room. This would be

PHOTOS BY CLAIRE CALLAGHAN

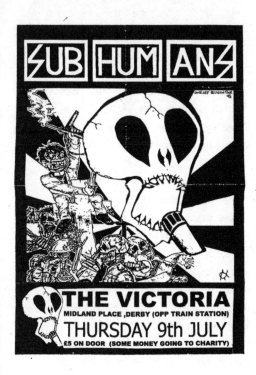

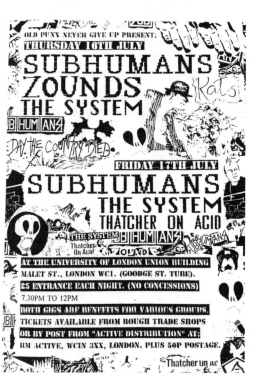

the Citizen Fish and Subhumans' creative nerve centre for the coming years. There was only minimal sound-proofing, and when we were practising you could hear it up the High Street, but thankfully the lovely staff in the shop downstairs were very tolerant.

"I'd gotten into home recording after the Subhumans had split in the '80s. Back then, you had to watch out for the squaddies in Warminster. I didn't have spikey hair or anything, I just looked like a student hippy at the time, so I didn't get too much grief. But if you were Pete The Roadie, walking around with a Mohawk or whatever, you'd get a lot more attention.

"Anyway, this one time, I'd had a late night, having some beer and eating some takeaway with some mates in the park; there were some squaddies there, and we were being stupidly friendly – they came over and jumped us, and one of them stamped on my leg, and broke my ankle. I didn't realise it was broken at the time, so hobbled home, all the way to the other side of town, and when I woke up in the morning – well, I didn't sleep actually – I went to the police, but they weren't interested at all. So, we went up the guard room at the camp, and they took it very seriously… they took it to court actually, and in the end, I got a load of compensation money and bought myself a Tascam eight-track cassette porta-studio, then progressed to getting an eight-track reel-to-reel.

"When Citizen Fish was working on the 'Active Ingredients' LP, I suggested asking Lookout Records for some money to buy some recording equipment to record it at my place, instead of paying for studio time. So I ended up getting a twenty-four-channel mixing desk and a sixteen-track ADAT recording set-up, which recorded digitally onto VHS tapes. This was all very high tech at the time, but within a couple of years they were already obsolete, as hard disk recording became available.

"With the Subhumans back in action, we thought it'd be nice to have something new to sell at the gigs so we dug up some silly old bits and recorded a few long-lost songs, that we re-learnt from old practice cassettes. These were songs that I remembered hearing at band practices in the early days, but I don't think I'd ever played them… except maybe 'Curl Up and Die'? I've always liked 'What's Your Number?' and 'Glad to Be Alive', with their awesome old Grant-era bass lines. It was fun to play and record them, and I think they came out great on the EP.

"For Dick's vocal, I've got a feeling I recorded him with the tape slightly slowed down in an attempt to make it sound like his youthful 1981 voice when played back at normal speed. And as a side point, since [their 2007 album] 'Internal Riot', we've detuned the guitars by a half-step to make it easier to catch some of those teenage high notes. That's E-flat tuning for the musical nerds.

"In the following years we'd record odds and sods in the home studio, which I'd called Phil's Roadside Café; local kids' bands would pop in and make demos, and some old punk mates would come over. Muckspreader from Bath recorded 'All Gone Dead' for the 'Still Can't Hear the Words' Subhumans covers album on the author's Blackfish label.

"I recall Nessun Dorma from Bristol – featuring Ju from Stupid Humans – came over to make a demo, armed with their portable gas stove for hot knives. They called it the 'San Marino Demo' after we'd watched England play San Marino on the box that night; England won 7–1, stunned by the unrated opposition's historic goal after only eight seconds... prompting howls of laughter.

"The most memorable recording session was Chaos UK, recording their EP 'Kanpai' for Vinyl Japan, when we bet bassist Jay [who would later stand-in for Subhumans] that he couldn't eat a Dave's Insanity Sauce sandwich. He took the bet and was obviously on fire and in great distress to everyone's amusement. Several gallons of water later, he'd just about recovered and thought he'd calm down with a smoke on his chillum pipe – only to discover that [Chaos UK guitarist] Gabba had covered the end of the pipe in the hot sauce!"

Armed with a new MCD to flog, Subhumans played nine UK gigs between July 9th and August 9th, 'ending' in Birmingham, at a sold-out Foundry, with Police Bastard, POA and Eastfield supporting – a gig that was captured on film and released on VHS video by Barn End Productions. It was strongly rumoured to be their last UK gig.

"I remember I got a phone call off Dick," says **Stu Pid**, who was then vocalist for Police Bastard. "'Pid, it's Dick – guess what?' 'What, Dick?' 'Subhumans are reforming, do you fancy putting the Birmingham gig on?' 'Fuckin' right I do, leave it with me!' Putting the phone down, I had this funny feeling it was gonna be big, and I was certainly gonna make it as massive as I could, so I booked The Foundry, and then Dick said he wanted to make it a benefit gig, and asked if I had any ideas about the best charity to raise money for...? Now, for a long time, one of our own, Chris Carthy AKA 'Chris Cripple' or 'Chris Packet', from Rugeley, had suffered in silence; he was born with a lot of disabilities, but I'd noticed for a while that he was slowing down and falling over more, but when I mentioned it to him, he would just say, 'I'm getting old, Pid...' So I rang Dick back and said, 'Wouldn't it be great to get Chris an electric wheelchair?' Cheryl knew of a second-hand one for sale; we just had to keep it quiet from Chris, who had Subhumans tattooed on his arm just like me... copycat, haha!

"I went to Derby for the first comeback gig of that tour, a sold-out gig, for 150 people, but then a few days later five or six hundred stormed the Foundry in Birmingham. It was a blistering gig, and Chris got a new pair of electric legs, haha! So hats off to Subhumans and POA, Eastfield and Police Bastard... our Chris remembers it as one of the most memorable days of his life..."

"That was certainly one of the hottest gigs we did," reckons **Dick**. "I remember for the first of not many times ever, I was singing the encores with no T-shirt on. I was halfway through getting changed into something less soaking wet when it was decided that we *would* play some more songs...

DICK, BLOODIED BUT UNBOWED, LONDON ULU, 1998 BY STEVE HYLAND

SAN BERNARDINO ARENA

137 SOUTH G ST. SAN BERNARDINO (909)276-7770

THERE IS WELL LIT PARKING AVAILABLE FOR YOU AT THE STADIUM NEXT DOOR * CALL FOR SHOW TIMES

FRIDAY, AUGUST 28

FROM THE **U.K.**

ALL ORIGINAL MEMBERS REUNION

SUB HUM ANS

$8

ONLY SOUTHERN CALIFORNIA APPEARANCE

ALL AGES / BUY YOUR TICKETS NOW BEFORE THEY SELL OUT!

TICKETMASTER

OR YOU CAN BUY TICKETS FROM THE SHOWCASE THEATRE
BOXOFFICE M-F / 10-7 OR DURING ANY SHOW AT SHOWCASE

FROM THE UK · ONE OFF REUNION · ORIGINAL LINEUP

SUBHUMANS US TOUR

AUGUST 98

W. 26 SACRAMENTO · BOJANGLES
Th. 27 SAN FRANCISCO · SLIMS
Fr. 28 SAN BERNADINO · ~~ARENA CACTUS~~ ORANGE PAVILION
S. 29 MESA ᴿ (AZ). THE NILE
Sn. 30 zoom zoom meep meep
M. 31 AUSTIN · ATOMIC CAFE

SEPTEMBER 98

T. 1 HOUSTON · THE ABYSS
W. 2 NEW ORLEANS · JIMMY'S
Th. 3 vroom vroom beep beep
Fr. 4 ST. PETERSBURG · STATE THEATRE
S. 5 FORT LAUDERDALE · THE FU BAR
Sn. 6 JACKSONVILLE · MILK BAR
M. 7 ATLANTA · THE POINT
T. 8 CANBORO (NC). CAT'S CRADLE
W. 9 WASHINGTON DC · CAPITOL BALLROOM
Th. 10 NEW YORK · CONEY ISLAND HIGH
Fr. 11 " " " " "
S. 12 PHILADELPHIA · TROCADERO
Sn. 13 PITTSBURGH · CLUB LAGA
M. 14 CLEVELAND · PEABODY'S
T. 15 DETROIT · ST. ANDREW'S HALL
W. 16 CINCINATTI · BOGART'S (FRONT ROOM)
Th. 17 ST. LOUIS · THE GALAXY
Fr. 18 CHICAGO · THE METRO
S. 19 GREEN BAY · CONCERT CAFE
Sn. 20 MINNEAPOLIS (ST. PAUL) NORTH STAR BALLROOM
M. 21 miaouwwww
T. 22 DENVER · AZTLAN THEATRE
W. 23 SALT LAKE CITY · DV8
Th. 24 putt putt fizz bang driver homicidal by now
F. 25 PORTLAND · LA LUNA
S. 26 SEATTLE · RKCNDY
S. 27 group therapy

all gigs $8 door
all gigs all ages

phone ahead to confirm
venues, door times,
support bands, ticket
availability, etc

'Unfinished Business'
new CD on sale at gigs
(recordings of old but
unreleased songs)

US FISH MUST
SWIM TOGETHER

U.S. TOUR 1998

"And it *would* have been the last of nine UK gigs, if we'd left it to just that tour. Then on the 26th of that month [August '98] we were over in the USA. And then we did Europe after that as well. Although I got a very angry letter with a big drawing of a middle finger about three foot high from a chap I won't name in Antwerp, saying 'Fuck you for playing the USA and not Europe!' I wrote back and said, 'Actually we are playing Europe, it'll be next year... hope you're okay with that?' I was like, 'Jeez!' I mean, if we hadn't been planning to play Europe, he would have had a point, obviously, but it was the only graphic 'fuck off' drawing I ever got in the post.

"Hate mail was a rare thing," he adds. "There was a chap called Paul Mendelowitz, who used to write for Flipside fanzine... I bet he loves me remembering his name all these years later, haha! But he sent me the only hate mail letter I ever got. He was slagging us off for saying one thing and doing another, not being real anarchists, preaching to the converted... all that sort of thing. I don't remember all the content, but he was very sarcastic. His writing for Flipside was fairly sarcastic too; he liked laying into bands for whatever reason, to build up his own cult of personality... whatever. Anyway, Paul, hope you're happy and well!

"And it was on that reformation UK tour in '98 [at the ULU in London] that I had a thankfully rare bloody nose from someone in the crowd, who was reacting to something I'd just said about not wearing leather; he was pissed off and pissed up, and wanted to grab the mic off me, and in the process of trying to keep hold of it, I got whacked in the face. It shook me up a fair bit. And it certainly put the brakes on the theory that anarcho punk bands are just 'preaching to the converted'! I've always resented that phrase; firstly, even if everyone in the room agrees with what's being said onstage, it doesn't hurt to have views reinforced or expanded now and then, and secondly, it's too cynical – it doesn't allow for differences or variations of opinion, and ignores the likelihood that there's someone in the room who is new to all this punk rock malarkey. And even if it's only one person walking out of a gig questioning so-called normality, it's always worth ranting a bit between songs..."

"Sadness, relief and relief again!" chuckles **Ruth Elias**, when recalling her feelings as the Subhumans split in '85, reformed briefly in '91 and then reformed again in '98. "If ever a band was meant to be onstage it was the Subhumans. By late '85, we were near to giving up ourselves, and other bands were imploding around us. Not many bands reformed within a few years of splitting up then, but most of our contemporaries had – or were reforming – by the time we did in 2011, and you'd be hard pressed to see the bands you loved in the '80s during the '90s or in the first decade of the millennium. In those fallow years, we could still catch up with the Subhumans though, marvel that Dick never seemed to grow older or run out of energy – as we still do now! – and, as a bonus, get to see our scattered friends. In fact, the Subhumans performed a public service in bringing us old punks together..."

The first gig of their twenty-nine-date US tour was in Sacramento, on August 26th, 1998, with San Francisco the next night, but it was the third gig – at the Orange Pavilion in San Bernardino, with Strychnine, Calavera and Narcoleptic Youth – that was to prove the most memorable of that tour, pulling in 4000 rabid punk fans.

"The idea of that first US tour was to play as many states as we could," recalls **Dick**, "One gig in each state basically, very simplistic, but not realising – or remembering – that California has all these huge places in that you could easily do a gig in each one – Sacramento, San Francisco, LA and San Diego, for instance, and we could do a large packed-out gig in each area. But we didn't think of it, and just scheduled this one Southern Californian gig. It was in some venue, I can't remember where, but it got moved like three times because it kept selling out, and we ended up in this airplane-hangar-sized place. It was just enormous – I stood in the corner and took a photo of the PA desk in the middle of it, and it looked tiny, just a little dot, amongst all this space.

"But everything about that gig was over the top. The age of the rider had arrived, and you could suddenly ask for a bottle of Jack Daniels and get it – for free… we eventually realised it's best to drink most of it *after* the gig! There was all this drink we hadn't even asked for – vodka, gin, rum, cognac, whiskey, yaddayadda… way more than a dozen bands could consume in a month! It was ridiculous. Every flavour of crisps… it was just mad. The amount of people was insane, the security out the front were insane, taking people's lighters off them, taking anything made of metal off their jackets… it was totally not good. There were between three and four thousand people in one room – no seats, no slope, all flat… there were three or four circle pits going simultaneously in various parts of the crowd.

"We had our merch set up at the side, these two little tables in all this space, and they were selling a shedload of T-shirts. We had to go out to the van and get more. Pete and [his wife] Paula were on the stall, helping out – apologies if I've forgotten who else was there – and a rumour got back to them that they were going to get robbed, of all the money they'd taken from the shirts, and that all the shirts were going to get nicked. So before we'd finished the gig, they were taking all the shirts out the back, scurrying down the side, and we were wondering what was going on.

"The stage was massive, a stupid size, so we had sort of gathered in the middle of it, with a huge space either side, so we could at least feel as if we were in a smaller space. A good few yards behind us, way behind all the kit, there was somewhere like 150 people stood behind Trotsky, watching the gig… just loads of people at the back. At some point, someone trod on an electrical connection or something, and the whole PA went down. Of course, I couldn't say anything about it down the mic, because the mic wasn't working, and I didn't know who was doing the monitors or anything, everyone was just miles away. And security were coming up to me, dressed like cops more or less, with batons, and saying, 'Right, you've got to get all these people behind you who are on the stage *off* the stage – before we let the gig carry on…' And I was like, 'Isn't that your job…?'

SAN BERNADINO, CALIFORNIA - EMPTY AND FULL, AUGUST 1998

The Sist Let

all done gead
dittish brizzees
baiste of wreath
KILLING
wet out of my gay ?!
URST FADE
thraitline stinking
1 lb. of BOMB DROPS
Messiness Bun
Banality is waiting for a Rusk
WÜRK ÉXPÉRIENSCHËN
Cig Bitty
Drink for yourhelf
Werk Rest Pley Dee
Jugs of Rugs of Mugs of Yoof
maybe No More Gigs

black and ''''''''''''''''

+ the rest of it

SILLY SET-LIST 1998

"So, out the front, we've got three or four thousand people chanting 'Bullshit! Bullshit! Bullshit!' and it's getting quite scary. And I couldn't even say anything, 'cos no one could hear me. I was walking over to all these people at the back of the stage, to see if they would move, and all they wanted to do was shake my hand and tell me how great the gig was… 'But can you please leave the stage?' And, of course, no one left!

"The power eventually came back on, and we carried on the gig. But it was off for a good five or ten minutes – and felt like a lot longer! We were on the wire, and there was literally nothing we could do about it… except maybe mime, haha! We've never done a gig as big as that since, and I don't really want to. We should have planned it out better and thought about it and done three gigs in California really. But I'm not complaining that we did an enormous gig there, because it was at least a massively memorable event."

"Oh, that was fucking insane!" concurs **Trotsky**. "The stage was bigger than most venues we play. The monitors were completely shit though, so you couldn't hear anything, but when you looked out across the crowd, you could see about five different mosh pits happening all at once. There were so many people onstage, probably 200 people or something – I looked around and was just surrounded by people, it was mental. They were standing all over Bruce's pedals. The atmosphere changed just like that when the PA went down and we had to get everyone off the stage, but we managed to carry on, and it all calmed down a bit. Later on, Pete was saying how he'd heard some people talking about rushing the stall, and if that had happened, the whole lot would have been gone just like that.

"But it was just incredible that so many people still wanted to see us out there, and by then, there were all these young kids coming to the gigs as well, who probably heard us listening to their mum and dad's record collection. It's mind-blowing really, and very humbling. Sometimes you see little kids who are seven or eight with their parents, all punked up with leather jackets and Mohicans and everything."

From there, Subhumans worked their way east, across Arizona, Texas, Louisiana, Florida and Georgia to Washington, where Chris Boarts Larson, who was the editor of the popular Slug & Lettuce fanzine, and took the photograph adorning the front cover of this book, first saw them.

"I grew up in central Pennsylvania, in a little town called State College," begins **Chris**. "In the mid-'80s I started reading zines like MRR and Flipside, and ordering more zines through those, ordering records, writing *lots* of letters – starting my decades of correspondence with pen pals. In the hometown, we had a pretty decent college punk scene, with some students booking shows and bringing some good touring bands through. I started hanging out, going to shows, taking photos, and eventually decided that I could contribute to the DIY underground by doing my own zine documenting the scene, which I started in 1986 when I was fifteen. I named it Slug & Lettuce after a pub I saw on a trip to England when the zine idea was brewing. I never actually went to that pub in Stratford-upon-Avon – I just saw it and thought it was a weird name.

390

"The Subhumans were one of my first early favourite bands I discovered in the mid-'80s, although I can't remember exactly how I first heard them, nor where or how exactly I got my first records. But it was likely at Eides in Pittsburgh, or through mail order. Amongst my groups of friends, the Subhumans were a real favourite. I remember making a long banner of Sub-Hum-Ans to hang in my friend's apartment. And incidentally we first ordered the Amebix record because it was associated with Bluurg Records.

"But I never interviewed Dick, nor the Subhumans, for S&L, or anywhere else. I absolutely loved Culture Shock, but found out about them a tad later and not when it was happening. However, when Citizen Fish first formed and came for their first tour to the USA, I was there, and that was a game- and life-changer. The first Citizen Fish show I saw at ABC NO RIO in NYC in September of 1990 was a pinnacle moment for me. I clearly remember being so very *in the moment*, looking around, feeling the energy, the love, the passion, the overall glee, and not just for a bunch of kids seeing the closest to their old favourite band the Subhumans, but – even better – being there for the beginning of something new. I remember thinking, 'This is really something special,' a very 'I'm here now' moment that I'll never forget. For once, I wasn't wishing I coulda been there, I *was* there. The present was now, and now was special, and very, very good.

"I met Dick at that show and that was another part of the amazing experience. If there was ever a punk rock idol in my world, it was Dick Lucas, but I met him and he became a friend. A real live person, who was in one of my favourite bands, but there were no barriers or walls; it was just us, and it was the greatest realisation ever.

"After that first show, Citizen Fish would come back and tour the States every year for a while, usually in the spring. Jasper, Phil and Trotsky all became good friends too. Richard the roadie was always with the Fish, and then Pete and Paula, and they too were part of the family crew. And so we had our annual Citizen Fish visit, and some friends and I would usually travel around to a few nearby shows each year. In 1996, a few friends and I took that 'following the Fish' thing even further out of the NE to more shows. And in 1997, Neil and I took the Tribal War distro on tour with Citizen Fish and Avail across the whole country and damn, that was seriously the best thing ever! Oh, we were so excited; I was thrilled.

"Like I said, at that point, Citizen Fish were friends and family, and the reunion of the Subhumans brought Bruce on guitar, switched Phil to bass, and Jasper to merch, so it still felt just like family, yet it was also one of our oldest, most favourite, most legendary punk bands playing those old songs in person! The first show of the reunion that I attended in DC, at the Capital Ballroom, was just so awesome. Robert joined Pete The Roadie... I don't think Richard was there for that first round? But all of those roadies – Richard, Pete and Paula, Robert and Karoline – are the best!

"I remember that first DC reunion show so well because of just how absolutely joyful everyone was. When I look at the photos from that show, all I see are smiling faces on

SUB HUM ANS UK

WITH: ONE COMMON VOICE ALL AGES
AND INSURRECTION 7PM
WED. SEPT. 2nd $8
JIMMY'S 8200 WILLOW

ADVANCED TICKETS AVAILABLE AT JIMMY'S, TICKET WEB, + UNDERGROUND SOUNDS. 586-1592-9050

FOR INFO: 283-4011
3336 MAGAZINE ST.

Devil Dolls Productions

SATURDAY, SEPTEMBER 12

SUB HUM ANS

the Boils

VIOLENT SOCIETY

AT THE
TROCADERO
on 10th and ARCH St. in Philadelphia

show starts at 7:30!!!!

SATURDAY SEPTEMBER 19

SUB HUM ANS

DIRECT FROM JOLLY OLE ENGLAND

FUNERAL ORATION   INFLICTED

8 BUCKS ALL AGES DOOR 6:30

POWERBOMB PRODUCTION

SHOW 7PM

CONCERT CAFE
1116 MAIN ST.
GREEN BAY, WI

INFO CALL (920) 435-0880 OR EMAIL AT
TIMEBOMBGB@AOL.COM

U.S. TOUR FLYERS, 1998

SUB HUM ANS

THE CRIMINALS
THE READYMEN
FRI. SEPT. 25
LA LUNA

9:30PM/ALL AGES/$8 ADVANCE

TICKETS @ ALL GI JOES/TICKETMASTER OUTLETS
OR CHARGE BY PHONE 224-4400

MONQUI PRESENTS

NEW ORLEANS, 2/9/1998

the punks, pure ecstasy – friends just losing their minds 'cos they were seeing a band they never thought they'd see. A band we/they all loved so much. And it was just so perfect. The reasons were right too; it all felt so natural that it happened.

"That first year in 1998, there was the DC Capital Ballroom, then the Trocadero in Philly. The DC show in particular was perfect 'cos everyone was just so blindingly happy. The Troc show was cool too – a lot of people were there from NYC, and the venue is a beautiful old theatre. I don't remember as much about that show though, other than the balcony view."

"I moved out to the US in 1998 with the wonderful Mrs Roadie," clarifies **Pete**. "She had lived with me in England for four years, and wanted to move back, so I went with her and have stayed ever since. When the Subhumans reformed in 1991, I roadied for them then, and Mrs Roadie and I did the US tour in 1998. I haven't done any recent tours as roadie for them, although I would always work for them when they played the Bay Area, or the BOB festivals.

"[Pete's own band] Kicker was formed in 2010, when I was persuaded to go over to the dark side, and it's been bloody brilliant – we've played loads of gigs in the US, UK, Europe and even Cuba. There's something to be said for being amplified with a mic in your hand, which is rather enjoyable – mind you, I do give my roadies somewhat of a hard time, and sometimes feel I'm quite a hindrance to the otherwise absolutely excellent musicians that make up the rest of the band.

"In 2016, Kicker did a USA West Coast tour with Subhumans, so a bit of double-duty for me most nights, which was very enjoyable. I don't think they've changed at all; they've still got the same great sense of humour, and are still just as almighty onstage."

"In 1995, I was living in Wisconsin, and I went down to Chicago to see Citizen Fish at the Fireside Bowl," recounts **Karoline Collins**. "I'd first met Dick in 1992, then me and a few other people had done a show for them in 1994, so we were in each other's orbit, and he knew who I was, even though I wasn't necessarily friends with them yet. The Fireside Bowl is this bowling alley, and at the one end they sell the merch off this plastic 1970s-style bench thing with a table in front of it... not the most convenient place to sell merch!

"I noticed that Dick was selling merch himself, and even though I didn't know him that well then, I thought it probably wasn't the best idea – because everyone wanted to talk to him. How can you sell, and have a conversation? And he was just being swarmed! Anyway, I'd toured with other bands before, and I'd done all sorts of punk merchandising, so I figured I should jump in. So, I started selling next to him, and then kept shoving him over bit by bit, until I got him over to the end where he could talk, and I was just selling the merch. And he looked over at me, as if to say, 'Alright?' And I was like, 'I'm good!' I'd basically given myself a job for the night.

"Then Richard the roadie came over, and was like, 'Alright!' And at the end of the night, they asked me if I wanted to go on the rest of the tour with them, and I was like, 'Yeah! Sure!' Paula hadn't been able to come on that tour, so they were winging it on the merch front, so it worked out great. And I went from the Midwest to the East Coast and down to Florida with them, and then I drove back with Richard, who I knew already. And that kinda morphed into me working with Richard and Avail. Then in 1998, there was an Avail tour in Europe, but that was at the same time as Subhumans were coming over here, which is when [Karoline's husband] Robert got hired – Richard was going to be in Europe with Avail, so he passed the baton to Robert to drive Subhumans."

Robert Collins: "So I'm here only by default and association, haha! I only did that tour because Richard and Karoline weren't available."

"Some of those tours were *hard*," continues **Karoline**. "I look back at the tour books, and there's twelve-hour drives… fifteen-hour drives… you'd be so excited to see a drive that was 'only' eight hours or five hours, y'know? Richard had this van called Behemoth, which belonged to Neurosis prior to that. It was an old U-Haul moving truck, and it definitely had a diesel leak on it somewhere, so sometimes you'd be in the back, thinking you were napping, but you'd actually passed out from the smell of the diesel leak." [laughs]

"I didn't grow up on Subhumans or anything," admits **Robert**. "I knew who they were – I'd seen the name around since forever – but they weren't really in my orbit. I got into punk through the US starter bands instead of the UK starter bands. So I knew that they were 'a thing' before we started that first tour, but at the first show I saw people literally losing their fucking minds, and it was only then that I realised the impact they have had on certain people. I was floored every night on that tour, not just by them as a band, but by watching other people have this experience – which I've been fortunate enough to continue having for the last twenty years! But seeing them for the first time, I was like a little kid, discovering them for the first time but as a thirty-year-old, if you know what I mean?

"Southern California is a whole different thing…," he ponders, on the band's cult status in the US. "They're very popular in the States, very influential, but in Southern California they're fucking gods! It's incredible! And you'll meet someone at every gig they play in that southwest part of the country – including Arizona and Nevada – who saw them in '84 or '85.

"So, we were two or three days in, and I was just starting to understand that they were a super big deal, right? We'd done San Francisco and Sacramento, and then there was this show in Orange [County], which was the only Southern California gig on that tour. It was in this absolutely massively colossal venue, and it was mayhem – the whole show was complete insanity, I've never seen anything like it.

"Paula was doing merch, and I believe her sister was helping her. I was helping out a bit as well, and a friend that I knew came up to me just after Subhumans started playing,

PHILADELPHIA (TOP), AND WASHINGTON (BOTTOM), 1998
BY CHRISTINE BOARTS LARSON

TROCADERO, PHILADELPHIA, 1998 BY CHRISTINE BOARTS LARSON

and pointed to a very large group of people who were all discussing robbing the merch stall. And they were going to take all the money and all the merch – very soon!"

Karoline: "We can laugh about it now, but what the fuck? Does that even happen at punk shows?"

Robert: "Me and Paula had thousands of dollars of cash wadded everywhere on our persons, and I was looking at this large group of people planning to jump us, and I said to my friend, 'Take this box and run!' And we started shovelling the merch backstage, shielding the people with the money, whilst kids were running towards the stall and just grabbing shit.

"They had three sets on that tour, if I remember, and they would rotate the sets – but they played all three sets that night, every song they had. There were several circle pits going on at any one time, some of them on the stage, no separation from the gear at all, and the sound guy was like, 'I'm done, I'm shutting this down…,' and Pete said to him, 'If you want to keep your PA, I suggest you let them finish playing!' There were like lines of riot cops outside, and helicopters… it was fucking chaos.

"During that first tour I did in '98, there was a gig in Atlanta, at a venue called The Point, and it's called that because the venue is literally a point, and there's no backstage access to the stage, you have to walk through the crowd to get onstage. The opening bands played, and everyone was onstage ready to go for the Subhumans set; it was totally packed out… me and Pete were onstage ready, but there was no Dick. No one knew where he was. And when you're onstage waiting to start in front of a full house, a few minutes feels like a really long time, so I got sent off to find Dick. He wasn't at the bar, and the sound guy didn't know where he was, so I went outside, and there was Dick, talking to the doorman, because there was a carful of kids who had driven for three hours to see the show, and the doorman wouldn't let them in because the show was sold out. And Dick wasn't being an asshole, he wasn't being a rock star, but he was insistent they were coming in, whether it was on the guest list or whatever, and he wasn't going to go in and play until they were let in. He had a room full of 500 people waiting to watch the band, but there were four kids outside without tickets who'd driven for hours to see Subhumans, and he wouldn't play until they were let in. I told this story to a friend of mine in Georgia some years ago, and he was like, 'Oh! That was me!'

"Also on the '98 tour, Dick got really, really drunk in Chicago, and we couldn't get him out of the van. Eventually we got him out though, and then he was leaning up against the back of the van, pretty much unresponsive, totally out of it, and Phil tapped him on the shoulder as we were trying to get him into the motel and said, 'But Dick, who's going to fight?' And Dick shouted, 'Not me!' And when he flopped onto his bed in the motel room, he hit his head on the table and started bleeding on the pillow… and I was like, 'Oh god, is this how it ends?'"

Thankfully it didn't end there (!) and the tour rumbled on, a great success, tracking back across country through Illinois, Minnesota, Colorado and Utah, before culminating with two large shows (1000-plus in attendance) in Portland and Seattle.

Karoline: "I remember when I was over in Europe with Avail in '98, and Rob was out with Subhumans here, and we'd arrange times to try and talk on the phone, because back in '98, you didn't know where there'd be a phone that you could actually talk to each other. And one of the first things I said to him was, 'How's 'Cradle to the Grave' live?' And he said, 'It kills the set!' I was like, 'No, that's not possible!' Haha! So when I got home from the Avail trip, I flew up to Portland and Seattle for the last dates of the Subs tour – they played 'Cradle' and he was right, the energy in the room really dropped. I mean, I loved hearing it 'n' all…"

Robert: "People would get amped to hear Phil start it, but then five minutes later, they're like, 'Meh…!'"

"One of the most memorable moments on the '98 tour was at the first of two nights at Coney Island High in New York," adds **Trotsky**. "It was my thirty-third birthday, and the crowd of 500 people sang me 'Happy Birthday', which was awesome. On the first couple of reformation US tours, we hired a big fuck-off RV for travelling in, and that was great; there was a table and seats in the back, where you could drink booze whilst on the road, which in the US is highly illegal if you are less than six feet away from the driver. But the RV was big enough to be six and a half feet away! As it was set up for 'happy campers', we had to find space for the gear and merch, which went in every available space, including the shower and toilet…

"Second time round, we had the Cargo version, which was much more practical, with an area for all the gear at the back, freeing up space up front. Robert later got a Dodge Sprinter which was so much cheaper on fuel, so we still use that. The RV was great, but rather impractical and expensive for a touring band.

"Drum-wise, I've been using the same kit in the US for the last twenty-seven years – a joint purchase between Citizen Fish and Richard the roadie in 1995. It's a Pearl wood shell (BLX) with a 22" bass drum, a 13" rack tom and 18" floor tom, the same sizes as I use here, but I always take over my cymbals, which are Zildjian Z3s, snare – a Pearl Free Floater, maple shell – and pedal, a DW 500."

After the very successful US trek, the Subhumans took a six-month break, before embarking upon the twenty-one-date European leg of their 'final' tour in March 1999. However, this trip was a bit more problematic, albeit another great success as regards the actual shows.

"There was a lot of drama," sighs **Bruce**, "With the van breaking down, and we had to get a train and everything – it was a bit like a tour from the old days, haha! It was a bit messy, lots of things went wrong. Paula, Pete's other half, put that tour on; she was getting into booking bands…

ALL THE ROADIES ON STAGE PLUS PHIL
RCKNDY, SEATTLE, 1998 BY KAROLINE COLLINS

RICHARD THE ROADIE AND PHIL, PORTLAND, SEPTEMBER 1998

LAST SHOW 1998 TOUR, SEATTLE, ROBERT AND PETE WORKING STAGE, DILDO IN CROWD, PIC BY KAROLINE COLLINS

MERCH CUSTOMER IN DIY SHIRT, SEATTLE, 1998, HOLDING WIFFLE THE WOMBAT, ONE OF DICK'S STUFFED TRAVEL COMPANIONS, PIC BY KAROLINE COLLINS

"Nowadays we go through Mary at Turbo Booking, who books the Restarts and various other bands. All these things get better as you get more together… and touch wood, our gigs in Europe are well attended, they pay well and always look after us alright. We seem to be very lucky now. But we've done all that: sleeping on floors, trying to get to sleep when there's a night club on downstairs… the Germans especially like to put lots of disco music on after the punk gig and party into the night. When we first got back together, we were super excited, and we were partying, and then you can sleep pretty much anywhere, so it wasn't that big a deal. But we've done it all before – and hopefully won't have to do it again!"

"Paula had been doing Euro tours for some US bands so had all the contacts," adds **Trotsky**. "There were some really good gigs on that trip, although there were a couple of howlers too. There was a squat gig in Italy next to a sewage works, and it fuckin' stank! The kit I was using was the worst piece of crap it's ever been my displeasure to use – partway through the set, the rack tom broke off, rolled across the stage and into the crowd! But overall, it was good, and at the last gig in Ghent we played for two hours – we just couldn't seem to stop."

"After the fever-pitch reaction to the '98 reformation tour in the US, with big sold-out venues, the Euro tour of '99 felt a lot more low-key," reckons **Phil**, "Smaller venues, smaller crowds and less fervour. Since the Subhumans tours in the '80s, which by that point felt a lifetime ago, Culture Shock and Citizen Fish had been pounding the Euro tour circuit on a yearly basis, so we'd previously played many of the towns on the tour, and we'd made a lot of long-time friends over the years, which always makes Euro-touring an enjoyable, family-feel experience.

"Jasper [from Culture Shock and Citizen Fish] and Silas [who would go on to drum for Citizen Fish] were onboard as merch and stage crew. I'd used my money from the US tour to buy myself a van, an old Renault Master, and this was to be our ride for the tour. I'd kitted it out nicely inside with a gas stove, benches and nice curtains, a real home from home, and a nice place to chill when you fancied a bit of p and q [i.e. 'peace and quiet']. It drove great, and had plenty of room for the gear; it just had a small oil drip from the sump, which I'd keep an eye on.

"The tour started off nicely, first gig being at the Lint Fabriek in Kontich, Belgium, hanging out with old Antwerp friends – Blauwers, the infamous punk goalkeeper for the Lunatics alternative football team and Herwin from the band Bad Influence. As with many of the Euro venues, sleeping accommodation was on-site, and the bar stayed open late after the show. Free beer, good company… we were in tour heaven.

"Fast forward a few days to the morning after a late night of heavy partying at the Karlsruhe gig. I'm sure one member of the entourage was found curled up under the van and subsequently named 'Pompeii Dog'? Bleary-eyed and feeling slightly the worst for wear, I topped up the oil and we jumped in the van and headed for Zurich.

"Chugging up a relentlessly steep mountain in Switzerland, the oil warning light came on and before I could pull over there was the loud, ominous sound of mangled engine. I think I felt physically sick, muttering, 'Fuck, fuck, fuck, my new van!' We called a tow truck to the nearest garage, and their instant diagnosis was that the engine was indeed completely fucked and would have to be replaced. We grabbed our guitars and a few essentials, and carried on by train.

"When we made it to Italy the following day, we rented a van and Silas returned to pick up the gear from my stricken Renault. I think we crammed into the back of our friend Chris Spurrell's tiny Ford van until Silas caught up with us.

"Unfortunately, the van had broken down in the most expensive country in Europe, and they quoted an astronomical figure to stick a reconditioned engine in. And thus, the van was left atop a Swiss mountain, to end its days amid the Edelweiss and clanking of cow bells, ha! So we finished off the tour in a turbo-charged Italian Fiat rental, a lesson learnt not to ignore oil leaks on the van. Doh.

"Despite the van problems, we'd had some great gigs and it felt great to be back touring Europe with Subhumans. At the last gig in Ghent, we were in party mood. Pid from Sensa Yuma was there and jumped up to sing along on a couple of songs. Riding high on end-of-tour euphoria, we were having too much fun by the end, and decided to just keep playing... I think we might even have played 'From the Cradle to the Grave' just for a laugh? Anyway, we played for ages, and two hours of Subhumans was more than enough for the Belgians, who drifted away sensing that this was some kind of (unfunny) band in-joke.

"I wasn't in quite such high spirits when we rolled home into Warminster and unloaded the gear: a few thousand quid out of pocket having ditched the van, facing a gruelling non-stop drive back to Milan to return the rental vehicle, and then a long trip home by train and ferry."

"I think when we first got back together again, we were all partying pretty hard," admits **Bruce**, "But as time went on, we realised we couldn't do that level of intoxication every night. Even though it's very tempting, because a lot of it is free – a lot of the booze is on the rider.

"When the band got back together, I gave up smoking. I did one night smoking at our first gig, at the Porter Butt, and that was it, no more cigarettes. I don't need cigarettes. The band is enough really... we're very lucky to be playing our own music, why do I need anything else? Why do I need a bonus on top of that? Why do I need nicotine and alcohol, on top of something that's so great anyway?

"Of course, the answer is, it gets boring, and cigarettes fill in the gap, and when you add alcohol to it, it's even more amazing that you're in a band, travelling the world playing your own songs, it really is. But you don't have to have it, and it really is enough of a buzz on its own.

A benefit for Mayday 2000 ......an orgy of anti-capitalism!

wattyler Petrograd **SUBHUMANS**

Saturday 15th April, at Chats Palace. 44 Brooksbys Walk, Hackney E9.
£4.50 in / £3.50 for cyclists. 8pm. Be there before they sell out!

SAT 17 APRIL 1999

SUBHUMANS LIVE

last belgium

WAR RISK III PUNK FROM BELGIUM + GUEST

DEMOCRAZY

SUBHUMANS → CULTURE SHOCK → CITIZEN FISH → SUBHUMANS

SUBHUMANS

DIAVOLO ★ ROSSO

28.3. JUGENDZENTRUM "Z"
FILDERSTADT
Tübingerstrasse 54

Enige concert in Nederland!!!!!

SUBHUMANS

EenmaligeReunieTour
HELLWORMS (USA)
Ex Victims Family

Vrijdag
16 April

Entree:f15,-
Aanvang:20.00 uur
THE BOOM (USA)
Freaky Jazzcore
Reserveren:072-5115076

PARKHOF

VICTORIEPARK 4 1811 ML ALKMAAR 072-5115076

ORCA 003: 'Still Can't Hear The Words (The Subhumans Covers album)'- 24 of England's finest Hardcore/Punk bands pay homage to the seminal UK Anarcho band... and raise money for Food Not Bombs and Sea Shepherd in the process. Featuring Assert, Bait, The Bungalow Band (members of Citizen Fish), Chokehold (ex-Broken Bones), Concrete Sox, Confusion Corporation, Cress, Decadence Within, The Dicklikkas (members of the Varukers, Hard To Swallow + Iron Monkey), Hellkrusher, Human Error (members of Stampin' Ground, Shutdown + Medulla Nocte), Imbalance, In The Shit, Knuckledust, LD50, Maggot Slayer Overdrive, Muckspreader (ex-Amebix, amongst others), POA, Police Bastard, Rectify, Statement, Ten Tennants, Wat Tyler, and Whippasnappa. 72 minutes of diverse noise, with a rather splendid 16 page booklet, out NOW. £6.50/$14 ppd, from Blackfish Records, PO Box 15, Ledbury, HR8 1YG, England.
No foreign cheques, please.

Still available, and still HOT: (ORCA 001) Unite 'Playing With Fire' MCD, and (ORCA 002) the Stampin' Ground/Knuckledust split MCD, 'The Dark Side Versus The East Side', both £4/$9 ppd. Coming next: Light Of The Morning MCD - an awesome return to the fray for these ex-members of Above All, Understand, Outbreak and Pepperman. Street date: May '99.

AD FOR 'STILL CAN'T HEAR THE WORDS - THE SUBHUMANS COVERS ALBUM' CD ON BLACKFISH RECORDS

"It's always been really good playing – that's the best bit about being in a band. It's just everything else that's never been so good... all the travelling and that. Unless you really like it. But sitting in the back of a van for hours when you're not hung over is much easier than when you are. You can read, write things, do stuff on your iPad... if you're hung over, it's miserable.

"Then again, if you're partying after the gigs, and in the bar afterwards, that's a lot of fun too, so you've got to weigh it up, haven't you? But we've had to cut down on hard liquor... well, I've had to, personally. That became a bit of a habit on the road... for all of us actually. So that's good, that we came out the other end of that."

Sometimes there is an expectation from fans of the band that you'll party with them into the small hours, and they don't realise you've got a mammoth drive the next day and weeks of hard road ahead of you.

"We've done that a little bit, and I'm sure Dick has some stories," says **Bruce**, "But usually it's mainly just drinking, and people forget what they wanted to ask you when they've had too many drinks, and it gets a bit boring. Unless you're Dick, who has people asking him stuff all the time – it must drive him a bit mad, he's answered so many of the same questions.

"We do sit backstage a lot of the time, where we can relax – you don't always feel like socialising every night – but Dick and Trotsky smoke, so they're going outside to smoke all the time, and they're getting nobbled when they're outside having a fag. It's a weird sort of thing, socialising when you're on the road..."

The 'Still Can't Hear the Words: Subhumans Covers Album' CD mentioned in the introduction to this book – and earlier by Phil – was released by your author on his DIY label, Blackfish Records, in 1999. Chris Willsher of the Plymouth punk band Bus Stations Loonies originally came up with the idea in 1995, but for various reasons it didn't come to fruition, so I picked it up and ran with it a few years later. As well as the covers Chris had collected initially, I bolstered the track-listing to twenty-four songs, which were then all mastered at the Whitehouse in Weston-super-Mare during February '99. It was a rag-tag but thoroughly enjoyable collection, a mixture of straight versions, cleaving close to the original songs, and some wildly imaginative deconstructions, from bands known (Concrete Sox, Wat Tyler, Police Bastard, Hellkrusher, Cress and the like) to the totally obscure (LD50, Human Error and the DickLikkas) – the one thing they all had in common was a love, or at least grudging respect, for the Subhumans. There were even contributions from the Subhumans' inner circle, with Jasper and Andy covering 'Somebody's Mother' as Ten Tennants and Silas's Bungalow Band doing a surreal take on 'Animal'. Robert 'Mid' Middleton from Deviated Instinct did the excellent cover art (his 'other' band Bait covered 'Zyklon B-Movie'), and Dick kindly provided some liner notes and lent his inimitable calligraphy for the back cover track-listing. It was a fun release, and several hundred pounds were raised for the Sea Shepherd Society and Food Not Bombs.

406

With the European tour under their belts, Subhumans returned to the back burner for the next year (allowing Citizen Fish back off their touring leash), their next gig not until April 2000, when they played Chats Palace in London, with Wat Tyler and Petrograd. And then they only played a total of eight gigs during 2000 and 2001, with no international trips, although they made their first two appearances at the annual Holidays in the Sun festival in Morecambe – which would soon morph into the Wasted festival, and then eventually the widely revered/reviled Rebellion festival.

"When it was first suggested, we really didn't want to do it," reveals **Bruce**, "Mainly because the line-up included lots of Oi! bands, and lots of bands that don't have very good principles. But in the end, we did do it, and it was okay, and it's sort of got better each time. As the festival itself got bigger, and the barriers started to come down a bit… I think the people broke the barriers down themselves. We thought we'd get a lot more trouble [as in *criticism*] from our audience for playing a festival like that, but we didn't – I think everyone has grown up a bit and mellowed, and punk has become this over-arching thing, and the violence has vanished for the most part.

"It's very healthy now. The Stranglers played after us last time we played, so it was a huge gig for us, and even more people came in for The Stranglers. They're one of my favourite bands, so it was great to watch them, but at the same time, as much as I'm influenced by The Stranglers, there's a lot of things I don't really like about The Stranglers from a lyrical point of view. And they came from that era before us when it was all a bit 'rock-star-ish'… so they wouldn't be happy with me wandering in their backstage area and saying 'Hi' and sharing a beer. In fact, there's a good chance you wouldn't get anywhere near their backstage area, and I find that attitude just unnecessary really. I suppose they might have to do something like that because they're so big and their fans might crash in and murder them or something, but it's not very punk. But you just have to park all that really, and just enjoy them for their music and what it means to you."

Another notable gig during those quiet few years after the millennium was at Fiddlers in Bristol, on July 13th, 2001, which was a benefit for the 2001 – A Football Oddity alternative Euro tournament. The gig was recorded and a rough 'n' ready (but extremely enjoyable) twenty-seven-song live CD released to further raise money for the cause.

"Well, Phil was captain of the Wessex Allstars," explains **Dick**, "Which was a football team, and along with the Easton Cowboys, another football team, from Bristol, and several other teams – there were some from Yorkshire, several from Germany, one from Antwerp – every summer they would have a tournament. And these weren't 'proper' football teams with stadiums and everything; these were punks basically, just forming a football team. Although the Easton Cowboys did take it one step further, and played benefit football for the Zapatistas, in Mexico… they really travelled and made a political statement out of the whole thing, and good on 'em. And they organised a lot of these

BRUCE AND DICK BY CHRISTINE BOARTS LARSON

tournaments, a different country every year, and that gig – and the CD of it that was put out – was to raise some money towards financing the next tournament, which I think was taking place in Somerset. It was the only time I've got sort of involved in football… but Phil's dead keen on football, and quite good at playing it too. My brother was in goal, and did pretty well at that; he saved a penalty or two. It was a mini football festival, with people bringing along tents and camping out… there was a marquee with bands playing, fires were lit, a lot of drinking went on, and football was played. It was all free to watch as well… not that that many people knew these matches were going on – some of the places they played would be like a field on the edge of the Alps or whatever.

"Citizen Fish were going quite well at that point," he continues. "We were busy, busy, busy, with loads and loads of gigs. And for the first few years, there were way more Citizen Fish gigs than there were Subhumans gigs, because Cit Fish was still like the main thing. And then we put the Fish on hold for a bit, in order to do more Subs gigs. For example, we only did five Subhumans gigs in 2000, and Citizen Fish were touring all over the place as usual. In 2001, we only did *three* gigs – Holidays in the Sun, that one in Bristol and one in Southend. So, we did carry on after those first three tours in '98 and '99, but we didn't really do much for the first few years. We laid low and just did very occasional gigs, but then in 2002 we started to play more – we did some more UK gigs, went to Canada and the US… from about 2002 onwards, we decided to put more energy into Subhumans and less into the Fish.

"The thing is, it wasn't balanced out right – Cit Fish were doing fifty gigs a year, and Subhumans were doing five, but more and more people were offering Subhumans gigs when they realised that we hadn't actually stopped after all. It just made sense to pause the Fish a little bit… I mean, we carried on, but the Subhumans just got a *lot* busier from 2002 onwards."

2002 — 2005

Subhumans activity really started to ramp up again in 2002, although the year started off fairly low-key with a gig at the Concorde, on the Brighton seafront at the end of March, which was something of a warm-up for a high profile gig a few weeks later at the London Astoria, playing main support to Conflict, on a stacked bill that also included Icons of Filth, Inner Terrestrials, Riot/Clone and Dezerter, from Poland. Apart from an intimate Warminster gig at the Weymouth Arms to celebrate Mel's birthday in May, the band's next gig wasn't until July 12th, when they flew out to Spain for the Festival Sans Nom.

"Ah yes, 'The Festival Without Name'," recalls **Dick**. "That was one of those rare, fly in/fly out 'one-off' gigs, with all sorts of bands – DOA… Dead Kennedys, without Jello… it was in some sort of cultural centre, I suppose, with all sorts of other stuff going on. There was food, and shops, and people wandering about all over the place… but it was pretty well packed out."

After another appearance at the Holidays in the Sun festival, which had migrated south from Morecambe to its now-traditional home in Blackpool, in July, they headed to Croatia for the Monte Paradiso festival in Pula in early August.

"That was quite extraordinary," says **Dick**. "The whole thing was set inside an old fort. John Active sorted that out, and got us over there with the Restarts… Subhumans and Citizen Fish played. There were two main stages, and two or three smaller stages, all sorts of stalls, people selling records, T-shirts, candles, whatever. Sort of like a mini-Glastonbury… very mini. And it didn't involve a field. But it was really good; we were there for the weekend, stayed in a hostel… it was a half-mile walk to the sea, the sun was out, it was very enjoyable."

At the end of October, Subhumans did seven gigs in Canada – in five days! If that doesn't compute, it's because they did matinee shows as well as evening ones in both Quebec and Montreal.

"I like Montreal, the French bit, because I like France," declares **Bruce**. "I like the attitude, and I like that the audience is listening, and it strikes me that French people – and Celtic people as well… people that have music and creativity in their psyche… they enjoy your playing in a different way, as well as just letting their hair down and jumping around to the choruses. They're also a bit crazy, which is always good, so you have the best of both worlds – they jump about *and* appreciate the finer points of what we're playing. Montreal is definitely a passionate audience, so it's always fun, always chaotic… having people just stand there watching you is never as much fun as having them hanging off the light shades!"

"We have been there and back a few times without going to the States," adds **Dick**. "It's actually much easier to get work permits for just Canada, because of the Commonwealth relationship… you need much less paperwork. Less permissions given, and it costs a lot less to get those permissions, to go in and play some gigs. There's even some gigs over there where they get bankrolled by the local state authority. Canada is much more regulation-free, put it that way, than the US… maybe more artistically minded in its culture. You take your bank account into your hands going to America – one thing goes wrong, you're in debt for a year.

"What makes Canada quite different though is the state of Quebec, which has got Montreal in it, and Quebec City, where they speak French a lot. And they just have an excess of wildness about them, that's most easily described as 'European'? It's a bit like playing in France, because of the accents, but it's also like playing mainland Europe because they do the food thing – they feed bands, and put you up in nice places… they look after you. There's a feeling of camaraderie, of unison, of all being in this punk scene together, and a lot less of the hero hierarchy stuff going on. And the crowds in Quebec State are just a little bit mad; they really go for it, stage invasions, stage diving…

"Like the Americans, they tend to say what they think, and say it quite loudly, but there's an extra subtlety about it, that makes it sort of European at the same time? Just to massively generalise, haha!"

And like America, there's some big distances to cover if you want to go coast to coast…

Dick: "We've never been to the middle of Canada, although it's possible if you do really long drives, to hop across the central states, doing one gig in each state. But we haven't done that, and we've only played the west coast properly, on tour, once. We did Vancouver, and then went up into the mountains and the plains, and played a small town called Rossland. There was one main street, one set of shops, and we played in one of the four bars, to fifty people. But they had a good time. There were mountains and signs about deer wandering around. It was a one-off for us and them, so it was treasurable.

"But we've been to the east several times; Ontario and Quebec states are great places to play. And there's a lot of history back in Canada, because I went out with a girl from Toronto for a few years, and went over and hung out with the punks in the scene there in the mid-Eighties. There was a band called Dayglo Abortions, who are still going, and I hung around with them a bit; there's still a few people left over from back then, which is great, that continuity."

As he had throughout the Nineties, **Trotsky** was still finding time to drum with other projects alongside the Subhumans:

"In the early Noughties I answered an advert in the local paper," he recounts. "I was living in Frome, Somerset, at the time, and it was for a groundsman to sort out someone's garden. As I'd always done garden/manual work for my crusts, I went along with my old rotovator and got to work. The guy whose garden it was came out after some time, and as we were chatting suddenly said, 'Aren't you Trotsky from Subhumans?' It turned out he was Alan Wilson from The Sharks, the rockabilly legends. He then asked me if I wanted to play on their next record, 'The Best of the Sharks'; I agreed at once, and as he had a studio in the house, over the next weeks, we recorded drums for two songs on that record.

"Then The Eccentrics were based in Lincoln – UK, not the US… there's an old soul band from Lincoln, Nebraska, called Eccentrics. My then-girlfriend Sandra was at university there and met them through Arthur from 999 and The Lurkers, whose house she was living at. They were looking for a drummer and guitarist, so it worked out well with me and Sandra, as I would travel to Lincoln most weekends from Somerset to visit. I don't think I've ever been in a band where we laughed so much, and the vocalist Shawn

411

was fuckin' hilarious. We did a lot of gigs, mostly around the Lincoln area, but also at BOB Fest in Bremen, and five or six shows with Subhumans in the US. That was me on drums, Sandra on guitar, Shawn on vocals and Vince on bass – great band, great people.

"I also got involved in the T4 Project. I had just moved to Bremen in 2005, and was contacted by Shannon Saint Ryan [ex–Meet the Virus]. He was writing songs for a record he wanted to make with a whole bunch of musicians from the punk scene. Being based in LA, he had access to a myriad of musicians there, but he asked me if I wanted to play drums on half the record, and could I recommend a second skins-man for the other half? I immediately put him in touch with Spike [ex–English Dogs/Damned/Morrisey etc.] who agreed to come onboard as well. Over the next weeks and months, Shannon would send me recordings of the songs with a drum machine track; I then practised to these songs over a PA in a local practice space, which was a WW2 bunker in Bremen with one-meter-thick concrete walls and blast doors... it was fuckin' freezing.

"After we felt ready, Shannon booked studio time at Southern Studios in London; he wanted that authentic historical punk sound for the rhythm section recording. It was, of course, the studio where Subhumans had recorded so much, and it was really nice to go back there again. Sadly, I believe it is now gone...?

"Anyway, Shannon flew over with Jay Bentley [Bad Religion], who was sharing bass duties with Tony Barber [Lack of Knowledge and Buzzcocks]. Spike drove down from Peterborough, and I drove to London from Bremen with my wife, Sandra, and our baby daughter, Lucy. I think we had about three days to get the drums and bass down, and it all went very smoothly with Harvey Birrel engineering.

"After we finished up, Shannon and Jay flew back to the US to complete the recording with all the others out there.

"Unfortunately, when it came to the point when it could be released, the two labels who had said they were interested both bailed, and it ended up coming out on a small label, Mental Records, but it was an amazing experience, and mega respect to Shannon whose dedication to the project was truly inspiring."

As mentioned earlier, in the '1983' chapter, Shannon was also instrumental in getting 'Susan' reinstated into the band's live set, albeit infrequently.

"Shannon just said, 'I'm going to bring a keyboard and we're going to play this song,' and he made it happen," says **Robert**. "But watching them sus it out during sound-check... having access to things like that, even in the context of working a big rock show or whatever, still makes me feel like a little kid. Watching a band that you know has completely flipped people's lives around re-learning a song... seeing that play out in front of you is just great."

"Cross Stitched Eyes were formed in Bremen around that time too," continues **Trotsky**. "Jason [Enemies] didn't want to drum and sing live, so they needed a drummer to play on tour. They had various member changes, but when I joined up it was Jason singing, Tim Trowbridge from Zygote on guitar, Chris from LA, and Stevie from Bremen band Cold Death. We did a bunch of rehearsals in the Bremen bunker room and hit the road. I did two tours with them and loved it; the music is so damn good, and they are all such excellent musicians. My only regret is that they didn't ask me to play on the record... ho hum!

412

"I once drum-checked for The Damned too, but I was very, very drunk, so probably best not mention it…"

Back to the Subhumans, who had taken the winter of 2002 – 2003 off, and were steeling themselves for their next US trek, that took in thirty shows in just under five weeks, and saw them recording the 'Live in a Dive' album at the Corona Showcase Theatre on April 3rd, 2003. It was well-timed: they were eight gigs into the tour and both nicely warmed up and firing on all cylinders, and consequently it's a cracking live album, all your favourite songs – and a load more for good measure – played pretty much perfectly. If a little faster than the studio versions, which just adds to the infectious energy of the whole thing. There was even a brand new (at that point in time) track, 'This Year's War', which bode well for new material from the band, and the enhanced CD version saw the twenty-six-song track-listing bolstered by the hidden 'New Age' track and an animated (as in lots of waving hands about, not a cartoon!) interview.

"I think that was the first professional-sounding record we did," enthuses **Trotsky**, "The sound is flawless, as far as I can tell. There was a recording truck at the back of the venue, this massive silver truck with a recording studio in the back. We did the full set in the sound-check, and then recorded the gig as well. It was absolutely top notch; they were off to record AC/DC at some festival after that… so they knew what they were doing, and it's no wonder it sounded so good."

"Fat Mike really wanted us to be a part of his 'Live in a Dive' series, which were basically live records by bands that he likes," elaborates **Dick**. "He does like the Subhumans a lot, so we said we'd do it, because we'd always toyed with the idea of a live album anyway, and until then that CD from Bristol was about as close as we'd got. A lot of live albums don't stand up for very long… although the Ramones did a good one. We had all these live tapes, and we'd be like, 'Would this make a good live record? Well, we didn't play very well on this song… or that song…'

"So, we set it up to happen at what became one of our favourite venues, the Corona Showcase, when we were on tour over there in April 2003. They brought along this truck which had a recording studio in the back of it, and set up about twenty-five microphones across the stage, and a couple above the crowd. Our sound-check consisted of playing through the entire set, which they recorded, just in case we had to replace a version of a track with another one. We extended the set quite a lot and played about twenty-seven songs, to get something off each album, and we played a few songs, like 'Somebody's Mother', that we haven't played for years.

"It turned out pretty good, although I had to re-do some of the vocals. I had a tickly throat, but then doing a twenty-seven-song sound-check and then a set later the same day, my voice was a bit shredded. So, much to my chagrin, I had to re-do the vocals, which is cheating really. This is the first time I've really mentioned this to anyone outside the circle, so to speak, because it wasn't the done thing – you shouldn't be doing the vocals again on a live album, because it's supposed to be a *live* album! But there was no choice really, the vocals sounded awful I couldn't hold any long notes, and I couldn't hit any high notes… [bursts into a croaky rendition of the 'Die' at the end of 'Religious Wars']. So it had to be done – it had all been recorded, and paid for, it was going ahead; we just had to make the most of it.

LIVE IN A DIVE ALBUM BACK COVER SHOT, 3/4/2003
BY SICKBOY PHOTOGRAPHY

DICK, APRIL 2003 BY CHRIS BOARTS LARSON

DICK, CHICAGO, 26/4/03 BY CHRIS BOARTS LARSON

"So we took it to a studio in Holt, a small village near Trowbridge, a few weeks after we got back off that tour and we had the rough mixes through and thought, 'Oh, shit! Okay…' Everything else sounded fine, except the vocals, so I just did those again. Which wasn't a problem, as we generally play all our songs at roughly the same speed every time we play them – which is usually faster than the recorded album versions, because the energy and excitement isn't in the studio, it's live. The studio is where the precision is. But the live one is actually a cracking recording, and in a sense is the best version of all those songs, as it's played at the live speed, with all the energy from the crowd, and with twenty-five mics you couldn't really go wrong on the mix."

"That was certainly an experience," concedes **Bruce**, "Because it was two full sets in one day, but it's a good album, I like it. The engineer [Ryan Greene] was an A-list producer who'd worked a lot with Fat Wreck… quite famous in his own right. It was recorded on a mobile studio truck called called Le Mobile – and it really is a truck, as in a big American truck, and it's got a great studio in the back of it. He even recorded on multi-track, as well as Pro Tools, so you had a choice. He was definitely the most expensive engineer we've had record us, haha! And he was noticing the difference between different speaker cabs… all this technical stuff. But then again, Steve [Evans] was doing that on the last recording we did, so I think engineers these days are much more clued up about what sounds good. So, all that was exciting. I think it's a bit of a hard album though… it's almost like the equipment was too good, and it sounds really quite harsh. It was only a small place, so it was a typical punk gig – no room, everything was jammed in.

"We recorded that when we still tuned to E, but we now tune down to E-flat. Which is a better key for Dick to sing in. There was a lot of pressure to get it right, and poor old Dick lost his voice. We were like, 'Whatever you do, don't get a cold…', and of course he got a cold. So we did have to re-do the vocals. But what are you going to do? It was a good experience, and it was a nice relaxed feeling with Fat Wreck Chords. We didn't take the whole project that seriously."

It was three weeks later, during the same US tour, that the band then recorded their 'All Gone Live' DVD, which was filmed April 26th – 28th at the Metro in Chicago, First Avenue in Minneapolis, and Globe East, Milwaukee, and released by Cleopatra Records.

"Oh yeah, that was a mixture of three different gigs," says **Dick**. "Kari from Cleopatra came along to all these gigs, and filmed us with two or three cameras at three gigs in a row. There's a surprising amount of editing – it's like watching a strobe light… we're changing T-shirts like five times a song, haha! And at first, it's a bit too much, you can't concentrate, but you kinda get used to it. And it sounds good."

"In 2003, I went out to meet up with my BFF Karoline – 'The Roadie' – Collins," **Chris Larson** remembers those gigs very well, "And we followed the Subhumans who were touring and playing with the Enemies from Oakland. We went to Chicago, then Minneapolis and then to Milwaukee. I got super stressed on the way to the Chicago show 'cos we were running late, but we made it just in time to see the Subhumans; we sat on the side of the stage and I got some great photos with that beautiful theatre stage background. I remember the Enemies guys had a whole little hand dance routine worked out to the 'Apathy' chorus, which was so much fun!

"Minneapolis was a good long overnight drive, of sleeping in the car, visiting the local coffee shop, checking out Extreme Noise [a much-loved Minneapolis record store], and the bookshop of the time, and eventually heading to the 7th Street Entry club to hang out with the dudes again. Great show, great town. Then it was back to Karoline's in Milwaukee, where the show was in a super tiny venue but was equally amazing; it really felt like all the shows had something totally unique about them."

More high profile (by UK punk standards at least) gigs followed, at the Boardwalk in Sheffield, with MDC, Leftover Crack, F-Minus, Goldblade, Broken Bones and Sick on the Bus, the London Astoria and the London Forum, the latter with Conflict, Inner Terrestrials and Lost Cherrees, before they trekked to Berlin for a one-off gig at the infamous Kopi.

"We've played there several times, and that is definitely a wild place," smiles **Dick**. "Several floors, a large squat, three sides of a square, multi-storey building, and it's a centre for squatters and anarchists and people who are making stuff, promoting its own existence and fighting to keep it open, fighting for the rights of people to come to the country and be refugees. It's one part of an amazingly together anarcho squat scene in Germany, as well as Holland and France and so on… central mainland Europe. And it's been putting on gigs for years and years, always four or five bands, that go onstage at one in the morning, and they want you to play for an hour and a half. You get to sleep there and wake up there. Although once when we woke up there, our van was covered in graffiti, which wasn't very good, but generally it's a very positive experience going there. The toilets are fairly horrendous, but you get used to that sort of thing… how much room is there in the book to talk about toilets and touring?

"And did I mention the seven necessary things for a good toilet experience? Me and Pete worked them out once. Toilet paper – totally number one on the list. A door, a lock on the door, a toilet seat, a light, a flush – and walls! I've seen toilets on tour where you can sit and have a shit, but everyone will witness it. Fuck that. But this only comes into play on tour, because most of our lives we control our own bathrooms. It's the subtextual stuff – like going to the toilet – that changes when you're on tour. It becomes a thing, because you do it so many times, in so many different toilets, in so many different venues…

"It's the same with eating. You don't get your regular meals, you don't get your favourite meals; you get what you're given – if you're given anything at all. If you're not, you have to work out how to be a vegetarian or vegan in service stations, and basically end up eating a lot of stuff that isn't very good for you, and not eating much stuff that is good for you.

"Trotsky doesn't eat fruit. Bruce has always got oranges and apples with him, and willingly shares them around, which is great, because just when you think, 'I feel terrible,' the best thing you can have is a tangerine. That'll sort you out. But Trots doesn't eat fruit. He's still relatively healthy despite that, but it doesn't seem to be in his metabolism to need it.

"A small square pillow that you can fit in your bag without taking up too much room is also essential, because even if you are sleeping on a floor, if your head is comfortable, the rest of your body will deal with it. You can be on a nice comfy mattress, but if your head is on a wooden block, you're not getting any sleep."

417

CHICAGO, 26/4/03 BY CHRIS BOARTS LARSON

MINNEAPOLIS, 27/4/03 BY CHRIS BOARTS LARSON

Subhumans started off 2004 with two local(ish) gigs, in Bristol and Bradford-on-Avon, before undertaking the first of two US tours that year, eighteen gigs starting in Texas and ending up on the West Coast, with support coming from Caustic Christ, Naked Aggression, New Mexican Disaster Squad and Frisk on the regional legs.

"Every single tour we do out in the States seems like one long highlight really," admits **Phil**. "We honestly feel blessed. I still can't believe that every year people come out for us. And the average age of the audience seems to remain around twenty-four or twenty-five. Electronic dance music has taken off there now, but punk has always been a thing with kids there – even when it died out over here. When the rave thing took off here, a lot of people lost interest in punk – the drugs were calling strong! – but over there it just kept going, there were always new kids coming through."

"The Adicts are massive over there – insanely massive," observes **Dick**. "They supported us once, I think, at the 100 Club, and yes, they're a punk band that dress up. But there was none of the 'Oh my god!'-ness that they get in America! They pull *thousands* of people to their gigs! But we have a small version of what they've got in America, which is nice, because 'small' in America is still 'quite big' compared to over here...

"Although the first or second time you do something like an American tour, it really settles into your memory. But by now, I must have been to America... I don't know how many times? And that's how much it doesn't stick in your head anymore – I don't even know how many times I've been there! If you said, 'What was it like the fifth time you went?', I'd have to go back to my diaries and check who the support bands were and see what I could remember of it. Unfortunately, things tend to fade with repetition..."

Subhumans seem really popular in California especially.

"A lot of bands probably find the same thing," ponders **Dick**. "In states like Kansas, Wisconsin, Omaha... the Bible Belt, the middle bit basically... beyond New York and Philadelphia, but before you've gone past Salt Lake City into California and Oregon... in that central block of America, roughly speaking, you can have a top crowd of 300, sometimes, but you'll probably average 120 people a gig... on the East Coast, it ranges between 200 and 500... but in California, it ranges between 300 and 800 – it's mad.

"It might be cynical to say this, but I put some of it down to the location of Hollywood, and the resonance Hollywood has had on American – and global – culture. Because of the nature of stage and film stars, and heroes being created by Hollywood, who ignore real life in order to present life as it might be if everything really was okay, and everyone could sing, and wanted to sing in harmony, and dance in the streets, and all cowboys really were good guys, rescuing people... and all that bullshit coming out of Hollywood has seeped through the culture, even the punk rock culture, to the point where I've met people in LA who are gushing to their mates about the fact that they are stood within ten yards of the singer of the Subhumans! 'Oh my god!'-ing it, like they've just won the lottery or summat! It's embarrassing, and a bit scary, and just weird, y'know? And so *not* punk rock, especially anarcho punk rock, it hurts. It's completely removed from the friendly chat I want to have with anybody that wants one.

"And the further away you get from LA, the less of that you get. And I'm not saying that all Californian punks are just shallow and freaked out on celebrities, because of course they're not. The vast majority are thinking people, like everywhere else, who care a lot about music and other people, and have a good time doing it.

"You go 3000 miles in one direction, and you get somewhere like New York, and *some* of the fanbase go, 'Oh my god!' But it's way less. And far more people stand there with their arms folded, working out whether they're actually into the band, rather than assuming they're great just because they're from the UK or whatever. Which makes you treat being in a band more seriously. You don't have to prove yourself exactly, but you have to make sure you're not too relaxed about the ease of doing a gig in front of people who are bound to like you. That can settle in, and that's worrying as well. You have to watch where your head is going when you're performing; you can easily get an inflated ego when you've got a lot of people saying how great you are. You can soon start to believe it… although I've got a lot of barriers against that sort of thing. I hate what that does to the culture – it fuels hierarchies based on talent, and perception of talent… which are two different things, but closely linked.

"And then you go even further east, over the sea and all the way to the Russian border, somewhere like Lithuania – we played a festival there, and no one knew who we were, no one shook your hand, and a couple of people said, 'Your concert was good, thank you!' And that was it, it was lovely. No pressure. It's a strange world. And it can be measured in terms of response, although there's a lot more to it than that, haha! But that's a side angle… on being in a band, and people's reaction to that.

"I suppose we started at the very top in terms of numbers and attention with the first Goldenvoice gig we did back in 1984.

"My theory is, anyone coming over from abroad, let alone the UK, to America in the early Eighties was a total rarity, apart from the likes of David Bowie and the Rolling Stones. But punk bands going over to America was quite a rarity. That garnered a bunch of attention on its own. That sort of adulation didn't fit the pattern of 'We're all united in this against the system…' We were put up on this instant pedestal, just for coming from the UK, for our weird accents before our music…"

"I can't put my finger on why they're so popular, why they hit so hard here compared to over there, but it might be exotic that they're foreign," offers **Robert**, "But tons of other bands are as well, y'know? It's specifically California though – they do great everywhere else, but it's totally different here. But there's such a difference – and I'm not just saying this because I know them – between them and most other bands that have reformed. They were obviously split up for ten years or whatever, but they never stopped playing, or doing what they were doing. And they're still writing new material… their live shows now are probably almost half new material, so they're not just coming over here and playing 'EP-LP' and walking offstage. People know the words to songs on 'Crisis Point' and 'Internal Riot' just like they do for the early records. And guess what? For someone who's twenty years old now, those are 'old' records, haha!"

It's a very healthy sign for them that they've managed to span generations, somehow staying vital and relevant despite the inevitable nostalgic attraction as well.

"If you go and see them over here, especially in LA, you'll see multiple generations going to the shows together," confirms **Karoline**. "Kids with their parents… even grandma! It's great."

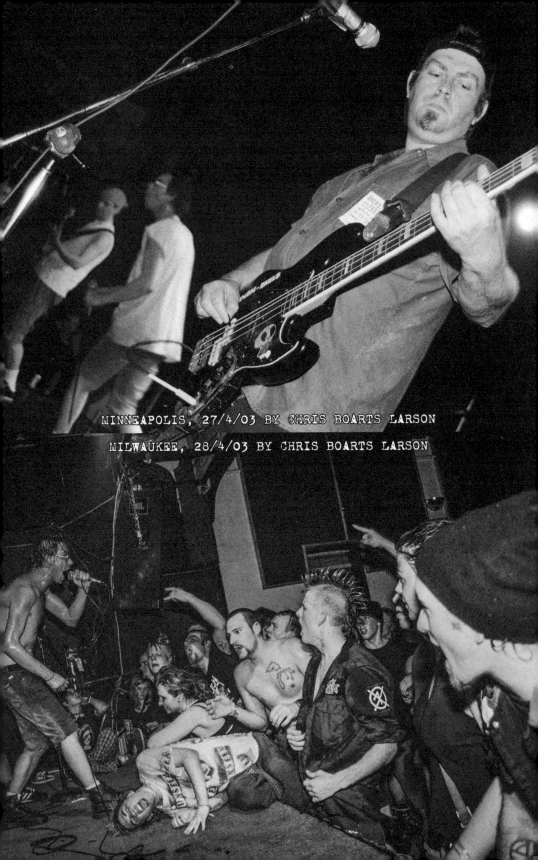

MINNEAPOLIS, 27/4/03 BY CHRIS BOARTS LARSON
MILWAUKEE, 28/4/03 BY CHRIS BOARTS LARSON

JASPER DOING MERCH ON U.S. TOUR, EARLY 2000s BY PHIL

PETE AND ROBERT ON STAGE DUTY

Robert: "At the last larger venue show in SoCal I did with them, I sold two 'The Day the Country Died' shirts to a guy who was already wearing a tattered 'TDTCD' shirt – the one he was wearing was his third 'TDTCD' shirt, so he was buying his fourth, and the other one was a second one for his kid!

"Another thing that separates them from other bands is, I don't think they're slogging through a thing that they hate, just for the money… they're doing a thing that they love, just doing what they do, but there's money to be made. They're just not dependent and focused on making money the same way some bands certainly are.

"There's definitely a line between acknowledging there is money there and not wanting to get ripped off, just wanting to be treated fairly… if you're doing a thing that obviously has a value, then you deserve your fair share – that's just being reasonable and not fucking yourself over. As opposed to, 'I want everything I can get!'

"Several years ago in Detroit, Subhumans were playing the same night as another big punk band from the UK, and some efforts were made to combine the two shows and not split the crowd, but for some reason that didn't happen. But essentially both bands were on very similar guarantees. The Subhumans show was $12 or $15 and was packed out, so they got a percentage on top of their guarantee, and we sold tons of merch and everything else – and the promoter made money too, so a great night. They had coordinated the start times of the two shows, so we went across to the other gig, in this much bigger venue, $25 or $30 door, and kind of a ghost town inside, maybe fifty people. The band got their money, but the promoter lost their ass! Two completely different show experiences, with the band walking away with the same amount of money…"

"There's a guy making skateboards in the States, right," says **Dick**, trying to articulate exactly where those imaginary lines that ultimately define some of their hard-fought principles lie (only they're not 'imaginary', because they *do* exist, but not in the tangible sense), "Who combined bits from all the covers into one picture to go on a skateboard deck, and he asked if he could sell them – he'd give us this percentage of the sales, and we were okay with that. But since then, he's been coming back with stuff like, 'There's a company that wants to make Subhumans watches…!' And he sent us a link to all these watches with band logos on, and they're selling for $99, and we weren't interested. Watches just don't come into the 'acceptable bracket' I've got in my head… I can't even explain what that bracket is, but there is good merchandise, and rip-off merchandise… and if the watch had been $10, it might have been different, but $99? And most people don't wear watches these days anyway.

"We've not had any backlash from people for merch decisions. I have a line in my head, and we haven't crossed it. Although I drew that line at Subhumans scarves, as I felt that would be exploiting the punters or whatever, but then we did 100 scarves, over in the States, where they like that sort of thing, and sold them all really quickly…! Do you go with what people want, or do you stick with what you think? Are we just pandering to commercialism sticking our name on scarves? Even though people ask for them? At least a scarf is useful when you're cold… but we sold quite a few of them in California, in the fucking desert, where it's never cold, and you'll never, ever need a scarf!

"It's a case of weighing up who's making them, how much they're making on them, how much people are getting charged for them. Shoes are useful – obviously – so they fall in the same bracket as T-shirts… and possibly scarves! But I don't want anything to do with Vans tours – they wanted to pay money to use something from 'Mickey Mouse' for something, but that puts us out there in this great big capitalist thing, which I just don't relate to at all. So, no watches, and no pillow cases, and no duvets…"

After playing one of those mini-Rebellion punk all-dayer type things at the horrible O2 Academy in Birmingham, standing out like a sore thumb (in a good way) on a bill comprising The Damned, the Buzzcocks, The Undertones, The Beat et al, Subhumans then played the Wasted festival in Morecambe, which was basically Rebellion before it was called Rebellion, but after it was called Holidays in the Sun (for the record, 2004 was the year it changed its name to Wasted, and it only became Rebellion in 2007). They then headed to a much more salubrious locale when they played the Puntala festival in Finland.

Dick: "It was definitely in the woods somewhere… but then again, everything is in the woods in Finland. It's all woods and lakes, and they drink this stuff, whatever it is, that you can't smell or see, because it's been totally distilled into as much alcohol as possible, and it's very, very strong… I assume it's some sort of vodka. I had one shot of it, or a glug out of a bottle, and sat on a stone, cross-legged, spacing out at all the trees. Feeling completely elevated for a while. And they're drinking *loads* of this stuff…! It's like, 'What?!'

"But the gig was good; there was a lot of people there… a lot of crusties, everyone wearing black sorta thing. In the deep countryside, all trees and the occasional lake. And of course, I got bitten by a mosquito on my lip somewhere…"

An unfortunate experience that informed the song 'Mosquitoes' on their next studio album, 'Internal Riot', perhaps?

"Absolutely," confirms **Dick**. "One of the practice sessions for that was at Trotsky's place, in Germany, and he had one or two mosquitoes – but you only need *one* – flying about the room I was sleeping in. And I woke up with a bite on my lower eye lid, and it was all itchy; I couldn't do nothing about it, and it all swelled up. Some people can trudge through a rain forest and not get bitten by anything, but I get one mosquito in the same room as me and that's it.

"John from AOS3 showed me his back once, when we were on tour in Germany, and oh my god, his back was covered in bites, he was really suffering… then other people don't get bitten at all. It's all to do with your chemical make-up and what you sweat…? I don't know.

"I've been bitten a couple of times where I've had to get antibiotics, because the bite went red, and the redness spread, and went off in a singular line, patently working its way along a vein or an artery towards my heart, all of it itching like mad, and I thought, 'Right, I better see a doctor about this…' This was in the States one year, and it was like, 'Yes, you need some antibiotics – that'll be fifty dollars!' So, me and mosquitoes don't get on very well, although touch wood, I've not been bitten – by anything – for about ten years now… so maybe I've evolved."

As mentioned by Dick, and as if they weren't seeing enough of the world already, the Subhumans also became a truly European band in 2004 (pre-Brexit, of course!), when Phil moved to Spain and Trotsky moved to Germany.

all ages blood bath presents:

SUB HUM ANS

with support from

TINY ELVIS

THE GREEN GUNS

22ND JULY
THE INVENTION ARTS CENTRE.
UPPER BOROUGH WALLS, BATH
DOORS: 7PM TILL 1AM. TAX: £7

SUB HUM ANS

2 SEPTEMBER
20:00
7 - CJP 6 - CKV
23:00 AFGELOPEN

PARKHOF

VICTORIEPARK 4 – ALKMAAR 072-5115076 WWW.GO.TO/PARKHOF

first uk tour in far too long

BUS STATION LOONIES

Energised singalong punk from Plymouth's finest

WILD HONEY PIE

Cutting edge rock from Torrington

BIDEFORD
LITTLEHAM Village Hall
2 miles south of Bideford

FRIDAY 28th OCTOBER

8–midnight > £5 < on the door
NO BAR! bring what you need

U.S. TOUR FLYERS, 1998

Oct 31st & Nov 1st
2 NIGHT
HALLOWEEN XTRAVAGANZA
WITH

SUB HUM ANS

special guests

OCT 31
THE UNSEEN
STOCKYARD STOICS

NOV 1
TOXIC NARCOTIC
SEVEN CROWNS

Knitting Factory
74 LEONARD ST.

BALTIMORE, 16/7/05 BY CHRIS BOARTS LARSON

"I got married to Sandra, then the guitarist of Korrupt from Bremen [she now plays with Sense]," explains **Trotsky**. "She came to live with me in England for a few years, and we were in The Eccentrics together for a while, then we decided to move out here. I'd always wanted to move to Germany; I've always loved the place, the whole vibe of it. We moved out here in 2004, had kids… but once a West Country lad, always a West Country lad, haha!

"I've got a practice room here, which is handy for when the band shows up. Usually, if we've got some gigs over here, they'll come back to our place for two or three days of intense practising and writing. It's the most convenient way to do it… do some gigs, do some practising, then go and finish the rest of the gigs. I'm out in the countryside, so there's no problems with noise. It's basically The Shed Mark II, haha!"

"None of us can do full-time jobs, because of touring," adds **Phil**. "Well, actually, back in '98 or '99, I did get a full-time job in Devizes, because I wanted to move to Spain. In fact, I did move to Spain for a while, and I had to get a job so I could get a loan and buy a house out there and stuff – a cheap one! So I got a job in this electrical place, and they were like, 'So you used to be in a band…?' And I replied, 'Those days are gone, I want to settle down now…' But then six months later I was off on tour again to the States! They actually held my job open for me for when I came back, which they never did for anyone, and then I went on tour again a year later. They were really good to me there, and I think they kept my job for me *again* – but then I moved to Spain, haha!

"And I stayed out there until 2010. I was an hour away from Alicante, and Trotsky was in Germany by then, so we were 'commuting'. We'd just meet up to go on tour, and like I said, we'd just rock up, no rehearsals, '1, 2, 3, 4!' and off we'd go. So we never practise before tours, we never have get-togethers for gigs, just when we're writing stuff. If you see us at a first gig on a tour, that is our practice! Trotsky will turn up, having got there from Germany – I might have driven there in the van, depending upon where it is – and we'll do a sound-check, which will be like one song, and then we'll get the set-list. Some songs we might leave out, 'cos it takes Bruce a few gigs to get his fingers really warmed up… there's some that he doesn't like doing straight away, on the first night, if they have lots of bendy guitar stuff in them…"

But never mind if they've got an insane bass run or crazy drum fills?

"Exactly!" laughs **Phil**. "Sometimes me and Trotsky will look at the set-list, and say, 'Oh, I don't fancy doing that straight off…' or 'That's a bit of a workout – can we skip that one for a couple of days?' The muscle memory for all the old songs that we've played hundreds of times comes back pretty quickly, but I quite often play along to some of our gigs on YouTube. There's one from the Fleece in Bristol which, unfortunately for anyone watching it, was filmed right next to me, so it's got really loud bass on it, but I can still hear everything else. If I play along to that, it's at full gig speed or whatever. The 'Live in a Dive' album we did on Fat Wreck is a good one too, because it's a good recording, and it's great to play along at our live speed…

"Sometimes I listen back to the records and think, 'Oh fuck, I don't play it like that!' But things evolve, and I'm not too precious about things like that – I'd rather put my own accent on things, and change stuff a bit… even my own bass lines, not just the Grant-era stuff. Nothing major, and nothing that would change the character of the song, but from night to night, I'll just play what I feel like really. I just feel confident enough, and happy enough, to do that; I don't like the idea of playing everything robotically, exactly the same every night.

"And you know we never tour a set-list, right? We write a fresh set-list every single night. Quite often, like James Brown or one of those legendary old bands, you don't know what you're going to play until you see the set-list. Bruce mostly writes them these days, but going back in time, I've wrote some years ago, and Dick would write some, but it's mainly Bruce now. So I make sure I'm around him when he's doing them, just so I don't end up with a shock onstage, haha! But he won't pull something out of the hat that we haven't done for years, y'know? If we decide we're going to reintroduce an old song, we'll do it in sound-check or something."

"We've got something like seventy songs we can call on," continues **Trotsky**. "Bruce has this moth-eaten piece of paper with all the songs written on it, that he carries around with him everywhere, and it's all held together with bits of Sellotape. It's the whole list of songs we can play. Of course, there's some songs we play every gig, like 'Religious Wars' and 'Mickey Mouse', but there's very few that we don't ever play, for various reasons... they might be songs that just don't work at a gig, like 'New Boy'. That's not a gig song... in fact, if we played that at a gig, everyone would fucking leave, haha!

"We've played some of these songs so many times now. When we reformed in '98, we had our first practice for seven years or whatever, and we played most of the songs just like that. It was curious how they all came back."

"Yes, I've got it in my pocket," exclaims **Bruce**, when asked about his list of songs, pulling it out of his wallet, "And I've got a copy of it in my guitar case as well. That's one of the things I enjoy doing, writing a set out; it's just an extra creative thing to do every day. It's all the songs we've written, and I've got the songs split into different speeds. It's not the only way to write a set-list, but you've got all the fast ones, and all the medium-paced ones... and those are what I call the 'bouncy' ones, and there's the real slow ones. Which we don't do very often. But you can get away with a slow one in each set, like 'Wake Up Screaming' or something. And the real long ones are there as well.

"What we find though is, with the ones we haven't played for a while, like say 'Process', we'd learn it for a couple of sound-checks and then we'd do it throughout the tour – only to find out it wasn't really going down that well anyway, haha! Maybe because we haven't been playing it enough, or maybe it just isn't a good song... but I really like songs like 'Sedated', and 'Straight Line Thinking', and I'd like to play them more. I keep them here, so we can maybe get them in the set again one day. We did 'Heads of State' on a tour recently, which was nice. And any of the songs that show Dick's emotional side are kind of great, rather than just the political spiel."

"But we're all aligned with it," interjects **Phil**, on the subject of the band's politics, that are admittedly 'set' as regards external perception by Dick, the singer/lyricist, "Although everybody has their individual takes on things. Some people are more knowledgeable on some things than other people, and sometimes other people in the band are more knowledgeable about certain things than Dick is. Everyone's different, and different people take interest in different things. Sometimes he might write something, and one of us will say, 'Actually that's not quite right', and he might change it. But obviously there's

429

STIG MEMORIAL CONCERT FEATURING:

ICONS OF FILTH

CONFLICT SUBHUMANS
THE OPPRESSED VARUKERS
INNER TERRESTRIALS LOST CHERREES

 NO CHOICE EXTINCTION OF MANKIND
ACTIVE SLAUGHTER

SATURDAY 5TH FEBRUARY 2005
LONDON THE FORUM
9-17 HIGHGATE ROAD, LONDON NW5. DOORS 3PM.

24 HR TICKET HOTLINES: 08701 500 044 / 0870 060 3777

BOOK ONLINE AT WWW.MEANFIDDLER.COM PLUS USUAL AGENTS.
NO BOOKING FEE FOR CASH AT THE ASTORIA AND JAZZ CAFÉ BOX OFFICES. INFO LINE: 020 8963 0940.

PUNTERS IS ENCOURAGED IN EVERYDAY BEING, PLEASE USE PUBLIC TRANSPORT
CENTRAL STAR BRIBED RAIL, UNDERGROUND & BUSES 134, 214 & C11. C2C PARKING IS AVAILABLE IN NEAR CARS.

ALL PROCEEDS FROM THE GIG WILL GO TO STIG'S FAMILY

A MEAN FIDDLER PRESENTATION

DICK WITH KAROLINE COLLINS, ABC NO RIO, 2005
BY KONSTANTIN SERGEYEV

no wild disparity in our beliefs – we're all pretty much in tune with each other really… there's no right-wing racists or Trump supporters in the band, haha! That just wouldn't work! There's not much we disagree about, to be honest; there's no wildly differing views on anything really."

"I've usually got a bit of a system," continues **Bruce**, on the ever-changing Subhumans set-list, "Depending upon whether it's the first night of the tour, when we don't want to play anything too tricky for anybody. And also, I've got some issues with my wrist now; I've got tendon problems, which is okay most of the time, but I can't go straight in playing some songs that have particular things in them, so I need to work my way into it a bit and warm up. I also like to spread everything out a bit. We don't do *every* song we've ever written, which I wish we did, because I wouldn't say any of them weren't worth doing, but not everybody wants to play them all, so we do a mixture…

"The thing about the songs you don't play very often, like 'Carry on Laughing', yeah, you can make the effort and learn it at practice, and when you're on tour you can play it, but then it doesn't go down that well at one of the gigs, and you don't bother with it again. It depends how much you want to play every song really – everyone has a different favourite song, and I know a few people who really like 'Carry on Laughing'. There's a guy in the States – Carl Santora, who has recorded loads of our shows over the years and become a good friend. He likes the obscure songs and always asks, 'Are you gonna play 'People Are Scared' tonight?' And we haven't played that in years!

"Personally, I really miss playing 'British Disease', and that's one of the ones we have worked up for a tour and then thought, 'Well, let's not bother!' Which is a shame. It's quite a workout for the bass, and definitely not one I'd put in there on the first night, haha! But they definitely haven't gone, we'll definitely pull them out again one day.

"But a song like 'New Boy' will never get played, because it's just too odd. We would probably get away with just playing what we wanted, like the whole new album and just one hit, but you have to have some popular songs in the set. As long as we played 'Religious Wars', we'd probably be alright.

"But it can work the other way too. When I saw Killing Joke last, at Rebellion, Dorothy, who really likes the 'Pandemonium' album (a record we'd listen to on family holidays with our kids, Alice and Lewis), was looking forward to hearing a few of those songs, because she never got into early Killing Joke – but that was one of the gigs where they decided to *only* play early Killing Joke songs, haha!

"When we first got back together and went to the States, I did work out three sets that hopped around a bit, but pretty much included every song we'd done. We had 'Set A', 'Set B' and 'Set C', and we rotated them. And 'From the Cradle to the Grave' was in there, every third night. But we don't have a particularly long set – you're only talking twenty-one songs, plus encores, per night.

"We did the whole of the 'Cradle…' album once; the organisers of the FunFunFun Fest in Austin wanted us to do the whole album for its thirtieth anniversary – so we did. It was an unusual thing to do, because it was a festival with all these other bands; it wasn't 'just' a punk festival at all, so it was a strange thing for them to request. But on the whole, it's great to mix it up, and we generally only play about four new ones in a set… or recent ones. But then some of the recent ones become 'hits' as well, and can go up in popularity a bit.

"I really think it's important to have the 'bouncy' songs in there – and not everyone agrees with my description! – like 'Germ' or 'Work Experience'… they're not fast, but they're relaxed and fun, and they get everybody moving. They always go down well, so you have to have a few of those in there, but not like a whole set. I've got all the songs separated out by speed – all the fast ones, and it's great fun to do a few of those together, so you've got all the energy and they flow into one another…

"And it's good to know where the talking points are in the set. You don't want a great big gap before a song that doesn't really need anything saying about it! What's Dick going to say about, I don't know, 'Germ'? Not loads – unless he's feeling very creative that night. But people like to listen to him, people like to listen to the singer, so it's good that he rants a bit.

"'Worlds Apart' is the most popular – or one of the most popular – of our albums in America, so we must have played a lot of those songs when we went over there in '85? Phil was new to the band still, and those 'Worlds Apart' songs were more Phil's than some of the older material, so we would definitely have played them, and perhaps that accounts for why it's so liked there?"

After eleven gigs around Belgium, France, Holland and Germany in September, that included another visit to Kopi, this time with Derby's Poundaflesh, Subhumans returned to the US East Coast for a dozen gigs in late October/early November. The opening band at half of those gigs was Seven Crowns, a Bath punk band with John Montague from A38 on vocals, who would eventually release two fine albums on Negative Press Records in 2017 and 2020.

Karoline recalls that one of those gigs (on November 4th, 2004) was with the UK Subs as main support: "They don't remember this, but Rob and I remember it as clear as day. The Subhumans were playing with the UK Subs in Atlanta, and on the drive to the show, Bruce and Phil were making a list of what songs they couldn't play because they are direct UK Subs rip-offs…"

Robert: "I spoke to Bruce about it later, and he was like, 'No, we never nicked stuff off Nicky…' And I was like, 'I'm not saying you did – I'm saying you said you did!'" [laughs]

"I *was* influenced by Nicky Garrett's down-strokes, by his technical ability to play the guitar," reveals **Bruce**, "And I was a big fan of the first UK Subs EP and LP… 'Live in a Car' and all that stuff was fantastic… so we might have borrowed a bit off them, I don't know! I think if you're inspired by a tune, and you feel you have to use that tune, you've got to do it – but we used to take them from stuff that wasn't just punk, and when it had been through the band, you wouldn't recognise it anyway. It was more about ideas and concepts as well."

On February 5th, 2005, Subhumans played an emotional gathering at the London Forum. The Stig Memorial gig was in memory of the late Icons of Filth singer, Andrew 'Stig' Sewell, who had tragically died unexpectedly the previous October, and also featured Conflict, Inner Terrestrials, the Restarts, Lost Cherrees, Extinction of Mankind, The Varukers, The Oppressed and No Choice. Icons of Filth headlined, with various guest vocalists taking on their favourite Icons songs, most poignantly Stig's son Calvin (who went on to front an incredible band of his own, Grand Collapse, but tragically passed away himself in March 2022), with Stig's father giving a moving speech at the very end of the night in tribute to his late son.

There was another appearance at the Wasted festival, before the band returned to the US for ten gigs running from St Louis to New York, although the trip started with one Canadian appearance, at the United Fest in Montreal with The Adicts, Dickies, Conflict and Anti-Nowhere League. Support for the US dates came mainly courtesy of Brooklyn's The World/Inferno Friendship Society and From Ashes Rise.

"In 2005, I got to see the Subhumans again in Philly with From Ashes Rise and Fighting Dogs at the Unitarian Church, which was a really perfect mix," reminisces **Chris Larson**. "It was also very cool to see the Subhumans in the Church, where all the best shows were happening at that time. The show in Baltimore [the day before] was a tough one to get to, I think? We got stuck in traffic in some epic rain storm, and almost missed the show entirely; we *did* miss From Ashes Rise, but got to see the Subhumans. What I find most interesting is the facial expressions in the photos from that show – I see a lot of young kids just sitting there, watching with blank faces. Compared to the blissful fanatics from 1998, it's an amazing difference, which I attribute to a whole new generation of kids that just didn't know the Subhumans in the same way."

A string of US gigs for Citizen Fish had been booked straight after the tour, but Trotsky had to head home after the Subhumans leg concluded, and Bruce stood in behind the drum kit for the CF dates, proving again his talent as a multi-instrumentalist.

"Well, I could play them, but I wasn't a great drummer," says **Bruce** modestly, "Although I had the coordination and all that. We'd finished a Subhumans tour in the States, and Citizen Fish had gigs booked straight after; Phil and Dick were in the band, and Jasper was selling our merch at the time, so we were all out there – Trotsky had left to go home, and I thought, 'I could just carry on and do some drums!' But it was really hard, even though I teach drums, and understand how to play drums… when you have to do it for real, it's a lot different to teaching theory!

"I had played drums with the A-Heads for a bit back in the Eighties, but it's a lot different now, and drummers have to have a lot more precision than they used to. I was just surprised at how much effort it takes to play drums compared to guitar – or bass. Drums really are a killer."

After two 'weekenders' in Europe during early September, the first taking in Holland and Belgium, the second Germany (including the Kopi for a third time, with Orang Utan supporting), Subhumans embarked on a twelve-date UK tour, that started in Penzance with Final Warning, and ended in Lancaster with Eastfield, taking in en route an assortment of venues and towns – including Littleham Village Hall on October 28th.

"What is the thing with smashing up toilets in venues?" asks **Dick**, incredulously. "It wasn't a particularly Eighties thing – it just seems to be a thing that happens, for some reason. We did this gig in Littleham Village Hall, which is in Devon, when I lived down that way in Barnstaple, and it was totally DIY, set up by a friend called Higgs. We had the Bus Station Loonies doing it too. Anyway, everyone locally was excited, like, 'What? The Subhumans are playing in Littleham?'… which has a population of 446. So, it was packed out, with 150 youths, and it said on the poster, 'No booze – bring your own', and it was like that was an *instruction*! Everyone brought booze, and drank most of it before they even got there, so there was a lot of drunk people, and both toilets got smashed up; we lost the deposit, mopped up the floor, and there were no more gigs there ever again – but that one time was a cracker."

After firmly re-establishing themselves on the live front since their reformation, as 2005 drew to a close, Subhumans were starting to think about a new studio record, confident they still had something relevant to offer as regards contemporary material and keen to prove that they were cut from a different cloth to the many other reformed punk acts content to just trot out the hits if the fee was right. But with the four of them now spread across three different countries, that would be easier said than done.

BRUCE'S SONG LIST

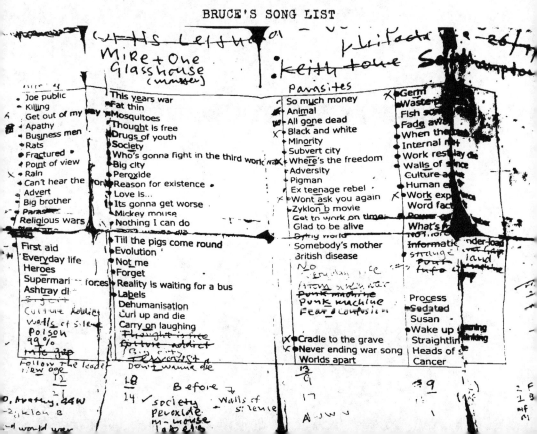

CITIZEN FISH WITH BRUCE DRUMMING, 2005
BY KONSTANTIN SERGEYEV

all ages blood bath presents:

ƧUB HUM ANƧ

with support from

TINY ELVIS

THE GREEN GUNS

22ND JULY

THE INVENTION ARTS CENTRE.
UPPER BOROUGH WALLS, BATH
DOORS: 7PM TILL 1AM. TAX: £7

FRIESENCREW PRESENTS..   from ENGLAND

ƧUB HUM ANƧ

MTV IS WATCHING YOU

CHAOT-X
from BREMEN

SAMSTAG
10.9
2005

FREIZI FRIESENSTR.

ƧUB HUM ANƧ
englische Kultpunkkapelle

in der

KØPI

HABEN Sie mich VERSTANDEN?

No Dogs!

SONNTAG 11. SEPT.

PUKE FANZINE PRESENTS

ƧUB HUM ANƧ

ANARCHO PUNK
SUBVERSIVES
PLUS
ANTIBODIES
CONCRETE ROCK

FALSE IDOL
ANGER IS AN ENERGY

RADIATION ANGELS
YOUNG N SAVAGE

LIVE @ EDWARDS No. 8

LOWER SEVERN STREET, BIRMINGHAM
(VERY NEAR NEW STREET STATION)

WEDNESDAY 2ND NOVEMBER 2005

£5 ON THE DOOR   DOORS 7PM

ALL AGES!   INFO: pukefanzine@yahoo.co.uk

2006 — 2010

Subhumans started off 2006 with a week in Spain mid-February; they played three gigs with Sensa Yuma – in Crevellente, Alicante and Alcoi – and knuckled down to the writing of their next studio album, 2007's 'Internal Riot'. The writing would be finished off later in the year, at Trotsky's place in Germany, and the album recorded in Bath the following summer.

"I was living out in Murcia, southern Spain," begins **Phil**, of that whole process. "With Trotsky living in Germany and me in Spain, it wasn't easy to get us all together to write new stuff – we never really practised by then; we'd just turn up for a tour and launch straight into it, using sound-checks to re-learn any song that we were rusty on but wanted to stick in the set.

"So, in February 2006, Dick, Bruce and Trotsky flew out to my place to work on the new record. We knew Pid [from Contempt and Police Bastard], who was living near Alicante and him and his [then-current] band Sensa Yuma booked a few gigs for us and them in the area, and also let us use their practice space for some writing sessions.

"We already had 'This Year's War' written – a live version had appeared on the Fat Wreck 'Live in a Dive' record – so we just gave it a little tweak. And 'Supermarket Forces' had been written as a thirty-second song for 'Short Music for Short People', which was also on Fat [a 1999 compilation that featured 101 bands playing songs averaging thirty seconds running time]. So, we extended that into a full-length song. Apart from those two, I think all the remaining songs were written fresh for 'Internal Riot' in 2006."

"As the years passed, I had got to know Trotsky, Phil and Bruce really well," explains **Pid**, "And with me being in Police Bastard and Sensa Yuma, we'd shared a few stages around Europe. I went to Dick's fortieth birthday party, near Bath, in 2001, and he came up to Birmingham to a crazy Hallowe'en party dressed like something from 'Psycho'! Trotsky had met and married Sandra and moved to Bremen, and I'd been out to visit them at their home. Then Phil moved to Spain, not far from where I was, and we eventually organised a Spanish tour for Subhumans and Sensa Yuma. Whilst on days off, Subhumans practised and wrote a lot of songs which ended up on the 'Internal Riot' LP… how mad is that? Writing an album whilst on tour? I remember the gig in Alicante well; they played some of the songs they had wrote the day before live, while Dick sang the songs off a piece of paper… it was great fun."

"Once we'd ironed out the kinks a bit, I think it's better now than it was before," says **Bruce**, of the dynamic in the band since they reformed, but he tempers that slightly by saying of the creative process, "Although writing new songs hasn't been as easy as it used to be. The best song-writing time was really when we were practising at The Shed regularly. Just practising regularly, come to think of it – it didn't matter where we were practising, as long as we were! And having lots of lyrics and lots of music and being very inspired. It's not that we're *not* inspired anymore, but I don't listen to music like I used to. When you're younger, you're listening to such a lot of music, and that inspires you, and that's why the first couple of albums by any band are usually the best. Times change, that's just the way it goes. I went through stages of listening to jazz, and classical, but I really like the old stuff, which I suppose is what everyone says at my age. Stuff from the Sixties and Seventies.

"That's quite an inspired album actually," he continues of 'Internal Riot'. "I remember writing the initial riff for 'Never-Ending War Song' very well – it came to me when I was teaching at school! I just picked up a guitar and played this flamenco-ish chord, and then a second chord, which I hung to a diminished chord, and then I worked out whether I could do the same melody over the two chords, F-sharp and G-diminished. I really like Spanish music, and I was just experimenting with things like that.

"We wrote most of that album either at Trotsky's, or Phil's place in Spain. We had a rehearsal place there for a week. And it went well, because we'd all started to work better together again by then. Ideally, we like to play songs live before we record them – it seems a better way of doing it, for lots of reasons. You can play them better for starters. And when we eventually went into the studio to record 'Internal Riot' in Bath, we'd just come off a tour, and we'd been playing most of the songs live, and we could play everything really well. We didn't have to write anything in the studio for that album."

On March 19th, 2006, Subhumans left for North America for a month, playing twenty-seven US gigs – with A Global Threat opening for the first leg, before making way for World/Inferno Friendship Society and then Clit 45 and Caustic Christ. The trip included four Canadian gigs with St. Catherines, and finished in Detroit and Chicago with Leftover Crack.

"The WIFS, as we called them, were hyper-different to all other bands," says **Dick**, of World/Inferno Friendship Society, "Or at least ones we'd played with! 'Unique' is the only accurate label for their music, as it mixes up skiffle, ska, punk, jazz... all sorts, with a singer, Jack – rest his shining soul – who had so much style and charisma, you could hang a hat on it – which he did! He was the anarchic side of well-dressed and well-spoken... he used to warm up his voice before playing, by running up and down a scale of seven notes. We would sing along to those notes with, 'Where-is-my-fuh-king-trac-tor?' Watching the WIFS had the same feeling as seeing Nomeansno or the Cardiacs for the first time – riveting and full of surprises!"

At the end of May, they played the Newcastle Academy, which was one of the venue's 'thirty years of punk anniversary celebrations' (AKA any excuse to hump the cash cow) Academy in the UK gigs, with The Damned, Rezillos, Upstarts, Penetration and all the usual suspects. Subhumans had missed the Birmingham event in April as they were in the US. They then headlined two stonking gigs in Sheffield and London in July, with Ignite and GBH as main supports, before heading out to Germany for three gigs with Police Bastard in early September. After playing Mulheim, Verden and Bielefeld, they hunkered down at Trotsky's to finish writing their all-important 'comeback' LP.

"When I think of my personal favourites from 'Internal Riot', or any of the records actually, there are some songs that I enjoy listening to that we don't often play," explains **Phil**, "Because we think they don't 'work' live or are too complicated to get around to re-learning; and some songs that I love to play live for their energy. 'Internal Riot', 'This Is Not an Advert' and 'Point of View' are all straightforward, short and bouncy songs that were written quickly, and I love playing them live because they get an instant

BRUCE'S 42ND BIRTHDAY, TAKEN ON THE ROOF OF PHIL'S PLACE IN MURCIA, SPAIN, 13/2/06

ULLSWATER, LAKE DISTRICT, 2006 - COURTESY OF PHIL

SUBHUMANS

EXEMPLARY PUNKROCK FOR THE DISCERNING PUNKROCKER. THIS GIG REALLY IS MANDATORY ATTENDANCE.

HARDSKIN

OI AS YOU HAVE NEVER SEEN BEFORE

GURKHA

TIS THE JOLLY OLD CRUSTPUNK FROM THE BRISTOL

+ EXTRA SPECIAL GUESTS

FRIDAY 14TH JULY

8-30PM TILL WAY PAST YOUR BEDTIME

@LAKOTA-STOKES CROFT-BRISTOL

TIX £8 ADVANCE-MORE ON DOOR!!!

FOR INFO & ADVANCE TIX
CALL MARYANNE 07944948156

BUCKLE UP DARLINGS,
IT'S GONNA
BE A FAST,
FAST RIDE!!!

BLIND DESTRUCTION RECORDS PROUDLY PRESENTS: U.K. PUNK LEGENDS...

SUBHUMANS

VICTIMS
HARDCORE
FROM
VENDEE
FRANCE

THIS SYSTEM KILLS
VETERAN
POLITICAL
VALLEYS
PUNKS

FRIDAY 26TH MAY 2006 AT: TJ'S, CLARENCE PLACE, NEWPORT
TICKETS £7.00 @TJ'S/ROCKAWAY/DAMAGED/BRISTOLTICKETSHOP.CO.UK
NOTE: EARLY DOORS: 7:00PM / BANDS 7:30PM / CLUB AFTER

WWW.TOXICPROMOTIONS.NET PRESENTS...

SUBHUMANS

WWW.CITIZENFISH.COM

DROPPIN BOMBS   EXCUSES

VOODOO LOUNGE
35-40 ARRAN QUAY

FRIDAY 1ST DECEMBER
8PM €15.00 WWW.TICKETS.IE

POO PROMOTIONS PROUDLY PRESENTS...

SUBHUMANS

LEGENDARY U.K. ANARCHO PUNK BAND
www.citizenfish

EXCUSES
FAST PUNK ROCK

ONLY FUMES AND CORPSES
GALWAY HARDCORE

THE DERELICTS
YOUNG SLIGO SNOTS

COOLERA HOUSE, SLIGO
SAT. 2ND DEC 2006

€12 DOORS 8 1ST BAND 9
STRICTLY OVER 18's · I.D. REQD

positive crowd reaction. And I think they were all written at Trotsky's place at the second 'Internal Riot' writing session we had in September 2006, or were developed from bass ideas that came out at that session.

"'Never-Ending War Song' is a great listen for me; it's got that Subhumans mix of power, dynamics and weird time signatures. It took a lot of work to put together, coming out of some Spanishy-sounding ideas that Bruce had. He's played and taught flamenco and Spanish guitar, and you can hear those influences in that song. We played it live after the record was released, but weighing in at nine and a half minutes, it doesn't make it into the set-list these days.

"There aren't any that I *don't* like on 'Internal Riot', but thankfully we don't often play 'Won't Ask You Again', 'cos that's a bit of a bit of a bass workout, haha!"

Late November saw them playing main support to Conflict, alongside Lost Cherrees and the Restarts, at both the Birmingham and London Academy, before wrapping 2006 up with four gigs in Ireland in early December.

Their 2007 campaign began in April at the Bath-hosted BOB Fest; that same month they also did a five-date UK tour with Barnyard Masturbator, and six Canadian gigs. In May they played eleven dates across Germany, Denmark and Holland, finishing at the Melkweg in Amsterdam for the Dutch leg of Rebellion, which was headlined by Conflict.

Two days later they were back in Bath, recording 'Internal Riot' at Riverside Studios, with engineer Tom Dalgety and producer Steve Evans.

"That was when I first got to know Steve Evans and his assistant, Tom," reveals **Bruce**, "But I think Phil and Dick had been doing stuff with him before. What I like about him is that he's very good with guitars, because, even though I play guitar and I'm really geeky about my sound, when it comes to being in the studio, I find it quite hard. That's the thing with recording guitar and bass: when you're stood in the room, you're not hearing the speaker, because your head's away from the speaker, and if you put your head right down next to the speaker, it sounds a bit too harsh. And in the studio, they put the microphone right by the speaker, or just off a bit, so you really get the sound of it... but these days they have mics further back now as well. For the last album he had mics going all the way up the stairs; he had a lot of mics on that guitar cab, in different places around the room. So, engineers are listening now; they're very clever, and can pretty much match a guitar sound if they're asked to. Anyway, Steve's a guitarist himself – he plays with a glam rock band actually – so he understands what it's about."

"Recording digitally on Pro Tools, Tom and Steve are super-fast and don't get bogged down in any – technical term – 'unnecessary indulgent fucking about', so that keeps our attention and focus," says **Phil**. "We've got memories of hours of fine tuning of reverbs and drum EQs at Southern in the Eighties, of falling asleep on the sofa, waking up drooling and John was still working on the same sound. To be fair, that was probably our low attention spans as teenagers, and we've just gotten more used to the studio environment as we got older.

"Ideally, we'd have liked to have played all the songs live before recording them, to get them bedded in and get a feel for what did and didn't work. But we'd given ourselves a deadline and weren't able to play them *all* live, and were still tweaking some bits right up to the last minute.

"The recording process is always a bit intense; the pressure's on, and it's your one chance to get the songs on record so you want it to be right, 'cos it's going to be out there… forever! Steve and Tom have always been great to work with, we find them easy to communicate with, and they get what we're trying to do. They always offer valuable input, and I'm very happy with how 'Internal Riot' came out."

Taking a break from the studio, six gigs were played in France and Belgium at the end of June, and it was on this tour that Phil was to first meet his future wife, Erika Ransom, formerly singer/guitarist with Boston DIY punk band The Profit$, who was at that time a Maximum Rocknroll columnist, in Europe collecting footage and interviews at Euro squats for a documentary project she was working on (the two hit it off, and Erika was invited to sell merch on their next US tour).

After four UK dates, they headed back into Riverside to finish recording and mixing the album, which was released soon after by Bluurg. Expectations were understandably high for the band's first proper studio offering in over twenty years, but 'Internal Riot' was classic Subhumans and didn't disappoint.

The album opens with the incredibly urgent 'This Year's War', which has all the elements of a perfect Subhumans composition – infectious energy, a clever arrangement, compelling dynamic, great musicianship, brilliant lyrics, subtle backing vocals – and it's bookended thematically by the closing song (well, if you discount the throwaway 'Mosquitoes', that feels somewhat tagged on the end), the aforementioned and rather epic 'Never-Ending War Song'. Which takes its sweet time unfolding a hypnotic eastern-tinged guitar hook, before exploding into a high-speed workout, complete with tight metallic picking from Bruce and a truly manic battery from Trotsky, and then the band throw in a curveball and a demented back-beat waltz segues into a pathos-laden breakdown. A discordant crescendo subsequently opens out into an enjoyably upbeat mid-section, before everything is twisted full circle to conclude quite possibly the band's most accomplished piece since the title track of their second album, complete with some of Dick's most poignant lyrics, digging beneath horribly rife Islamophobia to contemplate the real root causes of terrorism: 'Here is what you get for forcing us to buy your civilisation… war's the global empty face of loss and its retaliation.'

"I'm very glad you think so," says **Dick** happily, when told how highly I rate 'Internal Riot' in their catalogue. "I've never been *totally* sure about all the songs on there; they weren't practised that much before they were recorded, which has become a thing for us really, especially with [most recent album] 'Crisis Point', because we all live so far apart.

"'This Year's War' was one of the first songs invented for that record. People in the Middle East are just being bombed, and everything destroyed, by cultures entirely separate from theirs, claiming they're in charge of their security and peace. Whereas it's very much more about controlling their resources, and selling them arms. For example, you've got Russia and America both wanting to be in charge of what's going on in Syria, and on the one hand it's cultural interference by western – or Russian – civilisation into Middle Eastern civilisation; it's just interfering and pretending to be the global policeman. But nobody is safe under these policemen, storming in and wrecking everything in the name of democracy and peace. It's very Orwellian. And for Tony Blair and George Bush to more or less say that 'God told them to do it', to bring religion into it that way, you've

TAKEN AT THE PETRIFIED FOREST NATIONAL PARK,
ARIZONA, 2007 BY ERIKA

ERIKA AND ROBERT BY PHIL

got your ultimate escape clause – if God told me to do it, it's not my fault, it's God's fault, and if God is faultless, then it was the right thing to do. Yaddayaddayadda. Which again is why religion is such a dangerous thing, because people just use it as an excuse for mass slaughter.

"And then the lyrics in 'Never-Ending War Song' end up taking the viewpoints of different people involved in the so-called War on Terror. And right at the end it's like, 'This is what you get for crushing and exploiting someone else's civilisation!' And it's the view of the suicide bomber who has nothing left to live for, who's had everything taken away, and this is his act of finality and revenge. Which conveniently ignores the angle that suicide bombers are all brainwashed kids talked into their sacrifice by their leaders who are also using religion to get their underlings to go out and kill themselves and hundreds of people in the name of religion. It's all very twisted, and not at all a good thing, but I thought, I have to put a voice out there that maybe says, 'Could this be the reason we're blowing you up?' It's not because we like blowing things up, and we're mad and insane and sadists; it's because we've got nothing left, because you've destroyed everything we ever had – our infrastructure's gone, our property is destroyed, our buildings are dust, our families are dead, our government's bombing us because they're on your side, and you expect us to do what exactly…?

"So, I decided to have a two-sided perspective. You can't say all terrorists are wrong without inspecting why people become terrorists, or get labelled as terrorists in the first place… there's very much cause and effect going on."

By contrast, the rest of the album is slightly more simplistic, but nonetheless catchy, powerful and immediately recognisable as Subhumans, due to the unmistakable sound of Dick's voice and Bruce's inimitable punk/rock/prog guitar style, all powered by the best rhythm section in the whole of punkdom. And whilst many of the topics covered by Dick's lyrics have been covered before, his outlook has moved with the times, so we get new perspectives on frustratingly perennial issues; the focus seems less on changing the world and more on changing yourself for the better, through awareness and self-education, which should by extension have an incremental effect for the good on those around you. Whilst a song like 'Process' seems mellow by their standards, remember they've never been ones to paint themselves into familiar corners, as is evidenced by the lurching 'Sedated' (with some sublime backing vocals from Bruce), or the brilliant 'Too Fat, Too Thin', which counterpoints thrashy punk with some choppy reggae guitar and intricate bass runs, as Dick takes aim at societal programming about appearance and traditional precepts about what constitutes 'beauty'. A definite highlight is 'Fractured', where the three-chord verses sound disconcertingly generic at first, but the brooding chorus is one of the heaviest things the band have done, intellectually as well as musically, as Dick suggests, 'All we need is a whole lot less, of the voice saying "Here's some more…"'

"Whereas songs like 'This Year's War' and 'Never-Ending War Song' are – I think – classics, and amongst the best stuff we've ever done, a song like 'Sedated'… I'm only halfway into it," admits **Dick**. "It's surrounded by better songs, so therefore it comes across as weaker, but on its own, it stands up. That's only my opinion, of course – the rest of the band probably love it to death.

"'Too Fat, Too Thin' is an extraordinary song because of its subject matter; it's slightly political, as most of our songs are, but it's not your usual political song. It's the one

446

song I've written about body perception. Someone wrote, 'Oh, I'm really surprised the Subhumans are writing about this…?' Well, we are – deal with it.

"'This Is Not an Advert' is just an extension of 'Adversity' [off 'From the Cradle to the Grave'], but with more depth and thought behind it. So, in some ways, it's still the same old subject matter, but updated. Over the years, you pick up more thoughts about the same subjects, and try to cram in as much as you can. You start to analyse the nature of what advertising is, and does… the last verse of that song is another one of those long sentences that never stop!

"'Culture Addict' is all about our culture being summed up by advertising, in slogans, headline grabbing, attention grabbing, misleading stuff going on, and being addicted to that culture of instancy – the whole Facebook and social media thing. 'Fractured' reflects on the same temporal stuff that was going on, and is still going on, but much more so – getting my head around social media, and the massive expansion of electronic forms of advertising… it's no longer just the telly, it's your computer, your lap-top, your phone… and suddenly people aren't meeting up in person, but are meeting up over Instagram and Twitter and Facebook. Society has fractured into little parcels of people gaining nominal friends by pressing buttons; it's all become very shallow and false, and all-consuming yet empty. There's no emotional connection between people when they interact like that."

Now algorithms suggest who you should be friends with…

Dick: "Exactly! That sentence right there! What's an algorithm? What do you mean it 'suggests'? Is it talking to me? How does it know about me? Take yourself back forty years – and I know a lot of people reading this can't do that yet… but you will. Remember the days when there were books? When people spoke? The way it's going, all our fingers will atrophy, apart from one finger and one thumb, and our voices will disappear, because no one is saying anything anymore, they just type everything out…"

The album came wrapped in eye-catching artwork courtesy of Simon Gane, who **Dick** says, "Was a friend of ours from Bath, and did a comic strip zine called 'Arnie' about the adventures of a punk. He made the 'Subvert City' strip [for 'Live in a Dive'], and created the shattered version of my face that's on the front of 'Internal Riot', and went on to draw extensively for several magazines, mostly in the sci-fi bracket. He was – and no doubt, still is! – an inquisitive and happy chappie."

After four UK dates at the end of July, and the customary appearance at Rebellion, Blackpool, in August, Subhumans undertook a thirty-six-date US tour, which was lengthy even by their standards; it started in Milwaukee and ended in Chicago, but took in both coasts in between, with Witch Hunt as the main support for the first half, and World/Inferno Friendship Society the second.

"We used to do five or six weeks, to try and get around the whole country really," says **Bruce**, "And we like the idea of going to little out of the way places, rather than just what's easiest. Although we're veering towards that too! Because we're not getting any younger, and there's certain parts where you're guaranteed a good audience, so you have to try to hit those spots really. But the times you remember most are when you're in those out of the way places, where the people are a bit wacky and very excited to see you, y'know?

"We don't make enough from the band to say, 'Right, let's just do the band…', although we might be able to if we all agreed that was what we were going to do, and we could

What size are you supposed to be?
too fat too thin too scared all 3
pounds & ounces hierarchy
~~people~~ people in 3D
don't love yourself you need to starve
just to live up to their lies
all these smiles & patroneyes
are how your looks get stigmatized

Pressure to change to fit the size
that ~~...~~ shit they advertise

leads to a culture of disguise

& several teenage suicides

overstressed & underweight
or overweight + under rated

average

'TOO FAT, TOO THIN' - DICK'S ORIGINAL LYRIC SHEET

live! love! revolt! booking, samurai j sushi, & royal st. tattoo present

SUBHUMANS U.K.

ALL ORIGINAL MEMBERS

SUBHUMANS

THURSDAY
SEPT.
13TH

SOUL KITCHEN
MUSIC HALL
217 DAUPHIN ST.

LEFT HAND BREWING COMPANY
LONGMONT, COLORADO

www.myspace.com/liveloverevoltbooking
www.samuraij.com
www.royalstreettattoo.com

Asheville undead presents

SUB HUM ANS

punk rock from the UK

WORLD INFERNO
FRIENDSHIP SOCIETY
bizzaro gypsy punk caberet

THE HEART ATTACKS
glam rock from ATL

NEGATIVE FEEDBACK
Ashe. street punks

POX AMERICANA
local punk rock

sept. 16 (sun)
$30PM SHARP!!
@ ASHEVILLE ART CENTER
309 MERRIMON AVE
ALL AGES
NO ALCOHOL/NO ASSHOLES

SAT.SEPT
15
ALL AGES

WORLD/INFERNO
FRIENDSHIP
SOCIETY
LIBYAN
HIT SQUAD
NO PEACE
AT ALL

IRONFORGE
IRONFORGEPRESS.COM

SLAMMIE

STUDIO A
miami

SUB HUM ANS

SUB HUM ANS
WITCH HUNT
GET RAD

All Ages Show
(Alcohol Available W/ Proper I.D)
Fri. Aug. 24 6:00pm
The Miramar Theatre
2844 N. Oakland Ave
Milwaukee, Wi

Adv.Tkts: Atomic Records · www.madplanet.musictoday.com

tour a lot more. But we have to be sensible about how many times we could tour America without even Americans getting bored of us. It's a fine line.

"I'd be happy to do more. I'd be up for five- or six-week tours, because they make a lot of sense financially as well. Once you're there, you may as well do it. But people have different energy levels in the band, and different thoughts about it.

"Our agent in the States is Margie at Do It Booking, and she always asks us where we want to go, what we want to charge on the door, because she knows we're sensitive about that sort of thing. We've been working with her a long time, so she knows what we're about, and what bands she can put us with, who share similar political views and everything."

As mentioned earlier, Erika was selling merch on that tour, and she wrote a tour diary for the December 2007 issue of Maximum Rocknroll, a few excerpts from which are below, chosen because they capture the unpredictable mayhem of punk rock touring:

Last night, the show in Portland was brutally hot and the place was packed with sweaty punks. I was lucky to have a small merch booth where I could set up the T-shirts and CDs, protected from the wasted crowd. The place was so packed that people were everywhere, standing on booths at the back of the bar, crushed in together up front, falling into the tables. By the end, Witch Hunt's table was wiped out, pushed up against the wall, and punks were standing and sitting on it, trying to see the stage.

The Subs' set was fun; there was a massive circle pit larger than my apartment. I stood on my stool and watched the whole scene, singing along to myself, melting in the heat. At the end of the show the table was packed and busy; I slung T-shirts and CDs and gave out stickers, and afterwards I felt dazed, packing up the boxes and heading out to the van.

After a beer and a couple of shots, a smoke outside, cooling off, we had to get on the road again. It was already 1 am, but San Francisco was ten hours away, so we needed to cover some 100 miles tonight. Also, the Bay Bridge was closed for the weekend; we expected massive traffic, and at the very least, it would take an extra hour to get into the city.

So off we go into the van again. Phil sat up front, Robert drove as always, and I sat in the back but kept peeking my head up to the front between the seats, listening to their conversation about the tour, smiling at Phil and feeling good.

Dick, Trotsky and Bruce were sitting in the back of the van, making jokes that made us all laugh. Bruce stood up and started dusting everything in the van with a rag, proclaiming, 'Excuse me, dusting! Dust the drummer, dust the bag of chips, dust the bear claw that has been sitting here for a week, dust the water bottles on the floor...'

After a couple of hours on the road, we soon discovered that with the Memorial Day weekend travelers, there were no vacancies to be found in the cheap motels, anywhere. Robert called every place he could think of, doing a Google search through his phone, and Witch Hunt, who were traveling behind us in their van, did the same.

After stopping at five different motels on the side of the highway, around 5 am, we finally found a vacancy. It was an interesting place, and by far the scariest motel I've ever been to, reminding me of the setting of Bates Motel, except not so scenic or comfortable. The place was more redneck than motherly, more Hell's Angels on the run than an angry old woman in a rocking chair.

There was a row of rooms all facing the courtyard, a driveway with a few old wooden picnic tables on the grass, the interstate lanes about forty feet away. On one of the tables, I found a small metal sculpture, it seemed to be a long bullet attached to something else, bolted to the table. Odd.

Even at this late hour, almost dawn, a man was out in the yard, and came up to Nicole, asking her if she wanted to see his collection of stones, laid out in the yard in circles. I can't remember if she said yes or no, but the look on her face as she told us about it wasn't pleasant. It was all creepy as hell.

But we all desperately needed somewhere to rest for a few hours, not everyone could fit in the vans to sleep, there were too many people, and the place was cheap, so we decided to stay. Isn't this how bad horror movies begin?

A man in his boxers and no shirt came out of a trailer home that had a wooden sign that said 'office', and said he could give us a room for $40. Robert handed him two twenty-dollar bills; the man gave us a key, and pointed to a door. No paperwork, no signatures. I didn't want to think about what had gone on in the room before us. It was sinister, evoking images of old gunpowder, a dirty used condom, bags of bad drugs, lines on wasted faces, burned out people with nowhere else to go. Mould covered the ceiling, and rusty nails kept the sink together.

Four people slept on the two beds, two people camped out on the floor, and each van was filled with three people each. We woke up early, with about four hours of sleep, but it was enough that the people driving felt okay enough to get back on the road. Nightmares greeted me, a demon under my skin. Everyone else in the motel room also said they had bad dreams last night, it was eerie. We packed up quickly. Damn happy to be back in the van, back on the road!

We arrived in LA and drove down Hollywood Blvd. to the club. There are all the outlandish signs and tourist traps you can imagine. It looks like Disneyland on speed. The Knitting Factory is huge, an entire complex, and we loaded in through the back door. You go from the loading dock, down a long hallway, into the club itself.

Within an hour, the place was packed, and once again I was lucky to have a small spot behind the merch table, as everyone was crushed up front; there was hardly any room to move. Peligro Social played a good set, and the sound at the club reminded me of CBGBs, with a medium sized stage and a great house sound system. Witch Hunt played their usual right-on set, and then the Subs went on. The crowd was excited. There was a roar when then they got onstage and the energy was high. The set was fun and I danced behind the stall with Bridge, making funny '80s moves and having a good time.

After their set, there was a crazy hectic rush at the stall. Robert helped out, fending off the hundred punks screaming at us at once. In the end, the bouncers kicked the last of the drunk punks out, I had a smoke outside and then packed up the boxes. Phil came over, a Jack and cola in hand, smiling, bringing lots of hugs. Another show down!

This is when I remembered I was in Hollywood, and things got really strange. One of Jay's friends operates a limo service, and kindly offered to take us all down the street to a bar. It was a laugh! Totally ridiculous on all accounts – my first limo ride ever, and with anarcho punk legends, the Subhumans. We didn't know what to do but go ahead, take lots of dodgy photos, laugh and curse, and get inside the white stretch limo that waited for us

451

SACTO AREA PYRATE PUNX PREZENTS...
TUESDAY APRIL 8
EARLY SHOW YEAR OF NO LORD 2008
DOORS AT 5:30

SUB HUM ANS
CRIMINAL DAMAGE
ISONOMY
UNCUT: HURTS
R'N'DAMAGE
SILK BAR
DEL PASO BLVD

SUB HUM ANS

INTERNAL RIOT

VASTAVIRTA-KLUBI
TO 22.05
& RAKKAUS 10€

BATH PYRATE PUNX PRESENT:
XXX LIVE PUNK XXX

SUB HUM ANS
with F.U.K. and 7 CROWNS

AT BURDALL'S YARD
LONDON ROAD
BATH
on THURSDAY
18th SEPTEMBER
IN THE YEAR OF NO LORD 2008
FROM 7PM

DAMAGE £8
www.myspace.com/bathpyratepunxuk

SAMEDI 21 AVRIL 2007

SUB HUM ANS
+INVITÉS

SPECTACLE INTIME

20$
PRÉVENTE: BAR LE TRASH ET
FRÉQUENCES LE DISQUAIRE

BAR LE TRASH
470, MONDOR ST-HYACINTHE 450-252-0666

PHIL AND ALEC BAILLIE, LEFTOVER CRACK (RIP), 2008

SILAS (CITIZEN FISH) AND TROTSKY, BACKSTAGE MIGHTY SOUNDS FEST, CZECH REPUBLIC, 2008 BY PHIL

outside. We rode down the Boulevard, only a few blocks, hardly enough time to enjoy the three television screens, the bar, or stick our heads out the sunroof.

We arrived at a bar, operating after-hours, guests only. We were waved pass the security standing outside, a red velvet rope was opened, and we went inside into a plush large bar. It seemed to be the height of LA punk scenesters, very strange and surreal.

Two punk DJs played a good set of music, the place was dim, and a disco ball twirled overhead. We each bought a stiff drink, talked to the few people we knew, and enjoyed the weirdness of it all.

Robert, who had parked the van nearby, walked in on this scene about an hour later: Dick was laying on the floor listening to Metallica, being picked up by two bouncers (who said, 'You're not allowed to sit on the floor…'), everyone was wasted and Phil and I were making out on a leather couch in the corner. What a ridiculous sight, disco ball and all. Ah, good times! Luckily, being of sound mind and one of the best roadies in the world, within ten minutes he rounded us up, got us all in the van, and got us the hell out of Hollywood!

Driving through Texas, from El Paso to Dallas. The plains stretch on as far as I can see, bright green and yellow ground cover, low plants, dotted with darker green woody shrubs. Small oil pumps slowly bob their heads up and down, steel horses on the money trail, machines set on automatic, steadily riding along.

Last night the Subs played El Paso, a small town by the Mexican border. From the highway at night, we could see the lights of Juarez across the Rio. The Texas punks had warned us yesterday that the promoter tonight is well known for ripping off bands, and an all-around asshole ran this club. At this point there was nothing we could do but go and hope for the best.

The show itself was in a large room, bigger than my mom's house, probably used most often for disco dancing, judging from all the lights and the odd cages off to one side. At one end of the room was a large stage, and at the other end there was a bar, and a collection of tables and stools. I set up in the back, near the bar, where the club staff had given us a few tables for the bands.

The first band was terrible, probably the worst of the tour. One of their songs kept repeating in the chorus, 'He's a fag…', and I kept hoping it was a joke, or there was some point, or maybe they were queer, but in the end, it seemed they were just idiots who had managed to get their band on the show.

The show got even worse, when Witch Hunt went onstage and as Nicole was talking, she was heckled by a skinhead in the audience, 'Why don't you stop complaining? Take it all off! Take it off!' The kids in the crowd didn't want to start a fight with the large bonehead, and later we didn't either, as he was there with other large skinheads milling around, so the idiot stayed for the whole show, and no one told him off. Lame.

None of us by then were excited to be there, and just wanted to get the hell out of El Paso. But Phil came by the stall; we sat at one of the cocktail tables in front of the merch drinking Jack and colas, selling the odd T-shirt or sticker, and watched the Krum Bums, who impressed me with their high energy and enthusiasm. They play street punk that isn't cliché, which is hard to do. They are right on with the things they have to say onstage, sincere and still having fun, and their music is fast and furious. I'm wearing their T-shirt right now as I write this. So, get their record already, geez!

The Subs went on, and David and I talked behind the table, him telling me about El Paso punks, how he's looking forward to playing Austin, how excited they are to be on tour with the Subhumans for a few days. David is the type of person who I instantly like, the complete extrovert who tells stories, makes jokes, has too much energy and jumps around being silly, who is super friendly and welcoming to just about everyone. The first time I met him, he dove through a table of empty beer bottles onto the floor, just his way of saying hello. Punk fucking rock.

The stall was very slow, it was a small show, and there wasn't much for me to do except stand there to make sure things didn't get stolen. So, when the Krum Bums offered to smoke me out, I said 'Hell, yeah!', and Bridge was kind enough to watch the stall for a few minutes as I went out to the parking lot.

I don't smoke pot all the time, but every once in a while it's really nice, and I hadn't been stoned in quite some time. Ever since a fucking state trooper in Virginia caught me with a quarter ounce of weed, I make it a point not to travel with contraband. It's just too easy for cops to search you for no good reason at all. So, a quick smoke in their van, laughing at the fake pigeons they have riding on their roof, then running back to the show. The table was still dead by the last part of the Subs set, so I left Bridge to watch it one more time and went up front.

I was stoned, the music was loud but not deafening, and the place was big enough that I could easily make my way up front to the stage. The band sounded really on it; the two weeks of solid shows made their playing together and tight. The music kicked ass, and I remembered why I like the Subs so much as a band, how they are so great to see live. It was one of my favorite moments of tour, and I couldn't stop smiling.

For two weeks straight I had been trapped behind the stall, and now, at least for a few songs anyway, I was just another punk at the show. I almost didn't know what to do. Then I remembered what I've always loved to do at shows… I danced and sang along with everyone else up front. I loved the punks with the homemade Subs T-shirts, and the two young girls in front of me, probably fifteen or so, dancing in the pit, arms locked together, smiling to themselves. The sound of bass, drums and guitar marching on carried me in the music, Dick was fully into the thick of it, and the circle pit rushed around.

After the show, the promoter earned his reputation. When Robert asked for the Subs money at the end of the night, the guy gave him some of the money promised, but not all of it. When Robert tried to talk to him about his obligation, the guy replied, with all of his large security goons standing around in the office, 'Shut up and get the hell out of town…' So, with discretion the better part of valour, we did just that.

Despite all the drama about the promoter, the band was in a good mood. Bruce, Phil and I, sitting in the back of the van, decided to celebrate leaving El Paso with a tequila cocktail on the road. It was very civilized. A fine bottle of tequila someone had given them was stashed under the seat. We bought a bag of ice and a bottle of Sprite from a gas station down the road. We drank from plastic cups, sitting in the dark, and it was a nice end to the day. It was raining, making the van cool, the sound of raindrops hitting metal.

Once again, Robert was a driving champion, as we needed to make some miles towards Austin. I woke up in 'the loft' to lightning, a full storm on top of us, the windshield full of rain. At 4 am, we pulled into another cheap motel, everyone tired and spilling out into the night. Before going to sleep we stood on the motel balcony, looking at the sky, the storm off in another direction, dark clouds on the horizon, the energy still in the air.

455

SUBHUMANS UK PUNKS SINCE '80
LES SUCE-PENDUS NOISE PUNK AMIENS + QUASIMENT NEUF NEW WAVE PUNK-AMIENS
+ LEWIS KARLOF JAZZ CORE-LYON
+ SHUB POST PUNK-NÎMES

JEU DI 30 OCTObR
à L'ESPACE AUTOGERE des
TANNERIES
Bd Jo Chicago 5 Euros! 21H!

WALL STREET DESTROY & LA PENA FESTAYRE PRESENTENT
31 OCTOBRE DE 17H A 00H
10 EUROS + 1 CONSO
SUBHUMANS ANARKO PUNK LEGEND UK
LES ASSOIFFES ANARKO PUNK
HUMAN DOG FOOD STREET PUNK PAU
USUAL SUSPECTS FAST PUNK PAU, BEARNE
100 RAISONS PUNK PUNK, PARIS
PLUS SOIRÉE "JE N'AIME PAS HALLOWEEN" JUSQU'À 6H DU MAT
LA PENA FESTAYRE

FASLANE PEACE CAMP BENEFIT
SUBHUMANS
AUTONOMADS
I.C.H.
REFUSE/ALL
PAX
22ND May
8PM-3AM
£8 ENTRY
SUBVERT
WAGON & HORSES
ADDERLEY ST, DIGBETH
PUNK SKA FEMALE SOUND SYSTEM
DJS FRANNY ROOTS SKINNY CHRISTY

SØNDAG 14.JUNI
SUBHUMANS
LEGENDARISK ANARKOPUNK, ENGLAND
PKP
POLITISK HARDCORE, BERGEN
REST IN PISS
K(A)OSPUNK, ØSTBYEN
PRIS: 60 SPENN DØRA ÅPNER KL. 21.00
UFFA-HUS, INNHERREDSVEIEN 69C, 7042 TRONDHEIM WWW.UFFA.NO

the GATHERING of THE THOUSANDS

CONFLICT · SUB HUMANS
UK SUBS · ALTERNATIVE

Saturday 23 May 2009 ◎ 1pm - 1am ◎ +14 years · Queen Margaret Union ◎ 2 University Gardens
ticket price: £12.50 · t. 0141 339 9784

£125

JOCK, MEL AND JOHNNY BAINBRIDGE OF THE A-HEADS, NYC,
2009 BY PHIL

2007 ended with a twelve-date UK tour, that started in Bristol with Gurkha and wrapped at the Camden Underworld with Random Hand. Another UK tour followed relatively soon after in mid-February 2008, which included the band's first gig at the much-loved 1 in 12 Club in Bradford, a most important venue for DIY punk in the UK.

"It's a very good example over here of what they do in mainland Europe… and unfortunately a rare example too," says **Dick**. "They feed you, they'll put you up, they've got literature, a library, a café, a studio, and the venue itself, and they've been there for years and years. And it's self-organised, still DIY, not been bought out by anybody; they haven't had to sell themselves to keep themselves going. Totally recommended on an ideological level, but a great place to play as well. It's very much a social centre though, and gigs to them is just one of the types of event they run."

It should also be noted that sometimes the DIY scene can be more than a little unforgiving towards bands who play big commercial venues, like the Academy Group's O2 chain, or tour the States all the time… yet the Subhumans have seemingly maintained enough integrity to still have almost complete credibility with the subculture.

"Thankfully!" exclaims **Dick**. "I mean, typing up the list of gigs for the back of this book did demonstrate to me just how many times we've been over there, and just how many gigs we've done there compared to over here. Since we reformed in '98, we've averaged over one tour a year there. We go there a lot. But when you look at the crowd numbers, it might explain why – we're getting two or three times as many people at every show, with the average age of an American crowd still around twenty-three or twenty-four, whilst the average age of a European crowd is somewhere over forty. That's just the way it is, and I don't mind, but there is a difference there. Variety being the spice of life, and air travel being so *absolutely fucking fantastic*… I hate flying! You're just cattle. It's the most expensive form of transport, and you are treated like dirt, from the moment you get to the airport all the way until you get where you're going. Anyway, I'm not going to complain about being able to fly somewhere to tour, as it's quite a luxurious position to be in.

"Trotsky can only afford to go away for two weeks at a time max, due to his family situation. And everything is getting more expensive. We're planning to go over there again soon, so we'll find out whether it breaks even, once we've got our work permits and everything. We're not all in a position where we can afford to go there and lose money, so breaking even is bottom line really. It's a lot of fun touring there… it's a lot of fun touring, full-stop; it's where you build up a circle of friends, who you don't see very often, but when you do see them, it's like only last week, even though it's sometimes years apart.

"We played in Karlsruhe on our last European tour [November 2021] in a bar owned by a chap called Pluschi, who was putting on gigs in Karlsruhe twenty or thirty years ago. He still looks basically the same, he's just put on a bit of healthy weight, and he's still running the bar. And it's just great to see that continuity, because the continuity of punk rock, or a band, or a venue, whatever, is so important – it's vital to everybody's mental health. Especially these days [mid–COVID pandemic], when so many things have become discontinuous all at once. Things have stopped happening, and it's vital that things start happening again, especially gigs, and social events, things where people get together. And the repetition of that over time is definitely a strong base for staying sane.

"From a more cynical perspective, we've already 'sold out' multiple times by going to the States and not keeping our politics European, or British, or local, or whatever. But on that front, I personally feel that the process of politics and business is a global situation and a global problem, and can't be really lessened down to your own area – unless it's a very specific local issue, of course.

"In terms of playing corporate venues, usually it's a question of capacity: if we're playing an all-dayer with The Damned or Buzzcocks or Upstarts, say, then the only venues that can handle the numbers aren't part of the DIY ethic at all – but the promoters for such gigs are usually old punks doing a larger version of hiring the local village hall. You deal with business all the time, and there *is* a business end in punk rock... even running a DIY tape label, you are still exchanging one thing for another, money gets involved and you have to print this and distribute that... the *nature* of the business is the questionable thing, not the actual fact of doing business with people – that just has to happen if you want to function.

"But I think we're still welcome at places like the 1 in 12 because we still want to go there. We still give it the respect it deserves, and we're still very happy to play places like that. Happier, in fact, to play places like that than to play large halls where you can't have eye contact with 90% of the crowd. And more people turn up for us in America, which is why that's where those large gigs are more likely to happen."

And right on cue, the first two and a half weeks of April 2008 were spent back in the US, playing seventeen gigs down the West Coast and into Nevada and Arizona. Criminal Damage were main support at most of the shows.

"Subhumans are able to blur that line between band and audience, even when they're playing a massive show in front of a thousand people," reckons **Robert Collins**. "A highlight for me was during that 2008 tour, when they played Palmdale, California, a couple of hours north of LA in the high desert, and it was in a rented hall, a VFW [i.e. Veterans of Foreign Wars] hall. So we rolled up in the afternoon, assuming there might be a sound-check, and it was just heaving with kids outside already. It was in an isolated spot, so there was nowhere for kids to hang around apart from right there. And it was not a big room, with just a vocal PA and a kinda shitty drum riser. Which is fine for a little punk gig – but not for a gig that was going to be this rammed. I went back out to the van, after checking all this out, and said to them, 'The bad news is, you guys are going to hate this... the good news is, I'm about to have the time of my life!' It was probably the single best show where I had the most fun – I just got annihilated by the crowd; I was covered in bruises after the show. There was no 'working the stage' as such, because there was no stage. Phil and Dick were basically on their own, and I just tried to make a bridge over Bruce's pedals... everything else was a complete fucking free for all. It was mental, and probably sounded like shit – I know the drums got knocked over a couple of times – but it was absolutely great, because you don't get that very often. You can be a really good roadie, but 300 people will defeat you, haha!

"I remember they played a bigger theatre venue in Philadelphia once, and I don't recall what the schism was, but there was some sort of beef between the activist DIY community and the commercial big rock punk scene in Philly, so some people came to the show but wouldn't come in it. And they wanted the Subhumans to play a DIY warehouse show after the big rock show... I don't think they wanted to initially, but they

Phil 'n' Erika
New York City Wedding Weekend

9 JULY
Staten Island Ferry Ride

10 JULY
Get Married!! Central Park
Cake, Drinks @ Frying Pan
Party @ Trash Bar, Brooklyn

11 JULY
SUBHUMANS WITCHHUNT
A-HEADS @ Knitting Factory

12 JULY
CITIZEN FISH
A-HEADS
RAY GRADYS
@ Knitting Facto

PHIL AND ERIKA'S WEDDING WEEKEND, NYC, 2009
BY KONSTANTIN SERGEYEV

DICK AND PETE AT PHIL'S WEDDING, NYC, 2009 BY PHIL

ERIKA, DICK AND TROTSKY BY PHIL

did, and it was incredible. At some point during that show, Dick was playing drums…
he may not have been playing drums on Subhumans songs, but he *was* playing drums!

"For the most part, all their US tours have gone great, and they're just different
versions of the same best story. If there's a story to tell about touring on repeat, it should
be this one, because it's really good – more often than not, at the end of any show, one
or more of the band is just hanging out, having a conversation with someone they met
that night… and it's not a half-hearted, 'Okay, I'm in the band, I better talk to you' kinda
conversation, it's a real conversation."

Karoline: "And although you think you know, you have this expectation of what their
US tours are going to go like, and where the more successful spots are, you're constantly
surprised when you see kids who want to talk to this band so much. Which is great to
see. It's not even that they're especially humble, they're just real people. And we've
been around so many people who tour with bands who don't want to interact, who just
go backstage when they're done, and they're not going to talk to anyone. I just love the
dynamic in the Subs, and it was the same in Citizen Fish, and when I did the Culture
Shock tour up the West Coast. It's just lovely – it's like picking your family up at the
airport, you know how everyone is, and you know they're all good with interacting."

"They always wanted to keep it nice and tight and personal, working with close
friends," adds **Jock**. "Most of it was organised by Dick in the early days, but if he couldn't
do it himself, it would be people that he knew and respected… like the people they work
with in America, such nice, pleasant people, and an extension of the Subhumans family
really…"

"The thing that strikes me most is the humility of all of them," agrees **Kev**. "I've
never known Phil, Dick, Trotsky or Bruce be anything other than Phil, Dick, Trotsky or
Bruce. They've always got time for other people, they really have – even when they're
absolutely dog-tired, they'll make time to chat to people who want to talk to them."

A week after getting home from America, Subhumans flew out to Vienna, for the
Austrian leg of Rebellion, which was headlined by The Dwarves, and a month later they
were in Finland for three gigs over a long weekend, including one with Finnish hardcore
legends Rattus. After playing the Mighty Sounds festival in the Czech Republic, and
Rebellion, back in Blackpool, in July and August respectively, they then did a twelve-
date UK tour in September and a nine-date trek across France, Belgium and Germany
in October.

Their last gig of 2008 was as main support to a briefly reformed Flux of Pink Indians
at the Islington Academy on November 29th, a gig that is especially close to your author's
heart as I was playing bass for Flux at the time (their original bassist, Derek Birkett,
having no interest in the reformation), and it was quite surreal to have the Subhumans go
on *before* the band I was playing in. I was so excited by the whole occasion, I played the
bass intro to 'Tube Disaster' about twice as fast as it is on the record and got chastised by
Sid from Rubella Ballet (who were also on the bill, alongside the Restarts) who jumped
up to guest on it (he drummed for Flux on the original recording).

The year 2009 continued the pattern of sporadic bursts of gigging whenever the various
Subhumans could align their schedules, including a gig in Lodz, Poland, with The Real
MacKenzies and Dezerter, three dates in Italy in early March, and a Scandinavian mini-

462

tour in June, built around an appearance at the Punk Illegal festival in Sweden. Then it was back across the Atlantic, for seven gigs in Canada, and five US gigs, all with the Ray Gradys and some with Witch Hunt. This was a special trip for them as it climaxed in New York for Phil's wedding weekend, where he and Erika got married.

The A-Heads flew out to join in the celebrations and play a few gigs.

"Having decided to get married in New York, we thought it would be amazing to have the band and friends from the UK come over," explains **Phil**. "We set up a small Canadian/US tour with Witch Hunt and Ray Gradys before the wedding to cover the costs of the Subhumans folk, and we centred the wedding celebrations around some NYC gigs at the Knitting Factory. Our old Warminster mates A-Heads came over and played, so that helped towards their expenses. Mr and Mrs Roadie flew out from Oakland and, also from the East Bay, our good friend Kamala from Cringer.

"On the eve of the wedding, we all met up on the Staten Island Ferry and, wearing our green Liberty foam crowns, got to know each other over drinks and, of course, the punks and family members got on like a house on fire.

"The day of the wedding we were blessed with a glorious sunny day for the ceremony in Central Park. Roberto Miguel, our Citizen Fish US trombone player, serenaded us with mariachi on his guitar, and Erika's old mate Gretchen from Boston band Czolgosz officiated, having been ordained online as a wedding celebrant. We then headed off to Pier 66 on Manhattan's West Side for toasts and cake at the Frying Pan, an historic lightship. Jasper made a fantastic best man's speech, and we set up a free 'merch stall' with wedding posters, mugs and laminate passes.

"In the evening, the day was rounded off with a party/secret gig at the Trash Bar in Brooklyn, open to the public. Citizen Fish knocked out a few songs, and were joined onstage by Erika; the A-Heads played and to finish off the entertainment, we had the Punk Rock Karaoke band from the Tattooed Mom in Philly – featuring Mike Yak from Ray Gradys.

"By the end of the wedding day we were absolutely shattered, and the guests too, but over the next two days we still had two gigs to play at the Knitting Factory. Aaargh! At that point, we were thinking, 'Hang on, isn't this the point when we should be heading off on a relaxing, romantic honeymoon…?' [laughs]

"The first of the shows was Subhumans, with Witch Hunt and A-Heads; a brilliant celebratory atmosphere, we played in front of a 'Just Married' backdrop made by Erika's old Boston punk crew. The next day, Citizen Fish played with A-Heads – again! – and Ray Gradys. Being day three of the marathon wedding fest, everyone was just broken, poor Mel had completely lost her voice, and we all drew on our deepest reserves to get through it. We'd overdone it a bit by making it a three-day fest, but we'd had a fantastic, unforgettable wedding!"

"That was the first time we'd been to America," recounts **Mel**, "And we had three gigs – one at their wedding party, and two at the Knitting Factory. The first night was obviously the wedding, and the champagne was flowing, and we went on some boat and had lots of drinks. Anyway, the gig was great, and then we did the Knitting Factory gigs. Of course, we're playing with the Subhumans, and I can't help but sing along to them, so by the third night, I didn't have a voice. I got to the sound-check, and I'd been drinking tea all day, and I couldn't even sound-check, but about half hour before we went on, I

DEATHSTAR MUSIC PRESENTS

SUB HUM ANS

PLUS SPECIAL GUESTS

LONDON
&
VALDEZ

THURSDAY 3RD SEPTEMBER
£7.50 ADV / £9.50 DOOR   7.30PM

BIERKELLER

ALL SAINTS ST. BRISTOL. BS1 2NA
0117 9268514   www.bristolbierkeller.co.uk

SUB HUM ANS

WITCH HUNT, THE RAY GRADYS, & CODE ORANGE KIDS

JULY 7 · ALTAR BAR
1620 PENN AVE · PITTSBURGH, PA 15222 · IN THE STRIP · 6PM DOORS · 7PM SHOW · ALL AGES

DRUSKY
ENTERTAINMENT   TICKETMASTER OUTLETS, TICKETMASTER.COM, & 1-800-745-3000 FOR TICKETS

BLIND DESTRUCTION PRESENTS...

SUB HUM ANS

FOUR LETTER WORD
THE REJECTED

THE LEGENDARY TJ'S
CLARENCE PLACE NEWPORT
MONDAY AUGUST 24TH 2009
£7.00DOOR 8:00PM

FLYER CREATOR GRAPHICS

NEWPORT FLYER BY WELLY

SUB HUM ANS

MON 31ST AUG
WHITE
SWAN   8:30
             PM
TROWBRIDGE

SEPTEMBER 2009 BY WILL BINKS

SUBHUMANS
the dead class   stuntface★   The Mink

Saturday 12th December
Thatched House, Stourbridge
Doors. 7.30pm £8

was talking to the Ray Gradys, who were also playing, and they just told me to drink Jack Daniels. Which I did, and somehow got through our set. But yes, the Subhumans are very dangerous if you've got gigs with them and you're a massive fan... so now when we play with them, I just mouth the words, haha!

"That was the first time we went, just three gigs, but we did do a tour with them the following year as well, from San Francisco down through Las Vegas and all that. Every night was packed. Then we went back and toured with Seven Crowns, and it was like two completely different tours – with Subhumans, we were in really good venues, the sound was amazing, the crowds were brilliant... the next tour? Well, we barely played a full set! Electrocutions, tear gas, police stopping gigs... but that was great in its own way. I quite liked doing both tours. The one with Seven Crowns felt more real in a way – when we were with Subhumans, it felt like we were in this bubble."

With one less single member in their ranks, Subhumans flew home for their annual Rebellion appearance, before they played the Beautiful Days festival in Ottery St Mary at the end of August. That was with the Levellers, and drew 4000 people. It was also the first date of a three-week UK tour, that comprised eleven gigs in England, four in Ireland, two in Scotland and one in Wales. Another nine-date UK tour followed in December, albeit a rather low-key affair, although the Restarts and Moral Dilemma supported at a few of the gigs, before Subhumans took the winter off.

April 2010 saw a return to Belgium and Holland for six gigs, before a three-week tour of the States commenced in Austin on May 28th at the Chaos in Tejas festival. Cross Stitched Eyes played most of the gigs, including one at the Chapter House in Fort Defiance, which is on the Navajo Reservation in Apache County, Arizona.

"The Navajo's tribal name is 'Dine' as in D-Nay, or 'the people'," **Dick** wrote in his diary after the gig. "They are herded here, 6000 feet above sea level, where uranium and other deposits provide employment for exploitative corporations; their whole history and lives are of protest and retaliation, on a layer of poverty and enforced submission. This is what's left of real America. Support band Blackfire travel as a family: gran, band and children! They live in Flagstaff, and their songs are, as you'd expect, full of tribal calls to arms.

"There was a low turnout of about 50, possibly as there was a carnival going on at the same time. The venue felt like a large youth centre; we'd stopped to get supplies from a wholefood store on the way, which was just as well, as there was no food at the gig. Nor booze, as the reservation was alcohol free. We played well to a crowd happy to have us there, and it felt rewarding to have played a gig literally off the beaten track."

"The Navajo Nation gig was a big high point on that tour," confirms **Trotsky**. "It was a really rare honour to be asked to play there, and Blackfire were great, really lovely people. It was a small crowd, and felt a bit like playing a village gig back home with just the curious locals turning out, but it was great to play to some real Americans..."

"It was just another US tour for them... albeit without the riots that used to plague them, especially Citizen Fish... but for us, it was quite an eye-opener," admits **Jock** of the A-Heads, who joined the tour when they got to California. "At the first gig we did in Pomona, the police had to shut the whole area down because the Subhumans were in town. It was just mental, and we were thinking, 'Wow, these are the guys we used to rehearse with in the youth centre!'

"We had just flown in, done the eight-hour drive… and saw the town shut down within hours. Every authority associated with 911 were there. Just because of them! We honestly never thought that having the Humans in town would result in all the emergency services being called out in order to shut everything down. You couldn't move without the police breathing down your neck. I don't think there was another night like that, although the rest of the tour appeared to go by at light speed; it was an amazing experience. Watching Dick hold court with dozens of well-wishers brought home to us just how popular our close friends were, and what they meant to their fans. Watching your friends being a big part of somebody's life makes you proud. Amusing, but nevertheless joyful.

"There's a few videos of Dick getting pushed offstage and punched and what have you, but he literally took it on the chin; they never wanted heavy-handed security that were going to shout and scream at people, they surround themselves with people they know. Especially in America, where they have people they can trust on each coast, who'll get them from A to B and man the merch stall and stuff. I remember they travelled across the Nevada desert in a vehicle with no air con – we met them at the gig, opened the door… and promptly shut it again! Everyone was dripping sweat. But no big tour buses or anything – even when Citizen Fish toured with The Levellers, they would turn up in Phil's old van.

"But the most memorable moment of that tour was watching some methed-up guy standing on the rear bumper, or tailgate or whatever they call it, of the Humans' van from Santa Cruz to just outside San Francisco – mental times! Google maps will give you an idea of how far that dude hung on to the van [about seventy-five miles]. We passed them, thinking they had broken down, and they said, 'No, we've just been pulled by the police, because some fucking idiot has been hanging off the back of the van…'"

"We had loaded all the gear and were pulling away from the front of the venue in Santa Cruz," **Trotsky** picks up the story, "And a few punks out the front started waving and cheering at us – or so we thought, haha! – so we waved back and left. We had to drive to San Francisco, which is a two- or three-hour drive, and after we were on the highway for a while, we noticed all these cars passing us and flashing their lights… until one car that flashed its lights was a cop car! We pulled over and the cop came to the window asking if we were aware there was a person clinging onto the back of the van? Our jaws dropped. This guy had jumped onto the footplate on the back in Santa Cruz, and somehow held on for a couple of hours without being thrown off – it was fuckin' crazy. No idea what happened to him; the cops took him away, but they did say they didn't know what to charge him with..."

Jock: "Each date was different, but for us it was a joy to be part of what our mates were doing; we loved every minute of it. And I should mention that whilst in the States we were given a high percentage of the fee they got for each gig in order to help us get food, petrol and a bed. That's what mates do though, don't they? I'd do the same.

"It was amazing to do gigs with them over there, they're so popular; it's pretty mind-blowing really. We played Fresno on a Wednesday night, just the A-Heads, and they put something like 'ex-Subhuman member' on the poster just to try and get people in – but we didn't have an ex-Subhuman member on that tour anyway, and only about five people turned up, haha!"

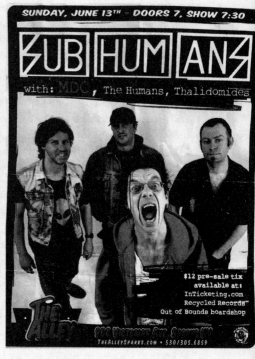

DICK AND PHIL, WITH AVOCADO MARGARITAS, IN
AUSTIN, TEXAS, FOR CHAOS IN TEJAS FEST, 2010

ROBERT AND JESSICA, 2010 BY PHIL

"I've seen them more times than I've seen any other band, and they're good every time," adds **Robert**. "I've obviously seen shows that are better than others, but they're great every single time. Off the record [whoops! – IG], there was a show in San Luis Obispo where Phil and Trots were *really* pissed, and got into a squabble with each other, about one of them playing too fast or too slow, and they were actively trying to throw the other off during the set. They didn't finish 'Society', and fucked up two or three other songs, but it was really fun to see. I was watching with a friend of mine, and said to them, 'You should really pay attention to this, because this is actually pretty special – this doesn't happen very often!'"

Karoline: "It's interesting to listen to the evolution of their music. I'm not one for analysing music the way some people do. Having driven Citizen Fish so much, when I listen to the newer Subs albums, I can't help think, 'Oh, that would have been a Citizen Fish song…!' Because there's a bit more reggae or ska in there. But it's cool to hear, and it's still what they want to do… it's fine either way."

June 6th, 2010, was a significant date in Subhumans' history, as it was the first time they ever performed 'Susan' live. As previously mentioned in the '1983' chapter, they were joined onstage by keyboardist Shannon Saint Ryan, much to the delight of those in attendance at the Echoplex in LA that particular night… and happily it wasn't to be a one-off.

"I was born in Blackburn, England, in 1979," **Shannon** begins. "I grew up in Clayton Brook, Preston, during the '80s and early '90s, with zero exposure to punk rock. My family moved to California in the early 1990s, where I met my best friend, Mike Carter, who exposed me to the punk scene – and changed my life. To me, punk rock was raw, honest, and made me feel that I could dive in and contribute. How did I learn of the Subhumans? Well, Mike and I had soon formed a band. I was playing drums, he was on bass and vocals, and our co-pilot Chris Campbell was on guitar. I had a drum kit with stickers plastered all over it, and Mike wanted to put a Subhumans sticker across my floor tom. I'd never heard of the Subhumans, so he grabbed a cassette and flooded the speakers with 'The Day the Country Died'. I was immediately drawn to their sound, the energy, their artwork, and all the handwritten lyrics…

"What made things worse for my new-found love affair though was the fact that the band had long since broken up, so there was no chance of ever seeing them live. As time went on, I had a cassette tape of 'Time Flies + Rats' that I would play obsessively. On there, sandwiched perfectly between all the heavy tracks, was the beautiful piano song, 'Susan'. It always seemed to draw me in closer. That cassette *lived* in my truck. A friend of mine that wasn't into punk loved it when I put that song on; she liked the way Dick said 'secretary' as '*sekretree*', as opposed to the way Americans say it, '*sekretary*'.

"Anyway, the years rolled by, and I went from playing the drums to the guitar, but I'd always thought about learning to play the piano. My grandma and granddad had both learned to play the organ at the age of fifty, so I always had it in the back of my mind that I'd play loud guitar-driven music 'til I turned fifty, then I'd learn the piano, get soft and eat bon bons. Fast forward to 2009, and I was now thirty years old, still involved with music, and enjoying life. For my day job, I was working in a warehouse and this new kid showed up, named Jimmy. He was originally from Guatemala. We got along from day one. He said, 'You seem to like the piano, I can show you how to play the basics, if you want?' I was twenty years ahead of schedule but thought, 'What the heck? He says he plays for his local church, so what could possibly go wrong for a punker?' So, he brought his plastic keyboard in and we spent an hour after work with him showing me how to make chords, and a basic scale. Now this was all news to me, as I had no music theory background, but having caught the piano bug, I made the leap and bought a digital one with proper weighted keys. I started spending hours every night, just playing, exploring, and affectionately being made fun of by close friends for putting down the guitar to hang out with a piano.

"After some time, Mike told me it was cool to see how much I was into it, and he could see an improvement. He said, 'You know what you should do? You should learn that 'Susan' song, get hold of the Subhumans and ask them why they don't ever play it live. They've never played that song in almost thirty years – you should play it with them!' I remember that moment; he was standing in the hallway to my room, and he wasn't joking, he was encouraging me, pushing me. He was right. Why not just ask? The worst they could say is no.

"So, I reached out to their drummer, Trotsky. My pitch was honest, respectful, straightforward and polite. I said, 'I see you guys are coming out to the US pretty soon – that's awesome – and you're heading up the West Coast for two and a half weeks. I have an idea, please, if you don't mind. I could learn the song 'Susan' on piano, take that entire two and a half weeks off work, and meet you guys down south at the first gig. We could try playing 'Susan' at sound-check, and if it sounds good, man, let's play it that night. If it's not ready, no worries at all, I'll pack up my gear and meet you at the next gig for sound-check. I'm sure by the time we've got all the way up to Seattle, 'Susan' will be ready to play for real. I promise you no stress; I'll be in my own truck with my own gear, so I won't be in your space at all…'

"Trotsky thought it was a decent proposal. He said, 'It makes sense, but you need to talk to Dick to see what he thinks…' He gave me Dick's number and said, 'Best of luck'. I called Dick and nervously repeated the same pitch. Dick paused for a moment, and to my surprise said, 'That's not a bad idea. Why not? We'll see you at the first gig!' You'd think that when I hung up the phone, I would've raised both arms high in the air and screamed with excitement, but no, I was immediately hit with a wave of nausea and thought, 'Dude, what have you just done?'

"As the clock slowly ticked down, I'd race home from work each night for the next month straight, learning the song as best I could, dissecting each part, trying to match every line, note for note. I can't read music, but I made some dots on staff paper to help me map it out. It's funny to look at those pages now. On the official recording of 'Susan', there's one part of the song where there's a weird extra beat in the measure, five beats instead of four. It took me ages to drill that into my brain without fumbling over it. As the first show drew closer, I finally had all the parts mapped out and could play it start to finish. But I was still a bundle of nerves. The time had arrived. I loaded my gear into the

SHANNON AND PHIL PLAYING 'SUSAN' AT THE OAKLAND METRO

PIANO NOTATION BY SHANNON, APRIL 2010

D.I.Y. HARDCORE PUNK FEST vol.6
9-10 lipca 2010

9.07 (piątek)
SUBHUMANS UK
DISTRESS Rosja
FAMILY MAN Niemcy
UTOPIA PL
edelweiss piraten PL
★NO-SE★ PL
GOVERNMENT FLU PL
Start: 18:00

10.07 (sobota)
DOOM UK
JUGGLING JUGULARS Finlandia
INSTINCT OF SURVIVAL Niemcy
el banda PL
ENUSJA PL
NEXT VICTIM PL
ANTIDOTUM PL
Start: 18:00

wjazd:
30 PLN / dzień

Przed koncertami D.I.Y. FilmFest

UCho
Gdynia
ul.Św.Piotra 2

szczegółowe info:
www.diyfest.prv.pl

FamEnts Present

SUBHUMANS

+ SUPPORT
constant state
of terror

TUESDAY 10TH AUGUST 2010
TICKETS £8 +BF ADV DOORS 7.30PM

Tickets on sale now at:
Rounder - Resident - Punkerbunker
www.ticketweb.co.uk / www.seetickets.co.uk / www.gigantic.co.uk

UPSTAIRS @ THE HYDRANT
75 LONDON ROAD BRIGHTON
TEL: 01273 608313 MYSPACE.COM/THEHYDRANTBRIGHTON
FACEBOOK: WHAT'S ON @ THE HYDRANT

SUBHUMANS

SLIT PROMOTIONS + PUMPKIN RECORDS
PRESENTS...

DECEMBER 2010

1st NORTHAMPTON - Labour Club
2nd LONDON - The Gaff
3rd BIRMINGHAM - Adam and Eve
5th MANCHESTER - Star and Garter
6th BRADFORD - 1in12 Club
7th CARLISLE - The Brickyard
8th EDINBURGH - Bannerman's
9th GLASGOW - Ivory Blacks
10th HUDDERSFIELD - The Parish

TICKETS + INFO AT WWW.SLIT.ME.UK

back of my truck and drove from Ventura to the Glass House in Pomona, California, a couple of hours from home. I got there early, way before any of the bands were to arrive. I made friends with the sound guy; he said it was okay to set up my gear onstage and run through the song if I liked. I took that opportunity. I had yet to hear what the piano sounds like running through a huge PA system. The stage was big. The building would soon be at capacity with almost 1000 punk rockers. Alone onstage, I sat down at my seat and began to play 'Susan'. It sounded so loud. Holy shit! The notes were echoing around the empty building and bouncing straight back at me. It was terrifying, like being under a microscope, all your imperfections turned up to eleven. This was a complete 180 from practising in the comfort of your own bedroom…

"I ran through the song a couple times, then thanked the sound guy for his generosity. When the Subhumans finally arrived, they asked me to set up in their room backstage, as the main room was now far too busy with activity and distractions. I set my gear up and settled into the seat. Each member of the Subhumans was now standing horseshoed around me, watching closely. This was not the time to screw it up, but I'm sure they could see my hands were shaking. I played through the song and Dick noticed I played the five beats on one single bar instead of four; he stepped back and said, 'I can't believe you played it note for note… that was a mistake on the record. Wow, you even learned the mistakes!' I was so relieved. They made me feel at ease. The ice was finally broken. We jammed it acoustically a few times right there in the room, but they asked me to play that single part as four beats instead of five. It was so hard for me to unlearn what I'd had to drill into my brain for the past month. I told them I would get it; I just needed a bit more repetition for it to sink in. They were happy and said, 'We'll play it again at sound-check in LA tomorrow afternoon, but let's not do it tonight.' I felt a weight lifted; I could relax, I had made it through the first hurdle. I pulled up at the next gig, at the Echoplex in Los Angeles. It was early and set to be another sold-out show, with 1000 hungry Subhumans fans. The Subs and I set up onstage for sound-check and we ran through 'Susan', but this time the whole band was amplified through the speakers of the house PA system. It was an unreal feeling just being there with them. And again, it felt so loud. With my piano tucked comfortably in the corner next to Phil's bass amp, I could hear every instrument and the vocals clearly, as the sound bounced around the empty venue and back to our ears. The song felt raw, much better now, but not yet quite ready. We played it through a few more times, ironing out the creases, but soon it was time to wrap up and clear the stage. The band looked at me calmly and said, 'Great! Let's do it!' I gulped, then found my words, 'Wait… shouldn't we practise it again at tomorrow's sound-check?' They said, 'No, it's good. If you mess up, just don't stop, make sure to keep playing…' They then happily left the stage. Sound advice from true warriors, but I felt like I was left standing there covered in children's paint and holding a cardboard sword.

"The Echoplex's doors officially opened and people starting rolling in. I found myself growing ever more nervous with each passing hour. The place was now packed. A sweat box. Nothing but a sea of spiked hair and studs. I spent most of the time hiding out alone in the parking lot out back, pacing around, hoping to come up with an excuse why I couldn't do it that night, but could tomorrow. I could hear another band finishing their set, and pretty soon the Subhumans would be up, and then I'd have to go up there too. The band had agreed it was best to play 'Susan' at the start of the encore, then they would play a few more and end the night.

"Showtime. When the Subhumans walked up onstage, I watched from the side as they ploughed through their set. Their energy was incredible, song after song, absolutely full throttle. I kept staring down at their set-list that was taped to the floor. I could see 'Susan' drawing closer and closer with each passing song. Finally, the band disappeared offstage as the packed venue chanted for more. The Subs walked right up to me, happy as ever and dripping with sweat. I stared back at them, also dripping with sweat but not quite looking the part. They said, 'You ready?' Before I could reply, 'No, absolutely not', I found myself sitting at the piano with my hands shaking above the keys, ready to play the first note. The Subs strapped on their guitars, gave me the nod, and I leapt off the diving board, freefalling for what felt like an eternity.

"Three seconds in however, I immediately realized that I couldn't hear shit. The venue was now packed full of bodies so the sound was no longer bouncing around and coming back to the stage as it had during sound-check. I could barely hear my piano, hardly any of Dick's vocals, and zero of Bruce's guitar, just a huge overwhelming amount of Phil's bass melting my right eardrum. I hung in there as best I could, and to be honest, I actually thought the band stopped halfway through the song. I was convinced they were now just staring at me, so I was about to stop also. But I remembered what they said, 'Just keep going, don't ever stop,' so I kept going, and when I looked up again, they were still playing too. I had just imagined it. Holy crap! I had been about to give up right in the middle of their song; I would've ruined it. Finally, the song came to its proper end. Dick looked so happy. I was just glad it was over. The audience was cheering. Bruce and Phil were smiling. 'Susan' had finally been played live, twenty-seven years after first being recorded. I loaded my truck and once again followed them to their next show for sound-check. We played 'Susan' again, to yet another packed audience of incredible fans, and without fail, I was the same bundle of nerves. But it was amazing to feel those emotions. To be vulnerable. Human. I drove and played the next few nights in a row with them. Then, to my surprise, the band pulled me aside and asked if I would ditch my truck and join them in the van for the rest of the tour. They would fly me back home from Seattle. And since 2010, I've played 'Susan' live with the Subhumans perhaps thirty or forty times, meeting up with them on several tours over the years, mostly of the western United States and England."

The rest of summer 2010 was rounded out with festivals such as the Ucho Punk Fest in Poland, the Endorsit festival in Sixpenny Handley (it's an oddly named village in Dorset… don't ask!), Rebellion festival (of course), and Boomtown in Hampshire. Subhumans then undertook a nine-date UK tour in late November/early December, including another gig at the 1 in 12 Club, Bradford; their last gig of the year was in Huddersfield at the Parish, with Total Bloody Chaos supporting, before they vanished into hibernation for another winter.

475

DICK AND JELLO BIAFRA BY JOCK MCCURDY

SUBHUMANS AND A-HEADS, CREW SHOT, 2010
COURTESY OF JOCK MCCURDY

TROTSKY, U.S. TOUR WITH CROSS STITCHED EYES

BRUCE WITH MATT FROM CITIZEN FISH,
BOOMTOWN 2010 BY PHIL

2011 — 2016

Spring 2011 saw the Subhumans back in the USA for twenty-three gigs with legendary hardcore punk band MDC as main support, a run that started in New York and finished in Oakland. These long stints of touring can be taxing on relationships within any band, being cooped up in restricted spaces together for hours on end, day after day, week after week, often irritable due to lack of sleep and 'regular' routine, but the Subhumans seem to have it all down to a tee.

"They really are as easy-going to tour with as you'd imagine," reveals **Robert Collins**. "They've got to have a hot breakfast in the morning, which is fair enough, and Bruce has to have milk for his tea – that's a thing that has to happen."

"It's always funny with the backstage food, because certain things are always on the rider," continues **Karoline**. "There's always lots of bananas… at the end of one of the tours, there were twenty-one bananas left in the tray, and the band were heading for the airport, so Robert and I ate twenty-one bananas! 'Have a banana?' 'I don't want a banana…' 'But you have to have a banana, they're on the rider…'"

Robert: "They're a really low-key bunch. Phil used to be really, really chatty – he was always up front with me, playing dance music, which was fine. That was when he was living in Spain, and he had a lot of things going on – every time we'd see each other for another tour, something had changed – where he was living, or other projects he was working on, and then he did The Knowledge [more on this mysterious 'Knowledge' later in this chapter…], but in the last several years, he seems to have settled, and now he just chills in the back and watches films – he's got his phone rubber-banded to the headrest, and we got him an auxiliary battery he can plug into."

"I do like dance, and electronic music," interjects **Phil**, on his eclectic tastes. "I was always into everything… give me as much music as you can, and I'll check everything out. When the whole acid house and rave started up, I had friends in Warminster, old punks, who got into it, and I even started messing around doing some Cubase stuff on an old Atari ST. Jungle drum 'n' bass was starting up, and I got quite into it, messing around on my own… I never released any of it, but it was a real outlet for me. A lot of it ended up in Jasper's Citizen Fish videos, like that 'Gaffer Tape' tour compilation… if you hear any vaguely electronic music in the background, it's probably something I did. I still do that… I've done some chill-out, dubby, ambient things for Michelle and Dick for their Bluurg TV. It's something totally different, but I enjoy doing that as much as I enjoy playing 4/4 bass.

"I'm probably the only one who does that sort of thing. I don't think any of the others are interested in that genre. Trotsky likes a bit of Rammstein… Bruce is very diverse, and I think he got into a bit of Chemical Brothers, and would listen to some stuff like that a bit. I listen to all sorts – I don't mind a bit of cheesy Ibiza house music, me! I even like disco… and Dick hates disco with an absolute passion. If he even hears a hint of it when we do anything in Citizen Fish, he's like, 'Argh, no disco!' Which is funny really, because he loves ska, which isn't a *million* miles away in vibe and feel. But like a lot of old punks, he knows what he likes, and he always hated disco.

478

"In the early Nineties, I did a really Prodigy-like song that ended up on the 'Psychological Background Reports' [out-takes] CD by Citizen Fish. That was called 'Brain Scanner' and was very Prodigy-esque!

"I used to like a lot of Groove Armada, because of the dub and reggae influences. The only thing I really can't take much of is the modern auto-tune pop music… ever since Cher did that song, and started the auto-tune thing, I had to draw the line there. I can't stand a lot of modern pop music, to be honest.

"But we all know what we like, and in many ways, we haven't changed that much. None of us are really into pop punk though… that melodic American punk doesn't do it for any of us. It's a fine line though, isn't it? Because some of our own songs, especially in Citizen Fish, aren't a million miles away. Come to think of it though, none of us listen to much punk when we're at home anyway, because we're doing it full-time. I enjoy watching a good band live, but even if I really like them, it's probably not something I'd listen to at home. I'm more likely to find myself listening to Neil Diamond or something!"

"I feel like Trotsky doesn't like the States that much?" **Robert** picks up the touring thread again. "He likes a lot of people in the States, but he doesn't like the long slog drives, and the US in general, for obvious reasons… which is why he lives in 'the loft' [the elevated cubbyhole in the van]! Well, that's changed the last few tours, but at one point he was definitely a loft troll… he would appear when we stopped to have a piss, and then he'd be straight back up into the loft when we'd start to drive again."

Karoline: "We used to call him The Loft Mess Monster! Because he used to be back in the loft, just lying down the whole day, not talking much. We have a newer Sprinter now, and there's two rows of seats… there *is* a loft in the back, but where everyone used to do rotation to go in the loft, now everyone sits on the seats. Even now, when I look round and see Trotsky sat in a seat, I'm startled, haha!"

Robert: "Dick has a routine. Every day… well, 90% of them. When we start driving, he'll first do the figures, logging everything from the night before, the door money, the merch money, he'll pay out everyone who needs to be paid out… cover the expenses and do the figures. And then he will write in his journal, where he has the gig list and set-lists and everything… and then he falls asleep."

Karoline: "I'll watch him peripherally, and sometimes he falls asleep with the pen in his hand. And he'll wake up moments later and go right back to writing! It's fascinating to watch, literally falling asleep mid-word… Rob and I are terrible instigators of documenting them falling asleep."

Robert: "I nailed one picture of him, asleep, with journal in hand, pen in hand, mid-word, with a huge line of drool coming down, haha! I used to post some of those pictures on Instagram, and when he finally signed up to that for his art account, he messaged me, 'Oh, really! This is what you've been doing!' Haha!"

Karoline: "Dick is always reading books. Before we had phones, we would play Scrabble in the van. Words are so important to that man, they're the fabric of his whole being. But he's constantly reading, and the input is massive, so it's no wonder the output is massive too, and stands the test of time. There's so much to dissect in his lyrics – it isn't just 'Blah blah blah, chorus!'

"At the start of a lot of the Citizen Fish tours, Dick would ask for the booklet from

Monday April 11th 2011

SUBHUMANS

M.D.C.

THE ZVILLS

7PM

$12 in advance
ALL AGES!
Mad Hatter 620 Scott Blvd.
Covington, KY. 41011

OAKLAND METRO OPERAHOUSE

630 3rd Street (Jack London Sq)

7PM DOORS – 1:00AM
$10/$12 or FESTIVAL PASS

BOB FEST
BREMEN BATH
OAKLAND
2011

SUBHUMANS (UK)
7 CROWNS (UK)
WWK (GERMANY)
FRACAS (OAKLAND)
BORN UGLIES (OAKLAND)

SUBHUMANS

B.O.B. FESTIVAL OAKLAND 2011

ANOTHER WINTER OF DISCONTENT

2012

SUBHUMANS DEADLINE

THE RESTARTS
ZOUNDS
INNER TERRESTRIALS
ANTISECT
SEX PISTOLS
NEWTOWN NEUROTICS
experience
Eastfield
Condition DEAD
LIBERTY
16 GUNS
HAGAR THE WOMB
bLAT OiDEA
ONE TRAX MINDS
FLOWERS (OF FLESH AND BLOOD)
VIRUS
LOUISE DISTRAS
SOCIAL SCISM
THE ASTRONAUTS
PUKES
ANDY T
RIIVA

1ST/2ND/3RD/4TH MARCH 2012 AT THE BOSTON ARMS
THE BOSTON ARMS (MUSIC ROOMS) 178 JUNCTION ROAD TUFNELL PARK LONDON N19 5QQ.
OPPOSITE TUFNELL PARK TUBE. BUS 134 & 390 AND C11

£40 FOR ALL FOUR DAYS OF THE FESTIVAL OR £12 FOR INDIVIDUAL NIGHTS
TICKETS AVAILABLE AT: WWW.AWOD2012.NET78.NET
FOR INFORMATION CONTACT: THEBIGRANANAPRESENTS@YAHOO.CO.UK

SUBHUMANS
ZEMEZLUC
THE WAR GOES ON
VAGIANT JARS

277 ZOR

SUB HUM ANS
legendary uk-anarcho-punk

THE WAR GOES ON
k-town punk, ex no hope for the kids & hjertestop

ZEMĚŽLUČ
punkrock from brno/cz since 86

+ KELLERSHOW:
JARS &
VAGIANT
2x post-punk/ noise-rock aus moskau

+ ANTIFA-SOLI-COCKTAILBAR
+ AFTERSHOW mit DJ KOJAK

27.07.
ZORO

NOISE
THERAPY
FESTIVAL
vol. 1

SUBHUMANS   SS-KALIERT

ROZPOR | DEZIPEKCH | SVINĚI
MARCH DUNKIN   TALES OF ERROR

11. 8. PRAHA · MODRÁ VOPICE

MINOVATION AND PUNK ROCK ROAD TRIPS PRESENT

SUB HUM ANS
AUSTRALIAN TOUR
SEPT 2012

WEDS 12TH
AMPLIFIER
PERTH

THURS 13TH
PRINCE OF WALES HOTEL
NUNDAH. BRISBANE

FRI 14TH
THE SANDRINGHAM HOTEL
NEWTOWN. SYDNEY

SAT 15TH
THE BENDIGO HOTEL
COLLINGWOOD. MELBOURNE

SUN 16TH
THE FORRESTERS AND SQUATTERS ARMS
THEBARTON. ADELAIDE

TICKETS FROM OZTIX WWW.OZTIX.COM.AU

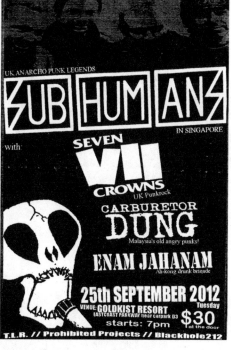

UK ANARCHO PUNK LEGENDS

SUB HUM ANS
IN SINGAPORE

with
SEVEN
VII
CROWNS
UK Punkrock

CARBURETOR
DUNG
Malaysia's old angry punks!

ENAM JAHANAM
Ah-kong drunk brigade

25th SEPTEMBER 2012
Tuesday
VENUE: GOLDKIST RESORT
EASTCOAST PARKWAY near Carpark D3
starts: 7pm $30
at the door

T.L.R. // Prohibited Projects // Blackhole212

THEE PARKSIDE, SAN FRANCISCO, APRIL 2011 BY SHANNON

MARGIE, THE BAND'S U.S. BOOKING AGENT, ROBERT, DICK, BRUCE, U.S., 2011 BY PHIL

BERKELEY, APRIL 2011, WITH SHANNON SAINT RYAN - LEFT

DICK SLEEPING IN VAN
BY ROBERT COLLINS

DICK, RAINY VAN DAY,
SEEKING SOLACE IN BANANAS
BY KAROLINE COLLINS

each CD, so he could reference the lyrics whenever he wanted... but of course – just how many words does that man have to memorise? [laughs] It's pretty insane."

There was a trip to Germany to play the Force Attack festival in Rostock at the end of July, then five UK dates in early August, starting with Rebellion. Five more gigs in September, including two in Scotland, were scheduled around an appearance at Durham University as part of the North East Calling festival, alongside Rezillos, Angelic Upstarts and UK Subs. The year 2011 was rounded out with five more UK gigs, including the Corporation Punk Fest in Sheffield with the Buzzcocks, Upstarts and King Kurt.

The next year, 2012, saw bursts of sporadic touring, including ten English gigs in late February/early March, ending at the Boston Arms in London (supported by Hagar the Womb, Zounds, Pukes, Lost Cherrees and Andy T), a nine-date tour of Holland, Germany and Belgium in July, and festival appearances in Frankfurt, Prague and Blackpool.

The most notable event for Subhumans in 2012 was their one and only excursion into the southern hemisphere that September; they played six gigs in Australia, four in New Zealand, and then hit Singapore and Java on the way home. The tour was booked by Min Stokes, an old friend of the band from Andover who emigrated to Australia in 1993, where she is now a flying instructor.

"I was born in Winchester, but grew up in the countryside near Andover," begins **Min**. "When punk began, I was at boarding school so it was all pretty inaccessible. I wanted more than the life that seemed to be mapped out for me and loved music, so it first began for me listening to John Peel. I left school and went to sixth form college to do A-levels and that was where I was more able to hang out with other punks, go to gigs, join a band etc. It was an amazing time to be a teenager, there really was something in the air back then, a tribe of like-minded people.

"My earliest Subhumans-related memories are of The Mental. I went to Peter Symonds [College] in Winchester to do my A-levels, and that's where I met Tony Delvalle, who was the drummer in The Mental. Through him I met Dick one day in The Fighting Cocks, the long-gone punk pub in Winchester... my enduring memory of him was how tall he was. Dick was one of the many of us who went to Stonehenge that fateful time in 1980 when the [Hell's] Angels decided they were going to kill all the punks and we ran for our lives. I saw Subhumans for the first time in 1982 in Andover, but after that I went to college, then travelled, and lost touch with a lot of people. The next time I saw Dick was at Rebellion in 2010, and he told me I still owed him a cigarette from that day at Stonehenge!

"The only time I saw the Subhumans in the Eighties though was at that gig in Andover in 1982; it was one of the last punk gigs of that era that I went to before I wandered off, and was one of those gigs in a hall, with no stage, bad sound, a lot of energy – it was brilliant. Dick just has something that connects with everyone, and of course the songs were great anthems of our time. The Mental EP was brilliant, I wish I still had my copy, but Subhumans were even better. I was finding that punk was starting to become uniform, and the music was getting very angry and rather boring, but Subhumans were on a different level, and still had the original spirit of punk. 'Demolition War' is one of the very best punk records ever made."

Min then goes on to explain how she came to book the band's 2012 tour 'down under': "I'd been involved in Steve Ignorant's Last Supper tour the year before; I was originally supposed to just be the financier, but ended up putting together the whole thing, with a lot of help from others, and then people started asking me to do another tour. Subhumans were a band that I knew would appeal to the older generation of Australian and ex-pat punks, as well as the younger ones, as well as being a favourite of mine. I'd also mentioned it to Dick at Rebellion and it looked doable, so we started to put it all together. It was great just working directly with Dick and not having to deal with managers and agents; we did it pretty much between us in true punk DIY style, with a lot of help from the Australian punk network I'd built up touring with Steve. It was really a collaboration between myself and several others, including Tim Edwards, who was booking the New Zealand leg of the tour, Cathy and Chris from Punkfest Brisbane, and Tom Brownrigg, who also came on the road with us and took care of all the technical details.

"I can safely say that it was the only tour I've done where there were no lows. There were only a few Spinal Tap moments, such as losing Bruce at an airport once, and water dripping through the ceiling onto the backline in Adelaide – which was quickly fixed by Tom and his trusty roll of gaffer tape. It all went smoothly because the band were all so easy to get along with, as well as being completely professional. The biggest problem was that we kept running out of merch! It's amazing what you can achieve when you have a big punk network on your side, and people moved mountains to get it printed and to various cities, although I did still end up with a book full of back orders and was sending out T-shirts for weeks after the tour.

"I think the Bendigo Hotel gig was the ultimate gig, just brilliant in every way – Melbourne was always the highlight of any tour – despite the death metal drum school going on downstairs just as I was trying to get a couple of hours kip before sound-check.

"They'd travelled about 15,000 miles in a week, flying for up to three hours every day, and did six gigs in six days before heading on to New Zealand; it was a pretty punishing schedule but that was how Dick wanted to do it, with no days off. Phil was also busy learning The Knowledge to be a London cabbie [yes, I promised more on this, and it's coming – be patient!]. We had a lot of fun and not a single tanty [i.e. tantrum] or missed lobby call. I recall 'The Ying Tong Song' being sung in various maxi-taxis between airports, hotels and venues.

"One high was in New Zealand, where I could relax as I went to Auckland as Dick's guest and Tim was running the shows. After the final gig in Auckland, we had a day trip with some old friends of the band that had moved there many years before, and I remember one of those amazing 'once in a lifetime' moments, of being on the other side of the world, looking out to sea at the island where Jaz Coleman has a house, hearing those lovely soft accents from home and knowing we had just done a really successful tour and made a lot of people very happy. We captured a time where there had been quite a punk revival, ex-pat old punks, some legendary original Australian punks and, of course, the many that had followed in our footsteps.

"I did some more tours after that, including The Members and Ruts DC; I also did some work for another promoter doing the Perth gigs on international tours, and was lucky enough to get to work with Killing Joke, who are one of my favourite bands of all

ANOTHER WINTER OF DISCONTENT
2013

CONFLICT · ANTI PASTI · THE MOB ·
SUBHUMANS · BROKEN BONES · NECK ·
BLYTH POWER · DRONGOS FOR EUROPE ·
THE CRAVATS · DISORDER · LOST CHERREES ·
THE ENEMY · THE SYSTEM ·
DIRT BOX DISCO ·
EASTFIELD · A HEADS ·
DECADENT FEW · DEFCON ZERO ·
SLUT MACHINE · LOUISE DISTRAS ·
TED DIBIASE & THE MILLION $ PUNK BAND ·
PAUL CARTER · ANDY T · BLATOIDEA · DOGSHITE ·
VIOLATION 69

£12 £15

TICKETS AVAILABLE FROM
HTTP://AWOEVENTS.CO.UK/TICKETS/ · WEGOTTICKETS.COM · ALLADES RECORDS, CAMDEN
FEBRUARY 28TH MUSIC ROOMS · MARCH 1ST THE DOME · MARCH 2ND MUSIC ROOMS · MARCH 3RD MUSIC ROOMS
BOSTON ARMS · 178 JUNCTION ROAD, KENTISH TOWN, LONDON N19 5QQ. TUFNELL PARK TUBE · BUS:134,490,C11.

THURSDAY, MAY 23RD · DOORS @ 8:00

SUBHUMANS
$13/$15   All Ages

TOTAL CHAOS

WITH OUT FOR WAR & PRISCILLA FORD

The ALLEY   906 VICTORIAN AVE, SPARKS NV
TheAlleySparks.com · 775/358.8891

CHARTA 77
SVERIGE
SUBHUMANS
UK

30. APRIL.

KVELDENS DJ-ER: SÆRHEIM OG BØREK AKA SISTEBØSSEN

VERKSTEDHALLEN
BILLETTPRIS: 200,- (BILLETTSERVICE) / PRIS I DØRA: 220 / DØRENE ÅPNER 21.00

15th ANNUAL
PUNK ROCK BOWLING & MUSIC FESTIVAL

MAY 24-27, 2013
DOWNTOWN LAS VEGAS

FEATURING:

DEVO   FLAG   BAD RELIGION
Original members Keith Morris, Chuck Dukowski,
and Bill Stevenson with Stephen Egerton
performing the music of Black Flag

THE DAMNED   TURBONEGRO   D.R.I
THE WEIRDOS   SUBHUMANS   LAGWAGON
BOUNCING SOULS   THE CASUALTIES
SWINGIN' UTTERS   U.S. BOMBS   LOWER CLASS BRATS
FUNERAL DRESS   CHANNEL 3   POUR HABIT
SEAN AND ZANDER   ·   RETOX
REVILERS   ·   TARTAR CONTROL   ·   PISS AND BLOOD
MOLOTOV COMPROMISE   ·   THE DIRTY PANTIES
SURROUNDED BY THIEVES   ·   AND MANY MORE!

WELCOME TO FABULOUS LAS VEGAS NEVADA

ALL AGES

TICKETS ON SALE
1/29 @ 10AM (PT)

PUNKROCKBOWLING

TICKETS · BOWLING REGISTRATION · HOTEL DEALS · POKER SIGN UP · AND FULL DETAILS AVAILABLE HERE

SUB HUM ANS

uk anarcho punk at it's finest

surgery without research

local punks

thursday 12th september

the three tuns
canterbury

FREE
ENTRY

SUB HUM ANS

LEGENDÁRNÍ ANARCHOPUNK z UK

KUTYA
HA-RAP
CRUST PUNK
VALAŠSKO

11.6.14.
STŘEDA
19:00

KLUB 007 STRAHOV

SUB HUM ANS

DARK THOUGHTS
ACHE

OCTOBER 17TH AT THE ACHERON
$15   8PM DOORS

FIFTHWHEEL PRESENTS

SUB HUM ANS

THE FREEZE

THE LINECUTTERS

Sunday, November 1st, 2015 at 7:00pm

NILE THEATER

DICK, WITH BUS STATION LOONIES,
PLYMOUTH VOODOO LOUNGE, 2011

PHIL, REBELLION, BLACKPOOL,
2011 BY ERIKA RANSOM

BRUCE, BORDERLINE, LONDON,
18-12-11 BY JOHN MARSHALL

DICK WITH CHRIS CONVERSE
FROM PUNKFEST IN BRISBANE,
13/9/2012 BY MIN STOKES

AIRPORT DIARY ENTRIES,
AUSTRALIA, 14/9/2012 BY
MIN STOKES

THE BAND WITH MIN STOKES,
17/9/2012

AT THE FORESTERS
AND SQUATTERS ARMS,
ADELAIDE, WITH MARK
HAYES FROM PERDITION,
16/9/2012 BY MIN STOKES

time, as well as three local gigs I did for The Selecter. The last one I did was the Perth gig for GBH's most recent Australian tour. I have met so many brilliant people, and reconnected with people I'd known from years before; it was a fun time, but I do believe in quitting while I am ahead, so I went back to just running my business and being a punter. Our band [SSA] broke up around the same time, so I decided to take life a bit easier as I was past fifty by that stage. I still love to go to gigs though, and try to get to Rebellion when I can."

"Singapore was a small 'normal' gig, with just a small stage for the drums and a vocal PA," adds **Dick**, of the two gigs they picked up on the way home from New Zealand. "It was us and Seven Crowns, and it was Liam from Seven Crowns' thirty-sixth birthday. John from Seven Crowns always had high praise for gigs in Indonesia, and I'm sure he told us they once had their band photo or something beamed onto the side of a skyscraper over there... something enormous like that anyway. So we thought there were going to be hundreds of people there, but it was not to be. It was a fairly quiet gig really, but never mind.

"We were being driven around in this small car. And we were being treated like royalty really. We went to this pizza place, and we were the only ones in there, because no one could afford to eat pizza basically. It felt like we were spending a month's wages on a meal.

"We then played in this park in Bandung [on Java], in the middle of the city. There was an art exhibition, and a bar; it was all outdoors. The cops had already tried to close it down, and the organisers somehow talked the cops into letting it go ahead. The stage was made out of planks and scaffold that they had put together, and if I jumped up and down, Bruce's mic would wobble and hit him in the face. It was all quite precarious, but everyone was so enthusiastic. We were a rare unexpected appearance. People were taking photographs of us endlessly, even just changing strings or writing the set out.

"But there was so much poverty. We were stuck in traffic after being picked up at the airport, going 1 mph or something, and a regular stream of people went by, banging on our window, playing their musical instruments and holding out their hats. People are very short of money over there. And all these young punks sorted out this outdoor gig, built the stage and everything... a phenomenal amount of effort had gone into it, and it was borderline whether they were going to get arrested for doing it, but they did it anyway. It was impressive, and I'm very glad we did that."

The year 2012 concluded with nine English gigs in December, plus a date for the Warzone collective in Belfast and a well-attended show at the Button Factory in Dublin with Paranoid Visions.

The next run of dates, around the UK again, was March 2013, the biggest being the Boston Arms in London, supporting Anti-Pasti, and BOB Fest in Bath, at the Komedia, with Slime from Germany and The Mob. These gigs were significant as they marked the live debut of Jay Whyte, who was depping on bass whilst Phil swotted for his Knowledge exam – as mentioned previously by Min, he had moved back to the UK and was training to be a London cabbie. The Knowledge is a stiff test all cabbies must pass, that involves them learning over 300 routes (and 25,000 streets!) around London, so Phil had to give it the respect it deserves. Interestingly enough, Jay was at the infamous Chippenham gig that directly contributed to the band splitting up in '85, and here he was helping keep them going nearly thirty years later.

"Jay's an old mate from Bath," explains **Phil**. "I'm a black cab driver in London, which is a perfect job for someone in a band, because I just rent a cab when I'm available, then drop it off when I go on tour. I've got no boss… 'no gods, no managers', haha! But I had to do The Knowledge first, which involves an insane amount of testing and exams, and once you start you can't really stop, because you have tests every few weeks, and you have to revise like fuck every day. I ended up doing like sixteen one-to-one examinations to get my cab badge, and I basically had to take a year out to get through that process, which is when Jay stood in. It was pretty gruelling, a real slog for a few years, but once you've got the badge, you've got it for life.

"I went to see them one night in St Albans, which was great – Jay's a real character – and I even got to see him do 'From the Cradle to the Grave'. I suggested him, because I knew he'd be able to work out all the bass lines, and he did a great job. But it was pretty bizarre being in the crowd watching someone else play the songs…"

"When Phil told us he had to take off time from the band for a couple of years, so he could get his Hackney Carriage Licence, it was like, 'Oh shit, what do we do now?'" recalls **Trotsky**. "Putting the band on ice was not really an option, so we had to find a stand-in, and fast. Luckily Jay was available and totally up for the job. He was an old mate and had toured a lot with Chaos UK, so he knew how it all worked, plus he's a really good bass player and a good chap t'boot! Bruce met up with him a few times in Bath, to go through the songs before we all had our first rehearsal together, which went really well; he had most of the songs sorted, and he'd been listening to them and seeing us live many times over the years too. It was a bit strange at first, to play live with a different bass player; you get so used to the way the other half of the rhythm section plays that sometimes you can just predict what the other will play next. But Jay stuck faithfully to Phil's bass lines, and didn't try to put his own mark on them or anything. He was a quieter player than Phil, which was probably the most notable difference – apart from the dreadlocks of course, haha!"

"I was born in 1969, and grew up in Calne, a small rural market town in Wiltshire, not far from Melksham," begins **Jay**. "How I got into punk is really easy to answer… the alternative was disco, new romantic or hair rock! So it was really, really easy to get into punk, haha! I had an older brother and sister, and my sister bought a few Ramones LPs when I was seven or eight years old, and my brother had a few Cockney Rejects and UK Subs records. So I was listening to them when I was really young.

"I went to school in Swindon for a while, and I met a kid who had a Crass patch on his bag. I used to see that patch every morning on the way to school, and every afternoon on the way home, and I wondered what it was – so I asked him one day, and he said, 'I could tell you… but it's better that I show you! Meet me here after school…' And we went to his house, where he played me 'Feeding of the 5000' – that was 1979, and you know, the rest is history.

"And then Lee [one of the vocalists in The Lumps of Merde, who supported that fateful night in Chippenham] got me into Discharge and Chaos UK a few years later, all the noisy bands. I can't remember if it was 1979 or 1980, but the first ever gig I went to

Dino and Luigi presents:
Thursday, October 22nd 2015
SUB HUM ANS
TØRSÖ
Korrosive
PAY NO MORE THAN 15$...

Thee Parkside
(1600 17th Street)
San Francisco CA
All Ages / Bar with ID
Enjoy Punk 8:30 PM

SUB HUM ANS
#POTATO PIRATES blood letters

MONDAY
NOV 2ND
2015

SAT 15TH DECEMBER AT THE GROSVENOR, STOCKWELL
SUB HUM ANS

The Eccentrics
HAGAR·THE·WOMB
+
ANTIDOTUM
alice rock
17 SIDNEY RD SW9 0TP DOORS 6PM DAMAGE 8 QUID

LIVE AT THE FROG AND FIDDLE CHELTENHAM
SUB HUM ANS
IDESTROY
THIS SYSTEM KILLS
FRIDAY 19TH FEBUARY - £10 OTD

WE ARE 138

AIRPORT CHECK-IN, AUSTRALIAN TOUR BY MIN STOKES

17-9-12, END OF AUSTRALIAN TOUR PISS UP, WITH
MIN STOKES AND MEMBERS OF VICIOUS CIRCLE - HEATH
WILLIAMS, ADAM SHIRLEY AND PAUL LINDSAY

17-9-12, NORTHCOTE SOCIAL CLUB, WITH AUSTRALIAN TOUR
ROADIE TOM BROWNRIGG BY MIN STOKES

INDONESIA, SEPTEMBER 2012 BY PHIL

MILE HIGH SUBS, AUSTRALIA BY MIN STOKES

JAY IN CHAOS U.K.

JAY IN THE WAZZOCKS

was at Gold Diggers in Chippenham; I was about ten years old, and it was Bad Manners and The Adicts. And it was full of skinheads because of Bad Manners. I went to see Crass in 1983, when I was fourteen; I went straight there from school in my school uniform, and I didn't tell my mum I was going, because she wouldn't have let me!

"I was never really into sitting downstairs and watching the telly with the family when I was a kid, so I had this homemade guitar with three strings on it, and I'd sit upstairs on my own playing that. I didn't want to sit and watch bloody 'Coronation Street' every night, did I? I picked it up pretty quick… I've got worse over the years – I used to be better then, than I am now.

"The first band I was in was The Fried Eggs, with Lee – that was pre–Lumps of Merde. I also played in Spite and Dumbstruck. I played guitar in a stoner rock band called The Rollbars. Then I was in a tribute to The Wurzels, called Adie White & The Wazzocks… within two months, we were packing places out; we were a Bristol phenomenon. We played this pub in Bristol, and there was 200 people outside who couldn't get in. I was in Cydernide too, and I was the longest-serving bassist in Chaos UK. Then I did FUK, which started when Chaos UK finished, because we all sort of left at the same time, but they couldn't keep bass players, so they asked me – and I did it, so I could go to Japan again."

When asked how he ended up in Subhumans, **Jay** replies: "We've known them for years. When I first moved to Bath, within six months of living here, I moved into a squat. I was living with a load of junkies, and eventually I'd been there the longest, so I threw 'em all out and got all my punk mates in. This legendary house in Pulteney Road in Bath, where I lived for four or five years or so, became quite a party house. So that was where we got to really know Dick. The Subhumans were the big local band when we were young – the words were so easy to pick up, it was really easy to sing along to. Their songs are all really catchy, but they're bass-driven… a lot of the melodies come from the bass. Which is quite unusual."

Lee: "But when we first saw the Subhumans, it was at the Court Mills in Trowbridge in 1984, and after the gig, they invited us to a party. Jay asked Trotsky for his drum sticks, because he was into drumming as well at the time – he gave them to him, but Jay left them at the party, haha!"

"I looked like I was nine when I was sixteen," laughs **Jay**. "I was always the youngest-looking kid at any gig we went to. Punk rock gigs were so scary back then. It's so easy for youngsters now, because there's not really any trouble at punk gigs these days, but that wasn't always the case. There was always fucking fighting and god knows what, and just 'cos we were kids, we weren't immune. You'd have full-grown twenty-five-year-old punk rockers having a right go at fourteen-year-old kids."

Lee: "We were queueing up to get into that Court Mills gig, and some punk bloke told me and Jay to get to the back of the queue! The gig was nearly sold out, and the queue was around the corner, so he thought he wasn't going to get in. We were scared of him, obviously, and we were about to fuck off, when a load of other punks came over and told *him* to fuck off, and pick on someone his own size."

"When Dick gave me the call," continues **Jay**, "I'd been on a couple of European tours with Citizen Fish before, selling merch, and they'd seen me play with FUK, who had played with Subhumans a couple of years earlier. I also did a four-track recording where I played every instrument, which Dick had really liked and wanted a copy of. So when he phoned me and said he needed a favour, I just assumed he was going to ask me to do the merch for them. When he said, 'How would you like to play the bass?', I was kind of in shock for a while. It was amazing, I was really honoured.

"My first gig was in Trowbridge [at The White Swan, on March 1st, 2013]. Whenever they do a UK tour, they always do the first gig in Trowbridge, because that's where they started. And it's like a practice without having to pay for a practice space, haha! And the second one was in Bath, the night after. I don't want to namedrop, but an old friend of ours, Bill Price, came to that first gig – he's the one that produced 'Never Mind the Bollocks' and the first Clash LP and stuff. I did tell the rest of the band that, but I don't think they cared.

"I wasn't stressed though. I'd had a few hours practice the two nights before – because I'd had to learn about eighty songs, it would take me about five hours to play along to them all, so I had two practises that were two and a half hours each! – and I nailed them all. Without any mistakes. So I knew I was ready.

"When I first joined, Bruce used to come over once a week and show me the songs. I had about three months to learn the songs before I did anything. I'd play him what I'd worked out so far, and you think you're playing it where you're hearing it, but he'd show me where it should be played. Which was usually quite different, with a few more notes than you thought there were, so it was more difficult. Bruce was the brains behind most of the music... the main song-writer, you know what I mean? Quite a genius really.

"I did feel at the time, when they asked me, that I might not be able to do it; I thought it might be a bit advanced for me. But once Bruce had pointed me in the right direction where I was going wrong on a few things, I didn't seem to have any problems. It's all well and good when you're practising, but when you're three weeks into a tour and hungover all to fuck, it's a bit different. And I suffer from insomnia too, so some of the gigs I think of that I didn't enjoy – like Boomtown – were where I didn't sleep a wink the night before. And I would be falling asleep on the stage and making mistakes, so I didn't enjoy that.

"And sometimes when you think you *can* sleep, you're sharing a room with some of your bandmates who are snoring, and if they fall asleep before you, you're in trouble. I might be talking about Trotsky... but I'm not confirming that, haha!

"Cheltenham was another bad gig for me too [November 21st, 2014]. If Phil could do a gig, he would, so if they played London, Phil would do it because he was there. And we'd done a gig in Norwich, where we finished off a couple of bottles of Jack Daniels between us, and after that was Brighton, which Phil was doing, and London, which Phil was doing, so I drank myself half to death those two nights. And then Cheltenham was the next day, and I was almost passing out; I think I had alcohol poisoning for that gig. And they decided to play 'Human Error' for the first time... I'd never played it before. And I thought, 'Oh shit, here we go!' I think I was playing different songs to them anyway!

"But they're professionals at what they do, and I didn't want to make *any* mistakes. I remember the first time Trotsky got really drunk, and was fucking up left, right and centre – that made me feel a whole lot better, haha!

LIVE WITH JAY

JAY, BRUCE, TROTSKY, DICK

KICKER SUPPORTING SUBHUMANS AT THE GROSVENOR,
LONDON, 27/3/2013 BY JOHN MARSHALL

PHIL TUNING HIS BASS,
AT THE GROSVENOR, LONDON, 27/3/2013
BY JOHN MARSHALL

DRIVING ACROSS NEVADA, 2013 BY SHANNON

PUNK ROCK BOWLING, LAS VEGAS, MAY 2013 BY LINDSAY BEAUMONT

OAKLAND 2013 BY CHIARA CORSARO

SUB HUM ANS

A-1

D-1 C-O

PLUS SUPPORT
19:00 £6 ADV

MONDAY 29TH FEB 2016
THE OWL SANCTUARY

ANARCHO-PUNK LEGENDS FROM THE UK RETURN!

SUB HUM ANS

WITH PEARS AND THE S/CKS
MON JUNE 6 6:30 PM ALL AGES, 21 TO DRINK $15
CATTIVO 146 44TH ST LAWRENCEVILLE
TIX: SOUND CAT, CALIBAN, DAVE'S, AND ONLINE AT
http://www.cattivopgh.com/event/1109587-subhumans-pittsburgh/

"'From the Cradle to the Grave' was obviously really difficult to learn. And I always thought 'Human Error' and 'When the Bomb Drops' were tricky to play. A lot of that is because it's quite repetitive, and then there's a little bit that you have to remember, and if you can't hear what Dick's saying, you can miss your cues. Strangely, the more difficult ones for me to get together to play really well were ones that Grant did… the older stuff. All the singles are fun to play, and the stuff on 'Cradle…' and 'Worlds Apart' was fun too, but a few of the older songs, like 'Subvert', have a few tricky bits, like the middle section where it gets all busy. And if you weren't on it, or you got a bit drunk…

"And drunkenness came into it in Europe especially, because sometimes you don't go on until two in the morning, and the amount of free beer they give you… well, I'm my own worst enemy – I'll drink until either there's nothing left or I fall over. And I think I was a bad influence on them, 'cos they were getting a lot drunker when I was in the band.

"Not long after I stepped in, we did a gig in St Albans, and Phil was there… he's the only current member of Subhumans that's ever *seen* them live. But he said to me afterwards, 'It's in safe hands!' Which was nice to hear. And we played 'From the Cradle to the Grave' that night too. But I know that song so well anyway… I remember we were coming back from a gig in Chippenham when we were younger – there were no late buses then, so we had to walk from Chippenham back to Calne, along the old railway track – and we sang that all the way home.

"But they never played the same set twice. They usually start with 'All Gone Dead' and finish up with 'Religious Wars', but always used to change it up in between. Which I loved. There's about fifteen songs that are favourites and they have to play at least five of those at every gig, but they rotate them, and make sure every album is represented. And everything was so much faster live than on record – so I learnt everything playing along to the records at home, but then it was twice as fast live. And with the later records, because Dick can't hit the higher notes anymore, they're tuned down, so I'd have to stop and retune my bass for the newer songs. No one in the audience really notices, but it's all dropped down a semi-tone."

Jay was soon heading for Scandinavia for three Norwegian gigs and two Swedish gigs, all with Charta 77, and a week later they did a one-off in Dublin, at The Button Factory, supporting Conflict. At the end of May, there was a five-date US tour that started in Sparks, Nevada, and ended at Punk Rock Bowling in Las Vegas, whilst June saw them back in Canada, for just one gig, the Amnesia Rock Fest in Montebello – but they squeezed in two NYC gigs the same weekend as well!

In early August, Subhumans played the Kanalrock festival in Helden, Norway, closely followed by Rebellion in Blackpool – by which time, Culture Shock had reformed, and all three of Dick's bands appeared over the course of the weekend.

"That's happened at most Rebellions for the last ten years," **Dick** points out. "Preferably playing on different days, but there's been a couple of occasions where two of them have played on the same day, which is a bit of a stretch on the energy."

Is it safe to say that Subhumans go down the best of the three?

"That's just inescapable fact," reckons **Dick**. "Whatever you do first, or whichever is the fastest, usually goes down best. Longevity has a lot to play in the 'pull factor', or whatever you call it. There is some crossover between the fans of the different bands… more than there used to be anyway. I don't know how much crossover there was between Subhumans and Culture Shock, because CS was so different from the Subhumans, and then a lot of people got attracted to Citizen Fish because the words 'ex-Subhumans' was all over the first 100 gigs' worth of posters, I guess. And quite a subsection of those people who turned up expecting to see something that sounded like the Subhumans, or a version of it, were disappointed. Quite a lot of people just don't like ska music, or didn't want it in their punk rock… they felt quite offended by it. I'm not sure how big that portion of people was, but Citizen Fish have never done the same, er, numbers, shall we say, as Subhumans.

"Whereas the first three years of Culture Shock was in a whole different time zone; it was the festival season, so to speak. A lot of festivals were going from the free gatherings that had existed so well up until the mid-Eighties when they got clamped down on by Thatcher and so on, and the rave scene was starting up at the same time, and we were doing gigs either side of that 'bridge' that was going on in the festival scene. We did a lot of that, and we were quite known for doing a lot of that.

"As to which band pulls the most, thirty years on at Rebellion, it's still the Subhumans… we can pack out the Empress Ballroom, which is about 3000 people, so I've heard. But Culture Shock or Citizen Fish can still pull 1000 or 1500, depending upon which venue we're in inside the Winter Gardens. I mean, Citizen Fish played at three o'clock in the afternoon on the Sunday once, and it was still full up."

Do you have to get yourself in a different head space for each band?

Dick: "Not really. It's more a case of, 'Do I remember all the songs in this set-list?' And if I don't, get the lyrics out, because I take all the lyrics with me to every gig, just in case someone pipes up, 'Oh, we're going to play this one tonight…' Because I got caught out like that when Citizen Fish were playing Berkeley, California, and Phil got a request to play 'Mind Bomb', a song we hadn't played for literally ages. I didn't have any lyrics on me, but Phil insisted… 'It'll be alright, they'll come back to you!' But I had my doubts. And, of course, it didn't come back to me. I had the first four lines in my head, but I had to make up the rest. It was… tricky. So I always take the lyrics now. And I revise the lyrics before gigs, because there's always a degree of nervousness about forgetting them. I can't let myself relax to the point of, 'You know these songs back to front, don't worry about singing them…' I have to at least look through the newer songs, or the ones we haven't played for ages, just to make sure, and subsequently it tends to go right.

"There's a sort of vocal muscle memory, because I can reach one second before the start of a verse, and I'm not quite sure what it is, and I haven't got time to think about it, but the words force their way through out of habit. Which is a bit of a lifesaver sometimes. The easiest ones to remember are where you've basically got a long sentence, that rhymes, with commas in it, and that's your verse, just this sentence with commas in it where one thing follows another naturally… much more difficult is where you've got four separate things in each verse that could interchange in that verse, or with any other verse in the song – that's tricky. It seems a daunting thing, but it's all about repetition."

"Seeing them at Rebellion was a real eye-opener for me," adds **Kev**. "I'd been living in London for years, and was used to seeing them in a pub in Camden or whatever, but I was

SUBHUMANS

ADOLESCENTS   DRUNKEN RAMPAGE   THE KRAYS

NORTHSIDE FESTIVAL

NEW YORK, 2013

MOMENTS BEFORE 'SUSAN',
THE OBSERVATORY, SANTA ANA,
MAY 2013 BY AMY ELKINS

DICK AND GREG DALY,
FUNFUNFUNFEST, 9/11/2013
BY KAROLINE COLLINS

ASYLUM RECORDS, TEMPE, ARIZONA,
NOVEMBER 2013 BY SCOTT ROBENALT

WILTSHIRE TIMES, DECEMBER 2013 BY GLENN PHILLIPS

THE GARAGE, LONDON, 8/12/13 BY JOHN MARSHALL

DICK, U.S. BOUND BY PHIL

LATVIA, JULY 2015
COURTESY OF JAY

JAY - COURTESY
OF JOCK MCCURDY

SLO BREW, SAN LUIS OBISPO, OCT 2015, WITH SHANNON
SAINT RYAN SEATED CENTRE BY AMY ELKINS

stood side of stage in the Empress Ballroom, and it was only seven o'clock or something, and the place was full. Absolutely packed. And the energy coming off the crowd, the energy coming off the stage, and the professionalism of the band playing on such a big stage... it took my breath away. They were like a machine, it was fantastic."

A long weekend in Europe in September, built around the Ratrock festival in Haralbeke, Belgium, was followed by yet more US dates undertaken in November, culminating at the Funfunfun Fest in Austin.

Karoline: "I did fly to Austin to see them play Funfunfun Fest, and they were playing before Ice T's band, Body Count. Looking over to side of stage and seeing Ice T watching Subhumans was definitely a 'Whoah!' moment, seeing a pop culture icon celebrity, or whatever, watching 'my' band... somewhere I have a shitty photo of Dick Lucas and Greg Daly under the Body Count banner, haha! Dick has often referred to me as the 'soul stealer' due to the number of pictures I take... 'Oh, stealing souls again, are you?'"

Nine UK dates in December rounded out 2013, the biggest supporting Conflict at the Camden Underworld, whilst the first gig of 2014 was the Grauzone Fest at the Milky Way, Amsterdam, on January 31st, with Peter Hook and Lydia Lunch, amongst others. Seven UK dates in early May were followed by nine European gigs in June, including the Melrock festival in Hotton, Belgium, before July saw two Canadian gigs followed by eight US gigs, with Mischief Brew in support.

"Mischief Brew was Erik [Petersen] from Philadelphia's band," elaborates **Dick**. "That was another sad loss to the punk world [Erik died in 2016]. They played folky punk, which is a genre I sort of half like, and half don't. But they did it very well, and they were very good people, so were very much liked. The fact that Eric is no longer with us is a tragic loss to the world of radical, DIY, independent free-thinking. He used to do solo stuff as well – just guitar and vocals – and he did a cover of 'Civilisation Street' at one point. But we did quite a few gigs with them, and they were a lovely bunch, and were refreshingly reminiscent of that Inner Terrestrials vibe."

August brought another long weekend in Blackpool, and then there was the Three Chords festival in Penzance with TV Smith and UK Subs later that month. Ten UK dates in November rounded off the year (including the drunken Cheltenham appearance Jay mentioned earlier), the largest at T-Chances in London with Grand Collapse as main support, although the Subhumans have never shied away from smaller gigs alongside some larger dates, philosophical in their approach about variable crowd sizes.

"Some small gigs are great, because they are perversely small," reasons **Dick**. "We did a gig in El Paso, on the Mexican border, and there was like twenty people there... actually that might have been Citizen Fish, come to think of it, not Subhumans, but the point is, there were so few people in quite a large space, it was like we were having a private party. So, 'The first song is for *you*... the next one is for you, hope you're well!' You just bring it down to the level it ends up at, and if there's not many there, you just have a laugh. You've got to play, otherwise the whole day has been wasted, so you make the most of it. Citizen Fish once played a basement in Kalamazoo to five people.

"If you haven't got many people, but it all sounds okay, you can have a good time playing; if you've not got many people, and the PA is shit, and there's loads of feedback, or other negative stuff going on, it's a bit of a downer. But generally, you take the good with the bad, which is why the good stuff seems so good. And you don't reflect too much on the bad gigs; you just move onto the next one… and more or less try to forget about them really."

The year 2015 started with two dates each in Germany and Denmark, closely followed by the Another Winter of Discontent festival in London, that was headlined by MDC. Ten European dates in May reached a suitably rowdy climax at the Kopi in Berlin, where the band played a street party to 700 revellers, and then the Pod Parou festival in Brno, Czech Republic, and the Labadaba festival in Riva, Latvia, both at the end of July, were closely followed by Rebellion and Boomtown.

Mid-October 2015 saw them embarking upon a three-week US tour, that included their first appearance in Mexico, with the last gig of that tour, and the last gig of the year, being at Funfunfun Fest in Austin again, this time alongside The Dwarves.

"There's so many of the same kind of highlights," admits **Robert**, when trying to zoom in on particularly memorable moments amongst the dizzying number of gigs he has done with them in the States, "Especially if a 'highlight' is sitting at the merch stall and meeting someone who is absolutely beside themselves at the impact this group of people that I consider my friends have had upon their life. They want to know *everything*, and it's not because they're being obsessive; they're just in absolute awe. That's always a highlight, but it's happened hundreds of times."

Karoline: "And to dovetail on that, you'll get the kid that wants to ask a million questions, and I'll see Dick right over there, so I'll say, 'Go talk to him, he's right over there…' And they might say, 'Oh no, I couldn't,' and I'm like, 'No, no, he *will* talk to you!' A lot of them don't, but then some of them do, and I feel a little bit bad because sometimes, once they've got past that initial fear, they won't leave him alone, haha!

"I always knew Dick was very approachable, having worked with Citizen Fish, but it was interesting on those early Citizen Fish tours, because at that time there was no concept that Subhumans were going to be a live, touring band again. So he'd be having people say to him, 'It's not political enough…' or 'Your voice is different…', and you'd see these teenagers trying to wrestle with the concept that the singer of their favourite band was now in a band that wasn't as punk, that wasn't as political – although it *was*, but in a different way. Just watching those teenage brains trying to get to grips with it… 'I wanted you to be like *this*, and you're not like this anymore!' And Dick would explain why, and I wonder if what he said to them resonated as they got older.

"I'm waffling, I know, but punk for me means that these people you might hold on a pedestal are approachable, and you can actually become a part of each other's lives – they're not like some celebrity you can't have access to. These are real people, talking about real things, and yes, we can talk to each other, and build a community – it's possible. A kid talks to someone like Dick and realises that it's possible, that punk is this ever-evolving scene, it's not where you just go to this huge $30 show once a year and pretend you're punk again. Even as we age, there's always these young kids coming through, and we can still all talk to each other."

Jay: "I remember someone asking Dick to sign something at a gig, and he wrote on there, 'I don't agree with this autograph thing, when all I do is write and sing!'"

The next year, 2016, got underway with a ten-date UK tour in February, the biggest of those gigs being Another Winter of Discontent at the Tufnell Park Dome, London, headlined by The Mob, and in early May, they played the Punk 40 festival in Tampere, Finland, with Anti-Pasti, amongst many others – which was Jay's last gig for them…

"I played about 150 gigs with them, over a three-and-a-bit-year period," says **Jay**, "In thirteen or fourteen countries – all across Europe, Scandinavia, Canada a couple of times, America… it seemed like every three or four months we'd go there! I did my first gig early 2013, and the last gig I did was in the summer of 2016. That was in Finland. I have a lot of old friends in Finland, going back over twenty years, and Phil knew that, so he said, 'I think you should do the gig in Finland…' So all my mates could come and see.

"When they first asked me, I honestly thought I wouldn't be able to do it, but I kind of surprised myself," he adds, pondering what he took from the experience of being a stand-in Subhuman. "I'm probably more accomplished than I think I am, haha!

"They're so relaxed, they very rarely argue amongst themselves," he continues, on what sets the band apart from others he's played in. "All the other bands I've been in would end up at each other's throats – we fought all the time in Chaos UK, it was mayhem – but the Subhumans are so chilled out and relaxed. And I think that's because they play so well together, they very rarely do any shit gigs to get pissed off about. You always come offstage at the end of the gig with a buzz. They just get on so well together. I *have* seen them fall out, mind, and it is unpleasant, but it doesn't last very long, and no grudges are held. And usually some booze is involved…"

At the end of May, with Phil all Knowledged up and back on bass full-time, they headed to the States once again for fifteen gigs, that started at Punk Rock Bowling in Las Vegas, with Flag and The Exploited, and finished at Punk Rock Bowling in Asbury Park, with The Descendents and Dag Nasty.

After playing the outside stage of Rebellion in August, they went back to the States in September, for eleven gigs down the West Coast with (Pete The Roadie's band) Kicker and Raukous in support. The second date of that run, in Portland, was the band's thousandth gig. Take a bow, gentlemen.

Eight UK gigs in November finished off the year, the biggest of those being Midlands Calling at the Wulfrun Hall, Wolverhampton, with Sham 69 and GBH, and the Koko in Camden, supporting Neurosis and Discharge.

January 2017 saw the Subhumans back at the 100 Club, with the A-Heads and Lost Cherrees supporting – just like the old days then! Seven dates in Germany and three in Holland followed in February, before a return to the US in April that comprised four dates in Florida with After the Fall, and then five dates in California with Love Songs, the final date of that run being the Oakland leg of BOB Fest.

That summer, Subhumans played the Ultrachaos Fest in Poland and Ieper Fest in Belgium, not to mention Rebellion, Another Winter of Discontent, Boomtown and Undercover in the UK. A ten-date UK tour at the end of September included a slot at North East Calling at Northumberland Uni, which was headlined by the Cockney Rejects, then five gigs in Canada supported by All Torn Up! rounded out the year in late November.

No doubt there was some déjà vu, as 2018 kicked off at the 100 Club again, this time supported by Criminal Mind and Desperate Measures. Soon after, they were main support to GBH at the Vive Le Rock festival in Athens during February, and a nine-date European tour followed in late March, which took in appearances at the Oilsjt Omploft Fest in Aalst and the Black Denim Fest in Rotterdam.

Five UK dates were arranged around an appearance at the Scotland's Calling Fest in Glasgow, which was headlined by the Buzzcocks and Cockney Rejects. In May, the Subhumans played a one-off in France at the Zikenstock festival, supporting Toy Dolls and Angelic Upstarts, before heading out to the USA again, for twelve gigs up the West Coast, starting at Punk Rock Bowling in Las Vegas, with support coming from – at various gigs – Final Conflict, Love Songs and Death Ridge Boys. That was followed immediately by four gigs in western Canada, with the Real Sickies supporting – including the Rossland gig previously mentioned by Dick.

"The Love Songs would readily admit they'd picked the worst band name in the world," smiles **Dick**, of the Oakland band. "If you call a band Love Songs, you immediately think they'll be cheesy and no good! But they were a fantastic band, like Nomeansno on acid… very good instrumentalists, and they would stop and start and mess around with the structure, speed and beat in their songs. They keep it non-flowing and full of surprises, and I like that in a band, where they keep waking you up three times a song…"

Four gigs in Germany and two in the Czech Republic in late June included the Fusion Fest in Lärz, then after Rebellion in August, it was back to the US in September for nine gigs with War on Women. October gigs in Belfast and Dublin with Paranoid Visions rounded off the year.

The first gig of 2019 was at the 100 Club again, for their increasingly traditional New Year bash, supported by Knock Off. The day after was in Bristol, with Warwound as main support – your author was the bassist in the reformed Warwound, and can confirm that the Subhumans were on fine form at a packed Fleece & Firkin, and were as approachable as ever backstage during the evening. Plymouth and Abertillery rounded out a long weekend in the south.

100 CLUB, LONDON, 11/1/2017 BY JOHN MARSHALL

In April 2019, they recorded their sixth studio album, 'Crisis Point', with Steve Evans at Nam Studios in Holt, near Trowbridge, which was released by Bay Area label Pirates Press Records.

"We kept bumping into Damon, who works at Pirates Press, and he'd always said they'd be up for doing a record with us if we ever wanted to do one with them… a live record or something, or if we ever wanted to re-release the old stuff," says **Dick**, of how 'Crisis Point' came to be on Pirates Press, and not Bluurg. "Their prime angle was that they wanted to re-release the stuff that was no longer available. And the situation had indeed arisen, where none of the stuff was available, especially the records, through us or Southern. There was a few CDs left, and that was it. The last pressing Southern did was 2008, or thereabouts, and that was only 500 of each album. Then it went very quiet, and they didn't repress any more… I don't really want to go into detail about what happened, but from my point of view, it was a very sad end to a very good relationship we had enjoyed with Southern all through the Eighties and Nineties. In order to get our own songs back, so Pirates Press could release them again, we had to sign a contract saying Southern owed us nothing whatsoever, in the same way we owed them nothing whatsoever, and that was the end of it – we'd get to own our own songs. And that's factual… you can put that in the book. But there's all sorts of ramifications to that statement – like, don't we own our own songs anyway? Apparently not! In UK law at least, in musical terms, whoever pays for a recording owns it… and Southern paid for it, because we didn't have any money. So, a prime piece of advice for any band is: beg, borrow and steal the money, and pay for your recordings yourself.

"Anyway, I kept seeing Damon at gigs and things, and having a chat, and eventually we thought, 'Why *not* do it through Pirates Press?' Because frankly, without Southern there anymore, Bluurg is basically down to what I can sell through mail order, and what I can do through social media… and I'm not brilliant at social media; I don't like it, and I refuse to be on Facebook. But Pirates Press are really on it. They release records, and all the bands they release are good, and more importantly the people there are very friendly, very together, and they do what they say they're going to do. They do it on time, and they're up for full discussion about what something looks like, when it should come out… all the details when you're releasing something, they're totally open for discussion; they're not dictatorial in any way about what happens, and when.

"So, it was the first non-Bluurg Subhumans record, apart from 'Live in a Dive', but it reached a point where Bluurg was basically me, and I couldn't afford to release records by anyone else, because they would lose money because I don't have the skills or money to do promotion properly, or advertise in the right places enough to get people to buy the record. John [Loder] didn't believe in advertising; he always said it was a waste of money, and word of mouth was the best advertising – and doing gigs. And I think he was quite right really."

16-02 I 2000 I 7/10 euro

DE ONDERBROEK

SUB HUM ANS *PERIOT*

LANDMINE
HEART

original drawing by alexander heir — after party at collectief cafe De Rijstand

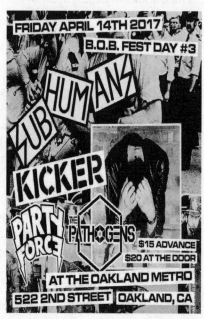

FRIDAY APRIL 14TH 2017

B.O.B. FEST DAY #3

SUB HUM ANS

KICKER

PARTY FORCE

THE PATHOGENS

$15 ADVANCE
$20 AT THE DOOR

AT THE OAKLAND METRO

522 2ND STREET I OAKLAND, CA

RMT MUSIC PRODUCTIONS PRESENT #RMT220

SUB HUM ANS

SPANNER · SKINNERS · HELL DEATH FURY · RAVETANK

7PM – 2AM
THE NEST   BATH
THURSDAY 7 SEPTEMBER
£8 ADV. VIA BRISTOL TICKET SHOP & SKIDDLE / £10 OTD.

RMT

CHIPPENHAM'S ANNUAL

PUNK FEST 2017

SATURDAY 18TH NOVEMBER

CONFLICT

ICONS OF FILTH

ANTI-SYSTEM.

ANDY T

VIRUS

hacksaw

The SetBacks

The Mistakes

Ambition Demolition

Jim Boo &
The Revolution

SUNDAY 19TH NOVEMBER

SUB HUM ANS

DEMOB

OMEGA TRIBE

THE A HEADS

BORROWED TIME

OI OI

50

Screaming Dead

Subject to Nothing

The Useless Rioters

DAY TICKETS £15 IN ADVANCE (£17 OTD)
WEEKEND TICKETS £25
TICKET HOTLINE 07849 491694. AVAILABLE FROM
CONSTI. CLUB OR
PAYPAL: DICKIECONCLUB@AOL.CO.UK

CONSTITUTIONAL CLUB CHIPPENHAM

THE FROG AND FIDDLE, IN ASSOCIATION WITH
MAGNETIC MUSIC PRESENTS

SUB HUM ANS

PLUS SUPPORT FROM

PIZZA TRAMP   AMBITION NO DEMOLITION   the setbacks

SATURDAY 13TH JANUARY 2018
FROG AND FIDDLE, CHELTENHAM

£10 IN ADVANCE // £12 ON THE DOOR // 8PM START // 18+ ONLY
TICKETS AVAILABLE NOW FROM WEGOTTICKETS.COM/FROGANDFIDDLE

REVOPROD & J.M.C. PRESENT ANARCHO-PUNK LEGENDS FROM ENGLAND

SUB HUM ANS
THE STRAPONES

28.3.18
20H

SEDEL
LUZERN

SUB HUM ANS

Anarcho-Punk / UK

Dt.-Punk / Karlsruhe
TERRORFETT

REFUSED
HC-Punk / CH

B.Blaser: 21:00

Sa 31.03.
AU
IN DER AU 14-16
Frankfurt (Rödelheim)

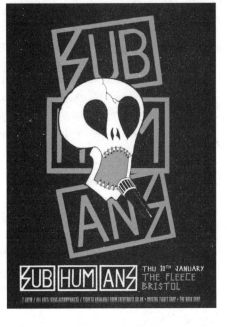

SUB HUM ANS
THU 10TH JANUARY
THE FLEECE
BRISTOL

7.30PM / ALL AGES (KIDS ACCOMPANIED) / TICKETS AVAILABLE FROM EVENTBRITE.CO.UK • BRISTOL TICKET SHOP • THE ROSE SHOP

"In 1994, Citizen Fish were playing in Northern California, and I interviewed Dick and Jasper for my college radio station," elaborates **Damon Bebe**, of Pirates Press Records. "After that interview, we kept in touch and I never missed a chance to catch a gig or say hello whenever they came through the Bay Area. They were always friendly, never pretentious, and exhibited a true DIY spirit.

"Then Subhumans reformed in 1998 and toured the USA, with the first show in Sacramento. The energy that night was through the roof: a band none of us ever thought we'd see, and we might not ever see again… everyone was singing their hearts out, and knew every lyric.

"Like that night, their shows still feel special, with fans from every corner of the scene, and beyond.

"While traveling Europe in 2000, I visited Bath and met up with Dick. He took me to a weekend party in Frome, about thirty minutes away, where Trotsky lived. That was a wild weekend, and gave me a chance to really just hang out with Dick on a casual level. It's funny now, looking back, but that weekend we talked about record labels. He asked for my honest opinion, as a fan, but also as someone who had some insight into what might be the pros and cons of signing to a label, and not just doing it themselves on Bluurg.

"In 2007, after just a few weeks of working at Pirates Press, I answered the phone, and was surprised to hear Dick on the other end. Dick, equally surprised, said, 'Oh hello, Damon, Subhumans are looking to put out a new record, called 'Internal Riot'. Can you help us make it?' Fast forward ten years, and I was at a Subhumans gig in San Francisco. Looking at their minimal merch offerings, I thought, 'That's not right! With multiple albums, tons of imagery for T-shirts and patches, these guys should have loads of merch…' So, I went backstage and that started a two-year-long dialogue with the band, trying to work out how we could use Pirates to help them.

"It turned out, they were not in possession of the music or artwork from any album prior to 'Internal Riot'. So, while I hadn't initially planned on trying to 'sign the band', I wanted to help them continue their legacy and continue to grow. Not only as a friend and a fan, but because they are important; important for the scene, and for the future.

"In early 2019, with all the material ready for a new record, I hopped on a long phone call with Dick, and we worked out a plan. Pirates Press Records would press their new album, 'Crisis Point', and repress 'Internal Riot', and we'd help them obtain all the materials and regain ownership of all their old records.

"Just months later, COVID hit, making it much more difficult to collect all the tapes and artwork to begin re-releasing the old albums. But, as of 2022, their entire catalogue is now available on Pirates Press Records. We have always been about friends and family, using our connections in the industry to help the bands we love and respect achieve their goals. And doing our best to have some fun along the way. I'm honored to call the Subhumans my friends, and proud that I could help this band I love and respect achieve some of their goals. And I've managed to have a blast along the way."

"I started working with Dick about six months after taking a job at Pirates Press Records, and it's been nothing but a joy," adds **Vique Martin**, PPR's label manager. "From figuring out what merch to take on tour, navigating digital distribution, and shipping his records out to him, we're in contact every single week and he's just a pleasure to work with!

"Writing the one sheet for 'Crisis Point' was a pretty surreal thing to do for a band that are such an important part of the history of punk. It was challenging, and stretched my creativity to do them justice, but I was proud of the end result and we sold a *lot* of records, so I think I did my job!

"I helped facilitate getting their back catalogue away from Southern, and have been working constantly with Dick towards getting the music back onto vinyl – the way it should be! We're due to have that come out by the end of 2022, and it's been a lot of fun dealing with the challenges that reissues always bring. I'm just so happy to be part of the fixing of all the wrongs certain record labels have done to such an important band. And to be helping make sure they are financially compensated for their art in a way that they always should have been."

"To be honest, I don't really have that deep an emotional connection with 'Crisis Point'," confesses **Phil**, "At least not as much as earlier records, though I'm still proud of the final result, and that we can still come up with a record that comes up to our own standards. Maybe I'm just a bit jaded after doing it for so long? Although 'Crisis Point' has maybe been better received of the two 'new' records, I think I prefer 'Internal Riot'. Pirates Press have been fantastic, and their upbeat enthusiasm and giving us a deadline to get it finished definitely helped to get our unfocused collective arse in gear! How many years did it take us to get this one written?

"Obviously, after so many years and so many records, it's hard to come up with something fresh, and you don't want it to sound like you're just going through the motions. So, in managerial wank-speak, the mission statement was to capture the vibrancy, urgency and energy of past days and not sound like a bunch of sad washed-up old fucks! And the feedback we got back, from the focus groups – joking, of course! – was that it had an old-school feel with a new take. So, I'm happy with that, and when we play the songs live, they go down great.

"As with 'Internal Riot', we arranged a writing session at Trotsky's place in Germany. He's got an outbuilding with a practice room and no neighbours; it's in beautiful countryside, so it's a lovely place to hang out with his family and dog while we try and grind out some new tunes. Most of the songs were written there, and the rest we got together at Crest Studios in our old spiritual homeland, Trowbridge.

"As always, it was a pleasure working with Steve Evans again. We tracked the songs at Nick Allen's Nam Studios in Holt; the studio is on the end of a terrace of old stone cottages, and Steve L. and I lived there with our friend Oz in the Eighties at the time of

SANTA ANA OBSERVATORY, 12/4/2017 BY ALBERT LICANO

T-CHANCES, LONDON, 22/9/2017 BY JOHN MARSHALL

'Split Vision'... that was Steve's sitar-playing phase, ha! Good times; we'd cycle into Trowbridge for a boozy night at Peewee's bar and amazingly make it home, past the Nestlés chocolate factory buzzing with workers on night shift, without falling in the hedge.

"I was excited to record with my new set-up. On a recent Canadian tour with All Torn Up!, I'd used their bassist Phillipe's amp – a Tech21 VT 500 – with the usual huge Ampeg SVT 'fridge' bass cab. I'd tried out some different mini/lightweight amps before, but they never had the bollocks to compete with Trotsky's Bonham-esque volume! This one sounded fucking ace, and I got a lovely growly tone off it, so I bought one when I got home. It weighs less than a bag of spuds and it fits in my backpack (in a foam case made from an old yoga mat). After a Brooklyn gig, our friend Alec Baillie [RIP], the bass player of Leftover Crack, messaged me in his faux cool young person speak, saying, 'Yo dog, what bass and amp were you using last night? Sorry to fanboy, but it sounded fucking sick!' Then he went out and got one too!

"As per usual, we played live together in a room with some screens placed to minimise spill, but still able to have eye contact. Priority was to get good drum takes, and they came out fantastic; Trotsky was on top form. I think most of the bass takes were kept too.

"Trotsky had done his bit, so he returned to Germany. Then, we went to Steve's own single room production studio next door to Crest in Trowbridge. Dick recorded his vocals there, set up next to Steve at the desk. Bruce set up and redid all his guitars, and we also did the backing vocals. A big part of the 'Subhumans sound' is Bruce's backing harmonies complementing Dick's vocal. I chipped in with a few, and Steve would offer up ideas when we were trying to work out bits: 'Why don't you try a really high one? Think you can manage it? Go on, give it a go!' As well as being a top bloke to record with, Steve's a great guitarist, who wrote, played and produced with Siouxsie in the 2000s, so he'd always have suggestions on tones, overdub parts and production if asked."

"For that last album, we did have to spend some time on one or two songs just before we went in the studio," sighs **Bruce**, a little frustratedly. "But it's finding time to get together to write... and I really hate the pressure of getting together *to write an album*. I prefer the creative process how we always used to do it, where you practise a lot, and you don't practise for any other reason than to write songs... so if you write songs, you write songs, and then you start to bring them into the set – it's a long process. What I don't like is, 'Let's write songs for the album!' That pressure is really horrible, and everyone in the band feels it, so it's really tense. Some people think it's important, so you have a reason to write them in the first place, but with me, I like time to think about these things – pressure can make you go in the wrong direction. If you feel the pressure as you're writing a song, you'll just go with that idea, because the pressure's there – whereas if you had the time, you might have thought that idea was actually crap, and you could have tried something else that was better – but you didn't have time! So it's not very good for creativity. Pressure makes you do stuff, makes you get things done, but no one's breathing down our necks – it's up to us when we want to record an album. It's not like we've got a record company saying, 'You have to do this!'"

"We had to argue a little bit about the end of [closing track] 'Thought Is Free'. It almost had more football chanting... well, not football chanting, but we wanted to get a lot of people singing 'Thought is free!' so we were thinking of getting a crowd to do it. But in the end, they just double-tracked it or something. And then it was going to carry on, echoing off into the distance, but we disagreed about that and went with something easier. But it's good stuff.

"I'd like to get together more... and when me and Phil get together, we come up with lots of ideas, which is nice to do, but we're geographically all over the place. We do practise at Trotsky's in Germany; we've rehearsed there quite a lot actually, to get songs together for albums. And that works okay. Having lots of lyrics is important – that makes the job so much easier. Usually there's more music than lyrics. Unless you do it the other way round – have just one lyric, and loads and loads of music, and then you can choose the best music for that lyric. That's the other way to do it... but you do need a lot of *something*, haha! Otherwise you're forced into using stuff that doesn't really work, and then you have to make it work, and that's how you end up with crap songs.

"We can go off, and think of a song, but when we get back together next, we might have had a completely different idea for it. But I think that's okay... although not everyone might agree on the new idea. But it's all about trying out those ideas. Then we also fundamentally disagree on certain things, and you have to watch out for that – you have to know when to duck out, or scrap the song.

"I usually have a real problem with kind of simple chord sequences, but it does depend upon how it's done. It's funny that, isn't it? I don't have a problem with 'pop' music as such, but I have a problem with music that sounds patronisingly simple, as if it's been designed that way. But sometimes that music can be great as well – and that's why it's confusing. It depends how you hear it, and in what context you're hearing it, I suppose.

"My only criticism of our recent writing is not having enough stuff to work with in the rehearsal room. Because that makes it a difficult situation sometimes. If we all had loads of material, we'd have plenty to work with and choose from. I'm a firm believer in having a lot of stuff. You can go in the rehearsal room and you've got a choice.

"Whenever I had a riff idea, I always used to record it onto a cassette in the old days, but nowadays I write them down. Anyway, I've got stacks of ideas in a file, just fragments of songs, and often, when we go to rehearse, I'll say, 'Oh, I like this...', and Phil might add a part or something. I don't usually add the extra bits, but it usually turns into something from there. It's a kick-start and we all decide what happens next, y'know? You've got to have something going on. I've usually got drum ideas to go with the riff, and sometimes I've got a bass idea, but no guitar riff... so it's a real mixture.

"We did try sending riffs to each other for 'Crisis Point', and Phil did come round here the one day so we could have a play-through, and I always enjoy it when we do that. I've had some sessions with Trotsky before recording, and even gone and done some playing with Dick, but that didn't seem to achieve much – I think singers need to hear the drums as well, to be inspired.

LOS ANGELES BY ALBERT LICANO

LOS ANGELES BY ALBERT LICANO

"The thing is, with being in a room altogether, when you start adding bits in, you can all talk about them, and you change it instantly, so it doesn't become just one person's vision. Sometimes these things need steering in the right direction if they're inappropriate for the band – and sometimes they're good because they *are* inappropriate!

"Or there might only be one person who's fired up for writing that day, and no one else is saying much, and that's alright too, because it introduces a bit of randomness into it. For example, 'Punk Machine' started with that bass line, which I basically wrote, but there was nothing else, no chorus or anything, and that only came when we were writing it together. So, that's an example of it all working well."

"'Crisis Point' was very undeliberated," **Dick**, er, deliberates. "We invented the songs, and most of them didn't have any time to evolve and grow by playing them live over and over again. But it's got a rawness to it as a result, which works really well.

"We recorded it with Steve Evans in Holt again, but he'd moved to Trowbridge by the time we mixed; he did both our last two albums, and also helped us with the vocals on 'Live in a Dive'.

"Most of the songs on 'Crisis Point' had not been played live at all. A lot of them were hammered out at Trotsky's place a month or so before we went into the studio. When we were on tour in Germany, we stopped there for five days between the weekend gigs, and practised at Trotsky's place, and the weekend gigs paid for the flights to do that.

"And then we came back and did a UK tour, and there were gaps during that we used to go into the studio, to practise and record. And then after that tour, we recorded some more as well. So, it was a bit of a patchwork of various appointments to practise and record quite quickly. 'Thought Is Free' was the oldest song on there, and that had been in existence for about three years before we recorded it. Although we hadn't played it very much, and we more or less reinvented it when we put it on the record.

"I thought it was a bit too rock," he adds, of the epic end-section of that song, which plays out the album. "And there were going to be some additional vocal harmonies at the end, where Phil and Bruce were going to do all these extra vocal bits, and it was like something Queen or Genesis would have done, so I was like, 'No!' I had to put my foot down, and say, 'They're my lyrics, please don't do that…' – with the emphasis being on, 'Don't do that!' Sometimes you have to pull a bit of weight, if you've got any. Because those occasions do pop up – I can plead with someone, 'Don't play that!' but it's their guitar, they do the music, and I can ask them not to play it all I want, it won't make any difference… but with lyrics, it's a different thing.

"Anyway, that would have made it even more rocky than it is. And we've played that song to crowds who've never heard it, and that ending has got surprisingly jaunty reactions – people jumping around and punching the air – so you just never can tell. It's completely different to the rest of the song… it had to be really, because the speed of the verses before it had used up its energy, and it had to totally go somewhere else."

More UK dates were also undertaken in April, the biggest being at the Manchester Punk Festival with Sonic Boom 6, and the last of that run being at the Bath edition of BOB Fest, with the brilliantly named Jewdriver, the A-Heads and Migraines, amongst others, at Bath Football Club, literally a stone's throw away from Dick's house – he could walk home after a gig for once!

In early May, they flew to Mexico (apologies for stating the bleedin' obvious, dear reader – how else would they get there?) for the Internacional Punkytud Festival, and a smaller gig in Mexico City with Cat Skull. Once back in the UK, they mixed 'Crisis Point' in mid-May.

"When it came to the mixing, we'd all headed back to home life and felt confident enough to leave it to Steve," reveals **Phil**. "He'd mix a few songs, then send them to us by Dropbox, and we'd offer feedback 'til we were happy with them. I was working the black cab in London and would get a ping from Steve, pull over and stick me headphones on, then send off my thoughts. It was a bit of a tortuous process, but we got there in the end, and were happy with the results.

"As usual, we were pulling our hair out over the cover art, probably the least enjoyable bit of putting out a record, with ideas flying about while we were on tour and staying at Carmel and Leon's in Yorkshire – HQ to our elite merchandising team. I came up with an idea which looked like a bad Simpsons cartoon, and that was thankfully given the thumbs down. Then our long-time artist friend Ron Conductor came up with the goods, and he has gone on to do covers for RDF and Culture Shock. The Pirates Press art team suggested the silvery monochrome finish which gives it a good gloomy look – a bit of a modern take on Kev's grey 'From the Cradle to the Grave' cover perhaps?"

In late May, Subhumans headed north for three Scottish gigs, and five northern gigs, culminating in the Northwest Calling festival at the Manchester O2, with Slaughter and the Dogs, UK Subs, Conflict and Discharge. And at the end of June, they made their first appearance on Guernsey at the Chaos Fest.

"Back in the Eighties, Guernsey had an impressive punk scene for a tiny island of twenty-four square miles and a population of just over 60,000 people," recalls **Rachel 'Baz' Ridley**. "I used to bring UK punk bands over, including Decadence Within, your author's old band. I have remained good friends with Ian ever since, and I am the person responsible for finding those little gems of spelling mistakes and grammatical errors before his books get published... so if you find any, blame me. Many leather jackets back in the day had SUB HUM ANS painted on them, in those three legendary squares. We would walk through town in a crowd, with a huge ghetto blaster bellowing out punk music, trying to look all menacing and making our presence known. It's quite funny looking back now, but at the time we all thought we were so cool.

"I first saw the Subhumans play at the Fulham Greyhound, on October 31st, 1985, with Steve L and Instigators. I had just turned sixteen, and it was my first time I had travelled

ROBERT, BRUCE AND TROTSKY, CANADA, 2018, BY KAROLINE COLLINS

BRITISH COLUMBIA, 2018, DICK ROCKING THE BANANA
PHONE BY KAROLINE COLLINS

GATESHEAD, 23/5/2019 BY WILL BINKS

to the UK. The gig was billed as their penultimate gig before they were splitting up. Little did that small punk girl, with the huge attitude – and Mohican! – know that the Subhumans would grace the shores of her beautiful island home of Guernsey over thirty years later, to play in a field nestled on the cliffs overlooking one of the most spectacular sea views the island has to offer.

"Anyway, in those thirty years we all – well, most of us – have grown up and got on with our busy lives. Although Guernsey is tiny, it's easy to not see fellow islanders for years. So when the Subhumans played, it was amazing. They drew everyone out of the woodwork; even my good friends Mary, Shaun and the Jersey crew came over to watch them play. There was such an air of nostalgia. Seeing all my old friends gathered together, singing along to all the songs, was such a great feeling. It really brought to mind the fact that we all developed such a strong bond during our youth, and although we may not have stayed in touch over the years, something like watching the Subhumans together rekindled that bond.

"My friend Lorna Chadwick and her husband, Ozy Chris, are both members of the Greenman MCC, who put on the Chaos festival every year. This is what Lorna had to say: 'From a personal point of view, I collected the band from the boat and took them up to the site. Some visiting bands have been so very demanding, so I cleared my weekend diary so I could make sure I could be there for anything they needed. Once we arrived at Pleinmont, they were taken aback by the beauty and the views. They had no demands at all, which was unheard of for me – one band had even made me drive to the co-op for carrot sticks and hummus! So, I gave them a parking clock and a Perry's guide map, and after their sound-check they went walking; the next time I saw them was onstage. Seriously, they were the most down to earth, well-mannered and easiest visiting band we have ever hosted. As for their set, it blew the roof off the marquee… unforgettable. They are welcome back here any time.'"

Nine European gigs followed in July, including the Back To Future Fest in Glaubitz, the Haltpop festival in Amsterdam, the Refuse Fest in Peine and the Loco Loco festival in Opwijk, by which time 'Crisis Point' was released by Pirates Press Records, complete with a fold-out poster and an old school stencil of the band's logo… just in case you fancied spray-painting it on any walls or jackets.

"It's pretty weird," ponders **Trotsky**. "I'm fifty-six now, and forty-two years of my life has been involved with Subhumans. It's been quite amazing. Although 2020 was our fortieth anniversary, but there was no anniversary tour for us because of COVID… I guess we'll just have to wait another eight years and celebrate for the fiftieth!

"But anyway, considering the time we've been back together, which is like four times longer than what we were together in the first place, it's not much to only release the two LPs, but a band that *doesn't* write any new material is just going through the motions really, so we've persevered. Obviously, we have certain situations to deal with, like me being in a different country, so it's difficult to practise, but I'm very happy with the last two records. It helps that recording technology is so much better than it was back in the Eighties too, so it's difficult to make a really bad record, haha! Sound-quality-wise at least. It takes that element of possible failure out of the equation."

Opener 'Terrorist in Waiting' is a high energy introduction to the album, with its slamming up-tempo drum intro, and Dick ranting, 'Everyone's a terrorist in waiting, one by one we all get redefined... our innocence is just a state of mind,' seemingly picking up the theme of 'This Year's War' and 'Never-Ending War Song' from 'Internal Riot'.

"This is more about the Criminal Justice Act and similar bills being passed in this country," reckons **Dick**, "And there's one going through Parliament right now [2021], which will make almost all protests illegal one way or another – even *talking about* having a protest will be seen as invoking violence and terror. They're going to make us all token terrorists in the name of being able to lock us up and keep us off the streets, or at least stop us gathering together to demonstrate against the anti-democratic processes going on in this country. People will believe the loudest lie. That song is about us all being potential terrorists, not because of what we do as far as outrageous acts of violence and revenge, but because of what we think and say and do in a peaceful way, in terms of communicating ideas that go against the system's idea of how things should be.

"And we're all connected to people who are connected to other people, and all these connections are out there because all the satellites know where everyone is at every fucking point of the day, and they can just draw lines between you and anybody else. If they exist, they can find them, and then it's, 'Sorry, mate, but that bloke you met down the pub last week is the cousin of someone married to someone who was seen with someone who was carrying a bomb...' You are now against the law because of your associations, your thought patterns... again, all very Orwellian. George Orwell was a fucking genius. They are coming to get you. And the really scary thing about it is that it's all in plain view. It's the brazenness of it, of how politicians lie, steal, are racist, misogynist, sexist, greedy, don't care... they're open about all that. They might have a little bit of paper covering over the cracks, and say the right thing for convenience – as long as they've said the right thing once, and it was on telly, they can quote that forever in the supportive right-wing newspapers, on the front page of the tabloids, people get it into their heads and think 'everything's okay'. All the other facts that come out of other media sources get brushed under the carpet. The sheer amount of bullshit and lying is fucking phenomenal. And yet the Tories can still win at the polls. I saw a nurse – working for the NHS – actually saying, 'Well, better the devil you know...' She'd rather vote for the Tories because she knows what they're like than vote for any other party that she's not sure about... like, what the fuck? I would say at this point that I fucking despair... but not all the time."

'Fear and Confusion' and 'Information Gap' are upbeat and catchy, with quirky chord progressions steering the band away from generic dead ends even at their most simplistic. 'Atom Screen War' is slightly more downbeat with its stop-start chorus and

CHAOS FEST, GUERNSEY, JUNE 2019

BY ANDREW LE POIDEVIN-WWW.TALLPICTURES.COM

lyrics bemoaning the hypnotic, dumbing-down 'qualities' of your television set, whilst the staccato 'Follow the Leader' is strident despite its tricky timing. 'Strange Land' is up next, and it's one of the stronger tracks on offer, stylistically a throwback to 'Worlds Apart' with its cascading bass line and choppy guitars; it also features possibly the most important lyric on the album, that addresses modern society's fixation on borders that places more value on nationality than human dignity. The plight of refugees is a heart-rending issue.

"Yes – coming over here and being spat on before you've even arrived," says **Dick**, with palpable emotion. "It sickens me, the racism that is still alive in this country. And still pushed by subtle – and not so subtle – means by 'The Sun' and the 'Express', and the 'Daily Mail', especially. Media and government hand in fucking hand, demonising whole chunks of humanity just because of the colour of their skin, and not because of their wealth, but because of their lack of it. We're going, 'Eat the rich…' and they're going, 'Eat the poor!'

"These people have got nothing. They've come away from where they grew up, left the whole history of their family behind, because that place gets destroyed; they've got nothing, totally alone sometimes, just the shirt on their back, and the guts to make it all the way to France, and then the final extra step to get over here and stay in this country is probably the hardest step of the whole journey. And it is shameful… people talk about 'true Brits', but it's just a cover for racism. All this talk of patriotism is based on racism, based on the commonwealth, which in itself was based on prejudice. Unfortunately, we haven't worked our way through to a cleaner conscience in this country… that'll probably take another fucking hundred years, and we don't have that long left anyway, before the planet heats up and everything gets twisted and destroyed… I thought I'd just drop that in there, haha!

"And the ones that made it over here previously are all going home. It's not just COVID scaring them off, it's this hostile environment… it's always been fairly shit wages, they were just fairly good compared to what they could earn back in Rumania or wherever… but now the shit wages over here, plus the negativity, and racism, and Brexit, means all these truck drivers and doctors and nurses, waiters, pub workers, and so on, all the people doing the jobs that most people who call themselves British in this country wouldn't do, have all gone home, and now we're fucked.

"And yet, there *are* good people here, treating refugees with the kindness and love they deserve, as human beings… there were some refugee children who were temporarily housed in Torrington [Devon] recently, and they'd been shown so much love by the people of Torrington, they didn't want to leave – there were tears when they had to go somewhere else. It was a really touching story, reported not in a mainstream newspaper but a local one, or online somewhere, and that's more representative of what actually happens when these people get put somewhere that isn't just a holding fucking pen.

"But it's disgusting the way we treat people. And it's illogical, because basically refugees are holding the strata of employment together. They should all be paid more to do less. People don't need that much looking after – we're all relying on service industries to deliver us everything instead of getting off our asses to get it ourselves. People are being paid to ring strangers up and ask them a question they don't want to answer. All these dehumanising jobs created out of thin air to promote and sell rubbish we don't need."

It's an angry album, and why wouldn't it be? Punk has always been a reaction against the bullshit foisted on the populace by government and mainstream media, and 'Crisis Point' was written against a backdrop of shamefully poor decisions in the UK and US – Brexit and Trump, respectively – dividing families and nations alike with their polarising politics. At the time of writing, the UK government are trying to push the Police, Crime, Sentencing and Courts Bill through, under the pretence it will protect hard-working citizens from pesky protesters.

"The bill is full of all sorts of stuff that is unbelievably restrictive," exclaims **Dick**. "It will be coming down hard on any travellers… people who don't have a fixed home, whose home is where they settle… and there will be way less places they can go to. No help for those who are just stuck and drifting… a lot more arrests will be made, a lot more homes will be confiscated and destroyed. That's not getting any publicity. In fact, the whole bill isn't getting much publicity. If they can shut down protests, there you go – dictatorship without any complaints attached."

Our tendency to be insular comes from our isolation as an island, and Brexit has magnified it…

"Well, it came from there," agrees **Dick**. "That was about twelve people in the establishment that got 52% of people to vote for it: Johnson and Murdoch and Dominic Cummins and Steve Bannon… and then there was Cambridge Analytica using Facebook… all these subversive mind control methods to get people to believe it was a good thing. It was just soundbites and subtle advertising and social media… and it worked, which is very scary. And it was all based on the 'British is best' mindset that comes from going to Eton and then getting into power with no real experience of life outside this little rich man's bubble that [Prime Minister] Boris Johnson and his ilk all live in. They literally have no idea what it's like on the other side of that fence, and yet there they are, making life considerably worse for the majority of people in this country for a long time to come."

By extension, why would a person below the poverty line in a depressed part of the USA vote for a billionaire to watch out for them?

Dick: "It's all just subtle hints, warped messages and one-sided bullshit, pretty much non-stop through social media, and the regular media. If you only watch one channel, you'll only get all the positives, whether they be true or not, but mostly negatives directed towards the other side. And they might have felt a little bit rebellious, seeing as they were voting for someone who isn't even a politician! Trump was a gameshow host before he moved into politics, and he lied and bullshitted and was sexist and racist, and suddenly all

DICK MAKING ROCK SCULPTURES, VENTURA, CALIFORNIA, OCTOBER 2019 BY SHANNON

DICK, 2019 BY KATE HOOS

HARD ROCK BANANA HALLWAY, LAS VEGAS, 2019
BY KAROLINE COLLINS

BROOKLYN, 10/9/2019 BY GREG DALY

the people who lie and bullshit and are sexist and racist had someone just like them they could vote for, and feel justified. Now all the assholes who make this world such a shit place to live in have someone they can believe in, and he's the biggest asshole of the lot. He represents not having to admit their own faults – of course they were going to vote for him, and he allows them to upgrade their faults into virtues. It's a twisted fucking world. And just the fact that could happen goes to show the undercurrent of racism and macho bullshit has only been just under the surface for the last thirty years or whatever. It didn't all magically disappear in the Nineties because Blair and Clinton came along and made it all seem, like, 'Yeah, easy, we play jazz…'"

What did you think about (Sex Pistols vocalist) John Lydon's vocal support for Trump?

"What was all that about, eh? From a shallow perspective, Trump was like the anarchist's dream – a non-politician who pretty much said, 'I'm gonna win anyway, fuck you all!' 'Yeah, this is what we want – a non-politician running the country…!' But then you quickly realise that he really is full of shit. If someone had said back in 2015 or whatever that someone was going to completely overturn American politics, you'd have thought, 'Fuck it! About time…' Whoops! And it's so weird… you almost start yearning for the bad old days, haha! When they were 'normal' – and they were shit when they were normal. But now they're more shit when they're abnormal! And you wonder what the answer is to it all? Do you want to go back to the Clinton days, or the Blair days, or whatever, just for that relative peace of mind, where you at least knew who your enemies are and where they are, but at least your enemies were being fairly… reasonable? Considering they're politicians!

"But so many people are suffering under Trump, so many people are suffering under Johnson, it puts all the previous political agitation into shadow really… the fascists are uprising. They are all assholes, they're all shouting the loudest – but empty vessels make the loudest sounds. They're controlling the narrative… if we let them. And there's the rub – to not let them, we have to be as vocal, as loud, almost to the point of being parodies of ourselves, to get the message across. And how do you defeat an enemy without turning into that enemy?

"In my case, I write lyrics. And talk like this. Everyone else can join in, but no one can dictate how to do something as radical as change the status quo. But everyone needs to wake up to the importance of what's going on. Politics affects everything – climate change… the world's running out of space, the land is running out of power to grow food – there's only so many harvests left in the land we're already using as much as we possibly can. We're not rotating crops anymore, and we're growing way too many crops to feed animals up for food, and we're pumping powdered concrete into cows to make them heavier so they make more money at market. We're feeding people poisoned dead animals, and the climate can't handle it, and it's going to burn us all up. The water will run out, the food will run out, and then the trouble's really going to start… if it hasn't started already! Sometimes I depress myself just talking about this shit, haha!"

'99%' is a blast, its seemingly throwaway verse opening out into a true earworm of a chorus, whilst 'Punk Machine' is an insistent number protesting the commodification of our beloved punk scene, and 'Poison' is jagged and chaotic and driven by a rollercoaster performance from Trotsky, its desperate lyric building to a frantic and depressingly inevitable climax. A short bass-driven instrumental interlude ushers in the final track, the aforementioned 'Thought Is Free', whose second act ('You can put a price on anything… but thought is free!') is one of the highlights of the band's whole catalogue. Ever. It gives me goosebumps every time I hear it, and it's reassuring to know that the band can still create music loaded with such power and pathos after four decades. The biggest drawback about 'Crisis Point' is that it's just too short.

"'Punk Machine' is an unusual song because it was specifically written for a film script that a mate of ours, Pete Isaacs, was putting together, with mostly Jasper, Silas and Matt, although John from Seven Crowns was in it too," interjects **Dick**, of the back story to said track. "Pete had written this script about this punk machine that turns crap musicians into really good punk bands [the film was actually released on DVD by Third Eye Films in 2011, but can be easily found in all its lo-fi glory on YouTube]. It was all very daft and silly, with novice actors; I had a small part in it, as the bloke who had the machine [Dr. Vile], so I was waving my hands around looking slightly evil. Jasper and Silas are in this crap band who can't play anything, and they look into this machine or whatever, and they get to play really well. So I wrote this song, 'Punk Machine', and we performed it once as the Hi-Fi Insectz – which is an anagram of Citizen Fish… and it basically *was* Citizen Fish, just all dressed up a bit silly in suits. We played one song at the start of somebody else's gig in Bath, which they filmed, and that was it. 'We're the Hi-Fi Insectz, we've got one song, called 'Punk Machine'!' Everyone was going, 'Huh?'

"The music wasn't the same as the way Subhumans eventually did it, but we kept the basic beat and flow, and some of the tune. But I wasn't going to write a song that I didn't believe had some meaning in it, and a lot of bands used to think the only way to fame and fortune was to look the part and get on Top of the Pops – which was just shallow nonsense. So the 'machine' in the song is basically the music industry…"

"I'm not so keen on the later records," admits **Bruce**, "Because we could have done with longer to write the songs – we're not getting the chance to really tour the songs before we record them. I've never liked rushing into a studio to record a song just after you've written it – a song needs to have its life on the road before it's recorded, to help gauge reaction to it… plus, you need to practise the song, so you may as well be out playing it. 'Internal Riot' was good, because we did a lot of touring before we went into the studio with that.

"Also, the latest one doesn't have enough songs on it, and I think the songs needed a bit more practice before we recorded them. It's okay though. And I really like the song 'Punk Machine', especially the work the engineer did helping me with some guitar ideas. 'Thought Is Free' was practised a lot too, and that's really good.

REBELLION, 2019 BY KEV TYDEMAN

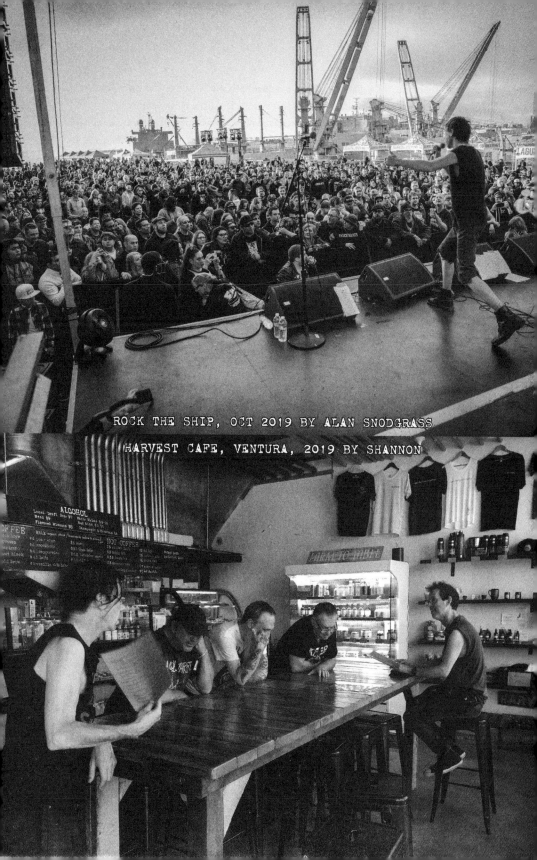

ROCK THE SHIP, OCT 2019 BY ALAN SNODGRASS

HARVEST CAFE, VENTURA, 2019 BY SHANNON

"But a song like '99%' just sounds too commercially punk. And unless I was leant on, I wouldn't have had a chorus line like that in a song... it's just a bit too poppy for me. And that's where me and some of the other band members sometimes cross swords, because there's a certain type of punk I don't like, and that's pop punk. It's okay when you're young and you can get into the mood of it, but really it's just music for the people to chant along to, and it's a bit too obvious. And I don't like that, but Phil and Trotsky do, so it can get a bit tricky. I personally can't stand American pop punk, all that stuff, even though it's done a lot for punk rock. It's all major key, and I'm a bit of a minor key person really..."

"That's my favourite track," says **Phil**, of '99%', "For its upbeat catchiness. I think it's the stand-out song on the record, and we haven't really got another song like it. 'Thought Is Free' is another favourite, for its, er, epic-ness and the brilliant-ness of the end section. Though I'm definitely not at all comfortable with self-congratulatory bigging-up of our own songs, which is very un-British, haha!

"My least favourite would be 'Follow the Leader'. The music came from a three-time 'Rain'-type bass idea and arrangement, and although I still like it, especially the guitar lead in the middle and the 'Could you be, would you be, out of control?' outro, it feels a bit one dimensional, especially when we've tried it live. That's a good example of a song that wasn't gigged before recording it. We tinkered with it right up to the last minute, sensing it wasn't quite right, but ran out of time and brain energy, and now it is what it is!

"But one of the things that has kept us going for so long is that we like what we play, and writing that music is fulfilling to us... and luckily other people like it as well. Although as time has gone on, there is definitely an element of 'What are people going to like?' It would be a lie to say we don't think about or care whether people will like it, y'know? After forty years or whatever, you get a feel about what works well, and on 'Internal Riot' and 'Crisis Point', we felt that we could write stuff that we like that is going to work live as well. And whenever we play songs off those records, they go down great live; they really fit in well and complement the set."

Blackpool beckoned in early August, and then they headed west in September for three Canadian gigs and twenty-five US shows, including the Sing Out Loud festival in St Augustine with Hot Water Music, and the Rock the Ship festival on the aircraft carrier USS Hornet in Alameda, with Cock Sparrer.

"Pirates Press were celebrating their fifteenth anniversary, so they were having a party on – most unusually – an old ex–aircraft carrier," explains **Dick**, "Which was moored in a bay near Oakland. So we did that, and then we did a secret gig that night in Oakland as well... which we couldn't really announce, in case it slightly dented the number of people going to the boat. But there was a lot of people on that boat.

"It was just the most curious venue you can imagine. A couple of people sent emails asking, 'How come you're playing on a warship? I thought you were against that sort of thing!' But don't be silly – it's only a warship if it's going to war... if it's full of soldiers and navy and weaponry, and about to attack someone. But right now, it's not a warship – it's a gig ship! It's just a fucking ship, and what humans load onto that ship is nothing to do with the ship itself... don't go getting semi-pissed-off because we're playing a 'warship' – it doesn't make any sense.

"I've never been on an aircraft carrier before, and they're huge. It had been demilitarised, but they hadn't redecorated it or anything, so it was all very grey. We were up on the top deck, and it was the size of a football field or something. Bands were on from about two or three in the afternoon, and it was a nice day for it. And there were stalls selling food, and you could watch the sun set over the sea – it was entirely pleasant... with a whole load of punk rock coming off the stage. We sort of stood out a bit, I think, as we were the only anarcho punk-orientated band on there, but we still went down alright – if you wanted to listen to some serious lyrics, you could, otherwise you could just dance around to the music.

"So that was a good set, and we came offstage about six or seven, then went over to Eli's, this very small bar in Oakland, where we were like 'special guests'. We were going on just before the curfew, at midnight, except by that time all the other bands had overrun, and it all got a bit chaotic, we only played for about quarter of an hour in the end... but it was fun trying!"

A one-off gig in Belgium, at the Magasin 4 in Brussels with Les Slugs, was a precursor to three in Cheltenham, Exeter and Chippenham... yikes! What could possibly go wrong?

The year 2020 dawned positively enough, with another gig at the 100 Club, with the brilliant Blunders, one of four gigs in January. There followed three gigs in March, including the Undercover Fest in Woking, with Johnny Moped, and then a certain global pandemic derailed this dedicated touring machine, and COVID-19 pulled the curtain down on live gigs for the next eighteen months. What should have been a busy year celebrating forty years of the band ended up a frustrating one, locked down and stifled by travel restrictions.

SUBHUMANS

REBELLION, 2019 BY KEV TYDEMAN

ONWARDS AND UPWARDS 2021 AND BEYOND

When looking back on the band's contribution to the worldwide punk scene, they've been incredibly consistent – they've hardly recorded a weak song, and you'll never hear anyone talk about them playing a bad gig. They take their craft seriously – with great power comes great responsibility, after all – but they don't take *themselves* too seriously, and they've always conducted their business – and continue to do so – in a highly principled manner, commanding and giving respect in equal measure. Musically and lyrically, they pour all of themselves into everything they do, their endearing sincerity transcending superficial barriers like language and race, and uniting the punk community in search of truth, change and a bloody great tune. It's no wonder they are much loved by everyone whose lives they've brightened along the way.

"No, I've never seen them have an off night either," agrees **Bill**. "Either that, or they're very good at covering it up, haha! But they clearly love what they're doing…

"Phil said something quite profound to me at a Culture Shock gig in London about ten years ago, when we were talking about their success in the US. He reckoned that no matter which band Dick had been in at that time – Subhumans, Citizen Fish or Culture Shock – they would have made it in America. And maybe there's something in that? Who knows? He has a lot of respect, and he's always stuck to his guns. He's only stating his opinions, but people can relate to them. That's why I'd never be a singer, haha! If you write something down and preach it, you've got to stick to it. That's why drumming's my thing – I'm not a politician… I'm not an anarchist or anything – I just want to enjoy my life, that's the bottom line. I just happened to fall in with Dick and the band, and there's a lot to be taken from them.

"It was the tunes as well – the catchy tunes. The lyrics were great, of course, but I'm a drummer, and for me it's always been about the music, the beat is paramount – Dick could have been singing about sheep and I would have still loved them. And actually knowing them, it meant more to me, 'cos I knew they meant it, and I could really relate to them.

"I was even in an X-Ray Spex band with Bruce four or five years back [so circa 2016], playing all of the 'Day Glo' album. It was just great to play in a band with him after all those years of knowing each other. We did three or four local gigs, around Bath and Warminster, and it was fucking brilliant. Mel was singing… Bruce's daughter was on sax. It was just a bit of fun, but sounded fucking brilliant."

Chris Larson: "Personally, my opportunities to see the Subhumans and Citizen Fish and hang out with Phil, Jasper, Trotsky and Dick, here, there and everywhere, are some of my most treasured memories. I love that I've seen them in basements, big clubs and small clubs, on hot days and cold days, and everything in between. I love those guys to the end of the earth.

"Dick's lyrics are genius. He's down to earth and real. And it translates through the music and all of the band members. They're real people, doing a thing they love. The songs are catchy yet diverse, thoughtful and thought-provoking. They have something to say that is universal and relatable, and just as poignant in 1985 as today! The lyrics are sing-a-longable and – who are we kidding? – Americans love that English accent. Dick is my hero... I'm also glad I can call him a friend."

"I think it's just their amazing energy and commitment," offers **Graham Burnett**, "And the fact they are basically free of the bullshit and nonsense that so many other musicians and bands get caught up in; they've always stayed true to the DIY ethos that punk was meant to be about....

"I occasionally bump into Dick here and there. Usually, it would have been at demos or protests or something like that, back in the 1980s, at things like Stop the City. I remember a few years later running into him at the big Reclaim the Streets protest at Parliament Square, on May Day 2000, when Winston Churchill received his turf Mohican haircut; then later the same day, in the bar at Charing Cross Station, where he gave me an 'Old punks never die, they just stand at the back' badge when we were both moaning about how we were getting too old for all this protest stuff...

"These days I run permaculture courses and am involved with a number of local community garden projects, as well as continuing to self-publish books and pamphlets about permaculture, food growing etc., so haven't really moved on that much since the fanzine-making days! Anyway, one day Mark [from The Mob] and Marta got in touch and asked me if I'd be interested in running a permaculture course over at Rockaway Park and suggested I come over for a look around. We were in the area a couple of weeks later as we were visiting my daughter at Cardiff University. I had a hired car, so I put the co-ordinates in the sat nav and drove over. I followed the directions up this narrow dirt track leading up a steep hill off some country road, and we came out into this yard full of all these Tesco home delivery vans. I thought, 'Oh, we've obviously made a mistake and ended up in a Tesco depot'; I was just about to turn around and drive off when the back of one of the trucks opened up and there was Mark with his unmistakable great big grin. Turned out he'd just bought a whole fleet of Tesco trucks that were being scrapped and was using them for parts, but also taking the delivery units off the back and doing these up to turn into self-contained workshop spaces that he could then hire out to artists and local craftspeople.

"Rockaway Park is an amazing place; as I say, the front is a big scrapyard area full of these amazing vehicles that look like they are from a Mad Max film, cars with rocket launchers soldered to the roof, trucks joined to aircraft bodies and all sorts of things like that, loads of amazing creative activity going on. Then you go down a little pathway into the main building where there is a big wooden door with a carving of the dove and the sun from the cover of the Mob's first album, and on the other side it's like you are suddenly in Hobbiton from Lord of the Rings, with loads of vegetable beds, sculptures, wooden panelling and carvings, and an amazing view out over the surrounding countryside through these big glass panel windows. Marta made us an amazing vegan meal and we had a discussion about doing the course, which happened a few months later, and was the basis for the new forest garden/orchard area they are now planting. They are currently raising the funds to create a community garden at Rockaway Park, and there is a great little documentary about that online which Dick asked me contribute to, for Bluurg TV…"

Ah yes, Bluurg TV, the YouTube channel dedicated to all things DIY, that kicked off in fine fashion with Culture Shock running through a rousing acoustic version of 'Civilisation Street' during August 2020 that was just what the plague doctor ordered during the coronavirus lockdown.

Dick: "It was in fact [Dick's partner] Michelle's idea. We were up at a studio in Melksham with Culture Shock, and she just had this brainwave about doing Bluurg TV. My initial reaction wasn't enthusiastic, because of the whole 'TV' thing… 'Bluurg TV' just felt like a total anathema to me, which didn't please anybody. Bill, Alex and Jasper were all like, 'Yeah! Great idea!'"

"But at that point, there were no gigs," recalls **Michelle**, "And they were recording an album around lockdown restrictions. You could only have like eight people in a space at a time, so we thought, 'Why don't we livestream gigs? We don't have to have a crowd!' And it started from there really… we filmed anything and everything, because we might be able to use it at some point. And the acoustic thing in Alex's garden was because Bill was taking ages with the drum kit, and Alex and Jasper were like, 'Let's just practise it now!' And it was a one-take wonder really."

Dick: "We were going to do three things a week, and for quite a long time, that was quite easy to do. Especially when we realised that you could easily blag stuff off other people's YouTube channels if you were polite about it, which we were, and you asked if you could use it, which we did. Some people said, 'Take everything you want…', whilst another bloke said we couldn't have anything. But we tried not to blag everything off other people, because it's better to do your own stuff, if you can. There were quite a lot of bands who had stuff, but didn't know what to do with it… or rather *did* know what to do with it, and threw it our way. Then we went off into punk poetry, and punk art… we didn't want it all to be music – well, we did, but we soon decided to expand it. Into these DIY chunks basically… chunks of creativity. And there's been some quite extraordinary

BATH, 7/9/2017 BY JESSIE SOUL MEDIA

'THE DAY THE COUNTRY DIED' INSPIRED GRAFFITI IN EUROPE

tales of independence. Most people haven't even addressed a camera before, and that can put you off, remembering what you have to say, and being natural when you say it, which takes a bit of practice."

Michelle: "But it's a lot of fun… driving around Bath at ten o'clock at night to find spots in the shadows for Dick to do poetry, one line at a time under various street lights, just to make it look a bit different from the line before. And just having fun with old footage to create trailers for 'And Another Thing…' People just really responded to it. And we want people to send in more stuff… anything that's DIY, we want to promote it. Things like the 'Cramond Island of Punk' documentary… that's a great story, so we got in touch, and they were happy for us to use it, and more people saw it as a result."

Dick: "It was a thing that happened during lockdown, because there were no gigs going on, and you weren't allowed out the house to do anything with anybody really, so everyone was staring at their screens, and we thought, 'We could put something up that's better than all this rubbish…' We assume everything is rubbish because we haven't watched it, haha! We don't watch TV… it's all shit until proven otherwise! So we wanted to share some good, honest, angry punk rock, quite often created by people stuck in their own houses. Like Uncivilised from Southsea, who did a great song called 'Lockdown'.

"But then we told everyone we were taking a break last December [2021], because we really needed some more stuff – we were running out – and that break has gone on for four months now. But that's because we've been busy – mostly with Michelle doing a lot of work for Rockaway, sorting out their website and everything, which is a really good endeavour to be involved in too."

"Subhumans are special on and offstage," reckons **Ruth Elias**, getting back to the topic at hand. "You come away from seeing them feeling like you've been through the wringer, even if you've just observed them from the back. It's the passion that's evident onstage, with those beautifully constructed lyrics spat out with every breath – and that charged energy they generate, that sweeps through the crowd and leaves us feeling changed. I always pack my inhaler for a Subhumans gig. And offstage, they are just decent lovely people who have never lost touch with their roots. They've always been firmly DIY, massively productive in their own output, but also in their unstinting efforts to promote other bands and the scene, so there has always been huge love and respect for them.

"We've had so much fun, without exception, playing with the Subhumans. We don't play much these days as other commitments get in the way, so it is a real treat to get to share a bill with them now. It's the pleasure of seeing those smiling faces again and suddenly we're transported back to our silly teenage selves again, but without the bad sleeping bag behaviour. I honestly can't tell the difference between now and then when they are onstage though, apart from the newer material, which is however still delivered at the same breakneck pace as the old. The only clue that we are firmly in the present is that I now get exhausted just *watching* them, whereas I used to get exhausted dancing to them."

Chris Knowles: "In my opinion, the reason for their longevity is because they've categorically never sold out. They retain an innate integrity that very few other bands can claim, and that to me is their most special quality. They play all the festivals, small gigs, underground events, never tried to 'go bigger' or change their sound to get more in tune with whatever else is out there. That is punk, and that ethos is the one I get up with every day still, and the Subhumans epitomise that more than any other band on the planet, which is why I have so much respect for them. They work hard and deliver every time. And they still sound awesome live, still have the same anger and energy.

"I took my mate Aaron – who DJs with me and really isn't into punk much, but resonates with the politics – to see Subhumans a few years back, at the Boston Arms in Tufnell Park, and he'd just finished reading 'The Establishment' [by Owen Jones]. After listening to the Subhumans, he said, 'Fuck, these guys have been saying all this stuff in their songs for the last thirty years that I've just read in this book that was written last week!' Not dissing that book though; it's well worth a read. He was blown away and went and bought all their albums the next day. They're still as current, and still as angry and potent. Hats off to them all, but Dick Lucas especially for those brilliantly spot-on lyrical observations."

"I think it was their song-writing ability and their musicianship, as well as Dick's devotion to the band and the music in general," suggests **Nut** from Lost Cherrees, when pondering their longevity. "I can't think of anyone else from a band of that era that has stuck to it quite as doggedly as Dick has. They also had something else over other punk bands of that time in that they weren't just four young herberts. Bruce is a great guitarist and obviously wasn't just listening to Crass and Discharge, and they had a long-haired hippy on drums, for gawd's sake! Thinking back to those early gigs, they had to put up with shitty amps and shitty PAs – if there even was one? – yet still managed to pull off a great sound. A finer bunch of blokes you'll be hard pushed to meet…"

Min Stokes: "Great songs, intelligent lyrics, powerful live performances, and what I love is the consistency. They never went wandering off in a different direction; although I love the other projects like Citizen Fish and Culture Shock, Subhumans has a formula that works and they stick to it. When you go to see them, you know exactly what you are going to get, and it will always be a professional quality show."

"I felt that 'Crisis Point' in particular was the best-sounding Subhumans release, and didn't have a weak moment on it," says **Peter Jones**, of Paranoid Visions. "I think it's the best one since 'The Day the Country Died'. 'Internal Riot' was also a wonderful record, and stacks up neatly beside the rest of the catalogue. Lyrically it's very astute and musically it's as good as anything they have done.

"I always feel that Dick is the benchmark for what is good, acceptable and correct. If one of his bands does it, then it's okay for everyone else to do it. They are the ultimate punk band with the most well-rounded, genuine, inclusive, informative, non-cliched, approachable and friendly attitude of any band I've ever met. Add to that they are a spectacular band with amazing music... tight and edgy as fuck, and so professional, it's a joy to watch."

"The Subhumans were special because, along with the likes of Magazine, The Ruts and Crass, they wrote – and still write – great music, which really stands the test of time," adds **Stew** from Shrapnel, who these days plays with his brother Paul in DaemoniK Fonce, "And as a lyricist, Dick is up there with the best of them. I'm afraid we haven't kept abreast of their later releases, but Paul has seen them fairly recently at Boomtown and Rebellion festivals, and said they were great at both. He also recommended some friends of ours in Wales to go and see them at the Clwb Ifor Bach in Cardiff, and at the end of the night, Simon – who initially turned us onto the band all those years ago – was onstage singing with them, therefore bringing the whole thing round full circle."

"I remained in contact with Dick on and off ever since we did the Sounds interviews," reveals **Richard Newson**. "He's a lovely chap. I like to think we share some kind of astral connection, a special bond, but that's probably just me. I've been to loads of Subhumans gigs over the years. Perhaps surprisingly, some of the best ones have been fairly recent. I saw them at the Boston Arms when they played the Winter of Discontent punk festival in 2012, and at the Camden Underworld the year before. They were amazing both times.

"Their songs seem to exist out of time, somehow always relevant. 'Religious Wars' stands out in this respect, so sharp lyrically. That line, 'The ultimate excuse is here, die for a cause, religion is fear'... it always resonates – and what a tune!

"And the other one that always hits home is from 'No', the line 'The system thrives on ignorance, what the public don't know, they can't reject'... I mean, how young was Dick when he wrote that? It's so simple and perfectly put, and so beyond the standard clichéd sloganeering of the times – he's singing about deception by omission, it could have been written about Blair's Iraq dossier, but that wasn't for another twenty years! Again, it always resonates and it's always relevant.

"This and the fact that they've stuck to their guns, plus their stubborn defiance in the face of fashion and their glorious, unaffected honesty – all this surely explains why they've lasted so long. And at those gigs in 2011 and 2012, not only was Dick still in great voice and full of energy, still exuding that lanky charisma, but by now the band were so tight musically, without losing any of the excitement... they were incredible. In fact, in some ways they were even better than when I first saw them in the early '80s.

"Around a decade ago, I had the title of their song 'Us Fish Must Swim Together' tattooed on my arm, because, as with so many Subhumans lyrics, it's such a perfect line. I think this would probably make Dick cringe if he knew.

"Things did get a bit awkward in January 1990, when I ended up with glass in my head thanks to some pissed crusty smashing a balcony window at Culture Shock's Queen Mary College gig, which I reviewed grumpily for Sounds, using my other pen name, Mr Spencer. But in the end Dick and I didn't let this spoil our beautiful relationship. Incidentally, I think that gig was that band's last before they called it a day?"

Sean Forbes: "Subhumans have integrity in spades, and you can't buy that. They were important then and are important now. Dick is a true punk lifer, next to Charlie Harper, GBH, Sned and a few others. He never dropped out; he just carried on in the bleak days of punk in the late '80s and early '90s. And for that he will always have my respect."

"From the first time I saw them, I was greatly impressed," reckons **Steve Bemand**, "And I enjoyed them every time I saw them... although I'm not always sure exactly when or where that was! They were just extremely tight, played catchy raunchy songs, and got a good live sound. Dick was always a brilliant front man, and you could actually hear and understand what he was singing, unlike many punky thrashy bands of the day. And the content of his lyrics was always enlightening, witty and wise.

"The 'Demolition War' EP was perfect punk, raw but controlled. And 'The Day the Country Died' expanded on that, even a bit quirky but still pretty explosive. It's hard to pick a 'worst' release by them, because it's all highly listenable and danceable, both live and on record, but I'm not so keen on 'Time Flies...', as more ska beats were creeping into some of the tracks, but I still think the album is brilliant... well, it's Dick and the lads, innit?"

"Subhumans were and still are great," adds **Andy 'Tez' Turner**. "They straddled the anarcho and what is now called UK82 without having to bow to anyone. And still do. I probably first heard them through tapes that were everywhere back in the early '80s, the 'Demolition War' stuff. Proper punk, but with thought-provoking lyrics which sideswiped quite a few people at the time, as they were moving so quickly from the early EPs and first album through one of the greatest punk singles of all time, 'Religious Wars' – as close to a perfect, dare I say it, 'pop' single as you're going to get in the punk world. Not too big, not too clever; it does everything it should in those couple of minutes – and then, hello what's this? 'From the Cradle to the Grave', which was almost touching on prog, but without the widdling. Upping the ante every release."

"I have come to praise Dick, not to bury him, and one day hope to get my socks back," laughs **Chris 'Wheelie' Willsher**, vocalist with The Bus Station Loonies, before reminiscing: "When, at the tail end of 1981, I moved with my folks to Devon, we spent the first few weeks living in a village on the edge of Dartmoor called Horrabridge. A place, perhaps most famed for being the location of the shop in the children's TV series

STEW AND PAUL, SHRAPNEL, 2021

DICK PLAYING KEYBOARDS WITH THE BUS STATION LOONIES AT
TRAMPS, PLYMOUTH, 2002 - COURTESY OF CHRIS WILLSHER

TRILLIANS, NEWCASTLE, 5/4/2022 BY WILL BINKS

'Bagpuss', but secondly, for the bus shelter which bore the artistic spray-painted legend 'Sub/Hum/Ans' divided on all three inside walls and clearly visible from the main road for a good couple of decades.

"From the point when the graffiti first appeared, I had promised myself I would find out more about the band, but it would be a couple of years later when the piggy bank was broken into and I paid no more than £3.25 on their life-changing debut album.

"A couple of years on, and more EP and LP buying later, it was one of those rare days I was on my way to catch the school bus with an intention of actually going to school – there must've been something good on the bill! Clutched in my eager hand was an envelope, just delivered by our postie, with my address written in a distinctive script I had already come to associate with things anarcho, rebellious and punk.

"I can still recall that excitement, at the age of fifteen, upon receiving a reply from Dick, singer with one of the best punk bands in the UK, if not the world, and certainly the whole of Wessex. That was part of the beauty of punk, especially with the emphasis upon the D, I and Y: any record or tape release worth its salt would include an address on the packaging. And not a fan club or corporate label address either, usually someone's home address. I think in this instance, Bluurg's Victoria Terrace was still the home of Dick's dear dad. I've often wondered how many unexpected visitors came a-knocking at his door over the years of his living there. My mum still gets the occasional punkers on pilgrimage popping over to Ruptured Ambitions HQ for a cup of tea, bless her.

"Once upon the school bus, I was able to fully take in the excited glory that the singer of the Subhumans had written to me – and as if it was a letter from an old mate. Always with my finger slightly off-the-pulse, it transpired the band had just split; 'Know anyone who needs a singer?' Dick enquired. As it happened, the band I was drumming with did, and I instantly began frantically puffing on the pipe-dreams of fantasy, little knowing at the time that Dick would guest in my band of the future, and we would still be gigging together nearly forty years on.

"By the time I'd written back with my flimsy plans of a replacement band, Dick had already gotten Culture Shock together and the demo tapes he kindly sent helped soften the blow. It wasn't until some three years – and countless letters and tape-swappings – later, that I was to meet Dick in person, steaming, and clad in a pair of green pants, at the end of a particularly hot 'n' sweaty Culture Shock gig in Plymouth, arranged by Tony Popkids, who would, himself, later become a permanent drum monkey fixture in The Bus Station Loonies. It had been hoped that I was to have recorded their set for inclusion on a compilation tape I was putting together, as the debut release on my new label, but the four-track I used was part of one of those all-in-one Amstrad music centres from the 1980s, and not the sort of thing it would've been easy for me to slip into my jacket pocket and take along on the bus.

"No matter though, as a couple of studio tracks were generously donated and what would become a (thus far) lifelong friendship was forged. Come the '90s, and Citizen

Fish became a staple band to put on, support and go and see. And, during this time, they became our favourite playmates with us Loonies, putting up with us getting shaving foam and silly string all over the place at gigs in various bouncing towns and cities in the UK.

"Then, of course, came the time when the Subhumans would reform, which, in itself, was a childhood dream come true, having never caught 'em in action the first time around, and even my crystal balls could not have foreseen us sharing a stage together. The reunited Subhumans at Bristol's Trinity Hall, along with Cult Maniax playing in between, has got to rank as one of my most magic moments. Complete with a brand new Sub/Hum/Ans skull logo backdrop, painted by my then-girlfriend Emma, which Dick seems to recall as 'appalling'... this either means he's recalling a different backdrop, or my nostalgic spectacles are so rose-tinted, I can envisage a work of art that no one else could see.

"Into the twenty-first century and our love affair with Dick, Subhumans, Citizen Fish, Culture Shock and The Bungalow Band has bounced along without abating. The beauty of the Sub/Culture/Fish family is that everyone who's been on board has been an absolute delight, and each time feels like catching up with an old chum. As, indeed, it is. Dick became something of a regular feature at Plymouth gigs with his unique brand of stand-up poetry in the early 2000s, and even briefly played with The Bus Station Loonies on keyboards and backing vocals, until he was pushed away from the microphone during a cover of 'Religious Wars', by a particularly frenzied 'Sweary' Mark – a Plymouth punk celebrity and ex-vocalist with the band Profane – who was determined to sing the whole thing, bless him.

"There have been impromptu arrivals on doorsteps, visits to comedy nights, birthday bashes and erecting tents in each other's gardens, philosophical debates and manic breakfasts, dancing in the kitchen to 'Banned from the Roxy', brandy, Jagermeister and home-baked bread... even plans for a 'super group', which never quite came to fruition, but you know, forty years on, it's still early days.

"I've much, much more to reflect upon and expose, but feel it unfair to take up any more room in this wonderful book. I'll save that for inclusion in my forthcoming memoirs. Suffice to say, the Subhumans and all who swim along have played a massive role within my own lucky life and for that, I am hugely grateful."

Jock: "The difference between them and us, as in the A-Heads and Organized Chaos, was that they just locked themselves away and practised. They were great musicians, Grant as well, and when Phil joined, he added another dimension too, because he was a solid guitarist already.

"There was always a natural chemistry there; they all clicked. It was an amazing thing to witness. You'd see Dick at the beginning of the gig, writing out sets and giving them to everybody. When Bruce was with the A-Heads as well, he was always writing out sheets of time structures for us, and figuring out the best way to play the set. Whereas when it was left to us, we'd all write out a different set-list and give it to each other, haha! It really highlighted how much more tuned in they were than the rest of us.

"To start with, when asked to talk about them for this book, I felt uncomfortable being asked to dish the dirt on my friends, y'know? But then I realised there's no dirt to dish, haha! The only issue we had was that Grant had a bladder the size of a very small petri dish. So we'd stop at a service station for a few beers, and five minutes later we'd be stopped on the side of the M5 and he's out there having a piss. And ten miles later, it would be the same.

"But I honestly can't think of any moment where I've thought, 'Oh, we've had an argument!' You can sit down with Dick, and he'll question things, he'll challenge you, but it's never in an aggressive way; he just wants to gain knowledge and understand why you've done something the way you have. He feeds off everything.

"I remember queuing outside the [public] phone box. Dick would be at the front of the queue with his carrier bag full of change, haha! He had a plastic policeman's helmet in his room, and all the money that went in there was used for the phone box. How he pulled off some of those gigs and tours is mind-blowing if you think about it now... the sheer amount of effort he used to put into it. It's so much easier nowadays.

"We've got such a small community of friends locally, and it's quite incredible how no one has really pissed anyone off. Well, except for when Bruce lost my beret at Trowbridge station! A proper French beret 'n' all... but that was 1981 – I've not let it go for over forty years, haha! I was glad to see the back of it actually..."

Kev: "Things were different back then; you were very limited as to what information you could get hold of – it was either the 'News at Ten' or 'The Sun' newspaper. And to have someone like Dick around, who was older, who was educated, talking about – and singing about – all these issues that you didn't really know about, was an eye-opener. And they just presented you with this information, that made you more aware, and it was up to you what you did with it – if anything.

"Even for me and Trotsky, who were drinking buddies, and it was all a bit of a laugh, it sunk in because we were around it. And I'll be forever thankful for that, because it changed my outlook... it helped shape the person I am. And I took that forward, the things I learned from not only Dick, but Trotsky, Phil, Bruce...

"One of my great pleasures in life was, once the gig started, plonking myself at the front of the stage, and your job was basically to keep the monitors on the stage. You would be constantly pulling the monitors back, and keeping people off them, but Subhumans would always let people who wanted to get onstage and dance do what they wanted. They would get very angry with bouncers who stopped people getting up. Within reason, of course, and you sometimes had to throw a few people off in good humour..."

"Subhumans played intelligent music. And had intelligent lyrics. No disrespect to anyone else either, but they could really play their instruments. They worked really hard at it. And on their segues as well. Instead of just playing their set, stopping after every song, there would always be these segues, a little bit of crash-bang-wallop, to run the songs together, whilst Dick would say his bit. They were all very much in tune with each other, even right from the start.

"There aren't many bands who've had so few members, who've kept such a tight unit around them. How many other bands do you see at Rebellion who have all original members? We've all known each other forty years, and I don't think there's ever been a bad word between any of us. And I don't think there ever will be. I've really enjoyed their friendship."

As a long-time friend of the whole band, **Jock** has some personal insights for all of them: "You should ask Dick about the Leeds United squad, 1972," he suggests. "I've never heard him talk about an interest in football, but have a fond memory of him naming the Leeds team of that era. He may well assume that everyone knew the team as he literally soaks up knowledge, and I doubt that he's a fan – but it would be nice to think so! I should ask him myself in all honesty, but football chit chat isn't the main topic of conversation when we meet. He may well be able to name the Man United squad of 1972 as well... I'd be disappointed, but not surprised. He has a random-knowledge jar of biscuits he can dip into when interacting in a conversation. An articulate way of life few of us adhere to. Another enduring memory of him is always having a plastic carrier bag full of books of knowledge, words and wisdom. Maybe that's what was in the briefcase in 'Pulp Fiction'...?

"Of course, Bruce was Mel's partner during the early '80s, and a backbone for our band when a drummer was needed. His musical knowledge was, and still is, of great benefit. To have a friend that would be part of what we were doing was amazing considering so much of his time was taken up by his own band. I'm forever grateful for his friendship, as I am for all of the band.

"I remember Trotsky arriving at the youth centre with long hair, a drum kit and wearing an Afghan coat. He'd occasionally smoke a pipe as per someone from the '30s, or he'd be smoking a roll-up which would contain more Rizla [i.e. rolling paper] than tobacco. I watched the Humans in Blackpool with a guest drummer doing one song, and I suddenly realised that nobody but nobody hits a drum harder than him. So solid and never misses a beat.

"Grant's a beautiful soul, who always came with a smile and knew how to play great bass riffs. I spent many hours listening to Joy Division whilst smoking odd herbs with him in Holland. We were either going to jump from the second-floor window or laugh uncontrollably throughout the night. We both chose the latter. He also knew how to stop the van on the motorway when wanting a piss...

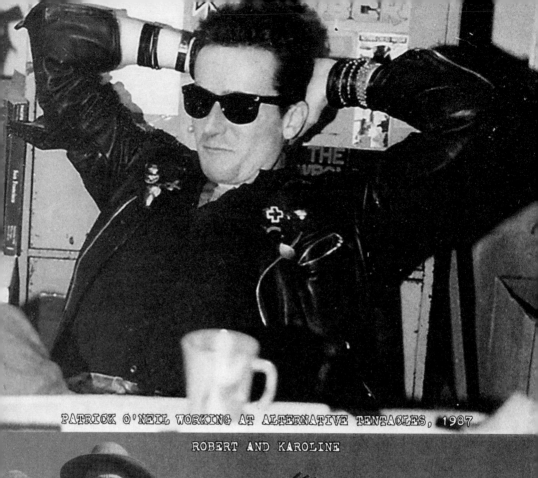

PATRICK O'NEIL WORKING AT ALTERNATIVE TENTACLES, 1987

ROBERT AND KAROLINE

PETE THE ROADIE
COURTESY OF MRS ROADIE

BRUCE'S GREAT GRANDAD
JOHN FIELD, 1900-ISH

BY CLAIRE CALLAGHAN

"I still see Andy occasionally and remain good friends with him. He was a solid drummer and we were glad he joined us. Nobody knew what our unwritten futures held.

"Of all the band though, Phil's my closest friend. A solid bassist who has had many compliments from those within the industry; he's actually lucky he still has fingers though, as his fiddling with my car stereo over the years whilst driving to watch Swindon Town nearly resulted in amputation. His invite to his and Erika's wedding in 2009 gave us our first taste of the States, a three-night residency in New York, which was fun. It gave us an insight as to how popular the guys from the youth centre were on another continent. He created the Wessex Allstars football team, which had its roots in downtime from Citizen Fish tours in Europe. A lot of friends became involved, a community developed, and a lot of laughs were – and are still – being had.

"All are close friends without egotistical traits. All are down to earth and are different from each other, but all have a gift of knocking out some great tunes with lyrics that cannot be dismissed."

Mel Bell: "All their songs were catchy, for a start. And there were all these little riffs in there that I'd heard before from my childhood, like Black Sabbath, that they'd given a twist to. They were so energetic though, and such good musicians – they played really well at every gig. Every gig I've ever seen them do was brilliant – and still is. I will never tire of seeing Subhumans; even when they have an 'off night', they're still really good.

"But I knew Subhumans had really 'made it' when they were on a jacket in 'The Mighty Boosh', with Noel Fielding. I think it was the second series [2005]? Noel Fielding's character gets into punk, and one of the punks has got 'Subhumans' on the back of his jacket. That was quite cool. I was made up actually."

"As far as bands go, Subhumans were unpretentious, with none of the usual ego that a lot of bands can have," recalls **Patrick O'Neil**. "We'd finish a show and they'd be just hanging out, drinking beers with the other bands and local punks. For a lead singer – who traditionally are usually the most problematic to deal with on the road [laughs] – Dick was super friendly and hilarious. We spent a lot of time talking during the long drives that make up touring America. Bruce and I butted heads the most; we had conflicting musical tastes. Trotsky was super cool, very reliable; he dealt with things logically. Phil just toured – nothing seemed to bother him.

"Pete The Roadie was a really good man, with a big heart. I had to get us across the Canadian border, which back then was notoriously hard for touring punk bands without work permits. I knew that Canadian customs were going to be highly scrutinizing of us, and I asked Subhumans to clean up a bit. Dick wasn't having it; he'd been perfecting his 'rat tails' haircut and didn't want to wash it out, let alone take off his shredded band shirt. Pete The Roadie not only washed out his two-foot-tall Mohawk, but he got everyone to look and dress the part, i.e. like tourists just wanting to see the big city of Toronto. The customs official looked at five UK passports and one American and hesitated; I thought we were fucked, but he eventually stamped them, and we were in…

"It's their music," he continues, trying to account for their longevity. "A lot of hardcore bands aren't melodic, but Subhumans can write *music*. Their sound is unique in a world of noise and two chord hardcore. Dick is a great front man. And you can't dismiss that they've been doing it for years, in one incarnation or another, and that kind of commitment says they're in this for life. Plus, they're still putting out new music. I don't want to name any of these bands by name… but a lot of the 'reunion bands' are still playing their catalogue of music that's twenty years old, and not putting anything new out. Subhumans are a working band. I'm involved with Razorcake, a non-profit magazine dedicated to DIY punk and independent culture, and they review every and anything Subhumans put out or play on, because they are still a viable band even for the younger punks that weren't around back in the '80s."

"If I had to take a guess at the Subhumans' secret to international success and longevity, it would be that they are just who they are," offers **Shannon Saint Ryan**, "As a band, and as individuals. They never sold out. They still set up their own gear, they rarely stay in motels, and for forty years they've maintained and solidified relationships with their fans, with other bands and promoters alike. They are caring, thoughtful, generous and humble. They would never claim to be 'the best'. Fans could say that for sure, but the band never would. Even after years of playing with them, I'd be lying if I told you I couldn't wait to get up onstage with them again, one of my all-time favourite bands. But to this day I'm still that scared little kid sitting next to his heroes, hands shaking at the piano. And in some weird way, I hope that feeling never fades."

Stu Pid: "My favourite lyric is, 'There's a scanner in the toilet, to watch you take a bath, and there's a picture of Hiroshima to make sure you never laugh' ['Big Brother']. Brilliant! After all these years I'm still invited to come onstage and sing 'Subvert City' with them, and I know I'm privileged to do so. They're one of my favourite bands in the world, but a band is only as good as the people in it… and the Subhumans are the real deal."

"Dick told us this story once," laughs **Robert Collins**, "About when, back in the early Eighties, someone had written to him, and sent him a demo, and that person's band was playing in another town. And Dick took a bus, a really long way, like 100 miles or something, to see the gig, but then couldn't find the gig when he got there. So he got drunk, and passed out on a bench somewhere, and took the bus home the next day. Which I guess might have been fairly normal behaviour in the Eighties, but I think sixty-year-old Dick would still do that…?"

"Oh, that!" recalls **Dick**. "That was 1980; I was swapping bootleg tapes with a bloke called Gary up in Kings Lynn, who said his band Exploding Hamsters were playing a gig there, and John Peel might turn up, so I went up there on various coaches with a bottle of whiskey for company and a bulky tape deck to record the gig. By the time I got to Kings Lynn, I'd missed the last bus, and half the whiskey was gone. According to my diary, I met a tramp in the bus station who said he assassinated politicians…! I then tried hitching, but ended up walking the ten miles to the village hall where the gig was, finishing the whisky on the way and only stopping to yell at passing cars. I missed the Hamsters, saw four other bands whose names I forgot, crashed out on a couple of wooden chairs, some twat started playing on the drum kit at four o'clock in the morning... and John Peel wasn't there! I got the coaches back the next morning, aching all over. Would the sixty-year-old me do that again? I don't think so!"

"I sometimes make this comparison… albeit mostly just to myself," continues **Robert**. "I like Van Halen, and the early records work, not just because of David Lee Roth's vocals alone; they work because of Dave Lee Roth playing off Mike Anthony's back-up vocals. And Dick is a great front person, but it's when Bruce comes in and sings back-ups… those are the parts that really grab you sonically, when they're working together. And I can't think of any other punk band that has a vocal relationship like that… certainly not in the more aggressive anarcho punk scene anyway. The way those two voices play off each other is priceless."

"I first heard the Subhumans in high school," recalls **Damon**, from Pirates Press, fondly. "Soon after a friend played them for me, I came across the entire discography on cassette and was instantly enthralled. The way the songs were composed, the sound, the vocals, was all so different from any other bands I listened to then – and to this day. There was such a poignant message, such a different way of thinking; those lyrics had a major effect on the way I began to think about myself and the world around me. Not only were they singing about atrocities and bad politicians, they looked inward, even at the punk scene itself. They didn't exclude themselves from their commentary on the idiosyncrasies and bad habits of human nature. For me, and for so many around the world, that is why we love them. The relevancy of their lyrics still holds true today. There is no other band like the Subhumans."

"Organized Chaos finished in '84, and I moved to Bristol in '91," explains **Julian**. "I joined Maggot Slayer Overdrive, and we became Night Terror Syndrome, but that didn't come to much. And then I did Nessun Dorma, who released a 12" and did a couple of tours in Germany. People always wanted to talk to me because I'd been in the Stupid Humans, not about what I was doing now, which was kinda funny at first, but became a little bit laborious. Then in 2006, Johnny Danger asked me if I wanted to do Crimewave Inc. [who've since appeared on Wild Arena's three 'Euthanasia' compilation CDs]. We even had Taf from Disorder on drums for a bit…

"They were good times [in the Stupid Humans]; we enjoyed ourselves, and it turned out to be very important. But the most important thing was that there were no rules, it was an open book, we could do what the hell we liked. And that's how we wanted it. I remember sitting in Bruce's bedroom when 'Drugs of Youth' was written… it's a Devo song played backwards, haha!

"Dick joining Subhumans changed everything really. He was like… our Gandalf really, he was our guiding light; he had something to say and he said it very articulately. He goes on a bit [laughs], but he has a strong philosophy on the right way to live your life.

"But I wrote the lyrics to 'All Gone Dead', 'Society', 'First Aid', 'Drugs of Youth', 'Killing'… and I didn't mind them using those songs. It wasn't about money or anything, it was about the attitude… Dick got me up onstage once to sing 'Society', and I did a very poor rendition, which I'm totally embarrassed about, ha! But I just wanted the songs to carry on, for the message to be out there. I'd rather have their friendship than anything else, you know what I mean?

"We always said that if we got to thirty, we'd be bloody lucky. Unfortunately, I'm sixty this year [2022], but I'm still here!"

"I have the Subhumans to thank for taking me on," exclaims **Pete The Roadie** gratefully. "At the time, I worked for other local punk bands, but went on to work for other bands, both in England and the USA, for the next forty years – which is how I met the wonderful Mrs Roadie. If it wasn't for the Subhumans, I don't know where I would be today? But certainly not this fantastic place in my life, so cheers, lads!"

"I've still got my bass, but I rarely touch it these days," reveals **Grant**. "But I carried on playing and jamming for a few years after I left. When I came back down – in '86, I think – I stayed with Bruce for a while until I got a place of my own again, and I was even in a crappy little band with him for a while, because the Subhumans had split up by then, which was quite proggy, but pretty poor, haha! I was playing keyboards, I wasn't playing bass, and I wasn't very good. Back then you'd try your hand at anything. I don't think we did any gigs… at least I hope we didn't play any gigs!

"I play the piano a bit these days, but only for my own entertainment, I would never inflict it on anyone else. I had piano lessons as a kid, probably got up to grade four or something – piano is a good one really, because it gives you a good overview of music, music theory, and rhythm, and how it all fits together… it may be an academic thing when you're a kid, and you're not really interested in it, so you just learn it, but it's very helpful if you go on to join a band or something. So I played piano as a kid, and then started learning guitar at school – and then you see other kids playing *cool* stuff on guitar, so you want to do what they're doing! My older brother played bass for a bit as well, so that might have been an influence…? But it all went from there.

"And it's all a glorious blur! All of us young punkers enjoying being teenagers and making music together. It felt great to be on the front cover of Sounds, to know that they liked what we were doing, to read all the positive write-ups they gave us. And it definitely helped with the roll of the band."

TRILLIANS, NEWCASTLE, 5/4/2022 BY WILL BINKS

REBELLION FESTIVAL 2022 BY CHRIS HILL, TCB PHOTOGRAPHY

TROTSKY, LOS ANGELES BY ALBERT LICANO

SUB HUM ANS

TROTSKY, JACK DANIELS AND DICK, OAKLAND METRO, 2018
BY KAROLINE COLLINS

2018
RO
STREET
LSHOWS.COM

"I don't play at all nowadays," **Andy Gale** told me in June 2021, "The kit is packed away. It's a bit sad really. I did have a few drum lessons off the guy that was in Big Country – for some reason, I wanted to learn how to read drum music… but that was a bit too heavy going for me, haha!

"My wife – my second wife now – can't believe she's never seen me drum, so I'm going to have to do something else one day. We had some low points, but I look back on that time very fondly; it was an exciting period. They were a good bunch of lads. And it's nice to see that youngsters are still tapping into the band even now."

As of early 2022 though, Andy has dusted off his kit and came out of retirement – to play in an as-yet-unnamed band with Bruce, which actually started off with them jamming covers of Status Quo and The Motors.

"The first Motors album ['1', 1977] was quite an influence on me," reveals **Bruce**, "And the Subhumans indirectly… well, me really – I don't know whether anyone else in Subhumans had any Motors stuff. They only did one good album; the next one was too pop and commercial for my taste. The Quo stuff I like from that era is the prog rock stuff, like 'Ring of a Change', which is really great – lots of stops and starts, and sixes, sevens and eights. We may even write some of our own songs in that style, as I've got stacks of riffs that are unused, and plenty of ideas to build on."

Bruce also has another interesting musical side-line in the works with his good friends Alan and Lorraine, as he explains: "Well, we've got a classical trio together, of violin, cello and classical guitar. I'm pretty sure my interest in playing classical music comes from a very old gene pool, as my grandparents – and their parents – were classical musicians. My great-grandad John Field even played concert harp on tour in America, with the pianist Ignacy Paderewski in the early twentieth century. So, the trio is different, and I like being different. It's a million miles away from punk rock, but probably the only way I'm ever going to get to play classical music. Although now I'm getting overly ambitious with it, and wanting to do something like Holst's 'The Planets'… it would be a very reduced version, with only three of us, but it's just an interesting thing to try and do, I think?

"My interest in the classical guitar really started to grow around 1985," he elaborates. "In fact, it was during the Subs split that I decided to gain more musical understanding and become a better reader/teacher. My grandmother, 'Win', helped me a lot, taking me through early method books, but it was through my old Kingdown school music teacher that I was introduced to my first guitar teacher, Chris Ross. As well as helping me through the grades, Chris introduced me to the 'Twelve Studies' by the twentieth-century art composer Heitor Villa-Lobos. These studies blew my mind, not just because of the virtuosity needed to play them, but the discords, Latin American rhythms and folk melodies. I'm still enjoying tackling these pieces some forty-five years later…!"

Happily unaffected by the unanimous praise heaped upon the Subhumans, **Bruce** then reflects on their longevity, and ambitions yet to be fulfilled:

"Well, we definitely get on well, which is important. I recognised what the success would be way back in 1980, when Julian left the Stupid Humans and I was without a singer, and I got to know Dick when he was in The Mental. And when The Mental broke up, it just seemed obvious that Dick would be really good in the Stupid Humans... his words and my music really, to be perfectly frank about it. I saw that potential and did fight for it a bit; I badgered Dick into joining. You could see that Dick's an intelligent bloke with a lot to say, in his own way, and he's grown this huge fanbase himself... a lot of the time it's pretty obvious some people are coming out to see him really, we kinda realised that. Especially in America.

"When we were teenagers, we were having lots of fun doing some of the stuff Dick was writing about, partying and all that, but as you get older, you stop doing that so much... 'What are we going to write about now we've stopped partying?' Haha! And you get a lot more serious, and start writing about politics. And I think the lyrics have really helped to keep the band going. Especially in America again, where the young people are still connecting with the lyrics. I think Dick was very forward-thinking when he wrote them; if the lyrics weren't still connecting with people, I don't think the music would have been enough on its own.

"I also like to think we've always tried to be original... well, as original as we can be. We try to make things interesting, for us, the people in the band as well as the listener – none of us want to be doing the same old thing. It works because we're doing our best to keep it fresh and different, and we've got something good to say.

"We sometimes wonder whether our longevity exists because we broke up for fifteen years, whether that actually helped? Because in that time we became legendary in some places... even though we didn't mean to. We did those two US tours in the Eighties that were very good – although we didn't really know that at the time, but we suspected the second one was – and then we broke up almost too soon, and there were lots of people that still wanted to see us. Breaking up created this kind of vacuum, especially in the States, so when we did go back again, people were pretty amazed. And it had almost become part of their heritage too.

"And I also think we were lucky Nick Lant did some covers for us, because the artwork has definitely helped. It's remained very iconic..."

"In brief summary, I moved around a bit, even living in London for a while," reveals **Nick**, of his journey since drawing Subhumans covers. "I carried on drawing in a similar vein, but a combination of loss of youthful idealism and my thoughts changing with life experience saw me reject the punk anarchist ideal as any realistic prospect for modern humanity. I struggle to label what replaced it... probably existentialism. My ethic remains that good old adage of doing unto others as you'd have done to yourself. My emphasis became human responsibility. We need values, ethics and laws if we are to have anything like social justice, and we each have a responsibility to engage with and shape

567

our lives and futures. I don't need to emphasise how much is wrong with the world; much of humanity remains selfish and greedy, and so it's a constant battle to organise society as fairly as possible.

"I had worked in a factory for a while then set up as an artist and signwriter, self-employed for about ten years, but couldn't compete with digitalisation so ditched it for employment again. It had to be something different so I chose public services. I moved back to my hometown area, married and stayed. We couldn't have children, and instead shared our lives with Jack Russell terriers.

"I've prioritised what matters to me. I've achieved my ambition to live back in the countryside and I'm close to the people I love. I work hard on making what surrounds me better. I'm happiest with my wife, walking a dog, or with my hands in the soil or on the handles of my bike.

"I have no contact with anyone from the punk period other than some of my peers from that time, but I still listen to the music, which takes me straight back. I listen when I ride, and I pedal fastest to punk.

"I have some very good memories of my subculture teens and early twenties. The opportunity to have created an iconic cover is an obvious highlight, and I suppose it gives me some sort of 'veteran status'… I wouldn't change that. There's stuff on a personal level I wish had been different, but to change it begs the age-old question of how that might have influenced where I'm at now. As I'm happy now, I'd have to say I wouldn't change.

"I think doing it as a business knocked the pleasure out of art for me. My eyesight has suffered with age and I rarely draw anymore. I keep saying I'll paint again, but the longer it gets, the less likely it looks. I have other hobbies that get priority, and I'm doing an old home and garden up, which leaves me very little time for anything else. Maybe one day?"

"But I would never have imagined we'd still be doing it forty years later," continues **Bruce**. "It's such a different world now as well. The future is just to keep on doing what we're doing – we've turned into quite a finely tuned machine with the support of our agents and the people who keep putting us on. In England we generally do our own gigs, but sorting out tours overseas would be hard work without them.

"We all enjoy it enough to keep on going. I'm not as ambitious as I used to be about writing new stuff, but that might happen – we just have to make the effort to get together a bit more. As musicians, we want to be writing new material if possible. I'd like to keep looking through the old songs and keep playing them too; I don't see any reason why we can't do that.

"And there's other little things I'd like to try. Like a pre-tour warm-up acoustically, where Dick talks about the songs in between? And that's because, when I'm warming up for a tour, practising on my own, I usually play through twenty songs or whatever, for the two or three nights leading up to the tour, and because I'm interested in all of the songs, I play some that we never play, and there's such a lot of memories that come off the songs. And I know Dick could talk about why he wrote that lyric as well, so with the right atmosphere that could be an interesting warm-up for a tour, discussing some of the Subhumans songs. But Dick isn't really into the idea of doing stuff acoustically, or quietly around a table, because he needs to get fired up by what's around him. As a guitar player, it's different, because you can sit there with your guitar and feel quite fired up immediately, because you've got all the notes going on.

"I'd like to do more on the radio too, because we never seem to do much of that. We never did that John Peel session that we always wanted to do, and I'm never going to be able to let go of that until I actually do a radio session. I know Citizen Fish did one for the punk show on BBC Radio 1, back in 2007, but we've never done anything like that, and I think it would be really cool, so that's what I'd like to do, something that would maybe reach a different audience.

"If we had the energy, I wouldn't mind ramping it up a bit somehow. I wouldn't mind doing a bit more when we go on tour… maybe slotting in some matinee shows or something. Using more of us, whilst we're still fit and healthy. Or at least using more of Dick, whilst he's still fit and healthy and legendary, haha! Just to make more of our time together when we are on tour? There's a lot of sitting around and you're only really playing fifty minutes a night, so why don't we play at the local school in the day or something? Or go on the radio? Just do something that's a bit different… but I don't think it'll happen though. It would just make everything more complicated, and we're a bit stuck in our ways. But we could definitely ditch sound-checks, so we could turn up later, and save some time there. Although I suppose playing more than one show in a day is a lot of work for the singer – and the drummer. I think guitars are the easiest instrument physically…

"I'm the only one who hasn't really suffered with my hearing as well, I think? The rest of them carried on after we split up, and damaged their hearing through all that touring… Trotsky having his kick drum banging in his monitor next to his ear and everything. Phil damaged his ears on a tour with Avail because their drummer was so loud. Dick doesn't seem too bad though – perhaps because he dances about and gets out of the way of the worst of it? Somehow he manages to not suffer too badly with it. But I've been wearing ear protection ever since we got back together, so I'm doing okay, although my right ear is about half the volume of my left – but my left is really good. I've been lucky with that. Of course, because some of us are a bit deaf, we sometimes play a bit loud, and we're battling each other volume-wise, so we can be a bit of a nightmare for engineers to mix us.

"At the end of the day, I would just like to write more songs – that would make me very happy to do that. Not necessarily for any reason, but just to all be in that frame of mind to write new music. But at the same time, I'm quite happy with the way things are going really – it's just so nice to play gigs where people are enjoying themselves and everything goes well… and that's been happening for us for a long time now. We've been very lucky in that way – I don't think we've had a terrible gig for a long time. Things are going really well… much better than they were at the end, back in Europe in '85. The punk scene is really, really good right now, and surprisingly healthy despite COVID."

"For a touring band to last this long, you've got to be able to all get on," ponders **Phil**, "Especially at our level where we're stuck together in small vans at close quarters and sharing rooms. There's no escape! That's the nuts 'n' bolts practical side of touring, but then there's the, er, 'artistic' considerations – that we all still enjoy playing the songs and get to throw in some of the newer songs every night to keep things fresh. I think we have to have the belief that we *will* write more songs and put out more records in the future; without that, it would feel a bit empty.

"Another factor that contributes to the band's longevity is that we don't overdo it – tours are never more than three weeks, we've never done that gruelling six months on tour thing. Six weeks in the States with Citizen Fish in the early '90s felt like hell by the end, so I'm happy with the balance that we've struck between touring and home life. I do get itchy feet to get on the road after a couple of months of cab work in London, and of course the COVID pandemic was a total head-fuck – no gigs for a year and a half, aargh! – so we were all pretty happy to finally get together for our little Euro tour at the end of 2021.

"We're fortunate to have enjoyed international success and that is, without doubt, hugely due to Dick being such a great front man; he's always engaging and gives it his all, 100% every night, whether it's to five people and a dog or a big festival. That, together with the band performing at a level of high intensity at every gig, has given us a reputation as a band that always delivers. We don't do 'half-arsed', ha!

"What haven't we achieved that we would still like to? Well, personally, I'd like to play in Japan… Robert and Karoline have been there, and Jay with Chaos UK, and they've recounted tales of great times. I'm always up for going somewhere new and different, for the experience. We came close to doing it a few times but for whatever reason it fizzled out and didn't happen, but I remain hopeful! Oh, and Iceland would be great – with a bit of tourist time thrown in.

"I don't think there'll be a new album on the horizon anytime soon, but it'd be nice to put some EPs out to keep things flowing, especially as we're now hooked up with the wonderful folks at Pirates Press. But who knows, maybe in a couple of years we'll find some time to get together and work on a new full-length studio album? With world events as they are, there's definitely no shortage of material for inspiration. And I'm definitely up for a song-writing vacation at Trotsky's rural retreat in Germany.

"As long as we all stay in good health – we ain't getting any younger – I can see us carrying on… indefinitely! We might have to tweak things a little, like asking for loaders to load our gear in to save our backs. Carrying heavy cabs down a wet, slippery fire escape after a gig in Cardiff recently had me thinking, 'Hang on, we're getting a bit old for this!'"

"I guess one of the reasons for our longevity is the lack of line-up changes," offers **Trotsky**, echoing Phil's sentiments. "We know each other so well that we manage to tolerate those annoying peculiarities which can exhibit themselves when you're all stuck together in a rattling metal box – i.e. a van! – for hours and hours *and hours* a day.

"As for our success, I would say that splitting up in '86 after only doing two tours in the States had a huge bearing on that. It was the right thing to do at the time – before we sucked!

"I still want to tour Japan. We have had a couple of offers over the years, but they never came to anything. The best things to achieve are sometimes the unexpected things... the thrill of surprise and all that. But next for the band is to get back to where we were before COVID. There *will* be another album sometime, but it may take a little while... watch this space!"

"We've been together since '83, but we just get on," reckons **Dick**. "We've rarely had any major bust-up type arguments. There's been a couple, of course, but only for one night, over one performance or something... then it's over the next day, and you carry on.

"But we don't make plans really, we never sit down and manifest our dreams or anything; we don't sit around a table and talk about it... we don't even sit in the back of a van on the way to gigs and talk about it. We've become quite quiet people really. We just wait to see how things develop. Since we reformed, and since Trotsky moved to Germany, it's become nigh on impossible to practise more than once or twice a year – and then we have to organise a European tour around that event.

"It's possibly because we are involved in things outside of the band much deeper than we've ever been before. Phil is now a cab driver, and he can do that whenever he wants – so, the ideal job. He's self-employed but he's got this majorly useful skill that he can use. He's fairly free, and I'm fairly free, to do whatever might come up, but Trotsky has got two kids, and needs to be there with them a lot, and Bruce is teaching guitar and drums at the school.

"People get more set in their life styles with kids and jobs, that sort of thing, and just getting all four of us free for any stretch of time at once is a rarer event. As you get older, you get more responsibilities, that involve more people, and life *changes*. Sometimes the fact that we are even still going at all is quite amazing in itself. Just having a drummer who doesn't live in the same country would probably kill off a lot of bands. And at one point Phil was in Spain as well...

"I can say with absolute certainty though that whatever happens next will be a continuation of what happened last time – we'll wait until we've had some practises, invented the songs, got enough for another record, and in the meantime keep playing as much as we can. We're coming out of an eighteen-month break due to the COVID stuff, which feels good, but we can't fill up loads of time with gigs because we're still unsure which way venues are going to go – it's all a bit foggy whether it will affect gigs more or less than it has done. Probably less though, as we're coming out of lockdown, and venues are still open, bands are still doing gigs… and thousands of people are still getting COVID! But the latest strain seems less fatal, probably due to the vaccine, or the nature of the strain of it, one or the other, which means that people are less freaked out by the thought of catching it. Plus the government has put business above everything and just told everybody to do what the fuck they want, in a major U-turn to their 'You can't do anything' stance. As if the threat has gone away – which it hasn't. But we're still booking gigs, and assuming they will go ahead; otherwise you'd just wait and wait and wait until you die for so-called normality to return.

"Quite honestly though," he continues, on the likelihood of further studio output from the Subhumans, "Doing an EP is a bit counterintuitive when you look at the cost of making records. A 7" costs about half what an album does, so you may as well make an album, and get more songs on it, so it's more to listen to. I'd rather get enough music for an EP, then get enough for another EP, and another one, and call it an album rather than an EP. Although we did cheat a bit with Crisis Point, because length-wise, it's quite short… but it does hold the attention long enough to be a proper album.

"People often talk to me about the impact our music has had on them. I'm now meeting people for the first time who are in my age bracket, who've been listening to Subhumans since they were eighteen or whatever, and they'll say our music changed their lives. And I'll say, 'Hopefully for the better!' or 'Sorry about that!' But yes, there has been an influence on people, that I find hard to comprehend… because I can't imagine saying that sort of thing to any other single band, to the extent where they actually changed my life. Although I did give full credit to Tim Smith [from The Adverts] when I met him – we were staying at the same house in Bradford, and there was me, and Tim Smith, and the guy whose house it was, who was thanking me for all the years of whatever, and I was thanking Tim for all the years of influence… in this lovely little chain, down through time… generations of punk rockers, haha! It's a nice feeling to be part of that continual influence of bands upon bands upon bands, upon the people who listen to the bands at every step.

"It's nice to be part of that, but I think it's wrong to take too much credit, because people credit bands with changing their lives with their music, when all that has really happened is that what was already inside them has been expressed. You like a band, or feel influenced by a band, because they express something you've never put into words, or failed to put into words, whatever… that's all it is really – the waking up of something already there. Influence is a two-way thing; there's the receiver and the giver, and the idea is that the receiver then gives it out to other people, and all these connections are spread about. To give too much credit to certain people in the scene, or to make heroes of them, is the antithesis of what actually happens. It's just a sheen put there through the influence of Disney and Hollywood, the cultural thing that has developed in the last hundred years due to television, and romanticism in films, that romanticises all things into being better than they actually are. And you have to keep away from all that nonsense, in order to remain realistic and relevant. Otherwise, you start to float off in your own bubble. I don't *mind* people saying we changed their life… but I do find it unusual, and a bit strange."

Strange it may be, but it's all in the eye – or ear – of the beholder. No one can deny that music is the soundtrack to our lives, and one band, or one song, can sometimes be forever associated with a particularly important moment in our short journey From the Cradle to the Grave. A lyric or musical hook can worm its way into your subconscious and nestle there as a constant companion to help guide you through turbulent times, and by virtue of their steadfast consistency – they've rarely put a foot wrong in either the studio or the live arena – Subhumans have no doubt provided that spark of inspiration and reassurance, when courage and conviction are desperately needed, for thousands of people around the world. If they didn't actually *change* those lives, they certainly illuminated them in some small but significant, meaningful way. Their intelligent lyrics and uplifting music have challenged our brains as much as they've moved our feet, their immutable presence in the underground music scene has been nothing but a positive energy for the greater good, and their approachable demeanour, self-deprecating humour and sincere humility, not to mention refreshing lack of machismo, has kept them healthily grounded and accessible to all. That's why we're still listening to them today, and that's why I wrote this book about them. At the beginning of which, I said, 'Every story has to start somewhere…', and inevitably every story has to eventually end somewhere too, but thankfully the Subhumans story has yet to reach its conclusion. When it does, I'm 100% sure it will be on their own terms – no compromise, ever! – but until then, long may they continue to put a smile on our faces and a question in our heads.

APPENDIX ONE
COMPLETE DISCOGRAPHY

7" EPs

'Demolition War'
Spiderleg, 1981 – cat. no. SPIDLE THREE / SDL3
First pressing – and one of the represses – had gatefold sleeve
Bluurg, 1983 – cat. no. XEP1
Reissued by Bluurg with fold-around sleeve
'Pay no more than 85p'

'Reason for Existence'
Spiderleg, 1982 – cat. no. SDL5
Bluurg, 1983 – XEP2
Fold-around sleeve
'No more than 85p'

'Religious Wars'
Spiderleg, 1982 – cat. no. SDL7
Bluurg, 1983 – XEP3
Fold-around sleeve
'Pay no more than 85p'

'Evolution'
Bluurg, 1983 – cat. no. FISH2
Fold-around sleeve
'85 pence'

'Rats'
Bluurg, 1984 – cat. no. FISH10
Fold-out poster sleeve
'Pay No More Than 90p'

'Unfinished Business'
Rugger Bugger/Bluurg, 2000 – cat. no. DUMP048 / FISH36
(CDEP released by Bluurg in 1998)
'Thanks to Gummidge and Sean'

'99%/1%' – split single with the Restarts
Pirates Press, 2019 – cat. no. PPR251
First 2000 on white vinyl

'Thought Is Free'
Pirates Press, 2019 – cat. no. PPR248F
Single-sided flexi-disc to promote the 'Crisis Point' album

12" EPs

'Time Flies… But Aeroplanes Crash'
Bluurg, 1983 – cat. no. FISH5
Came with one-sided lyric insert

ALBUMS

'The Day the Country Died'
Spiderleg, 1983 – cat. no. SDL9
Bluurg, 1983 – XLP1
Gatefold sleeve
'Pay no more than £3.25'
CD released by Bluurg in 1990, cat. XLP1CD

'From the Cradle to the Grave'
Bluurg, 1984 – cat. no. FISH8
Gatefold sleeve
'Pay no more than £3.50'
CD released by Bluurg in 1990, cat. FISH8CD

'Worlds Apart'
Bluurg, 1986 – cat. no. FISH12
Gatefold sleeve
'Pay no more than £4'
CD released by Bluurg in 1990, cat. FISH12CD

'EP-LP'
Bluurg, 1986 – cat. no. FISH14
Compilation of first four EPs, with lyric insert
'£3.00 or equivalent'
CD released by Bluurg in 1990, cat. FISH14CD

'29:29 Split Vision'
Bluurg, 1986 – cat. no. FISH16
With one-sided lyric insert
'Pay no more than £3.50'
CD released by Bluurg in 1990, cat.
FISH16CD

'Time Flies... But Aeroplanes Crash + Rats'
Bluurg, 1990 – cat. no. FISH25
Compilation of 'Time Flies' 12" and 'Rats' 7"
LP & CD, with lyric insert

'Live in Bristol 2001: Football Bootleg'
Label unknown, 2003 – no cat. #
Limited edition benefit CD for '2001 – A Football Oddity' alternative Euro tournament
Recorded live at Fiddlers, Bedminster, Bristol on July 13th, 2001
'£5.00'

'Live in a Dive'
Fat Wreck Chords, 2004
Double-LP, cat. FAT664-1,5 (with comic book)
CD, cat. FAT664-2,5 ('enhanced' CD with bonus track and interviews)
Recorded live at the Showcase Theatre, Corona, USA on April 3rd, 2003

'Internal Riot'
Bluurg, 2007 – cat. no. FISH50
LP with lyric insert
CD in digipack
Reissued on LP and CD by Pirates Press in 2019 – cat. PPR253

'Crisis Point'
Pirates Press, 2019 – cat. no. PPR248
LP & digipack CD – both with fold-out poster & stencil

COMPILATION APPEARANCES

'Wessex '82'
Bluurg, 1982 – cat. no. FISH1
First vinyl release on Bluurg – also featured A-Heads, Pagans & Organized Chaos
Subhumans track: 'No Thanks'

'We Don't Want Your Fucking War'
Fight Back, 1984 – cat. no. LP FIGHT 5
Reissued on CD by Mortarhate Records in 2003
Subhumans track: 'Rats'

'P.E.A.C.E.'
R Radical Records, 1984 – cat. no. RRR 1984
Double album, reissued as a double-CD by New Red Archives (USA) and We Bite Records (Europe) in 1997
Subhumans track: 'Rats'

'Life Is a Joke, Volume 2'
Weird System, 1986 – cat. no. WS022
Subhumans track: 'Human Error (Alternate Version)'

'Short Music for Short People'
Fat Wreck Chords, 1999 – cat. no. FAT591-1 (CD is FAT591-2)
Subhumans track: 'Supermarket Forces'

'Dangerously Unstable'
Suburban Voice, 1999 – cat. no. SVCD2
CD included with issue # 43 of 'Suburban Voice', benefit for Amnesty International
Subhumans track: 'Reason for Existence' (live)

'Angry Songs and Bitter Words'
Ruptured Ambitions, 2003 – cat. no. PC 1984
CD of covers of various bands that were on the Crass label
Subhumans track: 'Tube Disasters' (live)

'Anti-Floyd the Terrier State'
Fat Wreck Chords/Honest Don's, 2003 – no cat. #
Promo label sampler CD
Subhumans track: 'Apathy' (live)

'Punk Rawk Explosion #15'
Punk Rawk, 2004 – cat. no. PR011
Free CD with issue 15 of Punk Rawk
Magazine (March-April-May, 2004)
Subhumans track: 'Religious Wars' (live)

'Up Sampler 14'
Up Magazine, 2004 – cat. no. UPCD014
Free sampler CD with French magazine Up
Subhumans track: 'Religious Wars'

'Rock Sound Speciale #19 Punk Rock'
Rock Sound, 2004 – cat. no. RSCDSP19
Free sampler CD with issue 22 of Italian
magazine Rock Sound (June-July-August
2004)
Subhumans track: 'Religious Wars'

**'Anti-State (Anarcho Punk Compilation
Volume 2)'**
*Overground Records, 2005 – cat. no.
OVER 105VP CD*
Second in a series of four CDs mapping out
the anarcho punk movement
Subhumans track: 'So Much Money'

'G.A.M.H. & Slim's, Spring 2006'
Label unknown, 2006
Spring 2006 release of bands appearing at
sister venues Great American Music Hall
and Slim's in San Francisco
Subhumans track: 'Religious Wars'

'Canya De La Muntanya Vol. II'
*Canya De La Muntanya Records, 2007 –
cat. no. CMR-002*
Benefit CD for Spanish label Canya De La
Muntanya Records
Subhumans track: 'This Year's War'

'Angry Scenes Volume 3'
*Angry Scenes Records, 2008 – cat. no.
ASR010*
Subhumans track: 'This Is Not an Advert'

'Corruption of American Youth, Vol. 2'
*Crash Assailant Records, 2010 – cat. no.
CAR 020*
Subhumans track: 'This Year's War'

'And You Call This Civilization?'
*Pumpkin Records/Anarchistic Undertones,
2010 – cat. no. PUM023*
Double-CD dedicated to the memory of
Peter 'Pinguu' Williamson
Subhumans track: 'Point of View'

'Angry Scenes Volume 4'
*Angry Scenes Records, 2010 – cat. no.
ASR014*
A benefit CD in memory of 'Trogg' from
Contempt (R.I.P. 1964 – 2008)
Subhumans track: 'Point of View'

'South West Underground Vol. 1'
Riot Ska Records, 2012 – cat. no. RSR 021
CD of punk bands from the southwest UK
Subhumans track: 'Mosquitoes'

**'X Lat Ultra Chaos Pikniku Live
2016/2017'**
*No Pasaran Records, Melina Crew
Records, ZIMA, Black Wednesday Records,
83 Records, 2018 – cat. no. 062/BWR
044/83REC#37*
*CD released by ZIMA, 2018 – cat. no.
CD/Z 064*
Subhumans track: 'Religious Wars' (live)

**'Burning Britain – A Story of
Independent UK Punk 1980 – 1983'**
Cherry Red, 2018 – cat. no. CRCDBOX53
Four-CD 'book-set'
Subhumans track: 'Reason for Existence'

'Bluurg Records EPs '82 – '88'
Bluurg – cat. no. FISH45
CD compiling the 7" EPs released by
Bluurg in the Eighties
Subhumans track: 'No Thanks'

CASSETTES

'Demolition War Parts I – III'
Bluurg, 1981 – cat. BLUURG7
Re-released as a CDR by Bluurg, cat.
FISH42

'Community Centre Warminster Live 9-5-81'
Bluurg, 1981 – cat. BLUURG9
'Gig no. 8'

'Live Bath Walcot Village Hall 20.5.81'
Bluurg, 1981 – BLUURG10

'Live Melksham Youth Centre 15.7.81'
Bluurg, 1981 – BLUURG11
Split tape with Wild Youth

'Live in Swindon'
Bluurg, 1982 – cat. BLUURG14
Recorded live at Devizes Road Church
Hall, Swindon, 11th December, 1981

'Live Stevenage Bowes Lyon House 21.2.82'
Bluurg, 1982 – cat. BLUURG15

'Live Pub Crawl'
Bluurg, 1982 – cat. BLUURG16
Recorded live at Skunx, London, April 3rd,
1982, and the Ring O' Bells, Bath, April
10th, 1982

'Live London, Putney White Lion'
Bluurg, 1982 – cat. BLUURG19
Recorded live at the Putney White Lion,
July 1st, 1982

'Live London Moonlight'
Bluurg/96 Tapes, 1982 – cat. BLUURG21
Split with Faction
Recorded live at London Moonlight,
August 23rd, 1982

'Live + Practice'
Disforia (Italy), 1982 – cat. 03
Recorded live at Warminster Youth Centre,
December 9th, 1980, February 27th, 1981 &
March 21st, 1981

'Live London Finsbury Park George Robey'
Bluurg, 1983 – BLUURG23
Recorded live at the George Robey,
London, February 7th, 1983

'Subhumans Leeds'
Bluurg, 1983 – cat. BLUURG26
Recorded live at Leeds Brannigans, May
11th, 1983

'The Final Fling'
*Bluurg, 1983 – cat. BLUURG33 (also
released by Lively Tapes, no cat. #)*
Recorded live at Brannigans, Leeds, August
31st, 1983 and London, Fulham Greyhound,
September 1st, 1983 – so-called because it
was Grant's last gig

'Gateshead & Scarborough'
*Watergate Tapes, 1984 – cat. Watergate
Tapes 10*
Recorded live at The Station, Gateshead,
August 4th, 1984, & Rudies, Scarborough,
August 12th, 1984

'One Man's Fish Is Another Man's Poisson – Live in Paris'
Bluurg, 1984 – cat. BLUURG36
Recorded live at Usine Pali-Kou, Paris, on
October 8th, 1983

'Live at 100 Club 21.2.84'
*Discredit Our System Tapes, 1984 – cat.
D.O.S.027*
Recorded live at the 100 Club, London,
February 21st, 1984

'USAT4'
Bluurg, 1984 – cat. BLUURG41
Recorded live at 'On Broadway', San
Francisco, April 24th, 1984

'Live at Juz Korachstrasse, Hamburg 14.6.84'
Billie Bingham Tapes, 1984 – no cat. #
'Only available in West Germany'

'Live Bathgate'
Bluurg, 1984 – cat. BLUURG44
Recorded live at La Stradas, Bathgate,
August 9th, 1984

'USAT5'
Bluurg, 1985 – cat. BLUURG59
Recorded live at the Ritz, NYC, April 23rd, CBGBs, NYC, April 28th, Electric Banana, Pittsburgh, May 9th, and Mabuhay Gardens, San Francisco, May 22nd, 1985

'Leeds, Adam and Eves, 23-7-85'
Peaceville (UK)/Dasein Recordings (USA), 1985 – cat. no. p/v 50
Split release with Instigators

'Live Leeds'
Bluurg, 1985 – cat. BLUURG61
Recorded live at Adam & Eve's, Leeds, July 24th and October 23rd, 1985

'Worlds Apart – Live at the Station, Gateshead, 27-7-85'
Cowpat Tapes Ltd, 1985 – cat. no. PAT 3.

'Fulham Greyhound'
Bluurg, 1985 – cat. BLUURG62
Recorded live at the Fulham Greyhound, October 31st, 1985

'Everyday Live'
Musical Tragedies, 1985 – cat. MT-008
Recorded live in Darmstadt, West Germany, September 25th, 1985

'Adam & Eve's, Leeds, 6/2/85'
Watergate Tapes – no. cat. #
Recorded live at Adam & Eve's, Leeds, February 6th, 1985

'Live in Cassiopeia'
Atman-Music, 2017 – cat. 008
Recorded live at Cassiopeia, Berlin, February 13th, 2017

COMPILATION CASSETTE APPEARANCES

'Punk Ei Ole Kuollut'
P. Tuotanto, 1981 – no cat. # (Finland)
Reissued on CDR in 2013
Subhumans tracks: 'Drugs of Youth' / 'Sid' / 'Peroxide' (all live)

'New Criminals Volume 1'
New Crimes Tapes, 1981 – cat. no. NC2
Appearing as *The* Subhumans
Subhumans tracks: 'Parasites' / 'Drugs of Youth' / 'It's Gonna Get Worse'

'Kaaos'
Kaaos Fanzine, 1982 – no cat. # (Finland)
Free cassette with Finnish fanzine Kaaos
Subhumans tracks: 'All Gone Dead' / 'Germ' / 'Zyklon B-Movie'

'Religious Vomit'
Public Disturbance Tapes, 1983 – cat. no. P.D.1.
Subhumans tracks: 'song No. 35' / 'First Aid' (both live)

'Rising Free'
V.I.S.A., 1983 – cat. no. AF 009 (France)
Subhumans tracks: 'Big Brother'/'Waste of Breath'/'Rain'/'Zyklon B-Movie'/'Mickey Mouse Is Dead'

'Punk... The Acquired Taste!'
Rentaracket Records, 1983 – cat. no. RR 001
Subhumans tracks: 'Work-Rest-Play-Die'/'Evolution'

'Punk Belongs to the Punks'
Den Onde Sirkel, 1984 – no cat. # (Norway)
Subhumans tracks: 'Peroxide'/'So Much Money'

'Symphonies for the Disaffected'
Beer Belly Tapes, 1985 – no cat. #
Subhumans tracks: 'Zyklon B-Movie'/'Animal'/'Religious Wars'

'The Raw Power of Life... 2'
Alk, 1985 – cat. no. 002 (Germany)
Subhumans tracks: 'Fade Away'/'Walls of Silence'/'Can't Hear the Words'

'Tour De Farce #2'
Empty Records, 1987 – cat. no. MT-019 (Germany)
Subhumans track: 'Apathy'
International punk compilation released by DIY German label with 104-page fanzine

'The Return of Amicolings'
*Magnifica Productions, 1988 – no cat. #
(Spain)*
Subhumans track: 'Forget'

'E.K.H. Herbst 99 (Live Tape)'
Riot Tapes, 2000 – cat. no. RT 03 (Austria)
Subhumans track: 'Human Error' (live)

'News (S) Hit's January 2005'
*Funtomias Records, 2005 – no cat. #
(Germany)*
Subhumans track: 'I Don't Wanna Die'

'Vive Le Rock'
*Free cassette with Human Parasit fanzine,
2012 – no cat. # (Germany)*
Subhumans track: 'Not Me'

**'Tape's Not Dead Volume 3 (A Tapehead
City Mixtape)'**
*Tapehead City, 2020 – cat. no. THC-010
(USA)*
Subhumans track: 'Punk Machine'

'Endless Sickness'
*Endless Sickness, year not known? – no
cat. # (Germany)*
Subhumans track: 'Curl Up and Die'

'Real Deal Records Vol. 1'
*Real Deal Records, year not known – no
cat. # (Germany)*
Subhumans track: 'Rats'

'Acid Sound from United Kingdom, Vol 1'
*Acid Sound Distribution, year not known
– no cat. #*
Subhumans tracks: 'Fade Away' / 'Rats'
(both live)

'The Future Is Unwritten – The Second'
*Reflection Tapes, year not known – no cat.
(Germany)*
Subhumans track: 'Reason for Existence'

**'Yesterday's Bullshit Today's Manure
– A Benefit Tape for the Southern
California Anarchist Center'**
Label & year unknown, no cat. # (USA)
Subhumans track: 'Religious Wars' (live
1986)

'The Day You'll Be Lorned'
Label & year unknown, no cat. # (Germany)
Subhumans tracks: 'Fade Away' / 'Apathy'

**'Mad Monk Presents: Pleading for
Peace'**
*Bloody Monkers Tapes & Distribution,
year not known – cat. no. COMP.1*
Subhumans tracks: 'Pisshead' / 'Apathy'
(both live)

'Quand Des Voix S'Expriment...'
Label & year unknown, no cat. # (France)
Subhumans track: 'Zyklon B-Movie'

**'Is Charles Bronson Really the Sexiest
Man Alive?'**
*Peaceville Tapes/Not So Filthy Rich
Enterprises Inc., year not known – cat no.
P/V 23*
Subhumans tracks: 'Drugs of Youth'/
'Killing'/ 'Nothing I Can Do' / 'Trowbridge
Park'

'34 Punkowe Piosenki O Policji'
*Punk Tapes, year not known – no cat. #
(Poland)*
Subhumans track: 'British Disease'

VIDEOS

**'Live at Birmingham Foundry – 9th
August 1998'**
Barn End Productions – cat. no. BE329

DVDs

'All Gone Live'
*Cleopatra (US), 2005 – cat. no. 1437-9
Cherry Red Films (UK), 2005 – CRDVD102*
Recorded live at the Metro, Chicago, First
Avenue, Minneapolis, and Globe East,
Milwaukee, April 26th – 28th, 2003

APPENDIX TWO
SUBHUMANS GIGOGRAPHY

Where Subhumans headlined, supports are listed – where Subhumans were elsewhere on the bill, all the bands are listed in order, headliners first. The final figure is the attendance recorded in Dick's gig diary. A '?' means we're missing some information.

1.   19-9-80 BRADFORD-ON-AVON St Margaret's Hall + Wild Youth - 200
2.   22-11-80 TROWBRIDGE Park bandstand: Alarm Clox/Brain Flight/Subhumans/Wild Youth/Organized Chaos/Replacements - 70
3.   9-12-80 WARMINSTER Old Bell - 80
4.   21-2-81 TROWBRIDGE Court Mills + Wild Youth/Organized Chaos - 120
5.   1-4-81 WARMINSTER Kingdown School - 80
6.   11-4-81 WORCESTER Youth Centre + Wild Youth - 30
7.   30-4-81 BRADFORD-ON-AVON Youth Centre + Wild Youth/Organized Chaos - 100
8.   9-5-81 WARMINSTER Community Centre + Organized Chaos - 100
9.   13-5-81 DEVIZES Corn Exchange: Mob/Review/Null and Void/Subhumans - 40
10. 17-5-81 STEVENAGE Bowes Lyon House: Discharge/Mob/Subhumans - 400
11. 20-5-81 BATH Walcot Village Hall: Mob/Review/Null and Void/Subhumans/Organized Chaos - 30
12. 29-5-81 WARMINSTER Athenaeum: Mob/Review/Subhumans/Null and Void - 70
13. 4-6-81 BRADFORD-ON-AVON Youth Centre: Mob/Null and Void/Subhumans - 50
14. 15-7-81 MELKSHAM Canberra Youth Centre + Wild Youth - 40
15. 25-7-81 TROWBRIDGE Kenny's party - 20 [Trotsky's first gig]
16. 5-9-81 WIGAN Trucks: Flux of Pink Indians/Subhumans - 100
17. 19-9-81 LONDON Red Lion: Flux of Pink Indians/Subhumans/Rudimentary Peni - 350
18. 24-10-81 NOTTINGHAM Beeston Community Centre: Flux of Pink Indians/Subhumans/Fits/Verbal Warning/Anarchist Attack - 250
19. 28-11-81 LONDON Islington Pied Bull: Sinyx/Subhumans/Apostles/Terminal Disaster/Assassins of Hope/Flack - 250
20. 11-12-81 SWINDON Devizes Road Church Hall + Snipers/BSGs
21. 29-1-82 CODFORD fashion show - 150
22. 21-2-82 STEVENAGE Bowes Lyon House + Part One/Disrupters - 300
23. 5-3-82 TROWBRIDGE The Crown: Wasted Space/Subhumans/Pagans/A-Heads/Organized Chaos - 100
24. 25-3-82 WELLINGTON Gemini Club + Organized Chaos/Orinj 'n' Yella Kurtain Rayles - 36
25. 3-4-82 LONDON Skunx + Organized Chaos/Assassins of Hope - 220
26. 4-4-82 LONDON Centro Iberico Anarchist Centre + A-Heads/Organized Chaos/Hagar the Womb - 150
27. 10-4-82 BATH Ring O'Bells + Mob/A-Heads/Organized Chaos/Rebel Dance - 100
28. 13-4-82 BRISTOL Granary + Undead/Pagans - 60

29.	14-5-82 SWINDON Stratton Youth Centre + A-Heads/Sounds Depression/Apathy - 100
30.	18-5-82 BRADFORD-ON-AVON Youth Centre + A-Heads/Pagans/Assault - 60
31.	28-5-82 WELWYN GARDEN CITY Ludwig Family Club + Rudimentary Peni/Nightmare - 200
32.	3-6-82 TROWBRIDGE Julie's party - 40
33.	7-6-82 LONDON Camden Musician's Collective: Flux of Pink Indians/Conflict/Mob/ Subhumans/Rudimentary Peni - 500
34.	11-6-82 TROWBRIDGE Peewee's + A-Heads/Resistors - 75
35.	1-7-82 LONDON Putney White Lion: Flux of Pink Indians/System/Subhumans/Assassins of Hope - 250
36.	17-7-82 FAREHAM Technical College: Flux of Pink Indians/Subhumans/Polemic/11th Commandment - 170
37.	18-7-82 BATH Weston Centre 69: Flux of Pink Indians/Subhumans/Dead Popstars/Smart Pils - 150
38.	14-8-82 WESTWOOD Festival + Max Headroom & the Carparks/Rhythm Section/ Marshall Howe/White Spirit Blues Band/30,000 Frenchmen/The Divers - 200
39.	21-8-82 LONDON Skunx + A-Heads/Organized Chaos - 100
40.	22-8-82 LONDON Centro Iberico Anarchist Centre + Mob/A-Heads/Pagans - 200
41.	23-8-82 LONDON Moonlight Club + Faction/Flux of Pink Indians - 300
42.	24-8-82 GRAVESEND Red Lion + Mob/Faction - 80
43.	28-8-82 BATH Walcot Village Hall + Amebix/Smart Pils/Disorder/Rebel Dance - 100
44.	27-9-82 CARDIFF Central Hotel + Corruption/Politrix/Soldier Dolls - 170
45.	2-10-82 LEIGHTON BUZZARD Bossard Hall + State of Shock/Absconded - 200
46.	12-10-82 SOUTHAMPTON Stac Club + Ad Nauseam/Tears of Destruction - 120
47.	15-10-82 PORT TALBOT Sandfields Youth Centre + A-Heads/Resistance 77/Amebix/Ad Nauseam/Disorder/Skull Attack - 150
48.	16-10-82 EBBW VALE Catholic Church Hall + A-Heads/Anhrefn/Ad Nauseam/ Corruption/Decayed Youth/Soldier Dolls - 130
49.	26-11-82 LONDON Central Polytechnic: Dead Kennedys/MDC/Serious Drinking/ Subhumans - 400
50.	23-12-82 BISHOPS STORTFORD Triad + Burial/Animus/A-Heads/Emergency - 80
51.	2-1-83 STEVENAGE Bowes Lyon House + Destructors/Virus - 230
52.	8-1-83 LONDON Moonlight Club + Conflict/Naked - 370
53.	14-1-83 LIMPLEY STOKE Viaduct Hotel + Organized Chaos/A-Heads/Scum -100
54.	16-1-83 MANCHESTER Gallery + Andy T/The System - 120
55.	7-2-83 LONDON Sir George Robey + Organized Chaos/Lost Cherrees - 70
56.	8-2-83 LONDON 100 Club + A-Heads/Organized Chaos - 300
57.	4-3-83 LIMPLEY STOKE Viaduct Hotel + A-Heads/Disorder/Ad Nauseam/Amebix - 200
58.	11-3-83 WEYMOUTH St John's Ambulance Hall + Cult Maniax/Admass/Manix/Peace Heads - 120
59.	26-3-83 ANDOVER Avalon Hall + AWOL/Outrage/Black Easter - 150
60.	1-4-83 FELTHAM Football Club + Riot/Clone + Organized Chaos - 230
61.	9-4-83 NOTTINGHAM Union Club + Disorder/Chaos UK/Amebix/Antisect/Napalm Death - 350

62.   12-4-83 LONDON 100 Club + A-Heads/Naked/Part One - 420

63.   23-4-83 MANCHESTER Morrissey's + A-Heads/Organized Chaos/Warzone - 80

64.   30-4-83 CAMBRIDGE Sea Cadet Hall + Dead Man's Shadow/Reality - 250

65.   2-5-83 EAST WOODLANDS Church Hall + A-Heads/Organized Chaos - 80

66.   8-5-83 LONDON Streets + A-Heads/Organized Chaos - 150

67.   11-5-83 LEEDS Brannigan's + Anti-System/Underdogs - 200

68.   12-5-83 BRADFORD Palm Cove + Anti-System/Underdogs/Instigators - 150

69.   14-5-83 MELTHAM MILLS Fallout Shelter + Xtract/Two Fingered Approach/Corpse - 180

70.   15-5-83 BRADFORD Vaults + Instigators/Convulsions - 80

71.   27-5-83 HOLLAND - HENGELO Doe Wat Festival - 150

72.   31-5-83 - NIJMEGEN Sleeping Beauty + A-Heads/Holland's Glorie - 100

73.   1-6-83 - ZUTPHEN Youth Centre + Holland's Glorie/A-Heads - 35

74.   2-6-83 - AMSTERDAM Milky Way + A-Heads/Nick Toczek/Holland's Glorie - 250

75.   3-6-83 - GRONONGEN Simplon + A-Heads/Holland's Glorie - 80

76.   4-6-83 - HOORN De Troll: Holland's Glorie/Subhumans/A-Heads - 60

77.   10-6-83 WELLS YMCA Scout Hut squat + Phobia/Donnerstag - 70

78.   11-6-83 BOURNEMOUTH St Andrews Church Hall + Self Abuse/Parasites - 100

79.   14-6-83 LONDON 100 Club + Naked/Lost Cherrees/Lack of Knowledge - 200

80.   20-6-83 STONEHENGE Festival [by the van] + Polemic - 50

81.   25-6-83 LEIGHTON BUZZARD Bossard Hall + ? - 100

82.   27-6-83 HARROW-ON-THE-HILL Roxborough + Disrupters/Faction/Lost Cherrees/
        Four Minute Warning - 100

83.   15-7-83 LOWESTOFT Coleville House + Panorama in Black/Reality/Corrupted - 150

84.   22-7-83 BEDFORD Boy's Club + Organized Chaos/Legion of Parasites - 100

85.   29-7-83 FELTHAM Football Club + Naked/Lost Cherrees - 170

86.   17-8-83 WOLVERHAMPTON Queen's Hotel + Faction/Submission - 100

87.   19-8-83 NEWTOWN Church House + Faction/Subversives/Stoned Rayzens - 60

88.   20-8-83 NEWTOWN Upper Weeg cowshed party + Faction - 14

89.   21-8-83 WINSFORD Grange Youth Centre + Faction/Corpse - 70

90.   22-8-83 LIVERPOOL Pickwicks + Faction/Wartoys/Friction - 70

91.   23-8-83 MANCHESTER Jilly's + Faction/After Dark/Anarka and Poppy - 110

92.   26-8-83 BRADFORD Palm Cove + Faction/Instigators/Underdogs - 120

93.   27-8-83 GATESHEAD Station + Faction/Instigators/Blood Robots/Subvert - 150

94.   28-8-83 SHEFFIELD Marples + Faction/D & V - 200

95.   30-8-83 NOTTINGHAM Ad Lib Club + Faction/Verbal Warning/Kulturkampf/
        Scumdribblers - 120

96.   31-8-83 LEEDS Brannigans + Cult Maniax/Kulturkampf - 150

97.   1-9-83 LONDON Fulham Greyhound + Faction - 200

98.   8-10-83 FRANCE-PARIS Usine Pali-Kao + Faction/Berurier Noir/D & V [Phil's first gig] - 350

99.   16-10-83 LONDON Islington Peace Centre + Faction/Hagar the Womb - 150

100.   5-11-83 LUTON High Town Recreation Centre + Karma Sutra/Nightmare - 80

101.   11-11-83 ISLE OF SHEPPEY Little Oyster + Naked/Committed/Shadow Cabinet/Abandoned - 250

102. 18-11-83 TROWBRIDGE Tony's party + Organized Chaos/Wasted Space - 40
103. 25-11-83 ILFRACOMBE Collingwood Hotel + A-Heads/Wartoys/Krux - 150
104. 9-12-83 PURITON Village Hall + No Obligation/Spyin' for Brian/Organized Chaos/Exit 22/Shrapnel - 100
105. 11-12-83 STEVENAGE Bowes Lyon House + A-Heads/Organized Chaos - 150
106. 15-12-83 LONDON 100 Club + A-Heads/Naked/Instigators/Nick Toczek - 300
107. 17-12-83 SWINDON Salt and Light Building + Disturbance from Fear/Smart Pils/ Nursery/Scum - 60
108. 20-12-83 LONDON Stockwell Old Queen's Head + A-Heads/16 Guns - 150
109. 7-1-84 LUDGERSHALL Memorial Hall + AWOL/Organized Chaos/A-Heads/Black Easter - 150
110. 13-1-84 NOTTINGHAM Colwick Vale Social Club + A-Heads/Naked/Instigators/ Scumdribblers/Contempt/Seats of Piss - 200
111. 20-1-84 PORT TALBOT Rail and Transport Club + Organized Chaos/Shrapnel/Nux Vomica - 170
112. 28-1-84 OLDHAM Oddy's + Potential Victims/Mass of Black/Society's Problems - 170
113. 31-1-84 BOLTON Wheatsheaf Hotel + Mass of Black/Potential Victims - 150
114. 1-2-84 LEEDS Dortmunder Bierkeller + Instigators/Naked/Karl [poet]/Sick Vicars - 250
115. 4-2-84 HINTON ST GEORGE Village Hall + Self Abuse/Breakout/Wreck of the Hesperus - 150
116. 10-2-84 LONDON Stratford The Green Man + Lost Cherrees/3D Scream/Allegiance to No-one - 250
117. 21-2-84 LONDON 100 Club + Sears/Steve L./Smart Pils/Shrapnel - 327
118. 23-2-84 BRISTOL Trinity Hall: DOA/Subhumans/Toxic Shock/Spangles/Screaming Wild Spread - 300
119. 15-3-84 BRIGHTON Richmond Hotel + Exit-Stance/Crux/Rabid Dogs - 200
120. 21-3-84 EXETER Rougemont Hotel Caprice + Toxic Waste/Another Voice - 100
121. 22-3-84 PLYMOUTH Sound City + Toxic Waste/Blue Patrol - 120
122. 4-4-84 LEEDS Bierkeller: Hagar the Womb/A-Heads/Naked/Subhumans - 150
123. 13-4-84 USA - LOS ANGELES Olympic Auditorium + MDC/Dicks/Tourists/Red Scare/ New Regime - 2800
124. 14-4-84 - SAN FRANCISCO On Broadway + MDC/MIA/Trial/Atrocity - 500
125. 15-4-84 - SACRAMENTO Club Minimal + MIA/Trial/Satyagraha/X-Tal - 150
126. 19-4-84 - SALT LAKE CITY Indian Centre + Maimed for Life/Avon Calling - 300
127. 21-4-84 - DENVER Packing House + Bum Kon/Malibu Kens/Infanticide - 150
128. 24-4-84 - SAN FRANCISCO On Broadway + Angst/X-Tal/Sleeping Dogs/Treason/MJB - 250
129. 26-4-84 - RENO Sparks Elks Lodge + 7 Seconds/No Deal/Urban Assault - 200
130. 27-4-84 - SAN DIEGO Fairmount Hall + Red Scare/Killroy - 200
131. 28-4-84 - PASADENA Perkins Palace + Youth Brigade/MIA/Dr Know/Iconoclast - 800
132. 1-5-84 - KANSAS Fool Killer Theatre + Slabs/Names Don't Matter - 120
133. 3-5-84 - MINNEAPOLIS St Steven's Auditorium + Church Picnic/Lindberg's Baby - 50
134. 4-5-84 - MILWAUKEE Falcon Hall + Sacred Order - 150

135.   6-5-84 - CHICAGO Cubby Bear[afternoon] + 149 Dead Marines - 250

136.   6-5-84 - CHICAGO Cubby Bear[night] + 149 Dead Marines -100

137.   8-5-84 - HARRISBURG Paxtonia Fire Station + TSOL/Tom Terrific - 20

138.   9-5-84 - CLEVELAND Pop Shop: TSOL/Subhumans/Idiot Humans - 200

139.   10-5-84 - CINCINNATTI Newport Jockey Club + TSOL/Musical Suicide - 150

140.   11-5-84 - DETROIT Ann Arbor 7 Circle + TSOL/Ground Zero/Sudden Death - 100

141.   12-5-84 CANADA - TORONTO Desh Bhagat Temple: TSOL/Subhumans/Wrath - 400

142.   13-5-84 - QUEBEC Bar Univers + TSOL/Revolt - 250

143.   14-5-84 - MONTREAL The Cargo: TSOL/Subhumans/No Policy - 250

144.   16-5-84 USA - BALTIMORE Jules' Loft + Fear of God/Grey March - 100

145.   18-5-84 - PHILADELPHIA Long March + Freeze/Heart Attack/Adrenalin OD/FOD/
Kremlin Korps - 200

146.   20-5-84 - BOSTON Channel Club + Jerry's Kids/Killslug - 500

147.   14-6-84 GERMANY - HAMBURG Youth Centre + Public Disturbance/Die Jenigen - 100

148.   15-6-84 - HAMBURG Wutzrock Festival - 400

149.   18-6-84 HOLLAND - GRONINGEN Vera: Bougies/Ravioli Kids/Subhumans/ Gods Kods - 75

150.   19-6-84 - GRONINGEN Simplon - 150

151.   21-6-84 - AMSTERDAM Paradiso + Frites Modern - 200

152.   23-6-84 - UITHOORN [venue?] - 70

153.   28-6-84 PLYMOUTH Sound City + Wartoys/Contorted Vengeance/Steve L. - 100

154.   13-7-84 WESTBURY Youth Centre + Cult Maniax/Organized Chaos/Self Abuse - 170

155.   14-7-84 OLDHAM Oddy's + Mass of Black/Sears - 180

156.   16-7-84 BOLTON Duck and Firkin + Mass of Black/Instigators - 170

157.   22-7-84 BOURNEMOUTH Winton Continental Cinema + Self Abuse/Atrox/The Mad
Are Sane - 200

158.   26-7-84 LONDON 100 Club + Naked/D & V/Steve L./Blyth Power - 370

159.   1-8-84 WOLVERHAMPTON Queens + Sears/Contempt - 125

160.   2-8-84 ROCHDALE Youth Centre + Potential Victims/Mass of Black - 50

161.   4-8-84 GATESHEAD Station + Instigators/Faction/Phantoms of the Underground/Freak
Electric - 300

162.   6-8-84 GLASGOW Kelvin Centre + Last Rites/Toxic Reasons - 200

163.   9-8-84 BATHGATE La Stradas + Antisocial/Aliens - 170

164.   11-8-84 HULL Wellington Community Centre + Underdogs - 100

165.   12-8-84 SCARBOROUGH Rudie's + Sears - 100

166.   14-8-84 BRADFORD Palm Cove + Underdogs/Civilised Society? - 70

167.   15-8-84 MANCHESTER The Attik + Sick Vicars/Anarka and Poppy - 100

168.   17-8-84 LONDON Metropolitan + Sears/Wet Paint Theatre - 300

169.   20-8-84 BRISTOL Trinity Hall + Mau Maus/Onslaught/Organized Chaos - 200

170.   4-9-84 LONDON Ad Lib Club + Lost Cherrees/Steve L./Radical Elite - 130

171.   7-9-84 WARMINSTER Christchurch Hall + A-Heads - 150

172.   11-9-84 LONDON 100 Club + Sears/Legion of Parasites/Wartoys - 420

173.   14-9-84 TROWBRIDGE Court Mills + Organized Chaos/Steve L./A-Heads - 150

174.   15-9-84 AMESBURY Sports Centre + Do Easy/Opera for Infantry - 70

175.   26-9-84 LONDON Dickie Dirt's Warehouse + Dan Chumbawamba/Eat Shit/Toxic Waste/
        Conflict/Stalag 17 - 300

176.   5-10-84 IRELAND - DUBLIN Youth Expression Centre + Shrapnel - 120

177.   6-10-84 - DUBLIN Youth Expression Centre + Paranoid Visions/Mr Doom & Mrs Gloom - 100

178.   8-10-84 - BELFAST Manhattan's + Stalag 17/Asylum - 120

179.   9-10-84 - RATHCOOLE Fern Lodge + Toxic Waste/Shrapnel - 50

180.   10-10-84 - PORT STEWART Spuds + Self Destruct/Sterile Vision/Shrapnel - 100

181.   11-10-84 - DUBLIN Youth Expression Centre + Shrapnel/Paranoid Visions/Vicarious
        Living - 50

182.   13-10-84 - DUBLIN Youth Expression Centre + Vicarious Living/The Golden Horde/
        Paranoid Visions/Shrapnel - 120

183.   17-10-84 LEEDS Adam & Eve's + Steve L./Sears - 150

184.   19-10-84 PORTSMOUTH Hornpipe + Polemic/Ididid - 150

185.   25-10-84 SWEDEN - LINKOPING Grottan + Charta 77/Galler - 150

186.   27-10-84 - NORBERG Folketshus + Crude SS/Charta 77/Fear of War - 180

187.   29-10-84 - STOCKHOLM Birkagarden + Asta Kask - 160

188.   30-10-84 - HANDEN Ultra Huset + Zynthlakt - 75

189.   31-10-84 - HULTSFRED Lindblomshallen + Dom Dar/Sixteen Redlos - 70

190.   1-11-84 - VAXJO Rock Kallaren + Protest - 60

191.   2-11-84 - MALMO Stadt Hamburg + Moderat Liquidation/Puke - 120

192.   4-11-84 - BORAS Musikhusset + Jergens Fot - 100

193.   11-11-84 STEVENAGE Bowes Lyon House + Omega Tribe/Limbic System - 230

194.   25-11-84 BELFAST Labour Club + Disorder - 70

195.   27-11-84 LONDON 100 Club + Instigators - 320

196.   8-12-84 LONDON Interaction + Flowers in the Dustbin/Look Mummy Clowns - 400

197.   20-12-84 WARMINSTER King Arthur: Organized Chaos/Subhumans/Shrapnel/A-Heads - 180

198.   28-1-85 CARLISLE Stars and Stripes + Nightmare - 120

199.   1-2-85 SHETLAND Mossbank Hall + John Bibby's Dog - 250

200.   4-2-85 ABERDEEN 62 Club + Toxik Ephex - 80

201.   6-2-85 LEEDS Adam & Eve's + Mass of Black/TVOD - 200

202.   7-2-85 OLDHAM Oddy's + Instigators/Civilised Society?/Reprisal - 100

203.   8-2-85 WARWICK Liberal Club + Depraved/Sears - 200

204.   16-2-85 SUNDERLAND Bunker + Phantoms of the Underground/Toxic Waste - 100

205.   17-2-85 SHEFFIELD Lead Mill + D & V/Chumbawamba/Absit in Videa - 370

206.   21-2-85 LONDON 100 Club + Blyth Power/Steve L./Mass of Black - 350

207.   22-2-85 GILLINGHAM Red Lion + Organized Chaos/Virus/General Belgrano - 200

208.   1-3-85 COLWALL Horse and Jockey + Steve L./Decadence Within/Discarded Remnants
        of an Age No More/The Crows - 180

209.   3-3-85 OXFORD Co op Hall + Cremation Examples/Steve L./Stone the Crowz - 70

210.   3-4-85 LONDON Fulham Greyhound + Blyth Power/Push - 350

211.   6-4-85 SALISBURY Arts Centre + Don't Feed the Animals/Obvious Action/Grey Wolves - 350

212. 20-4-85 WARMINSTER Christchurch Hall Sharon's party + Steve L. - 60
213. 23-4-85 USA - NEW YORK Ritz: Scream/Subhumans/Murphy's Law - 175
214. 27-4-85 - BOSTON Paradise: Scream/Subhumans/The Not - 220
215. 28-4-85 - NEW YORK CBGB + Scream/Dr Know/MXJ - 250
216. 30-4-85 - WASHINGTON DC 930 Club: Pea Soup/Subhumans/Scream - 120
217. 1-5-85 - RICHMOND Rockitz [afternoon] + Scream/Judge Dread - 100
218. 1-5-85 - RICHMOND Rockitz [night] + Scream/Absence of Malice - 100
219. 2-5-85 - ATLANTA 688 [afternoon]: Scream/Subhumans - 100
220. 2-5-85 - ATLANTA 688 [night] + Scream - 100
221. 3-5-85 - COLUMBIA Striders + Scream - 120
222. 4-5-85 - GAINESVILLE American Legion Hall: Scream/Subhumans/Disorderly Conduct - 200
223. 5-5-85 - HOLLYWOOD The Cell + Scream/Drills - 250
224. 7-5-85 - NEWPORT Jockey Club: Scream/Subhumans/Poetic Justice - 80
225. 8-5-85 - CLEVELAND Underground + Raw Power/Scream/Breakouts - 250
226. 9-5-85 - PITTSBURGH Electric Banana: Scream/Subhumans/Half Life - 150
227. 10-5-85 - DETROIT Hungry Brain + Scream/Pagan Babies - 200
228. 12-5-85 - CHICAGO Cubby Bear: Scream/Subhumans - 250
229. 14-5-85 - MADISON Ocayz + Scream - 100
230. 17-5-85 - SANTA BARBARA Casa De La Raza + Scream/Detox/Rat Pack - 300
231. 18-5-85 - LOS ANGELES Olympic Auditorium + Scream/Bad Religion/Ill Repute/Detox
      - 3000
232. 19-5-85 - SUN VALLEY Sportsman's Hall + Scream/Caustic Cause/Johnny and the
      Dingbats - 150
233. 22-5-85 - SAN FRANCISCO Mabuhay Gardens + Scream/Boneless Ones - 200
234. 23-5-85 - SANTA CRUZ Club Culture + Scream/Blast/Christ on Parade/Mock - 150
235. 24-5-85 - SAN FRANCISCO The Farm: Dead Kennedys/Subhumans/Scream/Frightwig/
      Sea Hags - 600
236. 25-5-85 - SACRAMENTO Crest Theatre: Dead Kennedys/Subhumans/Frightwig/Blast/
      Junkwaffle - 400
237. 7-6-85 CHESTERFIELD Conservative Club + Chumbawamba/Toxic Toys - 200
238. 6-7-85 CHIPPENHAM Liberal Club + Organized Chaos/Smiles/Lumps of Merde - 70
239. 7-7-85 BRIGHTON Richmond Hotel + Rabid Dogs - 150
240. 12-7-85 LONDON Fulham Greyhound + Blyth Power/Paranoid Visions - 430
241. 24-7-85 LEEDS Adam & Eve's + Instigators/Miasma/Indian Dream - 250
242. 27-7-85 GATESHEAD Station + Instigators/Hex - 220
243. 31-7-85 DUDLEY Sugarhill Club + Sears/Contempt - 180
244. 11-8-85 WATERLOOVILLE Brambles Farm Peace Festival + Organized Chaos/Antisect/
      Polemic Attack/D.I.R.T... - 300
245. 16-8-85 PLYMOUTH Ziggy's + Virus
246. 30-8-85 UPTON Memorial Hall + Depraved/Decadence Within/Dismembered - 100
247. 31-8-85 COVENTRY Hand and Heart + Depraved/Sears - 150
248. 11-9-85 HOLLAND - AMSTERDAM Emma + Disgust - 400

249. 12-9-85 - GRONINGEN Vera - 150
250. 13-9-85 - ALKMAAR Parkhof - 100
251. 17-9-85 - NIJMEGEN Parapluie Fabrieken - 200
252. 19-9-85 - ZUTPHEN Debarak -100
253. 20-9-85 - STEENWIJK De Buze + Murder Inc./Funeral Oration - 80
254. 21-9-85 - ROTTERDAM Arena - 150
255. 22-9-85 - VENLO Bauplatz + Toxic Waste/Disgust - 200
256. 24-9-85 GERMANY - FREIBURG Fabrik - 150
257. 25-9-85 - DARMSTADT Arschgebuiden + Stromberg Polka - 200
258. 28-9-85 - BIELEFELD AJZ + Manson Youth/Velocet - 400
259. 29-9-85 - DUISBURG Eschhaus +? - 200
260. 23-10-85 LEEDS Adam & Eve's + Brigades/Organized Chaos/Shrapnel - 220
261. 31-10-85 LONDON Fulham Greyhound + Steve L./Instigators - 350
262. 10-11-85 WARMINSTER Athenaeum + Steve L./Organized Chaos - 275

----

263. 2-1-91 LONDON Venue + Zygote - 800
264. 3-1-91 LONDON Venue + Instigators - 1000

----

265. 20-2-98 BATH Porter Butt + Zero Tolerance/Ex-Mass - 250
266. 9-7-98 DERBY Victoria Inn + Roadrage - 200
267. 10-7-98 BRISTOL Trinity Hall + Cult Maniax/Bus Station Loonies - 370
268. 16-7-98 LONDON ULU + Zounds/System - 450
269. 17-7-98 LONDON ULU + System/Thatcher on Acid - 470
270. 23-7-98 NEWPORT TJ's + Muckspreader/Truth Decay/In the Shit - 100
271. 1-8-98 THORNCOMBE Alternative World Cup + Screamer/Hells Bells - 400
272. 6-8-98 GLASGOW Arena + Ex-Cathedra/Machine Gun Etiquette - 200
273. 7-8-98 BRADFORD Rio + TV Smith/P.A.I.N. - 400
274. 9-8-98 BIRMINGHAM Foundry + Police Bastard/POA/Eastfield - 470
275. 26-8-98 USA - SACRAMENTO Bojangles + Strychnine/Enemies - 511
276. 27-8-98 - SAN FRANCISCO Slim's + Strychnine/Enemies/Ding Dang - 750
277. 28-8-98 - SAN BERNARDINO Citrus Pavilion + Strychnine/Calovera/Narcoleptic Youth - 3971
278. 29-8-98 - MESA Nile Theatre + Retail Christ/Sam the Butcher - 900
279. 31-8-98 - AUSTIN Atomic Cafe + Ignorance Park - 513
280. 1-9-98 - HOUSTON Fitzgerald's + Fantastic Eddy/UTA - 202
281. 2-9-98 - NEW ORLEANS Jimmy's + One Common Voice/Insurrection - 252
282. 4-9-98 - ST PETERSBURG State Theater + Scams/Chamber/HCA - 560
283. 5-9-98 - FORT LAUDERDALE Fubar + Load/Beltones - 500
284. 6-9-98 - JACKSONVILLE Milk Bar + ?/Belik - 262
285. 7-9-98 - ATLANTA The Point + ? - 424
286. 8-9-98 CARRBOROUGH Cat's Cradle + Patriots/Louts - 427
287. 9-9-98 - WASHINGTON DC Capital Ballroom + Goons/Latchkey Kids - 441
288. 10-9-98 - NEW YORK Coney Island High + Unseen/Thulsa Doom - 550

289.	11-9-98 - NEW YORK Coney Island High + Anti-Flag/Casualties - 530
290.	12-9-98 - PHILADELPHIA Trocadero + Boils/Violent Society - 800
291.	12-9-98 - PHILADELPHIA Stalag 13 after-gig + members of Boils [+ bottle of Kahlua!] - 50
292.	13-9-98 - PITTSBURGH Laga + Submachine/Creeps - 582
293.	14-9-98 - CLEVELAND Peabody's + Spasms/Conservatives - 380
294.	15-9-98 - DETROIT St Andrew's Hall + Maloko Plus - 504
295.	16-9-98 - CINCINNATI Bogarts + Raw Power/SS20 - 635
296.	17-9-98 - ST LOUIS Galaxy + El Gordo's Revenge/Grumples - 320
297.	18-9-98 - CHICAGO Metro + Tossers/Funeral Oration - 863
298.	19-9-98 - GREEN BAY Concert Cafe + Funeral Oration - 295
299.	20-9-98 - ST PAUL Uni. of Minnesota + Code XIII - 542
300.	22-9-98 - DENVER Aztlan Theater + Criminals/Self Service - 715
301.	23-9-98 - SALT LAKE CITY DV8 + Criminals/We All Fall Down - 260
302.	25-9-98 - PORTLAND La Luna + Criminals/Readymen - 1139
303.	26-9-98 - SEATTLE RCKCNDY + Mark Bruback/David Koresh Choir - 1000
304.	25-3-99 BELGIUM - KONTICH Lint Fabriek + Charlie Don't Surf - 350
305.	26-3-99 GERMANY - AACHEN AJZ + Antidote/Tagtraum/Melangloomy - 300
306.	27-3-99 - FRANKFURT Exzess Cafe + WWK - 300
307.	28-3-99 - FILDERSTADT Jugundzentrum Z + Diavolo Rosso/Murder Disco Experience - 200
308.	29-3-99 - KARLSRUHE Schwartzwald + 10 Buck Fuck - 190
309.	30-3-99 SWITZERLAND - ZURICH Abart + Wicked - 83
310.	31-3-99 ITALY - MILAN Garibaldi + Berenica Beach - 300
311.	1-4-99 - TURIN El Paso + Plastination - 300
312.	2-4-99 - MODENA Scintilla + L'Huomo - 200
313.	3-4-99 - UDINE CSA + Elvis Jackson - 200
314.	5-4-99 SLOVENIA - ILIRSKA BISTRICA MKNZ + ? - 100
315.	6-4-99 AUSTRIA - VIENNA EKH + Petrograd/Grant - 200
316.	7-4-99 CZECH REPUBLIC - PRAGUE Ladronka + Wind of Pain - 400
317.	9-4-99 GERMANY - BERLIN Kopi + ? - 400
318.	10-4-99 POLAND - POZNAN Rozbart + Telefon - 250
319.	11-4-99 - WARSAW Culture Centre + Post Regiment/Telefon - 450
320.	13-4-99 GERMANY - POTSDAM Archiv + Resisters/Azotopakta - 200
321.	14-4-99 - HAMBURG Rota Flora + Stateless in the Universe/Ex-Cathedra - 500
322.	15-4-99 - BREMEN Schlachtof + Ex-Cathedra/Stateless in the Universe - 350
323.	16-4-99 HOLLAND - ALKMAAR Parkhof + Hellworms/Boom - 300
324.	17-4-99 BELGIUM - GENT Democrazy - 400
325.	15-4-00 LONDON - Chats Palace + Wat Tyler/Petrograd - 300
326.	15-7-00 DERBY - Victoria Inn punks' picnic + Bus Station Loonies/Hellkrusher/Assert/ MDM/Throw Bricks at Coppers/In the Shit/Amazing Screaming Willies - 250
327.	21-7-00 MORECAMBE Dome - Holidays in the Sun: Sic Boy Federation/Peter & Test Tube Babies/Subhumans/Vibrators etc. - 900
328.	7-10-00 MILTON KEYNES Sanctuary: Conflict/Subhumans/Steve Ignorant/P.A.I.N etc. - 2000

329.	22-12-00 PLYMOUTH Cooperage + Bus Station Loonies - 180
330.	8-7-01 MORECAMBE Dome - Holidays in the Sun + Hard Skin etc. - 1000
331.	13-7-01 BRISTOL Fiddlers + Far Cue/Bay 6 - 300
332.	22-12-01 SOUTHEND Image + P.A.I.N/Ex-Cathedra - 120
333.	29-3-02 BRIGHTON Concorde + MU330/Flatpig/Slaughterhouse 57/Shut Up Grandad/ No Comply - 350
334.	7-4-02 LONDON Astoria: Conflict/Subhumans/Icons of Filth/Inner Terrestrials/Dezerter/ Riot/Clone / La Fraction - 1700
335.	3-5-02 WARMINSTER Weymouth Arms - Mel's party - 60
336.	12-7-02 SPAIN - BARCELONA Festival Sans Nom: Dead Kennedys/Subhumans/DOA - 400
337.	21-7-02 BLACKPOOL Winter Gardens - Holidays in the Sun + GBH/MDC etc. - 600
338.	3-8-02 CROATIA - PULA Monte Paradiso Festival + Fack Off Bolan etc. - 1200
339.	30-10-02 CANADA - TORONTO Kathedral + Closet Monster - 220
340.	31-10-02 - TORONTO Kathedral + Lost - 240
341.	1-11-02 - LONDON Call the Office + ? - 152
342.	2-11-02 - MONTREAL Rainbow [afternoon] + Dead Generators - 600
343.	2-11-02 - MONTREAL Rainbow [night] + Dead Generators - 420
344.	3-11-02 - QUEBEC L'Anti [afternoon] + ? - 60
345.	3-11-02 - QUEBEC L'Anti [night] + ? - 412
346.	27-3-03 USA - SEATTLE Showbox + Mark Bruback/Enemies/Fitz of Depression - 1034
347.	28-3-03 - PORTLAND B Complex + Enemies/Voids - 650
348.	29-3-03 - SAN FRANCISCO Slim's + Enemies/Voids - 689
349.	30-3-03 - SACRAMENTO Colonial Theater + Enemies/Voids - 633
350.	31-3-03 - LOS ANGELES Roxy + Enemies/Voids - 500
351.	1-4-03 - LOS ANGELES Roxy + Meet the Virus/Enemies - 500
352.	2-4-03 - SAN DIEGO The Scene + Meet the Virus/Enemies - 634
353.	3-4-03 - CORONA Showcase Theatre + Meet the Virus/Enemies - 571
354.	4-4-03 - POMONA Glasshouse + Enemies/Meet the Virus - 409
355.	5-4-03 - SCOTTSDALE Cajun House + Enemies/Meet the Virus/Last Action Zeroes - 750
356.	7-4-03 - AUSTIN Emo's + Enemies/The Code - 354
357.	8-4-03 - HOUSTON Fitzgerald's + Enemies/The Code/Hates - 347
358.	9-4-03 - NEW ORLEANS in a bar… + Enemies/The Code - 214
359.	10-4-03 - TALLAHASSEE Beta Bar + Enemies/The Code - 150
360.	11-4-03 - ST PETERSBURG State Theatre + Enemies/The Code - 568
361.	12-4-03 - FORT LAUDERDALE Factory + Against All Authority/Enemies/The Code - 582
362.	13-4-03 - ORLANDO The Social + Enemies/The Code - 425
363.	14-4-03 - ATLANTA Cotton Club + Enemies/The Code - 580
364.	16-4-03 - RICHMOND Alley Katz + Enemies/Eccentrics - 198
365.	17-4-03 - PHILADELPHIA Trocadero Theatre + Enemies/Eccentrics - 593
366.	18-4-03 BOSTON Axis + Enemies/Eccentrics - 461
367.	19-4-03 - NEW YORK Knitting Factory + Enemies/Eccentrics - 421
368.	20-4-03 - NEW YORK Knitting Factory + Enemies/Eccentrics - 353

369.	21-4-03 - WASHINGTON DC Black Cat + Enemies/Suspect Device - 309
370.	22-4-03 - PITTSBURG Club Laga + Enemies - 362
371.	23-4-03 - CLEVELAND Agora Ballroom + Caustic Christ/Enemies - 325
372.	24-4-03 - DETROIT Magic Stick + Enemies/Caustic Christ - 366
373.	25-4-03 - CINCINNATI Bogarts + Tossers/Enemies - 511
374.	26-4-03 - CHICAGO Metro + Tossers/Enemies - 825
375.	27-4-03 - MINNEAPOLIS First Avenue + Tossers/Enemies - 866
376.	28-4-03 - MILWAUKEE Globe East + ? - 281
377.	16-5-03 SHEFFIELD Boardwalk + MDC/Leftover Crack/F-Minus/Goldblade/Broken Bones/Sick on the Bus - 600
378.	18-5-03 LONDON Astoria + ? - 700
379.	21-9-03 LONDON Forum: Conflict/Subhumans/Inner Terrestrials/Lost Cherrees - 600
380.	3-10-03 GERMANY - BERLIN Kopi + ? - 400
381.	6-12-03 LONDON Chat's Palace: Zounds/Subhumans/Lost Cherrees/ Restarts - 120
382.	13-12-03 DERBY Supanova + ? - 500
383.	30-1-04 BRISTOL Bierkeller + ? - 350
384.	6-2-04 BRADFORD-ON-AVON Riverside Inn + ? - 200
385.	17-2-04 USA - HOUSTON Mary Jane's + Caustic Christ/New Mexican Disaster Squad [N.M.D.S] - 207
386.	18-2-04 - AUSTIN Emo's + Caustic Christ/N.M.D.S./Storm the River - 351
387.	19-2-04 - DALLAS Trees + Caustic Christ/N.M.D.S - 393
388.	20-2-04 - OKLAHOMA CITY Green Door + Caustic Christ/N.M.D.S - 408
389.	21-2-04 - ALBUQUERQUE Launch Pad + Caustic Christ/N.M.D.S - 314
390.	22-2-04 - TEMPE Marquee Theater + Caustic Christ/N.M.D.S/Corrupt - 619
391.	24-2-04 - LAS VEGAS Jillian's + Caustic Christ/N.M.D.S/Loud Pipes - 377
392.	25-2-04 - CORONA Showcase + Naked Aggression/Caustic Christ - 500
393.	26-2-04 - CORONA Showcase + Naked Aggression/N.M.D.S - 540
394.	27-2-04 - SAN DIEGO Soma + Naked Aggression/Swindle/N.M.D.S - 1396
395.	28-2-04 - LOS ANGELES Roxy [1] + Naked Aggression/Frisk - 500
396.	29-2-04 - LOS ANGELES Roxy [2] + Naked Aggression/Frisk - 500
397.	2-3-04 - SAN FRANCISCO Bottom of the Hill + Frisk/Enemies - 380
398.	3-3-04 - SAN FRANCISCO Slim's + Naked Aggression/From Ashes Rise - 684
399.	4-3-04 - SACRAMENTO Colonial Theatre + Frisk/From Ashes Rise - 550
400.	5-3-04 - PORTLAND Crystal Ballroom + Frisk/From Ashes Rise/Observers - 1091
401.	6-3-04 - SEATTLE Graceland + Frisk/From Ashes Rise - 700
402.	7-3-04 - SEATTLE Graceland + Unseen/Virus – 777
403.	29-4-04 NEWCASTLE University + Sick on the Bus - 100
404.	30-4-04 GLASGOW G2 + Sick on the Bus - 250
405.	1-5-04 SHEFFIELD Corporation: Poison Idea/Subhumans/Peter & the Test Tube Babies/etc. - 350
406.	2-5-04 BIRMINGHAM Academy: Damned/Buzzcocks/Undertones/Meteors/Beat/ Slaughter & the Dogs/ Subhumans etc. - 2000
407.	3-5-04 LONDON Camden Underworld + ? - 250

408.	18-7-04 MORECAMBE Carlton - Wasted Festival + UK Subs/P.A.I.N etc. - 300
409.	22-7-04 BATH Invention Arts + Tiny Elvis - 250
410.	24-7-04 FINLAND - Puntala Rock festival - 1000
411.	2-9-04 HOLLAND - ALKMAAR Parkhof + ? - 70
412.	3-9-04 - ROTTERDAM Baroeg + No Hoodlums - 85
413.	4-9-04 - AMSTERDAM OCCII + Hatchetmen - 200
414.	5-9-04 GERMANY - HAMBURG Hafenklang + Panic DDH/Fatwahs - 150
415.	6-9-04 - BREMEN Schlachtof + ? - 150
416.	7-9-04 - BERLIN Kopi + Poundaflesh - 100
417.	8-9-04 - LEIPZIG Zorro + Poundaflesh/Sol - 80
418.	9-9-04 - GIESSEN Jokum: Poundaflesh/Subhumans/Restarts - 100
419.	10-9-04 FRANCE - ST BRIEUC Le Wagon + ? - 400
420.	11-9-04 - LISIEUX Alternatif Cafe - 100
421.	12-9-04 BELGIUM - KONTICH Lint Fabriek - 70
422.	26-10-04 USA - PITTSBURGH The World + Caustic Christ/Hero Dishonest - 270
423.	28-10-04 - SAYREVILLE Starland Ballroom + Unseen/Virus - 300
424.	29-10-04 - PHILADELPHIA First Unitarian Church + Unseen/Virus/Global Chaos - 486
425.	30-10-04 - BOSTON Axis + Unseen/Toxic Narcotic - 430
426.	31-10-04 - NEW YORK Knitting Factory + Unseen/Stockyard Stoics - 400
427.	1-11-04 - NEW YORK Knitting Factory + Toxic Narcotic/7 Crowns - 340
428.	2-11-04 - BALTIMORE Otto Bar + Casualties/Lower Class Brats/Monster Squad - 401
429.	3-11-04 - WEST COLUMBIA New Brookland Tavern + Caustic Christ/Seven Crowns - 170
430.	4-11-04 - ATLANTA Masquerade + UK Subs/Caustic Christ/Seven Crowns - 217
431.	5-11-04 - ST PETERSBURG State Theatre + Caustic Christ/Seven Crowns - 278
432.	6-11-04 - ORLANDO The Social + Caustic Christ/Seven Crowns - 361
433.	7-11-04 - FORT LAUDERDALE The Factory + ? - 235
434.	5-2-05 LONDON Forum: Icons of Filth/Subhumans/Conflict/Oppressed/Varukers/Inner Terrestrials/Lost Cherrees/Extinction of Mankind/Restarts/No Choice - 800
435.	20-5-05 LINCOLN Duke of Wellington + Eccentrics/MCD - 150
436.	21-5-05 MORECAMBE Wasted Festival: Stranglers/Angelic Upstarts/Undertones/Toyah/Subhumans/999/Oppressed/MDM - 1000
437.	8-7-05 CANADA - MONTREAL United Fest: Adicts/Dickies/ANWL/Conflict/Subhumans/..../ Citizen Fish - 800
438.	9-7-05 USA - ST LOUIS Creepy Crawl + Horrorshow Malchicks/Pubes - 200
439.	10-7-05 - CHICAGO Logan Auditorium + World/Inferno Friendship Society + From Ashes Rise + I Attack - 585
440.	11-7-05 - MINNEAPOLIS First Avenue + From Ashes Rise + World/Inferno Friendship Society + Rivethead + Building Better Bombs - 650
441.	12-7-05 - MILWAUKEE The Rave + World/Inferno Friendship Society + From Ashes Rise + SFN - 229
442.	14-7-05 - DETROIT Alvins + From Ashes Rise/Publife - 268
443.	15-7-05 - CLEVELAND Grog Shop + 9 Shocks Terror/From Ashes Rise/Beef Feeders - 423

444.	16-7-05 - BALTIMORE Otto Bar + Leftover Crack/From Ashes Rise/1905 - 493
445.	17-7-05 - PHILADELPHIA First Unitarian Church + Leftover Crack/From Ashes Rise/Fighting Dogs - 525
446.	18-7-05 - BOSTON Middle East + From Ashes Rise/? - 482
447.	19-7-05 - NEW YORK BB Kings + Leftover Crack + World/Inferno Friendship Society + From Ashes Rise - 1000
448.	2-9-05 HOLLAND - AMSTERDAM OCCII + Migra Violenta/Barnstorm Effect - 200
449.	3-9-05 BELGIUM - LIEGE C.P.C.R. + ? - 100
450.	10-9-05 GERMANY - BREMEN Friesenstrasse + Chaot-X - 150
451.	11-9-05 - BERLIN Kopi + Orang Utan - 200
452.	27-10-05 PENZANCE Club 2000 + Final Warning - 120
453.	28-10-05 LITTLEHAM Village Hall + Bus Station Loonies/Wild Honey Pie - 200
454.	29-10-05 BRADFORD-ON-AVON - St Margaret's Hall + Seven Crowns - 250
455.	30-10-05 BRISTOL Full Moon + ? - 200
456.	31-10-05 LONDON The Jamm + Eastfield - 300
457.	1-11-05 NOTTINGHAM Junktion 7 + Poundaflesh/Contempt - 200
458.	2-11-05 BIRMINGHAM Edward's No. 8 + Antibodies/Radiation Angels/False Idol - 200
459.	3-11-05 DERBY - Victoria Inn + Homebrew/Barnyard Masturbator - 150
460.	4-11-05 LIVERPOOL Heaven and Hell + MDM/Collective Responsibility/Rejected - 120
461.	5-11-05 LEEDS Cockpit + GBH/Goldblade/MDM/Milloy/Guilty Pleasures - 450
462.	6-11-05 EDINBURGH Wheatsheaf Inn + ? - 150
463.	7-11-05 LANCASTER Yorkshire House + Eastfield/Guilty Pleasures - 120
464.	11-2-06 SPAIN - CREVELLENTE Club 100 + Sensa Yuma/Estropizio - 120
465.	17-2-06 - ALICANTE Nave Iguana: Sensa Yuma/Subhumans/Weight of Government - 40
466.	18-2-06 - ALCOI El Barraro + Sensa Yuma - 150
467.	19-3-06 USA - MILWAUKEE Mad Planet + A Global Threat - 278
468.	20-3-06 - MINNEAPOLIS Triple Rock + A Global Threat/Disrespect/4 Minute Warning - 373
469.	21-3-06 - DES MOINES Hairy Mary's + A Global Threat/Black Market Foetus - 153
470.	22-3-06 - DENVER Bluebird Theatre + A Global Threat/Love Me Destroyer - 550
471.	23-3-06 - SALT LAKE CITY Club Sound + A Global Threat/Endless Struggle/All Systems Fail - 362
472.	24-3-06 - BOISE The Venue + A Global Threat/? - 278
473.	25-3-06 - SEATTLE El Corazon + A Global Threat + World/Inferno Friendship Society + Born/Dead - 800
474.	26-3-06 - TACOMA Hell's Kitchen + World/Inferno Friendship Society + Durango 9s + Syrens - 299
475.	27-3-06 - PORTLAND Loveland + World/Inferno Friendship Society + Born/Dead + Coldbringer - 690
476.	29-3-06 - SAN FRANCISCO Slim's + World/Inferno Friendship Society + Born/Dead - 600
477.	30-3-06 - SACRAMENTO Empire + World/Inferno Friendship Society + Born/Dead + Rebels Advocate - 500
478.	31-3-06 - CORONA Showcase + World/Inferno Friendship Society + Born/Dead + Rotting Stiffs - 500

479.	1-4-06 - SAN DIEGO Soma + Total Chaos + World/Inferno Friensdhip Society + Born/ Dead - 1348
480.	2-4-06 - LOS ANGELES Knitting Factory + World/Inferno Friendship Society + Born/ Dead - 559
481.	3-4-06 - LOS ANGELES Knitting Factory + Naked Aggression/Clit 45 - 561
482.	4-4-06 - TEMPE Clubhouse + Clit 45/Med-X/Ambivalent - 494
483.	6-4-06 - AUSTIN Emo's + Clit 45/Signal Lost/Storm the Tower - 348
484.	7-4-06 - DALLAS Galaxy + Clit 45/Signal Lost/Damage Case - 418
485.	8-4-06 - OKLAHOMA CITY Bricktown Ballroom + Clit 45/Signal Lost/Misread - 220
486.	10-4-0 - COLUMBUS The Basement + Caustic Christ/Signal Lost - 187
487.	11-4-06 - PITTSBURGH Rex + Caustic Christ/Signal Lost/Unarmed - 371
488.	12-4-06 - BALTIMORE Otto Bar + Gorilla Angreb/Caustic Christ/1905 - 358
489.	13-4-06 - PHILADELPHIA First Unitarian Church + Caustic Christ/Gorilla Angreb/ Signal Lost - 370
490.	14-4-06 - NEW YORK Knitting Factory + Caustic Christ/Gorilla Angreb - 400
491.	15-4-06 - BOSTON Axis + Caustic Christ/Gorilla Angreb/Mouth Sewn Shut - 320
492.	17-4-06 CANADA - MONTREAL Foufounes Electriques + St. Catherines/And the Saga Continues/Ventilators - 600
493.	18-4-06 - QUEBEC CITY L'Anti + Mop/St.Catherines - 364
494.	19-4-06 - OTTAWA Babylon + St. Catherines/Centre Town Insurgents/Bayonettes - 352
495.	20-4-06 - TORONTO Reverb + St. Catherines/Antics/Bayonettes - 309
496.	21-4-06 USA - DETROIT Magic Stick + Leftover Crack/St. Catherines/Bayonettes - 400
497.	22-4-06 - CHICAGO Logan's Square + Leftover Crack/St. Catherines/Siderunners - 500
498.	25-5-06 BOURNEMOUTH Neptune + Self Abuse/Toretz - 150
499.	26-5-06 NEWPORT TJs + Viktims/This System Kills - 200
500.	27-5-06 STOCKPORT Thatched House + Instant Agony/Blisterhead/3CR - 200
501.	28-5-06 NEWCASTLE Academy: Damned/Rezillos/Penetration/Angelic Upstarts/ Partisans/ Subhumans/GBH etc. – 2000
502.	29-5-06 NORTHAMPTON Racehorse + ? - 200
503.	13-7-06 BRISTOL Lakota + No Choice/Gurkha - 185
504.	15-7-06 SHEFFIELD The Plug + Ignite/GBH/Freaks Union/Peacocks/With Honour/ BXSXDX/Mingers/Black Radio - 280
505.	16-7-06 LONDON Mean Fiddler + Ignite/GBH [etc., as night before] - 280
506.	8-9-06 GERMANY - MULLHEIM AJZ + Police Bastard - 250
507	9-9-06 - VERDEN Juz + Police Bastard - 200
508.	10-9-06 - BIELEFELD AJZ + November 13th/Instinct of Survival - 40
509.	24-11-06 BIRMINGHAM Academy: Conflict/Subhumans/Restarts/Lost Cherrees - 350
510.	25-11-06 LONDON Islington Academy: Conflict/Subhumans/Lost Cherrees/Restarts - 500
511.	30-11-06 IRELAND - BELFAST Bunker + Excuses/Thousand Drunken Nights/ Hypocrites - 150
512.	1-12-06 - DUBLIN Voodoo Lounge + Droppin Bombs/Excuses - 300
513.	2-12-06 - SLIGO Coolera House + Excuses/Only Fumes and Corpses/Derelicts - 100

514.   3-12-06 - DERRY Mason's Bar + Antistate/Men Overbored - 30

515.   7-4-07 BATH B.O.B Fest, Invention Arts + ? [heaps of bands!] - 200

516.   10-4-07 LEICESTER The Shed + Barnyard Masturbator/The Nags/Wave of Fear/ Throbax/Charges - 70

517.   11-4-07 MANCHESTER Star and Garter + ? + Barnyard Masturbator - 175

518.   12-4-07 KETTERING Sawyers + Barnyard Masturbator/Rotten Agendas/Mutley - 80

519.   13-4-07 BOURNEMOUTH Railway Workers Social Club + Self Abuse/Barnyard Masturbator - 200

520.   14-4-07 LONDON Stepney Green, Dame Collett House squat + Barnyard Masturbator/ Defcon Zero/KADT - 200

521.   17-4-07 CANADA - OTTAWA Babylon + Fourstroke/Suicide Pilots/Bombed Out - 280

522   18-4-07 - MONTREAL Cafe Chaos + Ruffianz/Marshall Law - 170

523.   19-4-07 - QUEBEC L'Anti + Discordia/The Hunters/Defaillance - 270

524.   20-4-07 - MONTREAL Foufounes Electriques + Ripcordz/Hold a Grudge/Automatix - 450

525.   21-4-07 - SAINTE-HYACINTHE Le Trash + Heat Scores/ Hollerado - 200

526.   22-4-07 - TORONTO Reverb + 3 Tards/Antics - 100

527.   10-5-07 GERMANY - GOTTINGEN Juz + Maschinen Fest - 130

528.   11-5-07 - HAMBURG Hafenklang + ? - 150

529.   12-5-07 DENMARK - COPENHAGEN Loppen + Death Token - 300

530.   13-5-07 - AALBORG 1000 Fryd + Terveet Kadet/Hynkel Overskaeg/Totalickers - 40

531.   14-5-07 - ARHUS Studenterhusset + ? - 60

532.   15-5-07 GERMANY - BREMEN Schlachtof Magazinkeller + Filth Injection - 100

533.   16-5-07 - HANNOVER Stumpf + Bombenalarme - 200

534.   17-5-07 - FRANKFURT Exzess + ? - 400

535.   18-5-07 - DUSSELDORF Jugend + Heroes and Zeroes - 250

536.   19-5-07 HOLLAND - EINDHOVEN Ramblers + ? - 50

537.   20-5-07 - AMSTERDAM Melkveg, Rebellion Festival: Conflict/Subhumans/Deadline/ Hard Skin/Channel 3/Sonic Boom 6/Tat/Sick on the Bus/Sensa Yuma - 800

538.   20-6-07 BELGIUM - BRUSSELS Le Magazin 4 + Les Slugs - 150

539.   21-6-07 FRANCE - FOUGERES outdoor festival + loads of bands - 150

540.   22-6-07 - PARIS La Maroquinerie - Barricata Fest: Inner Terrestrials/Subhumans - 350

541.   23-6-07 - DIJON Les Tanneries + ? - 300

542.   24-6-07 BELGIUM - LIEGE La Zone + Vae Victis - 200

543.   25-6-07 FRANCE - LILLE Reve D'Hubert + ? - 150

544.   28-6-07 SOUTHAMPTON Nexus + Constant State of Terror/Social Parasites - 200

545.   29-6-07 CAMBRIDGE Cellar Bar + ? - 150

546.   30-6-07 FOLKESTONE Piper Club + Lost Cherrees + Refuse/All - 104

547.   1-7-07 BRISTOL Croft + A-Heads + War/System + Jesus Bruiser - 250

548.   10-8-07 BLACKPOOL Arena, Rebellion Festival - 2000

549.   24-8-07 USA - MILWAUKEE Miramar Theatre + Witch Hunt/Get Rad - 159

550.   25-8-07 - MINNEAPOLIS Triple Rock + Smoke or Fire/Witch Hunt - 277

551.   26-8-07 - OMAHA ? + Witch Hunt/Hercules - 120

552. 27-8-07 - DENVER Marquis Theatre + Witch Hunt/Clusterfux - 438
553. 28-8-07 - SALT LAKE CITY In the Venue + Witch Hunt - 200
554. 29-8-07 - MISSOULA The Other Side + Witch Hunt/Jacktop Town - 200
555. 30-8-07 - SEATTLE El Corazon + Witch Hunt/Skarp/Iron Lung - 524
556. 31-8-07 - PORTLAND Hawthorne Theatre + Witch Hunt/Embrace the Kill - 500
557. 1-9-07 - SAN FRANCISCO Slim's + Witch Hunt/Peligro Social - 670
558. 2-9-07 - SACRAMENTO Empire Theatre + Witch Hunt/Peligro Social - 275
559. 4-9-07 - LOS ANGELES Knitting Factory + Witch Hunt/Peligro Social - 650
560. 5-9-07 - LOS ANGELES Knitting Factory + MDC/Witch Hunt - 600
561. 6-9-07 - SAN DIEGO Soma + MDC/Witch Hunt/Career Soldiers/Peligro Social - 945
562. 7-9-07 - TEMPE Clubhouse + Witch Hunt/Peligro Social/Prosthetics - 517
563. 8-9-07 - ALBUQUERQUE Launch Pad + Krum Bums/Witch Hunt - 324
564. 9-9-07 - EL PASO Club 101 + Krum Bums/Witch Hunt - 100
565. 10-9-07- DALLAS Red Blood Club + Krum Bums/Witch Hunt/Sacred Shock - 240
566. 11-9-07- AUSTIN Emo's + Krum Bums/Witch Hunt/Sacred Shock - 300
567. 12-9-07- HOUSTON Walters on Washington + Krum Bums/Sacred Shock/Absence of Change - 294
568. 13-9-07 - MOBILE Soul Kitchen + World Inferno/Friendship Society + Libyan Hit Squad - 120
569. 14-9-07 - JACKSONVILLE Fuel + World/Inferno Friendship Society + Libyan Hit Squad + Grab Bag - 220
570. 15-9-07 - MIAMI Studio A + World/Inferno Friendship Society + Libyan Hit Squad + No Peace at All - 361
571. 16-9-07 - ORLANDO The Social + World/Inferno Friendship Society + Libyan Hit Squad - 356
572. 17-9-07 - CHARLESTON Map Room + World/Inferno Friendship Society + 33s - 292
573. 18-9-07 - ASHEVILLE Arts Centre + World/Inferno Friendship Society + Heart Attack + Pax Americana + Negative Feedback -310
574. 19-9-07 - CINCINNATI 20th Century Theatre + World/Inferno Friendship Society + Heart Attack - 250
575. 20-9-07 - PITTSBURGH Mr. Small's Theatre + World/Inferno Friendship Society + Caustic Christ + Last Hopes - 279
576. 21-9-07 - PHILADELPHIA First Unitarian Church + World/Inferno Friendship Society + Toxic Narcotic + Witch Hunt - 514
577. 22-9-07 - BALTIMORE Otto Bar + World/Inferno Friendship Society + Toxic Narcotic + Surroundings - 471
578. 23-9-07 - NEW YORK Knitting Factory + World/Inferno Friendship Society + Toxic Narcotic - 400
579. 24-9-07 - NEW YORK Knitting Factory + World/Inferno Friendship Society + I Object - 396
580. 25-9-07 - BOSTON Axis + World/Inferno Friendship Society + I Object + Mouth Sewn Shut - 310
581. 26-9-07 - ROCHESTER Water St. Music Hall + World/Inferno Friendship Society + I Object + Hounds of Hell - 200
582. 27-9-07 - CLEVELAND Grog Shop + World/Inferno Friendship Society + I Object - 184

583. 28-9-07 - DETROIT Magic Stick +World/Inferno Friendship Society + Caustic Christ + Attack of the... - 356

584. 29-9-07 - CHICAGO Logan Square Auditorium + World/Inferno Friendship Society + Caustic Christ + Calavera - 350

585. 5-12-07 BRISTOL Croft + Ghurka/SDFF - 100

586. 6-12-07 DERBY Victoria Inn + Mingers/Follow the White Line - 120

587. 7-12-07 SHEFFIELD Casbah + Bickle's Cab/Mingers/Follow the White Line - 120

588. 8-12-07 LEEDS Joseph's Well + Assert/Bug Central - 200

589. 9-12-07 GLASGOW Barfly + Repeaters/Dead Beat Heroes/The Void - 150

590. 10-12-07 EDINBURGH Cabaret Voltaire + ? - 150

591. 11-12-07 NEWCASTLE Trillians + Demon 340 - 130

592. 12-12-07 NOTTINGHAM Maze + Minus Society - 70

593. 13-12-07 PLYMOUTH White Rabbit + Bus Station Loonies/Profane - 120

594. 14-12-07 BARNSTAPLE Inn on the Square + Something Somethings/2 Sick Monkeys - 70

595. 15-12-07 SWINDON Furnace + 2 Sick Monkeys/Parodies - 100

596. 16-12-07 LONDON Camden Underworld + ?/Random Hand - 400

597. 9-2-08 CAMBRIDGE Barfly + Random Hand/? - 150

598. 10-2-08 LEICESTER Charlotte + Nags/Souvenirs - 80

599. 11-2-08 YORK Fibbers + ? - 60

600. 12-2-08 BRADFORD 1 in 12 + ? - 90

601. 13-2-08 LANCASTER Yorkshire House + ? - 80

602. 14-2-08 MANCHESTER Star and Garter + Bullet Kings/Revenge of the Psychotronic Man/Global Parasites – 111

603. 15-2-08 LONDON Hackney Chats Palace + Active Slaughter/Skints - 200

604. 16-2-08 BRISTOL Croft + ? - 120

605. 17-2-08 NORTHAMPTON Soundhouse + ? - 100

606. 2-4-08 USA - SEATTLE El Corazon + Snuggle/Society's Nurse - 280

607. 3-4-08 - TACOMA Hell's Kitchen + Insurgence/Red White and Die/CLR - 258

608. 4-4-08 - PORTLAND Hawthorn Theatre + Criminal Damage/Ether Circus - 502

609. 5-4-08 - BEND Domino Room + Criminal Damage/Larry and His Flask - 384

610. 6-4-08 - SAN FRANCISCO Slim's + Criminal Damage/Conquest for Death - 432

611. 7-4-08 - RENO Underground + Criminal Damage/Conquest for Death/Blood Brains/Beer - 360

612. 8-4-08 - SACRAMENTO Silk Bar + Criminal Damage/Rat Damage/Uncut Hunks/ Isonomy - 150

613. 9-4-08 - FRESNO The Exit + Criminal Damage + ? - 160

614. 10-4-08 - SANTA CRUZ Veterans Hall + Criminal Damage/Le Plebe - 360

615. 11-4-08 - PALMDALE Veterans Hall + Criminal Damage/Anima Mundi/Werfucht - 325

616. 12-4-08 - CORONA Showcase + Criminal Damage/Introspect/Hit Me Back - 561

617. 13-4-08 - CORONA Showcase + Resistance Culture/Ciril/Anima Mundi - 518

618. 14-4-08 - LAS VEGAS Canyon Club + Murder Majesty/Happy Campers - 302

619. 15-4-08 - LOS ANGELES The Echo + Naked Aggression/Ciril - 313

620.	16-4-08 - SAN DIEGO Soma + Resistance Culture/Introspect/Bumklaatt/Disabled Youth - 510
621.	17-4-08 - TUCSON The Rock + Besmirchers/Blues/The Last Act - 370
622.	18-4-08 - TEMPE Clubhouse + Howl of the Wolf/False Pride/Prosthetics - 304
623.	27-4-08 AUSTRIA - VIENNA Arena, Rebellion Festival: Dwarves/Subhumans/MDC/ Argy Bargy/Skeptic Eleptic/Los Fastidios/Sonic Boom 6/Exposed - 500
624.	21-5-08 FINLAND - TURKU Klubi + Rattus - 60
625.	22-5-08 - TAMPERE Vasta Virta + Rathaus - 120
626.	23-5-08 - HELSINKI Tavastia + ? - 250
627.	18-7-08 CZECH REPUBLIC Oparany, Mighty Sounds Festival +...Demented Are Go/ Citizen Fish/... - 1000
628.	9-8-08 BLACKPOOL Winter Gardens, Rebellion Festival - 1200
629.	12-9-08 POOLE Mr. C's + Virus/Toxic Suicide - 80
630.	13-9-08 LEEDS Fenton + Liberty/Police Bastard/Lowlife/Middle Finger Salute/One Man Down/Swine/Skank Agenda - 100
631.	14-9-08 NOTTINGHAM Rock City + Random Hand/Eccentrics - 70
632.	15-9-08 LANCASTER Yorkshire House + Random Hand/Eastfield - 70
633.	16-9-08 MANCHESTER Star and Garter + Sick 56/Whisky Bastards/Hydropaths/ Ambush UK - 94
634.	17-9-08 NEWPORT Le Pub + Resistance - 60
635.	18-9-08 BATH Burdall's Yard + FUK/7 Crowns - 170
636.	19-9-08 TAL-Y-BONT Hendre Hall + Instant Agony/Power Corrupts/Global Parasite/ Officer Down - 150
637.	20-9-08 DERBY Victoria Inn + ? - 120
638.	21-9-08 LEICESTER Charlotte + Nags/Insane Society/Tommy's Heroes/Mannix - 70
639.	22-9-08 BRIGHTON Engine Rooms + Flatpig/Geronimo/Arkwright - 190
640.	23-9-08 LONDON Camden Underworld + Love and a 45/The JB Conspiracy - 175
641.	23-10-08 SOUTHAMPTON Talking Heads + Social Parasites/Constant Fear/Haywire - 200
642.	25-10-08 HOLLAND - AMSTERDAM OCCII + Mondo Gecko - 250
643.	26-10-08 BELGIUM - ANTWERP Bar Mondial - 70
644.	27-10-08 GERMANY - DUSSELDORF AK47 + Van Helsing - 80
645.	28-10-08 - FRANKFURT AU + Sniper Alley - 70
646.	29-10-08 - SCHWABISCHE HELL Club Alpha + Gegen Stimme - 100
647.	30-10-08 FRANCE - DIJON Les Tanneries + Lewis Karloff/Les Suces Pendus/Shub - 70
648.	31-10-08 - PARIS La Pena Festayre: Assoiffes/Subhumans/Human Dog Food/Usual Suspects/100 Raisons - 300
649.	1-11-08 - PARIS Miroterie + Bad Influence/Unlogistic/Halal Vegan/Eurokunt - 150
650.	2-11-08 BELGIUM - LIEGE La Zone + Bad Influence - 60
651.	3-11-08 NORTHAMPTON Racehorse + Misspelt - 50
652.	27-11-08 BRISTOL Croft + Valdez/Goaterbikes - 80
653.	28-11-08 KETTERING Sawyers + London/Charred Hearts/The Pain - 60
654.	29-11-08 LONDON Islington Academy: Flux of Pink Indians/Subhumans/Rubella Ballet/ Restarts - 450

655.	7-2-09 POLAND - LODZ ? + Real Mackenzies/Dezerter - 500
656.	5-3-09 ITALY - TURIN United Club + HIV - 70
657.	6-3-09 - MODENA La Scintilla + No White Rag - 350
658.	7-3-09 - GORIZIA Pfieffe Factory + ? - 300
659.	22-5-09 BIRMINGHAM Wagon and Horses + Autonomads+I.C.H.+Refuse/All+Pax - 150
660.	23-5-09 GLASGOW Barrowland+Conflict+Refuse/All+Alternative/Meinhof/Fire Exit - 254
661.	24-5-09 MANCHESTER Star and Garter + Meinhof+Refuse/All+Warcoma+Rebel Conspiracy - 150
662.	10-6-09 SWEDEN - STOCKHOLM Kaffe 44 + Imperial Leather/PKP - 144
663.	11-6-09 - GOTEBORG Underground + PKP - 130
664.	12-6-09 - MUNKDAL Punk Illegal Festival: Moderat Likuidation/Subhumans/Wolf - 700
665.	13-6-09 NORWAY - OSLO Garage + PKP - 80
666.	14-6-09 - TRONDHEIM Uffa + PKP - 100
667.	28-6-09 CANADA - MONTREAL Foufounes Electriques + Business/Ripchordz/ Subsistence/La Couchette/Ray Gradys - 500
668.	29-6-09 - TROIS RIVIERES Le Complex + Ray Gradys/Kdense/We Don't Fight Fair - 50
669.	30-6-09 - QUEBEC CITY Casbah + Ray Gradys/Whiskey Trench - 200
670.	1-7-09 - ST HYACINTH Trash Bar + Kontort/Ray Gradys - 100
671.	2-7-09 - OTTAWA Mavericks + Ray Gradys/Putine - 171
672.	3-7-09 - TORONTO Kathedral + Witch Hunt/Ray Gradys/Delinquints - 214
673.	4-7-09 - LONDON Call the Office + Witch Hunt/Ray Gradys - 50
674.	5-7-09 USA - DETROIT Magic Stick + Witch Hunt/Ray Gradys - 150
675.	6-7-09 - CLEVELAND Now That's Class + Witch Hunt/Ray Gradys - 150
676.	7-7-09 - PITTSBURGH Altar Bar + Witch Hunt/Ray Gradys/Code Orange Kids - 180
677.	8-7-09 - PHILADELPHIA The Barbary + Witch Hunt/Ray Gradys - 206
678.	12-7-09 - NEW YORK Knitting Factory + Ray Gradys/A-Heads - 400
679.	7-9-09 BLACKPOOL Winter Gardens, Rebellion Festival - 1700
680.	23-8-09 OTTERY ST MARY Beautiful Days Festival: Levellers etc. etc. - 4000
681.	24-8-09 NEWPORT TJs + Rejected/Saturday's Kids - 50
682.	27-8-09 BRIGHTON Engine Rooms + Fish Brothers - 250
683.	28-8-09 LONDON Camden Underworld + Asshole Parade/Rachel - 200
684.	29-8-09 NOTTINGHAM Seven + Left for Dead/Section 13/Pax - 120
685.	30-8-09 IPSWICH Royal Oak + Dead Batteries/Fanny Pads - 120
686.	31-8-09 TROWBRIDGE White Swan - 60
687.	1-9-09 NORTHAMPTON Racehorse + Eastfield - 50
688.	2-9-09 LEICESTER Sumo + ? - 40
689.	3-9-09 BRISTOL Bierkeller + London/Valdez - 100
690.	4-9-09 SHEFFIELD Casbah + Rejected - 100
691.	5-9-09 BOLTON Soundhouse: Inner Terrestrials/Subhumans/2 Sick Monkeys/ Autonomads/Wonk Unit - 200
692.	6-9-09 NEWCASTLE Trillians + Restarts/Brain Worm - 100
693.	7-9-09 ABERDEEN Cafe Drummond + Skitzofrenik/Versificator/Heller State - 100

694. 8-9-09 GLASGOW Ivory Blacks + Prairie Dugs/Ceasefire - 100

695. 9-9-09 IRELAND - BELFAST Auntie Annie's + 1000 Drunken Nights+Lobotomies+A/Political - 120

696. 10-9-09 - GALWAY The Cellar + Space Monkeys - 100

697. 11-9-09 - DUBLIN Fibber Magees + Paranoid Visions/Setting Off Sirens/Momma's Slippers - 150

698. 12-9-09 - MYRTLEVILLE Pine Lodge - 70

699. 11-12-09 MILTON KEYNES Woughton Centre + Moral Dilemma/RSI/Powertones - 70

700. 12-12-09 STOCKPORT Thatched House + Dead Class/Stuntface/The Minx - 80

701. 13-12-09 BIRMINGHAM Wagon and Horses + ?/Comply or Die - 80

702. 14-12-09 DARLINGTON The Forum + Gimpfist/Zombie Headhunters - 40

703. 15-12-09 MANSFIELD Old Mill + Obnoxious UK/Rampton Release Date - 40

704. 16-12-09 KETTERING Sawyers + Faintest Idea/Washed Up/Powertones - 70

705. 17-12-09 DERBY Old Bell + Restarts/Moral Dilemma/Addictive Philosophy - 120

706. 18-12-09 SHEFFIELD Casbah + Restarts/Moral Dilemma - 80

707. 19-12-09 LONDON The Luminaire + Fuckshovel/Dirty Love - 80

708. 8-4-10 BELGIUM - ANTWERP Bar Mondial - 80

709. 9-4-10 HOLLAND - AMSTERDAM OCCII + Hummus - 170

710. 10-4-10 - LEEWARDEN Gloppe + Local Spastics/? - 80

711. 11-4-10 - ROTTERDAM Exit + Speckneck - 70

712. 14-4-10 BELGIUM - BRUSSELS Magazin 4 + The Furious - 200

713. 15-4-10 - LIEGE Carlo Levi + Restarts/Rene Biname/Suitside Vs Veda Plight - 100

714. 16-4-10 LONDON Brixton Jamm + Defcon Zero/Extinguishers/Kadt - 150

715. 17-4-10 ABERTILLERY Doll's House + Rectify - 40

716. 28-5-10 USA - AUSTIN Emo's Chaos in Tejas fest: Bastards/Walls/Subhumans/Rival Mob/Marked Men/Kim Phuc/Vaaska - 500

717. 30-5-10 - AUSTIN Beerland + Cross-Stitched Eyes/Mata Mata/Criaturas - 200

718. 31-5-10 - DALLAS Prophet Bar + Slang/Cross-Stitched Eyes/Unit 21/Dog Company - 180

719. 1-6-10 - OKLAHOMA CITY The Conservatory + Cross-Stitched Eyes/No Man's Slave - 120

720. 1-6-10 - OKLAHOMA CITY The Hi-Lo - 40

721. 2-6-10 - ALBUQUERQUE The Launch Pad + Cross-Stitched Eyes/80 Proof Piss/Coke Is Better With...- 170

722. 3-6-10 - FORT DEFIANCE [Navajo Reservation] Chapter + Cross-Stitched Eyes/Blackfire/Lo Cash Ninjas - 60

723. 4-6-10 - SCOTTSDALE Chasers + Cross-Stitched Eyes/Dogs of Ire/Prosthetics - 100

724. 5-6-10 - POMONA Glasshouse + Cross-Stitched Eyes/A-Heads/Godawfuls/Animalitos - 800

725. 6-6-10 - LOS ANGELES Echoplex + Cross-Stitched Eyes/A-Heads/Rayos - 805

726. 7-6-10 - LONG BEACH Alex's Bar + Cross-Stitched Eyes/A-Heads/Toys That Kill - 350

727. 8-6-10 - LAS VEGAS Box Office + Cross-Stitched Eyes/A-Heads/Hard Pipe Hitters/Murder Majesty/Burning Heads - 200

728. 9-6-10 - SAN LUIS OBISPO Downtown Brew + Cross-Stitched Eyes/A-Heads/Stop Breathing - 350

729.	10-6-10 - SANTA CRUZ Catalyst + A-Heads/Cross-Stitched Eyes - 330
730.	11-6-10 - BERKELEY Gilman Street + MDC/A-Heads - 602
731.	12-6-10 - SAN FRANCISCO Bottom of the Hill + Cross-Stitched Eyes/ A-Heads - 390
732.	13-6-10 - RENO The Alley + MDC/Thalidomides/Humans - 180
733.	14-6-10 - SACRAMENTO Shire Road Club + MDC/Rat Damage/Final Summation/ Dance for Destruction - 230
734.	15-6-10 - EUGENE Wow Hall + Arctic Flowers/Happy Bastards/Resist - 240
735.	16-6-10 - PORTLAND Hawthorn Theatre + Arctic Flowers/Salted City/Vivid Sekt - 350
736.	17-6-10 - SEATTLE Chop Suey + Arctic Flowers/Walls - 250
737.	9-7-10 POLAND - GDYNIA Ucho punk fest + Utopia/No Se/Government Flu/Distress/ Family Man - 350
738.	6-8-10 SIX PENNY HANDLEY Endorsit Festival: Eat Static/Subhumans/Vice Squad etc. - 1500
739.	8-8-10 BLACKPOOL Winter Gardens, Rebellion Festival - 1600
740.	10-8-10 BRIGHTON Hydrant + Flue Sniffers - 140
741.	11-8-10 LONDON Camden Underworld + Girlfixer/Condition:Dead - 290
742.	12-8-10 SOUTHAMPTON Joiners + Haywire/Social Parasites - 110
743.	13-8-10 DERBY Old Bell + ? - 130
744.	14-8-10 BOOMTOWN FESTIVAL + loads of bands - 500
745.	27-11-10 NEWPORT Meze Lounge + Spanner - 120
746.	1-12-10 NORTHAMPTON Labour Club + Mispelt - 50
747.	2-12-10 LONDON The Gaff + Refuse/All - 150
748.	3-12-10 BIRMINGHAM Adam and Eve + Rotunda - 70
749.	4-12-10 BURY ST EDMUNDS Old Malthouse + Global Parasite/Love Dump - 150
750.	5-12-10 MANCHESTER Star and Garter + Jay [Inner Terrestrials]/Love Dump - 170
751.	6-12-10 BRADFORD 1 in 12 Club + Jay [Inner Terrestrials]/Global Parasite/China Bull Shop - 50
752.	7-12-10 CARLISLE Brickhouse + ? - 50
753.	10-12-10 HUDDERSFIELD Parish + Total Bloody Chaos - 80
754.	1-4-11 USA - NEW YORK Santos + MDC/Death First/Cohones - 470
755.	2-4-11 - BALTIMORE Otto Bar + MDC/Scum Again/Deep Sleep - 331
756.	3-4-11 - ASBURY Asbury Lanes + MDC/Scandals - 216
757.	4-4-11 - PHILADELPHIA Barbary + MDC/Defect Defect/Sickoids - 210
758.	5-4-11 - PROVIDENCE Hell Club + MDC/Midnight Creeps/Week Teeth - 200
759.	6-4-11 - CAMBRIDGE Middle East + MDC/Libyans/War of Words - 300
760.	7-4-11 - BUFFALO Mohawk Bar + MDC/Plates - 170
761.	8-4-11 - PITTSBURGH Rex Theatre + MDC/Ratface/Code Orange Kids/Eat the Government - 310
762.	9-4-11 - CLEVELAND Grog Shop + MDC/Zero Defects/Masakari - 317
763.	10-4-11 - DETROIT Small's + MDC/UDI/Final Assault - 220
764.	11-4-11 - COVINGTON Mad Hatter + MDC/The Zvills - 240
765.	12-4-11 - ST LOUIS Firebird + MDC/Cardiac Arrest - 178

766. 13-4-11 - CHICAGO Reggies + MDC/Daylight Robbery/Neutron Bombs - 314

767. 14-4-11 - MINNEAPOLIS Triple Rock + MDC/Varix/Brain Tumour - 415

768. 15-4-11 - KANSAS Davey's Uptown + MDC/El Canero/At Your Throat - 280

769. 16-4-11 - DENVER Gothic Theatre + MDC/The Nervous - 717

770. 17-4-11 - ALBERQUERQUE Launch Pad + MDC/Domestic Violence - 179

771. 18-4-11 - TEMPE Clubhouse + MDC/The Grim/Rotten Youth - 320

772. 19-4-11 - POMONA Glasshouse + MDC/Gr'ups/Naked Aggression - 800

773. 20-4-11 - LOS ANGELES Echo [afternoon] + Seven Crowns/A-Heads - 340

774. 20-4-11 - LOS ANGELES Echo [night] + MDC/Naked Aggression - 350

775. 21-4-11 - SAN FRANCISCO Thee Parkside + MDC/Vacuum - 296

776. 23-4-11 - OAKLAND Metro + Seven Crowns/WWK/Fracas/Born Uglys - 600

777. 30-7-11 GERMANY - ROSTOCK Force Attack Festival + loads of bands - 400

778. 6-8-11 BLACKPOOL Winter Gardens, Rebellion festival - 1500

779. 8-8-11 NEWCASTLE-UNDER-LYME The Rigger + Anti Vigilante/Pedigree Skum - 30

780. 9-8-11 LONDON Camden Underworld + Luvdump/Flowers of Flesh and Blood - 100

781. 10-8-11 IPSWICH Royal Oak + Luvdump/Fanny Pads - 50

782. 11-8-11 SOUTHAMPTON Joiners + Liberty/Haywire - 130

783. 7-9-11 PRESTON New Continental + Mardi Gras Bombers/Addictive Philosophy/Dollface - 120

784. 8-9-11 GLASGOW Ivory Blacks + Happy Spastics/Razorblade Smile - 100

785. 9-9-11 EDINBURGH Bannermans + Restarts/Gin Goblins/Daddy No - 120

786. 10-9-11 DURHAM University, North East Calling: Rezillos/Angelic Upstarts/UK Subs/Subhumans/A.N.W.L./Goldblade/Restarts - 800

787. 11-9-11 WAKEFIELD The Hop + ? - 80

788. 14-12-11 BOURNEMOUTH Champions + Sporadics - 100

789. 15-12-11 BRISTOL Fleece + A-Heads/Bus Station Loonies - 200

790. 16-12-11 COVENTRY Kasbah + Army of Skanks/Dementias - 60

791. 17-12-11 SHEFFIELD Corporation Punk Fest: Buzzcocks/Angelic Upstarts/King Kurt/Subhumans/English Dogs etc. - 600

792. 18-12-11 LONDON Borderline + Moral Dilemma/Skits - 90

793. 24-2-12 BRIGHTON Hydrant + Headfuct/Flat Pig/Brain Jelly - 100

794. 25-2-12 BOURNEMOUTH Champions + Sporadics/A-Heads/Self Abuse/Headfuct - 100

795. 26-2-12 BIRMINGHAM Adam and Eve + ?/Merks - 100

796. 27-2-12 SHEFFIELD Corporation + Septic Psychos/Bones Park Rider - 100

797. 28-2-12 NEWCASTLE Trillians + The Fiend - 140

798. 29-2-12 DERBY Old Bell + Eccentrics/Ephemeral Foetus - 100

799. 1-3-12 ASHTON-UNDER-LYNE + Black Light Mutants - 90

800. 2-3-12 BUCKLEY Tivoli + 50 Hertz - 60

801. 3-3-12 BATH Green Park Tavern + Seven Crowns/Blunders - 150

802. 4 3 12 LONDON Boston Arms + Hagar the Womb/Zounds/Pukes/Lost Cherrees/Andy T. - 400

803. 9-6-12 GERMANY - FRANKFURT AU festival + Asta Kask/Union Jack/De Schwartzen Schaffe/Scheisse Minnelli - 700

804.	19-7-12 CANTERBURY 3 Tuns + ? - 100
805.	20-7-12 HOLLAND - TILBURG Little Devil + Tarantino - 74
806.	21-7-12 - AMSTERDAM OCCII + Gas - 160
807.	22-7-12 GERMANY - HAMBURG Stortebekker - 140
808.	26-7-12 - BREMEN Freisenstrasse - 70
809.	27-7-12 - LEIPZIG Zorro + Zemezluc/Jars/Vagiant - 200
810.	28-7-12 - BERLIN Kopi + ? - 450
811.	29-7-12 - POTTSDAM Archiv + Barroom Heroes - 50
812.	30-7-12 - KOLN Sonic Ballroom + Bad Influence - 85
813.	31-7-12 BELGIUM - ANTWERP De Rots Bar + Bad Influence - 150
814.	1-8-12 BRIGHTON The Haunt + Brain Jelly - 100
815.	2-8-12 BRISTOL Croft + Spanner/Grand Collapse - 100
816.	4-8-12 BLACKPOOL Winter Gardens, Rebellion Festival - 1500
817.	11-8-12 CZECH REPUBLIC - PRAGUE Noise Therapy festival + SS Kaliert/Rozpor/ Dezifekce/Svine/Marcel Duchon/Tales of Error - 200
818.	12-9-12 AUSTRALIA - PERTH Amplifier Bar + SSA/Scalphunter/The Lungs - 150
819.	13-9-12 - BRISBANE Prince of Wales + Mouthguard/50 Bags/Ahfuckthat - 200
820.	14-9-12 - SIDNEY Sandringham Hotel + Dark Horse/Unknown to God/Inebrious Bastard - 170
821.	15-9-12 - MELBOURNE Bendigo Hotel + Bloody Hammer/Wolfpack/12FU - 200
822.	16-9-12 - ADELAIDE Foresters and Squatters Arms + Perdition Vaginors/Suburban Standoff - 120
823.	17-9-12 - MELBOURNE Northcote Social Club + Vicious Circle/Spew n Guts/Dixon Cider - 110
824.	19-9-12 NEW ZEALAND - DUNEDIN Muso's Club + Bazookas/Conniption - 70
825.	20-9-12 - CHRISTCHURCH Dux Live + Gripper/Pistol Grip - 150
826.	21-9-12 - WELLINGTON Bodega + Rogernomix/Dead Vicious/Black Lick - 180
827.	22-9-12 - AUCKLAND The Kings Arms + Sex Pest/Big Jobs/Paul Hooli - 90
828.	25-9-12 SINGAPORE - Goldkist Resort + Seven Crowns/Carburretor Dung/Enam Jakanam - 60
829.	26-9-12 JAVA - BANDUNG Klub Racun + Seven Crowns - 200
830.	5-12-12 BIRMINGHAM Adam and Eve + Nurks/Lobster - 60
831.	6-12-12 LANCASTER Yorkshire House + Bad Transmission/Potential Victims/Dischord - 70
832.	7-12-12 IRELAND - DUBLIN Button Factory + Paranoid Visions - 300
833.	8-12-12 - BELFAST Warzone + Unfun/1000 Drunken Nights/Divisions - 150
834.	9-12-12 MANCHESTER Star and Garter + Epic Problem/Paper Towels/Holiday - 150
835.	10-12-12 SHEFFIELD Corporation + Acid Drop/Reverends - 70
836.	11-12-12 ST ALBANS The Horn + Rumour Mill/Brocker/Jesus Hooligan - 100
837.	12-12-12 KIDDERMINSTER Boar's Head + Screaming Abdabs - 60
838.	13-12-12 BRISTOL Fleece + Lost Cherrees/Area 51 - 170
839.	14-12-12 PONTYPOOL Hog and Hosper + This System Kills/Gone to Ruins - 60
840.	15-12-12 LONDON Grosvenor Inn + Antidotum/Hagar the Womb/Eccentrics/Alice Rock - 150
841.	1-3-13 TROWBRIDGE White Swan + ? - 80

842.	2-3-13 BATH Green Park Tavern + What's the Point?/Onanism - 100
843.	3-3-13 LONDON Boston Arms, Another Winter of Discontent: Anti-Pasti/Subhumans/ Lost Cherrees/Disorder - 450
844.	27-3-13 LONDON Grosvenor Inn + Kicker/Blatoidea/Fracas - 200
845.	29-3-13 BATH Komedia B.O.B. Fest + Slime/Mob - 500
846.	3-4-13 CARDIFF Koko Gorillaz + ? - 160
847.	4-4-13 BOURNEMOUTH Anvil + Sporadics/Zombie - 120
848.	5-4-13 PLYMOUTH Tramps + Bus Station Loonies - 70
849.	6-4-13 FALMOUTH Rugby Club + Bus Station Loonies/Chris Loonie's Harakiri Karaoke - 160
850.	30-4-13 NORWAY - TRONDHEIM Verkstedhallen: Charta 77/Subhumans - 450
851.	1-5-13 - OSLO Blitz + Charta 77/Polish Avant Gard - 170
852.	2-5-13 SWEDEN - STOCKHOLM Kake 44: Charta 77/Subhumans - 80
853.	3-5-13 NORWAY - HALDEN Feelgood + Charta 77/De Brisne/Stookers/Monotrons/ Pretty Shitty - 30
854.	4-5-13 SWEDEN - KOPING Ogir + Charta 77/Kottgrottorna/Total Egon/Rollands Gosskor - 300
855.	11-5-13 IRELAND - DUBLIN Button Factory: Conflict/Subhumans/Paranoid Visions/ Lost Cherrees - 450
856.	23-5-13 USA - SPARKS The Alley + Total Chaos/Out for War/Patricia Ward - 110
857.	24-5-13 - OAKLAND Metro + Total Chaos/Conquest for Death/Permanent Ruin - 350
858.	25-5-13 - LOS ANGELES The Vex + Total Chaos/Naked Aggression/Mundo Muerto - 800
859.	26-5-13 - SANTA ANA Observatory + Total Chaos/Generacion Suicida/ Fraude - 1000
860.	27-5-13 - LAS VEGAS Punk Rock Bowling fest: Flag/DRI/Subhumans/Casualties/etc. - 3000
861.	8-6-13 LONDON Pipeline + Eastfield - 150
862.	9-6-13 DERBY Victoria Inn + Happy Bastards - 30
863.	10-6-13 BIRMINGHAM Wagon and Horses + Eastfield/Brassick/Wet Ones - 80
864.	11-6-13 ST ALBANS The Horn + 16 Guns/Ministers Dead/Social Schism - 70
865.	14-6-13 CANADA - MONTEBELLO Amnesia Rock Fest + Adolescents/loads more - 1000
866.	15-6-13 USA - NEW YORK Bowery Ballroom + World/Inferno Friendship Society + Krays - 500
867.	16-6-13 - NEW YORK Williamsburg Music Hall + Adolescents/Drunken Rampage - 500
868.	3-8-13 NORWAY - HELDEN Kanalrock Festival - 1000
869.	9-8-13 BLACKPOOL Winter Gardens Rebellion festival - 2000
870.	12-9-13 CANTERBURY Three Tuns + Science Without Research - 35
871.	13-9-13 GERMANY - WIRMELSKIRCHEN AJZ Bahndamm + Bad Influence/Aftermath - 170
872.	14-9-13 BELGIUM - HARALBEKE Ratrock Fest: Toy Dolls/Subhumans/Bad Influence etc. - 1500
873.	15 9 13 FRANCE - PARIS Miroterie - 100
874.	3-11-13 USA - LOS ANGELES Los Globos + Grim/Dirty Kid Discount - 465
875.	4-11-13 - SAN DIEGO Casbah + Bumklaat/Sculpins - 250

876.   5-11-13 - POMONA Glasshouse + Reagan Youth/ACAD/38 Scars - 800
877.   6-11-13 - TEMPE Club Red + Grim/Rotten Youth - 300
878.   7-11-13 - DENVER Marquis Theatre + Negative Approach/R.O.A.C./Bad Engrish - 403
879.   8-11-13 - AUSTIN Mohawk + White Lung - 200
880.   9-11-13 - AUSTIN Fun Fun Fun Fest: ...Body Count/Subhumans... - 3000
881.   6-12-13 WELLINGBOROUGH The Horseshoe + Eastfield/Mispelt - 200
882.   7-12-13 LONDON Camden Underworld: Conflict/Dropping Bombs/Subhumans/Lost
       Cherrees/Liberty/Slug - 460
883.   8-12-13 LONDON Garage + Dropping Bombs/Lost Cherrees/Grand Collapse - 150
884.   10-12-13 TROWBRIDGE White Swan + Species/Area 53 - 80
885.   11-12-13 BIRMINGHAM Wagon and Horses + Alcohol Licks/Poor Old Dogs - 80
886.   12-12-13 BRADFORD Vampires + ? - 40
887.   13-12-13 SHEFFIELD Penelope's + Brain Freeze/Chewed Up - 81
888.   14-12-13 BRISTOL Exchange + Cydernide - 80
889.   15-12-13 SOUTHAMPTON Joiners + ? - 70
890.   31-1-14 HOLLAND - AMSTERDAM Milky Way, Grauzone Fest: Peter Hook/Lydia
       Lunch/Subhumans etc. - 400
891.   2-5-14 LONDON Pipeline + Slug/Blatoidea - 90
892.   3-5-14 BRISTOL O2 Academy: Buzzcocks/A.N.W.L./Mob/GBH/Subhumans/Eddie
       Tenpole etc - 180
893.   7-5-14 NEWPORT Le Pub + Bring to Ruin - 50
894.   8-5-14 DERBY Hairy Dog + Ephemeral Foetus/Apocalypse Babies - 60
895.   9-5-14 LIVERPOOL Blade Factory + Seven Crowns/Luvdump/Dead Subverts/2 Sick Monkeys - 130
896.   10-5-14 GATESHEAD 3 Tuns + ? - 140
897.   11-5-14 WAKEFIELD Warehouse 23 + ? - 150
898.   7-6-14 HOLLAND - ENSCHEDE Attak + Drongos for Europe/Neuroot/Rat Patrol - 300
899.   8-6-14 BELGIUM HOTTON Melrock festival: Funeral Dress/Subhumans/Joy De Vivre/
       Stigmate/Skating Teenagers/Les Michels Galabis/Mad Farmers/Hand of Shadows - 200
900.   9-6-14 GERMANY - BONN Kult 41 + Aftermath - 90
901.   10-6-14 - HANNOVER Stumpf + Reset/Mankind - 120
902.   11-6-14 CZECH REPUBLIC - PRAGUE 007 + Kutya Harap - 100
903.   12-6-14 GERMANY - BERLIN Tommyhaus + Scrapyard/Baccos Punk - 230
904.   13-6-14 - KIEL Alte Maierei + 2015 - 160
905.   14-6-14 - BREMEN Schlachthof + ? - 70
906.   21-6-14 BELGIUM - ANTWERP Blauwers 50th party - 150
907.   18-7-14 CANADA - MONTREAL Foufounes Electriques + Mischief Brew/Ab Irato/
       Society Ills - 424
908.   19-7-14 - TORONTO Horseshoe Tavern + Mischief Brew/School Damage - 379
909.   20-7-14 USA - DETROIT Magic Stick + Mischief Brew/? - 251
910.   21-7-14 - CHICAGO Reggies + Mischief Brew/Warrior Tribes - 260
911.   22-7-14 - CLEVELAND Grog Shop + Mischief Brew/Kill the Hippies - 187
912.   23-7-14 - PITTSBURGH Rex Theatre + Mischief Brew/Sicks/Wrathcobra/Pressinon - 283

913.	24-7-14 - BALTIMORE Otto's Bar + Mischief Brew/Station - 288
914.	25-7-14 - BOSTON Brighton Music Hall + Mischief Brew/? - 367
915.	26-7-14 - PHILADELPHIA Voltage Lounge + Mischief Brew/Nightbirds/Latex - 240
916.	27-7-14 - NEW YORK Poisson Rouge + Sheer Terror/Mischief Brew/? - 250
917.	9-8-14 BLACKPOOL Winter Gardens, Rebellion Festival: Jaya the Cat/Paranoid Visions & Steve Ignorant/Subhumans/ATV/Cravats/Rubella Ballet/Eastfield/Part 1/Lost Cherrees/ A-Heads - 1000
918.	22-8-14 SOUTHAMPTON Lennon's + Atterkop/? - 60
919.	23-8-14 PENZANCE Three Chords Festival + TV Smith/UK Subs - 800
920.	13-11-14 TROWBRIDGE White Swan + A-Heads/Onanism - 70
921.	14-11-14 PRESTON New Continental + Anarka and Poppy/Kill Pretty - 160
922.	15-11-14 MANCHESTER Star and Garter + Billy Club/Xtract/Wonk Unit - 100
923.	16-11-14 BIRMINGHAM Adam and Eve + Rotunda/The Vile/etc. - 100
924.	17-11-14 NORWICH Owl Sanctuary + Fireside Collective/Blatoidea - 150
925.	18-11-14 SOUTHEND Chinnery's + Dogtown Rebels/Knockoff - 120
926.	19-11-14 BRIGHTON Sticky Mike's Frog Bar + Feroxity/? - 100
927.	20-11-14 LONDON T Chances + Grand Collapse/Permawar/Brutal Regime - 250
928.	21-11-14 CHELTENHAM Frog and Fiddle + Officer Down/Noise Agents - 170
929.	22-11-14 BRISTOL Exchange + Grand Collapse - 100
930.	11-2-15 GERMANY - HAMBURG Hafenklang + Future Kill - 200
931.	12-2-15 DENMARK - COPENHAGEN Stengarde + Dead Action - 160
932.	13-2-15 - AALBORG 1000 Fryd + Night Fever/Extended Suicide - 60
933.	14-2-15 GERMANY - FLENSBURG Hafemarkt + Cholera Tarantula - 50
934.	28-2-15 LONDON Tufnell Park Dome, Another Winter of Discontent fest: MDC/Restarts/ Subhumans/Sick on the Bus/Anti-System/Hagar the Womb - 400
935.	6-3-15 BIRKENHEAD Hotel California + Vermin Suicide/Biteback/Dead Blends - 300
936.	7-3-15 WAKEFIELD The Hop + ? - 120
937.	14-5-15 HOLLAND - DRECHTEN Iduna + Oi Polloi/Wugah Wugah - 100
938.	15-5-15 - ARNHEM Willemeen + Doodskoop/Likker - 150
939.	16-5-15 GERMANY - FRANKFURT AU + Nervous Assistant - 120
940.	17-5-15 - REGENSBURG Alte Metzerai + ? - 40
941.	18-5-15 - STUTTGART Kellar Klub + Uberdosis - 50
942.	19-5-15 - KOLN Sonic Ballroom + Aftermath - 100
943.	20-5-15 - JENA Kassablanka + Blackbird Raum - 140
944.	21-5-15 - HANNOVER Stumpf + Peuison Idea - 60
945.	22-5-15 - RUHRPOTT Rodeo Fest + Bloodsucking Zombies from Outer Space - 270
946.	23-5-15 - BERLIN Kopi street party - 700
947.	30-7-15 CZECH REPUBLIC - BRNO Pod Parou festival - 400
948.	31-7-15 LATVIA - RIVA Labadaba Festival - 600
949.	7-8-15 BLACKPOOL Wintergardens, Rebellion festival - 1200
950.	15-8-15 WINCHESTER Boomtown Festival - 500
951.	17-10-15 USA - NEW YORK Acheron + Dark Thoughts/Ache - 200

952. 18-10-15 - NEW YORK Acheron + Opposition Rising/Orphans - 200
953. 19-10-15 - DENVER Marquis Theatre + Joy Subtraction/ROAC/Self Service - 385
954. 20-10-15 - SEATTLE Chop Suey + RVIVR/Mysterious Skin - 395
955. 21-10-15 - PORTLAND Hawthorn Theatre + RVIVR/Arctic Flowers - 474
956. 22-10-15 - SAN FRANCISCO Thee Parkside + Torso/Korrosive/Closet Fiends - 295
957. 23-10-15 - OAKLAND Metro + La Plebe/Love Songs - 600
958. 24-10-15 - SANTA ANA Beach Goth Festival - 2000
959. 25-10-15 - SAN LUIS OBISPO Slo Brew + Love Songs/Stop Breathing - 110
960. 26-10-15 - SACRAMENTO Barfly + La Plebe/Love Songs - 233
961. 27-10-15 - SANTA CRUZ Catalyst + Love Songs/Infirmaries - 194
962. 28-10-15 - FRESNO Strummers + Love Songs - 176
963. 29-10-15 - LOS ANGELES Los Globos + Blazing Eye/Liberate - 410
964. 30-10-15 - LOS ANGELES Los Globos + Generacion Suicida/Death March - 430
965. 31-10-15 MEXICO - TIJUANA You Revolucion + Biocrisis/Helldandys/DFMK - 300
966. 1-11-15 USA - MESA Nile Theatre + Freeze/Linecutters - 400
967. 2-11-15 - DALLAS Three Links + Potato Pirates/Blood Letters - 172
968. 3-11-15 - SAN ANTONIO Korova + Lower Class Brats/Potato Pirates/Equinox - 270
969. 4-11-15 - HOUSTON Walters + Potato Pirates/Equinox/Ballistics - 220
970. 5-11-15 - BROWNSVILLE Bam + Potato Pirates/Equinox/Muk - 100
971. 6-11-15 - AUSTIN Sidewinders Fun Fun Fun Fest + Dwarves/Dirty Kid Discount - 300
972. 18-2-16 TROWBRIDGE White Swan + Blunders - 100
973. 19-2-16 CHELTENHAM Frog and Fiddle + I Destroy/This System Kills - 200
974. 20-2-16 PLYMOUTH Underground + Bus Station Loonies/51st State - 150
975. 23-2-16 CARDIFF Moon Club + Poetic Justice/Bluff - 60
976. 24-2-16 LEEDS Brudenell Club + Burning Flag/Mammoth Tank - 200
977. 25-2-16 LANCASTER Apothecary + Maniacs/John Player Specials/Hexed - 40
978. 26-2-16 MANCHESTER Star and Garter + Xtract/Bite Back - 200
979. 27-2-16 DERBY Hairy Dog + Mammoth/W.O.R.M./Sophie Sparham - 160
980. 28-2-16 LONDON Tufnell Park Dome, Another Winter of Discontent fest: Mob/
      Subhumans/Yalla Yallas/Rabies Babies/Autopsy Boys/Kill Pretty/Healthy Junkies - 350
981. 29-2-16 NORWICH Owl Sanctuary + Lost Pirates/Tick Turds - 150
982. 7-5-16 FINLAND - TAMPERE Punk 40 Festival + Anti-Pasti/Riisteyt/HC Andersons - 400
983. 28-5-16 USA - LAS VEGAS Punk Rock Bowling: Flag/Exploited/Subhumans/etc. - 3000
984. 29-5-16 - SALT LAKE CITY Urban Lounge + Pears/All Systems Fail - 140
985. 30-5-16 - DENVER Bluebird Theatre + Pears/Rotten Blue Menace/In Loo - 452
986. 31-5-16 - KANSAS CITY Riot Room + Pears/M.A.D. - 100
987. 1-6-16 - MINNEAPOLIS Triple Rock + Pears/Bonefire - 400
988. 2-6-16 - CHICAGO Double Door + Pears/La Armada - 400
989. 3-6-16 - ST LOUIS Firebird + Pears/Spiders - 220
990. 4-6-16 - DETROIT Magic Stick downstairs + Pears/Break Anchor - 200
991. 5-6-16 - CLEVELAND Grog Shop + Pears/Party Plates - 150
992. 6-6-16 - PITTSBURGH Cattivo + Pears + S/cks - 130

993.   7-6-16 - BALTIMORE Metro Gallery + Pears/Children of Earth - 120
994.   8-6-16 - NEW HAVEN Cafe 9 + Pears/M13 - 111
995.   9-6-16 - BOSTON Brighton Music Hall + Pears/Trophy Lung - 242
996.   10-6-16 - NEW YORK Brooklyn Virus Lounge + Pears/Zings - 225
997.   11-6-16 - ASBURY Punk Rock Bowling: Descendents/Dag Nasty/Subhumans/H2O/88 Fingers Louie - 3000
998.   5-8-16 BLACKPOOL Winter Gardens, Rebellion festival [outside stage] - 1000
999.   7-9-16 USA - SEATTLE Crocodile Club + Kicker/Raukous - 403
1000.   8-9-16 - PORTLAND Hawthorne Theatre + Kicker/Raukous/Rendered Useless - 520
1001.   9-9-16 - SAN FRANCISCO Thee Parkside + Isotope/Sterile Mind - 262
1002.   10-9-16 - OAKLAND Metro + Kicker/Raukous - 379
1003.   11-9-16 - RENO Studio on 4th + Kicker/Raukous - 105
1004.   12-9-16 - SANTA CRUZ Constellation + Kicker/Raukous - 140
1005.   13-9-16 - FRESNO Strummers + Kicker/Raukous - 189
1006.   14-9-16 - VENTURA The Garage + Kicker/Raukous - 293
1007.   15-9-16 - SAN DIEGO Brick by Brick + Kicker/Raukous - 300
1008.   16-9-16 - SANTA ANA Observatory + Kicker/Raukous - 900
1009.   17-9-16 - LOS ANGELES Los Globos + Kicker/Raukous - 450
1010.   1-11-16 TROWBRIDGE White Swan + Rage DC - 80
1011.   2-11-16 HEREFORD Booth Hall + Teddy's Leg - 92
1012.   3-11-16 LIVERPOOL Don't Drop the Dumbells - ? - 70
1013.   4-11-16 STOKE Underground + Destination Venus/Herbie Jacks - 114
1014.   5-11-16 WOLVERHAMPTON Wulfrun Hall, Midlands Calling: Sham 69/GBH/Angelic Upstarts/UK Subs/Subhumans/999 - 800
1015.   6-11-16 WELLINGBOROUGH Horseshoe Inn + Wreckage/Healer of Bastards - 60
1016.   7-11-16 NORWICH Owl Sanctuary + Midnight Parasite/Dissociates/Rampton Disco - 100
1017.   8-11-16 LONDON Camden Koko: Neurosis/Discharge/Subhumans - 700
1018.   11-1-17 LONDON 100 Club + A-Heads/Lost Cherrees - 200
1019.   12-1-17 BRISTOL Fleece + A-Heads/? - 200
1020.   13-1-17 BRIGHTON Prince Albert + The Fleas - 70
1021.   14-1-17 SOUTHAMPTON Talking Heads + ? - 170
1022.   10-2-17 GERMANY - BREMEN Friesenstrasse + Sense/Temple of Death Moth - 120
1023.   11-2-17 - WERMELSKIRCHEN AZ Bahndamm + Profit and Murder/ Aftermath - 140
1024.   12-2-17 - BONN Bla + Bloodstains - 60
1025.   13-2-17 - BERLIN Cassiopeia + WAYL/Them Bailers - 200
1026.   14-2-17 - HAMBURG Hafenklang + Sense - 180
1027.   15-2-17 HOLLAND - AMSTERDAM OCCII + Cracked Up - 220
1028.   16-2-17 - NIJMEGEN Onderbroek + Periot/Landmine Heart - 70
1029.   17-2-17 GERMANY - BIELEFELD Forum + Hirnsaule/HC Baxxter - 100
1030.   18 2 17   KIEL Alte Meierei + Nasty Jeans - 130
1031.   19-2-17 HOLLAND - GRONINGEN Bambara + Uneasy Peace/Systembastard - 120
1032.   6-4-17 USA - ST PETERSBURG Local 662 + After the Fall/Slade and the Wasters - 239

1033.   7-4-17 - GAINESVILLE The Atlantic + After the Fall/Vaga - 140

1034.   8-4-17 - ORLANDO Back Booth + After the Fall/Coma Club - 202

1035.   9-4-17 - MIAMI Churchills + After the Fall/? - 224

1036.   10-4-17 - LOS ANGELES Los Globos + Love Songs/Dis - 400

1037.   11-4-17 - SAN DIEGO Observatory + Love Songs/Raukous - 325

1038.   12-4-17 - SANTA ANA Observatory + Love Songs/Raukous - 856

1039.   13-4-17 - LOS OSOS Sweet Springs + Love Songs/Bear Cats - 200

1040.   14-4-17 - OAKLAND Metro B.O.B Fest + Kicker/Pathogens - 300

1041.   28-4-17 BIRMINGHAM Ceol Castle + Borrowed Time/Molotov Souls/Mutiny - 60

1042.   29-4-17 MANCHESTER Star and Garter + ? - 120

1043.   30-4-17 WAKEFIELD Warehouse 23: UK Subs/Subhumans - 270

1044.   24-6-17 POLAND - BILGORAJ Ultrachaos Fest: Inner Terrestrials/Subhumans... - 400

1045.   4-8-17 BLACKPOOL Winter Gardens, Rebellion Festival - 3000

1046.   11-8-17 BELGIUM - YPRES Ieperfest: Hatebreed/Memoriam/Napalm Death/Subhumans/
         Havok/Sheer Terror... - 350

1047.   12-8-17 LONDON Boston Arms, Another Winter of Discontent + Inner Terrestrials/Lost
         Cherrees/Virus - 150

1048.   13-8-17 WINCHESTER Boomtown Festival + Inner Terrestrials/RDF/Back to the
         Planet... - 400

1049.   7-9-17 BATH The Nest + Spanner/Skinners/Hell Death Fury - 150

1050.   8-9-17 SOUTHAMPTON Talking Heads + Armoured Flu Unit/Watch You Drown - 200

1051.   9-9-17 MARGATE Dreamland, Undercover Festival: Doctor & the Medics/Angelic
         Upstarts/Ruts DC/Subhumans/RDF... - 250

1052.   10-9-17 TROWBRIDGE White Swan + Setbacks - 60

1053.   22-9-17 LONDON T Chances + Coitus/Dread Messiah/In Evil Hour/Flatpig - 350

1054.   23-9-17 NORTHWICH Salty Dog + Flat Back Four/Dead Objectives - 50

1055.   24-9-17 GRIMSBY Equinox Festival - 200

1056.   25-9-17 LEICESTER Musician + Wronguns/Try Subversion - 80

1057.   26-9-17 NORWICH Epic Studios + Skraelings - 130

1058.   27-9-17 YORK Fulford Arms + Hospital Food - 130

1059.   28-9-17 GLASGOW Audio + Hatefuls/Decibel Freaks - 220

1060.   29-9-17 EDINBURGH Bannermans + AOA/Happy Spastics/Disturbed/Iron System - 200

1061.   30-9-17 NEWCASTLE Northumberland Uni, North East Calling fest: Cockney Rejects/
         Angelic Upstarts/A.N.W.L/Ruts DC/Peter & the Test Tube Babies/ Subhumans/Gimpfist/
         Dirtbox Disco/Zounds - 900

1062.   1-10-17 DERBY Hairy Dog + Addictive Philosophy/Bones Park Rider - 60

1063.   18-11-17 PLYMOUTH Underground + ?/CDS - 120

1064.   19-11-17 CHIPPENHAM Consti Club Punk Fest + Conflict/Omega Tribe/
         A-Heads... - 250

1065.   22-11-17 CANADA - OTTAWA 27 Club + All Torn Up! - 130

1066.   23-11-17 - TORONTO Lee's Palace + All Torn Up! - 220

1067.   24-11-17 - MONTREAL Katacombes [1] + All Torn Up! - 300

1068.   25-11-17 - MONTREAL Katacombes [2] + All Torn Up! - 300

1069.   26-11-17 - QUEBEC CITY Le Cirque + All Torn Up! - 200

1070.   10-1-18 LONDON 100 Club + Criminal Mind/Desperate Measures - 170

1071.   11-1-18 BRISTOL Fleece + Criminal Mind/Blunders - 300

1072.   12-1-18 ABERTILLERY Doll's House + Pizza Tramp/Drunken Marksman/Social Experiment- 100

1073.   13-1-18 CHELTENHAM Frog and Fiddle + Pizza Tramp/Borrowed Time/Setbacks - 120

1074.   16-2-18 GREECE - ATHENS Tres, Vive Le Rock festival: GBH/Subhumans/Project Youth/Green Goblins - 500

1075.   17-2-18 ITALY - ROME CSO Ricomino Del Faro + Into the Baobab/Rake Off/The Radsters/Sect Mark/Education - 400

1076.   23-3-18 GERMANY - OSNABRUCK Substanz + ? - 150

1077.   24-4-18 BELGIUM - AALST Oilsjt Omploft Festival: Extreme Noise Terror/Negative Approach/Siberian Meat Grinder/Subhumans/Svetlanas... - 400

1078.   25-3-18 HOLLAND - ROTTERDAM Baroeg, Black Denim Fest + Disorder/Diesel Breath/Sick of Stupidity/Slavery Farm - 400

1079.   26-3-18 GERMANY - KOLN Sonic Ballroom + Grabowskis - 80

1080.   27-3-18 - STUTTGART Keller Klub + Kubala/Krime - 120

1081.   28-3-18 SWITZERLAND - LUCERNE Sedel + Strapones - 170

1082.   29-3-18 AUSTRIA - BREGENZ Between + Strapones - 75

1083.   30-3-18 FRANCE - LE THILLOT Mediatheque OK Chaos fest + Les Villains Clowns/ Hysterie Collective - 200

1084.   31-3-18 GERMANY - FRANKFURT AU + Terrorfett/Defused - 180

1085.   26-4-18 WORCESTER Marr's Bar + Brassick/Drunk in Charge - 110

1086.   27-4-18 MANCHESTER Star & Garter + ? - 200

1087.   28-4-18 GLASGOW ABC, Scotland's Calling: Buzzcocks/Cockney Rejects/Angelic Upstarts/UK Subs/GBH/Ruts DC/Subhumans/Dirtbox Disco/Fire Exit - 1500

1088.   29-4-18 GATESHEAD Black Bull + Born Equal/Force Fed Lies - 80

1089.   30-4-18 YORK Fulford Arms + Jaded Eyes/Pink Candle - 80

1090.   12-5-18 FRANCE - LECATEAU-CAMBRESIS, Zikenstock festival: Toy Dolls/Angelic Upstarts/Batmobile/Subhumans/Inner Terrestrials - 600

1091.   26-5-18 USA - LAS VEGAS Fremont Country Club, Punk Rock Bowling + Unseen/ Noise/Two Man Advantage - 900

1092.   27-5-18 - PHOENIX Rebel Lounge + Corrupted Youth/Flossies - 330

1093.   28-5-18 - SAN DIEGO Casbah + Final Conflict/Karbonite - 230

1094.   29-5-18 - SANTA ANA Observatory + Final Conflict/Rats in the Wall - 700

1095.   30-5-18 - LOS ANGELES Los Globos + Apocalyse/Nausea/Generacion Suicida - 400

1096.   31-5-18 - VENTURA Garage + Final Conflict - 200

1097.   1-6-18 - SACRAMENTO Holy Diver + Love Songs/? - 300

1098.   2-6-18 - OAKLAND Metro + Love Songs/Screaming Fist - 450

1099.   3-6-18 - EUREKA Siren's Song + Love Songs/Chain Links - 150

1100.   4-6-18 - EUGENE Whirled Pies + Death Ridge Boys/Bad Channels/Hippie Fight - 230

1101.	5-6-18 - PORTLAND Hawthorne Theatre + Death Ridge Boys/Corrupted Youth - 358
1102.	6-6-18 - SEATTLE El Corazon + Death Ridge Boys/Corrupted Youth/Dreadful Children - 262
1103.	7-6-18 CANADA - VANCOUVER Rickshaw Theatre + Vicious Cycles/Real Sickies - 450
1104.	8-6-18 - ROSSLAND Flying Steam Shovel + Real Sickies/Nelson - 110
1105.	9-6-18 - EDMONTON Starlite Room + Real Sickies/Chips Ov Oy - 225
1106.	10-6-18 - CALGARY Dickens + Real Sickies/Border Guard - 250
1107.	22-6-18 GERMANY - HAMBURG Hafenklang + Eat the Bitch - 110
1108.	23-6-18 - BERLIN Clash + Antibastards - 350
1109.	28-6-18 CZECH REPUBLIC - PRAGUE Rock Cafe + Kung Fu Girls - 115
1110.	29-6-18 - VSETIN Vesmir + Zemezluc/Obscene Revenge - 120
1111.	30-6-18 GERMANY - DRESDEN Chemiefabrik + Last Decay - 30
1112.	1-7-18 - LARZ, Fusion Fest - 400
1113.	3-8-18 BLACKPOOL Winter Gardens, Rebellion Festival – 2000
1114.	7-9-18 USA - MILWAUKEE Cactus Club + Assault & Battery/Curbsitter - 181
1115.	8-9-18 - CHICAGO Cobra Lounge + War on Women/Ugly Bones - 259
1116.	9-9-18 - CINCINNATI Northside Yacht Club + War on Women/Canadian Rifle - 200
1117.	10-9-18 - FERNDALE Loving Touch + War on Women/Womb - 101
1118.	11-9-18 - CLEVELAND Now That's Class + War on Women/Snakes - 146
1119.	12-9-18 - PITTSBURGH Spirit Hall + War on Women/Empty Beings - 181
1120.	13-9-18 - PHILADELPHIA First Unitarian Church + War on Women/Dark Thoughts/Brood - 400
1121.	14-9-18 - WASHINGTON DC Black Cat + Mike Watt/Ted Leo/Des Demonas/Digger Moon/Scanners/Honey - 480
1122.	15-9-18 - NEW YORK Knitting Factory + War on Women/All Torn Up! - 350
1123.	28-9-18 HOLLAND - HAARLEM Paronat - 150
1124.	19-10-18 IRELAND - BELFAST Voodoo + ? - 220
1125.	20-10-18 - DUBLIN Voodoo Lounge + Menace/Paranoid Visions... - 140
1126.	9-1-19 LONDON 100 Club + Knock Off - 150
1127.	10-1-19 BRISTOL Fleece + Warwound/Ambition Demolition - 350
1128.	11-1-19 PLYMOUTH Underground + 51st State/Piss Midget/Po-Lice/Space Tourettes - 150
1129.	12-1-19 ABERTILLERY Doll's House + In Evil Hour/Social Experiment/System Reject - 90
1130.	6-4-19 STAFFORD Red Rum + In Evil Hour/Mannequin Factory - 150
1131.	11-4-19 BIDEFORD Palladium + Falling Apart/Sinful Maggie - 150
1132.	12-4-19 BRISTOL Exchange + A-Heads/Rage DC - 180
1133.	13-4-19 LONDON New Cross Inn + Aerial Salad/Left for Dead/Terminal Heads/Butane Regulators - 300
1134.	14-4-19 BEDFORD Esquires + Tendons - 120
1135.	18-4-19 WAKEFIELD Warehouse 23 + Infa-Riot/Billy Club - 150
1136.	19-4-19 MANCHESTER Bread Shed, Punk Festival: Sonic Boom 6/Subhumans.... - 350
1137.	20-4-19 BATH Football Club, B.O.B. Fest + Jewdriver/Sense/A-Heads/Meekers/Nebenwirkung/ Migraines - 150

1138.	4-5-19 MEXICO - Internacional Punkytud Festival - 700
1139.	5-5-19 - MEXICO CITY Cat Skull - 200
1140.	23-5-19 GATESHEAD Black Bull + Born Equal/Sanction This - 100
1141.	24-5-19 DUNDEE Church + ? - 40
1142.	25-5-19 EDINBURGH Bannermans + Sanction This/Happy Spastics/Subvision - 170
1143.	26-5-19 GLASGOW Audio + Hateful/Cuttin Edge - 150
1144.	27-5-19 BOLTON Alma Inn + Bone Idols/Incisions/Litterbug/Crash Mats - 30
1145.	30-5-19 YORK Fullerton Arms + Yada Yadas/Almighty Uprisers - 60
1146.	31-5-19 LEEDS Brudenell Rooms + In Evil Hour/A Time to Stand - 150
1147.	1-6-19 MANCHESTER O2, North East Calling: Slaughter & the Dogs/UK Subs/ A.N.W.L./Conflict/Discharge/Subhumans/Dirt Box Disco/Peter & the Test Tube Babies/ Crashed Out/Kid Klumsy/Vomit/Litterbug - 1000
1148.	27-6-19 BOURNEMOUTH Anvil + Self Abuse - 100
1149.	28-6-19 GUERNSEY Chaos Fest - 400
1150.	29-6-19 SOUTHAMPTON 1865 Club + ? - 250
1151.	19-7-19 GERMANY - GLAUBITZ, Back To Future Fest: Briefs/Lokalmatadore/Marky Ramone/Nashville Pussy/Barstool Preachers/Subhumans/Fckr/Omixhl/Get Dead.... - 400
1152.	20-7-19 - HAMBURG Hafenklang - 130
1153.	21-7-19 HOLLAND - AMSTERDAM Haltpop Festival: Toasters/?/Pears/?/ Subhumans/?... - 400
1154.	22-7-19 - GRONINGEN Bambara + ? - 70
1155.	23-7-19 GERMANY - KOLN Sonic Ballroom + Alien Fight Club - 150
1156.	24-7-19 - SCHWERTE Rattenloch + ? - 80
1157.	25-7-19 - WEINHEIM Cafe Central + ? - 40
1158.	26-7-19 - PEINE Refuse Festival - 350
1159.	27-7-19 BELGIUM - OPWIJK Loco Loco Festival - 400
1160.	2-8-19 BLACKPOOL Winter Gardens, Rebellion Festival - 3000
1161.	5-9-19 CANADA - TORONTO Horseshoe Tavern + Fea/Brutal Youth - 225
1162.	6-9-19 - MONTREAL Foufounes Electriques + Fea/Meh/Fractured - 500
1163.	7-9-19 - QUEBEC CITY, Envolet Macadam Festival + Bigwig/Monoc Serge... - 3000
1164.	8-9-19 USA - PORTLAND Port City Hall + Fea/Savage Head - 184
1165.	9-9-19 - SOMERVILLE Once + Fea/Savage Head - 222
1166.	10-9-19 - NEW YORK Brooklyn Kingsland + Fea/Soul Glo -200
1167.	11-9-19 - BALTIMORE Otto Bar + Fea/Soul Glo/Glue Traps - 228
1168.	12-9-19 - DURHAM Motorco + Fea/Drug Charge - 273
1169.	13-9-19 - ATLANTA Masquerade + Fea/Drug Charge - 414
1170.	14-9-19 - ST AUGUSTINE Sing Out Loud Festival: Hot Water Music/Menzingers/?/ Subhumans... - 1400
1171.	15-9-19 - ORLANDO Will's Pub + Fea - 240
1172.	19-10-19 USA ALAMEDA aircraft carrier Rock the Ship fest: Cock Sparrer/Subhumans/ Street Dogs/Monster Squad - 2000
1173.	19-10-19 - OAKLAND Eli's + Kicker - 150

1174. 20-10-19 - FRESNO Strummers + Neighbourhood Brats - 70

1175. 21-10-19 - VENTURA Discovery + Neighbourhood Brats/Detoxi - 150

1176. 22-10-19 - LOS ANGELES Echoplex + Neighbourhood Brats/Smut/Fissure - 650

1177. 23-10-19 - SAN DIEGO Soma + Neighbourhood Brats/Agonista - 500

1178. 24-10-19 - POMONA Glasshouse + Love Songs/Neighbourhood Brats - 805

1179. 25-10-19 - LAS VEGAS Hard Rock Hotel + Neighbourhood Brats/Love Songs - 250

1180. 26-10-19 - PHOENIX Rebel Lounge + Neighbourhood Brats/Love Songs - 326

1181. 27-10-19 - LANCASTER American Legion Hall + Neighbourhood Brats/Love Songs - 70

1182. 28-10-19 - MORRO BAY Siren + Neighbourhood Brats/Bad Breeding - 100

1183. 29-10-19 - SAN FRANCISCO DNA Lounge + Neighbourhood Brats/Plot 66 - 96

1184. 30-10-19 - SACRAMENTO Holy Roller + Neighbourhood Brats/Plot 66 - 237

1185. 31-10-19 - ARCATA Rampart Skate Park + Neighbourhood Brats/Bad Breeding - 358

1186. 1-11-19 - EUGENE Whirled Pies + Neighbourhood Brats/Bad Breeding - 155

1187. 2-11-19 - PORTLAND Bossanova + Neighbourhood Brats/Bad Breeding - 451

1188. 3-11-19 - SEATTLE El Corazon + Neighbourhood Brats/Bad Breeding - 280

1189. 20-11-19 BELGIUM - BRUSSELS Magasin 4 + Les Slugs/Donder Hell/Hagel - 300

1190. 6-12-19 CHELTENHAM Frog and Fiddle + Terminal Rage/Drunk in Charge - 120

1191. 7-12-19 EXETER Cavern + 51st State/? - 150

1192. 8-12-19 CHIPPENHAM Neeld Hall + Liabilities/Das Ghoul - 70

1193. 9-1-20 LONDON 100 Club + Blunders - 150

1194. 10-1-20 CARDIFF Clwb Ifor Bach + Blunders - 120

1195. 11-1-20 BRISTOL Fleece + Blunders - 400

1196. 12-1-20 SOUTHAMPTON 1865 Club + Acid Attack/Self Abuse - 140

1197. 6-3-20 HASTINGS Crowley Club + Werecats/Butane Regulators - 150

1198. 7-3-20 WOKING Undercover Fest: Johnny Moped/Subhumans/Hot Rods... - 300

1199. 8-3-20 PORTSMOUTH Milton Arms + The Dinz - 100

1200. 24-9-21 BARNSTAPLE Golden Lion Tap + Jolly Roger/Landspeeder - 80

1201. 25-9-21 LONDON New Cross Inn + Dread Messiah/Butcher Baby/Jawless/Radioactive
       Rats/Tystvar/Chain of Panic/Anymal Function/Robaki - 150

1202. 26-9-21 BRIGHTON Pipeline + Exit-Stance/Austerity/Credentials - 40

1203. 22-10-21 GERMANY - OTTERSBURG AZ + Frontalangriff/Sense - 150

1204. 23-10-21 HOLLAND - AMSTERDAM OCCII + Kutland - 150

1205. 24-10-21 BELGIUM - LIEGE La Zone + Werly - 120

1206. 25-10-21 HOLLAND - ROTTERDAM Baroeg + Bottlecaps - 120

1207. 27-10-21 GERMANY - ESSEN Don't Panic - 78

1208. 28-10-21 - OSNABRUCK Bastard Club + Saint Nudes - 140

1209. 29-10-21 - HAMBURG Hafenklang + Crackmeier - 150

1210. 30-10-21 - KASSEL Gold Rube + Beta Blocker - 86

1211. 31-10-21 - SCHWERTE Rattenloch + Tricky Woo/Dead Kardashians - 200

1212. 2-11-21 - KOLN Sonic Ballroom + Alien Fight Club - 40

1213. 3-11-21 - KARLSRUHE Alte Hackerei - 130

1214. 4-11-21 - STUTTGART Goldmarks + Murder Disco - 120

1215.	5-11-21 SWITZERLAND - SOLOTHURN Kofmehl + Pig Sweat - 100
1216.	6-11-21 GERMANY - FRANKFURT AU - 100
1217.	30-3-22 SOUTHAMPTON The 1865 + Dinz/Sodds - 90
1218.	31-3-22 FROME 23 Bath St + Far Cue - 135
1219.	1-4-22 GUILDFORD Holroyd, Undercover Festival + Rage DC/Menace/Omega Tribe/ Girls Like Us - 200
1220.	2-4-22 CORBY Shire Horse + Eastfield/Julie's Dead - 150
1221.	3-4-22 WIGAN Boulevard + the Big I Am/Dry Retch - 170
1222.	4-4-22 EDINBURGH Legends + Subversion/Reality Asylum - 140
1223.	5-4-22 NEWCASTLE Trillians + Deadbeat by Dawn - 150
1224.	6-4-22 LEEDS Brudenall Rooms + Deadbeat by Dawn/Eryx London - 130
1225.	10-6-22 WAKEFIELD Vortex + Krayons/Skiprat -130
1226.	11-6-22 MANCHESTER O2 Ritz, Northwest Calling fest: Ruts DC/Steve Ignorant/ Subhumans/Outcasts/Goldblade... - 600
1227.	12-6-22 LONDON New Cross Inn, London's Burning fest + Sick on the Bus/Drongos for Europe/Rabies Babies... - 80
1228.	15-7-22 USA - SAN FRANCISCO Great American Music Hall + Generacion Suicida/ Kanta Kanta - 650
1229.	16-7-22 - LOS ANGELES Regent Theatre + Generacion Suicida/Prision Postumo - 871
1230.	17-7-22 - SAN DIEGO Casbah + Generacion Suicida/Blinding Glow - 230
1231.	18-7-22 - TUCSON Congress Hotel + Generacion Suicida/Get a Grip - 272
1232.	19-7-22 - PHOENIX Rebel Lounge + Generacion Suicida/Skull Drug - 325
1233.	20-7-22 - LAS VEGAS Rockstar Bar + Generacion Suicida/Hard Pipe Hitters - 200
1234.	21-7-22 - SAN PEDRO Sardines + Generacion Suicida/Sweat - 200
1235.	22-7-22 - POMONA Glasshouse + Generacion Suicida/Cemento - 872
1236.	23-7-22 - VENTURA Gigi's + Generacion Suicida/Headcut - 220
1237.	24-7-22 - MORRO BAY Siren + Generacion Suicida/Hot Tina - 175
1238.	25-7-22 - BAKERSFIELD Tumblor Brew + Generacion Suicida/Plot 66 - 400
1239.	26-7-22 - SACRAMENTO Harlow's + Generacion Suicida/Monster Squad - 400
1240.	27-7-22 - RENO Virginia St Brew + Generacion Suicida/Beer Can! - 230
1241.	28-7-22 - EUREKA Veterans Hall + Generacion Suicida/Tick - 220
1242.	29-7-22 - EUGENE Whirled Pies + Generacion Suicida+Rot/Woven - 350
1243.	30-7-22 - PORTLAND Bossanova + Generacion Suicida/Red Dons - 630
1244.	31-7-22 - SEATTLE Madame Lou's + Generacion Suicida/Red Dons - 300
1245.	5-8-22 BLACKPOOL Winter Gardens, Rebellion Festival: Steve Ignorant/Subhumans/ TV Smith & The Bored Teenagers/Moscow Death Brigade... - 2500
1246.	22-9-22 TEMPLE CLOUD Rockaway Park + Autonomads/Human Error - 150
1247.	23-9-22 MANCHESTER Star and Garter + Kicked in the Teeth/Afflicted - 120
1248.	24-9-22 NEWCASTLE University, North East Calling - Skids/Ruts DC/GBH/Subhumans/ Gimp Fist/Outcasts - 500
1249.	25-9-22 LEEDS Boom + N/A Political - 64
1250.	26-9-22 BLACKPOOL Scream and Shake + Hot Pink Sewage/Dischord - 90

1251.   27-9-22 READING Face Bar + Uncle Peanut - 150

1252.   28-9-22 BRISTOL Exchange + Blunders/Migraines - 250

1253.   29-9-22 EXETER Cavern + Blunders - 200

1254.   30-9-22 LEWES Con Club + Meffs/Zero Again - 150

1255.   1-10-22 CARDIFF Clwb Ifor Bach + Pizza Tramp/Zero Again - 140

1256.   31-10-22 USA - NEW YORK Brooklyn Market Hotel + All Torn Up!/Atruth - 330

1257.   1-11-22 - PHILADELPHIA First Unitarian Church + All Torn Up!/Fuckin Lovers/Delco MFS - 260

1258.   2-11-22 - BALTIMORE Otto Bar + All Torn Up!/Pearl - 191

1259.   3-11-22 - PITTSBURGH Spirit + All Torn Up!/Peace Talks? - 234

1260.   5-11-22 - SILVERADO Canyon Park, Punk in the Park Fest: Bad Religion/Face to Face/
Vandals/Adolescents/7 Seconds/Manic Hispanic/Subhumans/Bronx/Flatliners/Dead Boys/Briefs/
Love Canal/Suzi Moon - 8000

1261.   6-11-22 - LOS ANGELES Teragram + Abuso De Poder/No Plan - 630

1262.   9-12-22 BRISTOL Fleece - UK Subs/GBH/Subhumans - 450

1263.   10-12-22 DUBLIN Button Factory - Paranoid Visions/Subhumans/Dangerous Dave/Nils - 400

SUBHUMANS

DUBLIN, DECEMBER 2022

SUBHUMANS

TIME FLIES
BUT AEROPLANES CRASH

SUBHUMANS

THE DAY THE COUNTRY DIED

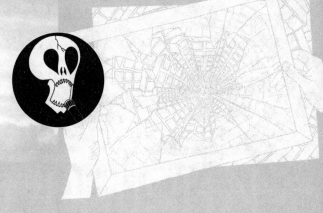

SUBHUMANS

SUBHUMANS   WORLDS APART

SUBHUMANS

internal riot

SUBHUMANS

crisis point

ABOUT THE AUTHOR

IAN, ABOUT TO UNDERTAKE THE VERY FIRST
INTERVIEW FOR THIS BOOK, WITH DICK, 10/5/2021

Ian Glasper has been writing about punk since 1986, when he first started his own fanzine, 'Little Things Please Little Minds'. Although it only ran for five issues, it helped him realise that he could indeed string a few words together, and gave him the confidence – in the early Nineties – to start writing reviews for Record Collector, and a hardcore punk column for Terrorizer, the extreme music magazine that he contributed to for the next twenty years. In 2003, he got fed up of reviewing books about the Sex Pistols and The Clash and decided to write a book about the particular era of the UK punk scene that was closest to his own heart, the second wave of punk during the early Eighties – or UK82, as it became more affectionately known. The resultant 'Burning Britain' tome, published by Cherry Red in 2003 to much critical acclaim, flew off the shelves and is now widely regarded as the definitive document on that period.

It was followed by 'The Day the Country Died: A History of Anarcho Punk 1980 – 1984' (2006), 'Trapped in a Scene: UK Hardcore 1985 – 1989' (2009) and 'Armed with Anger: How UK Punk Survived the Nineties' (2012). After then covering the last forty years of UK thrash metal with 'Contract in Blood: A History of UK Thrash' (2018), Glasper joined the Earth Island Books family and gave us 2020's celebrated 'The Scene That Would Not Die: Twenty Years of Post-Millennial Punk in the UK'.

During the whole of this time, Glasper has also been busy writing, recording and touring with his own punk and hardcore bands, keeping his finger firmly on the pulse and staying in touch with the grassroots DIY element of the punk scene that so drew him to it in the first place. Since 1983, he has played bass for Ammonia 77, Decadence Within, Burnside, Stampin' Ground, Human Error, Suicide Watch, Flux of Pink Indians, Freebase, Betrayed by Many, Thirty Six Strategies and Warwound, and he currently plays with Bristol-based anarcho punkers Zero Again, whose debut album is due in 2023.

A father of two, and a lifelong vegetarian/vegan, he writes for Down for Life and Fistful of Metal magazines, as well as regularly penning liner notes for retrospective punk and metal releases. He is tentatively working on the next book in his ongoing overview of the UK punk scene...

PM Press is an independent, radical publisher of books and media to educate, entertain, and inspire. Founded in 2007 by a small group of people with decades of publishing, media, and organizing experience, PM Press amplifies the voices of radical authors, artists, and activists. Our aim is to deliver bold political ideas and vital stories to all walks of life and arm the dreamers to demand the impossible. We have sold millions of copies of our books, most often one at a time, face to face. We're old enough to know what we're doing and young enough to know what's at stake. Join us to create a better world.

PM PRESS
PO BOX 23912
OAKLAND
CA 94623

510-658-3906
WWW.PMPRESS.ORG

PM PRESS IN EUROPE

EUROPE@PMPRESS.ORG
WWW.PMPRESS.ORG.UK

FRIENDS OF PM

These are indisputably momentous times—the financial system is melting down globally and the Empire is stumbling. Now more than ever there is a vital need for radical ideas.

In the many years since its founding—and on a mere shoestring—PM Press has risen to the formidable challenge of publishing and distributing knowledge and entertainment for the struggles ahead. With hundreds of releases to date, we have published an impressive and stimulating array of literature, art, music, politics, and culture. Using every available medium, we've succeeded in connecting those hungry for ideas and information to those putting them into practice.

Friends of PM allows you to directly help impact, amplify, and revitalize the discourse and actions of radical writers, filmmakers, and artists. It provides us with a stable foundation from which we can build upon our early successes and provides a much-needed subsidy for the materials that can't necessarily pay their own way. You can help make that happen—and receive every new title automatically delivered to your door once a month—by joining as a Friend of PM Press. And, we'll throw in a free T-shirt when you sign up.

Here are your options:

- **$30 a month** Get all books and pamphlets plus 50% discount on all webstore purchases
- **$40 a month** Get all PM Press releases (including CDs and DVDs) plus 50% discount on all webstore purchases
- **$100 a month Superstar**—Everything plus PM merchandise, free downloads, and 50% discount on all webstore purchases

For those who can't afford $30 or more a month, we have **Sustainer Rates** at $15, $10, and $5. Sustainers get a free PM Press T-shirt and a 50% discount on all purchases from our website.

Your Visa or Mastercard will be billed once a month, until you tell us to stop. Or until our efforts succeed in bringing the revolution around. Or the financial meltdown of Capital makes plastic redundant. Whichever comes first.

THE DAY THE COUNTRY DIED
A HISTORY OF ANARCHO PUNK
1980–1984

IAN GLASPER

ISBN: 978-1-60486-516-5
$24.95 • 496 pages

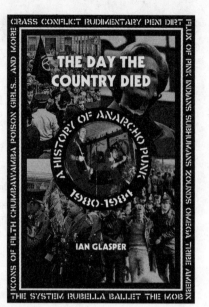

The Day the Country Died features author, historian, and musician Ian Glasper exploring in minute detail the influential, esoteric, UK anarcho punk scene of the early eighties.

If the colorful '80s punk bands captured in *Burning Britain* were loud, political, and uncompromising, those examined in *The Day the Country Died* were even more so, totally prepared to risk their liberty to communicate the ideals they believed in so passionately.

With Crass and Poison Girls opening the floodgates, the arrival of bands such as Zounds, Flux of Pink Indians, Conflict, Subhumans, Chumbawamba, Amebix, Rudimentary Peni, Antisect, Omega Tribe, and Icons of Filth heralded a brand-new age of honesty and integrity in underground music. With a backdrop of Thatcher's Britain, punk music became self-sufficient and considerably more aggressive, blending a DIY ethos with activism to create the perfectly bleak soundtrack to the zeitgeist of a discontented British youth.

It was a time when punk stopped being merely a radical fashion statement and became a force for real social change; a genuine revolutionary movement, driven by some of the most challenging noises ever committed to tape. Anarchy, as regards punk rock, no longer meant "cash from chaos." It meant "freedom, peace, and unity." Anarcho punk took the rebellion inherent in punk from the beginning to a whole new level of personal awareness.

All the scene's biggest names, and most of the smaller ones, are comprehensively covered with new, exclusive interviews and hundreds of previously unseen photographs.

"The oral testimony assembled here provides an often-lucid participant's view of the work of the wider anarcho-punk milieu, which demonstrates just as tellingly the diversity as well as the commonality by which it was defined. The collection hints at the extent to which—within a militant antiwar, antiwork, antisystem framework—the perception and priorities of the movement's activists differed: something the movement's critics (who were always keen to deride the uniformity of the 'Crass punks') rarely understood."
—Rich Cross, *Freedom*

"With a backdrop of Thatcher's Britain, punk music became self-sufficient and considerably more aggressive, blending a DIY ethos with activism to create the perfectly bleak soundtrack to the zeitgeist of a discontented British youth. Including such iconic bands as Crass, Conflict, Flux of Pink Indians, Subhumans, Chumbawamba, Oi Polloi, Amebix, Rubella Ballet, and Zounds to name but a few, Ian Glasper's history of punk stands out as an important and relevant history of the genre."
—Dave Faulds, *Dulwich Books Review*

BURNING BRITAIN
THE HISTORY OF UK PUNK
1980–1984

IAN GLASPER

ISBN: 978-1-60486-748-0

$24.95 • 456 pages

As the Seventies drew to a close and the media declared punk dead and buried, a whole new breed of band was emerging from the gutter. Harder and faster than their '76–'77 predecessors, not to mention more aggressive and political, the likes of Discharge, the Exploited, and G.B.H. were to prove not only more relevant but arguably just as influential.

Several years in the making and featuring hundreds of new interviews and photographs, *Burning Britain* is the true story of the UK punk scene from 1980 to 1984 told for the first time by the bands and record labels that created it. Covering the country region by region, author Ian Glasper profiles legendary bands like Vice Squad, Angelic Upstarts, Blitz, Anti-Nowhere League, Cockney Rejects, and the UK Subs as well as more obscure groups like Xtract, The Skroteez, and Soldier Dolls.

The grim reality of being a teenage punk rocker in Thatcher's Britain resulted in some of the most primal and potent music ever committed to plastic. Burning Britain is the definitive overview of that previously overlooked era.

"Ian Glasper's chatty, engaging history follows the regional lines along which UK punk's 'second wave' scene divided, as well as talking about the record labels involved and what the main protagonists, from the Anti-Nowhere League to Vice Squad, are up to now."
—Iain Aitch, *The Guardian*

"Glasper is thorough and democratic. He lets everyone speak, tell their own story, edits out the rambling and bullshit, and presents a fair picture of all the main bands from all over the UK and Ireland. Geographically divided up, it's an encyclopaedic but down-to-earth reference book, full of detail and anecdotes."
—Ged Babey, LouderThanWar.com

THE STORY OF CRASS

GEORGE BERGER

ISBN: 978-1-60486-037-5

$20.00 • 304 pages

Crass was the anarcho-punk face of a revolutionary movement founded by radical thinkers and artists Penny Rimbaud, Gee Vaucher, and Steve Ignorant. When punk ruled the waves, Crass waived the rules and took it further, putting out their own records, films, and magazines and setting up a series of Situationist pranks that were dutifully covered by the world's press. Not just another iconoclastic band, Crass was a musical, social, and political phenomenon.

Commune dwellers who were rarely photographed and remained contemptuous of conventional pop stardom, their members explored and finally exhausted the possibilities of punk-led anarchy. They have at last collaborated on telling the whole Crass story, giving access to many never-before-seen photos and interviews.

"Lucid in recounting their dealings with freaks, coppers, and punks the band's voices predominate, and that's for the best."
—*The Guardian*

"Thoroughly researched … chockful of fascinating revelation … it is, surprisingly, the first real history of the pioneers of anarcho-punk."
—*Classic Rock*

"They (Crass) sowed the ground for the return of serious anarchism in the early eighties."
—Jon Savage, *England's Dreaming*

THE LAST OF THE HIPPIES

AN HYSTERICAL ROMANCE

PENNY RIMBAUD

ISBN: 978-1-62963-103-5

$12.00 • 128 pages

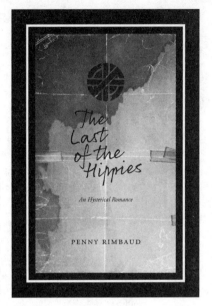

First published in 1982 as part of the Crass record album *Christ: The Album*, Penny Rimbaud's *The Last of the Hippies* is a fiery anarchist polemic centered on the story of his friend, Phil Russell (aka Wally Hope), who was murdered by the State while incarcerated in a mental institution.

Wally Hope was a visionary and a freethinker whose life had a profound influence on many in the culture of the UK underground and beyond. He was an important figure in what may loosely be described as the organization of the Windsor Free Festival from 1972 to 1974, as well providing the impetus for the embryonic Stonehenge Free Festival.

Wally was arrested and incarcerated in a mental institution after having been found in possession of a small amount of LSD. He was later released, and subsequently died. The official verdict was that he committed suicide, although Rimbaud uncovered strong evidence that he was murdered. Rimbaud's anger over unanswered questions surrounding his friend's death inspired him in 1977 to form the anarchist punk band Crass.

In the space of seven short years, from 1977 to their breakup in 1984, Crass almost single-handedly breathed life back into the then-moribund peace and anarchist movements. *The Last of the Hippies* fast became the seminal text of what was then known as anarcho-punk and which later blossomed into the anti-globalization movement.

This revised edition comes complete with a new introduction in which Rimbaud questions some of the premises that he laid down in the original.

The Primal Screamer

Nick Blinko

ISBN: 978-1-60486-331-4
$15.95 • 128 pages

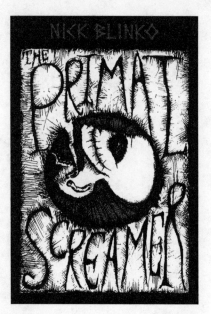

A Gothic horror novel about severe mental distress and punk rock. The novel is written in the form of a diary kept by a psychiatrist, Dr. Rodney H. Dweller, concerning his patient, Nathaniel Snoxell, brought to him in 1979 because of several attempted suicides. Snoxell gets involved in the nascent UK anarcho-punk scene, recording EPs and playing gigs in squatted Anarchy Centers. In 1985, the good doctor himself "goes insane" and disappears.

This semi-autobiographical novel from Rudimentary Peni singer, guitarist, lyricist, and illustrator Nick Blinko plunges into the worlds of madness, suicide, and anarchist punk. Lovecraft meets Crass in the squats and psychiatric institutions of early '80s England. This new edition collects Blinko's long-sought-after artwork from the three previous incarnations.

"Dense, haunted, shot through with black humour."
—*Raw Vision*

"Nick Blinko is a madman. That's not intended as pejorative opinion but rather a statement of plain fact."
—*Maximum Rocknroll*

"The insights it offers into the punk scene and into the unsettling landscapes of its author's mind are fascinating. The whole book has a distinct sense of coming from a mind unlike most we are used to."
—*The Big Issue*

"An intensely written and authentically Gothic look at the life of a man suffering extreme mental distress."
—*Detour*

"Fascinating and compelling."
—*Kerrang!*

THE SPITBOY RULE
TALES OF A XICANA IN A FEMALE PUNK BAND

MICHELLE CRUZ GONZALES

FOREWORD BY MARTÍN SORRONDEGUY
PREFACE BY MIMI THI NGUYEN

ISBN: 978-1-62963-140-0
$15.96 • 160 pages

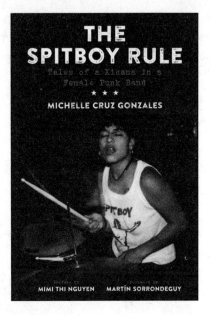

Michelle Cruz Gonzales played drums and wrote lyrics in the influential 1990s female hardcore band Spitboy, and now she's written a book—a punk rock herstory. Though not a riot grrrl band, Spitboy blazed trails for women musicians in the San Francisco Bay Area and beyond, but it wasn't easy. Misogyny, sexism, abusive fans, class and color blindness, and all-out racism were foes, especially for Gonzales, a Xicana and the only person of color in the band.

Unlike touring rock bands before them, the unapologetically feminist Spitboy preferred Scrabble games between shows rather than sex and drugs, and they were not the angry man-haters that many expected them to be. Serious about women's issues and being the band that they themselves wanted to hear, a band that rocked as hard as men but sounded like women, Spitboy released several records and toured internationally. The memoir details these travels while chronicling Spitboy's successes and failures, and for Gonzales, discovering her own identity along the way.

Fully illustrated with rare photos and flyers from the punk rock underground, this fast-paced, first-person recollection is populated by scenesters and musical allies from the time, including Econochrist, Paxston Quiggly, Neurosis, Los Crudos, Aaron Cometbus, Pete the Roadie, Green Day, Fugazi, and Kamala and the Karnivores.

"*The Spitboy Rule* is a compelling and insightful journey into the world of '90s punk as seen through the eyes of a Xicana drummer who goes by the nickname Todd. Todd stirs the pot by insisting that she plays hardcore punk, not riot grrrl music, and inviting males to share the dance floor with women in a respectful way. This drummer never misses a beat. Read it!"
—Alice Bag, singer for the Bags, author of *Violence Girl: East L.A. Rage to Hollywood Stage, a Chicana Punk Story*

"Best punk memoir that I've ever had the privilege of reading. In a punk scene dominated by middle-class white males, you can't forget Spitboy, four brave women playing music with the intensity of an out-of-control forest fire. Gonzales's involvement and presence in the punk scene, in particular, was significant because she represented a radical, feminist person of color, and she reflected a positive change in the scene for the Bay Area. Her memoir, chronicling her unique experience and perspective, occupies an important moment in the punk saga. This is a must-read for anyone still dedicated to social justice and change."
—Wendy-O Matik, author of *Redefining Our Relationships: Guidelines for Responsible Open Relationships*

QUEERCORE
HOW TO PUNK A REVOLUTION: AN ORAL HISTORY

EDITED BY LIAM WARFIELD, WALTER CRASSHOLE, AND YONY LEYSER

INTRODUCTION BY ANNA JOY SPRINGER AND LYNN BREEDLOVE

ISBN: 978-1-62963-796-9
$18.00 • 208 pages

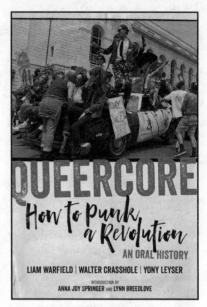

Queercore: How to Punk a Revolution: An Oral History is the very first comprehensive overview of a movement that defied both the music underground and the LGBT mainstream community.

Through exclusive interviews with protagonists like Bruce LaBruce, G.B. Jones, Jayne County, Kathleen Hanna of Bikini Kill and Le Tigre, film director and author John Waters, Lynn Breedlove of Tribe 8, Jon Ginoli of Pansy Division, and many more, alongside a treasure trove of never-before-seen photographs and reprinted zines from the time, *Queercore* traces the history of a scene originally "fabricated" in the bedrooms and coffee shops of Toronto and San Francisco by a few young, queer punks to its emergence as a relevant and real revolution. *Queercore* is a down-to-details firsthand account of the movement explored by the people that lived it—from punk's early queer elements, to the moment that Toronto kids decided they needed to create a scene that didn't exist, to Pansy Division's infiltration of the mainstream and the emergence of riot grrrl—as well as the clothes, zines, art, film, and music that made this movement an exciting middle finger to complacent gay and straight society. *Queercore* will stand as both a testament to radically gay politics and culture and an important reference for those who wish to better understand this explosive movement.

"Finally, a book that centers on the wild, innovative, and fearless contributions queers made to punk rock, creating a punker-than-punk subculture beneath the subculture, Queercore. Gossipy and inspiring, a historical document and a call to arms during a time when the entire planet could use a dose of queer, creative rage."
—Michelle Tea, author of *Valencia*

"*Queercore: How to Punk a Revolution* delivers a deeply invested history of the forgotten roots of queercore. While to some punk was inherently gay as fuck, the actual queer revolution came few and far between bands, scenes, and eras whose intersections were small, yet wildly significant. With voices ranging from Penny Arcade to Brontez Purnell, we hear a vast history from around the globe, echoing everything queer, dirty, and true."
—Cristy C. Road, frontwoman of Choked Up and author of *Spit and Passion*

LEFT OF THE DIAL
CONVERSATIONS WITH PUNK ICONS

DAVID ENSMINGER

ISBN: 978-1-60486-641-4
$20.00 • 296 pages

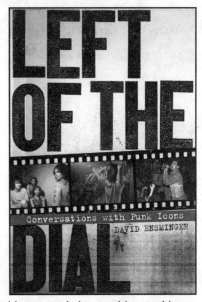

Left of the Dial features interviews by musical journalist, folklorist, educator, and musician David Ensminger with leading figures of the punk underground: Ian MacKaye (Minor Threat, Fugazi), Jello Biafra (Dead Kennedys), Dave Dictor (MDC), and many more. Ensminger probes the legacy of punk's sometimes fuzzy political ideology, its ongoing DIY traditions, its rupture of cultural and social norms, its progressive media ecology, its transgenerational and transnational appeal, its pursuit of social justice, its hybrid musical nuances, and its sometimes ambivalent responses to queer identities, race relations, and its own history. Passionate, far-reaching, and fresh, these conversations illuminate punk's oral history with candor and humor.

Rather than focus on discographies and rehashed gig memories, the interviews aim to unveil the secret history of punk and hardcore ideologies and values, as understood by the performers. In addition, Ensminger has culled key graphics from his massive punk flyer collection to celebrate the visual history of the bands represented. The book also features rare photographs shot by Houston-based photographer Ben DeSoto during the heyday of punk and hardcore, which capture the movement's raw gusto, gritty physicality, and resilient determination.

Interviews include Peter Case (Nerves, Plimsouls), Captain Sensible (The Damned), Tony Kinman (The Dils), El Vez, Charlie Harper (UK Subs), The Deaf Club (an oral history of the landmark San Francisco club), Mike Palm (Agent Orange), Gregg Turner (Angry Samoans), Ian MacKaye (Minor Threat, Fugazi), Jello Biafra (Dead Kennedys), Gary Floyd (Dicks, Sister Double Happiness), Mike Watt (Minutemen, fIREHOSE), Shawn Stern (Youth Brigade), Kira Roessler (Black Flag, Dos), Jack Grisham (TSOL), Keith Morris (Circle Jerks, Off!), Fred "Freak" Smith (Beefeater), U-Ron Bondage (Really Red), Vic Bondi (Articles of Faith), Lisa Fancher (Frontier Records), Dave Dictor (MDC), and Thomas Barnett (Strike Anywhere).

"David Ensminger is the right mix of intellectual and real-ass emotional punk. He is a historian and has walked the life ... I recommend everything this man is up to!"
—Dave Dictor, MDC

"David is one of the rare scene insiders who also has a depth of knowledge of the social and political context for the punk and hardcore moment. His love for the scene and understanding of its importance is unique, well-researched, and valuable."
—Vic Bondi, Articles of Faith

ALSO BY THE AUTHOR

The Scene That Would Not Die:
Twenty Years of Post-Millennial Punk In The UK

Ian Glasper

A PASSIONATE AND COMPREHENSIVE OVERVIEW
OF THE UK'S CONTEMPORARY DIY PUNK SCENE

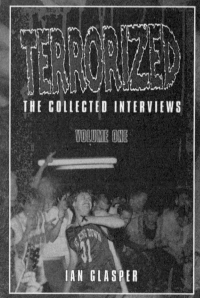

TERRORIZED
THE COLLECTED INTERVIEWS
VOLUME ONE
IAN GLASPER

TERRORIZED
THE COLLECTED INTERVIEWS
VOLUME TWO
IAN GLASPER

TWO HUGE VOLUMES COMPILING ALL 300 INTERVIEWS GLASPER
UNDERTOOK FOR TERRORIZER MAGAZINE BETWEEN 1993 AND 2018

AVAILABLE AT: WWW.EARTHISLANDBOOKS.COM